KARL MARX
FREDERICK ENGELS

COLLECTED WORKS
VOLUME
12

KARL MARX
FREDERICK ENGELS

Volume
12

MARX AND ENGELS: 1853-54

1979
LAWRENCE & WISHART
LONDON

This volume has been prepared jointly by Lawrence & Wishart Ltd., London, International Publishers Co. Inc., New York, and Progress Publishers, Moscow, in collaboration with the Institute of Marxism-Leninism, Moscow.

ISBN 0 85315 357 4

Printed in the Union of Soviet Socialist Republics

Contents

KARL MARX AND FREDERICK ENGELS

WORKS

March 1853-February 1854

1853

March

April

October-beginning of December

November

December

ILLUSTRATIONS

TRANSLATORS

CLEMENS DUTT: Article 64

RODNEY LIVINGSTONE: Article 8

JOAN and TREVOR WALMSLEY: Articles 63, 82

Preface

Volume 12 of the *Collected Works* of Marx and Engels contains articles and reports written between March 22, 1853, and February 10, 1854. Most of the articles were published in the *New-York Daily Tribune,* for which Marx began to work in August 1851.

Writing for the *Tribune* became for Marx and also Engels, whom Marx enlisted to write some of the articles, an important part of their revolutionary activity. In the climate of political reaction which prevailed on the European continent in the 1850s, the opportunity to propagate revolutionary communist ideas in the columns of a popular American newspaper was one not to be missed. Marx had no hesitation about contributing to this bourgeois newspaper in view of the progressive role it was then playing in the social life of the USA. It condemned slavery and supported the abolitionist movement at a time when the conflict between the bourgeois North and the slave-owning South was coming to a head; and since this stand corresponded to the mood of broad sections of the population, it attracted many readers to the paper.

Marx's and Engels' articles aroused great interest in America. Many of them, in addition to appearing in the daily issues of the *Tribune,* were reprinted in special supplements: the *New-York Semi-Weekly Tribune* and the *New-York Weekly Tribune.* Eventually it became editorial practice to publish these articles and reports in the form of leaders.

The articles by Marx and Engels in the *New-York Daily Tribune* became known in Europe as well. Thus, in a speech in the House of Commons on July 1, 1853, the leader of the Free Traders, John

Bright, mentioned Marx's *New-York Daily Tribune* article on Gladstone's budget (see this volume, p. 176).

At the same time Marx and Engels tried to use for revolutionary propaganda the then very few organs of the proletarian press. Thus, Marx published a number of articles in the Chartist *People's Paper*, which began to appear in May 1852 with Ernest Jones as editor. It also reproduced some articles by him written for the *Tribune*. Marx also supported the New York working-class paper *Die Reform*, which came out from 1853 to 1854 in German and played a considerable part in the dissemination of communist ideas in the USA. Joseph Weydemeyer and Adolph Cluss were among its most active contributors. Marx did all he could to help his German-American friends with the work of editing *Die Reform*. He allowed them to print gratis in the newspaper translations of his articles from the *Tribune*. His letters to Cluss and Weydemeyer often contained ready-made material for articles. Thus, Cluss included in his article "The 'Best Paper in the Union' and Its 'Best Men' and Political Economists" extracts from Marx's letters criticising the economic theory of Carey, then in fashion in the USA and acclaimed by the bourgeois editors of the *Tribune*. The article "David Urquhart" published in *Die Reform* reproduced in its entirety the text of a letter from Marx to Cluss which has not survived.

Marx and Engels used their journalistic activity to expose reactionary regimes in Europe, to reveal the contradictions of capitalist society, to criticise the different trends of bourgeois ideology, and to formulate the position of the working class and revolutionary democracy on major political questions. Although after the disbandment of the Communist League there was no international working-class organisation on which they could lean, they set themselves the task of preserving international links between the representatives of the working-class movement in different countries, uniting them on the platform of scientific communism, and preparing the conditions for the creation of a proletarian party. By their articles in the press and by other means, they sought to show the more politically conscious elements of the proletariat how unstable was the reign of reaction and to strengthen their belief in the advent of a new revolutionary upsurge.

The journalistic activity of Marx and Engels was closely linked with their theoretical research and rested largely on the results obtained by Marx in his studies of political economy and world history, and by Engels in his research on military science, Oriental studies, philology and history. The extant notebooks contain numerous copied extracts showing that in addition to accumulating a vast amount of material for his economic work, Marx made a special study of a large number of sources for his articles and reports (these sources are given in the notes to the individual articles). Conversely, Marx's continuous interest in current economic questions broadened the base for his work on general economic theory. The materials quoted by Marx in his articles for the *New-York Daily Tribune* were later used by him in the *Economic Manuscripts of 1857-58* (the *Grundrisse*), and also in Volume I of *Capital*.

In this period, 1853-54, Marx's and Engels' attention was centred on three questions: the economic condition of the European countries, in particular of the most developed one, England, and the consequent prospects for a new upsurge of the democratic and working-class movements; the colonial policy of the capitalist powers and the national liberation struggle of the oppressed peoples; and, finally, international relations.

Analysing the economic position of the European countries, Marx devoted a number of articles—"The War Question.—British Population and Trade Returns.—Doings of Parliament", "Political Movements.—Scarcity of Bread in Europe", "The Western Powers and Turkey.—Symptoms of Economic Crisis", and many others—to the state of industrial production, primarily in England, agriculture, domestic and foreign trade, market prices, foreign exchange rates, etc. He distinguished different phases in the current trade and industrial cycle and gave concrete expression to the thesis he had propounded as early as the 1840s on the cyclical nature of the development of production under capitalism. Marx revealed laws actually operating in a capitalist economy, and so refuted the arguments of bourgeois apologists who represented capitalism as a never-changing, harmonious system which ensures the well-being of all classes of society. The whole secret of bourgeois political economy, he observed, "consists simply in transforming transitory social relations belonging to a determined epoch of history and corresponding with a given state of material production, into eternal, general, never-changing laws, natural laws, as they call them" (see this volume, p. 247). At the same time, Marx called attention to specific features in the different economic schools and doctrines current in the various countries. Thus, Carey's views were influenced by specific features of social-economic development in the USA, and his attacks on

British industrialists and economists, Ricardo in particular, reflected the struggle between the American and British capitalists. What Carey had in common with the French economist Bastiat and a number of British followers of the classical school, however, was his preaching of the harmony of class interests under capitalism and his defence of the foundations of the capitalist system.

Marx's articles include a sharp, critical description of the economic and political liberalism proclaimed by the British Free Traders. The hypocritical phrases of the Free Traders about "freedom" and prosperity concealed a defence of the unlimited exploitation of the workers, and their pacifist propaganda expressed not their love of peace, but the belief of the British industrial bourgeoisie in Britain's ability to retain its monopoly of world industry and trade by peaceful means, without the onerous expenditure of waging war.

The falsity of the Free Traders' argument that free trade would lead to a development of capitalism without crises was strikingly revealed at the end of 1853, when a phase of prosperity gave way to a period of stagnation in industry and trade. Emphasising the growing influence of British industry and its periodic crises on the world market and on the world economy as a whole, Marx concluded that the symptoms of crisis observable in 1853-54 were inevitably bound to develop into a universal economic crisis, which did in fact break out in 1857.

A number of articles in the present volume, e.g. "The Russian Victory.—Position of England and France" and "The Fighting in the East.—Finances of Austria and France.—Fortification of Constantinople", dealt with the position of France. In them Marx called attention to the political consequences in France of economic difficulties, poor harvests, the rising cost of living, financial mismanagement, and so on. The discontent of the masses, particularly a section of the peasantry, with the measures of Louis Bonaparte's government bore witness to the instability of the Second Empire (see this volume, pp. 540-42). The decisive blow against this counter-revolutionary regime, Marx predicted, would be dealt by the French workers. The time would come "when general causes and the universal discontent of all other classes" would enable the workers of France "to resume their revolutionary work anew" (see this volume, p. 541).

Closely related to the economic reviews were Marx's articles on financial questions: "The New Financial Juggle; or Gladstone and the Pennies", "Achievements of the Ministry", "*L.S.D.*, or Class

Budgets and Who's Relieved by Them", and others. Some of these were written for the Chartist *People's Paper.* In this series of articles Marx showed up the class nature of the economic policy of the bourgeois state and of the financial and fiscal measures taken by the British Government, which was always careful, on this as on other questions, not to overstep the limit "beyond which the working man would gain—the aristocrat and middle classes lose" (see this volume, p. 66). The budget of Gladstone, the Chancellor of the Exchequer in the Coalition Cabinet, is described by Marx as "a middle-class Budget—written by an aristocratic pen" (see this volume, p. 63).

Describing the destitution of the English workers and the aggravation of contradictions between the bourgeoisie and the proletariat, manifested in large-scale class conflicts, strikes and lock-outs, Marx made a profound analysis of the strike movement. He gave a detailed description of the strikes which were taking place in the industrial areas of Britain in his articles "English Prosperity.—Strikes.—The Turkish Question.—India", "Russian Policy Against Turkey.—Chartism", "Panic on the London Stock Exchange.—Strikes", and others, noting a new and positive phenomenon—the participation of unorganised workers in strikes. An analysis of the results of the mass strikes in 1853 and early 1854 helped Marx to give more concrete expression to conclusions on the different forms of the class struggle of the proletariat which he and Engels had drawn in the *Manifesto of the Communist Party* and other works. Marx showed that strikes are natural phenomena in capitalist society, that they serve as a means of restraining the arbitrary behaviour of factory owners and ensuring that the vital needs of the workers are satisfied. He stressed the influence of the capitalist economic cycle, the fluctuations in the state of the market and the level of wages, in exacerbating social antagonisms and the growth of the class consciousness of the proletariat. "Without the great alternative phases of dullness, prosperity, over-excitement, crisis and distress, which modern industry traverses in periodically recurring cycles, with the up and down of wages resulting from them, as with the constant warfare between masters and men closely corresponding with those variations in wages and profits, the working classes of Great Britain, and of all Europe, would be a heart-broken, a weak-minded, a worn-out, unresisting mass, whose self-emancipation would prove as impossible as that of the slaves of Ancient Greece and Rome" (see this volume, p. 169—written by Marx in English).

Marx saw the prime importance of strikes in the political and moral influence which they have on workers, increasing their spirit of resistance and further promoting their class solidarity and organisation.

Describing the working-class movement in Britain, Marx concluded that the workers should not confine themselves to waging an economic struggle, important as it might be, but must combine it with a political struggle as the main means of liberating the working people from wage slavery. He constantly emphasised the need to organise the proletariat on a national scale, form a mass political party of the working class and wage a struggle for the conquest of political power. The trade unions—class organisations often created by the workers in the course of the strikes themselves—would, he said, assume particularly great importance for the working class when "their activity will ... be carried over to the *political field*" (see this volume, p. 334). In Marx's view, to overcome the idea that trade unions were not concerned with politics and to draw them into political life was one of the ways of achieving a higher form of class organisation of the British proletariat—of creating a proletarian party.

Marx assigned an important role in this to the revolutionary Chartists led by Ernest Jones, then a small but highly active detachment of the British working-class movement. In the articles "The Labor Question", "Prosperity.—The Labor Question", "Manteuffel's Speech.—Religious Movement in Prussia.—Mazzini's Address.—London Corporation.—Russell's Reform.—Labor Parliament", and others, Marx wrote with great sympathy of Jones' attempts to strengthen the influence of the Chartists among the masses, his tours of industrial areas and his agitation among strikers, trade union members and unorganised workers. In many cases Marx reproduced reports of workers' meetings and Jones' speeches at them, in which one can sense the influence of Marx's own ideas. Marx welcomed the Chartist proposal to convene a representative Labor Parliament as a step towards the founding of a national workers' organisation capable not only of co-ordinating the sporadic strikes, but also of directing the political actions of the masses.

Marx and Engels did all they could to support the endeavours of Jones and other revolutionary Chartist leaders to revive the Chartist movement on a new basis, combining the struggle for the People's Charter with the propaganda of revolutionary socialism. They attached great importance to the struggle of the British workers for universal suffrage. At a time when the British proletariat already constituted the majority of the population, and the ruling classes did not yet possess a sufficiently powerful military and bureaucratic machine, universal suffrage could help the proletariat to win political power as an essential prerequisite for achieving socialism in Britain.

Marx pointed to symptoms of revolutionary ferment not only in Britain and France, but also in other European countries—Prussia, Austria, and Italy. For him they were signs of the imminent new revolutionary events. Even the Prussian Government, he noted, "smells the breath of Revolution in midst of the apparent apathy" (see this volume, p. 30). The realisation that the situation in Europe was fraught with a new upsurge of the revolutionary movement impelled Marx and Engels to return to tactical problems and to criticise false tactical premises, particularly those of a conspiratorial and adventurist nature. Thus, criticising the tactics of the Italian revolutionary Mazzini, Marx stressed the mistaken and utopian nature of his view that an Italian revolution "is not to be effected by the favorable chances of European complications, but by the private action of Italian conspirators acting by surprise" (see this volume, p. 512).

Marx's pamphlet *The Knight of the Noble Consciousness*, the text of which includes a letter from Engels, was also aimed against adventurism and sectarianism in the revolutionary movement. In this work, as in two earlier ones—*The Great Men of the Exile* and *Revelations Concerning the Communist Trial in Cologne*—Marx and Engels exposed the petty-bourgeois pseudo-revolutionism and phrase-mongering, the demagogic playing at revolutions and conspiracies, in which the leaders of the petty-bourgeois émigrés indulged. The pamphlet unmasks August Willich, one of the leaders of the sectarian faction of the Communist League, who used the émigré democratic press to attack working-class revolutionaries. Analysing Willich's "revolutionary" plans, Marx sharply criticised the voluntarism and subjectivism characteristic of the supporters of conspiratorial tactics, their reluctance and inability to make a sober assessment of the situation, and their political vacillation.

A new and important feature in the theoretical and journalistic work of Marx and Engels at this period was their deep interest in the historical fate of the colonial peoples. At this time they began to publish articles systematically in the press about the situation in the colonial countries of the East, exposing the predatory policy of the capitalist states in relation to these countries. Whereas earlier Marx had treated colonial problems on a general theoretical plane, explaining the general laws of capitalist development and the place which colonial exploitation occupied in it, in the 1850s he began to pay far more attention to the history of the colonies and dependent countries, colonial policy, and the methods and consequences of colonial rule. And he made extensive use of the results of his studies in his journalistic writings. Marx's articles on this subject proclaimed the ideas of proletarian internationalism, and of the solidarity of the working class with the oppressed peoples of the colonies and dependent countries.

This approach to the colonial question enabled Marx to give a new interpretation of the history of the peoples of the oppressed countries, to reveal the interrelation and interdependence of the historical development of the countries where capitalism was well established and the economically backward countries of the East, of the metropolises and the colonies. Marx regarded colonial policy as an expression of the most repulsive and cruel aspects of the capitalist system. "The profound hypocrisy and inherent barbarism of bourgeois civilization lies unveiled before our eyes, turning from its home, where it assumes respectable forms, to the colonies, where it goes naked" (see this volume, p. 221).

Marx devoted considerable space in his works to India. The position and history of this great country, which had fallen under the rule of British colonialism, was examined by him in a series of articles, "The British Rule in India", "The East India Company—Its History and Results", "The Future Results of British Rule in India", and others, in which he traced the most important stages and methods of the colonial enslavement of India by Britain.

A major role in the subjugation of India, with its colossal natural resources and ancient culture, as Marx shows in his articles, was played by the East India Company—"merchant adventurers, who conquered India to make money out of it" (see this volume, p. 179). Over the decades, the Company robbed the peoples of Hindustan, annexing one region after another, and using the resources it had seized to organise aggressive incursions into neighbouring territories—Afghanistan, Burma and Persia. The Company made wide use of the Ancient Roman principle *divide et impera* (divide and rule), which, as Marx stressed, was one of the main methods of effecting colonial conquests in the capitalist age as well. The colonialists took advantage of India's political fragmentation, its communal heterogeneity, and the strife between the local rulers, and bribed members of the local aristocracy to win their support. Binding the native sovereign princes to them by a system of subsidiary treaties, promissory notes and other bonds of "alliance", they turned them into the Company's puppets. "After having won over their allies in the way of ancient Rome, the East India Company executed them in the modern manner of Change-Alley," wrote Marx, comparing the methods of the colonialists to the practices of one of the centres of usury in London (see this volume, p. 197). The robbery and usurpation committed by the Company in India served as a source of wealth and strength for the land-owning magnates and money-lords in Britain itself.

While revealing the essence and methods of colonial policy, Marx at the same time showed by his analysis of the internal situation in India and other Eastern countries the reason for their retarded historical development in the periods preceding conquest. He saw the source of their backwardness and weakness, as a result of which they became easy prey for conquerors, in the isolated nature of the small village communities, in the concentration of considerable means of production in the hands of despotic rulers, which impeded the emergence of a capitalist economy, and in other specific features of the social system of the Asian countries, which had at one time attained a high level of civilisation.

Marx gives a vivid portrayal of the British colonialists' predatory rule in India and its appalling consequences for the peoples of that country. Having inherited from the Eastern rulers such branches of administration as the financial and war departments, and using them to rob and oppress the people, the British rulers of India disregarded a third branch, to which even the Eastern despots devoted attention—the department of public works. As a result, irrigated farming in India fell into total decline. The competition of British manufactures was disastrous for local handicraft production, particularly hand-spinning and hand-weaving, and doomed millions of people to poverty and death. A great burden was put upon the population by the land and salt taxes and the whole system of financial extortion practised by the colonialists. While destroying old patriarchal forms of communal land-owning, the British retained in India's social and political system numerous feudal forms which hampered the country's progressive development.

Marx showed that the system of land-tenure and land taxes introduced by the British in India essentially consolidated pre-capitalist relations in the countryside and adapted them to the interests of the colonialists. It strengthened the various forms of shackling tenure in India's agrarian system, and increased the exploitation of the peasants by the landowners, land middlemen and tax collectors to the absolute limit. As a result, Marx remarks, "the Ryots—and they form 11/12ths of the whole Indian population—have been wretchedly pauperized" (see this volume, p. 215).

Pre-capitalist forms of exploitation flourished under colonial rule in other enslaved countries too—in particular, Ireland, which Marx and Engels considered the first British colony. In the article "The Indian Question.—Irish Tenant Right", for example, Marx vividly compared the extortion practised by landlords on the enslaved Irish tenants—an extortion legalised by the British—with the relations "between the robber who presents his pistol, and the traveler who presents his purse" (see this volume, p. 160).

In the article "Revolution in China and in Europe" Marx also showed the pernicious consequences of the intervention of European capital in the internal life of the Asian countries. He pointed to the destructive influence of the competition of British goods on Chinese local industry, to the drain of silver from the country as a result of the import of opium, which threatened to ruin the Chinese economy, and to the enormous growth of taxes in connection with the payment of the indemnity imposed on China by Britain at the end of the First Opium War.

The colonial administrative, legal and military apparatus was a parasite on the body of the oppressed country. Marx showed that under the extraordinarily confused and cumbersome system of government in India true power was wielded by a clique of officials from the head office of the East India Company in London. "...The real Home Government of India are the permanent and irresponsible *bureaucracy*" (see this volume, p. 183).

Marx used the example of British rule in India to show the contradictoriness and double-faced nature of the bourgeois system as a whole, and revealed the reverse side of progress under the rule of the exploiters. The period of the rule of the bourgeoisie, he pointed out in the article "The Future Results of British Rule in India", was in general to create the material basis for a new, socialist society. However, these material prerequisites, the powerful productive forces which constitute the foundation of bourgeois civilisation, are created at the cost of incredible sufferings on the part of the masses. Whole peoples are doomed by the bourgeois age to follow the bitter path of blood and filth, poverty and humiliation. Only after the socialist revolution, he wrote, will "human progress cease to resemble that hideous pagan idol, who would not drink the nectar but from the skulls of the slain" (see this volume, p. 222).

At a time when the colonial system of capitalism was still in the process of formation, Marx saw that it bore the seeds of its own destruction. He noted, for example, that the British colonialists of India, who were motivated solely by the pursuit of profit, would be compelled, against their will, to promote the development of elements of capitalism in their colony, in particular, to commence railway construction and create related branches of industry. By permitting, albeit in a colonially distorted form, the birth of capitalist economy, the colonialists were bringing to life forces which threatened their rule—a local proletariat and a national bourgeoisie, which were capable of giving a more organised and stable character to the growing resistance of the masses to colonial oppression. These processes had barely begun at that time, but Marx was already fully aware of their significance for the future of the colonial world. He foresaw the growth of the opposition of the masses to the colonialists in India and other oppressed countries. In the article "Revolution in China and in Europe" he noted, in particular, the great successes of the Taiping peasant rebellion. The Taiping movement was ostensibly directed against the oppression of the foreign Manchu nobility. At the same time, like other progressive liberation movements in the East, it was an anti-colonial movement. Its advent was accelerated by "English cannon forcing upon China that soporific drug called opium" (see this volume, p. 93).

Marx saw in the liberation struggle of the enslaved peoples and the victory of the proletariat in the metropolis the two conditions for freeing the oppressed countries from colonial oppression and for their true social rebirth. The population of India, he wrote, would be unable to benefit from the fruits of modern civilisation "till in Great Britain itself the now ruling classes shall have been supplanted by the industrial proletariat, or till the Hindoos themselves shall have grown strong enough to throw off the English yoke altogether" (see this volume, p. 221).

Thus, Marx saw two possible paths for the future liberation of the colonies, which he by no means regarded as mutually exclusive. He considered the struggle of the working class for proletarian revolution in the capitalist countries and the national liberation movement as two interconnected aspects of the revolutionary process.

His discovery of the profound inner connection between the processes of revolutionary ferment in the colonial world and the maturing of the prerequisites for proletarian revolution in the West was perhaps the most important result of Marx's study of colonial problems. In his articles he showed that the drawing of the colonial and dependent countries into the orbit of capitalist relations would inevitably sharpen the antagonisms of the capitalist world, and that the national liberation movement in these countries, by inflicting blows on the capitalist colonial system, would weaken the position of capitalism in the metropolis. Marx referred to the revolutionary processes in the East as a spark thrown into the "overloaded mine of the present industrial system" (see this volume, p. 98). Conversely, as all Marx's articles on India, Ireland and China show, the working class of the capitalist countries must in the long term benefit from the destruction of the colonial system, and should render all possible assistance to the liberation of the colonies.

Marx's studies of national and colonial problems in his articles of 1853 and subsequent years were vital contributions to revolutionary theory and provided the foundation for working-class policy on the colonial question. They were the point of departure for Lenin's subsequent analysis of imperialism, and of the liberation movement in the colonial and dependent countries as an integral part of the world-wide anti-imperialist revolutionary process.

Marx and Engels examined problems of international relations in the context of prospects for the proletarian and national liberation movement. The articles on these questions constitute a considerable section of the present volume. The experience of the revolution of 1848-49 convinced Marx and Engels of the important role of diplomacy and foreign policy. Diplomatic means were used extensively by the reactionary forces of absolutist states and the ruling bourgeoisie for the achievement of counter-revolutionary ends. Marx and Engels considered, as Marx later formulated it in the "Inaugural Address of the Working Men's International Association", that one of the most important tasks of proletarian revolutionaries was to understand the secrets of international politics and to expose the machinations of the diplomacy of the ruling classes and their aggressive designs. In the working class they saw a real social force capable of effectively counteracting the aggressive policies of governments. They stressed the need for the working class to pursue its own revolutionary line in international conflicts, aimed at thorough-going bourgeois-democratic transformations in Europe and the preparation of the conditions for a victorious proletarian revolution. It was from this position, the position of the "Sixth Power", as Marx and Engels called the European revolution, contrasting it with the five "Great Powers" of the day (see this volume, p. 557), that they approached all international questions.

In their numerous articles on these subjects Marx and Engels exposed the whole system of international relations which had taken shape since the Congress of Vienna in 1815. They saw this system as an obstacle to the progressive development of Europe, the liberation of the oppressed nations, and the national unification of politically disunited countries. Statesmen and diplomats clung to this decrepit system, but not from any belief in the principle of observing international agreements. Marx showed in many of his articles that the treaties of 1815 were constantly violated by the rulers of European states when it suited their purpose. Thus the traditional cunning methods of the diplomacy of the ruling classes continued to flourish on the basis of established international relations. Marx and Engels in their articles condemned its practice of setting nations against one another, of intimidation and blackmail, and blatant interference in the internal affairs of small states. In the article "Political Position of the Swiss Republic", in particular, Engels pointed out that the declared neutrality of the small states had in fact become a pure formality and that the existing "European political system" doomed these states to the role of lackeys of the counter-revolutionary forces and the "scapegoat" in the diplomatic game of the Great Powers (see this volume, p. 86).

At the centre of the attention of Marx and Engels at that time were the contradictions between the European powers in the Middle East, the struggle for the partition of the Turkish Empire, for control of the Bosphorus and the Dardanelles, and for predominance in the Balkans and the countries of Asia Minor. A long series of articles by Marx and Engels is devoted to "the Eastern question", the aggravation of which led to the outbreak of the Crimean War. Already in the first articles on this subject, which were written by Engels—the section "Turkey" in the article "British Politics.—Disraeli.—The Refugees.—Mazzini in London.—Turkey", the articles "The Real Issue in Turkey", "The Turkish Question", and "What Is to Become of Turkey in Europe?"—Marx's and Engels' position on this question was substantially outlined. Their point of view was further developed in Marx's articles "The Turkish Question.—*The Times*.—Russian Aggrandizement", "The War Question.—Doings of Parliament.—India", "The Western Powers and Turkey", and others.

Analysing the position in the Middle East and the Balkans, Marx and Engels revealed the economic, political and military causes of the rivalry between the European powers in this region. The complexity of the problem, in their opinion, lay in the fact that this competition was linked with international confrontations caused by the liberation movement of the Balkan peoples against the rule of feudal Turkey.

In contrast to West European politicians and diplomats, who concealed their aggressive aims in the Middle East behind the doctrine of maintaining the *status quo* as established by the

Congress of Vienna and the pretence of defending the inviolability of the feudal Ottoman Empire, Marx and Engels saw that Empire as a great obstacle to historical progress and the development of the Balkan peoples who were under the rule of the Ottoman conquerors. The revolutionary-democratic solution to the Eastern question lay, in their opinion, first and foremost, in the granting of independence and the right to choose the form of their future state system to the Southern Slavs and all the peoples of the Balkan Peninsula. Marx wrote that the choice would depend on the concrete historical conditions. He did not exclude the possibility of the creation in the Balkans of a Federal Republic of Slavonic States (see this volume, p. 212).

A genuine solution to the Middle East crisis, Marx and Engels stressed, should not be expected from the Western politicians. "The solution of the Turkish problem is reserved, with that of other great problems, to the European Revolution," wrote Engels (see this volume, p. 34). Moreover he foresaw the possibility of the revolution spreading eastwards. Already in 1789 the boundaries of revolution had begun steadily to extend further and further. "The last revolutionary outposts were Warsaw, Debreczin, Bucharest; the advanced posts of the next revolution must be Petersburg and Constantinople" (see this volume, p. 34).

Marx and Engels denounced in particular the policy of Tsarist autocracy, its role of gendarme in Europe, its striving for aggrandisement. Tsarism, they stressed, sought to use for counter-revolutionary and aggressive aims the sincere sympathy which the peoples of the Balkan Peninsula felt for Russia, particularly since its victory in the wars with Turkey had actually facilitated the liberation of those peoples from Turkish oppression. But Tsarist autocracy, the oppressor of the Russian people and the other peoples of the Russian Empire, was the worst enemy of revolution. The strengthening of Tsarism presented a serious threat to the democratic and working-class movement in Europe.

Marx's and Engels' detestation of Tsarism was shared by the progressive representatives of revolutionary democracy, first and foremost, by the Russian revolutionaries themselves. "Half a century ago," Lenin wrote in 1903, "Russia's reputation as an international gendarme was firmly established. In the course of the last century our autocracy rendered no small support to various reactionary causes in Europe even to the point of crushing by downright military force the revolutionary movements in neighbouring countries. One has only to recall the Hungarian campaign of Nicholas I, and the repeated repressions of Poland, to understand why the leaders of the international socialist proletariat from the forties onward denounced tsarism so often to the European workers and European democrats as the chief mainstay of reaction in the whole civilised world.

"Beginning with the last three decades or so of the nineteenth century, the revolutionary movement in Russia gradually altered this state of affairs. The more tsarism was shaken by the blows of the growing revolutionary movement at home, the weaker it became as the enemy of freedom in Europe" (Lenin, *Collected Works*, Vol. 15, p. 461).

Marx and Engels regarded the exposure of the self-seeking, anti-democratic position of the ruling circles of the Western powers, above all, of Britain and France, as one of the main aims of their articles on the Eastern question.

In their view the essence of the foreign policy of these powers was to strive to weaken Russia as a rival in the struggle for supremacy in the Middle East and the Balkans, while at the same time seeking to preserve Tsarism as a dependable weapon and bulwark of counter-revolutionary regimes in Europe. The desire to prevent the revolutionary consequences of the collapse of Tsarism and to avoid a decisive clash with Tsarism on the assumption that it would continue to perform the services of a gendarme in the future revealed, to quote Marx, "the mean and abject spirit of the European middle classes" (see this volume, p. 590). However, he stressed that all the ambiguous manoeuvres and tricks of Western diplomacy—the provocative incitement of the Sultan to offer resistance to Tsarist Russia, while at the same time conniving with the Tsar, and the attempt to perform a mediatory role as "peace-maker"—could only aggravate the situation and precipitate the impending military conflict. Western diplomats and politicians, Marx stated, "will not get rid of their embarrassment in this sneaking way" (see this volume, p. 561). The hostilities between Russia and Turkey which began in October 1853 were inevitably developing into a European war.

The France of Napoleon III, Marx stressed, played the role of one of the main instigators of the Crimean War. "The Bonapartist usurpation, therefore," he pointed out, "is the true origin of the present Eastern complication" (see this volume, p. 615). In the article "The London Press.—Policy of Napoleon on the Turkish Question", and others Marx exposed the adventurism and dynastic aims of Louis Bonaparte and his supporters in the Eastern question. For the ruler of the Second Empire foreign adventures were a means of preserving the counter-revolutionary Bonapartist dictatorship and a way for the usurper of the imperial throne of France to gain recognition from the European monarchs as one of those who decided the fate of Europe.

Marx's articles "Urquhart.—Bem.—The Turkish Question in the House of Lords", "The Turkish Question in the Commons", "The Quadruple Convention.—England and the War", "The Czar's Views.—Prince Albert", "Russian Diplomacy.—The Blue Book on the Eastern Question.—Montenegro". and many others dealt with the position of the British ruling circles on the Eastern question. They contain a scathing criticism of the foreign policy of the British Government which, as Marx and Engels frequently stressed, was dictated by the interests of the bourgeois-aristocratic oligarchy. The founders of Marxism saw this policy as a manifestation of the counter-revolutionary role which Britain played in Europe during the wars against the French Revolution of 1789-94 and in 1848-49, when the British bourgeoisie in league with Tsarism and other reactionary forces acted as the suppressor of the revolutionary movement. Marx and Engels stressed that British ruling circles were especially apprehensive lest the conflict with Russia on the Eastern question should develop into a general revolutionary conflagration on the continent, which might find a response among the mass of the people in Great Britain. This factor, they noted, left its mark on the whole of British diplomacy.

By their criticism of the British ruling oligarchy, which was acting as a counter-revolutionary force not only in Great Britain itself, but also in the international arena, Marx and Engels sought to promote the democratic struggle for a change in the domestic and foreign policy of Great Britain. This was the aim, in particular, of a series of revealing articles by Marx entitled "Lord Palmerston", which were printed in *The People's Paper* and, in part, in the *New-York Daily Tribune.* Some of the articles in this series were reprinted in Britain in the form of pamphlets.

"Lord Palmerston" is a brilliant *exposé* written on the basis of a detailed study of numerous diplomatic documents, parliamentary debates and the press. In this work Marx draws a remarkably accurate and witty portrait of the eminent statesman of bourgeois-aristocratic Britain. His description of Palmerston actually contains an assessment of the whole British system of government, the whole political course of official Britain, the characteristic features of its diplomacy, its striving to exploit other nations for its own ends, its provocative role in many European conflicts, and its perfidious attitude to its allies. Marx revealed the class roots of this system, showing that British statesmen of the Palmerston type were concerned above all that no clouds should darken "the bright sky of the landlords and moneylords" (see this volume, p. 351).

Analysing Palmerston's stand on the Irish question and his attitude towards the Italian, Hungarian and Polish national movements, Marx revealed the anti-democratic, anti-revolutionary character of British policy which was demagogically concealed by liberal phrases and hypocritical expressions of sympathy for the victims of despotism. A self-proclaimed supporter of "constitutionalism", Palmerston was in Britain itself the initiator of repressive measures and the opponent of all progressive reforms, while in Europe—in Greece, Spain and Portugal—he supported the reactionary monarchist governments and flirted with Bonapartist circles in France.

Palmerston, Marx emphasises, possessed remarkable political cunning, and an actor's ability to play the role required by this or that situation, in keeping with the British two-party system and the constant polemics between representatives of the government party and the opposition. Marx regarded as one of the main features of Palmerston's political art the ability to represent actions taken in the interest of bourgeois-aristocratic circles as national policy, his feigned concern for the well-being and prestige of the British nation. Palmerston proclaimed himself everywhere as a "truly English minister".

In stressing the similarity between the counter-revolutionary aspirations of Russian Tsarism and of the British oligarchy, however, Marx somewhat exaggerated Palmerston's subservient role in relation to the Tsarist autocracy. The position of Palmerston, as of other leading British statesmen, on the Eastern question was determined not only by fear of revolution and the desire to make use of the Russian autocracy in the struggle against it, but also by the British ruling class's own aggressive aspirations in the Middle East, its expansionist ambitions with respect to the Caucasus, and its plans to build up its own supremacy at the expense of Tsarist Russia. This was, indeed, one of the main causes of the Crimean War.

In writing the pamphlet against Palmerston, and in a number of other works, Marx made use of factual material from the articles and brochures of David Urquhart, then a leading figure in propaganda about "the Russian menace" to Britain. And this caused several newspapers, and also bourgeois historians of a later period, to conclude that Marx and Urquhart shared the same position on the Eastern question. However, in fact, as the works in the present volume show, Marx and Engels disagreed radically with Urquhart and regarded his views as on the whole reactionary. Particularly noteworthy in this respect is the article "David Urquhart", published in *Die Reform.* In it Marx attacked the emotional attitudinising of David Urquhart, "who is basically conservative", his arbitrary interpretation of revolutionary events as, allegedly, the result of the machinations of Tsarist diplomacy, his Russophobia, and his idealisation of the feudal Ottoman Empire and the reactionary Empire of the Habsburgs. Marx also emphatically refutes Urquhart's conception of history as "more or less exclusively the work of diplomacy" (see this volume, p. 478). Marx regarded Urquhart's denunciation of the foreign policy of Palmerston and the Tsarist government as the only positive aspect of his activity.

When the Crimean War began, Marx and Engels followed its course with the greatest attention. Engels wrote a number of reviews on the fighting on the Danubian and Caucasian fronts, and also on the Black Sea ("The Holy War", "The War on the Danube", "The Last Battle in Europe", and others). These reviews were written immediately after the events in question and some of them inevitably show traces of the influence of the one-sided and sometimes also tendentious information about them in the Western press, which Engels could not immediately check from other sources. As a result of this, his assessment of, in particular, the sea-battle of Sinope on November 30, 1853, in the article "Progress of the Turkish War", was inaccurate. In his reviews (see this volume, pp. 471-73, 520-22) Engels amended some exaggerated statistics about the strength of the Russian troops on the Danube which he had quoted in the articles "The Russians in Turkey" and "Movements of the Armies in Turkey" on the basis of information in the Western press. Nevertheless, Engels' long series of articles on the Crimean War, published in this volume, and also in Volumes 13 and 14 of the present edition, occupies an important place in his writings on military theory. It contains important observations and conclusions on questions of the art of warfare, military strategy and tactics. In analysing the political and military aspects of the Crimean War Marx and Engels worked out a general tactical line for the revolutionary proletariat in this major European military conflict. They arrived at the conclusion that the policy of the ruling classes, whose aggressive aims had plunged the peoples into bloodshed, should be contrasted with the idea of a revolutionary war against Tsarism in the name of the democratic reorganisation of Europe, the liberation of the Poles, Hungarians, Southern Slavs and other oppressed peoples, and the national unification of Germany and also Italy by revolutionary means. Such a war, in their opinion, would inflict a telling blow on Tsarist autocracy, facilitate the liberation of the peoples of Russia, and lead to the collapse of counter-revolutionary regimes in Western

Europe, France and Britain included, and thereby advance the victory of the West European working class.

In this volume four works by Marx are published for the first time in English—"Hirsch's Confessions", "David Urquhart", *The Knight of the Noble Consciousness,* and "Apropos Carey". The articles by Marx and Engels written in English, mainly from the *New-York Daily Tribune,* are published for the first time in the language of the original in collected form (publication in part of a number of them in the collection *The Eastern Question,* London, 1897, is indicated in the notes).

As Marx and Engels repeatedly pointed out in their correspondence, the editors of the *New-York Daily Tribune* treated their articles in a somewhat arbitrary fashion, particularly those which were printed, unsigned, in the form of editorials. During the preparation of this volume editorial insertions were discovered in some of these articles. These insertions are reproduced in the present edition in notes to the relevant passages in the given article. Parallel publications in the *New-York Daily Tribune* and *The People's Paper* have been collated. Important divergencies between the two texts are indicated in footnotes. Rare instances of discrepancies in the texts of the *New-York Daily Tribune* and its special issues—the *New-York Semi-Weekly Tribune* and *New-York Weekly Tribune*—are also indicated in footnotes, with the exception of corrections of misprints made in the main issue. In this case corrections are made in the text without special mention. Obvious misprints in quotations, proper names, geographical names, numbers, dates, etc., discovered in the text of the *New-York Daily Tribune* and other newspapers, have been corrected after checking with the sources used by Marx and Engels. The articles are published under the titles under which they appeared in the newspapers. In cases when an article bore no title in the original, the editorial heading is given in square brackets.

The volume was compiled and the preface, notes, subject index and the index of quoted and mentioned literature written by Tatyana Vasilyeva and edited by Lev Golman (CC CPSU Institute of Marxism-Leninism). The indexes of names and of periodicals were prepared by Galina Kostryukova (CC CPSU Institute of Marxism-Leninism).

The translations were made by Clemens Dutt, Rodney Livingstone, and Joan and Trevor Walmsley and were edited by Maurice Cornforth and Nicholas Jacobs (Lawrence and Wishart) and Victor Schneierson (Progress Publishers).

The volume was prepared for the press by the editors Tatyana Grishina, Victor Schnittke, Lyudgarda Zubrilova and Alla Varavitskaya, and the assistant editors Nadezhda Korneyeva and Alexander Strelnikov for Progress Publishers, and Vladimir Mosolov, scientific editor, for the Institute of Marxism-Leninism of the CC CPSU.

KARL MARX
and
FREDERICK ENGELS

WORKS

March 1853-February 1854

NEW-YORK DAILY TRIBUNE.

VOL. XII......NO. 3,736. NEW-YORK, THURSDAY, APRIL 7, 1853. PRICE TWO CENTS.

Karl Marx and Frederick Engels

BRITISH POLITICS.—DISRAELI.— THE REFUGEES.—MAZZINI IN LONDON.—TURKEY[1]

London, Tuesday, March 22, 1853

The most important event in the contemporaneous history of parties is Disraeli's deposition from the leadership of the "great Conservative" minority.[2] Disraeli, it has transpired, was himself prepared to throw overboard his former allies eight or nine weeks before the dissolution of the Tory Cabinet, and desisted from his resolution only at the urgent instance of Lord Derby. He in his turn, is now dismissed and has been formally replaced by Sir John Pakington, a safe character, cautious, not altogether wanting in administrative ability, but a mournful man otherwise, the very incarnation of the worn-out prejudices and antiquated feelings of the old English squireocracy. This change in leadership amounts to a complete, and perhaps to the final transformation of the Tory party.—Disraeli may congratulate himself on his emancipation from the landed humbugs. Whatever be our opinion of the man, who is said to despise the aristocracy, to hate the *bourgeoisie*, and not to like the people; he is unquestionably the ablest member of the present Parliament, while the flexibility of his character enables him the better to accommodate himself to the changing wants of society.

In reference to the Refugee question I told you in my last,[a] that after Lord Palmerston's speech in the House of Commons, the Austrian journals declared it to be useless to ask for redress from a Cabinet corrupted by Palmerstonian influence. But scarcely was Aberdeen's declaration in the House of Lords telegraphed to

[a] K. Marx, "Kossuth and Mazzini.—Intrigues of the Prussian Government.—Austro-Prussian Commercial Treaty.—*The Times* and the Refugees" (see present edition, Vol. 11, pp. 535-41).—*Ed.*

Vienna when the aspect of things changed again.[3] The same journals now assert that "Austria trusts to the honor of the English Cabinet," and the semi-official *Oesterreichische Correspondenz* publishes the following from its Paris Correspondent:

"Lord Cowley, on his return to Paris, stated to the Emperor of the French,[a] that the diplomatic representatives of England at the Northern Courts had been formally instructed to employ all their efforts to deter the Northern Powers from forwarding a collective note to the British Government, and to urge, as the ground for such abstention, that that Government would be the better enabled to *comply with the demand of those powers,* the more it could keep up, in all eyes of England, the appearance of *acting freely and voluntarily in the matter....*

"The British Ambassador, Lord Cowley, urged the Emperor of the French to place implicit confidence on the British Cabinet, the more so as the Emperor would always be at liberty to take any steps he might consider proper in the event of that confidence not having been justified.... The Emperor of the French, while reserving to himself full freedom of action for the future, was induced *to put the sincerity of the British Cabinet to the proof,* and he is now endeavoring to persuade the other powers to follow his example."

You see what is expected from "*ce cher Aberdeen,*" as Louis Philippe used to call him, and what promises he must have made. These promises are actually already followed up by deeds. Last week the English Police drew up a list of the Continental refugees residing in London. Several detectives, in plain clothes, walked from square to square, from street to street, and from house to house, making notes on the personale of the refugees, addressing themselves in the majority of cases to the publicans in the neighborhood, but entering in some instances, under the pretense of the pursuit of criminals, the very domiciles and searching the papers of some exiles.

While the Continental Police is vainly hunting after Mazzini, while at Nuremberg the magistrates have ordered the closure of the gates in order to catch him—no man being hanged there before he is caught, according to the old German proverb—while the English press publishes reports after reports as to his supposed sojourn, Mazzini has for the past few days been safe and sound at London.

Prince Menchikoff, after reviewing the Russian forces stationed in the Danubian Principalities, and after an inspection of the army and fleet at Sebastopol, where he caused manoeuvres of embarking and disembarking troops to be executed under his own eyes, entered Constantinople in the most theatrical style on Feb. 28,

---

[a] Napoleon III.—*Ed.*

attended by a suite of 12 persons, including the Admiral of the Russian squadron in the Black Sea,[a] a General of Division,[b] and several staff officers, with M. de Nesselrode, Jr., as Secretary of the Embassy. He met with such a reception from the Greek and Russian inhabitants as he were the orthodox Czar himself entering *Tsarigrad* to restore it to the true faith. An enormous sensation was created here and at Paris, by the news that Prince Menchikoff, not satisfied with the dismissal of Fuad Effendi, had demanded that the Sultan should abandon to the Emperor of Russia, not only the protection of all the Christians in Turkey, but also the right of nominating the Greek patriarch; that the Sultan had appealed to the protection of England and France; that Colonel Rose, the British Envoy, had dispatched the steamer *Wasp* in haste to Malta to request the immediate presence of the English fleet in the Archipelago, and that Russian vessels had anchored at Kilia, near the Bosphorus.[c] The Paris *Moniteur* informs us that the French squadron at Toulon had been ordered to the Grecian waters.[d] Admiral Dundas, however, is still at Malta. From all this, it is evident, that the Eastern Question is once more on the European "*ordre du jour*," a fact not astonishing for those who are acquainted with history.

Whenever the revolutionary hurricane has subsided for a moment, one ever-recurring question is sure to turn up: the eternal "*Eastern Question*." Thus, when the storms of the first French revolution had passed, and Napoleon and Alexander of Russia had divided, after the peace of Tilsit, the whole of Continental Europe[4] betwixt themselves, Alexander profited by the momentary calm to march an army into Turkey, and to "give a lift" to the forces that were breaking up from within that decaying empire. Again, no sooner had the revolutionary movements of Western Europe[5] been quelled by the Congresses of Laybach and Verona, than Alexander's successor, Nicholas, made another dash at Turkey. When a few years later, the revolution of July, with its concomitant insurrections in Poland, Italy, Belgium, had had its turn, and Europe, as remodeled in 1831, seemed out of the reach of domestic squalls, the Eastern Question, in 1840, appeared on the point of embroiling the "great Powers" in a general war.[6] And now, when the shortsightedness of the ruling

[a] V. A. Kornilov.—*Ed.*
[b] A. A. Nepokoichitsky.—*Ed.*
[c] The *New-York Daily Tribune* erroneously has "Dardanelles".—*Ed.*
[d] *Le Moniteur universel*, No. 79, March 20, 1853.—*Ed.*

pigmies prides itself in having successfully freed Europe from the dangers of anarchy and revolution, up starts again the everlasting topic, the never-failing difficulty: What shall we do with Turkey?

Turkey is the living sore of European legitimacy.[7] The impotency of legitimate, monarchical government, ever since the first French Revolution, has resumed itself in the one axiom: Keep up the *status quo.* A *testimonium paupertatis,* an acknowledgment of the universal incompetence of the ruling powers, for any purpose of progress or civilization, is seen in this universal agreement to stick to things as by chance or accident they happen to be. Napoleon could dispose of a whole continent at a moment's notice; aye, and dispose of it, too, in a manner that showed both genius and fixedness of purpose; the entire "collective wisdom" of European legitimacy, assembled in Congress at Vienna, took a couple of years to do the same job, got at loggerheads over it, made a very sad mess, indeed, of it, and found it such a dreadful bore that ever since they have had enough of it, and have never tried their hands again at parceling out Europe. Myrmidons of mediocrity, as Béranger calls them,[a] without historical knowledge or insight into facts, without ideas, without initiative, they adore the *status quo* they themselves have bungled together, knowing what a bungling and blundering piece of workmanship it is.

But Turkey no more than the rest of the world remains stationary; and just when the reactionary party has succeeded in restoring in civilized Europe what they consider to be the *status quo ante,* it is perceived that in the meantime the *status quo* in Turkey has been very much altered, that new questions, new relations, new interests have sprung up, and that the poor diplomatists have to begin again where they were interrupted by a general earthquake some eight or ten years before. Keep up the *status quo* in Turkey! Why, you might as well try to keep up the precise degree of putridity into which the carcass of a dead horse has passed at a given time, before dissolution is complete. Turkey goes on decaying, and will go on decaying as long as the present system of "balance of power" and maintenance of the "status quo" goes on, and in spite of Congresses, protocols and ultimatums it will produce its yearly quota of diplomatic difficulties and international

---

[a] P. J. Béranger, *Les Mirmidons, ou les funérailles d'Achille.* There is a pun in the title of this allegory: "les mirmidons" meaning a warlike Thessalian race who accompanied Achilles to the Trojan War, and "mirmidon" also denotes "shorty, dwarf, good-for-nothing".—*Ed.*

squabbles quite as every other putrid body will supply the neighborhood with a due allowance of carburetted hydrogen and other well-scented gaseous matter.

Let us look at the question at once. Turkey consists of three entirely distinct portions: the vassal principalities of Africa, viz. Egypt and Tunis; Asiatic Turkey, and European Turkey. The African possessions, of which Egypt alone may be considered as really subject to the Sultan, may be left for the moment out of the question; Egypt belongs more to the English than to anybody else, and will and must necessarily form their share in any future partition of Turkey. Asiatic Turkey is the real seat of whatever strength there is in the Empire; Asia Minor and Armenia, for four hundred years the chief abode of the Turks, form the reserved ground from which the Turkish armies have been drawn, from those that threatened the ramparts of Vienna, to those that dispersed before Diebitsch's not very skillful manoeuvers at Kulevcha.[8] Turkey in Asia, although thinly populated, yet forms too compact a mass of Mussulman fanaticism and Turkish nationality to invite at present any attempts at conquest; and in fact whenever the "Eastern Question" is mooted, the only portions of this territory taken into consideration, are Palestine and the Christian valleys of the Lebanon.

The real point at issue always is, Turkey in Europe—the great peninsula to the south of the Save and Danube. This splendid territory has the misfortune to be inhabited by a conglomerate of different races[9] and nationalities, of which it is hard to say which is the least fit for progress and civilization. Slavonians, Greeks, Wallachians, Arnauts,[a] twelve millions of men, are all held in submission by one million of Turks, and up to a recent period it appeared doubtful whether, of all these different races, the Turks were not the most competent to hold the supremacy which, in such a mixed population, could not but accrue to one of these nationalities. But when we see how lamentably have failed all the attempts at civilization by Turkish authority—how the fanaticism of Islam, supported principally by the Turkish mob in a few great cities, has availed itself of the assistance of Austria and Russia invariably to regain power and to overturn any progress that might have been made; when we see the central, *i.e.* Turkish authority weakened year after year by insurrections in the Christian provinces, none of which, thanks to the weakness of the Porte and to the intervention of neighboring States, is ever

[a] The Turkish name for Albanians.—*Ed.*

completely fruitless; when we see Greece acquire her independence, parts of Armenia conquered by Russia—Moldavia, Wallachia, Serbia, successively placed under the protectorate of the latter power,—we shall be obliged to admit that the presence of the Turks in Europe is a real obstacle to the development of the resources of the Thraco-Illyrian Peninsula.

We can hardly describe the Turks as the *ruling class* of Turkey, because the relations of the different classes of society there are as much mixed up as those of the various races. The Turk is, according to localities and circumstances, workman, farmer, small freeholder, trader, feudal landlord in the lowest and most barbaric stage of feudalism, civil officer, or soldier; but in all these different social positions he belongs to the privileged creed and nation—he alone has the right to carry arms, and the highest Christian has to give up the footpath to the lowest Moslem he meets. In Bosnia and the Herzegovina, the nobility, of Slavonian descent, has passed over to Islam, while the mass of the people remain Rayahs, *i.e.* Christians. In this province, then, the ruling creed and the ruling class are identified, as of course the Moslem Bosnian is upon a level with his co-religionist of Turkish descent.

The principal power of the Turkish population in Europe, independently of the reserve always ready to be drawn from Asia, lies in the mob of Constantinople and a few other large towns. It is essentially Turkish, and though it finds its principal livelihood by doing jobs for Christian capitalists, it maintains with great jealousy the imaginary superiority and real impunity for excesses which the privileges of Islam confer upon it as compared with Christians. It is well known that this mob in every important *coup d'état* has to be won over by bribes and flattery. It is this mob alone, with the exception of a few colonized districts, which offers a compact and imposing mass of Turkish population in Europe. And certainly there will be, sooner or later, an absolute necessity of freeing one of the finest parts of this continent from the rule of a mob, compared to which the mob of Imperial Rome was an assemblage of sages and heroes.

Among the other nationalities, we may dispose in a very few words of the Arnauts, a hardy aboriginal mountain people, inhabiting the country sloping toward the Adriatic, speaking a language of their own, which, however, appears to belong to the great Indo-European stock. They are partly Greek Christians, partly Moslems, and, according to all we know of them, as yet very unprepared for civilization. Their predatory habits will force any neighboring government to hold them in close military subjection, until industrial progress in the surrounding districts shall find them employment as hewers of wood and drawers of water, the same as has been the case with the Gallegas[a] in Spain, and the inhabitants of mountainous districts generally.

The Wallachians or Daco-Romans, the chief inhabitants of the district between the Lower Danube and the Dniester, are a greatly mixed population, belonging to the Greek Church and speaking a language derived from the Latin, and in many respects not unlike the Italian. Those of Transylvania and the Bukovina belong to the Austrian, those of Bessarabia to the Russian Empire; those of Moldavia and Wallachia, the two only principalities where the Daco-Roman race has acquired a political existence, have Princes of their own, under the nominal *suzeraineté* of the Porte and the real dominion of Russia. Of the Transylvanian Wallachians we heard much during the Hungarian War[10]; hitherto oppressed by the feudalism of Hungarian landlords who were, according to the Austrian system, made at the same time the instruments of all Government exactions, this brutalized mass was in like manner as the Ruthenian serfs of Galicia in 1846,[11] won over by Austrian promises and bribes, and began that war of devastation which has made a desert of Transylvania. The Daco-Romans of the Turkish Principalities have at least a native nobility and political institutions; and in spite of all the efforts of Russia, the revolutionary spirit has penetrated among them, as the insurrection of 1848 well proved.[12] There can hardly be a doubt that the exactions and hardships inflicted upon them during the Russian occupation since 1848 must have raised this spirit still higher, in spite of the bond of common religion and Czaro-Popish superstition which has hitherto led them to look upon the imperial chief of the Greek Church as upon their natural protector. And if this is the case, the Wallachian nationality may yet play an important part in the ultimate disposal of the territories in question.

The Greeks of Turkey are mostly of Slavonic descent, but have adopted the modern Hellenic language; in fact, with the exception of a few noble families of Constantinople and Trebizond, it is now generally admitted that very little pure Hellenic blood is to be found even in Greece. The Greeks, along with the Jews, are the principal traders in the seaports and many inland towns. They are also tillers of the soil in some districts. In all cases, neither their numbers, compactness, nor spirit of nationality, give them any

[a] An ancient mountain people of Galicia.—*Ed.*

political weight as a nation, except in Thessaly and perhaps Epirus. The influence held by a few noble Greek families as dragomans (interpreters) in Constantinople, is fast declining, since Turks have been educated in Europe and European legations have been provided with attachés who speak Turkish.

We now come to the race that forms the great mass of the population and whose blood is preponderant wherever a mixture of races has occurred. In fact it may be said to form the principal stock of the Christian population from the Morea to the Danube, and from the Black Sea to the Arnaut Mountains. This race is the Slavonic race, and more particularly that branch of it which is resumed under the name of Illyrian (Ilirski), or South Slavonian (Jugoslavenski). After the Western Slavonian (Polish and Bohemian), and Eastern Slavonian (Russian), it forms the third branch of that numerous Slavonic family which for the last twelve hundred years has occupied the East of Europe. These southern Slavonians occupy not only the greater part of Turkey, but also Dalmatia, Croatia, Slavonia and the south of Hungary. They all speak the same language, which is much akin to the Russian, and by far to western ears, the most musical of all Slavonic tongues. The Croatians and part of the Dalmatians are Roman Catholics, all the remainder belong to the Greek Church. The Roman Catholics use the Latin alphabet, but the followers of the Greek Church write their language in the Cyrillian character,[13] which is also used in the Russian and old Slavonic or Church language. This circumstance connected with the difference of religion, has contributed to retard any national development embracing the whole south Slavonic territory. A man in Belgrade may not be able to read a book printed in his own language at Agram[a] or Betch,[b] he may object even to take it up, on account of the "heterodox" alphabet and orthography used therein; while he will have little difficulty in reading and understanding a book printed at Moscow, in the Russian language, because the two idioms, particularly in the old Slavonic etymological system of orthography, look very much alike, and because the book is printed in the "orthodox" (pravoslavni) alphabet. The mass of the Greek Slavonians will not even have their bibles, liturgies and prayer books printed in their own country, because they are convinced that there is a peculiar correctness and orthodoxy and odor of sanctity about anything printed in holy Moscow or in the imperial printing establishment

[a] Zagreb.— *Ed.*
[b] The Serbian name for Vienna.— *Ed.*

of St. Petersburg. In spite of all the panslavistic efforts of Agram and Prague enthusiasts,[14] the Serbian, the Bulgarian, the Bosnian Rayah, the Slavonian peasant of Macedonia and Thrace, has more national sympathy, more points of contact, more means of intellectual intercourse with the Russian than with the Roman Catholic south Slavonian who speaks the same language. Whatever may happen, he looks to St. Petersburg for the advent of the Messiah who is to deliver him from all evil; and if he calls Constantinople his *Tsarigrad* or Imperial City, it is as much in anticipation of the orthodox Tsar coming from the north and entering it to restore the true faith, as in recollection of the orthodox Tsar who held it before the Turks overrun the country.

Subjected in the greater part of Turkey to the direct rule of the Turk, but under local authorities of their own choice, partly (in Bosnia) converted to the faith of the conqueror, the Slavonian race has, in that country, maintained or conquered political existence in two localities. The one is Serbia, the valley of the Morava, a province with well defined natural lines of frontier, which played an important part in the history of these regions six hundred years ago. Subdued for a while by the Turks, the Russian war of 1806[15] gave it a chance of obtaining a separate existence, though under the Turkish supremacy. It has remained ever since under the immediate protection of Russia. But, as in Moldavia and Wallachia, political existence has brought on new wants, and forced upon Serbia an increased intercourse with Western Europe. Civilization began to take root, trade extended, new ideas sprang up; and thus we find in the very heart and stronghold of Russian influence, in Slavonic, orthodox Serbia, an anti-Russian, progressive party (of course, very modest in its demands of reform), headed by the ex-Minister of Finances Garašanin.[16]

There is no doubt that, should the Greco-Slavonian population ever obtain the mastery in the land which it inhabits and where it forms three-fourths of the whole population (seven millions), the same necessities would by and by give birth to an anti-Russian, progressive party, the existence of which has been hitherto the inevitable consequence of any portion of it having become semi-detached from Turkey.

In Montenegro, we have not a fertile valley with comparatively large cities, but a barren mountain country of difficult access. Here a set of robbers have fixed themselves, scouring the plains and storing the plunder in their mountain fastnesses. These romantic but rather uncouth gentlemen have long been a nuisance in Europe, and it is but in keeping with the policy of Russia and Austria that they should stick up for the rights of the Black Mountain people (Tsernogorci) to burn down villages, murder the inhabitants and carry off the cattle.

Written between March 12 and 22, 1853

First published in the *New-York Daily Tribune*, No. 3736, and the *Semi-Weekly Tribune*, No. 821, April 7, 1853; reprinted in the *New-York Weekly Tribune*, No. 604, April 9, 1853

Signed: *Karl Marx*

Reproduced from the *New-York Daily Tribune*

Frederick Engels

THE REAL ISSUE IN TURKEY[17]

We are astonished that in the current discussion of the Oriental Question the English journals have not more boldly demonstrated the vital interests which should render Great Britain the earnest and unyielding opponent of the Russian projects of annexation and aggrandizement. England cannot afford to allow Russia to become the possessor of the Dardanelles and Bosphorus. Both commercially and politically such an event would be a deep if not a deadly blow at British power. This will appear from a simple statement of facts as to her trade with Turkey.

Before the discovery of the direct route to India, Constantinople was the mart of an extensive commerce. And now, though the products of India find their way into Europe by the overland route through Persia, Turan[a] and Turkey, yet the Turkish ports carry on a very important and rapidly increasing traffic both with Europe and the interior of Asia. To understand this, it is only necessary to look at the map. From the Black Forest to the sandy hights of Novgorod Veliki, the whole inland country is drained by rivers flowing into the Black or Caspian Sea. The Danube and the Volga, the two giant-rivers of Europe, the Dniester, Dnieper and Don, all form so many natural channels for the carriage of inland produce to the Black Sea—for the Caspian itself is only accessible through the Black Sea. Two-thirds of Europe—that is, a part of Germany and Poland, all Hungary, and the most fertile parts of Russia, besides Turkey in Europe, are thus naturally referred to the Euxine[b] for the export and exchange of their produce; and

[a] The old name of the Turkestan Lowland.—*Ed.*
[b] Pontus Euxinus—ancient name of the Black Sea.—*Ed.*

the more so, as all these countries are essentially agricultural, and the great bulk of their products must always make water-carriage the predominant means of transport. The corn of Hungary, Poland, Southern Russia, the wool and the hides of the same countries appear in yearly increasing quantities in our Western[a] markets, and they all are shipped at Galatz, Odessa, Taganrog, and other Euxine ports. Then there is another important branch of trade carried on in the Black Sea. Constantinople, and particularly Trebizond, in Asiatic Turkey, are the chief marts of the caravan trade to the interior of Asia, to the valley of the Euphrates and Tigris, to Persia, and Turkestan. This trade, too, is rapidly increasing. The Greek and Armenian merchants of the two towns just named import large quantities of English manufactured goods, the low price of which is rapidly superseding the domestic industry of the Asiatic harems. Trebizond is better situated for such a trade than any other point. It has in its rear the hills of Armenia, which are far less impassable than the Syrian desert, and it lies at a convenient proximity to Bagdad, Shiraz, and Teheran, which latter place serves as an intermediate mart for the caravans from Khiva and Bokhara. How important this trade, and the Black Sea trade generally is becoming, may be seen at the Manchester Exchange, where dark-complexioned Greek buyers are increasing in numbers and importance, and where Greek and South-Slavonian dialects are heard along with German and English.

The trade of Trebizond is also becoming a matter of most serious political consideration, as it has been the means of bringing the interests of Russia and England anew into conflict in Inner Asia. The Russians had, up to 1840, an almost exclusive monopoly of the trade in foreign manufactured goods to that region. Russian goods were found to have made their way, and in some instances even to be preferred to English goods, as far down as the Indus. Up to the time of the Afghan war, the conquest of Scinde and the Punjab,[18] it may be safely asserted that the trade of England with Inner Asia was nearly null. The fact is now different. The supreme necessity of a never-ceasing expansion of trade—this *fatum* which, specter-like, haunts modern England, and, if not appeased at once, brings on those terrible revulsions which vibrate from New-York to Canton, and from St. Petersburg to Sidney—this inflexible necessity has caused the interior of Asia to be attacked from two sides by English trade: from the Indus

[a] The *New-York Weekly Tribune* has "English".—*Ed.*

and from the Black Sea; and although we know very little of the exports of Russia to that part of the world, we may safely conclude from the increase of English exports to that quarter, that the Russian trade in that direction must have sensibly fallen off. The commercial battle-field between England and Russia has been removed from the Indus to Trebizond, and the Russian trade, formerly venturing out as far as the limits of England's Eastern Empire, is now reduced to the defensive on the very verge of its own line of custom-houses. The importance of this fact with regard to any future solution of the Eastern Question, and to the part which both England and Russia may take in it, is evident. They are, and always must be, antagonists in the East.

But let us come to a more definite estimate of this Black Sea trade. According to the London *Economist*,[a] the British exports to the Turkish dominions, including Egypt and the Danubian Principalities, were:

In 1840	£1,440,592	In 1846	£2,707,571
In 1842	2,068,842	In 1848	3,626,241
In 1844	3,271,333	In 1850	3,762,480
In 1851	£3,548,959		

Of these amounts, at least two-thirds must have gone to ports in the Black Sea, including Constantinople. And all this rapidly increasing trade depends upon the confidence that may be placed in the power which rules the Dardanelles and the Bosphorus, the key to the Black Sea. Whoever holds these can open and shut at his pleasure the passage into this last recess of the Mediterranean. Let Russia once come into possession of Constantinople, who will expect her to keep open the door by which England has invaded her commercial domain?

So much for the commercial importance of Turkey, and especially the Dardanelles. It is evident that not only a very large trade, but the principal intercourse of Europe with Central Asia, and consequently the principal means of re-civilizing that vast region, depends upon the uninterrupted liberty of trading through these gates to the Black Sea.

Now for the military considerations. The commercial importance of the Dardanelles and Bosphorus at once makes them

---

[a] "Turkey and Its Value", *The Economist*, No. 498, March 12, 1853.—*Ed.*

first-rate military positions, that is, positions of decisive influence in any war. Such a point is Gibraltar, and such is Helsingör[a] in the Sound. But the Dardanelles are, from the nature of their locality, even more important. The cannon of Gibraltar or Helsingör cannot command the whole of the strait on which they are situated, and they require the assistance of a fleet in order to close it; while the narrowness of the strait at the Dardanelles and of the Bosphorus is such that a few properly-erected and well-armed fortifications, such as Russia, once in possession, would not tarry an hour to erect, might defy the combined fleets of the world if they attempted a passage. In that case, the Black Sea would be more properly a Russian lake than even the Lake of Ladoga, situated in its very heart. The resistance of the Caucasians would be starved out at once; Trebizond would be a Russian port; the Danube a Russian river. Besides, when Constantinople is taken, the Turkish Empire is cut in two; Asiatic and European Turkey have no means of communicating with or supporting each other, and while the strength of the Turkish army, repulsed into Asia, is utterly harmless, Macedonia, Thessaly, Albania, outflanked and cut off from the main body, will not put the conqueror to the trouble of subduing them; they will have nothing left but to beg for mercy and for an army to maintain internal order.

But having come thus far on the way to universal empire, is it probable that this gigantic and swollen power will pause in the career? Circumstances, if not her own will, forbid it. With the annexation of Turkey and Greece she has excellent seaports, while the Greeks furnish skillful sailors for her navy. With Constantinople, she stands on the threshold of the Mediterranean; with Durazzo and the Albanian coast from Antivari to Arta, she is in the very center of the Adriatic, within sight of the British Ionian islands, and within 36 hours' steaming of Malta. Flanking the Austrian dominions on the North, East and South, Russia will already count the Hapsburgs among her vassals. And then, another question is possible, is even probable. The broken and undulating western frontier of the Empire, ill-defined in respect of natural boundaries, would call for rectification, and it would appear that the natural frontier of Russia runs from Dantzic or perhaps Stettin to Trieste. And as sure as conquest follows conquest, and annexation follows annexation, so sure would the conquest of Turkey by Russia be only the prelude for the annexation of Hungary, Prussia, Galicia, and for the ultimate

---

[a] The *New-York Weekly Tribune* gives the English name "Elsinore".—*Ed.*

realization of the Slavonic Empire which certain fanatical Pan-slavistic philosophers have dreamed of.

Russia is decidedly a conquering nation, and was so for a century, until the great movement of 1789 called into potent activity an antagonist of formidable nature. We mean the European Revolution, the explosive force of democratic ideas and man's native thirst for freedom. Since that epoch there have been in reality but two powers on the continent of Europe—Russia and Absolutism, the Revolution and Democracy. For the moment the Revolution seems to be suppressed, but it lives and is feared as deeply as ever. Witness the terror of the reaction at the news of the late rising at Milan.[19] But let Russia get possession of Turkey, and her strength is increased nearly half, and she becomes superior to all the rest of Europe put together. Such an event would be an unspeakable calamity to the revolutionary cause. The maintenance of Turkish independence, or in case of a possible dissolution of the Ottoman Empire, the arrest of the Russian scheme of annexation is a matter of the highest moment. In this instance the interests of the revolutionary Democracy and of England go hand in hand. Neither can permit the Czar to make Constantinople one of his Capitals, and we shall find that when driven to the wall, the one will resist him as determinedly as the other.

Written between March 23 and 28, 1853

First published in the *New-York Daily Tribune*, No. 3740, April 12, 1853, as a leader; reprinted in the *New-York Weekly Tribune*, No. 605, April 16, 1853

Reproduced from the *New-York Daily Tribune*

Karl Marx

THE LONDON PRESS.—POLICY OF NAPOLEON ON THE TURKISH QUESTION[20]

London, March 25th, 1853

Until this morning no further authentic news has been received from Turkey. The Paris Correspondent of *The Morning Herald*, of to-day, asserts that he has been informed by responsible authority that the Russians have entered Bucharest. In the *Courrier de Marseille* of the 20th inst. we read:

"We are in a position to convey to the knowledge of our readers the substance of the note which has already been presented to the Sublime Porte by M. d'Ozeroff immediately after the departure of Count Leiningen, and before the brutal 'sortie' of the Prince Menchikoff in the midst of the Divan. The following are the principal points referred to in this diplomatic note. The Count de Nesselrode complained in the most lively terms that the Porte, in spite of its formal promise not to attack the Montenegrins, had carried on a sanguinary war against that people, which had given the greatest dissatisfaction to the Cabinet of St. Petersburg. In order, now, to secure a sufficient protection to the Montenegrins, and for their preservation from new disasters, Russia would invite the Porte to recognize the *independence of Montenegro*. The note contained also a protest against the blockade of the Albanian Coast, and in conclusion it pressed the demand upon the Sultan[a] to dismiss those ministers whose doings had always occasioned misunderstandings between the two governments. On the receipt of this note Turkey is said to have shown a disposition to yield, although with regret, to that one point relating to the dismission of ministers, particularly of Fuad Effendi, the Sultan's brother-in-law, who has actually been replaced by Rifaat Pasha, a partisan of Russia. The Porte, however, refused to acknowledge the independence of Montenegro. It was then that Prince Menchikoff, without previously paying the usual compliments to the Minister of Foreign Affairs, presented himself in the Divan, to the neglect of all diplomatic forms, and intimated in a bullying manner to that body to subscribe to his demands. In consequence of this demand the Porte invoked the protection of England and France."

---

[a] Abdul Mejid.—*Ed.*

In ancient Greece, an orator who was paid to remain silent, was said to have an *ox on his tongue*. The *ox*, be it remarked, was a silver coin imported from Egypt.[21] With regard to *The Times*, we may say that, during the whole period of the revived Eastern Question, it had also an ox on its tongue, if not for remaining silent, at least for speaking. At first, this ingenious paper defended the Austrian intervention in Montenegro, on the plea of Christianity. But afterwards, when Russia interfered, it dropped this argument, stating that the whole question was a quarrel between the Greek and Roman Churches, utterly indifferent to the "subjects" of the Established Church of England. Then, it dwelt on the importance of the Turkish commerce for Great Britain, inferring from that very importance, that Great Britain could but gain by exchanging Turkish Free-Trade for Russian prohibition and Austrian protection. It next labored to prove that England was dependent for her food upon Russia, and must therefore bow in silence to the geographical ideas of the Czar.[a] A gracious compliment this to the commercial system exalted by *The Times*, and a very pleasant argumentation, that to mitigate England's dependence on Russia, the Black Sea had to become a Russian lake, and the Danube a Russian river. Then, driven from these untenable positions, it fell back on the general statement that the Turkish Empire was hopelessly falling to pieces,—a conclusive proof this, in the opinion of *The Times*, that Russia presently must become the executor and heir of that Empire. Anon, *The Times* wanted to subject the inhabitants of Turkey to the "pure sway" and civilizing influence of Russia and Austria, remembering the old story that wisdom comes from the East, and forgetting its recent statement that "the state maintained by Austria in the provinces and kingdoms of her own Empire, was one of arbitrary authority and of executive, tyranny, regulated by no laws at all." In conclusion, and this is the strongest bit of impudence, *The Times* congratulates itself on the "brilliancy" of its Eastern leaders[b]!

The whole London Press, Morning Press and Evening Press, Daily Press and Weekly Press rose as one man against the "leading journal." *The Morning Post* mocks at the intelligence of its brethren of *The Times*, whom it accuses of spreading deliberately false and absurd news. *The Morning Herald* calls it "our Hebraeo-Austro-Russian contemporary," *The Daily News* more shortly the "Brun-

---

[a] Nicholas I.—*Ed.*

[b] See the leader in *The Times*, No. 21383, March 23, 1853.—*Ed.*

now organ."[a] Its twin-brother, *The Morning Chronicle* heaves at it the following blow:

"The journalists who have proposed to surrender the Turkish Empire to Russia, on the score of the commercial eminence of a dozen large [Anglo-]Greek firms, are quite right in claiming for themselves the monopoly of brilliancy!"[b]

The Morning Advertiser says:

"*The Times* is right in stating that it is isolated in its advocacy of Russian interests.... It is printed in the English language. But that is the only thing English about it. It is, where Russia is concerned, Russian all over."[c]

There is no doubt that the Russian bear will not draw in his paws, unless he be assured of a momentary "entente cordiale" between England and France.[22] Now mark the following wonderful coincidence. On the very day when *The Times* was trying to persuade my lords Aberdeen and Clarendon, that the Turkish affair was a mere squabble between France and Russia, the "roi des drôles"[d] as Guizot used to call him, M. Granier de Cassagnac, happened to discover in the *Constitutionnel*, that it was all nothing but a quarrel between Lord Palmerston and the Czar.[e] Truly, when we read these papers, we understand the Greek orators with Macedonian oxen on their tongues, at the times when Demosthenes fulminated his Philippics.

As for the British aristocracy represented by the Coalition Ministry, they would, if need be, sacrifice the national English interests to their particular class interests, and permit the consolidation of a juvenile despotism in the East in the hopes of finding a support for their valetudinarian oligarchy in the West. As to Louis Napoleon he is hesitating. All his predilections are on the side of the Autocrat, whose system of governing he has introduced into France, and all his antipathies are against England, whose parliamentary system he has destroyed there. Besides, if he permits the Czar's plundering in the East, the Czar will perhaps permit him to plunder in the West. On the other hand he is as quite sure of the feelings of the Holy Alliance with regard to the "parvenu Khan." Accordingly he observes an

[a] *The Morning Post*, No. 24726, March 22, 1853; *The Morning Herald*, No. 22115, March 25, 1853, and *The Daily News*, No. 2133, March 23, 1853.—*Ed.*

[b] *The Morning Chronicle*, No. 26910, March 24, 1853.—*Ed.*

[c] *The Morning Advertiser*, March 24, 1853.—*Ed.*

[d] King of the buffoons.—*Ed.*

[e] A. Granier de Cassagnac, "Des Affaires d'Orient", *Le Constitutionnel*, No. 83, March 24, 1853.—*Ed.*

ambiguous policy, striving to dupe the great powers of Europe as he duped the parliamentary parties of the French National Assembly. While fraternizing ostentatiously with the English ambassador for Turkey, Lord Stratford de Redcliffe, he simultaneously cajoles the Russian Princess de Lieven with the most flattering promises, and sends to the court of the Sultan M. De la Cour, a warm advocate of an Austro-French alliance, in contradistinction to an Anglo-French one. He orders the Toulon fleet to sail to the Grecian waters, and then announces the day afterward, in the *Moniteur*, that this had been done without any previous communication with England. While he orders one of his organs, the *Pays*, to treat the Eastern Question as most important to France, he allows the statement of his other organ, the *Constitutionnel*, that Russian, Austrian and English interests are at stake in this question, but that France has only a very remote interest in it, and is therefore in a wholly independent position. Which will outbid the other, Russia or England? that is the question with him.

Written on March 25, 1853

First published in the *New-York Daily Tribune*, No. 3739, April 11, 1853; reprinted in the *Semi-Weekly Tribune*, No. 822, April 12, 1853

Signed: *Karl Marx*

Reproduced from the *New-York Daily Tribune*

Frederick Engels

THE TURKISH QUESTION[23]

It is only of late that people in the West of Europe and in America have been enabled to form anything like a correct judgment of Turkish affairs. Up to the Greek insurrection[24] Turkey was, to all intents and purposes a *terra incognita*, and the common notions floating about among the public were based more upon the *Arabian Nights' Entertainments* than upon any historical facts. Official diplomatic functionaries having been on the spot, boasted a more accurate knowledge, but this, too, amounted to nothing, as none of these officials ever troubled himself to learn Turkish, South Slavonian, or modern Greek, and they were one and all dependent upon the interested accounts of Greek interpreters and Frank[a] merchants. Besides, intrigues of every sort were always on hand to occupy the time of these lounging diplomatists, among whom Joseph von Hammer, the German historian of Turkey,[b] forms the only honorable exception. The business of these gentlemen was not with the people, the institutions, the social state of the country; it was exclusively with the Court, and especially with the Fanariote Greeks,[25] wily mediators between two parties either of which was equally ignorant of the real condition, power and resources of the other. The traditional notions and opinions, founded upon such paltry information, formed for a long while, and strange to say, form to a great extent even now, the ground-work for all the action of Western diplomacy with regard to Turkey.

---

[a] Franks is the name commonly used in the Middle East for West-Europeans.—*Ed.*

[b] Jos. Hammer, *Geschichte des Osmanischen Reiches.*—*Ed.*

But while England, France, and for a long time even Austria, were groping in the dark for a defined Eastern policy, another power outwitted them all. Russia herself semi-Asiatic in her condition, manners, traditions and institutions, found men enough who could comprehend the real state and character of Turkey. Her religion was the same as that of nine-tenths of the inhabitants of Turkey in Europe; her language almost identical with that of seven millions of Turkish subjects; and the well-known facility with which a Russian learns to converse in, if not fully to appropriate a foreign tongue, made it an easy matter for her agents, well paid for the task, to acquaint themselves completely with Turkish affairs. Thus at a very early period the Russian Government availed itself of its exceedingly favorable position in the South-east of Europe. Hundreds of Russian agents perambulated Turkey, pointing out to the Greek Christians, the Orthodox Emperor as the head, the natural protector, and the ultimate liberator of the oppressed Eastern Church, and to the South Slavonians especially, pointing out that same Emperor as the almighty Czar who was sooner or later to unite all the branches of the great Slavic race under one sceptre, and to make them the ruling race of Europe. The clergy of the Greek Church very soon formed themselves into a vast conspiracy for the spread of these ideas. The Servian insurrection of 1804,[26] the Greek rising in 1821 were more or less directly urged on by Russian gold and Russian influence; and wherever among the Turkish pashas the standard of revolt was raised against the Central Government, Russian intrigues and Russian funds were never wanting; and when thus, internal Turkish questions had entirely perplexed the understanding of Western diplomatists who knew no more about the real subject than about the man in the moon, then war was declared, Russian armies marched toward the Balkan, and portion by portion the Ottoman Empire was dismembered.

It is true that during the last thirty years much has been done toward general enlightenment concerning the state of Turkey. German philologists and critics have made us acquainted with the history and literature, English residents and English trade have collected a great deal of information as to the social condition of the Empire. But the diplomatic wiseacres seem to scorn all this, and to cling as obstinately as possible to the traditions engendered by the study of Eastern fairy-tales, improved upon by the no less wonderful accounts given by the most corrupt set of Greek mercenaries that ever existed.

And what has been the natural result? That in all essential

points Russia has steadily, one after another, gained her ends, thanks to the ignorance, dullness, and consequent inconsistency and cowardice of Western governments. From the battle of Navarino[27] to the present Eastern crisis, the action of the Western powers has either been annihilated by squabbles among themselves, mostly arising from their common ignorance of Eastern matters, and from petty jealousies which must have been entirely incomprehensible to any Eastern understanding—or that action has been in the direct interest of Russia alone. And not only do the Greeks, both of Greece and Turkey, and the Slavonians, look to Russia as their natural protector; nay, even the Government at Constantinople, despairing, time after time, to make its actual wants and real position understood by these Western ambassadors, who pride themselves upon their own utter incompetency to judge by their own eyes of Turkish matters, the very Turkish Government has in every instance been obliged to throw itself upon the mercy of Russia, and to seek protection from that power which openly avows its firm intention to drive every Turk across the Bosphorus and plant the cross of St. Andrew upon the minarets of the Aya-Sofiyah.

In spite of diplomatic tradition, these constant and successful encroachments of Russia have at last roused in the Western Cabinets in Europe a very dim and distant apprehension of the approaching danger. This apprehension has resulted in the great diplomatic nostrum, that the maintenance of the *status quo* in Turkey is a necessary condition of the peace of the world. The magniloquent incapacity of certain modern statesmen could not have confessed its ignorance and helplessness more plainly than in this axiom which, from having always remained a dead letter, has, during the short period of twenty years, been hallowed by tradition, and become as hoary and indisputable as King John's Magna Charta.[28] Maintain the *status quo*! Why, it was precisely to maintain the *status quo* that Russia stirred up Servia to revolt, made Greece independent, appropriated to herself the protectorate of Moldavia and Wallachia, and retained part of Armenia! England and France never stirred an inch when all this was done, and the only time they did move was to protect, in 1849, not Turkey, but the Hungarian refugees.[29] In the eyes of European diplomacy, and even of the European press, the whole Eastern question resolves itself into this dilemma, either the Russians at Constantinople, or the maintenance of the *status quo*—anything beside this alternative never enters their thoughts.

Look at the London press for illustration. We find *The Times* advocating the dismemberment of Turkey, and proclaiming the unfitness of the Turkish race to govern any longer in that beautiful corner of Europe. Skilful as usual, *The Times* boldly attacks the old diplomatic tradition of the *status quo*, and declares its continuance impossible. The whole of the talent at the disposal of that paper is exerted to show this impossibility under different aspects, and to enlist British sympathies for a new crusade against the remnant of the Saracens. The merit of such an unscrupulous attack upon a time-hallowed and unmeaning phrase which, two months ago, was as yet sacred to *The Times*, is undeniable. But whoever knows that paper, knows also that this unwonted boldness is applied directly in the interest of Russia and Austria. The correct premises put forth in its columns as to the utter impossibility of maintaining Turkey in its present state, serve no other purpose than to prepare the British public and the world for the moment when the principal paragraph of the will of Peter the Great,[30] the conquest of the Bosphorus, will have become an accomplished fact.

The opposite opinion is represented by *The Daily News*, the organ of the Liberals. *The Times* at least seizes a new and correct feature of the question, in order afterwards to pervert it to an interested purpose. In the columns of the Liberal journal, on the other hand, reigns the plainest sense, but merely a sort of *household sense*. Indeed, it does not see farther than the very threshold of its own house. It clearly perceives that a dismemberment of Turkey *under present circumstances* must bring the Russians to Constantinople, and that this would be a great misfortune for England; that it would threaten the peace of the world, ruin the Black Sea trade, and necessitate new armaments in the British stations and fleets of the Mediterranean. And in consequence, *The Daily News* exerts itself to arouse the indignation and fear of the British public. Is not the partition of Turkey a crime equal to the partition of Poland[31]? Have not the Christians more religious liberty in Turkey than in Austria and Russia? Is not the Turkish Government a mild, paternal government, which allows the different nations and creeds and local corporations to regulate their own affairs? Is not Turkey a paradise compared to Austria and Russia? Is not life and property safe there? And is not British trade with Turkey larger than that with Austria and Russia put together, and does it not increase every year? And then goes on in dithyrambic strain, so far as *The Daily News* can be dithyrambic, an apotheosis of Turkey, the Turks and everything Turkish, which must appear quite incomprehensible to most of its readers.

The key to this strange enthusiasm for the Turks is to be found in the works of David Urquhart,[a] Esq., M.P. This gentleman, of Scotch birth, with medieval and patriarchal recollections of home, and with a modern British civilized education, after having fought three years in Greece against the Turks, passed into their country and was the first thus to enamour himself of them. The romantic Highlander found himself at home again in the mountain ravines of the Pindus and Balkan, and his works on Turkey, although full of valuable information, may be summed up in the following three paradoxes, which are laid down almost literally thus: If Mr. Urquhart were not a British subject, he would decidedly prefer being a Turk; if he were not a Presbyterian Calvinist, he would not belong to any other religion than Islamism; and thirdly, Britain and Turkey are the only two countries in the world which enjoy self-government and civil and religious liberty. This same Urquhart has since become the great Eastern authority for all English Liberals who object to Palmerston, and it is he who supplies *The Daily News* with the materials for these panegyrics upon Turkey.

The only argument which deserves a moment's notice, upon this side of the question is this: "It is said that Turkey is decaying; but where is the decay? Is not civilization rapidly spreading in Turkey and trade extending? Where you see nothing but decay, our statistics prove nothing but progress." Now it would be a great fallacy to put down the increasing Black Sea trade to the credit of Turkey alone, and yet this is done here, exactly as if the industrial and commercial capabilities of Holland, the high road to the greater part of Germany, were to be measured by her gross exports and imports, nine-tenths of which represent a mere transit. And yet, what every statistician would immediately, in the case of Holland, treat as a clumsy concoction, the whole of the liberal press of England, including the learned *Economist*, tries, in the case of Turkey, to impose upon public credulity. And then, who are the traders in Turkey? Certainly not the Turks. Their way of promoting trade, when they were yet in their original nomadic state, consisted in robbing caravans, and now that they are a little more civilized it consists in all sorts of arbitrary and oppressive exactions. The Greeks, the Armenians, the Slavonians and the Franks established in the large seaports, carry on the whole of the trade, and certainly they have no reason to thank

[a] This evidently refers to David Urquhart's books published in the 1830s: *Turkey and Its Resources* and *The Spirit of the East.*—*Ed.*

Turkish Beys and Pashas for being able to do so. Remove all the Turks out of Europe, and trade will have no reason to suffer. And as to progress in general civilization, who are they that carry out that progress in all parts of European Turkey? Not the Turks, for they are few and far between, and can hardly be said to be settled anywhere except in Constantinople and two or three small country districts. It is the Greek and Slavonic middle class in all the towns and trading posts who are the real support of whatever civilization is effectually imported into the country. That part of the population are constantly rising in wealth and influence, and the Turks are more and more driven into the background. Were it not for their monopoly of civil and military power, they would soon disappear. But that monopoly has become impossible for the future, and their power is turned into impotence, except for obstructions in the way of progress. The fact is, they must be got rid of. To say that they cannot be got rid of except by putting Russians and Austrians in their place, means as much as to say, that the present political constitution of Europe will last forever. Who will make such an assertion?

Written at the end of March 1853

First published in the *New-York Daily Tribune*, No. 3746, April 19, 1853, as a leader; reprinted in the *New-York Weekly Tribune*, No. 606, April 23, 1853

Reproduced from the *New-York Daily Tribune*

Karl Marx

THE BERLIN CONSPIRACY

London, Friday, April 1, 1853

At length, the fifth of the "Great Powers," Prussia, enjoys the good fortune of having added of her own to the great discoveries made by the Austrian Police,[32] with respect to the "demagogical machinations" of the revolutionists.

"The Government," we are assured by its official organs, "having obtained proof that the chiefs of the Democratic party held continued relations with the revolutionary *propaganda*, ordered domiciliary visits to be made, on the 29th of March, at Berlin, and succeeded in arresting 40 individuals, among whom were Streckfuss, and the ex-members of the Prussian N. Assembly, Berends, Waldeck, etc. Domiciliary visits were made in the houses of eighty persons suspected of participation in a conspiracy. Arms and amunition were found."[a]

Not content with publishing these "startling facts" in its official papers, the Prussian Government thought proper to forward them by telegraph to the British Foreign Office.

In order to lay bare the mystery of this new police farce, it is necessary to go somewhat back. Two months after the *coup d'état* of Bonaparte, Mr. Hinckeldey, the *Polizei Praesident* of Berlin, and his inferior, Mr. Stieber, the *Polizei Rath*, conspired together, the one to become a Prussian *Maupas*, and the other to become a Prussian *Piétri*. The glorious omnipotence of the French police, perhaps, disturbed their slumbers. Hinckeldey addressed himself to Herr von Westphalen, the Minister of the Interior, making unjust representation to that weak-minded and fanatical reaction-

[a] See "Prussia", *The Morning Post*, No. 24734, March 31, 1853.—*Ed.*

ist (Herr von Westphalen being my brother-in-law I had ample opportunity of becoming acquainted with the mental powers of the man), on the necessity of concentrating the whole police force of the Prussian State in the hands of the *Polizei Praesident* of Berlin. He stated, that in order to accelerate the action of the police, it must be made independent of the Minister of the Interior and intrusted exclusively to himself. The minister von Westphalen, represents the ultra Prussian aristocracy and the President of the ministry, Herr von Manteuffel, represents the old bureaucracy; the two are rivals, and the former beheld in the suggestion of Hinckeldey, although it apparently narrowed the circle of his own department, a means of inflicting a blow on his rival, whose brother, M. von Manteuffel, was the director in the ministry of the Interior, and especially charged with the control of the entire police. Herr von Westphalen therefore submitted his proposition to a council of State, presided over by the King himself.[a]

The discussion was very angry. Manteuffel, supported by the Prince of Prussia, opposed the plan of establishing an independent ministry of police. The King inclined to the proposition of Herr von Westphalen, and concluded with the Solomonian sentence, that he would follow the example of Bonaparte and create a ministry of police, "if the necessity of that step were proved to him by facts." Now, the affair of the Cologne Communists was chosen by Hinckeldey and Stieber to furnish these facts. You are aware of the heroic performances of those men in the Cologne trials.[33] After their conclusion the Prussian Government resolved to elevate the openly-perjured Stieber, the man who had been hissed wherever he showed himself in the streets of Cologne—to the dignity of a *Polizei-Director* of Cologne. But M. de Bethmann-Hollweg and other well-meaning conservative deputies of Rhenish Prussia, intervened, representing to the ministers that such an open insult to the public opinion of that province might have very ominous consequences at a moment when Bonaparte coveted the *natural limits* of France.[34] The Government yielded, contenting itself with the nomination of Stieber as *Polizei-Director* of Berlin, in reward for his perjuries committed at Cologne and his thefts committed at London. There, however, the affair stopped. It was impossible to accomplish the wishes of Mr. Hinckeldey and to create for him an independent ministry of police on the ground of the Cologne trial. Hinckeldey and Stieber watched their time.

[a] Frederick William IV.—*Ed.*

Happily there came the Milan insurrection. Stieber at once made twenty arrests at Berlin. But the thing was too ridiculous to be proceeded with. But then came Libeny, and now the King was ripe. Overwhelmed with fearful apprehensions he saw at once the necessity of having an independent ministry of police, and Hinckeldey saw his dreams realized. A royal ordinance created him the Prussian *Maupas,* while the brother of Herr von Manteuffel tendered his resignation. The most astounding part of the comedy, however, was yet to come. Scarcely had Mr. Hinckeldey rushed into his new dignity when the "great Berlin conspiracy" was discovered directly. This conspiracy, then, was made for the express purpose of proving the necessity of Mr. Hinckeldey. It was the present Mr. Hinckeldey made over to the imbecile King in exchange for his newly-gained police-autocracy. Hinckeldey's adjunct, the ingenious Stieber, who had discovered at Cologne that whenever letters were found terminating with the words "*Gruss*" and "*Bruderschaft,*"[a] there was unquestionably a Communist conspiracy, now made the discovery that there appeared at Berlin for some time since an ominous quantity of "Calabrese hats," and that the Calabrese hat was unquestionably the "rallying sign" of the revolutionists. Strong upon this important discovery, Stieber made on the 18th of March several arrests, chiefly of workmen and foreigners, the charge against whom was the wearing of Calabrese hats. On the 23d ejusdem domiciliary visits were made in the house of Karl Delius, a merchant at Magdeburg and brother of a member of the Second Chamber, who had also an unhappy taste for Calabrese hats. Finally, as I informed you at the beginning of this letter, on the 29th ultimo the great *coup d'état* against the Calabrese hats was struck at Berlin. All those who know anything of the milk-and-water opposition of Waldeck, Berends,&c., will laugh at the "arms and munition" found in the possession of these most inoffensive Brutuses.

But futile as this police comedy may appear to be got up, as it were, by mere personal motives of Messrs. Hinckeldey & Stieber, it is not without significance. The Prussian Government is exasperated at the passive resistance it meets with in every direction. It smells the breath of Revolution in midst of the apparent apathy. It despairs at the want of a tangible form of that specter, and feels alleviated, as it were, from the nightmare every time the police

[a] "Greeting" and "Fraternity".—*Ed.*

affords bodily shapes to its ubiquitous but invisible antagonist. It attacks, it will go on attacking, and it will successfully convert the passive resistance of the people into an active one.

Written on April 1, 1853

First published in the *New-York Daily Tribune*, No. 3745, April 18, 1853; reprinted in the *Semi-Weekly Tribune*, No. 824, April 19, 1853

Signed: *Karl Marx*

Reproduced from the *New-York Daily Tribune*

Frederick Engels

WHAT IS TO BECOME OF TURKEY IN EUROPE?

We have seen how the obstinate ignorance, the time-hallowed routine, the hereditary mental drowsiness of European statesmen, shrinks from the very attempt to answer this question. Aberdeen and Palmerston, Metternich and Guizot, not to mention their republican and constitutional substitutes of 1848 to 1852—who will ever be nameless—all despair of a solution.

And all the while Russia advances step by step, slowly, but irresistibly, towards Constantinople, in spite of all the diplomatic notes, plots and manoeuvres of France and England.

Now this steady advance of Russia, admitted by all parties, in all countries of Europe, has never been explained by official statesmen. They see the effect, they see even the ultimate consequence, and yet the cause is hidden from them, although nothing is more simple.

The great motive power which speeds Russia on towards Constantinople, is nothing but the very device, designed to keep her away from it; the hollow, the never-enforced theory of the *status quo.*

What is this *status quo*? For the Christian subjects of the Porte, it means simply the maintenance for ever and a day, of Turkish oppression over them. As long as they are oppressed by Turkish rule, the head of the Greek Church, the ruler of sixty millions of Greek Christians, be he in other respects what he may, is *their natural liberator and protector.* Thus it is, that ten millions of Greek Christians in European Turkey, are forced to appeal to Russian aid, by that very diplomatic scheme, invented in order to prevent Russian encroachments.

Look at the facts as history records them. Even before the reign of Catherine II Russia never omitted an opportunity of obtaining favorable conditions for Moldavia and Wallachia. These stipulations, at last, were carried to such a length in the Treaty of Adrianople (1829)[35] that the above-named principalities are now more subject to Russia than to Turkey. When, in 1804, the Servian revolution broke out, Russia took the rebel Rayahs at once under her protection, and in two treaties, after having supported them in two wars, guaranteed the internal independence of their country.[36] When the Greeks revolted, who decided the contest? Not the plots and rebellions of Ali Pasha of Janina, not the battle of Navarino, not the French army in the Morea,[37] not the conferences and protocols of London, but the march of Diebitsch's Russians across the Balkan into the valley of the Maritza.[38] And while Russia thus fearlessly set about the dismemberment of Turkey, western diplomatists continued to guarantee and to hold up as sacred the *status quo* and the inviolability of the Ottoman territory!

So long as the tradition of the upholding, at any price, of the status quo and the independence of Turkey in her present state is the ruling maxim of Western diplomacy, so long will Russia be considered, by nine-tenths of the population of Turkey in Europe, their only support, their liberator, their Messiah.

Now, suppose for a moment that Turkish rule in the Graeco-Slavonian peninsula were got rid of; that a government more suitable to the wants of the people existed; what then would be the position of Russia? The fact is notorious, that in every one of the States which have sprung up upon Turkish soil and acquired either total or partial independence, a powerful anti-Russian party has formed itself. If that be the case at a time when Russian support is their only safeguard against Turkish oppression, what, then, are we to expect, as soon as the fear of Turkish oppression shall have vanished?

But to remove Turkish authority beyond the Bosphorus; to emancipate the various creeds and nationalities which populate the peninsula; to open the door to the schemes and machinations, the conflicting desires and interests of all the great powers of Europe;—why is not this provoking universal war? Thus asks diplomatic cowardice and routine.

Of course, it is not expected that the Palmerstons, the Aberdeens, the Clarendons, the Continental Foreign Secretaries, will do such a thing. They cannot look at it without shuddering. But whosoever has, in the study of history, learned to admire the eternal mutations of human affairs in which nothing is stable but instability, nothing constant but change; whosoever has followed up that stern march of history whose wheels pass relentlessly over the remains of empires, crushing entire generations, without holding them worthy even of a look of pity; whosoever, in short, has had his eyes open to the fact that there was never a demagogic appeal or insurgent proclamation, as revolutionary as the plain and simple records of the history of mankind; whoever knows how to appreciate the eminently revolutionary character of the present age, when steam and wind, electricity and the printing press, artillery and gold discoveries cooperate to produce more changes and revolutions in a year than were ever before brought about in a century, will certainly not shrink from facing a historical question, because of the consideration that its proper settlement may bring about a European war.

No, diplomacy, Government according to the old fashion will never solve the difficulty. The solution of the Turkish problem is reserved, with that of other great problems, to the European Revolution. And there is no presumption in assigning this apparently remote question to the lawful domain of that great movement. The revolutionary landmarks have been steadily advancing ever since 1789. The last revolutionary outposts were Warsaw, Debreczin, Bucharest; the advanced posts of the next revolution must be Petersburg and Constantinople. They are the two vulnerable points where the Russian anti-revolutionary colossus must be attacked.

It would be a mere effort of fancy to give a detailed scheme as to how the Turkish territory in Europe might be partitioned out. Twenty such schemes could be invented, every one as plausible as the other. What we have to do is, not to draw up fanciful programmes, but to seek general conclusions from indisputable facts. And from this point of view the question presents a double aspect.

Firstly, then, it is an undeniable reality that the peninsula, commonly called Turkey in Europe, forms the natural inheritance of the South-Slavonian race. That race furnishes seven millions out of twelve of its inhabitants. It has been in possession of the soil for twelve hundred years. Its competitors—if we except a sparse population which has adopted the Greek language, although in reality of Slavonic descent—are Turkish or Arnaut barbarians, who have long since been convicted of the most inveterate opposition to all progress. The South-Slavonians, on the contrary, are, in the inland districts of the country, the exclusive representatives of civilization. They do not yet form a nation, but they have a powerful and comparatively enlightened nucleus of nationality in Servia. The Servians have a history, a literature of their own. They owe their present internal independence to an eleven years' struggle, carried on valiantly against superior numbers. They have, for the last twenty years, grown rapidly in culture and the means of civilization. They are looked upon by the Christians of Bulgaria, Thrace, Macedonia and Bosnia as the center, around which, in their future efforts for independence and nationality, all of them must rally. In fact, it may be said that, the more Servia and Servian nationality has consolidated itself, the more has the direct influence of Russia on the Turkish Slavonians been thrown into the background; for Servia, in order to maintain its distinct position as a Christian State, has been obliged to borrow from the West of Europe its political institutions, its schools, its scientific knowledge, its industrial appliances; and thus is explained the anomaly, that, in spite of Russian protection, Servia, ever since her emancipation, has formed a constitutional monarchy.

Whatever may be the bonds which consanguinity and common religious belief may draw between the Russian and the Turkish Slavonians, their interests will be decidedly opposite from the day the latter are emancipated. The commercial necessities arising from the geographical position of the two countries explain this. Russia, a compact inland country, is essentially a country of predominant agricultural, and perhaps, one day, manufacturing production. The Graeco-Slavonian peninsula, small in extent, comparatively, with an enormous extent of shore on three seas, one of which it commands, is now essentially a country of commercial transit, though with the best capacities for independent production. Russia is monopolizing, South Slavonia is expansive. They are, besides, competitors in Central Asia; but while Russia has every interest to exclude all but her own produce, South Slavonia has, even now, every interest to introduce into the Eastern markets the produce of Western Europe. How, then, is it possible for the two nations to agree? In fact, the Turkish South Slavonians and Greeks have, even now, far more interests in common with Western Europe than with Russia. And as soon as the line of railway, which now extends from Ostende, Havre and Hamburg to Pesth, shall have been continued to Belgrade and Constantinople (which is now under consideration), the influence of Western civilization and Western trade will become permanent in the South-east of Europe.

Again: The Turkish Slavonians especially suffer by their

subjection to a Mussulman class of military occupants whom they have to support. These military occupants unite in themselves all public functions, military, civil and judicial. Now what is the Russian system of government, wherever it is not mixed up with feudal institutions, but a military occupation, in which the civil and judicial hierarchy are organized in a military manner, and where the people have to pay for the whole? Whoever thinks that such a system can have a charm for the South Slavonians, may study the history of Servia since 1804. Kara-George, the founder of Servian independence, was abandoned by the people, and Miloš Obrenović, the restorer of that independence, was ignominiously turned out of the country, because they attempted to introduce the Russian autocratic system, accompanied with its concomitant corruption, half-military bureaucracy and pasha-like extortion.

Here then is the simple and final solution of the question. History and the facts of the present day alike point to the erection of a free and independent Christian State on the ruins of the Moslem Empire in Europe. The next effort of the Revolution can hardly fail to render such an event necessary, for it can hardly fail to inaugurate the long-maturing conflict between Russian Absolutism and European Democracy. In that conflict England must bear a part, in whatever hands her Government may for the moment happen to be placed. She can never allow Russia to obtain possession of Constantinople. She must then, take sides with the enemies of the Czar and favor the construction of an independent Slavonian Government in the place of the effete and overthrown Sublime Porte.[39]

Written at the beginning of April 1853

First published in the *New-York Daily Tribune*, No. 3748, April 21, 1853, as a leader; reprinted in the *New-York Weekly Tribune*, No. 607, April 30, 1853

Reproduced from the *New-York Daily Tribune*

Karl Marx

THE BERLIN CONSPIRACY.—LONDON POLICE.—MAZZINI.—RADETZKY

London, Friday, April 8, 1853

At the time of writing my last letter concerning the great conspiracy discovered by Mr. Stieber,[a] I could not anticipate, that my views on that affair would be more or less confirmed by two Conservative Berlin papers. The *Preussisches Wochenblatt*, the organ of the Conservative faction headed by Mr. von Bethmann-Hollweg, was confiscated on April 2d for recommending its readers "not to believe too hastily in the tales of the police respecting the late arrests."[b] But of far greater importance is an article in the *Zeit*, the semi-official journal belonging to the section of the Prussian Ministry headed by M. von Manteuffel. The *Zeit* is compelled to make the following admission:

> "Whosoever is not struck with blindness, cannot but be aware that the numerous and inextricable complications presented by the general situation of Europe must lead in a given time, to a violent explosion, which the sincere endeavors of the Great Powers of Europe may postpone for a while, but to prevent which in a permanent way they are utterly unable, notwithstanding all human exertions.... It is for us the accomplishment of a duty not to dissimulate any longer, that discontent is spreading wider and wider and *is the more dangerous and the more deserving of serious attention, as it appears not at the surface but conceals itself more and more in the depth of men's minds.* This discontent, we must say without paraphrase, is created by the efforts to bring about a counter-revolution in Prussia latterly paraded with an incredible *étourderie.*"[c]

The *Zeit* is only mistaken in its conclusion. The Prussian counter-revolution is not now about to be commenced, it is to be ended. It is not a thing of recent growth, but began on March 20th,

---

[a] See this volume, pp. 28-31.—*Ed.*

[b] "Die neuesten Verhaftungen und Haussuchungen in Berlin", *Preussisches Wochenblatt*, No. 25, April 2, 1853.—*Ed.*

[c] "Die Contre-Revolution", *Die Zeit*, No. 77, April 3, 1853.—*Ed.*

1848,[40] and has been steadily advancing ever since that day. At this very moment the Prussian Government is hatching two very dangerous projects, the one of limiting the free sub-division of real property, the other subjecting public instruction to the Church. They could not have selected two objects more appropriate to alienate the peasantry of Rhenish Prussia and the middle classes throughout the monarchy. As a curious incident, I may also mention the forced dissolution of the Berlin Hygienic Society (A Mutual Benefit Sick Club), in consequence of the "great discovery." This society was composed of nearly 10,000 members, all belonging to the working classes. The Government, it appears, are convinced, that the present constitution of the Prussian State is incompatible with "hygienics."

The London press, till now unconscious of the doings of the London police, are surprised by statements in the Vienna *Presse* and the *Emancipation*,[a] the leading reactionary journal of Belgium, that the police of London have drawn up a list of all the political refugees in that city, with a variety of details relating to their private circumstances and conduct.

"Once such a system is tolerated with regard to foreigners," exclaims *The Morning Advertiser*, "it will be employed whenever deemed advisable by the Government, or any member of it, in order to become acquainted with the details of the private lives of our own countrymen.... Is it not saddening to think that the London police should be called upon to play the infamous part assigned to their continental colleagues?"

Besides these statements in Belgian and other papers, the London press is this day informed by telegraphic dispatch from Vienna,[b]

"that 'the Refugee question is settled: the British Government has promised to keep a strict guard on the refugees, and to visit them with the full severity of the law whenever it should be proved that they have taken part in revolutionary intrigues.'"

"Never before," remarks *The Morning Advertiser*, "did England appear in so humiliating a situation as she does now, in having prostrated herself to the feet of Austria. No degradation could equal this. It was reserved for the Coalition Cabinet."[c]

I learn from a very creditable source that the law officers of the Crown will institute a prosecution against Mazzini as soon as his

---

[a] *L'Emancipation*, No. 94, April 4, 1853.—*Ed.*

[b] The report cited below was published in *The Times*, No. 21395, April 6,1853 and reprinted in several other newspapers on April 7.—*Ed.*

[c] *The Morning Advertiser*, No. 19279, April 7, 1853.—*Ed.*

sojourn at London shall be ascertained. On the other hand I hear that the Ministers will be interpellated in the House of Commons with regard to their scandalous transactions with Austria, and their intentions on the refugee question in general.

I have stated in a former letter that Radetzky was glad to have been afforded, by the Milan insurrection, a pretext for "obtaining money under false pretenses."[a] This view of the matter has since been confirmed by an act not to be misunderstood. In a recent proclamation Radetzky has declared null and void all loans or mortgages contracted since 1847 on the security of the sequestrated estates of the Lombard emigrants. This confiscation can have no other possible excuse than the *horror vacui*[b] of the Austrian exchequer. The sentimental bourgeoisie have everywhere sacrificed the revolution to their god called Property. The counter-revolution now repudiates that god.

A sub-marine telegraphic dispatch of to-day brings the news that Prince Menchikoff has concluded a convention with the Porte, that the Russian armies have received orders to retire from the Turkish frontiers, and that the Eastern question is once more settled.

Written on April 8, 1853

First published in the *New-York Daily Tribune*, No. 3748, April 21, 1853; reprinted in the *Semi-Weekly Tribune*, No. 825, April 22, 1853

Signed: *Karl Marx*

Reproduced from the *New-York Daily Tribune*

[a] K. Marx, "The Attack on Francis Joseph.—The Milan Riot.—British Politics.—Disraeli's Speech.—Napoleon's Will" (see present edition, Vol. 11, pp. 513-21).—*Ed.*

[b] Fear of vacuity.—*Ed.*

Karl Marx

HIRSCH'S CONFESSIONS

Hirsch's "Confessions",[41] as I see it, are valid only insofar as they are confirmed by other facts. If only because they contradict themselves. On returning from his mission to Cologne he declared at a workers' public meeting that Willich was his accomplice. Naturally, this ostensible confession was thought too contemptible to record in the minutes. Various people let me know—whether with or without Hirsch's instructions I cannot tell—that Hirsch was willing to make a full confession to me. I turned the offer down. Later, I learned that he was living in the utmost penury. I have no doubt, therefore, that his "very latest" confessions have been written in the interest of the party that is *paying* him at the moment. Strangely, there are people who find it necessary to seek the protection of a person like Hirsch.

For the present, I shall confine myself to a few marginal comments. We have had other spy confessions, those from Vidocq, Chenu, de la Hodde,[a] and so on.[42] There is one point on which they tally. None of them are ordinary spies, but are spies in a higher sense, all of them successors of "Cooper's spy."[b] Their confessions are inevitably just so many apologies.

Hirsch, too, tries to make out, for example, that it was not he but Colonel Bangya who informed Greif, and Fleury through Greif, of the day my party comrades held their meetings. These

---

[a] F. Vidocq, *Mémoires*, T. I-IV; A. Chenu, *Les Conspirateurs. Les sociétés secrètes. La préfecture de police sous Caussidière. Les corps francs*; L. de la Hodde, *La naissance de la république en février 1848.—Ed.*

[b] Harvey Birch, the main character of James Fenimore Cooper's novel *The Spy*, performed his work out of patriotic motives.—*Ed.*

took place on Thursdays on the few occasions when Hirsch attended, but on Wednesdays after Hirsch was excluded from them. The false minutes[43] of before and after Hirsch's attendances are dated Thursday. Who but Hirsch could have committed this "misstatement"!

Hirsch is luckier on another point. He claims Bangya has repeatedly disclosed information bearing on my correspondence with Germany. And since all the relevant data in the Cologne court records are false, it is certainly impossible to determine who invented them. Now to Bangya.

Spy or no spy, Bangya could never become dangerous either to me or to my party comrades, because I *never* spoke to him about *my* party affairs, and Bangya himself—as he reminds me in one of his exculpatory letters—had always avoided broaching any of these matters. Hence, spy or no spy, he could betray nothing, because he knew nothing. The Cologne records bear this out.[44] They show that apart from confessions made in Germany itself and documents seized there, the Prussian police knew nothing of the party to which I belong and were therefore compelled to serve up the silliest cock-and-bull.

But Bangya sold a pamphlet by Marx "about the refugees" to the police, did he not?[a]

Bangya learned from me in the presence of other persons that Ernst Dronke, Frederick Engels and I were contemplating a publication about the German refugees in London which was to appear in several instalments. He assured me that he could find a publisher in Berlin. I asked him to see about it at once. Eight or ten days later he announced that a Berlin publisher named Eisermann was prepared to put out the *first* instalment on condition that its authors remain anonymous, since otherwise he feared confiscation. I agreed, but stipulated for my part that the fee should be payable at once on delivery of the manuscript, because I did not wish to repeat the experience I had with the *Revue of the Neue Rheinische Zeitung*, and that the manuscript should be printed on delivery. I then went to see Engels in Manchester where the pamphlet was written. In the meantime, Bangya brought my wife a letter from Berlin in which Eisermann agreed to my conditions with the reservation that the publication of the second instalment would depend on the sales of the first. On my return, Bangya received the manuscript, and I my fee.

[a] K. Marx and F. Engels, *The Great Men of the Exile* (see present edition, Vol. 11, pp. 227-326).—*Ed.*

But the printing was delayed on various plausible pretexts. I became suspicious. Not of the manuscript having been given to the police in order that the police should print it. I am now ready to surrender my manuscripts even to the Russian Emperor, so long as he, for his part, should be willing to print them the following day. No, what I feared was suppression of the manuscript.

It attacked the pulpiteers of the day—not, of course, as revolutionaries dangerous to the state, but as windbags of counter-revolution.

My suspicions were confirmed. Georg Weerth, whom I had asked to inquire about Eisermann in Berlin, wrote that no Eisermann could be discovered. Dronke and I went to see Bangya. Eisermann had now become merely Jacob Collmann's manager. Anxious to obtain Bangya's statements in writing, I insisted that he should repeat them in my presence in a letter to Engels in Manchester, giving Collmann's address. I also wrote a few lines to Bruno Bauer, asking him to inquire about who lived in the house that Bangya said belonged to Collmann, but received no answer. The alleged publisher replied to my reminders that no printing date had been *contractually* stipulated. He claimed to be the best judge of the most suitable time. In a subsequent letter he feigned offence. Finally, Bangya informed me that the publisher was refusing to print the manuscript and would return it. He himself disappeared to Paris.

The Berlin letters and Bangya's letters containing the whole negotiations, along with Bangya's exculpatory efforts, are in my possession.

But why was I not put off by the suspicions of Bangya cast about by the refugees? Simply because I knew their "pre-history". And for the time being I propose to leave this pre-history in the obscurity it merits.

Because I *knew* that Bangya had done laudable things as an officer of the revolution in the Hungarian war. Because he corresponded with Szemere, whom I respect, and was on friendly terms with General Perczel. Because I had myself seen a diploma in which *Kossuth* appointed him police chief *in partibus*,[a] countersigned by Count Szirmay, Kossuth's confidant, who lived in the same house as Bangya. This post with Kossuth also explained his inevitable relationship with policemen. If I am not mistaken, Bangya is at present still Kossuth's agent in Paris.

[a] *In partibus infidelium*—here in the sense of "in exile". Literally: in the land of infidels. This phrase was added to the title of Catholic bishops appointed to purely nominal dioceses in non-Christian countries.—*Ed.*

The Hungarian leaders must have known their man. And what was I risking compared to them? Nothing worse than suppression of a copy to which I had retained the original.

Later, I asked Lizius, a publisher in Frankfurt am Main, and other publishers in Germany whether they would publish the manuscript. They said this was not possible in the present circumstances. Lately, an opportunity has arisen to have it printed outside Germany.

Following these explanations, which I am certainly not addressing to Herr Hirsch, but to my countrymen in America, does not there remain the "open question": what interest did the Prussian police have in suppressing a pamphlet against Kinkel, Willich and the other "great men of the exile"?

Solve for me, o Oerindur,
This riddle of Nature![a]

London, April 9, 1853

First published in the *Belletristisches Journal und New-Yorker Criminal-Zeitung*, No. 8, May 5, 1853

Signed: *Karl Marx*

Printed according to the newspaper

Translated from the German

Published in English for the first time

[a] A. Müllner, *Die Schuld*, Act II, Scene 5.—*Ed.*

THE
People's Paper
THE CHAMPION OF
POLITICAL JUSTICE AND UNIVERSAL RIGHT.

50] LONDON, SATURDAY, APRIL 16, 1853. [Price Fourpence.

Karl Marx

THE NEW FINANCIAL JUGGLE; OR GLADSTONE AND THE PENNIES[45]

Our readers know, to their cost, and have learned, to the tune of their pockets, that an old financial juggle has imposed a National Debt of £800,000,000 on the people's shoulders. That Debt was chiefly contracted to prevent the liberation of the American colonies, and to counteract the French Revolution of the last century. The influence of the increase of the National Debt on the increase of the national expenditure, may be gathered from the following tabular analysis[a]:—

1. *National Debt*

	£
When Queen Anne succeeded to William (1701)[46]	16,394,702
When George I ascended the Throne (1714)	54,145,363
When George II began his Reign (1727)	52,092,235
When George III assumed the reins of Government (1760)	146,682,844
After the American War (1784)	257,213,043
At the end of the Anti-Jacobin War (1801)	579,931,447
In January, 1810 (during the Napoleonic War)	811,898,082
After 1815 ....about	1,000,000,000

[a] The figures for the following table were taken mainly from W. Cobbett's book, *Paper against Gold*, pp. 21-25.—*Ed.*

2. *National Expenditure*

	£
When Queen Anne succeeded to William (1701), all expenses, including the interest of the National Debt, amounted to	5,610,987
When George I ascended the Throne (1714)	6,633,581
When George II began his Reign (1727)	5,441,248
When George III assumed the reins of power (1760)	24,456,940
At the end of the Anti-Jacobin War (1801)	61,278,018[a]

3. *National Taxation*

Queen Anne (1701)	4,212,358
George I (1714)	6,762,643
George II (1727)	6,522,540
George III (1760)	8,744,682
After the American War (1784)	13,300,921
After the Anti-Jacobin War (1801)	36,728,971
1809	70,240,226
After 1815	about 82,000,000

The people well know, from personal pocket-experience, what is the weight of taxation resulting from the National Debt—but many are not aware of the peculiar forms under which this Debt has been contracted, and actually exists. The "State," that jointocracy of coalesced land and money mongers, wants money for the purpose of home and foreign oppression. It borrows money of capitalists and usurers, and in return gives them a bit of paper, pledging itself to pay them so much money in the shape of interest for each £100 they lend. The means of paying this money it tears from the working classes through the means of taxation—so that the people are the security for their oppressors to the men who lend them the money to cut the people's throats. This money has been borrowed as a debt under various denominations—sometimes to pay 3 per cent., $3^1/_2$ per cent., 4 per cent., &c., and according to that percentage and other accidents the funds have various denominations, as the 3 per cents., &c.

Every Chancellor of the Exchequer, with the exception of the Whigs, as not only the working classes, but the manufacturers and

[a] *The People's Paper* erroneously gave £82,027,288 here as national expenditure for 1809. The figure has been corrected according to W. Cobbett's book.—*Ed.*

landlords also, have to pay a portion of this interest, and wish to pay as little as possible, tries accordingly, in some way or other, to alleviate the pressure of this incubus.

On the 8th of April, before the Budget of the present Ministry was brought forward, Mr. Gladstone laid before the House a statement of several resolutions dealing with the Public Debt—and before this statement had been made *The Morning Chronicle* announced that resolutions of the utmost importance were to be proposed, "heralded by rumours of great interest and magnitude."[a] The funds rose on these rumours; there was an impression that Gladstone was going to pay off the National Debt. Now, "what was all this pother about?"[b]

The ultimate aim of Mr. Gladstone's proposals, as stated by himself, was to reduce the interest on the various public stocks to $2^1/_2$ per cent. Now, in the years 1822-3, 1824-5, 1830-1, 1844-5, there had been reductions, from 5 per cent. to $4^1/_2$, from $4^1/_2$ to 4, from 4 to $3^1/_2$, from $3^1/_2$ to 3, respectively. Why should there not be a reduction from 3 to $2^1/_2$?

Now, let us see in what manner Mr. Gladstone proposes to achieve this end.

Firstly. He proposes with respect to certain stocks amounting to £9,500,000, chiefly connected with the old South Sea Bubble,[47] to bring them under one single denomination, and to reduce them compulsorily from 3 per cent. to $2^3/_4$ per cent. This gives a permanent annual saving approaching to £25,000. The invention of a new general name of various stocks, and the saving for £25,000 on an annual expense of £30,000,000, does not merit any particular admiration.

Secondly. He proposes to issue a new financial paper, called Exchequer Bonds, not exceeding the amount of £30,000,000, transferable by simple delivery, without cost of any kind, bearing interest at $2^3/_4$ per cent., up to the 1st of September, 1864, and then $2^1/_2$ per cent. up to the 1st of September, 1894. Now this is simply the creation of a new financial instrument for the comfort of the monied and mercantile class. He says "without cost," that is, without cost to the City Merchant. At the present moment there are £18,000,000 of Exchequer Bills at $1^1/_2$ per cent. Is it not a loss to the country to pay 1 per cent. more upon the Exchequer *Bonds* than upon the Exchequer Bills? At all events the second

[a] *The Morning Chronicle*, No. 26922, April 7, 1853.—*Ed.*
[b] Here and below the quotations are from Benjamin Disraeli's speech in the House of Commons on April 8, 1853 (*The Times*, No. 21398, April 9, 1853).—*Ed.*

proposition has nothing to do with the reduction of the National Debt. The Exchequer *Bills* can circulate only in Great Britain, but the Exchequer *Bonds* are transferable as common Bills, therefore it is a mere measure of convenience to the City Merchants, for which the people pay a high price.

Now, finally, we come to the only important matter—to the 3 per cent. consols, and the "3 per cent. reduced," amounting together to a capital of nearly 500,000,000. As there exists a Parliamentary provision forbidding these stocks to be reduced compulsorily, except on twelve months notice, Mr. Gladstone chooses the system of voluntary commutation, offering various alternatives to the holders of the 3 per cent. stock for exchanging them at option with other stocks to be created under his resolutions. The holders of the 3 per cent. stocks shall have the option of exchanging each £100 3 per cent. in one of the three following forms:—

1.—Semi-Exchange, every £100 of the 3 per cent. with an Exchequer Bond for the like amount carrying interest at the rate of £2 15s. until 1864, and then at the rate of £2 10s. until 1894. If the whole of the £30,000,000 of Exchequer Bonds at $2^1/_2$ per cent. replaced £30,000,000 of 3 per cents., there would be a saving in the first ten years of £75,000; and after the first ten years of £150,000; together £225,000; but the Government would be bound to repay the whole of the £30,000,000, after forty years. In no respect is this a proposition dealing largely, or even at all, with the National Debt. For what is a saving of £225,000 in an annual expense of £30,000,000?

2.—The second proposal is, that the holders of stock shall retain for every £100 in 3 per cents., £82 10s. in new stock of $3^1/_2$ per cent., which would be paid at the rate of £3 10s. per cent. until the 5th of January, 1894. The result of that would be to give a present income to the persons accepting the $3^1/_2$ per cent. stock, of £2 17s. 9d., instead of £3—reduction of 2s. 3d. on the interest of every £100. If the £500,000,000 were all converted under this proposal, the result would be that, instead of paying, as at present, £15,000,000 per annum, the nation would only pay £14,437,500, and this would be a gain of £562,500 a year. But, for this saving of £562,500 Parliament would tie up its hands for half a century, and grant higher interest than 2 four-fifths per cent. at a time of transition and of utter insecurity of every rate of interest! One thing, however, would be gained for Gladstone—at the expiration of forty years there would be, in the place of the 3 per cent. stock being now *defended* by twelve months' notice, a $3^1/_2$ per cent. stock redeemable at par by Parliament. Gladstone proposes not to fix any limit on that $3^1/_2$ per cent. stock.

3.—The third proposal is, that the holders of every £100 3 per cent. shall receive £110 in a new stock of $2^1/_2$ per cent. until 1894. When Mr. Gladstone first introduced his plan in the House of Commons, on the 8th of April, he had not limited the amount of the new $2^1/_2$ per cent. to be issued, but Mr. Disraeli having pointed out that, contrasting this proposal with the two other ones, every man in his senses would choose the conversion of £100 3 per cent. into £110 $2^1/_2$ per cent.; and that by the conversion of the £500,000,000 3 per cent. into the new stock, the nation would gain on one side, £1,250,000 per annum, but be saddled on the other hand with an addition to the Public Debt of £50,000,000, Mr. Gladstone, on the following day, altered his proposition, and proposed to limit the new $2^1/_2$ per cent. stock to £30,000,000. By this limitation, his proposal loses almost all effect on the great stock of the Public Debt, and augments its capital only by £3,000,000.

Now you know "one of the most important and gigantic financial proposals that ever has been brought forward."[a] There exists, perhaps, in general, no greater humbug than the so-called finance. The simplest operations relating to the Budget and the Public Debt, are clothed by the adepts of that "occult science" in abstruse terminology, concealing the trivial manoeuvres of creating various denominations of stocks, the commutation of old stocks for new ones, the diminishing the interest, and raising the nominal capital—the raising the interest and reducing the capital, the instalment of premiums, bonuses, priority shares—the distinction between redeemable and irredeemable annuities—the artificial graduation in the facility of transferring the various papers—in such a manner that the public understanding is quite bamboozled by these detestable stock-jobbing scholastics and the frightful complexity in details; while with every such new financial operation the usurers obtain an eagerly-seized opportunity for developing their mischievous and predatory activity. Mr. Gladstone is, without any doubt, a master in this sort of financial alchemy, and this proposal cannot be better characterised than by the words of Mr. Disraeli:—

> More complicated and ingenious machinery to produce so slight a result, appeared to him never to have been devised by the subtlety and genius of the most

[a] A quotation from the speech of Edward Ellice, M.P. from Coventry, cited by Benjamin Disraeli in his House of Commons speech on April 8, 1853.—*Ed.*

skilful casuist. In Saint Thomas Aquinas[a] there was a chapter that speculated upon the question of how many angels could dance on the point of a needle. It was one of the rarest productions of human genius; and he recognised in these resolutions something of that master mind.

You will remember that we have stated that the ultimate end of Gladstone's plan was the establishment of a "normal" $2^1/_2$ per cent. fund. Now, in order to achieve this end, he creates a very limited $2^1/_2$ per cent. fund, and an illimited $3^1/_2$ per cent. stock. In order to create his limited $2^1/_2$ per cent. stock, he reduces the interest by a half per cent., and augments the capital by a bonus of 10 per cent. In order to rid himself of the difficulty of all legislation on the 3 per cents. being defended by twelve months' notice, he prefers legislating for half a century to come; in conclusion, he would, if successful, cut off all chance of financial liberation for half a century from the British people.

Every one will confess, that if the Jewish Disabilities Bill was a little attempt at establishing religious tolerance—the Canada Reserves Bill a little attempt at granting colonial self-government[48]—the Education Resolution[b] a little attempt at avoiding National Education—Gladstone's financial scheme is a mighty little attempt at dealing with that giant-monster, the National Debt of Britain.

Written on April 12, 1853

First published in *The People's Paper*, No. 50, April 16, 1853

Signed: *C. M.*

Reproduced from the newspaper

[a] Thomas Aquinas, *Summa Theologica*.—*Ed.*

[b] See this volume, pp. 51-52.—*Ed.*

Karl Marx

ACHIEVEMENTS OF THE MINISTRY

London, Tuesday, April 12, 1853

The best thing perhaps that can be said in favor of the Coalition Ministry is that it represents impotency in power at a moment of transition, when not the reality, but only the appearance of government, is possible, with evanescent old parties and not yet consolidated new ones.

The "administration of all the talents," what has it accomplished during its first quarter's trial? Two readings of the Jewish Disabilities Bill and three of the Canada Clergy Reserves Bill.[49] The latter enables the Canadian Legislature to dispose of a certain portion of the proceeds of the land-sales hitherto reserved exclusively for the benefit of the favorite churches of England and Scotland. When first laid before the House by Lord John Russell, it consisted of three clauses, the third clause repealing the enactment by which the consolidated fund was charged to supply the deficiency, if in any year the Canada land-sales could not produce £9,285. This bill had been carried through a second reading, but on the House going into Committee[50] upon it (March 18) Lord John suddenly moved the withdrawal of his own third clause. Now, if the Canadian Legislature were to secularize the Clergy Reserves, about £10,000 per annum would be taken out of the pockets of the British people for the maintenance of a sect thousands of miles away. The Radical Minister, Sir W. Molesworth who disclaims all ecclesiastical endowments, appeared himself to have become a convert to Lord John's doctrine "that British Colonies were not to be freed from the incubus of the Established Church, except at the cost and risk of the British people at home."

Three Radical resolutions were proposed during the first quarter's trial. Mr. Collier moved the abolition of the Ecclesiastical

Courts, Mr. Williams the extension of the legacy and probate-duty to real property, and Mr. Hume the extinction of all "strictly protective" duties. The Ministry, of course, opposed all these "sweeping" reforms. But the Coalition Ministry opposes them in quite a different manner from the Tories. The latter resolutely announced their decision to resist the "encroachments of Democracy." The former actually do the same, but do it under the pretence of attending to reform measures more carefully. They live on reforms, as the others lived on abuses. Apparently eagerly engaged in reforms they have contrived a perfect system of postponing them. One day it is "advisable to await the result of an impending inquiry." Then "a Commission has just been appointed and nothing can be done till it has given its decisions." Again "the object is just under the consideration of the Government," who expect not to be interrupted in their lucubrations. Next, "the subject deserves the attention of the House—when a fitting opportunity shall occur." "The proper season has not yet arrived." "The time is not far distant when something must be done." Particular measures must be postponed in order to readjust entire systems, or entire systems must be conserved in order to carry out particular measures. The "policy of abstention" proclaimed on the Eastern question is also the Ministerial policy at home.

When Lord John Russell first[a] announced the programme of the Coalition Ministry, and when it was received amid general consternation, his adherents exclaimed, "We must have something to be enthusiastic at. Public education shall be the thing. Our Russell is breeding a wonderful Education scheme. You will hear of it."

Now we have heard of it. It was on the 4th of April that Russell gave a general description of his intended Educational Reform. Its principal features consist in enabling the municipal councils to levy a local rate for the assistance of *existing* schools in which the Church of England doctrines are required to be taught. As to the Universities, those pet-children of the State Church, those chief opponents to every reform, Lord John hopes "that the Universities will reform themselves."[b] The malversation of the charities destined for educational establishments is notorious. Their value may be guessed from the following:

---

[a] February 10, 1853.—*Ed.*

[b] Here and below John Russell's speech is quoted from *The Times*, No. 21394, April 5, 1853.—*Ed.*

"There are 24 of £2,000 a year and under £3,000, 10 of £3,000 and under £4,000, 4 of £4,000 and under £5,000, 2 of £5,000 and under £6,000, 3 of £8,000 and under £9,000, and single ones of £10,000, £15,000, £20,000,£29,000, £30,000 and £35,000 a year each."

It needs no great sagacity to conceive why the oligarchs living on the malversation of these funds are very cautious in dealing with them. Russell proposes:

"Charities are to be examined into, those under £30 per annum in the County Courts, those above by the Master of the Rolls. But *no suit* in either of those Courts is to be instigated *without the permission of a Committee of the Council appointed for the purpose.*"

The *permission* of a committee is necessary to institute a suit in the Imperial Courts to redress the plunder of the charities originally destined for the education of the people. A permission! But Russell, even with this reservation, feels not quite sure. He adds:

"If the administration of a school is *found* to be corrupt, *nobody but the Committee of Council shall be allowed to interfere.*"

This is a true Reform in the old English sense of the word. It neither creates anything new, nor abolishes anything old. It aims at conserving the old system, by giving it a more reasonable form and teaching it, so to say, new manners. This is the mystery of the "hereditary wisdom" of English oligarchical legislation. It simply consists in making abuses hereditary, by refreshing them, as it were, from time to time, by an infusion of new blood.

If everybody must confess that the Jewish Disabilities Bill was a *little* attempt at establishing religious tolerance, the Canada Reserves Bill a *little* attempt at granting Colonial Self-Government, the Education Bill a *little* attempt at avoiding public education, Gladstone's financial scheme is, undoubtedly, a *mighty little* attempt at dealing with that giant monster, the National Debt of Great Britain.

On the 8th of April, before the promulgation of the budget, Mr. Gladstone laid before the House of Commons a statement of several resolutions dealing with the public debt, and, before this statement had been made, *The Morning Chronicle* had made a special announcement that resolutions of the utmost importance were about to be proposed, "heralded by rumors of great interest and magnitude."[a] The funds rose on this rumor. There was an

[a] *The Morning Chronicle,* No. 26922, April 7, 1853 (cf. this volume, pp. 48-49).—*Ed.*

impression that Gladstone was going to pay off the National Debt; but on the 8th of April, the moment the Committee met for deliberation on these resolutions, Mr. Gladstone suddenly altered them, and in such a manner as to divest them both of "magnitude and interest." Now, let us ask, with Mr. Disraeli, "what was all this pother about?"[a]

The ultimate aim of Mr. Gladstone's propositions, as stated by himself, was to reduce the interest on the public stocks to the standard rate of $2^1/_2$ per cent. Now, in the years 1822-23-24-25, 1830-31, 1844-45, reductions were made from 5 per cent. to $4^1/_2$ per cent., from $4^1/_2$ to 4 per cent., from 4 to $3^1/_2$ per cent., from $3^1/_2$ to 3 per cent. respectively. Why should there not be a reduction from 3 per cent. to $2^1/_2$ per cent.? Mr. Gladstone's proposals are as follows:

Firstly. With respect to various stocks amounting to £9,500,000, and chiefly connected with the old South Sea bubble,[51] to bring them under one single denomination, and to reduce them compulsorily from 3 to $2^3/_4$ per cent. This would give a permanent annual saving approaching to £25,000. The invention of a new common name for various stocks, and the saving of £25,000 on an annual expense of £30,000,000, is certainly not to be boasted of.

Secondly. He proposes the issue of a new financial paper called *Exchequer Bonds*, not exceeding in amount £30,000,000, transferable by simple delivery without costs of any kind, bearing interest at $2^3/_4$ per cent. up to Sept. 1, 1864, and then $2^1/_2$ per cent. up to Sept. 1, 1894. Now this is merely the creation of a new financial instrument limited in its use by the wants of the monied and mercantile classes. But how can he keep £18,000,000 of Exchequer Bills at $1^1/_2$ per cent. in circulation, with Exchequer Bonds at $2^1/_2$ per cent.? And is it not a loss to the country to pay 1 per cent. more upon Exchequer Bonds than upon Exchequer Bills? Be this as it may, this second proposition has at least nothing to do with the reduction of the public debt.

Thirdly and lastly. We come to the chief object, the only important point of Gladstone's resolutions, to the 3 per cent. consols and the 3 per cent. reduced, amounting together to a capital of nearly £500,000,000. *Hic Rhodus, hic salta!*[b] As there exists a Parliamentary provision forbidding these stocks to be

---

[a] Here and below the quotations are from Benjamin Disraeli's speech in the House of Commons on April 8, 1853 (*The Times*, No. 21398, April 9, 1853).— *Ed.*

[b] Words addressed to a braggart in a tale by Aesop. He boasted of his leaps on the Island of Rhodes.— *Ed.*

reduced compulsorily, *except on twelve months notice*, Mr. Gladstone chooses the system of voluntary commutation, offering various alternatives to the [option] holders of the 3 per cent. stocks for exchanging them at option with other stocks to be created under his resolutions. They are to have the option of exchanging every £100 of the 3 per cent. stock in one of the following ways.

1. They may exchange every £100 of 3 per cent. stock for an Exchequer Bond of the like amount, bearing interest at the rate of $2^3/_4$ per cent. until 1864, and then at the rate of $2^1/_2$ per cent. until 1894. If the whole of the £30,000,000 Exchequer Bonds at $2^1/_2$ per cent. should thus replace £30,000,000 of 3 per cent. there would be a saving in the first ten years of £75,000, and after the first ten years of £150,000—together £225,000; but Government would be bound to repay the whole of the £30,000,000. In any case this is not a proposition to deal largely with the public debt.

2. The second proposal is, that the holders of stock shall obtain for every £100 in 3 per cent. £82 10s. in new stock at $3^1/_2$ per cent., which shall be paid at the rate of $3^1/_2$ per cent. until the 5th January, 1894. The result of this would be to give a present income to the persons accepting the $3^1/_2$ per cent. stock of £2 17s. 9d., instead of £3. Here then is a reduction of 2s. 3d. annually in every £100. If the £500,000,000 were all converted upon this proposal, the result would be that instead of paying as at present £15,000,000 a-year, the nation would only pay £14,437,500, and this would be a gain of £562,500 a-year. But for this small saving of £562,500 Parliament would tie up its hands for half a century and guaranty a higher interest than 2 4-5 per cent. at a time of transition and of utter uncertainty as to the future standard rate of interest. On the other hand, one thing at least would be gained for Mr. Gladstone. At the expiration of 40 years, he would not be troubled with a 3 per cent. stock, being defended, as now, by a twelve months' notice. He would only have to deal with the $3^1/_2$ per cent. stock redeemable at par by Parliament. Gladstone proposes not to fix any limit on his $3^1/_2$ per cent. stock.

3. The third proposal is that the holders of every £100 3 per cent. should receive £110 in a new stock of $2^1/_2$ per cent. until 1894. When Mr. Gladstone introduced his plan in the House of Commons on the 8th April, he had not limited the amount (the $2^1/_2$ per cents.) to be issued. But Mr. Disraeli having pointed out that, contrasting this proposal with the two other modes proposed, every man in his senses would choose the conversion of £100 into $2^1/_2$ per cents., and that by the conversion of the whole £500,000,000 3 per cents. into the new stock, the country would

gain on one side £1,250,000 per annum, but be saddled on the other side with an addition to the capital of the public debt of £50,000,000, Mr. Gladstone on the following day altered this proposition and proposed to limit this new $2^1/_2$ stock to £30,000,000. By this alteration the whole of the third proposal loses its significance with respect to the public debt. The capital of that debt would be augmented only by £3,000,000.

Here you have "one of the most important and gigantic financial proposals that has ever been brought forward."[a] There exists perhaps in general no greater humbug than the so-called Finance. The most simple operations on the Budget and the Public Debt are clothed by the adepts of that occult science in an abstruse terminology, concealing the trivial maneuvers of creating various denominations of stocks—the commutation of old stocks into new ones, the diminishing the interest and raising the nominal capital, the raising the interest and reducing the capital, the installing of premiums, of bonus, priority-shares, the distinctions between redeemable and irredeemable annuities, the artificial graduation in the facility of transferring the various descriptions of paper—in a manner which quite bamboozles the public with these detestable stock-jobbing scholastics and frightful complexity of details, while the usurers obtain with every such new scheme an eagerly seized opportunity for developing their mischievous and predatory activity. On the other hand, the political economist finds in all this apparent intricacy of commutations, permutations and combinations, not so much a matter of financial policy as a simple question of arithmetic or of mere phraseology.

Mr. Gladstone is certainly a master in this sort of financial alchymics, and his scheme cannot be better characterized, than in the words of Mr. Disraeli:

> "More complicated and ingenious machinery, to produce so slight a result, appeared to him never to have been devised by the subtlety and genius of the most skilful casuist. In St. Thomas Aquinas[b] there was a chapter that speculated upon the question of how many angels could dance on the point of a needle. It was one of the rarest productions of human genius; and he recognised in these resolutions something of that master mind."

You will remember that I stated that the end of Mr. Gladstone's plan was the establishment of a "normal" $2^1/_2$ per cent. stock. Now, in order to achieve this end, he creates a very limited $2^1/_2$

[a] A quotation from the speech of Edward Ellice, M.P. from Coventry, cited by Benjamin Disraeli in his House of Commons speech on April 8, 1853.—*Ed.*

[b] Thomas Aquinas, *Summa Theologica*.—*Ed.*

per cent. stock and an unlimited $3^{1}/_{2}$ per cent. stock. In order to create his small $2^{1}/_{2}$ per cent. stock, he reduces the interest by $^{1}/_{2}$ per cent., and gives on the other hand a bonus of 10 per cent. for the purpose of accomplishing that reduction. In order to rid himself of the difficulty of the 3 per cent., being "defended" by a twelve-months notice, he prefers legislating for the 40 years next to come, and in conclusion he would, if successful, bereave two generations of all possible fortunate chances in their financial affairs.

The position of the Coalition Ministry in the House, is clearly shown by the statistics of votes. On the question of Maynooth[52] in a large house, it had but the narrow majority of 30. On the Jewish Disabilities Bill (not yet carried through the third reading), in a house of 439 members, its majority amounted not even to 30 votes. In the Canada Reserves Bill, when Russell withdrew his own third clause, the Ministers were saved by the Tories from their own supporters. Their majority was almost entirely supplied from the benches of the Conservatives.

I shall not dwell on the internal dissensions of the Cabinet, which appeared in the debates on the Canada Bill, in the hot controversy of the ministerial papers with regard to the Income-Tax, and above all, in their foreign policy. There is not one single question to which the Coalition Ministry might not answer, as did Gaysa, the Magyar king, who, after having been converted to Christianity, continued, notwithstanding, to observe the rites of his ancient superstition. When questioned to which of the two faiths he really belonged, he replied: "I am rich enough to belong to two sorts of faith."

Written on April 12, 1853

First published in the *New-York Daily Tribune,* No. 3753, April 27, 1853; reprinted in the *Semi-Weekly Tribune,* No. 827, April 29, 1853

Signed: *Karl Marx*

Reproduced from the *New-York Daily Tribune*

Karl Marx

FEARGUS O'CONNOR.— MINISTERIAL DEFEATS.—THE BUDGET

London, Tuesday, April 19, 1853

The Commission which met last week to examine into the state of mind of Feargus O'Connor, late M.P. for Nottingham, returned the following verdict:

"We find that Mr. Feargus O'Connor has been insane since the 10th of June, 1852, without any lucid intervals."[a]

As a political character O'Connor had outlived himself already in 1848. His strength was broken, his mission fulfilled, and unable to master the proletarian movement organised by himself, he had grown almost a hindrance to it. If historical impartiality oblige me not to conceal this circumstance, it also obliges me in justice to the fallen man, to lay before the same public, the judgment given on O'Connor, by Ernest Jones, in *The People's Paper*:

"Here was a man who broke away from rank, wealth, and station; who threw up a lucrative and successful practice; who dissipated a large fortune, not in private self-denial, but in political self-sacrifice; who made himself an eternal exile from his own country, where he owned broad acres and represented one of its largest Counties; who was hated by his family because he loved the human race; whose every act was devotion to the people; and who ends almost destitute after a career of unexampled labor.... There is his life. Now look at his work: At a time of utter prostration, of disunion, doubt and misery, he gathered the millions of this country together, as men had never yet been gathered. O'Connell rallied the Irish, but it was with the help of the priests; Mazzini roused the Italians, but nobles and traders were on his side; Kossuth gathered the Hungarians, but Senates and armies were at his back; and both the Hungarians and Italians were burning against a foreign conqueror. But O'Connor, without noble, priest or trader, rallied and upheld one downtrodden class against them all! without even the leverage of national feeling to

[a] *The People's Paper*, No. 50, April 16, 1853; below is cited a passage from Ernest Jones' article "The People's Friend" published in this issue.—*Ed.*

unite them! La Fayette had the merchants, Lamartine had the shopkeepers. O'Connor had the people! But the people in the nineteenth century, in Constitutional England, are the weakest of all. He taught them how to become the strongest."

Last week was a week of defeats for the Coalition Cabinet. It met for the first time with a Coalition Opposition. On Tuesday the 12th inst., Mr. Butt moved to maintain for the Irish soldiers the Asylum of Kilmainham Hospital. The Secretary at War[a] opposed the motion; but it was carried against the Government by 198 against 131. On this occasion it was beaten by a Coalition of the Irish Brigade[53] with the Conservative Opposition. On the following Thursday it was defeated by a Coalition of the Conservatives and the Manchester School.[54] Mr. Milner Gibson having brought in his yearly motion for the abolition of the "Taxes on Knowledge," the repeal of the Advertisement Duty was voted,[55] notwithstanding the protestations of Gladstone, Russell and Sidney. They lost, by 200 against 169. Bright, Gibson and MacGregor voted side by side with Disraeli, Pakington, etc., and Mr. Cobden made the formal declaration, "That he accepted the assistance of Mr. Disraeli and his friends with all his heart."[b] But by far the greatest defeat the Government has sustained was brought upon it, not by a division in the House, but by an act of its own.

Of the Kossuth rocket affair[c] full particulars will already have reached the readers of the *Tribune*, but in order to prove that the whole of it was a premeditated affair between Palmerston and the Foreign Powers, it is merely necessary to state what his own official journal, *The Morning Post*, contains with regard to the occurrence:

"The promptitude and vigilance of the course adopted by Government will give confidence to those foreign powers who have doubted the efficacy of our laws in repressing mischief among our troublesome guests."[d]

This business will have its serious consequences for the Coalition Ministry. Already, and this is of great significance, it has demasked old Palmerston's revolutionary dandyism. Even his most credulous but honest admirer, *The Morning Advertiser*, openly disavows him. Palmerston's star began to pale at the time when he bestowed his sympathies on the hero of the 2d December and of the plain of

[a] S. Herbert.— *Ed.*

[b] Richard Cobden's speech in the House of Commons on April 14 is quoted from the leading article published in *The Times*, No. 21403, April 15, 1853.— *Ed.*

[c] See this volume, pp. 82-84.— *Ed.*

[d] *The Morning Post*, April 18, 1853.— *Ed.*

Satory; it has vanished, since he became professedly an "Austrian Minister."[56] But, the mission of the Coalition Ministry is precisely the demoralization of all the current talents and *renommées* of the old Oligarchy. And this problem it is resolving with an admirable perseverance. Should Palmerston's Ministry survive this catastrophe, then he may indeed, with a slight alteration of the saying of Francis I, jocosely proclaim "Nothing is lost except honor."[a]

I come now to the event of the day—Mr. Gladstone's budget—laid before the House of Commons in its yesterday's sitting, in a speech which occupied no less than five hours.[b] It is a Coalition Budget, elaborated in an encyclopedical manner, exceedingly fitted for an article in *Ersch & Gruber's* voluminous Dictionary of Arts and Sciences. You know that the era of encyclopedists arrives always when facts have become bulky, and genius remains proportionably small.

In every budget the principal question is the relation between income and expenditure, the balance in the shape of a surplus or a deficiency prescribing the general conditions of either a relaxation or an increase to be established in the taxation of the country. Mr. Disraeli had estimated the revenue for the year 1852-53 at £52,325,000, and the expenditure at £51,163,000. Now, Mr. Gladstone informs us that the actual revenue has been £53,089,000, and the real expenditure only £50,782,000. These figures show an actual surplus of income over expenditure amounting to £2,460,000. Thus far, Mr. Gladstone would seem to have improved Mr. Disraeli. The latter could only boast of a surplus of £1,600,000; Gladstone comes with a saving of £2,460,000. Unfortunately, unlike Disraeli's surplus, that of Mr. Gladstone, on nearer examination, dwindles down to the moderate amount of £700,000, the millions having already found their way out of his pocket by various votes of the House of Commons and other extraordinary expenditure; and, as Mr. Gladstone cautiously adds:

> "It must be remembered that £215,000, out of the £700,000, is derived from occasional and not permanent sources of income."

Then, the only basis of operations left to Mr. Gladstone is a surplus of £485,000. Accordingly any proposed remission of old

---

[a] After his defeat and capture at Pavia in 1525, in the war against the King of Spain and the Emperor of Germany, Charles V, Francis I wrote in a letter to his mother: "All is lost except honour."—*Ed.*

[b] The reference is to William Gladstone's speech in the House of Commons on April 18, 1853, quoted below from the report in *The Times*, No. 21406, April 19, 1853.—*Ed.*

taxes beyond this amount has to be balanced by the imposition of new ones.

Mr. Gladstone opened his speech with the "*question brûlante*" of the Income Tax. He said that it was possible to part with that tax at once, but that the Government were not prepared to recommend its immediate abandonment. The first thing to which he called attention was, that "we draw from this tax £5,500,000." Next he attempted a "brilliant" vindication of the effects of this tax, on the history of which he expended a good deal of breath.

> "The Income Tax," he remarked, "has served in a time of vital struggle to enable you to raise the income of the country above its expenditure for war and civil government.... If you do not destroy the efficacy of this engine, it affords you the means, should unhappily hostilities again break out, of at once raising your army to 300,000 men, and your fleet to 100,000, with all your establishments in proportion."

Further Mr. Gladstone observed, that the Income Tax had not only served in carrying on the Anti-Jacobin war, but also the free-trade policy of Sir Robert Peel. After this apologetic introduction we are suddenly startled by the announcement that "the Income Tax is full of irregularities." In fact, Mr. Gladstone admits, that in order to preserve the tax, it must be reconstructed so as to avoid its present inequalities; but that in order to remove these inequalities, you must break up the whole set. Strangely contradicting himself, he is afterwards at great pains to show that there exist no such inequalities at all, and that they are merely imaginary. As to the question of realized and precarious incomes, he reduces it to a question of "land and of trade," and tries to persuade people, through some awkward calculations, that land actually pays 9d. in the pound, while trade only pays 7d. He then adds:

> "that the assessment on land and houses does not depend on the returns of the owners, whereas in trade the returns of income are made by the holders themselves, and in many cases in a fraudulent manner."

With regard to fundholders, Mr. Gladstone asserts that to tax the capitalised value of their income, would be a gross breach of the public faith. Any distinction, in short, between realized or precarious income, as proposed by Mr. Disraeli, is flatly rejected by Mr. Gladstone. On the other hand he is ready to extend the Income Tax to Ireland, and an income above £100, the limit of its area having hitherto been at £150 a year. Quite inconsistently, however, with his just pronounced doctrine, that "it is impossible to distinguish between the respective value of intelligence, labor and property, and to represent these relations in arithmetical results," he proposes to subject incomes between £100 and £150 to a rate of only 5d. in the pound. Lastly, in order to reconcile his admiration for the Income Tax, with the avowed necessity of its abolition, Mr. Gladstone proposes

"to renew the tax for two years, from April, 1853, at 7d. in the pound; for two years more, from April, 1855, at the rate of 6d. in the pound; and for three years more, from April, 1857, at the rate of 5d. in the pound; under which proposal the tax would expire on 5th April, 1860."

Having thus conferred, what he imagines to be a boon, [on] the landed aristocracy and the fundholders, by his refusal to acknowledge the principle of distinction between realized and precarious incomes, Mr. Gladstone, on the other hand, is careful to hold out a similar bait to the Manchester School by the adjustment of the legacy duty, extending it to all kinds of property, but declining to deal with the probates.

"I have no doubt," he remarked, "that this tax, if adjusted by the House, will add £500,000 more to our permanent means in 1853-'54; will add £700,000 more in 1854-'55; £400,000 in 1855-'56; and £400,000 more in 1856-'57; making a total addition to the permanent means of the country of £2,000,000."

Respecting Scotland, Mr. Gladstone proposed, that 1/ should be added to the present Spirits' Duty of 3/8 (the gain would be £318,000), and also an increased impost on the licenses of tea-dealers, brewers, maltsters, tobacco-manufacturers and dealers, and soap-boilers.

The whole amount of the increased taxes available for the year 1853-'54 would thus be:

Upon the Income Tax	£295,000
Upon the Legacy Duty	500,000
Upon Spirits	436,000
Upon Licenses	113,000
Total	£1,344,000
Which with the surplus of	805,000
Would give us for the remission of taxes a sum amounting to	£2,149,000

Now, what are the propositions of Mr. Gladstone with respect to the remission of old taxes? I shall restrain myself, of course, from entering too deeply into this labyrinth. It cannot be fathomed in a moment. Accordingly I shall touch merely on the principal points, which are:

1. The abolition of the duty on Soap, the gross amount of which is actually £1,397,000.

2. Gradual reduction of the duties on Tea, when the descent from $2/2^{1}/_{4}$ to 1/ is to be brought about in about three years.

3. Remission of the duties upon a large number of minor articles.

4. Relaxation of the £4,000,000 owed by Ireland in the shape of Consolidated Annuities.

5. Reduction of the Attorney's Certificate Duty by one-half, according to the motion of Lord R. Grosvenor, which abolished the whole.

6. Reduction of the Advertisement Duty to /6, according to the motion of Mr. Gibson (the House having, however, already noted its entire abolition).

Lastly:

7. Abolition of the Stamp Duty on Newspaper Supplements (a huge *pièce de réjouissance*[a] for *The Times*, the only paper issuing Supplements).

These are, in short, the principal features of the budget which Mr. Gladstone has been hatching now for more than four months. The debate in the House of Commons, fixed for Monday next, will afford me the opportunity of further commenting upon that coalition product.

Written on April 19, 1853

First published in the *New-York Daily Tribune*, No. 3758, May 3, 1853

Signed: *Karl Marx*

Reproduced from the newspaper

[a] Enjoyment.— *Ed.*

Karl Marx

L. S. D., OR CLASS BUDGETS, AND WHO'S RELIEVED BY THEM

Gladstone has brought forth his Budget. We have heard two cocks on a barn floor crowing against each other, in style somewhat similar to that of the two Chancellors of the Exchequer—Ex[a] and Actual—on the floor of the House of Commons—with this difference, that the Whig Bantam has borrowed some of the notes of the Conservative Turkey. Last week we analysed that portion of Mr. Gladstone's financial plan which deals with the National Debt, and showed how it was a miserable paltering with the question, and a mere matter of convenience to usurers, stockjobbers, and merchants, to facilitate and cheapen their transactions.[b] We shall see, on the present occasion, that the Budget is a class Budget—a middle class Budget—written by an aristocratic pen. We will, first, give a brief outline of this notable affair:—

I.—As to Expenditure and Revenue:

The Chancellor states that the National Expenditure for the present year will exceed that of the last, by £1,400,000!! A promising way of opening a Budget of Financial Reform. The cause of the increase is not less encouraging.

It comprises an increase in our naval force of £617,000; in the army and commissariat of £90,000; for the ordnance £616,000; for the militia £230,000. While education, the arm of enlightenment and the defence of knowledge, receives an increase of only £100,000. The total estimated expenditure of the country for

---

[a] Benjamin Disraeli.—*Ed.*

[b] See this volume, pp. 44-49.—*Ed.*

the current year, is placed at £52,183,000. The total income is estimated at £52,990,000—showing a surplus of £807,000, from which, however, £100,000 is deducted for the packet service, and altogether an available surplus predicted of £500,000.

We now approach

II.—The Financial Scheme.

Here the Chancellor deals:—*Firstly.* With the Income Tax; and makes no distinction between fixed and precarious incomes. He proposes to reduce, after two years, the tax from 7d. to 6d. in the pound. Then, after two years more, from 6d. to 5d. for three years—to extend the tax to Ireland, and to lower it so as to embrace incomes of £100 per annum. This, he says, "will not touch upon the ranks of labour." The incomes between £100 and £150 are to pay only 5d. in the pound. The effect of this will be, to lighten the burdens of the rich, and cast that alleviation as a weight upon the less rich. The wealthy tradesman is to pay less, but, to make up for it, the poor tradesman is to pay where he did not pay directly before. This is strange justice—for four years, it is true, the man of £100 is to pay 2d. in the pound less than he of £150, or £150,000—but after that period they pay the same—while after two years the rich man comes into the benefit of a reduction effected by taxing the poorer one. Our notion of taxation would far sooner incline to a graduated scale in which the percentage increased with the amount of the income, for 10,000 fivepences are less to the man of £10,000 per annum, than 100 fivepences to him of £100. So much for Whig Finance—with a specious, paltry, and roundabout tinkering, it gradually but surely lightens the burdens of the rich and increases the burdens of the poor. As to saying that the Income Tax does not affect the working man, it is a patent absurdity, for under our present social system of employer and employed, the middle class man generally indemnifies himself for additional taxation in diminished wages or increased prices.

Secondly. The Chancellor proceeds to the legacy duties. Here he relieves the sons-in-law and daughters-in-law from the "relations'" duty of 10 per cent. reducing theirs to 7 per cent.—infinitesimal boon!—and includes all property within the operations of the tax, the succession to rateable property being taxed on the life interest. By this means he adds £2,000,000 to the taxation of the country, and takes credit to himself for supporting skill and industry as against property. This clause recognises a principle, and is a significant concession, extorted by industrial and commercial development from propertied monopoly. It is, we repeat, a concession; but one the evasion of which is not only easy, but may possibly have been borne in mind by the propertied legislators of the financial world.

Thirdly. The stamp duties for receipts are to be repealed, and the affixing of a penny postage stamp to a receipt of any amount is in future to be sufficient. A great measure of convenience—to the rich—in which the increased use of stamps is supposed to counterbalance the loss of revenue, but in which, again, no benefit is conferred on the working classes, in but very few of whose transactions matter of sufficient value (£5) to demand a stamp ever comes under consideration.

Fourthly. The Advertisement Duty is reduced to 6d., instead of 1s. 6d., as now. This is another instance of miserable tinkering. No sound reason can be advanced for keeping the sixpence if you give up the shilling—inasmuch as the cumbrous and expensive machinery for collecting the sixpence will eat up the proceeds of the tax! But the reason may possibly be, not to have to give up the posts and appointments connected with the levying of that impost. Supplements to newspapers containing advertisements only—are to go free by post. Both these clauses are a concession to the middle class—while the retention of the newspaper stamp still fronts with its massive barrier the spread of Democratic education. "The present papers shall have advantages," says the Chancellor, "but new ones, and cheaper ones, shall not be started."

Fifthly. The Tax on Life Assurance is reduced from 2s. 6d. to 6d.—another instance of the same paltering spirit; indentures of apprenticeship, without consideration, from £1 to 2s. 6d.; attorneys' certificates from £12 and £8 to £9 and £6; and the articles of clerks from £120 to £80. The first and two last items of the above are again a manifest relief to the middle class, but not the shadow of a benefit to the poor—while the tax of 6d. is kept on advertisements, the Newspaper Stamp Duties and the Taxes on Paper are retained, in order that those on servants, dogs, and horses, may be reduced to benefit the rich.

Sixthly. In Scotland and Ireland an addition is to be made to the Spirit Duties—and the distillers are to have an allowance for "waste."

Seventhly. Tradesmen's Licences (another boon to the middle class) are to be more equalised.

Eighthly. The Soap Duties, and a host of others, are to be dealt with, and the Duty on Tea is to be reduced from 2s. $2^1/_4$ d. to 1s. 10d. up to '54; to 1s. 3d. to '56; and to 1s. after that date.

Such is a fair outline of the Whig Budget; and we ask our readers whether a more contemptible piece of "Penny Legislation," to use the Chancellor's own expression, ever emanated from the Treasury Bench? It is plausible, specious, and sets forth some showy points; but what real benefit, what real relief, is conferred on the working classes of this country? The reduction of the duties on soap and tea are the only features at which one can catch; but small indeed is the relief thus conferred. The margin has everywhere been nicely measured, beyond which the working man would gain—the aristocrat and middle classes lose; and the transgression of that margin has been studiously avoided. The Budget is likely to catch the thoughtless among the people: "Reduction of Advertisement Duty to 6d. and Suppression of the Supplement Stamp!" But what does it practically amount to for the people? Nothing! "Penny Receipt Stamps!" But what is that to the wages-slaves who "receive" starvation? Absolutely nothing. "Life Assurances reduced from 2s. 6d. to 6d." What is it to the toiler at 6s., 8s., 10s., per week—who cannot insure his life from the crushing slavery of Manchester? Ay, or even to him at £1 and 30s? Nothing! What is it to the workingman that attorneys can get certificates for £3 less? Or clerks be articled for £80 instead of £40 more? What to them is the lightening of the legacy duty in one item, and its general extension so easily avoided? Does it ease their burthen by the weight of a single feather? What is it to them that the shopkeepers' licences shall be more equalised, while their profits on labour's wants find no equality with labour's wage? "Financial Reform" was the one cry out of two which seated this Parliament and raised this ministry. There you have it—the Reform of Whigs, aristocrats, and moneymongers. Something was necessary—some slight concession—the task was to make it so slight, that it should scarcely be perceptible, and admirably has the financial artist succeeded in his attempt. In his own words—to use his own expressions—Gladstone's Budget is framed "for the convenience of the trading classes," and yet it is but a piece of "Penny Legislation."

Written about April 20, 1853

First published in *The People's Paper*, No. 51, April 23, 1853

Reproduced from the newspaper

Karl Marx

RIOT AT CONSTANTINOPLE.— GERMAN TABLE MOVING.—THE BUDGET[57]

London, Friday, April 22, 1853

A telegraphic dispatch has been received to the effect that on the 12th inst. there was a great tumult at Constantinople and the vicinity, fifteen Christians having been killed or wounded by the fanatic Turkish mob.

"Order was immediately restored by means of the military force."

Another dispatch from Copenhagen states that the Chamber or Folketing has rejected the ministerial message on the proposed succession of the Danish Crown. This we may consider as an important check to the diplomacy of Russia, whose interests the message represented, according to the London protocol acknowledging Russia as ultimate heir of the Danish kingdom.[58]

From the Hague we learn that an agitation similar to that which visited England two years ago in the shape of "Roman Catholic aggression,"[59] has now taken hold of the Netherlands, and led to the formation of an ultra-Protestant ministry. Concerning Germany, or rather that portion of it formerly known under the name of the Empire,[60] nothing can be more significant of the present state of mind prevailing through the educated middle-class, than a declaration of the editor of *The Frankfort Journal*, under date of April 19. For the edification of your readers I give you a translation of it:

"The communications we receive by every post, on the subject of table-moving (*Tisch-Rücken*),[a] are assuming an extent to which, since the memorable 'Song on the Rhine,' by Nic. Becker, and the first days of the revolution of March, 1848, we

[a] The reference is to spiritism, very much in vogue in Germany at the time.—*Ed.*

have seen nothing equal. Satisfactory as these communications are, since they prove better than any political *raisonnement*, in what *harmless and innocent* times we again find ourselves, we regret that we cannot take further notice of them, fearing that they might entirely overwhelm our readers and ourselves, and absorb in the end all the space of this journal."

"*An Englishman*"[a] has addressed a letter to *The Times*, and Lord Palmerston, on the latest Kossuth affair, at the conclusion of which he says:

"When the Coalition Cabinet is gathered to its fathers, or its uncles, or grandfathers, we would delicately hint to the noble lord a new edition of *Joe Miller*. In fact we opine we shall hear no more of Joe. Palmerston will be the word. It is long. That is a fault! We believe, however, it has already been improved into the Anglo-Saxon *Pam*. This will suit verse as well as prose, and rhyme with 'sham, flam, and cram.'"[b]

In my letter of Tuesday last[c] I gave you a rough sketch of Mr. Gladstone's budget. I have now before me an official publication, filling 50 pages in folio: "The Resolutions to be proposed by the Chancellor of the Exchequer," and "An expository Statement to accompany the Resolutions," but I shall only touch on those details which would be of interest to foreign readers in the event of their becoming the law of Great Britain.

The most important resolutions are those concerning the Customs. There is a proposal to abolish the duties on 123 minor articles, yielding about £55,000 per annum, and including all furniture woods with four exceptions, as well as fixtures and frames, bricks and tiles. There is to be a reduction, firstly, on the tea duties from 2/2¼ to 1/10 till 5th April, 1854; secondly, on 12 articles of food. The present duty on almonds is to be reduced to 2/2 per cwt.; upon cheese from 5/ to 2/6 per cwt.; on cocoa from 2d. to 1d. per lb.; on nuts from 2/ to 1/ per bushel; on eggs from 10d. to 4d. a hundred; on oranges and lemons to 8d. a bushel; on butter from 10/ to 5/ per cwt.; on raisins from 15/9 to 10/ per cwt.; and on apples from 2/ to 3d. per bushel. The whole of these articles yield, at present, a revenue of £262,000. There is, in the third place, to be a reduction on 133 articles of food, yielding a revenue of £70,000. Besides, a simplification is to be applied on a number of articles by the levy of specific instead of *ad valorem* duties.

---

[a] The pen-name of A. Richards.—*Ed.*

[b] Quoted from the anonymous article "*The Times* and the New Gunpowder Plot" by A. Richards, published in *The Morning Advertiser*, No. 19291, April 21, 1853.—*Ed.*

[c] See this volume, pp. 57-62.—*Ed.*

As to the Excise, I have already stated the proposed abolition of the soap tax, and the increase in the scale of licenses to brewers and dealers in tea, coffee, tobacco and soap.

As to the Stamps, besides the reduction on attorneys' certificates, and in the advertisement duty, there is to be a reduction of the duty on life assurances, on receipt stamps, on indentures of apprenticeship, and on hackney carriages.

As to Assessed taxes, there is to be a reduction of the taxes on men-servants, private carriages, horses, ponies and dogs, and a reduction of $17^1/_2$ per cent. in the charge for redemption of land tax.

As to the Post-Office, there is to be a reduction of colonial postages to a uniform rate of 6d.

A general feature of the budget deserving note, is the circumstance of most of its provisions having been forced on the Coalition Ministry, after an obstinate opposition to them in the course of the present session.

Mr. Gladstone proposes *now* to extend the legacy duty to real property; but on the 1st of March he still opposed Mr. Williams's motion, that real property should be made to pay the "same probate and legacy duties as are now payable on personal property!" He affirmed on that occasion, as the Tory journals do at this very moment, that the exemption was only apparent, and counterbalanced by other duties peculiar to real property. It is equally true, that on the same 1st of March, Mr. Williams threatened Mr. Gladstone with "being replaced by Mr. Disraeli, if he were not to give way on that point."

Mr. Gladstone proposes *now* to abolish or reduce the protective duties on about 268 minor articles; but on the 3d of March he still opposed Mr. Hume's motion, of "speedily repealing the strictly protective duties on about 285 articles." It is also true that Mr. Disraeli declared on that day that

> "we could not cling to the rags and tatters of the Protective System."

Mr. Gladstone proposes now to reduce the advertisement duty by one half; but only four days before he brought out his Budget he opposed Mr. Milner Gibson's motion, to repeal that duty. It is true that he was defeated by a division of the House.

It would be easy to augment this enumeration of concessions made by the Coalition Ministry to the Manchester School.[61] What do these concessions prove? That the industrial bourgeoisie, weakly represented as it is in the House, are yet the real masters of the situation, and that every Government, whether Whig, Tory, or Coalition, can only keep itself in office, and the bourgeoisie out of office, by doing for them their preliminary work. Go through the records of British legislation since 1825, and you will find that the bourgeoisie is only resisted politically by concession after concession financially. What the Oligarchy fail to comprehend, is, the simple fact that political power is but the offspring of commercial power, and that the class to which they are compelled to yield the latter, will necessarily conquer the former also. Louis XIV himself, when legislating through Colbert in the interest of the manufacturers, was only preparing the revolution of 1789, when his "*l'état c'est moi*" was answered by Sieyès with "*le tiers état est tout.*"[a]

Another very striking feature of the budget is the strict adoption of the policy of Mr. Disraeli, "that reckless adventurer" who dared to affirm in the House that the necessary result of commercial free-trade was a financial revolution, that is to say, the gradual commutation of indirect into direct taxation. Indeed, what does Mr. Gladstone propose? He strengthens and extends the system of direct taxation, in order to weaken and to contract the system of indirect taxation.

On the one side he renews the income-tax unaltered for seven years. He extends it to a whole people, to the Irish. He extends it by copying Mr. Disraeli, to a whole class, to the holders of incomes from £100 to £150. He accepts, partially, the extension of the house-tax, proposed by Mr. Disraeli, giving it the name of an altered license-tax and raising the charge for licenses in proportion to the size of the premises. Lastly, he augments direct taxation by £2,000,000, by subjecting real property to the legacy-duty, which was also promised by Mr. Disraeli.

On the other side he attacks indirect taxation under the two forms of Customs and of Excise; in the former by adopting Disraeli's reduction of the tea duties, or by abolishing, reducing, or simplifying the customs duties on 268 articles; in the latter by entirely abolishing the soap-tax.

The only difference between his budget and that of his predecessor, is this, that the one was the author, and that the other is the plagiary; that Disraeli removed the excise-duties in favor of the land-interest, and that Gladstone removes them in

---

[a] This refers to the following passage from Emmanuel Sieyès' *Qu'est-ce que le tiers-état?*: "What is the third estate? Everything.—What was it until now politically? Nothing.—What is it striving for? To be something."—*Ed.*

favor of the town-interest; that Disraeli proclaimed the principle, but was forced by his exceptional position to falsify the practice, while Gladstone, opposed to the principle, is enabled by his coalition character to carry details through a series of compromises.

What will be the probable fate of the Coalition budget, and what will be the probable attitude assumed by the respective parties?

There are, in general, but three points on which the battle can be fought—the Income-Tax, the Legacy-Duty, and Ireland.

The Manchester School has pledged itself to oppose any prolongation of that "horrid inequality," the present Income-Tax. The oracle of Printinghouse-square,[a] *The Times*, has thundered for ten years against that same "monstrosity," and the public prejudice of Great Britain in general has doomed the present system of charging equally all descriptions of income. But on this one point Mr. Gladstone repudiates compromise. As Mr. Disraeli, when Chancellor of the Exchequer, proposed to modify the Income-Tax by establishing a distinction between precarious revenues and realized property, charging the former with 5d. and the latter with 7d. in the pound, the Income-Tax would seem to become the rallying point for the common opposition of the Conservatives, the Manchester School and the "general opinion" represented by *The Times*.

But will the Manchester men redeem their pledge? This is very doubtful. They are in the commercial habit of pocketing the present profits, and of letting principles shift for themselves. And the present profits offered by Mr. Gladstone's budget are by no means contemptible. Already the tone of the Manchester organs has become very moderate and very conciliatory with regard to the Income-Tax. They begin to comfort themselves with the prospect held out by Mr. Gladstone, that "the whole Income-Tax shall expire in seven years,"[b] forgetting at the opportune moment that, when the late Sir Robert Peel introduced it in 1842, he promised its expiration by the year 1845, and that the extension of a tax is a very awkward way toward its ulterior extinction.

As to *The Times*, that is the only journal which will profit by Mr. Gladstone's proposal of abolishing the stamp on newspaper supplements. It has to pay for double supplements every day that it publishes them during the week 40,000 pence, or £166 3s. The

---

[a] The square in London where *The Times* had its main offices.—*Ed.*

[b] Quoted from William Gladstone's speech in the House of Commons on April 18, 1853, published in *The Times*, No. 21406, April 19, 1853.—*Ed.*

whole of the 40,000d. remitted by Mr. Gladstone will go into its coffers. We can then conceive that the Cerberus will be soothed down into a lamb, without Mr. Gladstone being metamorphosed into a Hercules. It would be difficult to find in all the Parliamentary history of Great Britain, a more undignified act than this of Mr. Gladstone, buying up the support of a journal by inserting a special provision for it in the budget. The abolition of the Taxes on Knowledge was chiefly asked for with a view to break down the monopoly of the newspaper-leviathans. The "unctuous" Mr. Gladstone adopts only so much of that measure as tends exactly to double the monopoly of *The Times*.

In principle, we contend that Mr. Gladstone is right in rejecting all distinctions between the sources from which income is derived. If you distinguish between the quality of incomes you must also distinguish between quantity, as in 99 cases out of 100, the quantity of an income constitutes its quality. If you distinguish between their quantities you arrive unavoidably at progressive taxation, and from progressive taxation you tumble directly into a very trenchant sort of Socialism, a thing certainly abhorred by the opponents of Mr. Gladstone. With the narrow and interested interpretation of the difference between fixed and precarious incomes, as made by the Manchester School, we arrive at the ridiculous conclusion that the income of the richest class of England, the trading class, is only a precarious one. Under the pretence of philanthropy they aim at changing a portion of the public burdens from their own shoulders to the backs of the land-owners and fundholders.

As to the extension of the legacy-duty to real property the country party, as cannot be doubted, will vehemently resist it. They naturally desire to receive their successions as heretofore, untaxed; but Mr. Disraeli, as Chancellor of the Exchequer, has acknowledged the injustice of that exception, and the Manchester men will vote as one man with the Ministers. *The Morning Advertiser* in its number of yesterday[a] informs the country party that should they be imprudent enough to take their stand on the legacy duty, they must abandon all idea of being supported by the Liberals. There exists hardly any privilege to which the British middle class are more bitterly opposed, and there exists also no more striking instance of oligarchic legislation. Pitt introduced in 1796 two bills, the one subjecting personal property to the probate and legacy-duty, and the other imposing the same duties on real

[a] April 21, 1853.—*Ed.*

property. The two measures were separated because Pitt apprehended a successful opposition from members of both houses to subjecting their estates to those taxes. The first bill passed the House with little or no opposition. Only one division took place, and only 16 members voted against it. The second bill was proceeded with through all its stages, until it came to the third reading, when it was lost by a division of 30 against 30. Pitt, seeing no chance of passing the bill through either house, was forced to withdraw it. If the probate and legacy-duties had been paid on real property since 1796, by far the greater portion of the public debt might have been paid off. The only real objection the country party could now make is the plea that the fundholders enjoy a similar exemption, but they would, of course, not strengthen their position by rousing against them the fundholders, who are gifted with a particular taste for fiscal immunities.

There remains then but one probable chance of successfully opposing the Coalition budget, and this is a coalition of the country party with the Irish Brigade.[62] It is true Mr. Gladstone has endeavored to induce the Irish to submit to the extension of the Income-Tax to Ireland, by making them the gift of four millions and a half of Consolidated Annuities. But the Irish contend that three out of these four and a half millions, connected with the famine of 1846-47,[63] were never intended to constitute a national debt, and have never been acknowledged as such by the Irish people.

The ministry itself seems not to be quite sure of success, since it menaces an *early dissolution* of the House, unless the budget be accepted as a whole. A formidable suggestion this for the great majority of members whose "pockets have been materially affected by the *legitimate* expenses of the last contest," and for those Radicals who have clung as closely as possible to the old definition of an Opposition; namely, that it does, in the machine of Government, the duty of the safety-valve in a steam-engine. The safety-valve does not stop the motion of the engine, but preserves it by letting off in *vapor* the power which might otherwise blow up the whole concern. Thus they let off in vapor the popular demands. They seem to offer motions only to withdraw them afterward, and to rid themselves of their superfluous eloquence.

A dissolution of the House would only reveal the dissolution of the old parties. Since the appearance of the Coalition Ministry, the Irish Brigade has been split up into two factions—one governmental, the other independent. The country party is likewise split up into two camps—the one led by Mr. Disraeli, the other by Sir

John Pakington; although now, in the hour of danger, they both rally again around Disraeli. The Radicals themselves are broken up into two sets—the Mayfair-men[64] and the Manchester-men. There is no longer any power of cohesion in the old parties, but at the same time there is no power of real antagonism. A new general election would not mend, but only confirm this state of things.

By the election-disclosures the Lower House is sunk as low as it can possibly go. But simultaneously, week after week, it has denounced the rottenness of its foundation, the thorough corruption of the *constituencies* themselves. Now after these disclosures, will the ministry venture on an appeal to these branded constituencies—an appeal to the country? To the country at large they have nothing to offer, holding in one hand the refusal of parliamentary reform, and in the other an Austrian patent, installing them as general informers of the continental police.[65]

Written on April 22, 1853

First published in the *New-York Daily Tribune*, No. 3761, and the *New-York Semi-Weekly Tribune*, No. 829, May 6, 1853

Signed: *Karl Marx*

Reproduced from the *New-York Daily Tribune*

Karl Marx

SOAP FOR THE PEOPLE, A SOP FOR *THE TIMES*.— THE COALITION BUDGET

Everybody knows that a Budget is simply an estimate of the probable Revenue and Expenditure of Government for the year current, which estimate is based on the financial experience, i.e., on the balance sheet for the past year.

The first thing, therefore, for Mr. Gladstone was to produce the balance sheet for the year 1852-3. Mr. Disraeli, in his statement as Chancellor of the Exchequer, has estimated the probable income for 1852-3 at £52,325,000, and the Expenditure for the same period at £51,163,000, thus anticipating a surplus of £1,162,000. Mr. Gladstone, in making up the actual balance from the books, discovers that the real amount of Revenue for the past year was £53,089,000, and the real Expenditure only £50,782,000, showing an actual surplus of £2,307,000, or, as Mr. Gladstone calculates (we know not in what way) £2,460,000.

As it is the fashion, or rather as Parliament affects, to consider the Chancellor of the Exchequer as the mysterious conjuror who, by nobody knows what secret tricks, contrives to produce the whole yearly Revenue of the nation, it is no wonder that that personage, whoever he happens to be, takes care not to discountenance so flattering a delusion. Consequently, if the nation, by increasing the rate of production, is found to have swelled the amount of Tax Revenues above the estimate, it is taken for granted that the Minister of Finance who, by this process, can present more than double the surplus his predecessor had promised, is undoubtedly the man of the greater financial capacities. This was the cheerful idea of Mr. Gladstone, cheerfully received and appreciated by the supporters of the Coalition Oligarchy in the House.

Two Millions Four Hundred and Sixty Thousand Pounds Surplus! But not a farthing out of the two millions will the House permit to go to the people. Where, then, are they to go to? Mr. Gladstone explains it:

"Favourable as this statement may seem, the House must not forget that it has already largely drawn on this surplus by various extraordinary votes on the estimates of the current year."[a]

The House knew from Mr. Disraeli that there would be at all events a surplus of more than one million of pounds. Accordingly, on going into Committee of Ways and Means,[66] it voted merrily the following additional sums above and beyond the ordinary surplus:—

	£
For the Navy, including Packet Service	617,000
Army and Commissariat	90,000

To these sums, as Mr. Gladstone announced, will have to be added:—

For the Kaffir war[67] (no peace?)	270,000
Increase on Ordnance	616,000
Increase on Militia	230,000
Public (read private) Education	100,000
Making a total of	£1,923,000

Mr. Gladstone again (probably by omitting the Kaffir war item on account of its uncertainty) calculates the total at only £1,654,000. Deducting this sum from the original (barely figurative) surplus of £2,460,000, there would remain an actual surplus of £806,000, or, still calculating with Mr. Gladstone, £807,000. Yet, even from this moderate sum the House is warned to deduct £220,000, accruing from precarious, and not recurring sources of Revenue. Thus the original two millions, so cheerfully announced, are after all but £587,000, by no means a very extensive basis for any even the most moderate reform of taxation. As, however, the country is assured that it has a Ministry of Reform, Reforms there must be; and Mr. Gladstone forthwith engages to bring out these Reforms.

An ordinary Free Trader, a Mr. Hume for instance, would perhaps have advised the Chancellor of the Exchequer to do good

[a] Here and below William Gladstone's speech in the House of Commons on April 18, 1853 is quoted from *The Times*, No. 21406, April 19, 1853.—*Ed.*

with his surplus, by the abolition of duties on such foreign articles, the revenue of which, as shown by the Customs' Returns, would balance exactly the £587,000. What a vulgar, commonplace, profane suggestion to so learned and profound a financial alchemist as Mr. Gladstone! Do you think that the man who contemplates nothing short of the suppression of the entire public debt, would gratify his ambition by the simple remission of £500,000 of taxes? Surely, for so small a purpose, Sancho Timber needed not have been removed to his Indian Barataria,[a] to make room for the great Don Quixote of coalition finance.

Gladstone's Taxation Reform bears the proud Oxford Street shop-frontispiece of—

"Immense Reduction!

"Five millions, and several odd thousand pounds, forthwith to be dispensed with!"

There is something to attract the people, and to beguile even the most protected Parliamentary old female.

Let us enter the shop. "Mr. Gladstone, your bill of fare, if you please. What is it really that you mean, Sir? Five millions of pounds reduction?" "Decidedly, my dear Sir," answers Mr. Gladstone. "Would you like to look at the figures? Here they are:—

1. Abolition of the entire Soap Tax	1,126,000
2. Reduction of duty on Life Assurances, from 2s. 6d. to 6d.	29,000
3. Reduction of duty on Receipt Stamps to uniform rate of 1d.	155,000
4. Reduction on duty on Apprentice Indentures, from 20s. to 2s. 6 d. 5. Reduction on duty on Attorney's Certificates	50,000
6. Reduction on duty on Advertisements, from 1s. 6d. to 6d.	160,000
7. Reduction on duty on Hackney Carriages, from 1s. 5d. to 1s. per day	26,000
8. Reduction on duty on Men Servants to £1 1s. for those above eighteen years, and 10s. 6d. for those under	87,000

[a] Allusion to the appointment of Charles Wood, Chancellor of the Exchequer in the Whig Cabinet of 1846-52, as President of the Control Council on India. Barataria is a fictitious island given over to Sancho Panza in Cervantes' *Don Quixote.—Ed.*

9. Reduction on duty on Private Carriages	95,000
10. Reduction on duty on Horses, Ponies, and Dogs	108,000
11. Reduction on duty on Post Horses, by substituting licenses to charge on mileage	54,000
12. Reduction on duty on Colonial Postage (6d. a letter) ...	40,000
13. Reduction on duty on Tea, from 2s. 2¼d. to 1s. 10d. till 5th of April, '54, to 1s. 6d. in 1855, to 1s. 3d. in 1856, and to 1s. thereafter	3,000,000
14. Reduction on duty on Apples, Cheese, Cocoa, Eggs, Butter, and Fruit	262,000
15. Reduction on duty on 133 minor articles	70,000
16. Abolition of duty on 123 minor articles	53,000
Total	5,315,000

Why, a remission of £5,315,000 taxes would unquestionably be a handsome thing. But is there no drawback in this most liberal Budget? To be sure, there is. Else, how could it be called a Reform? Constitutional Reforms and Oxford Street shops, handsome as they both look, are sure to have always a very handsome drawback.

Of all clever tricks men contrive in the end to catch the secret. Mr. Gladstone, with only *half a million* in his bag, bestows a donation on the public of *five million and a half.* Whence does he get it? Ay, from the same blindfold public whom he bewilders with his generosity. He makes them a present, but invites them to return the favour. Of course, not in a direct or petulant manner, nor even from the same people whom it is his purpose to win over now. There are various customers with whom he intends to deal, and Russell, the juggler, has taught the adept Gladstone how to redeem his liberality of to-day by a revenge on to-morrow.

Gladstone remits old taxes to the amount of £5,315,000. Gladstone imposes new ones to the amount of £3,139,000. Still Gladstone would give to us a benefit of £2,176,000. But Gladstone is, at the best, but the Minister of the year; and the amount of his contemplated reduction for the year is only £2,568,000, which will cause a loss to the Revenue of £1,656,000, to be balanced by the anticipated yield of the new taxes for the year, viz., £1,344,000, leaving a deficiency of £312,000, which, set off against the actual surplus, as stated in the Budget, of £807,000, would still show a favourable balance of £495,000.

These are the principal features of the Coalition Budget. We shall now state to our readers what are the points of which the Ministry hope to make the most—what objections are most likely to be raised against it by the various Parliamentary parties in opposition—and, in conclusion, what is our own opinion of the question.

Gladstone, in all his anxiety to create a sensation, and to secure to himself both financial notoriety and popular favour by a large remission of taxes, felt the necessity of introducing his proposal for an increase of £3,139,000, under some plausible and apparently rational pretence. He was aware that he would not be permitted to nibble with the whole system of taxation, for the sole purpose of an uncalled for and unwarranted personal gratification, without some show of what Parliamentary and middle class men call "principle and justice." Accordingly, he astutely resolved to take the legislating Pecksniffs by what he knew to be their weakest side, adroitly screening his intended augmentation of the public burdens behind the pleasant and acceptable phrase of a "just extension of certain taxes, with a view to their final and lasting equalisation." The imposts he chose for that object were:—

1. The Legacy Duty.
2. The Spirits Excise; and,
3. The Income Tax.

The Legacy Duty he demands to embrace equally all kinds of property. As landed property was heretofore exempted, this proposal is expected to gratify the commercial and manufacturing interests. The Spirits Excise is to be extended to Scotland and Ireland, so as to bring them more on a par with distilling England.

Lastly, the Income Tax is to extend, in its area, to incomes between £150 and £100; and also to Ireland. The Income Tax proposal is certainly not one of the points on which Gladstone can expect, or will obtain, much applause. But of that anon, when we come to the objections.

Besides the Legacy and Spirits proposition, the Free Trade reductions on a vast number of import articles are undoubtedly considered by Ministers as the most attractive bait; and some favourable clamour is likely to be got up on this point by the shopkeepers, housewives, and the small middle class in general, before they discover that, with regard to Tea, at least, a very trifling benefit will accrue to the consumers, the profit of the holders and the monopoly of producers tending to absorb the greater part of the advantage. But, then, there is the entire abolition of the duty on Soap—a measure by which he hopes to enable the country to wash away not only its own dirty, filthy, and miserable appearance, by making all faces clean, comfortable and happy; but also to entirely abolish black slavery, and make an end to the misfortunes of numberless Uncle Toms, by the impulse given to "legitimate trading and production of African palm oil." Assured by this, Gladstone bids fair to out-puff the fastest haberdasher and the most bombastic quack doctor. To these attractive features he adds a good number of minor bribes, including one of several millions to the Irish Brigade,[68] in the shape of a remission of the famine loan, and to *The Times*, the big supporter of the "good Aberdeen," and his colleagues of the Coalition. This latter bribe consists in the abolition of the Stamp on Newspaper Supplements, containing advertisements only, *The Times* being notoriously the only journal issuing any of the kind to any extent.

We come now to the objections that are most likely to be raised against the Budget from oppositional quarters. The discussion on Monday last, in the House, having been only an introductory skirmish, we must glean, if possible, from the daily papers the intentions of parties. And here we are very scantily supplied. *The Times, Chronicle*, and *Post*, are actually in the bonds of the Coalition Government, and *The Daily News* can scarcely be regarded as the organ of the Manchester School.[69] Besides, it is still vacillating, and apparently much tempted by the Free Trade propositions. But if we look at *The Herald*, the Tory-Conservative paper, we already find its judgment given; and with a truly unusual frankness:—

> "The whole Budget of Mr. Gladstone," it says, "is nothing but a contemptible admixture of bribes and jobs."[a]

The Tories, therefore, are sure to oppose the scheme of Gladstone, from whom Disraeli will not fail to revindicate the stolen feathers of the Legacy and Income Tax extension, the Tea reduction, and other impudently-appropriated merits of his own. The landed aristocracy desire, at all events, if they must submit to a further loss of privileges, to reserve to themselves the merit of a voluntary surrender. But as they cannot well take their stand on the Legacy Duty, Mr. Disraeli will cause them to rally around the principle of distinction between real and precarious incomes, on which ground he will have a considerable portion of the Brigade fighting alongside with him. It is obvious that the Irish can and will never acknowledge the obligation of a debt, forced by the English upon their country only in consequence of the previous ruin of its population. Besides, for all practical purposes, the

---

[a] Marx's rendering of the statement from *The Morning Herald*, No. 22137, April 20, 1853.—*Ed.*

remission of the interest from £3,000,000 imaginary capital, must appear to them a very inadequate concession for the imposition of a Spirit Excise and an Income Tax. As far as the Manchester School is concerned, although they are pledged to their constituents, if not on the abolition, at least on the transformation of the Income Tax, it is not to be expected that they will act otherwise than as business men, *i.e.* without any political honour, but with a very due regard to profit. And the profit on the side of Mr. Gladstone's Budget, as a "whole," is by no means despicable, as far as those gentlemen are concerned.

Now, as to our opinion on the question at issue, we desire most eagerly to see a ministry defeated, which deserves equal contempt for its reactionary deceitful dodgery at home, as for its cowardly subservient policy abroad. And we think we are the more right in doing so, as such an event would certainly promote the interests of the people. One thing is clear: as long as an aristocratic coalition does the work required from them by the manufacturing and trading class, the latter will neither make any political effort themselves, nor allow the working class to carry their own political movement. If, however, the country party once more obtain the upper hand, the middle class cannot get rid of them without remodelling the rotten oligarchic parliament, and then it is no longer in their power to agitate for a limited reform, but they must go the whole length of the people's demands. The people, of course, can never, without abandoning both their principles and interests, join and appeal to the middle classes: but for the *bourgeoisie*, it would not be the first time that they are forced to throw themselves on the shoulders of the people. And such a contingency would lead to a very decided revolution in the present financial system. Already, it is evident that even middle class society inevitably tends towards the substitution of one direct property-tax in lieu of the traditional fiscal *olla podrida*. The Manchester School has long since registered, Disraeli has acknowledged, and even the oligarchic coalition has confirmed, the principle of direct taxation. But let the machinery of a direct property-tax be once properly established, and the people, with political power in their hands, have only to put that engine into motion, in order to create the

Budget of Labour.

Written about April 25, 1853

First published in *The People's Paper*, No. 52, April 30, 1853

Reproduced from the newspaper

Karl Marx and Frederick Engels

THE ROCKET AFFAIR.— THE SWISS INSURRECTION[70]

London, Friday, April 29, 1853

The notorious *Polizei-Director* Stieber, accompanied by the Police Lieutenant, Goldheim, and the *Criminal-Rath*, Nörner, arrived here a few days ago, from Berlin, on the special mission of connecting the Rotherhithe gunpowder-plot with the Calabrian hat-conspiracy at Berlin.[a] I know, from private information, that they met at Kensington, in the house of Fleury, and that the ex-clerk Hirsch was also present at that meeting. A day later the same Hirsch had a secret interview with Mr. Kraemer, the Russian consul. If your readers recollect my letter on the Cologne trials,[b] they must be aware, that the identical personages who concocted that plot, are again at work.

On Saturday, 23d inst., proceedings were commenced, before Mr. Henry, the Bow-st. Police Magistrate, against Mr. Hale, the proprietor of the Rotherhithe rocket manufactory, where the Government seizure had been made. On that day, the question discussed was merely relating to the point, whether the explosive material under seizure was gunpowder, or not. Mr. Henry who had reserved his decision until yesterday, has now pronounced, contradictorily to Mr. Ure, the celebrated chemist's opinion, that it was gunpowder. Accordingly, he fined Mr. Hale 2s. for every pound of gunpowder, beyond the legal allowance, found in his possession, which quantity amounted to 57 lbs. W. Hale, R. Hale, his son, and J. Boylin, then appeared at the side bar to answer the charge of having, at various intervals, between Sept. 13, 1852 and

---

[a] See this volume, pp. 28-31.—*Ed.*

[b] F. Engels, "The Late Trial at Cologne" (see present edition, Vol. 11, pp. 388-93).—*Ed.*

April 13, 1853, made or caused to be made divers large quantities of rockets. Mr. Bodkin, the Government solicitor, stated that Mr. W. Hale had made several unsuccessful applications to the British Government with regard to his rockets, that from October, 1852, a great number of workmen had been employed by him, some of whom were foreign refugees; that the whole of their proceedings had been carried on in the greatest possible secrecy, and that the shipping records at the Customs refuted Mr. Hale's statement of having been an exporter through the Customs. At the conclusion he said:

"The cost of the rockets found in possession of Mr. Hale, was estimated at from £1,000 to £2,000. Where did the money come from? Mr. Hale was only lately a bankrupt, and superseded his bankruptcy by paying only 3s. in the pound."[a]

J. Saunders, a sergeant of the Detective Police, stated, that he took possession of

"1,543 loaded rockets, 3,629 rocket heads, 2,482 rocket bottoms, 1,955 empty rockets, 22 iron shot, 2 instruments for firing rockets."

A witness, Mr. Usener, next appeared, who said that he had been for 15 years an officer in the Prussian artillery, and served in the Hungarian war as Major of the staff. He was employed by the Messrs. Hale in making rockets at Rotherhithe. Before going to the factory he had been in prison for theft for five or six months at Maidstone, to which step he declared he had been driven by utter destitution. The most important part of his deposition was literally as follows:

"I was introduced to the Hales by M. Kossuth; I first saw M. Kossuth on the subject last summer, on his return from America; about the middle of September I saw the elder Mr. Hale in the company of M. Kossuth, at the house of the latter; a Hungarian, the adjutant, was also there; M. Kossuth said to Mr. Hale, 'This person was in the Hungarian service, and a late officer of the Prussian artillery, and I can recommend him to your employ to assist in making *our* rockets, or *your* rockets,' I don't remember which was the word he said; M. Kossuth said my wages should be 18s. per week, and he recommended me to keep the affair quite secret; Mr. Hale, he said, would point out what I was to do; M. Kossuth spoke partly in the Hungarian and partly in the English language; I believe Mr. Hale does not understand the German language. The word *secret* was said to me in German; [...] I was sent to Pimlico by R. Hale to see M. Kossuth; I saw M. Kossuth at Pickering Place; W. Hale and another Hungarian were there; we went to try a firing machine; when we were all together, the machine was set up, and a trial was made with the rockets; the conversation took place partly in English, and chiefly about the quality of the rockets, etc.; we were there an hour and a half, and when it was

[a] Here and below the authors quote from the article "The War Rocket Factory and the Government", *The Times*, No. 21415, April 29, 1853.—*Ed.*

all over, M. Kossuth and Mr. Hale desired us to leave the house carefully, one by one, and Mr. Hale joined us at the corner of the street; on this occasion M. Kossuth repeatedly told us to keep his connection with the rockets secret."

W. Gerlach, another German, was then examined through an interpreter. He was employed at Mr. Hale's factory, in making rockets. There were, besides him, three Hungarians. He was recommended to Mr. Hale by M. Kossuth, but he never saw them in company together.

Mr. Henry, who had the alternative of committing summarily in the penalty of £5, or sending the case before the Assizes, adopted the latter course, but was willing to accept bail for each of the Hales. Mr. W. Hale declared that he would not ask any friend to become bail, either for himself or for his son, and accordingly the defendants were removed to Horsemonger-lane Jail.

The depositions of the witnesses, it is clear, are in strong contradiction with the letter of Mr. Hale, Jr.; the substance of which I have already communicated to you,[71] and, with the letters addressed by Kossuth to Captain Mayne Reid and Lord Dudley Stuart,[a] wherein he affirmed he knew nothing either of Mr. Hale, or his rockets. It would be unjust, however, to draw any inference from this circumstance, before further explanations shall have been given by M. Kossuth. As to Mr. Usener, is it not a shame that a talented countryman of ours in exile, and a man most willing to labor, as is proved by the fact of his agreeing to become an ordinary workman at 18s. a week, should have been driven by mere destitution to theft, while certain German refugees, notorious idlers, assume the privilege of squandering the small funds destined for the revolutionists, in self-imposed missionary trips, ridiculous plots, and public house *conciliabules*?

On Friday, the 22d inst., an insurrection broke out again at Fribourg, in Switzerland, the fifth, already, since the late Sonderbund war.[72] The insurrection was to be commenced simultaneously all over the surface of the canton; but at the given moment, the majority of the conspirators did not come forward. Three "colonnes," who had promised their cooperation in the affair, remained behind. The insurgents, who actually entered the town, were chiefly from the district of Farvagny, and from the communes of Autigny, Prez, Torny [le Grand], Middes, and other neighborhoods. At $4^1/_2$ a. m., the body of 400 peasants, all wearing the colors of the Sonderbund, and carrying the emblem of the Virgin on their standard, moved towards Fribourg, on the road

[a] See *The Times*, No. 21412, April 26, 1853.—*Ed.*

from Lausanne, headed by Colonel Perrier, and the notorious peasant Carrard, the chief of the insurrection of 1851, who had been amnestied by the Grosse-Rath. About 5 o'clock they entered the town, by the "Porte des Etangs," and took possession of the College and the Arsenal, where they seized 150 guns. Alarm having been beaten, the town council immediately declared the state of siege, and Major Gerbex assumed the command of the assembled civic guard. While he ordered the streets at the back of the college to be occupied with cannon, he pushed a body of riflemen forward, to attack the insurgents in front. The riflemen advanced up the two flights of steps, leading to the college, and soon dislodged the peasants from the windows of the buildings. The combat had lasted for about an hour, and the assailants already numbered eight dead and eighteen wounded, when the insurgents, attempting in vain to escape through the back streets, where they were received with grape shot, sent forth a priest with a white flag, declaring their readiness to surrender.

A Committee of the Civic Guard instantly formed a Court-martial, which condemned Col. Perrier to thirty years' imprisonment, and which is still sitting. The number of prisoners is about two hundred, among whom Messrs. Wuilleret, Weck and Chollet. M. Charles, the president of the well-known Committee at Posieux, has been seen at the gate of Romont, but not captured. Besides the parson of Torny le Grand, two other priests are included in the number of prisoners. As to the expenses of the affair, the canton appears to be safe, half the property of the patrician, Mr. Weck, being sufficient for that object.

Written on April 26-29, 1853

First published in the *New-York Daily Tribune*, No. 3768, May 14, 1853; reprinted in the *New-York Semi-Weekly Tribune*, No. 832, May 17, 1853

Signed: *Karl Marx*

Reproduced from the *New-York Daily Tribune*

Frederick Engels

POLITICAL POSITION OF THE SWISS REPUBLIC[73]

London, May 1, 1853

Royal families formerly used to employ whipping-boys, who had the honor of receiving condign punishment on their profane backs, whenever any of the scions of royalty had committed an offense against the rules of good behavior. The modern European political system continues this practice, in a certain degree, in the erection of small intermediate States, which have to act the scapegoat in any domestic squabble by which the harmony of the "balance of power" may be troubled. And in order to enable these smaller States to perform this enviable part with suitable dignity, they are, by the common consent of Europe "in Congress assembled,"[74] and with all due solemnity, declared "*neutral.*" Such a scapegoat, or whipping-boy, is Greece—such is Belgium and Switzerland. The only difference is this—that these modern political scapegoats, from the abnormal conditions of their existence, are seldom quite undeserving of the inflictions they are favored with.

The most conspicuous of this class of States has of late been Switzerland,

> Quicquid delirant reges, plectuntur—[a]

the Swiss. And wherever the *people* of any European State came into collision with their rulers, the Swiss were equally sure to come in for their share of the trouble; until since the beginning of this year, Switzerland, after having made itself gratuitously contempti-

---

[a] Q. Horatii Flacci, *Epistolarum*, Liber Primus, Epistola II, Ad Lollium; the line ends with "Achivi"—Achaeans.—*Ed.*

ble to the revolutionary party, has been placed in a sort of interdict by the rulers of Continental Europe. Squabbles about refugees with the Emperor Bonaparte, for whose sake Switzerland once came very near risking a war; squabbles with Prussia on account of Neuchâtel; squabbles with Austria about Tessinese and the Milan insurrection[75]; squabbles with the minor German States about subjects which nobody cares for; squabbles on all hands, threatening notes, expulsions, passport chicanes, blockades, raining down upon poor Switzerland thick as hailstones in a storm, and yet, such is human nature, the Swiss are happy, contented and proud in their own way, and feel more at home in this shower of abuse and insult, than if the political horizon was cloudless and bright.

This honorable political position of Switzerland is, by the popular mind of Europe, rather vaguely and clumsily expressed in the common saying: Switzerland has been invented by the rulers of Europe in order to bring republican governments into contempt; and certainly, a Metternich or Guizot may have often said: If Switzerland did not exist, we should have to create it. To them, a neighbor like Switzerland, was a real god-send.

We cannot be expected to repeat the multifarious charges brought of late, against Switzerland and Swiss institutions, by real or would be revolutionists. Long before the movements of 1848, the organs of the revolutionary Communist party of Germany analyzed that subject, they showed why Switzerland, as an independent State, must ever be lagging behind in the march of European progress, and why that country, with all its republican shows, will ever be reactionary at heart.[a] They were even violently attacked, at that time, by divers democratic spouters and manufacturers of clandestine declamation, who celebrated Switzerland as their "model-republic," until the model institutions were once tried upon themselves. The subject is now as trite as can be; nobody disputes the fact, and a few words will suffice to put the matter in its true light.

The mass of the Swiss population follow either pastoral or agricultural pursuits; pastoral, in the high mountains, agricultural wherever the nature of the ground admits of it. The pastoral tribes, for tribes you may call them, rank among the least civilized populations of Europe. If they do not cut off heads and ears like the Turks and Montenegrins, they perform acts of hardly less

[a] The reference is to Engels' article "The Civil War in Switzerland", *Deutsche-Brüsseler-Zeitung*, November 1847 (see present edition, Vol. 6, pp. 367-74).— *Ed.*

barbarity by their judicial assemblies; and what cruelty and beastly ferocity they are capable of, the Swiss mercenaries at Naples and elsewhere have proved.[76] The agricultural population is quite as stationary as the pastoral; they have nothing in common with the agricultural population of the American Far West, whose very aliment is change, and who clear every twelvemonth an amount of land far larger than all Switzerland. The Swiss peasant tills the patch of ground his father and grandfather tilled before him; he tills it in the same slovenly way as they did; he earns about as much as they did; he lives about as they did, and consequently he thinks very nearly in the same way as they did. Had it not been for feudal burdens and imposts levied upon them, partly by aristocratic families, partly by patrician corporations in the towns, the Swiss peasantry would always have been quite as stationary in their political existence as their neighbors, the cowherds, are up to the present day. The third components of the Swiss people, the industrial population, although necessarily far more advanced in civilization than the two classes mentioned before, yet live under circumstances which exclude them in a great degree from the progressive giant impulse which the modern manufacturing system has imparted to Western Europe. Steam is hardly known in Switzerland; large factories exist in a few localities only; the cheapness of labor, the sparseness of the population, the abundance of small mountain-streams fit for mills; all these and many other circumstances tend to produce a petty and sporadic sort of manufactures mixed up with agricultural pursuits, the most eligible industrial system for Switzerland. Thus watch-making, ribbon-weaving, straw-plaiting, embroidery, &c. are carried on in several cantons, without ever creating or even increasing a town; and Geneva and Basle, the richest, and with Zurich, the most industrial towns, have hardly increased for centuries. If, then, Switzerland carries on her manufacturing production almost exclusively upon the system in practice all over Europe *before* the invention of steam, how can we expect to find other than corresponding ideas in the minds of the producers; if steam has not revolutionized Swiss production and intercommunication, how could it overthrow the hereditary ways of thinking?

The Hungarian Constitution bears a certain resemblance to that of Great Britain, which circumstance has been turned to good account by Magyar politicians, who thence would make us jump to the conclusion that the Hungarian nation is almost as advanced as the English; and yet there are many hundreds of miles and of years between the petty tradesman of Buda and the Cotton lord of

Lancashire, or between the traveling tinker of the Puszta[a] and the Chartist working-man of a British manufacturing metropolis. Thus, Switzerland would give itself the airs of a United States on a smaller scale; but barring the superficial resemblance of political institutions, no two countries are more unlike than ever-moving, ever-changing America, with a historical mission whose immensity people on both sides of the Atlantic are but just beginning to divine, and stationary Switzerland, whose never-ending petty distractions would result in the perpetual round-about motion within the narrowest circle, were she not in spite of herself dragged forward by the industrial advance of her neighbors.

Whoever doubts this, will be satisfied after a perusal of the history of Swiss railways. Were it not for the traffic from south to north moving round Switzerland on both sides, not a railroad would ever have been constructed in that country. As it is, they are made twenty years too late.

The French invasion of 1798, and the French revolution of 1830, gave occasion to the peasantry to throw off their feudal burdens; to the manufacturing and trading population to throw off the mediaeval yoke of patrician and corporative control. With this progress the revolution of *Cantonal* Government was completed. The more advanced cantons had obtained constitutions to suit their interests. This Cantonal revolution reacted upon the Central Representation Assembly[b] and Executive. The party vanquished in the individual cantons was here strong; the struggle was fought over again. The general political movement of 1840-'47, which everywhere in Europe brought about preliminary conflicts, or prepared decisive collisions, was in all second- and third-rate States—thanks to the jealousies of the great powers—favorable to the opposition, which may be described as the middle-class party. It was the case, too, in Switzerland; the moral support of Britain, the indecision of Guizot, the difficulties which kept Metternich at bay in Italy, carried the Swiss over the Sonderbund war[77]; the party which had been victorious in the liberal cantons in 1830, now conquered the Central Powers. The revolutions of 1848 made it possible for the Swiss to reform their feudal constitutions in accordance with the new political organization of the majority of the cantons[78]; and now we may say that Switzerland has attained the highest political development of which she, as an independent State, is capable. That the new

[a] Hungarian steppe.—*Ed.*
[b] The Federal Diet.—*Ed.*

federal constitution is quite adequate to the wants of the country, the constant reforms in the monetary system, the means of communication, and other legislative matters affecting the industry of the country, abundantly show; but, alas! these reforms are of a nature that any other State would be ashamed of, on account of the mass of traditionary nuisances, and the antediluvian state of society, the existence of which, up to that date, they disclose.

What, at most, can be said in favor of the Swiss Constitution 1848 is this: that by its enactment the more civilized portion of the Swiss declared themselves willing to pass, to a certain extent, from the Middle Ages into modern society. Whether, however, they will at any time be able to do away with privileged trades' corporations, guilds, and such-like mediaeval amenities, must remain very doubtful to any one who has the least knowledge of the country, and who has seen in a single instance the strenuous efforts with which respectable "vested interests" oppose even the most matter-of-course reform.

Thus we see the Swiss, true to their character, moving on quietly in their own restricted domestic circle while the year 1848 uprooted all the stability of the European Continent around them. The revolutions of Paris, of Vienna, of Berlin, of Milan, were by them reduced to as many levers of Cantonal intrigue. The European earthquake had even for the radical Swiss no other interest but this—that it might vex some conservative neighbor by upsetting his crockery. In the struggle for Italian independence Sardinia solicited an alliance with Switzerland, and there is no doubt that an addition to the Sardinian army of 20 or 30,000 Swiss would have very soon driven the Austrians out of Italy. When 15,000 Swiss in Naples were fighting against Italian liberty it certainly might be expected that Switzerland, in order to maintain her boasted "*neutrality*," should send an equal number to fight for the Italians; but the alliance was rejected and the cause of Italian independence was lost as much through Swiss as through Austrian bayonets. Then came the disasters of the revolutionary party, and the wholesale emigration from Italy, from France, from Germany, to the *neutral* Swiss soil. But there neutrality ceased; Swiss radicalism was satisfied with what it had achieved, and the very insurgents, who, by holding in check the tutors and natural superiors of Switzerland, the absolutist governments of the Continent, had enabled the Swiss to carry out their internal reform undisturbed—these very insurgents were now treated in Switzerland with every possible insult and turned out of the country at the first bidding of their persecutors. Then began that series of degradation and insult which one neighboring government after another heaped upon Switzerland, and which would make the blood of every Swiss boil if Swiss nationality had any foundation and Swiss independence any existence other than in boast or fame.

Never has such treatment been offered to any people as the Swiss have been made to submit to by France, Austria, Prussia, and the minor German States. Never were demands half as humiliating made upon any country, without being resented by a struggle for life or death. The surrounding Governments, by their agents, presumed to exercise the office of Police upon the Swiss territory; they exercised it not only over the refugees, but over the Swiss Police officers also. They laid complaints against subaltern agents, and demanded their dismissal; they even went so far as to hint at the necessity of changes in the Constitutions of several cantons. As for the Swiss Government, to every bolder demand, it gave an humbler reply; and whenever its words breathed a spirit of opposition, its acts were sure to make up for it by increased subserviency. Insult after insult was pocketed, command after command was executed, until Switzerland was brought down to the lowest level of European contempt,—till she was more despised than even her two "neutral" rivals, Belgium and Greece. And now, when the demands of her chief assailant, Austria, have reached that hight of impudence which even a statesman of the temper of M. Druey could hardly swallow, without some show of resistance—now, in her most recent, most spirited notes to Vienna, she shows how far she is reduced.

The champions of Italian independence,—men who, far from showing any wicked Socialist or Communist tendencies, would, perhaps, not even go to the length of wishing for Italy the same Constitution as that under which Switzerland lives,—men who have and make no claim to the demagogical celebrity even of Mazzini, are there treated as assassins, incendiaries, brigands, and upsetters of all social order. As to Mazzini, the language is of course far stronger; and yet everybody knows that Mazzini, with all his conspiracies and insurrections, is as much a supporter of social order, as at present constituted, as M. Druey himself. Thus, the result of the whole exchange of notes is, that, in principle, the Swiss give in to the Austrians. How, then, is it to be expected they will not give in in practise?

The fact is this: Any bold and persistent Government can get from the Swiss what it likes. The isolated life which the mass of them lead, deprives them of all sense of their common interest as a nation. That a village, or a valley, or a canton should stick together is no wonder. But, to stick together as a Nation for a common purpose, be what it may, they never will. In all invasions, as soon as the danger becomes serious, as in 1798, one Swiss has betrayed the other, one canton abandoned the next. The Austrians have expelled 18,000 Tessinese from Lombardy, without any cause. The Swiss make a great outcry about it and collect money for their unfortunate confederates. Now, let Austria hold out, and continue to prohibit the return of these Tessinese, and in a very short time you will see a wonderful change in Swiss opinion. They will get tired of collecting money, they will say that the Tessinese always meddled in Italian politics and deserved no better; in fact they are no true Swiss confederates (*Keine guten Eidgenossen*). Then the expelled Tessinese will settle in the other cantons of Switzerland and "turn the natives out of employment." For in Switzerland a man is not a Swiss, but a native of such and such a canton. And when that comes to pass then you will see our brave confederates muster up their indignation, then you will see intrigues of all sorts directed against the victims of Austrian despotism, then you will see the Tessinese Swiss as much hated, persecuted, calumniated as the foreign refugees were during their time in Switzerland, and then Austria will obtain everything she wants and a great deal more if she takes the trouble to ask for it.

When the nations of Europe have recovered their faculty of free and normal action they will take into consideration what is to be done with these petty "*neutral*" States, which while subservient to counter-revolution when it is ascendant, are neutral and even hostile to every revolutionary movement and yet pass themselves off as free and independent Nations. But, perhaps, by that time, not a trace will be left of these excrescences of an unsound body.

Written about April 26, 1853

First published in the *New-York Daily Tribune*, No. 3770, May 17, 1853 and in abridged form in German in *Die Reform*, Nos. 18 and 19, June 1 and 4, 1853

Signed: *Karl Marx*

Reproduced from the *New-York Daily Tribune*

Karl Marx

REVOLUTION IN CHINA AND IN EUROPE

A most profound yet fantastic speculator on the principles which govern the movements of Humanity,[a] was wont to extol as one of the ruling secrets of nature, what he called the law of the contact of extremes. The homely proverb that "extremes meet" was, in his view, a grand and potent truth in every sphere of life; an axiom with which the philosopher could as little dispense as the astronomer with the laws of Kepler or the great discovery of Newton.

Whether the "contact of extremes" be such a universal principle or not, a striking illustration of it may be seen in the effect the Chinese revolution[79] seems likely to exercise upon the civilized world. It may seem a very strange, and a very paradoxical assertion that the next uprising of the people of Europe, and their next movement for republican freedom and economy of government, may depend more probably on what is now passing in the Celestial Empire,—the very opposite of Europe,—than on any other political cause that now exists,—more even than on the menaces of Russia and the consequent likelihood of a general European war. But yet it is no paradox, as all may understand by attentively considering the circumstances of the case.

Whatever be the social causes, and whatever religious, dynastic, or national shape they may assume, that have brought about the chronic rebellions subsisting in China for about ten years past, and now gathered together in one formidable revolution, the occasion of this outbreak has unquestionably been afforded by the English cannon forcing upon China that soporific drug called opium.[80]

[a] G.W.F. Hegel.—*Ed.*

Before the British arms the authority of the Manchu dynasty fell to pieces; the superstitious faith in the eternity of the Celestial Empire broke down; the barbarous and hermetic isolation from the civilized world was infringed; and an opening was made for that intercourse which has since proceeded so rapidly under the golden attractions of California and Australia.[81] At the same time the silver coin of the Empire, its lifeblood, began to be drained away to the British East Indies.

Up to 1830, the balance of trade being continually in favor of the Chinese, there existed an uninterrupted importation of silver from India, Britain and the United States into China. Since 1833, and especially since 1840, the export of silver from China to India has become almost exhausting for the Celestial Empire. Hence the strong decrees of the Emperor against the opium trade, responded to by still stronger resistance to his measures. Besides this immediate economical consequence, the bribery connected with opium smuggling has entirely demoralized the Chinese State officers in the Southern provinces. Just as the Emperor was wont to be considered the father of all China, so his officers were looked upon as sustaining the paternal relation to their respective districts. But this patriarchal authority, the only moral link embracing the vast machinery of the State, has gradually been corroded by the corruption of those officers, who have made great gains by conniving at opium smuggling. This has occurred principally in the same Southern provinces where the rebellion commenced. It is almost needless to observe that, in the same measure in which opium has obtained the sovereignty over the Chinese, the Emperor and his staff of pedantic mandarins have become dispossessed of their own sovereignty. It would seem as though history had first to make this whole people drunk before it could rouse them out of their hereditary stupidity.

Though scarcely existing in former times, the import of English cottons, and to a small extent of English woollens, has rapidly risen since 1833, the epoch when the monopoly of trade with China was transferred from the East India Company to private commerce, and on a much greater scale since 1840, the epoch when other nations, and especially our own, also obtained a share in the Chinese trade. This introduction of foreign manufactures has had a similar effect on the native industry to that which it formerly had on Asia Minor, Persia and India. In China the spinners and weavers have suffered greatly under this foreign competition, and the community has become unsettled in proportion.

The tribute to be paid to England after the unfortunate war of 1840, the great unproductive consumption of opium, the drain of the precious metals by this trade, the destructive influence of foreign competition on native manufactures, the demoralized condition of the public administration, produced two things: the old taxation became more burdensome and harassing, and new taxation was added to the old. Thus in a decree of the Emperor,[a] dated Peking, Jan. 5, 1853, we find orders given to the viceroys and governors of the southern provinces of Wu-chang and Hang-Yang to remit and defer the payment of taxes, and especially not in any case to exact more than the regular amount; for otherwise, says the decree, "how will the poor people be able to bear it?"

> "And thus, perhaps," continues the Emperor, "will my people, in a period of general hardship and distress, be exempted from the evils of being pursued and worried by the tax-gatherer."[b]

Such language as this, and such concessions we remember to have heard from Austria, the China of Germany, in 1848.

All these dissolving agencies acting together on the finances, the morals, the industry, and political structure of China, received their full development under the English cannon in 1840, which broke down the authority of the Emperor, and forced the Celestial Empire into contact with the terrestrial world. Complete isolation was the prime condition of the preservation of Old China. That isolation having come to a violent end by the medium of England, dissolution must follow as surely as that of any mummy carefully preserved in a hermetically sealed coffin, whenever it is brought into contact with the open air. Now, England having brought about the revolution of China, the question is how that revolution, will in time react on England, and through England on Europe. This question is not difficult of solution.

The attention of our readers has often been called to the unparalleled growth of British manufactures since 1850. Amid the most surprising prosperity, it has not been difficult to point out the clear symptoms of an approaching industrial crisis. Notwithstanding California and Australia, notwithstanding the immense and unprecedented emigration, there must ever without any particular accident, in due time arrive a moment when the extension of the markets is unable to keep pace with the extension

[a] Hsien Fêng.—*Ed.*

[b] Quoted from the article "China", *The Economist*, No. 505, April 30, 1853.—*Ed.*

of British manufactures, and this disproportion must bring about a new crisis with the same certainty as it has done in the past. But, if one of the great markets suddenly becomes contracted, the arrival of the crisis is necessarily accelerated thereby. Now, the Chinese rebellion must, for the time being, have precisely this effect upon England. The necessity for opening new markets, or for extending the old ones, was one of the principal causes of the reduction of the British tea-duties, as, with an increased importation of tea, an increased exportation of manufactures to China was expected to take place. Now, the value of the annual exports from the United Kingdom to China amounted, before the repeal in 1833 of the trading monopoly possessed by the East India Company, to only £600,000; in 1836, it reached the sum of £1,326,388; in 1845, it had risen to £2,394,827; in 1852, it amounted to about £3,000,000. The quantity of tea imported from China did not exceed, in 1793, 16,167,331 lbs.; but in 1845, it amounted to 50,714,657 lbs.; in 1846, to 57,584,561 lbs.; it is now above 60,000,000 lbs.

The tea crop of the last season will not prove short, as shown already by the export lists from Shanghai, of 2,000,000 lbs. above the preceding year. This excess is to be accounted for by two circumstances. On one hand, the state of the market at the close of 1851 was much depressed, and the large surplus stock left has been thrown into the export of 1852. On the other hand, the recent accounts of the altered British legislation with regard to imports of tea, reaching China, have brought forward all the available teas to a ready market, at greatly enhanced prices. But with respect to the coming crop, the case stands very differently. This is shown by the following extracts from the correspondence of a large tea-firm in London:

> "In Shanghai the terror is extreme. Gold has advanced upward of 25 per cent., *being eagerly sought for hoarding*; silver has so far disappeared that *none could be obtained* to pay the China dues on the British vessels requiring port clearance; and in consequence of which Mr. Alcock has consented to become responsible to the Chinese authorities for the payment of these dues, on receipt of East India Company's bills, or other approved securities. *The scarcity of the precious metals* is one of the most unfavorable features, when viewed in reference to the immediate future of commerce, as this abstraction occurs precisely at that period when their use is most needed, to enable the tea and silk buyers to go into the interior and effect their purchases, for which a *large portion of bullion is paid in advance, to enable the producers to carry on their operations*.... At this period of the year it is usual to begin making arrangements for the new teas, whereas at present nothing is talked of but the means of protecting person and property, all transactions being at a stand.... If the means are not applied to secure the leaves in April and May, the early crop,

which includes all the finer descriptions, both of black and green teas, will be as much lost as unreaped wheat at Christmas."[a]

Now the means for securing the tea leaves, will certainly not be given by the English, American or French squadrons stationed in the Chinese seas, but these may easily, by their interference, produce such complications, as to cut off all transactions between the tea-producing interior and the tea-exporting sea ports. Thus, for the present crop, a rise in the prices must be expected—speculation has already commenced in London—and for the crop to come a large deficit is as good as certain. Nor is this all. The Chinese, ready though they may be, as are all people in periods of revolutionary convulsion, to sell off to the foreigner all the bulky commodities they have on hand, will, as the Orientals are used to do in the apprehension of great changes, set to hoarding, not taking much in return for their tea and silk, except hard money. England has accordingly to expect a rise in the price of one of her chief articles of consumption, a drain of bullion, and a great contraction of an important market for her cotton and woolen goods. Even *The Economist*, that optimist conjuror of all things menacing the tranquil minds of the mercantile community, is compelled to use language like this:

"We must not flatter ourselves with finding as extensive a market for our exports to China as hitherto.... It is more probable that our export trade to China should suffer, and that there should be a diminished demand for the produce of Manchester and Glasgow."

It must not be forgotten that the rise in the price of so indispensable an article as tea, and the contraction of so important a market as China, will coincide with a deficient harvest in Western Europe, and, therefore, with rising prices of meat, corn, and all other agricultural produce. Hence contracted markets for manufactures, because every rise in the prices of the first necessaries of life is counterbalanced, at home and abroad, by a corresponding deduction in the demand for manufactures. From every part of Great Britain complaints have been received on the backward state of most of the crops. *The Economist* says on this subject:

"In the South of England not only will there be left much land unsown, until too late for a crop of any sort, but much of the sown land will prove to be foul, or otherwise in a bad state for corn-growing. On the wet or poor soils destined for

[a] Here and below the quotations are from the article "China and the Tea Trade", *The Economist*, No. 508, May 21, 1853.—*Ed.*

wheat, signs that mischief is going on are apparent. The time for planting mangel-wurzel may now be said to have passed away, and very little has been planted, while the time for preparing land for the turnip is rapidly going by, without any adequate preparation for this important crop having been accomplished.... Oat-sowing has been much interfered with by the snow and rain. Few oats were sown early, and late sown oats seldom produce a large crop.... In many districts losses among the breeding flocks have been considerable."[a]

The price of other farm-produce than corn is from 20 to 30, and even 50 per cent. higher than last year. On the Continent, corn has risen comparatively more than in England. Rye has risen in Belgium and Holland full 100 per cent. Wheat and other grains are following suit.

Under these circumstances, as the greater part of the regular commercial circle has already been run through by British trade, it may safely be augured that the Chinese revolution will throw the spark into the overloaded mine of the present industrial system and cause the explosion of the long-prepared general crisis, which, spreading abroad, will be closely followed by political revolutions on the Continent. It would be a curious spectacle, that of China sending disorder into the Western World while the Western powers, by English, French and American war-steamers, are conveying "order" to Shanghai, Nanking, and the mouths of the Great Canal. Do these order-mongering powers, which would attempt to support the wavering Manchu dynasty, forget that the hatred against foreigners and their exclusion from the Empire, once the mere result of China's geographical and ethnographical situation, have become a political system only since the conquest of the country by the race of the Manchu Tartars[82]? There can be no doubt that the turbulent dissensions among the European nations who, at the later end of the 17th century, rivaled each other in the trade with China, lent a mighty aid to the exclusive policy adopted by the Manchus. But more than this was done by the fear of the new dynasty, lest the foreigners might favor the discontent existing among a large proportion of the Chinese during the first half century or thereabouts of their subjection to the Tartars. From these considerations, foreigners were then prohibited from all communication with the Chinese, except through Canton, a town at a great distance from Peking and the tea-districts, and their commerce restricted to intercourse with the Hong[83] merchants, licensed by the Government expressly for the foreign trade, in order to keep the rest of its subjects from all connection

[a] "Backwardness of the Season", *The Economist*, No. 507, May 14, 1853.—*Ed.*

with the odious strangers. In any case an interference on the part of the Western Governments at this time can only serve to render the revolution more violent, and protract the stagnation of trade.

At the same time it is to be observed with regard to India, that the British Government of that country depends for full one seventh of its revenue on the sale of opium to the Chinese, while a considerable proportion of the Indian demand for British manufactures depends on the production of that opium in India. The Chinese, it is true, are no more likely to renounce the use of opium than are the Germans to forswear tobacco. But as the new Emperor is understood to be favorable to the culture of the poppy and the preparation of opium in China itself, it is evident that a death-blow is very likely to be struck at once at the business of opium-raising in India, the Indian revenue, and the commercial resources of Hindostan. Though this blow would not immediately be felt by the interests concerned, it would operate effectually in due time, and would come in to intensify and prolong the universal financial crisis whose horoscope we have cast above.

Since the commencement of the eighteenth century there has been no serious revolution in Europe which had not been preceded by a commercial and financial crisis. This applies no less to the revolution of 1789 than to that of 1848. It is true, not only that we every day behold more threatening symptoms of conflict between the ruling powers and their subjects, between the State and society, between the various classes; but also the conflict of the existing powers among each other gradually reaching that hight where the sword must be drawn, and the *ultima ratio* of princes be recurred to. In the European capitals, every day brings dispatches big with universal war, vanishing under the dispatches of the following day, bearing the assurance of peace for a week or so. We may be sure, nevertheless, that to whatever hight the conflict between the European powers may rise, however threatening the aspect of the diplomatic horizon may appear, whatever movements may be attempted by some enthusiastic fraction in this or that country, the rage of princes and the fury of the people are alike enervated by the breath of prosperity. Neither wars nor revolutions are likely to put Europe by the ears, unless in consequence of a general commercial and industrial crisis, the signal of which has, as usual, to be given by England, the representative of European industry in the market of the world.

It is unnecessary to dwell on the political consequences such a crisis must produce in these times, with the unprecedented extension of factories in England, with the utter dissolution of her official parties, with the whole State machinery of France transformed into one immense swindling and stock-jobbing concern, with Austria on the eve of bankruptcy, with wrongs everywhere accumulated to be revenged by the people, with the conflicting interests of the reactionary powers themselves, and with the Russian dream of conquest once more revealed to the world.

Written on May 20-21, 1853

First published in the *New-York Daily Tribune,* No. 3794, June 14, 1853, as a leader; reprinted in the *New-York Weekly Tribune,* No. 615, June 25, 1853

Reproduced from the *New-York Daily Tribune*

Karl Marx

AFFAIRS IN HOLLAND.—DENMARK.— CONVERSION OF THE BRITISH DEBT.— INDIA, TURKEY AND RUSSIA[84]

London, Tuesday, May 24, 1853

The general elections in Holland, necessitated by the late dissolution of the States-General, are now completed, and the result has been the return of a majority of 12 in favor of the Ultra-Protestant and Royalist ministry.

Denmark is by this time inundated with anti-governmental pamphlets, the most prominent of which are the *Dissolution of Parliament Explained to the Danish People,* by Mr. Grundtvig, and one anonymous entitled *The Disputed Question of the Danish Succession; or What Is to Be Done by the Powers of Europe.* Both these pamphlets aim at proving that the abolition of the ancient law of succession as demanded by the ministry and stipulated in the London protocol,[85] would turn to the ruin of the country, by converting it, in the first instance, into a province of Holstein, and later into a dependency of Russia.

Thus, it appears, the Danish people have at last become aware of what their blind opposition to the demands for independence raised by the duchies of Schleswig-Holstein in 1848 has brought over them. They insisted upon their country's permanent union with Holstein, for which purpose they made war on the German revolution—they won in that war, and they have retained Holstein. But, in exchange for that conquest, they are now doomed to lose their own country. The *Neue Rheinische Zeitung* in '48 and '49 never ceased to warn the Danish democrats of the ultimate consequences of their hostility to the German revolution.[86] It distinctly predicted that Denmark, by contributing to disarm revolution abroad, was tying itself forever to a dynasty which, as the legitimate course of succession had obtained its sanction and validity through their own consent, would surrender their nationality to the "bon plaisir"[a] of the Russian czar. The Danish democracy refused to act upon that advice, and are now receiving the same price for their short-sighted folly as the Bohemian Sclaves did, who, in order to "preserve their nationality against the Germans," rushed to the destruction on the Viennese revolutionists, their only possible liberators from that German despotism which they hated. Is not this a grave lesson which is now being received by these two peoples, who allowed themselves to be arrayed in self-destructive warfare against the cause of the revolution, by the intrigues of the counter-revolution?

Now that Mr. Gladstone's scheme for the reduction of the public debt has passed through Parliament, and is undergoing its practical test, his apologists—and almost the entire London press seemed highly to approve of that famous scheme—have all of them become mute at once. Mr. Gladstone's three alternatives for voluntarily converting the five hundred millions of 3 per cents., turn out so very innocent, that none of them has as yet met with an acceptation worth mentioning.—As to the conversion of the South Sea[87] stock, up to the evening of May 19 only £100,000 out of the £10,000,000 had been converted into new stock. It is a general rule that such operations, if not effected in the first weeks, lose every day something of the probability of their being carried out at all. Besides, the rate of interest is just rising in slow but steady progression. It is, therefore, almost an exaggeration to suppose that ten millions of old paper will be converted into new stock within the time fixed for that operation. But even in this case, Mr. Gladstone will have to repay at least eight millions of pounds to those holders of South Sea Funds, who are unwilling to convert them into his new stock. The only fund he has provided for such an eventuality is the public balance at the Bank of England, amounting to about eight or nine millions. As this balance, however, is no excess of income over expenditure, but is only lodged in the Bank, because the public income is paid a few months in advance of the time when it is necessary to expend it, Mr. Gladstone will find himself at a future moment in a very heavy financial embarrassment, which will produce, at the same time, a most serious disturbance in the monetary transactions of the Bank and in the money market in general, the more so as a presumed deficient crop will cause a more or less extensive drain of bullion.

[a] Caprice.—*Ed.*

The charter of the East India Company expires in 1854. Lord John Russell has given notice in the House of Commons, that the Government will be enabled to state, through Sir Charles Wood, their views respecting the future Government of India, on the 3d of June. A hint has been thrown out in some ministerial papers, in support of the already credited public rumor, that the Coalition have found the means of reducing even this colossal Indian question to almost Lilliputian dimensions. *The Observer* prepares the mind of the English people to undergo a new disenchantment.

> "Much less," we read in that confidential journal of Aberdeen, "than is generally supposed will remain to be done in the new organization for the Government of our Eastern Empire."[a]

Much less even than is supposed, will have to be done by my lords Russell and Aberdeen.

The leading features of the proposed change appear to consist in two very small items. Firstly, the Board of Directors will be "refreshed" by some additional members, appointed directly by the Crown, and even this new blood will be infused "sparingly at first." The cure of the old directorial system is thus meant to be applied, so that the portion of blood now infused with "great caution" will have ample time to come to a standstill before another second infusion will be proceeded upon. Secondly, the union of Judge and of Exciseman in one and the same person, will be put an end to, and the Judges shall be educated men. Does it not seem, on hearing such propositions, as if one were transported back into that earliest period of the Middle Ages, when the feudal lords began to be replaced as Judges, by lawyers who were required, at any rate, to have a knowledge of reading and writing?

The "Sir Charles Wood" who, as President of the Board of Control, will bring forward this sensible piece of reform, is the same timber who, under the late Whig Administration, displayed such eminent capacities of mind, that the Coalition were at a dreadful loss what to do with him, till they hit upon the idea of making him over to India. Richard the Third offered a kingdom for a horse[b];—the Coalition offers an ass for a kingdom. Indeed, if the present official idiocy of an Oligarchical Government be the expression of what England *can* do now, the time of England's ruling the world must have passed away.

---

[a] *The Observer*, May 22, 1853.—*Ed.*
[b] Shakespeare, *King Richard III*, Act V, Scene 4.—*Ed.*

On former occasions we have seen that the Coalition had invariably some fitting reason for postponing every, even the smaller measure. Now, with respect to India their postponing propensities *are* supported by the public opinion of two worlds. The people of England and the people of India simultaneously demand the postponement of all the legislation on Indian affairs, until the voice of the natives shall have been heard, the necessary materials collected, the pending inquiries completed. Petitions have already reached Downing-st., from the three Presidencies,[88] deprecating precipitate legislation. The Manchester School have formed an "Indian Society,"[89] which they will put immediately into motion, to get up public meetings in the metropolis and throughout the country, for the purpose of opposing any legislation on the subject for this session. Besides, two Parliamentary Committees are now sitting with a view to report respecting the state of affairs in the Indian Government. But this time the Coalition Ministry is inexorable. It will not wait for the publication of any Committee's advice. It wants to legislate instantly and directly for 150 millions of people, and to legislate for 20 years at once. Sir Charles Wood is anxious to establish his claim as the modern Manu. Whence, of a sudden, this precipitate legislative rush of our "cautious" political valetudinarians?

They want to renew the old Indian Charter for a period of 20 years. They avail themselves of the eternal pretext of Reform. Why? The English oligarchy have a presentiment of the approaching end of their days of glory, and they have a very justifiable desire to conclude such a treaty with English legislation, that even in the case of England's escaping soon from their weak and rapacious hands, they shall still retain for themselves and their associates the privilege of plundering India for the space of 20 years.

On Saturday last dispatches were received by telegraph from Brussels and Paris, with news from Constantinople to May 13. Immediately after their arrival a Cabinet-Council was held at the Foreign-Office, which sat 3 hours and a half. On the same day orders were sent by Telegraph to the Admiralty at Portsmouth, directing the departure of two steam-frigates, the *London* 90, and *Sanspareil* 71, from Spithead for the Mediterranean. The *Highflyer* steam-frigate 21, and *Oden* steam-frigate 16, are also under orders for sea.

What were the contents of these dispatches which threw ministers into so sudden an activity, and interrupted the quiet dulness of England?

You know that the question of the Holy Shrines had been settled to the satisfaction of Russia,[90] and according to the assurances of the Russian Embassy at Paris and London, Russia asked for no other satisfaction than a priority share in those holy places. The objects of Russian diplomacy were merely of such a chivalric character, as were those of Frederick Barbarossa and Richard Cœur de Lion. This, at least, we were told by *The Times*.

"But," says the *Journal des Débats*, "on the 5th of May the Russian steam-frigate *Bessarabia* arrived from Odessa, having on board a Russian Colonel with dispatches for Prince Menchikoff, and on Saturday, 7th inst., the Prince handed to the Ministers of the Porte the draught of a convention or special treaty, in which the new demands and pretentions were set forth. This is the document called the ultimatum, since it was accompanied by a very brief note, fixing Tuesday, 10th May, as the last day on which the refusal or the acceptance of the Divan could be received. The note terminated in nearly the following words: 'If the Sublime Porte should think proper to respond by refusal, the Emperor would be compelled to see in that act the complete want of respect for his person, and for Russia, and would receive intelligence of it with *profound regret*.'"[a]

The principal object of this treaty was to secure to the Emperor of Russia the Protectorate of all Greek Christians subject to the Porte. By the treaty of Kutshuk-Kainardji, concluded at the close of the 18th century, a Greek chapel was allowed to be erected at Constantinople, and the privilege was granted to the Russian Embassy of interfering in instances of collision of the priests of that chapel with the Turks. This privilege was confirmed again in the treaty of Adrianople.[91] What Prince Menchikoff now demands, is the conversion of that exceptional privilege into the general Protectorate of the whole Greek Church in Turkey, i.e., of the vast majority of the population of Turkey in Europe. Besides, he asks that the patriarchs of Constantinople, Antiochia, Alexandria, and Jerusalem, as well as the metropolitan archbishops, shall be immovable, unless proved guilty of high-treason (against the Russians), and then only upon the consent of the Czar,—in other words, he demands the resignation of the Sultan's[b] sovereignty into the hands of Russia.

This was the news brought by the telegraph on Saturday: firstly, that Prince Menchikoff had granted a further delay until 14th inst., for the answer to his *ultimatum*; that then a change in the Turkish Ministry ensued, Reshid Pasha, the antagonist of

[a] Quoted from an editorial by X. Raymond in the *Journal des Débats*, May 23, 1853. The editorial gave the wrong date of handing the note to the Ministers. It was handed on May 5, 1853 (see this volume, p. 110).—*Ed.*

[b] Abdul Mejid.—*Ed.*

Russia, being appointed Minister of Foreign Affairs, and Fuad Effendi reinstated in his office; lastly, that the *Russian ultimatum had been rejected.*

It would have been impossible for Russia to make more extensive demands upon Turkey, after a series of signal victories. This is the best proof of the obstinacy with which she clings to her inveterate notion, that every interregnum of the counter-revolution in Europe constitutes a right for her to exact concessions from the Ottoman Empire. And, indeed, since the first French revolution, Continental retrogression has ever been identical with Russian progress in the East. But Russia is mistaken in confounding the present state of Europe with its condition after the congresses of Laybach and Verona, or even after the peace of Tilsit.[92] Russia herself is more afraid of the revolution that must follow any general war on the Continent, than the Sultan is afraid of the aggression of the Czar.[a] If the other powers hold firm, Russia is sure to retire in a very decent manner. Yet, be this as it may, her late maneuvers have, at all events, imparted a mighty impetus to the elements engaged in disorganizing Turkey from within. The only question is this; Does Russia act on her own free impulse, or is she but the unconscious and reluctant slave of the modern *fatum*, Revolution? I believe the latter alternative.

Written on May 24, 1853

First published in the *New-York Daily Tribune*, No. 3790, June 9, 1853; reprinted in the *New-York Semi-Weekly Tribune*, No. 839, June 10, 1853

Signed: *Karl Marx*

Reproduced from the *New-York Daily Tribune*

[a] Nicholas I.—*Ed.*

Karl Marx

MAZZINI.—SWITZERLAND AND AUSTRIA.— THE TURKISH QUESTION[93]

London, Friday, May 27, 1853

The presence of M. Mazzini in England is now, at last, confirmed by a quasi-official announcement in a London paper connected with him.

The trial of the Messrs. Hale, on account of the "gunpowder-plot,"[a] will not be brought before the present assizes, but will take place in August next, the Coalition Government being anxious to let time and oblivion interpose between its "discoveries" and the judicial discussion of their value.

Count Karnicky, the Austrian Chargé d'Affaires at Berne, received orders from his Government, on the 21st inst., to quit his post immediately, and return to Vienna, after notifying the President of the Helvetic Confederation[b] of the rupture of diplomatic relations between Austria and Switzerland. The *Bund*, of the 23d, states, however, that the Austrian Envoy had already previously received permission to take a discretionary *congé* when he should think proper. The ultimatum of Count Karnicky is declared by the same journal to be the answer of Austria to the note of the *Bundesrath*,[c] of May 4. That the ultimatum contained something beside a mere answer, may be inferred from the fact, that the Bundesrath has just called upon the Fribourg Government to account for their "extreme" measures recently taken against the defeated rebels. The English journals publish the following dispatch from Berne, dated May 23:

"In consequence of the notification made by the Austrian Chargé d'Affaires to the President of the Helvetic Confederation of the rupture of diplomatic relations

[a] See this volume, pp. 82-84.—*Ed.*

[b] Wilhelm Naeff.—*Ed.*

[c] Federal Council.—*Ed.*

between Austria and Switzerland, the Federal Council has decided on putting an immediate end to the functions of the Swiss Envoy at Vienna."

The substance of this dispatch is, however, refuted by the following article in *La Suisse,* dated May 23:

"We are about in the same situation as Piedmont.[94] The negotiations between the two countries are interrupted.... The Austrian Legation remains at Berne for the disposal of the ordinary current of business. The *Bund* says that the recall of the Swiss Chargé d'Affaires at Vienna was desirable, since he drily managed there his own affairs on pretext of transacting those of the nation, for he was merely engaged in the silk trade. Mr. Steiger is but a diplomatist of the second-hand order, and we happen to know that he understands a great deal more about silk-worms than about his official business. There was, then, no necessity for recalling such a diplomatist, since he had never been commissioned, but was already at Vienna on his own account."[a]

Let nobody imagine, therefore, that the Swiss are recalling to their memory the celebrated motto with which Loustallot adorned, in 1789, his *Révolutions de Paris*:

Les grands ne sont pas grands,
Que parce que nous sommes à genoux.
—Levons nous![b]

The mystery of the Swiss courage is sufficiently explained by the presence of the Duke of Genoa[c] at Paris, and that of the King of Belgium[d] in Vienna and perhaps no less by an article in the French *Moniteur* of May 25th.

"No other nation must ever interpose between France and Switzerland; all other considerations must subside before this fundamental condition."

The hopes of the Prussian King[e] for the recovery of Neuchâtel, thus obtain no great encouragement. A rumor prevails, even of the formation of a French *corps d'observation* on the frontiers of Switzerland. Louis Napoleon, of course, would be but too glad of having an opportunity to revenge himself on the Emperors of Russia and Austria, and the Kings of Prussia and Belgium, for the contempt and ridicule with which they have loaded him during the latter months.[95]

---

[a] *La Suisse,* No. 120, May 24, 1853.—*Ed.*
[b] The great are only great
Because we are kneeling.
Let us rise!—*Ed.*
[c] Ferdinando Alberto Amedeo.—*Ed.*
[d] Leopold I.—*Ed.*
[e] Frederick William IV.—*Ed.*

The intelligence I transmitted to you in my last,[a] of the rejection of the Russian ultimatum and of the formation of an anti-Russian Ministry at Constantinople has since been fully confirmed. The most recent dispatches are from Constantinople, of May 17.

"On assuming office, Reshid Pasha requested from Prince Menchikoff a delay of six days. Menchikoff refused, declaring diplomatic relations broken off, and adding that he would remain at Constantinople three days more, to make the necessary preparations for his departure, and he exhorted the Porte to reflection and to profit by the short time he should be detained."

Under date of Constantinople, May 19, we further learn:

"On the 17th, a meeting of the Divan was held, at the issue of which it was definitively resolved that the convention, as proposed by Prince Menchikoff, could not be accepted. Nevertheless, on this being notified to Prince Menchikoff, he did not quit Constantinople. On the contrary, he has opened new communications with Reshid Pasha. The day of the departure of the Russian Embassy is *no longer fixed*."

Contradictorily to the latter dispatch, the French Government evening organ, *La Patrie*, positively announces that the Government has received intelligence that Prince Menchikoff has taken his departure for Odessa, and that the occurrence had occasioned but little sensation at Constantinople. The *Pays* agrees with this statement, but is contradicted by the *Presse.*[b] Girardin adds, however, that if the news was correct, it might easily be accounted for.

"If Prince Menchikoff really departed from Bujukdere[96] for Odessa, the fact is that, having failed in his mission (manqué son effet), no alternative was left to him but to withdraw, from station to station."

Some papers assert that the fleet of Admiral Delasusse has passed the Dardanelles, and is now at anchor in the Golden Horn, but this assertion is contradicted by *The Morning Post*. The *Triester Zeitung* assures its readers that, before giving an answer to Prince Menchikoff, the Porte had asked Lord Redcliffe and M. De la Cour whether it could eventually count upon their support. To this *The Times* gives its solemn contradiction.

I now give you a literal translation from the Paris *Siècle*, containing some curious details with respect to the negotiations from May 5 to 12th at Constantinople—an exposure of the ridiculous behaviour of Prince Menchikoff, who, in the whole of this transaction, has combined in a most disgusting style, Northern

[a] See this volume, pp. 105-06.—*Ed.*

[b] The reference is to Charles Schiller's report published in *La Patrie*, No. 146, May 26, 1853 and confirmed by the article of J. Augier in *Le Pays*, No. 146, May 26, 1853, and by E. de Girardin's article in *La Presse*, May 27, 1853, quoted below.—*Ed.*

barbarity with Byzantine duplicity, and has succeeded in making Russia the laughing-stock of Europe. This "Grec du Bas-Empire"[a] presumed to conquer the sovereignty over a whole empire by mere theatrical performances. For Russia there remains no step from the sublime to the ridicule—a ridicule which can only be wiped out by blood. But these days of stockjobbing moneyocracy are not the days of chivalrous tournaments. The article in the *Siècle*[b] runs thus:—

"On Thursday, the 5th of May, the day of departure of the French steam-packet, the Sublime Porte communicated copies of the firman resolving the question of the Holy Places to M. De la Cour and Prince Menchikoff. The day passed away without any declamation, without any *démarche* on the part of Prince Menchikoff, and all the ambassadors, thinking that question to be settled, profited by the departure of the French steamer, for the announcement of the happy turn of affairs to their respective governments. Prince Menchikoff, however, who had just accepted the firman respecting the Holy Places, dispatched, as soon as midnight had arrived, a common *cavas*, i.e. a gens'-d'arme, to the Minister of Foreign Affairs,[c] with an ultimatum in which he demanded a *sened* (treaty) containing the solution of the Holy Shrines' question *and* the future guaranty of the privileges and immunities of the Greek Church, i.e. the most extensive protectorate of that Church for the benefit of Russia, such as would establish two distinct Emperors in Turkey—the Sultan for the Mussulmans, and the Czar for the Christians. For answering this ultimatum, the Prince allowed only four days to the Porte, requiring, besides, an immediate acknowledgment of the receipt of his ultimatum by a government officer. The Minister of Foreign Affairs returned him a kind of receipt by his aga, an inferior officer of the gendarmery. The Prince dispatched a steamer for Odessa in the course of the same night. On Friday, 6th, the Sultan,[d] having been informed of the presentation of the ultimatum by such an unusual proceeding, called together the Divan, and gave official notice to Lord Redcliffe and M. De la Cour of what had happened. Those two ambassadors immediately concerted measures for a common policy, advising the Porte to reject the ultimatum with the greatest moderation in language and terms. M. De la Cour, besides, is said to have most formally declared that France should oppose every Convention infringing the rights secured to her by the treaty of 1740, respecting the Holy Places. Prince Menchikoff, in the meantime, had retired to Bujukdere (like Achilles to his tent). Mr. Canning, on the 9th, there requested an interview with the Prince with a view of engaging him to a more moderate conduct. Refused. On the 10th the Ministers of War[e] and of Foreign Affairs, were at the Grand Vizir's,[f] who had invited Prince Menchikoff to join him there for the purpose of attempting to arrive at a reasonable arrangement. Refused. Nevertheless, Prince Menchikoff had intimated to the Porte that he was inclined to grant a further delay of three days. Then, however, the Sultan and his Ministers replied, that their

[a] A Byzantine of the Eastern Roman Empire.—*Ed.*

[b] Below is quoted H. Lamarche's article "Affaires d'Orient.—Rejet de l'Ultimatum Russe", *Le Siècle*, May 26, 1853.—*Ed.*

[c] Rifaat Pasha.—*Ed.*

[d] Abdul Mejid.—*Ed.*

[e] Mehemed Mutergim Pasha.—*Ed.*

[f] Mehemet Ali Pasha.—*Ed.*

resolutions were taken and that time would not modify them. This negative answer of the Porte was sent toward midnight on the 10th, to Bujukdere, where the whole of the Russian Embassy was collected, and where demonstrations for an approaching departure had been made for several days past. The Turkish Ministry, informed of this circumstance, was just about to yield, when the Sultan dismissed it and formed a new Administration."

I conclude my report on Turkish affairs by an excerpt from the *Constitutionnel*, showing the conduct of the Greek clergy during all these transactions.

"The Greek clergy, so deeply interested in this question, had pronounced in favor of the *status quo*, i.e., in favor of the Porte. They are protesting *en masse* against the protectorate threatened to be imposed on them by the Emperor of Russia.[a] Generally speaking, the Greeks desire the support of Russia, but only on condition of not being subject to her direct domination. It is repulsive to their minds to think that the Oriental Church, which is the mother of the Russian Church, should ever become subordinate to the latter, a thing which of necessity would happen, if the designs of the Petersburg Cabinet should be accepted."[b]

Written on May 27, 1853

First published in the *New-York Daily Tribune*, No. 3791, June 10, 1853; reprinted in the *New-York Semi-Weekly Tribune*, No. 840, June 14, 1853

Signed: *Karl Marx*

Reproduced from the *New-York Daily Tribune*

[a] Nicholas I.—*Ed.*

[b] Quoted from the editorial by L. Boniface in *Le Constitutionnel*, No. 146, May 26, 1853.—*Ed.*

Karl Marx

THE TURKISH QUESTION.—*THE TIMES*.— RUSSIAN AGGRANDIZEMENT[97]

London, Tuesday, May 31, 1853

Admiral Corry's fleet has been seen in the Bay of Biscay on the way to Malta, where it is to reinforce the squadron of Admiral Dundas. *The Morning Herald* justly observes:

"Had Admiral Dundas been permitted to join the French squadron at Salamis, several weeks ago, the present state of affairs would be quite different."[a]

Should Russia attempt, were it only for the salvation of appearances, to back up the ridiculous demonstrations of Menchikoff by actual maneuvers of war, her first two steps would probably consist in the re-occupation of the Danubian Principalities, and in the invasion of the Armenian province of Kars and the port of Batum, territories which she made every effort to secure by the treaty of Adrianople. The port of Batum being the only safe refuge for ships in the eastern part of the Black Sea, its possession would deprive Turkey of her last naval station in the Pontus and make the latter an exclusively Russian Sea. This port added to the possession of Kars, the richest and best cultivated portion of Armenia, would enable Russia to cut off the commerce of England with Persia by way of Trebizond, and afford a basis of operations against the latter power, as well as against Asia Minor. If, however, England and France hold firm Nicholas will no more carry out his projects in that quarter, than the Empress Catherine carried out hers against Aga Mahmed, when he commanded his slaves to drive the Russian Ambassador Voinovich

---

[a] *The Morning Herald*, No. 22168, May 26, 1853.—*Ed.*

and his companions with scourges to their ships, away from Astrabad.

In no quarter did the latest news create greater consternation than in Printing-House-square.[a] The first attempt made by *The Times* to lift up its head under the terrible blow, was a desperate diatribe against the electric telegraph, that "most extraordinary" instrument. "No correct conclusions could be drawn," it exclaimed, "from that mendacious wire." Having thus laid its own incorrect conclusions to the fault of the electric wire, *The Times,* after the statement of Ministers in Parliament, endeavors now also to get rid of its ancient "correct" premises. It says:

"Whatever may be the ultimate fate of the Ottoman Empire, or rather of that Mohammedan Power which has ruled it for four centuries, there can be no difference of opinion between *all* parties in this country and in Europe, that the gradual progress of the indigenous Christian population toward civilization and independent government is the interest of the world, and that these races of men ought never to be suffered to fall under the yoke of Russia, and to swell her gigantic dominions. On that point we confidently hope, that the resistance offered to these pretensions of Russia would be not only that of Turkey, but of all Europe; and this spirit of annexation and aggrandizement needs but to display itself in its true shape to excite universal antipathy and an insurmountable opposition, in which the Greek and Sclavonian subjects of Turkey are themselves prepared to take a great part."[b]

How did it happen, that the poor *Times* believed in the "good faith" of Russia toward Turkey, and her "antipathy" against all aggrandizement? The good will of Russia toward Turkey! Peter I proposed to raise himself on the ruins of Turkey. Catherine persuaded Austria, and called upon France to participate in the proposed dismemberment of Turkey, and the establishment of a Greek Empire at Constantinople, under her grandson,[c] who had been educated and even named with a view to this result. Nicholas, more moderate, only demands the *exclusive Protectorate* of Turkey. Mankind will not forget that Russia was the *protector* of Poland, the *protector* of the Crimea, the *protector* of Courland, the *protector* of Georgia, Mingrelia, the Circassian and Caucasian tribes. And now Russia, the protector of Turkey! As to Russia's antipathy against aggrandizement, I allege the following facts from a mass of the acquisitions of Russia since Peter the Great.

---

[a] The square in London where *The Times* had its main offices.—*Ed.*
[b] *The Times,* No. 21440, May 28, 1853.—*Ed.*
[c] Constantine.—*Ed.*

The Russian frontier has advanced.

Toward Berlin, Dresden and Vienna about	700 miles
Toward Constantinople	500 "
Toward Stockholm	630 "
Toward Teheran	1,000 "

Russia's acquisitions from Sweden are greater than what remains of that Kingdom; from Poland nearly equal to the Austrian Empire; from Turkey in Europe, greater than Prussia (exclusive of the Rhenish Provinces); from Turkey in Asia, as large as the whole dominion of Germany proper; from Persia equal to England; from Tartary to an extent as large as European Turkey, Greece, Italy and Spain, taken together. The total acquisitions of Russia during the last 60 years are equal in extent and importance to the whole Empire she had in Europe before that time.

Written on May 31, 1853

First published in the *New-York Daily Tribune*, No. 3794, June 14, 1853

Signed: *Karl Marx*

Reproduced from the newspaper

Karl Marx

THE RUSSIAN HUMBUG.—GLADSTONE'S FAILURE.— SIR CHARLES WOOD'S EAST INDIAN REFORMS[98]

London, Tuesday, June 7,[a] 1853

According to a dispatch from Berne, the *Bundesrath*[b] has cancelled the judgment pronounced by the Court Martial at Fribourg against the late insurrectionists, ordering them to be brought before the Ordinary Courts, *unless* they should be pardoned by the Cantonal Council. Here, then, we have the first of the heroic deeds accompanying the "rupture between Switzerland and Austria," the infallible result of which I traced in a former letter on the European "Model Republic."[c]

In transmitting to you the news of the Prussian Government having ordered several Artillery officers on furlough abroad to return immediately to their duties, I stated, by mistake, that those officers were engaged in instructing the Russian army, while I intended to have said the Turkish artillery, in field-practice.[99]

All the Russian Generals, and other Russians residing at Paris have received orders to return to Russia without delay. The language adopted by M. de Kisseleff, the Russian Envoy at Paris, is rather menacing, and letters from Petersburg are ostentatiously shown by him, in which the Turkish question is treated *assez cavalièrement*.[d] A rumor has issued from the same quarter, reporting that Russia demands from Persia the cession of the territory of Astrabad, at the south-eastern extremity of the Caspian Sea. Russian merchants, at the same time, dispatch, or are *reported* to have dispatched, orders to their London agents, "*not* to press any sales of grain at the present juncture, as prices were expected to rise in the imminent eventuality of a war." Lastly, confidential hints are being communicated to every newspaper, that the Rus-

---

[a] The *New-York Daily Tribune* erroneously has "Saturday, May 7".— *Ed.*
[b] Federal Council.— *Ed.*
[c] See this volume, pp. 107-08.— *Ed.*
[d] Too freely.— *Ed.*

sian troops are marching to the frontiers—that the inhabitants of Jassy are preparing for their reception—that the Russian Consul at Galatz[a] has bought up an immense number of trees for the throwing of several bridges across the Danube, and other *canards*, the breeding of which has been so successfully carried on by the *Augsburg Gazette*[b] and other Austro-Russian journals.

These, and a lot of similar reports, communications, etc., are nothing but so many ridiculous attempts on the part of the Russian agents to strike a wholesome terror into the western world, and to push it to the continuance of that policy of extension, under the cover of which Russia hopes, as heretofore, to carry out her projects upon the East. How systematically this game of mystification is being played, may be seen from the following:

Last week, several French papers notoriously in the pay of Russia, made the discovery, that the

> "real question was less between Russia and Turkey than between Petersburg and Moscow—*i.e.* between the Czar and the Old-Russian party; and that for the autocrat, there would be less danger in war, than in the vengeance of that conquest-urging party, which has so often shown how it deals with monarchs that displease it."[c]

Prince Menchikoff, of course, is the "head of this party." *The Times* and most of the English papers did not fail to reproduce this absurd statement, the one in consciousness of its meaning; the others, perhaps, its unconscious dupes. Now, what conclusion was the public intended to draw from this novel revelation? That Nicholas, in retreating under ridicule, and abandoning his warlike attitude against Turkey, has won a victory over his own warlike Old-Russians, or that Nicholas, in actually going to war, only does so from the necessity of yielding to that (fabulous) party. At all events, "there would only be a victory of Moscow over Petersburg, or of Petersburg over Moscow;" and, consequently, *none of Europe over Russia.*

Respecting this famous Old-Russian party, I happen to know from several well-informed Russians, aristocrats themselves, with whom I have had much intercourse at Paris, that it has long been entirely extinct, and is only occasionally called back into apparent existence, when the Czar stands in need of some bugbear to frighten the West of Europe into passive endurance of his arrogant claims. Hence the resurrection of a Menchikoff, and his appropriate outfit in the

---

[a] M. Cola.—*Ed.*
[b] *Allgemeine Zeitung.*—*Ed.*
[c] Quoted, with slight changes, from *The Times*, No. 21446, June 4, 1853.—*Ed.*

fabulous Old-Russian style. There is but one party among the Russian nobles actually feared by the Czar—the party whose aim is the establishment of an aristocratico-constitutional system, after the pattern of England.

Besides these different spectres conjured up by Russian diplomacy, for the misguidance of England and France, another attempt to bring about the same result has just been made, by the publication of a work entitled, *L'Empire Russe depuis le Congrès de Vienne*, by Viscount de Beaumont-Vassy. It will be sufficient to extract one sentence only, for the purpose of characterising this *opusculum*:

"It is well known that a deposit of coin and ingots exists in the cellar of the fortress of St. Peter and St. Paul. This *hidden treasure* was officially estimated, on the 1st of January, 1850, at 99,763,361 silver rubles." [a]

Has any one ever presumed to speak of the *hidden treasure* in the Bank of England? The "hidden treasure" of Russia is simply the metal reserve balancing a three times larger circulation of *convertible* notes, not to speak of the *hidden* amount of inconvertible paper issued by the Imperial Treasury. But, perhaps, this treasure may yet be called a "hidden" one, inasmuch as nobody has ever seen it, except the few Petersburg merchants selected by the Czar's Government for the annual inspection of the bags which hide it.

The chief demonstration of Russia in this direction is, however, an article published in the *Journal des Débats*, and signed by M. de St.-Marc Girardin, that old Orleanist sage. I extract:

"Europe has two great perils, according to us: *Russia*, which menaces her independence; and the *Revolution*, which menaces her *social order*. Now, she cannot be saved from one of these perils except by exposing herself entirely to the other. [...] Does Europe believe that the knot of her independence, and especially of the independence of the Continent, is at Constantinople, and that it is there that the question must be boldly decided; then, that is war against Russia. In that war France and England would struggle to establish the independence of Europe. What would Germany do? We know not. But what we know is, *that in the present state of Europe, war would be the social revolution*."

As a matter of course, M. de St.-Marc Girardin concludes in favor of peace on any condition against the social revolution, forgetting, however, that the Emperor of Russia has, at least, as much "horreur" of the revolution as he himself and his proprietor, M. Bertin.

Notwithstanding all these soporifics, administered by Russian diplomacy to the Press and people of England, "that old and

[a] A quotation from Viscount de Beaumont-Vassy's book as cited by *The Times*, No. 21446, June 4, 1853.—*Ed.*

obstinate" Aberdeen has been compelled to order Admiral Dundas to join the French fleet on the coast of Turkey, and even *The Times*, which, during the last few months, knew only how to write Russian, seems to have received a more English inspiration. It talks now very big.

The Danish (once Schleswig-Holstein) question is beginning to create considerable interest in England, since the English Press, too, has at length discovered that it involves the same principle of Russian extension, as supplies the foundation of the Eastern complication. Mr. Urquhart, M.P., the well-known admirer of Turkey and Eastern Institutions, has published a pamphlet on the Danish Succession,[a] of which an account will be given in a future letter.[100] The chief argument put forward in this publication is that the Sound is intended by Russia to perform the same functions for her in the North as the Dardanelles in the South, viz., the securing her maritime supremacy over the Baltic, in the same manner as the occupation of the Dardanelles would do with regard to the Euxine.

Some time since I gave you my opinion that the rate of interest would rise in England, and that such an occurrence would have an unfavorable effect on Mr. Gladstone's financial projects.[b] Now, the minimum rate of discount has in the past week been actually raised by the Bank of England from 3 per cent. to 3 1/2 per cent., and the failure I predicted for Mr. Gladstone's scheme of conversion has become already a fact, as you may see from the following statement:

BANK OF ENGLAND, Thursday, June 2, 1853

Amount of new stock accepted until this day:

3 1/2 per cent	£138,082	0/ 3
2 1/2 per cent	1,537,100	10/10
Exchange Bonds	4,200	0/ 0
Total	£1,679,382	11/1

SOUTH SEA HOUSE,[101] Thursday, June 2, 1853

Amount of convertible annuities till this day:

For 3 1/2 per cent annuities	£17,504	12/8
For 2 1/2 per cent annuities	986,528	5/7
Exchequer Bonds	5,270	18/4
Total	£1,009,303	16/7

[a] The reference is to the section, "The Danish Succession", in David Urquhart's pamphlet, *Progress of Russia in the West, North and South*.—*Ed.*

[b] See this volume, p. 102.—*Ed.*

Thus, of the whole amount of South Sea annuities offered for conversion, only one-eighth has been taken, and of the twenty millions new stock created by Mr. Gladstone, only one-twelfth has been accepted. Mr. Gladstone will, therefore, be obliged to contract for a loan at a time when the rate of interest has increased and will most likely continue to increase, which loan must amount to £8,157,811. Failure! The saving of £100,000 anticipated from this conversion, and already placed to the credit of the Budget, has, accordingly, to be dispensed with. Respecting the great bulk of the Public Debt, viz.: the £500,000,000 of 3 per cents., Mr. Gladstone has obtained, as the only result of his financial experiment, that another year will have elapsed on the 10th of Oct., 1853, during which he has been unable to give notice of any conversion. The greatest mischief, however, is this, that £3,116,000 must be paid in money in a few days to holders of Exchequer Bills, who refuse to renew them on the terms offered by Mr. Gladstone. Such is the financial success of the Government of "all the talents."

Lord John Russell, in the debate on the Ecclesiastical Revenues of Ireland (House of Commons, 31st ult.), expressed himself as follows:

"It has been evident, of late years, that the Roman Catholic Clergy—looking to its proceedings in this country—looking to that church acting under the direction of its head,[a] who himself a foreign sovereign, has aimed at political power [hear! hear!], which appears to me to be at variance with the due attachment to the Crown of this country [hear! hear!]—with the due attachment to the general cause of liberty—with the due attachment to the duties a subject of the State should perform toward it—now, as I wish to speak with as much frankness as the honorable gentleman who spoke last,[b] let me not be misunderstood in this House. I am far from denying that there are many members of this House, and many members of the Roman Catholic persuasion, both in *this country* and in Ireland, who are attached to the Throne, and to the liberties of *this country*; but what I am saying, and that of which I am convinced, is, that if the Roman Catholic clergy had increased power given to them, and if they, as ecclesiastics, were to exercise greater control and greater political influence they do now, that power would not be exercised in accordance with the *general freedom* that prevails in *this country*—[Hurrah!]—and that neither in respect of political power, nor upon other subjects, would they favor that *general freedom* of discussion and that activity and energy of the human mind, that belongs to the spirit of the constitution of *this country*. [Flourish of trumpets!] I do not think that, in that respect, they are upon a par with the Presbyterians of Scotland [bagpipes!], the Wesleyans of *this country*,[102] and the Established Church of *this country*. [General rapture.] ... I am obliged, then, to conclude, most unwillingly to conclude, but most decidedly, that the endowment of

---

[a] Pope Pius IX.—*Ed.*
[b] F. Lucas.—*Ed.*

the Roman Catholic Religion in Ireland, in the place of the endowment of the Protestant Church in *that country*, in connection with the State, is not an object which the Parliament of *this country* ought to adopt or to sanction."[a]

Two days after this speech of Lord John, in which he attempted for the six-thousandth time, to make a show of his love of "general freedom," by his zealous genuflexions before particular sects of Protestant bigotry, Messrs. Sadleir, Keogh, and Monsell gave in their resignations to the Coalition Ministry, in a letter addressed by Mr. Monsell to My Lord Aberdeen. My Lord Aberdeen in his answer dated 3d June, assures these gentlemen that

"The reasons given by Lord John Russell and the sentiments of which you complain, are not shared by me, nor by many of my colleagues.... Lord John Russell desires me to say, that he did not impute want of loyalty to the Roman Catholics."[b]

Messrs. Sadleir, Keogh and Monsell accordingly withdrew their resignations, and the arrangements for a general reconciliation passed off last night in Parliament, "to the greatest satisfaction of Lord John Russell."

The last India Bill of 1783 proved fatal to the Coalition Cabinet of Mr. Fox and Lord North. The new India Bill of 1853 is likely to prove fatal for the Coalition Cabinet of Mr. Gladstone and Lord John Russell. But if the former were thrown overboard, because of their attempt to abolish the Courts of Directors and of Proprietors, the latter are threatened with a similar fate for the opposite reason. On June 3, Sir Charles Wood moved for leave to bring in a bill to provide for the Government of India. Sir Charles commenced by excusing the anomalous length of the speech he was about to deliver, by the "magnitude of the subject," and "the 150,000,000 of souls he had to deal with."[c] For every 30,000,000 of his fellow-subjects, Sir Charles could do no less than sacrifice one hour's breath. But why this precipitate legislation on that "great subject," while you postpone it "for even the most trifling matters?" Because the Charter of the East India Company expires on the 30th April, 1854. But why not pass a temporary

[a] John Russell's speech is quoted, with slight changes, from the report in *The Times*, No. 21443, June 1, 1853.—*Ed.*

[b] See *The Times*, No. 21447, June 6, 1853.—*Ed.*

[c] Here and below Charles Wood's speech is quoted from the report in *The Times*, No. 21446, June 4, 1853.—*Ed.*

continuance bill, reserving to future discussion more permanent legislation? Because it cannot be expected that we shall ever find again "such an opportunity of dealing quietly with this vast and important question"—i.e., of burking it in a Parliamentary way. Besides, we are fully informed on the matter, the Directors of the East India Company express the opinion that it is necessary to legislate in the course of the present session, and the Governor-General of India, Lord Dalhousie, summons the Government by an express letter by all means to conclude our legislation at once. But the most striking argument wherewith Sir Charles justifies his immediate legislation, is that, prepared as he may appear to speak of a world of questions, "not comprised in the bill he proposed to bring in," the

"*measure* which he has to submit is, so far as legislation goes, *comprised in a very small compass.*"

After this introduction Sir Charles delivered himself of an apology for the administration of India for the last twenty years. "We must look at India with somewhat of an Indian eye"—which Indian eye seems to have the particular gift of seeing everything bright on the part of England and everything black on the side of India.

"In India you have a race of people slow of change, bound up by religious prejudices and antiquated customs. There are [...],in fact, [...] all obstacles to rapid progress."

(Perhaps there is a Whig Coalition party in India.)

"The points," said Sir Charles Wood, "upon which the greatest stress has been laid, and which are the heads of the complaints contained in the petitions presented to the Committee, relate to the administration of justice, the want of public works, and the tenure of land."

With regard to the Public Works, the Government *intends* to undertake some of "the greatest magnitude and importance." With regard to the tenure of lands, Sir Charles proves very successfully that its three existing forms—the *Zemindari*, the *Ryotwari*, and the *Village* systems—are only so many forms of fiscal *exploitation* in the hands of the Company,[a] none of which could well be made general, nor deserved to be made so. An idea of establishing another form, of an altogether opposite character, does not in the least preoccupy the mind of Sir Charles.

---

[a] See this volume, pp. 213-16.—*Ed.*

"With regard to the *administration of justice*," continues he, "the complaints relate principally to the inconvenience arising from the technicalities of English law, to the alleged incompetency of English judges, and to the corruption of the native officers and judges."

And now, in order to prove the hard labor of providing for the administration of justice in India, Sir Charles relates that already, as early as 1833, a Law Commission was appointed in India. But in what manner did this Commission act, according to Sir Charles Wood's own testimony? The first and last result of the labors of that Commission was a *penal code*, prepared under the auspices of Mr. Macaulay. This code was sent to the various local authorities in India, which sent it back to Calcutta, from which it was sent to England, to be again returned from England to India. In India, Mr. Macaulay having been replaced as legislative counsel by Mr. Bethune, the code was totally altered, and on this plea the Governor-General, not being then of opinion "that delay is a source of weakness and danger," sent it back to England, and from England it was returned to the Governor-General, with authority to pass the code in whatever shape he thought best. But now, Mr. Bethune having died, the Governor-General thought best to submit the code to a third English lawyer,[a] and to a lawyer who knew nothing about the habits and customs of the Hindoos, reserving himself the right of afterward rejecting a code concocted by wholly incompetent authority. Such have been the adventures of that yet unborn code. As to the technical absurdities of the law in India, Sir Charles takes his stand on the no less absurd technicalities of the English law-procedure itself; but while affirming the perfect incorruptibility of the English judges in India, he nevertheless is ready to sacrifice them by an alteration in the manner of nominating them. The general progress of India is demonstrated by a comparison of the present state of Delhi with that under the invasion of Khuli-Khan. The salt-tax is justified by the arguments of the most renowned political economists, all of whom have advised taxation to be laid on some article of first necessity. But Sir Charles does not add what those same economists would have said, on finding that in the two years from 1849-'50, and 1851-'52, there had been a decrease in the consumption of salt, of 60,000 tuns, a loss of revenue to the amount of £415,000, the total salt revenue amounting to £2,000,000. The measures proposed by Sir Charles, and "comprised in a very small compass," are:

[a] B. Peacock.—*Ed.*

1. The Court of Directors, to consist of eighteen instead of twenty-four members, twelve to be elected by the Proprietors, and six by the Crown.

2. The revenue of Directors to be raised from £300 to £500 a year, the Chairman to receive £1,000.

3. All the ordinary appointments in the civil service, and all the scientific in the military service of India, to be thrown open to public competition, leaving to the Directors the nomination to the Cadetships in the Cavalry-of-the-Line.

4. The Governor-Generalship to be separated from the Governorship of Bengal, and power to be given to the Supreme Government to constitute a new Presidency in the districts on the Indus.

5. And lastly, the whole of this measure only to continue until the Parliament shall provide otherwise.

The speech and measure of Sir Charles Wood was subjected to a very strong and satirical criticism by Mr. Bright, whose picture of India ruined by the fiscal exertions of the Company and Government did not, of course, receive the supplement of India ruined by Manchester and Free Trade. As to last night's speech of an old East-Indiaman, Sir J. Hogg, Director or ex-Director of the Company, I really suspect that I have met with it already in 1701, 1730, 1743, 1769, 1772, 1781, 1783, 1784, 1793, 1813, etc., and am induced, by way of answer to his directorial panegyric, to quote merely a few facts from the annual Indian accounts published, I believe, under his own superintendence.

Total Net-Revenues of India

1849-'50	£20,275,831	Loss of Revenue within three years, £348,792
1850-'51	20,249,932	
1851-'52	19,927,039	

Total Charges

1849-'50	£16,687,382	Increase of expenditure within three years, £1,214,284
1850-'51	17,170,707	
1851-'52	17,901,666	

Land-Tax

Bengal oscillated in last four years from	£3,500,000	to	£3,560,000
North West oscillated in last four years from	4,870,000		4,900,000
Madras oscillated in last four years from	3,640,000		3,470,000
Bombay oscillated in last four years from	2,240,000		2,300,000

	Gross Revenue in 1851-52	Expenditure on Public Works in 1851-52
Bengal	£10,000,000	£87,800
Madras	5,000,000	20,000
Bombay	4,800,000	58,500
Out of	£19,800,000	not £166,300

have been expended on roads, canals, bridges and other works of public necessity.

Written on June 7, 1853

First published in the *New-York Daily Tribune*, No. 3801, June 22, 1853; reprinted without the section "The Russian Humbug" in the *New-York Weekly Tribune*, No. 615, June 25, 1853

Signed: *Karl Marx*

Reproduced from the *New-York Daily Tribune*

Karl Marx

THE BRITISH RULE IN INDIA[103]

London, Friday, June 10, 1853

Telegraphic dispatches from Vienna announce that the pacific solution of the Turkish, Sardinian and Swiss questions, is regarded there as a certainty.

Last night the debate on India was continued in the House of Commons, in the usual dull manner. Mr. Blackett charged the statements of Sir Charles Wood and Sir J. Hogg with bearing the stamp of optimist falsehood. A lot of Ministerial and Directorial advocates rebuked the charge as well as they could, and the inevitable Mr. Hume summed up by calling on Ministers to withdraw their bill. Debate adjourned.

Hindostan is an Italy of Asiatic dimensions, the Himalayas for the Alps, the Plains of Bengal for the Plains of Lombardy, the Deccan for the Apennines, and the Isle of Ceylon for the Island of Sicily. The same rich variety in the products of the soil, and the same dismemberment in the political configuration. Just as Italy has, from time to time, been compressed by the conqueror's sword into different national masses, so do we find Hindostan, when not under the pressure of the Mohammedan, or the Mogul,[104] or the Briton, dissolved into as many independent and conflicting States as it numbered towns, or even villages. Yet, in a social point of view, Hindostan is not the Italy, but the Ireland of the East. And this strange combination of Italy and of Ireland, of a world of voluptuousness and of a world of woes, is anticipated in the ancient traditions of the religion of Hindostan. That religion is at once a religion of sensualist exuberance, and a religion of self-torturing asceticism; a religion of the Lingam and of the Juggernaut; the religion of the Monk, and of the Bayadere.[105]

I share not the opinion of those who believe in a golden age of Hindostan, without recurring, however, like Sir Charles Wood, for the confirmation of my view, to the authority of Khuli-Khan.[a] But take, for example, the times of Aurangzeb; or the epoch, when the Mogul appeared in the North, and the Portuguese in the South; or the age of Mohammedan invasion, and of the Heptarchy in Southern India[106]; or, if you will, go still more back to antiquity, take the mythological chronology of the Brahman himself, who places the commencement of Indian misery in an epoch even more remote than the Christian creation of the world.

There cannot, however, remain any doubt but that the misery inflicted by the British on Hindostan is of an essentially different and infinitely more intensive kind than all Hindostan had to suffer before. I do not allude to European despotism, planted upon Asiatic despotism, by the British East India Company, forming a more monstrous combination than any of the divine monsters startling us in the Temple of Salsette.[107] This is no distinctive feature of British Colonial rule, but only an imitation of the Dutch, and so much so that in order to characterise the working of the British East India Company, it is sufficient to literally repeat what Sir Stamford Raffles, the *English* Governor of Java, said of the old Dutch East India Company:

> "The Dutch Company, actuated solely by the spirit of gain, and viewing their [Javan] subjects, with less regard or consideration than a West India planter formerly viewed a gang upon his estate, because the latter had paid the purchase money of human property, which the other had not, employed all the existing machinery of despotism to squeeze from the people their utmost mite of contribution, the last dregs of their labor, and thus aggravated the evils of a capricious and semi-barbarous Government, by working it with all the practised ingenuity of politicians, and all the monopolizing selfishness of traders."[b]

All the civil wars, invasions, revolutions, conquests, famines, strangely complex, rapid, and destructive as the successive action in Hindostan may appear, did not go deeper than its surface. England has broken down the entire framework of Indian society, without any symptoms of reconstitution yet appearing. This loss of his old world, with no gain of a new one, imparts a particular kind of melancholy to the present misery of the Hindoo, and separates

---

[a] See this volume, p. 122.—*Ed.*

[b] Th. S. Raffles, *The History of Java*, Vol. 1, p. 151.—*Ed.*

Hindostan, ruled by Britain, from all its ancient traditions, and from the whole of its past history.

There have been in Asia, generally, from immemorial times, but three departments of Government; that of Finance, or the plunder of the interior; that of War, or the plunder of the exterior; and, finally, the department of Public Works. Climate and territorial conditions, especially the vast tracts of desert, extending from the Sahara, through Arabia, Persia, India, and Tartary, to the most elevated Asiatic highlands, constituted artificial irrigation by canals and water-works the basis of Oriental agriculture. As in Egypt and India, inundations are used for fertilizing the soil in Mesopotamia, Persia, &c.; advantage is taken of a high level for feeding irrigative canals. This prime necessity of an economical and common use of water, which, in the Occident, drove private enterprise to voluntary association, as in Flanders and Italy, necessitated, in the Orient where civilization was too low and the territorial extent too vast to call into life voluntary association, the interference of the centralizing power of Government. Hence an economical function devolved upon all Asiatic Governments, the function of providing public works. This artificial fertilization of the soil, dependent on a Central Government, and immediately decaying with the neglect of irrigation and drainage, explains the otherwise strange fact that we now find whole territories barren and desert that were once brilliantly cultivated, as Palmyra, Petra, the ruins in Yemen, and large provinces of Egypt, Persia, and Hindostan; it also explains how a single war of devastation has been able to depopulate a country for centuries, and to strip it of all its civilization.

Now, the British in East India accepted from their predecessors the department of finance and of war, but they have neglected entirely that of public works. Hence the deterioration of an agriculture which is not capable of being conducted on the British principle of free competition, of *laissez-faire* and *laissez-aller*.[a] But in Asiatic empires we are quite accustomed to see agriculture deteriorating under one government and reviving again under some other government. There the harvests correspond to good or bad government, as they change in Europe with good or bad seasons. Thus the oppression and neglect of agriculture, bad as it is, could not be looked upon as the final blow dealt to Indian

---

[a] *Laissez-faire, laissez-aller* was the formula of the advocates of free trade and non-intervention of the state in economic relations.—*Ed.*

society by the British intruder, had it not been attended by a circumstance of quite different importance, a novelty in the annals of the whole Asiatic world. However changing the political aspect of India's past must appear, its social condition has remained unaltered since its remotest antiquity, until the first decennium of the 19th century. The hand-loom and the spinning-wheel, producing their regular myriads of spinners and weavers, were the pivots of the structure of that society. From immemorial times, Europe received the admirable textures of Indian labor, sending in return for them her precious metals, and furnishing thereby his material to the goldsmith, that indispensable member of Indian society, whose love of finery is so great that even the lowest class, those who go about nearly naked, have commonly a pair of golden ear-rings and a gold ornament of some kind hung round their necks. Rings on the fingers and toes have also been common. Women as well as children frequently wore massive bracelets and anklets of gold or silver, and statuettes of divinities in gold and silver were met with in the households. It was the British intruder who broke up the Indian hand-loom and destroyed the spinning-wheel. England began with driving the Indian cottons from the European market; it then introduced twist into Hindostan, and in the end inundated the very mother country of cotton with cottons. From 1818 to 1836 the export of twist from Great Britain to India rose in the proportion of 1 to 5,200. In 1824 the export of British muslins to India hardly amounted to 1,000,000 yards, while in 1837 it surpassed 64,000,000 of yards. But at the same time the population of Dacca decreased from 150,000 inhabitants to 20,000. This decline of Indian towns celebrated for their fabrics was by no means the worst consequence. British steam and science uprooted, over the whole surface of Hindostan, the union between agriculture and manufacturing industry.

These two circumstances—the Hindoo, on the one hand, leaving, like all Oriental peoples, to the Central Government the care of the great public works, the prime condition of his agriculture and commerce, dispersed, on the other hand, over the surface of the country, and agglomerated in small centers by the domestic union of agricultural and manufacturing pursuits—these two circumstances had brought about, since the remotest times, a social system of particular features—the so-called *village system,* which gave to each of these small unions their independent organization and distinct life. The peculiar character of this system may be judged from the following description, contained in an old official report of the British House of Commons on Indian affairs:

NEW-YORK DAILY TRIBUNE, SATURDAY, JUNE 25, 1853.

French Princess married King Leopold. It seems that Napoleon is eager to pick a quarrel with King Leopold, who has thrown himself under the protection of Russsia and Austria, instead of suing for peace at Paris, as the Kings of Holland and Sardinia, and the Swiss Republic have done. Spain, too, is not looked at favorably by the Emperor; her royal honse is too much allied with the Orleans family, not to be disliked by a Bonaparte. A rising, therefore, would not be suppressed by French Intervention, and such a rising is not altogether impossible in Spain, where royalty has lost its dignity by the personal behaviour of the Queen-Mother and of the Queen.

A. C. C.

The British Rule in India.

Correspondence of The N. Y. Tribune

LONDON, Friday, June 10, 1853.

Telegraphic dispatches from Vienna announce that the pacific solution of the Turkish, Sardinian and Swiss questions, is regarded there as a certainty.

Last night the debate on India was continued in the House of Commons, in the usual dull manner. Mr. Blackett charged the statements of Sir Charles Wood and Sir J. Hogg with bearing the stamp of optimist falsehood. A lot of Ministerial and Directorial advocates rebuked the charge as well as they could, and the inevitable Mr. Hume summed up by calling on Ministers to withdraw their bill. Debate adjourned.

Hindostan is an Italy of Asiatic dimensions, the Himalayas for the Alps, the Plains of Bengal for the Plains of Lombardy, the Deccan for the Appenines, and the Isle of Ceylon for the Island of Sicily. The same rich variety in the products of the soil, and the same dismemberment in the political configuration. Just as Italy has, from time to time, been compressed by the conqueror's sword into different national masses, so do we find Hindostan, when not under the pressure of the Mohammedan, or the Mogul, or the Briton, dissolved into as many independent and conflicting States as it numbered towns, or even villages. Yet, in a social point of view, Hindostan is not the Italy, but the Ireland of the East. And this strange combination of Italy and of Ireland, of a world of voluptuousness and of a world of woes, is anticipated in the ancient traditions of the religion of Hindostan. That religion is at once a religion of sensualist exuberance, and a religion of self-torturing ascetism; a religion of the Lingam and of the Juggernaut; the religion of the Monk, and of the Bayadere.

I share not the opinion of those who believe in a golden age of Hindostan, without recurring, however, like Sir Charles Wood, for the confirmation of my view, to the authority of Khuli-Khan. But take, for example, the times of Aurung-Zebe; or the epoch, when the Mogul appeared in the North, and the Portuguese in the South; or the age of Mohammedan invasion, and of the Heptarchy in Southern India; or, if you will, go still more back to antiquity, take the mythological chronology of the Brahman himself, who places the commencement of Indian misery in an epoch even more remote than the Christian creation of the world.

There cannot, however, remain any doubt but that the misery inflicted by the British on Hindostan is of an essentially different and infinitely more intensive kind than all Hindostan had to suffer before. I do not allude to European despotism, planted upon Asiatic despotism, by the British East India Company, forming a more monstrous combination than any of the divine monsters startling us in the Temple of Salsette. This is no distinctive feature of British Colonial rule, but only an imitation of the Dutch, and so much so that in order to characterise the working of the British East India Company, it is sufficient to literally repeat what Sir Stamford Raffles, the *English* Governor of Java, said of the old Dutch East India Company:

"The Dutch Company, actuated solely by the spirit of gain, and viewing their subjects, with less regard or consideration than a West India planter formerly viewed a gang upon his estate, because the latter had paid the purchase money of human property, which the other had not, employed all the existing machinery of despotism to squeeze from the people their utmost mite of contribution, the last dregs of their labor, and thus aggravated the evils of a capricious and semi barbarous Government, by working it with all the practised ingenuity of politicians, and all the monopolizing selfishness of traders."

All the civil wars, invasions, revolutions, conquests, famines, strangely complex, rapid, and destructive as the successive action in Hindostan may appear, did not go deeper than its surface. England has broken down the entire framework of Indian society, without any symptoms of reconstitution yet appearing. This loss of his old world, with no gain of a new one, imparts a particular kind of melancholy to the present misery of the Hindoo, and separates Hindostan, ruled by Britain, from all its ancient traditions, and from the whole of its past history.

There have been in Asia, generally, from immemorial times, but three departments of Government; that of Finance, or the plunder of the interior; that of War, or the plunder of the exterior; and, finally, the department of Public Works. Climate and territorial conditions, especially the vast tracts of desert, extending from the

personal influence and minute acquaintance with the situation and concerns of the people render him the best qualified for this charge. The *kurnum* keeps the accounts of cultivation, and registers everything connected with it. The *tallier* and the *totie*, the duty of the former of which consists in gaining information of crimes and offenses, and in escorting and protecting persons traveling from one village to another; the province of the latter appearing to be more immediately confined to the village, consisting, among other duties, in guarding the crops and assisting in measuring them. The *boundary-man*, who preserves the limits of the village, or gives evidence respecting them in cases of dispute. The Superintendent of Tanks and Watercourses distributes the water for the purposes of agriculture. The Brahmin, who performs the village worship. The schoolmaster, who is seen teaching the children in a village to read and write in the sand. The calendar-brahmin, or astrologer, &c. These officers and servants generally constitute the establishment of a village; but in some parts of the country it is of less extent, some of the duties and functions above described being united in the same person; in others it exceeds the above-named number of individuals. Under this simple form of municipal government, the inhabitants of the country have lived from time immemorial. The boundaries of the villages have been but seldom altered; and though the villages themselves have been sometimes injured, and even desolated by war, famine or disease, the same name, the same limits, the same interests, and even the same families have continued for ages. The inhabitants gave themselves no trouble about the breaking up and divisions of kingdoms; while the village remains entire, they care not to what power it is transferred, or to what sovereign it devolves; its internal economy remains unchanged. The potail is still the head inhabitant, and still acts as the petty judge or magistrate, and collector or rentor of the village."

These small stereotype forms of social organism have been to the grester part dissolved, and are disappearing, not so much through the brutal interference of the British tax-gatherer and the British soldier, as to the working of English steam and English free trade. Those family-communities were based on domestic industry, in that peculiar combination of hand-weaving, hand-spinning and hand-tilling agriculture which gave them self-supporting power. English interference having placed the spinner in Lancashire and the weaver in Bengal, or sweeping away both Hindoo spinner and weaver, dissolved these small semi barbarian, semi-civilized communities, by blowing up their economical basis, and thus produced the greatest, and to speak the truth, the only *social* revolution ever heard of in Asia.

Now, sickening as it must be to human feeling to witness those myriads of industrious patriarchal and inoffensive social organizations disorganized and dissolved into their units, thrown into a sea of woes, and their individual members losing at the same time their ancient form of civilization, and their hereditary means of subsistence, we must not forget that these idyllic village-communities, inoffensive though they may appear, had always been the solid foundation of Oriental despotism, that they restrained the human mind within the smallest possible compass, making it the unresisting tool of superstition, enslaving it beneath traditional rules, depriving it of all grandeur and historical energies. We must not forget the barbarian egotism which, concentrating on some miserable patch of land, had quietly witnessed the ruin of empires, the perpetration of unspeakable cruelties, the massacre of the population of large towns, with no other consideration bestowed upon them than on natural events, itself the helpless prey of any aggressor who deigned to notice it at all. We must not forget that this undignified, stagnatory, and vegetative life, that this passive sort of existence evoked on the other part, in contradistinction, wild, aimless, unbounded forces of destruction and rendered murder itself a religious rite in Hindostan. We must not forget that these little communities were contaminated by distinctions of caste and by slavery, that they subjugated man to external circumstances instead of elevating man the sovereign of circumstances, that they transformed a self-developing social state into never changing natural destiny, and thus brought about a brutalizing worship of nature, exhibiting its degradation in the fact that man, the sovereign of nature, fell down on his knees in adoration of Kanuman, the monkey, and Sabbala, the cow.

England, it is true, in causing a social revolution in Hindostan, was actuated only by the vilest interests, and was stupid in her manner of enforcing them. But that is not the question. The question is, can mankind fulfil its destiny without a fundamental revolution in the social state of Asia? If not, whatever may have been the crimes of England she was the unconscious tool of history in bringing about that revolution.

Then, whatever bitterness the spectacle of the crumbling of an ancient world may have for our personal feelings, we have the right, in point of history, to exclaim with Göethe:

"Sollte diese Qual uns quälen
Da sie unsre Lust vermehrt,
Hat nicht myriaden Seelen
Timuris Herrschaft aufgezehrt?"

KARL MARX.

TURKEY AND RUSSIA

Part of a page of the *New-York Daily Tribune* with Marx's article "The British Rule in India"

"A village, geographically considered, is a tract of country comprising some hundred or thousand acres of arable and waste lands; politically viewed it resembles a corporation or township. Its proper establishment of officers and servants consists of the following descriptions: The *potail*, or head inhabitant, who has generally the superintendence of the affairs of the village, settles the disputes of the inhabitants, attends to the police, and performs the duty of collecting the revenue within his village, a duty which his personal influence and minute acquaintance with the situation and concerns of the people render him the best qualified for this charge. The *kurnum* keeps the accounts of cultivation, and registers everything connected with it. The *tallier* and the *totie*, the duty of the former of which consists [...] in gaining information of crimes and offenses, and in escorting and protecting persons traveling from one village to another; the province of the latter appearing to be more immediately confined to the village, consisting, among other duties, in guarding the crops and assisting in measuring them. The *boundary-man*, who preserves the limits of the village, or gives evidence respecting them in cases of dispute. The Superintendent of Tanks and Watercourses distributes the water [...] for the purposes of agriculture. The Brahmin, who performs the village worship. The schoolmaster, who is seen teaching the children in a village to read and write in the sand. The calendar-brahmin, or astrologer, &c. These officers and servants generally constitute the establishment of a village; but in some parts of the country it is of less extent, some of the duties and functions above described being united in the same person; in others it exceeds the above-named number of individuals. [...] Under this simple form of municipal government, the inhabitants of the country have lived from time immemorial. The boundaries of the villages [...] have been but seldom altered; and though the villages themselves have been sometimes injured, and even desolated by war, famine or disease, the same name, the same limits, the same interests, and even the same families have continued for ages. The inhabitants gave themselves no trouble about the breaking up and divisions of kingdoms; while the village remains entire, they care not to what power it is transferred, or to what sovereign it devolves; its internal economy remains unchanged. The potail is still the head inhabitant, and still acts as the petty judge or magistrate, and collector or renter of the village." [a]

These small stereotype forms of social organism have been to the greater part dissolved, and are disappearing, not so much through the brutal interference of the British tax-gatherer and the British soldier, as to the working of English steam and English free trade. Those family-communities were based on domestic industry, in that peculiar combination of hand-weaving, hand-spinning and hand-tilling agriculture which gave them self-supporting power. English interference having placed the spinner in Lancashire and the weaver in Bengal, or sweeping away both Hindoo spinner and weaver, dissolved these small semi-barbarian, semi-civilized communities, by blowing up their economical basis,

[a] "Report of the Committee of the House of Commons" published in 1812; quoted from Th. S. Raffles' *The History of Java*, Vol. 1, p. 285.—*Ed.*

and thus produced the greatest, and to speak the truth, the only *social* revolution ever heard of in Asia.

Now, sickening as it must be to human feeling to witness those myriads of industrious patriarchal and inoffensive social organizations disorganized and dissolved into their units, thrown into a sea of woes, and their individual members losing at the same time their ancient form of civilization, and their hereditary means of subsistence, we must not forget that these idyllic village-communities, inoffensive though they may appear, had always been the solid foundation of Oriental despotism, that they restrained the human mind within the smallest possible compass, making it the unresisting tool of superstition, enslaving it beneath traditional rules, depriving it of all grandeur and historical energies. We must not forget the barbarian egotism which, concentrating on some miserable patch of land, had quietly witnessed the ruin of empires, the perpetration of unspeakable cruelties, the massacre of the population of large towns, with no other consideration bestowed upon them than on natural events, itself the helpless prey of any aggressor who deigned to notice it at all. We must not forget that this undignified, stagnatory, and vegetative life, that this passive sort of existence evoked on the other part, in contradistinction, wild, aimless, unbounded forces of destruction and rendered murder itself a religious rite in Hindostan. We must not forget that these little communities were contaminated by distinctions of caste and by slavery, that they subjugated man to external circumstances instead of elevating man the sovereign of circumstances, that they transformed a self-developing social state into never changing natural destiny, and thus brought about a brutalizing worship of nature, exhibiting its degradation in the fact that man, the sovereign of nature, fell down on his knees in adoration of Kanuman, the monkey, and Sabbala, the cow.

England, it is true, in causing a social revolution in Hindostan, was actuated only by the vilest interests, and was stupid in her manner of enforcing them. But that is not the question. The question is, can mankind fulfil its destiny without a fundamental revolution in the social state of Asia? If not, whatever may have been the crimes of England she was the unconscious tool of history in bringing about that revolution.

Then, whatever bitterness the spectacle of the crumbling of an ancient world may have for our personal feelings, we have the right, in point of history, to exclaim with Goethe:

"Sollte diese Qual uns quälen
Da sie unsre Lust vermehrt,
Hat nicht myriaden Seelen
Timur's Herrschaft aufgezehrt?"[a]

Written on June 10, 1853

First published in the *New-York Daily Tribune*, No. 3804, June 25, 1853; reprinted in the *New-York Semi-Weekly Tribune*, No. 844, June 28, and the *New-York Weekly Tribune*, No. 616, July 2, 1853

Signed: *Karl Marx*

Reproduced from the *New-York Daily Tribune*

[a] "Should this torture then torment us
Since it brings us greater pleasure?
Were not through the rule of Timur
Souls devoured without measure?"
From Goethe's "An Suleika", *Westöstlicher Diwan*.—*Ed.*

Karl Marx

ENGLISH PROSPERITY.—STRIKES.— THE TURKISH QUESTION.—INDIA[108]

London, Friday, June 17, 1853

The declared value of British exports for the month of

April, 1853, amounts to	£7,578,910
Against, for April, 1852	5,268,915
For four months ending April 30 [1853]	27,970,633
Against the same months of 1852	21,844,663

Showing an increase, in the former instance, of £2,309,995, or upward of 40 per cent.; and in the latter of £6,125,970, or nearly 28 per cent. Supposing the increase to continue at the same rate, the total exports of Great Britain would amount, at the close of 1853, to more than £100,000,000.

The Times, in communicating these startling items to its readers, indulged in a kind of dithyrambics, concluding with the words: "We are all happy, and all united."[a] This agreeable discovery had no sooner been trumpeted forth, than an almost general system of strikes burst over the whole surface of England, particularly in the industrial North, giving a strange echo to the song of harmony tuned by *The Times*. These strikes are the necessary consequence of a comparative decrease in the labor-surplus, coinciding with a general rise in the prices of the first necessaries. 5,000 hands struck at Liverpool, 35,000 at Stockport, and so on, until at length the very police force was seized by the epidemic, and 250

[a] *The Times*, No. 21449, June 8, 1853.—*Ed.*

constables at Manchester offered their resignation. On this occasion the middle-class press, for instance *The Globe*, lost all countenance, and foreswore its usual philanthropic effusions. It calumniated, injured, threatened, and called loudly upon the magistrates for interference, a thing which has actually been done at Liverpool in all cases where the remotest legal pretext could be invoked. These magistrates, when not themselves manufacturers or traders, as is commonly the case in Lancashire and Yorkshire, are at least intimately connected with, and dependant on, the commercial interest. They have permitted manufacturers to escape from the Ten-Hours Act, to evade the Truck Act,[109] and to infringe with impunity all other acts passed expressly against the "unadorned" rapacity of the manufacturer, while they interpret the Combination Act[110] always in the most prejudiced and most unfavorable manner for the workingman. These same "gallant" free-traders, renowned for their indefatigability in denouncing government interference, these apostles of the bourgeois doctrine of *laissez-faire*, who profess to leave everything and everybody to the struggles of individual interest, are always the first to appeal to the interference of Government as soon as the individual interests of the workingman come into conflict with their own class interests. In such moments of collision they look with open admiration at the Continental States, where despotic governments, though, indeed, not allowing the bourgeoisie to rule, at least prevent the workingmen from resisting. In what manner the revolutionary party propose to make use of the present great conflict between masters and men, I have no better means of explaining than by communicating to you the following letter, addressed to me by Ernest Jones, the Chartist leader, on the eve of his departure for Lancashire, where the campaign is to be opened:

"*My Dear Marx*: ... To-morrow, I start for Blackstone-Edge, where a camp-meeting of the Chartists of Yorkshire and Lancashire is to take place, and I am happy to inform you that the most extensive preparations for the same are making in the North. It is now seven years since a really national gathering[111] took place on that spot sacred to the traditions of the Chartist movement, and the object of the present gathering is as follows: Through the treacheries and divisions of 1848, the disruption of the organization then existing, by the incarceration and banishment of 500 of its leading men—through the thinning of its ranks by emigration—through the deadening of political energy by the influences of brisk trade—the national movement of Chartism had converted itself into isolated action, and the organization dwindled at the very time that social knowledge spread. Meanwhile, a labor movement rose on the ruins of the political one—a labor movement emanating from the first blind gropings of social knowledge. This labor movement showed itself at first in isolated cooperative attempts; then, when these were found to fail, in an energetic action for a ten-hour's bill, a restriction of the moving power, an abolition of the stoppage system in wages, and a fresh interpretation of the Combination Bill. To these measures, good in themselves, the whole power and attention of the working classes was directed. The failure of the attempts to obtain legislative guaranties for these measures has thrown a more revolutionary tendency in the labor-mind of Britain. The opportunity is thus afforded for rallying the masses around the standard of real Social Reform; for it must be evident to all, that however good the measures above alluded to may be, to meet the passing exigencies of the moment, they offer no guaranties for the future, and embody no fundamental principle of social right. The opportunity thus given for a movement, the power for successfully carrying it out, is also afforded by the circumstances of the present time—the discontent of the people being accompanied by an amount of popular power which the comparative scarcity of workingmen affords in relation to the briskness of trade. Strikes are prevalent everywhere and generally successful. But it is lamentable to behold that the power which might be directed to a fundamental remedy, should be wasted on a temporary palliative. I am, therefore, attempting, in reorganizing with numerous friends, to seize this great opportunity for uniting the scattered ranks of Chartism on the sound principles of social revolution. For this purpose I have succeeded in reorganizing the dormant and extinct localities, and arranging for what I trust will be a general and imposing demonstration throughout England. The new campaign begins by the camp-meeting on Blackstone-Edge, to be followed by mass meetings in all the manufacturing Counties, while our agents are at work in the agricultural districts, so as to unite the agricultural mind with the rest of the industrial body, a point which has hitherto been neglected in our movement. The first step will be a demand for the Charter,[112] emanating from these mass meetings of the people, and an attempt to press a motion on our corrupt Parliament for the enactment of that measure, expressly and explicitly as the only means for Social Reform—a phase under which it has not yet been presented to the House. If the working classes support this movement, as I anticipate, from their response to my appeal, the result must be important; for, in case of refusal on the part of Parliament, the hollow professions of sham-liberals and philanthropic Tories will be exposed, and their last hold on popular credulity will be destroyed. In case of their consenting to entertain and discuss the motion, a torrent will be loosened which it will not be in the power of temporising expediency to stop. For you must be aware, from your close study of English politics, that there is no longer any pith or any strength in aristocracy or moneyocracy to resist any serious movement of the people. The governing powers consist only of a confused jumble of worn-out factions, that have run together like a ship's crew that have quarreled among themselves, join all hands at the pump to save the leaky vessel. There is no strength in them, and the throwing of a few drops of bilge water into the democratic ocean will be utterly powerless to allay the raging of its waves. Such, my friend, is the opportunity I now behold—such is the power wherewith I hope to see it used, and such is the first immediate object to which that power shall be directed. On the result of the first demonstration I shall again write to you.

"Yours truly, *Ernest Jones.*"

That there is no prospect at all of the intended Chartist petition being taken into consideration by Parliament, needs not to be proved by argument. Whatever illusions may have been entertained on this point, they must now vanish before the fact, that

Parliament has just rejected, by a majority of 60 votes, the proposition for the ballot introduced by Mr. Berkeley, and advocated by Messrs. Phillimore, Cobden, Bright, Sir Robert Peel, etc. And this is done by the very Parliament which went to the utmost in protesting against the intimidation and bribery employed at its own election, and neglected for months all serious business, for the whim of decimating itself in election inquiries. The only remedy, purity Johnny[a] has yet found out against bribery, intimidation and corrupt practices, has been the disfranchisement, or rather the narrowing of constituencies. And there is no doubt that, if he had succeeded in making the constituencies of the same small size as himself, the Oligarchy would be able to get their votes without the trouble and expense of buying them. Mr. Berkeley's resolution was rejected by the combined Tories and Whigs, their common interest being at stake: the preservation of their territorial influence over the tenants at will, the petty shopkeepers and other retainers of the land-owner. "Who has to pay his rent, has to pay his vote," is an old adage of the glorious British Constitution.

Last Saturday *The Press*, a new weekly paper under the influence of Mr. Disraeli, made a curious disclosure to the public of England, as follows:

> "Early in the spring Baron Brunnow communicated to Lord Clarendon the demand which the Emperor of Russia[b] was about to make on the Porte, that he did so with a statement that the object of the communication was to ascertain the feeling of England on the subject—that Lord Clarendon made no objection, nor in any way discouraged the intended course, and that the Muscovite diplomatist communicated to his imperial master that England was not indisposed to connive at his designs on the Golden Horn."[c]

Now, *The Times* of yesterday had an elaborate and official article emanating from the Foreign Office, in answer to the grave charge of Mr. Disraeli, but which, in my opinion, tends rather to strengthen than to refute that charge. *The Times* asserts that, early in the spring, before the arrival of Prince Menchikoff at Constantinople, Baron Brunnow made a complaint to Lord John Russell, that the Porte had revoked the privileges conferred on the Greek clergy by treaty, and that Lord John Russell, conceiving the matter only to concern the Holy Places, gave his assent to the designs of the Czar. But *The Times* is compelled at the same time to concede that after Prince Menchikoff's arrival at Constan-

---

[a] Allusion to John Russell.—*Ed.*

[b] Nicholas I.—*Ed.*

[c] Rendering of a passage from a report in *The Press*, No. 6, June 11, 1853.—*Ed.*

tinople, and when Lord John Russell had been replaced by Lord Clarendon at the Foreign Office, Baron Brunnow made a further communication to Lord Clarendon "purporting to convey the sense of his instructions, and some of the expressions used in the letter of credentials of which Prince Menchikoff was the bearer from the Emperor of Russia to the Sultan.[a]" Simultaneously, *The Times* admits that "Lord Clarendon gave his assent to the demands communicated by Baron Brunnow." Evidently this second communication must have contained something more than what had been communicated to Lord John Russell. The matter, therefore, cannot stop with this declaration. Either Baron Brunnow must turn out a diplomatical cheat, or my Lords Clarendon and Aberdeen are traitors. We shall see.

It may be of interest to your readers to become acquainted with a document concerning the Eastern question, which was recently published in a London newspaper.[b] It is a proclamation issued by the Prince of Armenia, now residing in London, and distributed among the Armenians in Turkey:

"Leo, by the grace of God, sovereign Prince of Armenia, &c., to the Armenians in Turkey:

"Beloved brothers and faithful countrymen.—Our will and our ardent wish is that you should defend to the last drop of your blood your country and the Sultan against the tyrant of the North. Remember, my brothers, that in Turkey there are no knouts, they do not tear your nostrils and your women are not flogged, secretly or in public. Under the reign of the Sultan, there is humanity, while under that of the tyrant of the North there are nothing but atrocities. Therefore place yourselves under the direction of God, and fight bravely for the liberty of your country and your present sovereign. Pull down your houses to make barricades, and if you have no arms, break your furniture and defend yourselves with it. May Heaven guide you on your path to glory. My only happiness will be to fight in the midst of you against the oppressor of your country, and your creed. May God incline the Sultan's heart to sanction my demand, because under his reign, our religion remains in its pure form, while, under the Northern tyrant, it will be altered. Remember, at least, brothers, that the blood that runs in the veins of him who now addresses you, is the blood of twenty kings, it is the blood of heroes—Lusignans—and defenders of our faith; and we say to you, let us defend our creed and its pure form, until our last drop of blood."

On the 13th inst. Lord Stanley gave notice to the House of Commons that on the second reading of the India Bill (23d inst.) he would bring in the following resolution:

"That in the opinion of this House further information is necessary to enable Parliament to legislate with advantage for the permanent government of India, and

[a] Abdul Mejid.—*Ed.*
[b] *The Daily News*, No. 2207, June 17, 1853.—*Ed.*

that at this late period of the session, it is inexpedient to proceed into a measure, which, while it disturbs existing arrangements, cannot be regarded as a final settlement."[a]

But in April, 1854, the Charter of the East India Company will expire, and something accordingly must be done in one way or the other. The Government wanted to legislate permanently; that is, to renew the Charter for twenty years more. The Manchester School wanted to postpone all legislation, by prolonging the Charter at the utmost for one year.—The Government said that permanent legislation was necessary for the "best" of India. The Manchester men replied that it was impossible for want of information. The "best" of India, and the want of information, are alike false pretences. The governing oligarchy desired, before a Reformed House should meet, to secure at the cost of India, their own "best" for twenty years to come. The Manchester men desired no legislation at all in the unreformed Parliament, where their views had no chance of success. Now, the Coalition Cabinet, through Sir Charles Wood, has, in contradiction to its former statements, but in conformity with its habitual system of shifting difficulties, brought in something that looked like legislation; but it dared not, on the other hand, to propose the renewal of the Charter for any definite period, but presented a "settlement," which it left to Parliament to unsettle whenever that body should determine to do so. If the Ministerial propositions were adopted, the East India Company would obtain no renewal, but only a suspension of life. In all other respects, the Ministerial project but apparently alters the Constitution of the India Government, the only serious novelty to be introduced being the addition of some new Governors, although a long experience has proved that the parts of East India administered by simple Commissioners, go on much better than those blessed with the costly luxury of Governors and Councils. The Whig invention of alleviating exhausted countries by burdening them with new sinecures for the paupers of aristocracy, reminds one of the old Russell administration, when the Whigs were suddenly struck with the state of spiritual destitution, in which the Indians and Mahommedans of the East were living, and determined upon relieving them by the importation of some *new Bishops*, the Tories, in the plenitude of their power, having never thought more than one to be necessary. That resolution having been agreed upon, Sir John Hobhouse, the then Whig President of the Board of Control, discovered

[a] Quoted from a report in *The Times*, No. 21454, June 14, 1853.—*Ed.*

immediately afterwards, that he had a relative admirably suited for a Bishopric, who was forthwith appointed to one of the new sees. "In cases of this kind," remarks an English writer, "where the fit is so exact, it is really hardly possible to say, whether the shoe was made for the foot, or the foot for the shoe." Thus with regard to the Charles Wood's invention; it would be very difficult to say, whether the new Governors are made for Indian provinces, or Indian provinces for the new Governors.

Be this as it may, the Coalition Cabinet believed it had met all clamors by leaving to Parliament the power of altering its proposed act at all times. Unfortunately in steps Lord Stanley, the Tory, with his resolution which was loudly cheered by the "Radical" Opposition, when it was announced. Lord Stanley's resolution is nevertheless self-contradictory. On one hand, he rejects the Ministerial proposition, because the House requires more information for permanent legislation. On the other hand, he rejects it, because it is no permanent legislation, but alters existing arrangements, without pretending to finality. The Conservative view is, of course, opposed to the bill, because it involves a change of some kind. The Radical view is opposed to it, because it involves no real change at all. Lord Stanley, in these coalescent times has found a formula in which the opposite views are combined together against the Ministerial view of the subject. The Coalition Ministry affects a virtuous indignation against such tactics, and *The Chronicle*, its organ, exclaims:

"Viewed as a party-move the proposed motion for delay is in a high degree factious and discreditable.... This motion is brought forward solely because some supporters of the Ministry are pledged to separate in this particular question from those with whom they usually act."[a]

The anxiety of Ministers seems indeed to be serious. *The Chronicle* of to-day, again recurring to the subject, says:

"The division on Lord Stanley's motion will probably be decisive of the fate of the India Bill; it is therefore of the *utmost importance* that those who feel the *importance* of early legislation, should use every exertion to strengthen the Government."[b]

On the other hand, we read in *The Times* of to-day:

"The fate of the Government India Bill has been more respectively delineated.... The danger of the Government lies in the entire conforming of Lord

[a] *The Morning Chronicle*, No. 26981, June 15, 1853.—*Ed.*
[b] *The Morning Chronicle*, No. 26983, June 17, 1853.—*Ed.*

Stanley's objections with the conclusions of public opinion. Every syllable of this amendment tells with deadly effect against the ministry."[a]

I shall expose in a subsequent letter,[b] the bearing of the Indian Question on the different parties in Great Britain, and the benefit the poor Hindoo may reap from this quarreling of the aristocracy, the moneyocracy and the millocracy about his amelioration.

Written on June 17, 1853

First published in the *New-York Daily Tribune,* No. 3809, and the *New-York Semi-Weekly Tribune,* No. 845, July 1, 1853; reprinted without the last two subsections in the *New-York Weekly Tribune,* No. 617, July 9, 1853

Signed: *Karl Marx*

Reproduced from the *New-York Daily Tribune*

[a] *The Times,* No. 21457, June 17, 1853.—*Ed.*

[b] See this volume, pp. 148-56.—*Ed.*

Karl Marx

TURKEY AND RUSSIA.— CONNIVANCE OF THE ABERDEEN MINISTRY WITH RUSSIA.—THE BUDGET.— TAX ON NEWSPAPER SUPPLEMENTS.— PARLIAMENTARY CORRUPTION[113]

London, Tuesday, June 21, 1853

In the year 1828, when Russia was permitted to overrun Turkey with war, and to terminate that war by the Treaty of Adrianople, which surrendered to her the whole of the Eastern coast of the Black Sea, from Anapa in the North to Poti in the South (except Circassia), and delivered into her possession the islands at the mouth of the Danube, virtually separated Moldavia and Wallachia from Turkey, and placed them under Russian supremacy—at that epoch Lord Aberdeen happened to be Minister of Foreign Affairs in Great Britain. In 1853 we find the very same Aberdeen as the chief of the "composite ministry" in the same country. This simple fact goes far to explain the overbearing attitude assumed by Russia in her present conflict with Turkey and with Europe.

I told you in my last letter that the storm aroused by the revelations of *The Press* respecting the secret transactions between Aberdeen, Clarendon and Baron Brunnow,[a] was not likely to subside under the hair-splitting, tortuous and disingenuous pleading of Thursday's[b] *Times. The Times* was even then forced to admit in a semi-official article, that Lord Clarendon had indeed given his assent to the demands about to be made by Russia on the Porte, but said that the demands as represented in London, and those actually proposed at Constantinople, had turned out to be of quite a different tenor, although the papers communicated by Baron Brunnow to the British Minister purported to be "*literal extracts*" from the instructions forwarded to Prince Menchikoff. On

[a] See this volume, pp. 137-38.—*Ed.*
[b] June 16, 1853.—*Ed.*

the following Saturday, however, *The Times*[a] retracted its assertions—undoubtedly in consequence of remonstrances made on the part of the Russian Embassy—and gave Baron Brunnow a testimonial of perfect "candor and faith." *The Morning Herald* of yesterday puts the question "whether Russia had not perhaps given false instructions to Baron Brunnow himself, in order to deceive the British Minister?"[b] In the meantime, fresh disclosures, studiously concealed from the public by a corrupt daily press, have been made, which exclude any such interpretation, throwing the whole blame on the shoulders of the "composite ministry," and quite sufficient to warrant the impeachment of Lords Aberdeen and Clarendon before any other Parliament than the present, which is but a paralytic produce of dead constituencies artificially stimulated into life by unexampled bribery and intimidation.

It is stated that a communication was made to Lord Clarendon, wherein he was informed that the affair of the Shrines was *not* the *sole object* of the Russian Prince.[c] In that communication the general question was entered into, the question of the Greek Christians of Turkey, and of the position of the Emperor of Russia with respect to them under certain treaties. All these points were canvassed, and the course about to be adopted by Russia explicitly stated—the same as detailed in the projected convention of the 6th of May.[114] Lord Clarendon, with the assent of Lord Aberdeen, in no wise either disapproved or discouraged that course. While matters stood thus in London, Bonaparte sent his fleet to Salamis, public opinion pressed from without, Ministers were interpellated in both Houses, Russell pledged himself to the maintenance of the integrity and independence of Turkey, and Prince Menchikoff threw off the mask at Constantinople. It now became necessary for Lords Aberdeen and Clarendon to initiate the other Ministers in what had been done, and the Coalition was on the eve of being broken up, as Lord Palmerston, forced by his antecedents, urged a directly opposite line of policy. In order to prevent the dissolution of his Cabinet, Lord Aberdeen finally yielded to Lord Palmerston, and consented to the combined action of the English and French fleets in the Dardanelles. But at the same time, in order to fulfill his engagements toward Russia, Lord Aberdeen intimated through a private dispatch to St. Petersburg

---

[a] Clauses of the Balta-Liman Convention and the *Times* commentaries to them are quoted from Issue No. 21458, June 18, 1853.—*Ed.*
[b] *The Morning Herald*, No. 22189, June 20, 1853.—*Ed.*
[c] A. S. Menshikov.—*Ed.*

that he would not look upon the occupation of the Danubian Principalities by the Russians as a *casus belli,* and *The Times* received orders to prepare public opinion for this new interpretation of international treaties. It would be unjust to withhold the testimonial that it has labored hard enough to prove that black is white. This same journal, which had all along contended that the Russian *protectorate* over the Greek Christians of Turkey would not be of any political consequence at all, asserted at once that Moldavia and Wallachia were placed under a divided allegiance, and formed in reality no integral portions of the Turkish Empire; that their occupation would not be an invasion of the Turkish Empire in the "strict sense of the word," inasmuch as the treaties of Bucharest and Adrianople had given to the Czar a Protectorate over his co-religionists in the Danubian Provinces.[115] The Convention of Balta-Liman, concluded on May 1, 1849,[116] distinctly stipulates:

"1. That the occupation of those provinces, if it occurs, shall only be by a joint one of Russian and Turkish forces.

"2. That the sole plea for it shall be in grave events taking place in the principalities."

Now as no events at all have taken place in those Principalities, and moreover, as Russia has no intention to enter them in common with the Turks, but precisely against Turkey, *The Times* is of opinion, that Turkey ought to suffer quietly the occupation by Russia alone, and afterward enter into negotiations with her. But if Turkey should be of a less sedate temper and consider the occupation as a *casus belli, The Times* argues that England and France must not do so; and if, nevertheless, England [and] France should do so, *The Times* recommends that it should be done in a gentle manner, by no means as belligerents against Russia, but only as defensive allies of Turkey.

This cowardly and tortuous system of *The Times,* I cannot more appropriately stigmatise than by quoting the following passage from its leading article of to-day. It is an incredible combination of all the contradictions, subterfuges, false pretences, anxieties and lâchetés[a] of Lord Aberdeen's policy:

"Before proceeding to the last extremities the Porte may, if it think fit, protest against the occupation of the principalities, and with the support of all the Powers of Europe, may still negotiate. It will remain with the Turkish government, acting in concert with the ambassadors of the four Powers, to determine this momentous point, and especially to decide whether the state of hostilities is such as to cause the

---

[a] Baseness.—*Ed.*

Dardanelles to be opened to foreign ships of war, under the Convention of 1841.[117] Should that question be decided in the affirmative, and the fleets be ordered to enter the Straits, it will then remain to be seen whether we come there as mediating Powers or as belligerents; for supposing Turkey and Russia to be at war, and foreign vessels of war to be admitted, *casus foederis* (!) they do not necessarily acquire a belligerent character, and they have a far greater interest in maintaining that of mediating Powers, inasmuch as they are sent not to make war but to prevent it. Such a measure does not of necessity make us principals in the contest."

All the leaders of *The Times* have been to no purpose. No other paper would follow in its track—none would bite at its bait, and even the Ministerial papers, *The Morning Chronicle, Morning Post, Globe,* and *Observer* take an entirely different stand, finding a loud echo on the other side of the channel, where only the legitimist *Assemblée nationale* presumes to see no *casus belli* in the occupation of the Danubian Principalities.

The dissension in the camp of the Coalition Ministry has thus been betrayed to the public by the clamorous dissension in their organs. Palmerston urged upon the Cabinet to hold the occupation of Moldavia and Wallachia as a declaration of war, and he was backed up by the Whig and Sham-Radical members of the composite ministry. Lord Aberdeen, having only consented to the common action of the French and English fleets upon the understanding that Russia would not act at the Dardanelles but in the Danubian Provinces, was now quite "outwinded." The existence of the Government was again at stake. At last, at the pressing instances of Lord Aberdeen, Palmerston was prepared to give a sullen assent to the unchallenged occupation of the Principalities by Russia, when suddenly a dispatch arrived from Paris announcing that Bonaparte had resolved to view the same act as a *casus belli.* The confusion has now reached its highest point.

Now, if this statement be correct, and from our knowledge of Lord Aberdeen's past, there is every reason to consider it as such—the whole mystery of that Russo-Turkish tragi-comedy that has occupied Europe for months together, is laid bare. We understand at once, why Lord Aberdeen would not move the British fleet from Malta. We understand the rebuke given to Colonel Rose for his resolute conduct at Constantinople,[118] the bullying behavior of Prince Menchikoff, and the heroic firmness of the Czar who, conceiving the warlike movements of England as a mere farce, would have been glad to be allowed, by the uncontroverted occupation of Moldavia and Wallachia, not only to withdraw from the stage as the "master," but to hold his annual grand maneuvers at the cost and expense of the subjects of the Sultan. We believe that, if war should break out, it will be because Russia had gone too far to withdraw with impunity to her honor; and above all, we believe her courage to be up to this notch simply because she has all the while counted on England's connivance.

On this head the following passage is in point from the last letter from *The Englishman*[a] on the Coalition Ministry:

"The coalition is shaking at every breeze that flows from the Dardanelles. The fears of the good Aberdeen and the miserable incompetence of Clarendon, encouraged Russia, and have produced the crisis."

The latest news from Turkey is as follows: The Turkish Ambassador at Paris has received by telegraph, via Semlin, a dispatch from Constantinople, informing him that the Porte has rejected the last ultimatum of Russia,[119] taking its stand on the memorandum forwarded to the Great Powers. The *Sémaphore*, of Marseilles, states that news had been received at Smyrna of the capture of two Turkish trading vessels on the Black Sea by the Russians; but that, on the other hand, the Caucasian tribes had opened a general campaign against the Russians, in which Shamyl had achieved a most brilliant victory, taking no less than 23 cannons.

Mr. Gladstone has now announced his altered proposals, with regard to the Advertisement Duty. He had proposed, in order to secure the support of *The Times*, to strike the duty off supplements containing advertisements only. He now proposes, intimidated by public opinion, to let all single supplements go free, and to tax each double supplement $^1/_2$d. Imagine the fury of *The Times*, which, by this altered proposition, will only gain £20,000, instead of £40,000 a year, besides seeing the market thrown open to its competitors. This consistent journal which defends to the utmost the taxes upon knowledge, and the duty on advertisements, now opposes any tax on supplements. But it may console itself. If the Ministry, after having carried the greater part of the budget, feel no longer any necessity for cajoling *The Times*, the Manchester men, as soon as they have secured their share of the budget, will no longer want the Ministry. This is what the latter apprehend, and that very apprehension accounts for the fact of the budget discussion extending over the whole period of the session. It is characteristic of the compensating justice of Mr. Gladstone, that while he reduces the newspaper advertisement

---

[a] The pen-name of A. Richards.—*Ed.*

duty from 1s. 6d. to 1s. 3d., he proposes to tax the literary advertisements inserted at the end of most books and reviews, 6 pence each.

To-night the House of Commons will be occupied on two cases of bribery. During the present session 47 Election-Committees have been sitting, out of which, 4 are yet sitting, 43 having concluded their investigations, by finding the majority of the unseated members guilty of bribery. To show the respect in which this Parliament, the offspring of corruption and the parent of Coalitions, is held by public opinion, it is sufficient to quote the following words of to-day's *Morning Herald*:

> "If want of clear aim and object, and still more, the tottering and quavering attack, be symptomatic of imbecility, then it must be confessed that this Parliament, the child of six months, has fallen already into second childishness. [...] It is already subsiding and curdling away into small knots of spiritless and purposeless coteries."

Written on June 21, 1853

First published in the *New-York Daily Tribune*, No. 3814 and the *New-York Semi-Weekly Tribune*, No. 847, July 8, 1853

Signed: *Karl Marx*

Reproduced from the *New-York Daily Tribune*

Karl Marx

THE EAST INDIA COMPANY— ITS HISTORY AND RESULTS

London, Friday, June 24,[a] 1853

The debate on Lord Stanley's motion to postpone legislation for India, has been deferred until this evening. For the first time since 1783 the India question has become a ministerial one in England. Why is this?

The true commencement of the East India Company cannot be dated from a more remote epoch than the year 1702, when the different societies, claiming the monopoly of the East India trade, united together in one single Company. Till then the very existence of the original East India Company was repeatedly endangered, once suspended for years under the protectorate of Cromwell, and once threatened with utter dissolution by Parliamentary interference under the reign of William III. It was under the ascendancy of that Dutch Prince when the Whigs became the farmers of the revenues of the British Empire, when the Bank of England[120] sprung into life, when the protective system was firmly established in England, and the balance of power in Europe was definitively settled, that the existence of an East India Company was recognized by Parliament. That era of apparent liberty was in reality the era of monopolies not created by Royal grants, as in the times of Elizabeth and Charles I, but authorized and nationalized by the sanction of Parliament. This epoch in the history of England bears, in fact, an extreme likeness to the epoch of Louis Philippe in France, the old landed

[a] The *New-York Daily Tribune* gave an erroneous dateline: "Saturday, June 21" (June 21 was a Tuesday). Here it is corrected according to Marx's notebook, in which mailing of the article is dated June 24.—*Ed.*

aristocracy having been defeated, and the bourgeoisie not being able to take its place except under the banner of moneyocracy, or the "*haute finance*." The East India Company excluded the common people from the commerce with India, at the same time that the House of Commons excluded them from Parliamentary representation. In this as well as in other instances, we find the first decisive victory of the *bourgeoisie* over the feudal aristocracy coinciding with the most pronounced reaction against the people, a phenomenon which has driven more than one popular writer, like Cobbett, to look for popular liberty rather in the past than in the future.

The union between the Constitutional Monarchy and the monopolizing monied interest, between the Company of East India and the "glorious" revolution of 1688 [121] was fostered by the same force by which the liberal interests and a liberal dynasty have at all times and in all countries met and combined, by the force of corruption, that first and last moving power of Constitutional Monarchy, the guardian angel of William III and the fatal demon of Louis Philippe. So early as 1693, it appeared from Parliamentary inquiries, that the annual expenditure of the East India Company, under the head of "gifts" to men in power, which had rarely amounted to above £1,200 before the revolution, reached the sum of £90,000. The Duke of Leeds was impeached for a bribe of £5,000, and the virtuous King himself convicted of having received £10,000. Besides these direct briberies, rival Companies were thrown out by tempting Government with loans of enormous sums at the lowest interest, and by buying off rival Directors.

The power the East India Company had obtained by bribing the Government, as did also the Bank of England, it was forced to maintain by bribing again, as did the Bank of England. At every epoch when its monopoly was expiring, it could only effect a renewal of its Charter by offering fresh loans and by fresh presents made to the Government.

The events of the Seven-Years-War transformed the East India Company from a commercial into a military and territorial power.[122] It was then that the foundation was laid of the present British Empire in the East. Then East India stock rose to £263, and dividends were then paid at the rate of $12^1/_2$ per cent. But then there appeared a new enemy to the Company, no longer in the shape of rival societies, but in the shape of rival ministers and of a rival people. It was alleged that the Company's territory had been conquered by the aid of British fleets and British armies, and that no British subjects could hold territorial sovereignties independent of the Crown. The ministers of the day and the people of the day claimed their share in the "wonderful treasures" imagined to have been won by the last conquests. The Company only saved its existence by an agreement made in 1767 that it should annually pay £400,000 into the National Exchequer.

But the East India Company, instead of fulfilling its agreement, got into financial difficulties, and, instead of paying a tribute to the English people, appealed to Parliament for pecuniary aid. Serious alterations in the Charter were the consequence of this step. The Company's affairs failing to improve, notwithstanding their new condition, and the English nation having simultaneously lost their colonies in North America, the necessity of elsewhere regaining some great Colonial Empire became more and more universally felt. The illustrious Fox thought the opportune moment had arrived, in 1783, for bringing forward his famous India bill, which proposed to abolish the Courts of Directors and Proprietors, and to vest the whole Indian government in the hands of seven Commissioners appointed by Parliament. By the personal influence of the imbecile King[a] over the House of Lords, the bill of Mr. Fox was defeated, and made the instrument of breaking down the then Coalition Government of Fox and Lord North, and of placing the famous Pitt at the head of the Government. Pitt carried in 1784 a bill through both Houses, which directed the establishment of the Board of Control, consisting of six members of the Privy Council, who were

> "to check, superintend and control all acts, operations and concerns which in any wise related to the civil and military Government, or revenues of the territories and possessions of the East India Company."

On this head, Mill, the historian, says[b]:

> "In passing that law two objects were pursued. To avoid the imputation of what was represented as the heinous object of Mr. Fox's bill, it was necessary that the principal part of the power should *appear* to remain in the hand of the Directors. For ministerial advantage it was necessary that it should in *reality* be all taken away. Mr. Pitt's bill professed to differ from that of his rival, chiefly in this very point, that while the one destroyed the power of the Directors, the other left it almost entire. Under the act of Mr. Fox the powers of the ministers would have been avowedly held. Under the act of Mr. Pitt, they were held in secret and by fraud. The bill of Fox transferred the powers of the Company to Commissioners appointed by Parliament. The bill of Mr. Pitt transferred them to Commissioners appointed by the King."

---

[a] George III.—*Ed.*

[b] J. Mill, *The History of the British India*; the passage above is also quoted from this book.—*Ed.*

The years of 1783 and 1784 were thus the first, and till now the only years, for the India question to become a ministerial one. The bill of Mr. Pitt having been carried, the Charter of the East India Company was renewed, and the Indian question set aside for twenty years. But in 1813 the Anti-Jacobin war, and in 1833 the newly introduced Reform Bill[123] superseded all other political questions.

This, then, is the first reason of the India question's having failed to become a great political question, since and before 1784; that before that time the East India Company had first to conquer existence and importance; that after that time the Oligarchy absorbed all of its power which it could assume without incurring responsibility; and that afterwards the English people in general were at the very epochs of the renewal of the Charter, in 1813 and 1833, absorbed by other questions of overbearing interest.

We will now take a different view. The East India Company commenced by attempting merely to establish factories for their agents, and places of deposit for their goods. In order to protect them they erected several forts. Although they had, even as early as 1689, conceived the establishment of a dominion in India, and of making territorial revenue one of their sources of emolument, yet, down to 1744, they had acquired but a few unimportant districts around Bombay, Madras, and Calcutta. The war which subsequently broke out in the Carnatic had the effect of rendering them after various struggles, virtual sovereigns of that part of India. Much more considerable results arose from the war in Bengal and the victories of Clive. These results were the real occupation of Bengal, Bihar, and Orissa.[124] At the end of the Eighteenth Century, and in the first years of the present one, there supervened the wars with Tippoo Saib, and in consequence of them a great advance of power, and an immense extension of the subsidiary system.[125] In the second decennium of the Nineteenth Century the first convenient frontier, that of India within the desert, had at length been conquered. It was not till then that the British Empire in the East reached those parts of Asia, which had been, at all times, the seat of every great central power in India. But the most vulnerable point of the Empire, from which it had been overrun as often as old conquerors were expelled by new ones, the barriers of the Western frontier, were not in the hands of the British. During the period from 1838 to 1849, in the Sikh and Afghan wars, British rule subjected to definitive possession the ethnographical, political, and military frontiers of the East Indian Continent, by the compulsory annexation of the Punjab and of Scinde.[126] These were possessions indispensable to repulse any invading force issuing from Central Asia, and indispensable against Russia advancing to the frontiers of Persia. During this last decennium there have been added to the British Indian territory 167,000 square miles, with a population of 8,572,630 souls. As to the interior, all the native States now became surrounded by British possessions, subjected to British *suzeraineté* under various forms, and cut off from the sea-coast, with the sole exception of Guzerat and Scinde. As to its exterior, India was now finished. It is only since 1849, that the one great Anglo-Indian Empire has existed.

Thus the British Government has been fighting, under the Company's name, for two centuries, till at last the natural limits of India were reached. We understand now, why during all this time all parties in England have connived in silence, even those which had resolved to become the loudest with their hypocritical peace-cant, after the *arrondissement* of the one Indian Empire should have been completed. Firstly, of course, they had to get it, in order to subject it afterward to their sharp philanthropy. From this view we understand the altered position of the Indian question in the present year, 1853, compared with all former periods of Charter renewal.

Again, let us take a different view. We shall still better understand the peculiar crisis in Indian legislation, on reviewing the course of British commercial intercourse with India through its different phases.

At the commencement of the East India Company's operations, under the reign of Elizabeth, the Company was permitted for the purpose of profitably carrying on its trade with India, to export an annual value of £30,000 in silver, gold, and foreign coin. This was an infraction against all the prejudices of the age, and Thomas Mun was forced to lay down in *A Discourse on Trade from England to the East Indies*, the foundation of the "mercantile system," admitting that the precious metals were the only real wealth a country could possess, but contending at the same time that their exportation might be safely allowed, provided the *balance of payments* was in favor of the exporting nation. In this sense, he contended that the commodities imported from East India were chiefly re-exported to other countries, from which a much greater quantity of bullion was obtained than had been required to pay for them in India. In the same spirit, Sir Josiah Child wrote *A Treatise Wherein It Is Demonstrated That the East India Trade Is the*

Most National Trade of All Trades. By-and-by the partisans of the East India Company grew more audacious, and it may be noticed as a curiosity, in this strange Indian history, that the Indian monopolists were the first preachers of free trade in England.

Parliamentary intervention, with regard to the East India Company, was again claimed, not by the commercial, but by the industrial class, at the latter end of the 17th century, and during the greater part of the 18th, when the importation of East Indian cotton and silk stuffs was declared to ruin the poor British manufacturers, an opinion put forward in John Pollexfen: *England and India Inconsistent in Their Manufactures,* London, 1697,[127] a title strangely verified a century and a half later, but in a very different sense. Parliament did then interfere. By the Act 11 and 12 William III, cap. 10, it was enacted that the wearing of wrought silks and of printed or dyed calicoes from India, Persia and China should be prohibited, and a penalty of £200 imposed on all persons having or selling the same. Similar laws were enacted under George I, II and III, in consequence of the repeated lamentations of the afterward so "enlightened" British manufacturers. And thus, during the greater part of the 18th century, Indian manufactures were generally imported into England in order to be sold on the Continent, and to remain excluded from the English market itself.

Besides this Parliamentary interference with East India, solicited by the greedy home manufacturer, efforts were made at every epoch of the renewal of the Charter, by the merchants of London, Liverpool and Bristol, to break down the commercial monopoly of the Company, and to participate in that commerce, estimated to be a true mine of gold. In consequence of these efforts, a provision was made in the Act of 1773 prolonging the Company's Charter till March 1, 1814, by which private British individuals were authorized to export from, and the Company's Indian servants permitted to import into England, almost all sorts of commodities. But this concession was surrounded with conditions annihilating its effects, in respect to the exports to British India by private merchants. In 1813 the Company was unable to further withstand the pressure of general commerce, and except the monopoly of the Chinese trade, the trade to India was opened, under certain conditions, to private competition. At the renewal of the Charter in 1833, these last restrictions were at length superseded, the Company forbidden to carry on any trade at all—their commercial character destroyed, and their privilege of excluding British subjects from the Indian territories withdrawn.

Meanwhile the East India trade had undergone very serious revolutions, altogether altering the position of the different class interests in England with regard to it. During the whole course of the 18th century the treasures transported from India to England were gained much less by comparatively insignificant commerce, than by the direct exploitation of that country, and by the colossal fortunes there extorted and transmitted to England. After the opening of the trade in 1813 the commerce with India more than trebled in a very short time. But this was not all. The whole character of the trade was changed. Till 1813 India had been chiefly an exporting country, while it now became an importing one; and in such a quick progression, that already in 1823 the rate of exchange, which had generally been 2/6 per rupee, sunk down to 2/ per rupee. India, the great workshop of cotton manufacture for the world, since immemorial times, became now inundated with English twists and cotton stuffs. After its own produce had been excluded from England, or only admitted on the most cruel terms, British manufactures were poured into it at a small and merely nominal duty, to the ruin of the native cotton fabrics once so celebrated. In 1780 the value of British produce and manufactures amounted only to £386,152, the bullion exported during the same year to £15,041, the total value of exports during 1780 being £12,648,616, so that the India trade amounted to only 1-32 of the entire foreign trade. In 1850 the total exports to India from Great Britain and Ireland were £8,024,000, of which cotton goods alone amounted to £5,220,000, so that it reached more than $^1/_8$ of the whole export, and more than $^1/_4$ of the foreign cotton trade. But, the cotton manufacture also employed now $^1/_8$ of the population of Britain, and contributed 1-12th of the whole national revenue. After each commercial crisis the East Indian trade grew of more paramount importance for the British cotton manufacturers, and the East India Continent became actually their best market. At the same rate at which the cotton manufactures became of vital interest for the whole social frame of Great Britain, East India became of vital interest for the British cotton manufacture.

Till then the interests of the moneyocracy which had converted India into its landed estates, of the oligarchy who had conquered it by their armies, and of the millocracy who had inundated it with their fabrics, had gone hand in hand. But the more the industrial interest became dependent on the Indian market, the more it felt the necessity of creating fresh productive powers in India, after having ruined her native industry. You cannot continue to inundate a country with your manufactures, unless you enable it to give you some produce in return. The industrial interest found that their trade declined instead of increasing. For the four years ending with 1846, the imports to India from Great Britain were to the amount of 261 million rupees; for the four years ending 1850 they were only 253 millions, while the exports for the former period 274 millions of rupees, and for the latter period 254 millions. They found out that the power of consuming their goods was contracted in India to the lowest possible point, that the consumption of their manufactures by the British West Indies, was of the value of about 14s. per head of the population per annum, by Chile, of 9s. 3d., by Brazil, of 6s. 5d., by Cuba, of 6s. 2d., by Peru, of 5s. 7d., by Central America, of 10d., while it amounted in India only to about 9d. Then came the short cotton crop in the United States, which caused them a loss of £11,000,000 in 1850, and they were exasperated at depending on America, instead of deriving a sufficiency of raw cotton from the East Indies. Besides, they found that in all attempts to apply capital to India they met with impediments and chicanery on the part of the India authorities. Thus India became the battle-field in the contest of the industrial interest on the one side, and of the moneyocracy and oligarchy on the other. The manufacturers, conscious of their ascendency in England, ask now for the annihilation of these antagonistic powers in India, for the destruction of the whole ancient fabric of Indian government, and for the final eclipse of the East India Company.

And now to the fourth and last point of view, from which the Indian question must be judged. Since 1784 Indian finances have got more and more deeply into difficulty. There exists now a national debt of 50 million pounds, a continual decrease in the resources of the revenue, and a corresponding increase in the expenditure, dubiously balanced by the gambling income of the opium tax, now threatened with extinction by the Chinese beginning themselves to cultivate the poppy, and aggravated by the expenses to be anticipated from the senseless Burmese war.[128]

"As the case stands," says Mr. Dickinson, "as it would ruin England to lose her Empire in India, it is threatening our own finances with ruin, to be obliged to keep it."[a]

---

[a] J. Dickinson, *The Government of India under a Bureaucracy*, p. 50.—*Ed.*

I have shown thus, how the Indian question has become for the first time since 1783, an English question, and a ministerial question.

Written on June 24, 1853

First published in the *New-York Daily Tribune*, No. 3816, July 11, 1853; reprinted in the *New-York Semi-Weekly Tribune*, No. 848, July 12, 1853

Signed: *Karl Marx*

Reproduced from the *New-York Daily Tribune*

Karl Marx

THE INDIAN QUESTION.—IRISH TENANT RIGHT

London, June 28, 1853

The debate on Lord Stanley's motion with respect to India commenced on the 23d, continued on the 24th, and adjourned to the 27th inst., has not been brought to a close. When that shall at length have arrived, I intend to resume my observations on the India question.

As the Coalition Ministry depends on the support of the Irish party, and as all the other parties composing the House of Commons so nicely balance each other that the Irish may at any moment turn the scales which way they please, some concessions are at last about to be made to the Irish tenants. The "Leasing Powers (Ireland) Bill," which passed the House of Commons on Friday last, contains a provision that for the improvements made on the soil and separable from the soil, the tenant shall have at the termination of his lease, a compensation in money, the incoming tenant being at liberty to take them at the valuation, while with respect to improvements in the soil, compensation for them shall be arranged by contract between the landlord and the tenant.[129]

A tenant having incorporated his capital, in one form or another, in the land, and having thus effected an improvement of the soil, either directly by irrigation, drainage, manure, or indirectly by construction of buildings for agricultural purposes, in steps the landlord with demand for increased rent. If the tenant concede, he has to pay the interest for his own money to the landlord. If he resist, he will be very unceremoniously ejected, and supplanted by a new tenant, the latter being enabled to pay a higher rent by the very expenses incurred by his predecessors, until he also, in his turn, has become an improver of the land, and is replaced in the same way, or put on worse terms. In this easy way a class of absentee landlords has been enabled to pocket, not merely the labor, but also the capital, of whole generations, each generation of Irish peasants sinking a grade lower in the social scale, exactly in proportion to the exertions and sacrifices made for the raising of their condition and that of their families. If the tenant was industrious and enterprising, he became taxed in consequence of his very industry and enterprise. If, on the contrary, he grew inert and negligent, he was reproached with the "aboriginal faults of the Celtic race." He had, accordingly, no other alternative left but to become a pauper—to pauperise himself by industry, or to pauperise by negligence. In order to oppose this state of things, "Tenant Right" was proclaimed in Ireland—a right of the tenant, not in the soil but in the improvements of the soil effected at his cost and charges. Let us see in what manner *The Times*, in its Saturday's leader, attempts to break down this Irish "Tenant Right:"

"There are two general systems of farm occupation. Either a tenant may take a lease of the land for a fixed number of years, or his holding may be terminable at any time upon certain notice. In the first of these events, it would be obviously his course to adjust and apportion his outlay so that all, or nearly all, the benefit would find its way to him before the expiration of his term. In the second case it seems equally obvious that he should not run the risk of the investment without a proper assurance of return."[a]

Where the landlords have to deal with a class of large capitalists who may, as they please, invest their stock in commerce, in manufactures or in farming, there can be no doubt but that these capitalist farmers, whether they take long leases or no time leases at all, know how to secure the "proper" return of their outlays. But with regard to Ireland the supposition is quite fictitious. On the one side you have there a small class of land monopolists, on the other, a very large class of tenants with very petty fortunes, which they have no chance to invest in different ways, no other field of production opening to them, except the soil. They are, therefore, forced to become tenants-at-will.[130] Being once tenants-at-will, they naturally run the risk of losing their revenue, provided they do not invest their small capital. Investing it, in order to secure their revenue, they run the risk of losing their capital, also.

"Perhaps," continues *The Times*, "it may be said, that in any case a tenantry could hardly expire without something being left upon the ground, in some shape

[a] *The Times*, No. 21464, June 25, 1853.—*Ed.*

or another, representing the tenant's own property, and that for this compensation should be forthcoming. There is some truth in the remark, but the demand thus created [...] ought, under proper conditions of society, to be easily adjusted between landlord and tenant, as it might, at any rate, be provided for in the original contract. We say that the conditions of society should regulate these arrangements, because we believe that no Parliamentary enactment can be effectually substituted for such an agency."

Indeed, under "proper conditions of society," we should want no more Parliamentary interference with the Irish land-tenant, as we should not want, under "proper conditions of society," the interference of the soldier, of the policeman, and of the hangman. Legislature, magistracy, and armed force, are all of them but the offspring of improper conditions of society, preventing those arrangements among men which would make useless the compulsory intervention of a third supreme power. Has, perhaps, *The Times* been converted into a social revolutionist? Does it want a *social* revolution, reorganizing the "conditions of society," and the "arrangements" emanating from them, instead of "Parliamentary enactments?" England has subverted the conditions of Irish society. At first it confiscated the land, then it suppressed the industry by "Parliamentary enactments,"[131] and lastly, it broke the active energy by armed force. And thus England created those abominable "conditions of society" which enable a small *caste* of rapacious lordlings to dictate to the Irish people the terms on which they shall be allowed to hold the land and to live upon it. Too weak yet for revolutionizing those "social conditions," the people appeal to Parliament, demanding at least their mitigation and regulation. But "No," says *The Times*; if you don't live under proper conditions of society, Parliament can't mend that. And if the Irish people, on the advice of *The Times*, tried to-morrow to mend their conditions of society, *The Times* would be the first to appeal to bayonets, and to pour out sanguinary denunciations of "the aboriginal faults of the Celtic race," wanting the Anglo-Saxon taste for pacific progress and legal amelioration.

"If a landlord," says *The Times*, "deliberately injures one tenant, he will find it so much the harder to get another, and whereas his occupation consists in letting land, he will find his land all the more difficult to let."

The case stands rather differently in Ireland. The more a landlord injures one tenant, the easier he will find it to oppress another. The tenant who comes in, is the means of injuring the ejected one, and the ejected one is the means of keeping down the new occupant. That, in due course of time, the landlord, beside injuring the tenant, will injure himself and ruin himself, is not only a probability, but the very fact, in Ireland—a fact affording, however, a very precarious source of comfort to the ruined tenant.

"The relations between the landlord and tenant are those between two traders," says *The Times*.

This is precisely the *petitio principii* which pervades the whole leader of *The Times*. The needy Irish tenant belongs to the soil, while the soil belongs to the English Lord. As well you might call the relation between the robber who presents his pistol, and the traveler who presents his purse, a relation between two traders.

"But," says *The Times*, "in point of fact, the relation between Irish landlords and tenants will soon be reformed by an agency more potent than that of legislation. [...] The property of Ireland is fast passing into new hands, and, if the present rate of emigration continues, its cultivation must undergo the same transfer."

Here, at least, *The Times* has the truth. British Parliament does not interfere at a moment when the worked-out old system is terminating in the common ruin, both of the thrifty landlord and the needy tenant, the former being knocked down by the hammer of the *Encumbered Estates* Commission, and the latter expelled by compulsory emigration. This reminds us of the old Sultan of Morocco. Whenever there was a case pending between two parties, he knew of no more "potent agency" for settling their controversy, than by killing both parties.

"Nothing could tend," concludes *The Times* with regard to Tenant Right, "to greater confusion than such a *communistic distribution of ownership*. [...] The only person with any right in the land, is the landlord."

The Times seems to have been the sleeping Epimenides of the past half century, and never to have heard of the hot controversy going on during all that time upon the claims of the landlord, not among social reformers and Communists, but among the very political economists of the British middle-class. Ricardo, the creator of modern political economy in Great Britain, did not controvert the "right" of the landlords, as he was quite convinced that their claims were based upon fact, and not on right, and that political economy in general had nothing to do with questions of right; but he attacked the land-monopoly in a more unassuming, yet more scientific, and therefore more dangerous manner. He proved that private proprietorship in land, as distinguished from the respective claims of the laborer, and of the farmer, was a relation quite superfluous in, and incoherent with the whole frame-work of modern production; that the economical expression of that relationship, the rent of land, might, with great advantage, be appropriated by the State; and finally that the interest of the landlord was opposed to the interest of all other classes of modern society. It would be tedious to enumerate all the conclusions drawn from these premises by the Ricardo School against the landed monopoly. For my end, it will suffice to quote three of the most recent economical authorities of Great Britain.

The London *Economist*, whose chief editor, Mr. J. Wilson, is not only a Free Trade oracle, but a Whig one, too, and not only a Whig, but also an inevitable Treasury-appendage in every Whig or composite ministry, has contended in different articles that exactly speaking there can exist no title authorizing any individual, or any number of individuals, to claim the exclusive proprietorship in the soil of a nation.

Mr. Newman, in his *Lectures on Political Economy*, London, 1851, professedly written for the purpose of refuting Socialism, tells us:

"No man has, or can have, a natural right to *land*, except so long as he occupies it in person. His right is to the use, and to the use only. All other right is the creation of artificial law (or parliamentary enactments as *The Times* would call it).... If, at any time, land becomes needed to *live upon*, the right of private possessors to withhold it comes to an end." [Pp. 137, 141.]

This is exactly the case in Ireland, and Mr. Newman expressly confirms the claims of the Irish tenantry, and in lectures held before the most select audiences of the British aristocracy.

In conclusion let me quote some passages from Mr. Herbert Spencer's work, *Social Statics*, London, 1851, also, purporting to be a complete refutation of Communism, and acknowledged as the most elaborate development of the Free Trade doctrines of modern England.

"No one [...] may use the earth in such a way as to prevent the rest from similarly using it. [...] Equity, therefore, does not permit property in land, or the rest would live on the earth by sufferance only. The landless men might equitably be expelled from the earth altogether.... It can never be pretended, that the existing titles to such property are legitimate. Should any one think so let him look in the Chronicles. [...] The original deeds were written with the sword, rather than with the pen. Not lawyers but soldiers were the conveyancers: blows were the current coin given in payment; and for seals blood was used in preference to wax. Could valid claims be thus constituted? Hardly. And if not, what becomes of the pretensions of all subsequent holders of estates so obtained? Does sale or bequest generate a right where it did not previously exist?... If one act of transfer can give no title, can many?... At what rate per annum do invalid claims become valid?... The right of mankind at large to the earth's surface is still valid, all deeds, customs and laws notwithstanding. [...] It is impossible to discover any mode in which land can become private property.... We daily deny landlordism by our legislation. Is a canal, a railway, or a turnpike road to be made? We do not scruple to seize just as many acres as may be requisite. [...] We do not wait for consent.... The change required would simply be a change of landlords.... Instead of being in the possession of individuals, the country would be held by the great corporate body—society. Instead of leasing his acres from an isolated proprietor, the farmer would lease them from the nation. Instead of paying his rent to the agent of Sir John, or His Grace, he will pay to an agent, or deputy-agent of the community. Stewards would be public officials, instead of private ones, and tenantry the only land tenure.... Pushed to its ultimate consequences, a claim to exclusive possession of the soil involves land-owning despotism." [Pp. 114-16, 122-23, 125.][132]

Thus, from the very point of view of modern English political economists, it is not the usurping English landlord, but the Irish tenants and laborers, who have the only right in the soil of their native country, and *The Times*, in opposing the demands of the Irish people, places itself into direct antagonism to British middle-class science.

Written on June 28, 1853

First published in the *New-York Daily Tribune*, No. 3816, July 11, 1853; reprinted in the *New-York Semi-Weekly Tribune*, No. 848, July 12, 1853

Signed: *Karl Marx*

Reproduced from the *New-York Daily Tribune*

Karl Marx

RUSSIAN POLICY AGAINST TURKEY.— CHARTISM[133]

London, Friday, July 1, 1853

Since the year 1815 the Great Powers of Europe have feared nothing so much as an infraction of the *status quo.* But any war between any two of those powers implies subversion of that *status quo.* That is the reason why Russia's encroachments in the East have been tolerated, and why she has never been asked for anything in return but to afford some pretext, however absurd, to the Western powers, for remaining neutral, and for being saved the necessity of interfering with Russian aggressions. Russia has all along been glorified for the forbearance and generosity of her "august master," who has not only condescended to cover the naked and shameful subserviency of Western Cabinets, but has displayed the magnanimity of devouring Turkey piece after piece, instead of swallowing it at a mouthful. Russian diplomacy has thus rested on the timidity of Western statesmen, and her diplomatic art has gradually sunk into so complete a *mannerism,* that you may trace the history of the present transactions almost literally in the annals of the past.

The hollowness of the new pretexts of Russia is apparent, after the Sultan[a] has granted, in his new firman to the Patriarch of Constantinople,[b] more than the Czar himself had asked for—so far as religion goes. Now was, perhaps, the "pacification of Greece"[134] a more solid pretext? When M. de Villèle, in order to tranquilize the apprehensions of the Sultan,[c] and to give a proof of the pure intentions of the Great Powers, proposed "that the

[a] Abdul Mejid.—*Ed.*
[b] Germanos.—*Ed.*
[c] Mahmud II.—*Ed.*

allies ought above all things to conclude a Treaty by which the actual *status quo* of the Ottoman Empire should be guaranteed to it," the Russian Ambassador at Paris[a] opposed this proposition to the utmost, affirming

"that Russia, in displaying *generosity in her relations with the Porte,* and in showing *inappreciable respect* for the wishes of her allies, [...] had been obliged, nevertheless, to reserve exclusively to herself to determine her own differences with the Divan; [...] that a general guarantee of the Ottoman Empire, independently of its being unusual and surprising, would wound the *feelings of his master* and the *rights* acquired by Russia, and the principles upon which they were founded."[b]

Russia pretends now to occupy the Danubian principalities, without giving to the Porte the right of considering this step as a *casus belli.*

Russia pretended, in 1827, "to occupy Moldavia and Wallachia *in the name of the three Powers.*"

While Russia proclaimed the following in her declaration of war of April 26, 1828:

"Her allies would always find her ready to concert her march with them, in execution of the Treaty of London,[135] and ever anxious to aid in a work, which her *religion* and all the sentiments honorable to humanity recommended to her active solicitude, always disposed to profit by her actual position *only* for the purpose of accelerating the accomplishment of the Treaty of July 6th,"[c]

while Russia announced in her manifesto, A. D. 1st October, 1829:

"Russia has remained constantly a stranger to every desire of conquest—to every view of aggrandizement."

Her Ambassador at Paris was writing to Count Nesselrode.

"When the Imperial Cabinet examined the question, whether it had become expedient to take up arms against the Porte, [...] there might have existed some doubt about the urgency of this measure in the eyes of those who had not sufficiently reflected upon the *effects of the sanguinary reforms,* which the Chief of the Ottoman Empire has just executed with such tremendous violence. [...]

"*The Emperor has put the Turkish system to the proof, and his Majesty has found it to possess a commencement of physical and moral organization which it hitherto had not.* If this Sultan had been enabled to offer us a more determined and regular resistance, while he had scarcely assembled together the elements of his new plan of reform and ameliorations, how formidable should we have found him had he had time to give it more solidity. [...] Things being in this state, we must congratulate ourselves upon having attacked them before they became more dangerous for us, for delay

---

[a] K. O. Pozzo di Borgo.—*Ed.*

[b] "Copy of a Despatch from Count Pozzo di Borgo, dated Paris, 22nd Dec. 1826", *The Portfolio,* 1843, No. II, p. 130.—*Ed.*

[c] *The Portfolio,* 1836, No. VII, pp. 347-50.—*Ed.*

would only have made our relative situation worse, and prepared us greater obstacles than those with which we meet."

Russia proposes now to make an aggressive step and then to talk about it. In 1829 Prince Lieven wrote to Count Nesselrode:

"We shall confine ourselves to generalities, for every circumstantial communication on a subject so delicate would draw down real dangers, and if once we discuss with our allies the articles of treaty with the Porte, we shall only content them when they will *imagine* that they have imposed upon us irreparable sacrifices. It is in the midst of our camp that peace must be signed and it is when it shall have been concluded that Europe must know its conditions. Remonstrances will then be too late and it will then patiently suffer what it can no longer prevent."[a]

Russia has now for several months been delaying action under one pretence or another, in order to maintain a state of things, which, being neither war nor peace, is tolerable to herself, but ruinous to the Turks. She acted in precisely the same manner in the period we have alluded to. As Pozzo di Borgo said:

"It is our policy to see that nothing new happens during the next four months and I hope we shall accomplish it, *because men in general prefer waiting*; but the fifth must be fruitful in events."[b]

The Czar, after having inflicted the greatest indignities on the Turkish Government, and notwithstanding that he now threatens to extort by force the most humiliating concessions, nevertheless raises a great cry about his "friendship for the Sultan Abdul Mejid" and his solicitude "for the preservation of the Ottoman Empire." On the Sultan he throws the "responsibility" of opposing his "just demands," of continuing to "wound his friendship and his feelings," of rejecting his "note," and of declining his "protectorate."

In 1828, when Pozzo di Borgo was interpellated by Charles X about the bad success of the Russian arms in the campaign of that year, he replied, that, not wishing to push the war *à outrance* without absolute necessity, the Emperor had hoped that the Sultan would have profited by his *generosity*, which *experiment* had now failed.

Shortly before commencing her present quarrel with the Porte Russia sought to bring about a general coalition of the Continental Powers against England, on the Refugee question, and having failed in that experiment, she attempted to bring about a coalition with England against France. Similarly, from 1826 to 1828, she

---

[a] *The Portfolio*, 1843, Vol. I, No. I, p. 24.—*Ed.*

[b] *The Portfolio*, 1836, Vol. I, Nos. VIII-IX, p. 473.—*Ed.*

intimidated Austria by the "ambitious projects of Prussia," doing simultaneously all that was in her power to swell the power and pretensions of Prussia, in order to enable her to balance Austria. In her present circular note she indicts Bonaparte as the only disturber of peace by his pretensions respecting the Holy Places[136]; but, at that time, in the language of Pozzo di Borgo, she attributed

"all the agitation that pervaded Europe to the agency of Prince Metternich, and tried to make the Duke of Wellington himself perceive that the deference which he would have to the Cabinet of Vienna would be a drawback to his influence with all the others, and to give such a turn to things that it would be no longer Russia that sought to compromise France with Great Britain, but Great Britain who had repudiated France, in order to join the Cabinet of Vienna."[a]

Russia would now submit to a great humiliation if she retreated. That was identically her situation after the first unsuccessful campaign of 1828. What was then her supreme object? We answer in the words of her diplomatist:

"A second campaign is indispensable in order to acquire the superiority requisite for the success of the negotiation. [...] When this negotiation shall take place we must be in a state to dictate the conditions of it in a prompt and rapid manner.... *With the power of doing more* His Majesty would consent to *demand less.* [...] To obtain this superiority appears to me what ought to be the aim of all our efforts. *This superiority has now become a condition of our political existence,* such as we must establish [...] and maintain in the eyes of the world."[b]

But does Russia not fear the common action of England and France? Certainly. In the Secret Memoirs on the Means possessed by Russia for breaking up the alliance between France and England, revealed during the reign of Louis Philippe, we are told:

"In the event of a war, in which England should coalesce with France, Russia indulges in no hope of success, unless that union [...] be broken up; so that at the least England should consent to remain neutral during the continental conflict."[c]

The question is: Does Russia believe in a common action of England and France? We quote again from Pozzo di Borgo's dispatches:

"From the moment that the idea of the ruin of the Turkish Empire ceases to prevail, it is not probable that the British Government would risk a general war for the sake of exempting the Sultan from acceding to such or such condition, above all in the state in which things will be at the commencement of the approaching campaign, when everything will be as yet uncertain and undecided. These

---

[a] *The Portfolio,* 1836, Vol. II, pp. 210-11.—*Ed.*
[b] *The Portfolio,* 1836, Vol. I, pp. 364, 361.—*Ed.*
[c] *The Portfolio,* 1836, Vol. II, pp. 294-95.—*Ed.*

considerations would authorize the belief that we have no cause to fear an open rupture on the part of Great Britain; and that she will content herself with counseling the Porte to beg peace, and with lending the aid of the good offices in her power during the negotiation if it takes place, without going further, should the Sultan refuse or we persist."[a]

And as to Nesselrode's opinion of the "good" Aberdeen, the Minister of 1828, and the Minister of 1853, it may be well to quote the following from a dispatch by Prince Lieven:

"Lord Aberdeen reiterated in his interview with me the assurance that at no period it had entered into the intentions of England to seek a quarrel with Russia—that he feared that the position of the English Ministry was not well understood at St. Petersburg—that he found himself in a delicate situation. Public opinion was always ready to burst forth against Russia. The British Government could not constantly *brave* it; and it would be dangerous to excite it on questions [...] that touched so nearly the national prejudices. On the other side we could reckon with entire confidence upon the [...] friendly dispositions of the English Ministry which struggled against them."[b]

The only thing astonishing in the note of M. de Nesselrode, of June 11, is not "The insolent mélange of professions refuted by acts, and threats veiled in declaimers," but the reception Russian diplomatical notes meet with for the first time in Europe, calling forth, instead of the habitual awe and admiration, blushes of shame at the past and disdainful laughter from the Western world at this insolent amalgamation of pretensions, finesse and real barbarism. Yet Nesselrode's circular note, and the "ultimatissimum" of June 16, are not a bit worse than the so much admired master-pieces of Pozzo di Borgo and Prince Lieven. Count Nesselrode was at their time, what he is now, the diplomatical head of Russia.

There is a facetious story told of two Persian naturalists who were examining a bear; the one who had never seen such an animal before, inquired whether that animal dropped its cubs alive or laid eggs; to which the other, who was better informed, replied: "That animal is capable of anything." The Russian bear is certainly capable of anything, so long as he knows the other animals he has to deal with to be capable of nothing.

En passant, I may mention the signal victory Russia has just won in Denmark, the Royal message having passed with a majority of 119 against 28, in the following terms:

"In agreement with the 4th paragraph of the Constitution d. d. June 5, 1849, the United Parliament, for its part, gives its consent to the arrangement by His

[a] *The Portfolio,* 1836, Nos. VIII-IX, pp. 444-45.—*Ed.*
[b] *The Portfolio,* 1843, No. I, pp. 17-19.—*Ed.*

Majesty of the succession to the whole Danish Monarchy in accordance with the Royal message respecting the succession of Oct. 4, 1852, renewed June 13, 1853."

Strikes and combinations of workmen are proceeding rapidly, and to an unprecedented extent. I have now before me reports on the strikes of the factory hands of all descriptions at Stockport, of smiths, spinners, weavers, etc., at Manchester, of carpet-weavers at Kidderminster, of colliers at the Ringwood Collieries, near Bristol, of weavers and loomers at Blackburn, of loomers at Darwen, of the cabinet-makers at Boston, of the bleachers, finishers, dyers and power-loom weavers of Bolton and neighborhood, of the weavers of Barnsley, of the Spitalfields broad-silk weavers, of the lace makers of Nottingham, of all descriptions of workingmen throughout the Birmingham district, and in various other localities. Each mail brings new reports of strikes; the turn-out grows epidemic. Every one of the larger strikes, like those at Stockport, Liverpool, etc., necessarily generates a whole series of minor strikes, through great numbers of people being unable to carry out their resistance to the masters, unless they appeal to the support of their fellow-workmen in the Kingdom, and the latter, in order to assist them, asking in their turn for higher wages. Besides it becomes alike a point of honor and of interest for each locality not to isolate the efforts of their fellow-workmen by submitting to worse terms, and thus strikes in one locality are echoed by strikes in the remotest other localities. In some instances the demands for higher wages are only a settlement of long-standing arrears with the masters. So with the great Stockport strike.

In January, 1848, the mill-owners of the town made a general reduction of 10 per cent. from all descriptions of factory-workers' wages. This reduction was submitted to upon the condition that when trade revived the 10 per cent. was to be restored. Accordingly the work-people memorialized their employers, early in March, 1853, for the promised advance of 10 per cent.; and as they would not come to arrangements with them, upward of 30,000 hands struck. In the majority of instances, the factory-workmen affirmed distinctly their *right* to *share* in the prosperity of the country, and especially in the prosperity of their employers.

The distinctive feature of the present strikes is this, that they began in the lower ranks of unskilled labor (not factory labor), actually trained by the direct influence of emigration, according to various strata of artizans, till they reached at last the factory people of the great industrial centers of Great Britain; while at all former periods strikes originated regularly from the heads of the factory-workers, mechanics, spinners, &c., spreading thence to the lower classes of this great industrial hive, and reaching only in the last instance, to the artizans. This phenomenon is to be ascribed solely to emigration.

There exists a class of philanthropists, and even of socialists, who consider strikes as very mischievous to the interests of the "workingman himself," and whose great aim consists in finding out a method of securing permanent average wages. Besides, the fact of the industrial cyclus, with its various phases, putting every such average wages out of the question. I am, on the very contrary, convinced that the alternative rise and fall of wages, and the continual conflicts between masters and men resulting therefrom, are, in the present organization of industry, the indispensable means of holding up the spirit of the laboring classes, of combining them into one great association against the encroachments of the ruling class, and of preventing them from becoming apathetic, thoughtless, more or less well-fed instruments of production. In a state of society founded upon the antagonism of classes, if we want to prevent Slavery in fact as well as in name, we must accept war. In order to rightly appreciate the value of strikes and combinations, we must not allow ourselves to be blinded by the apparent insignificance of their economical results, but hold, above all things, in view their moral and political consequences. Without the great alternative phases of dullness, prosperity, over-excitement, crisis and distress, which modern industry traverses in periodically recurring cycles, with the up and down of wages resulting from them, as with the constant warfare between masters and men closely corresponding with those variations in wages and profits, the working-classes of Great Britain, and of all Europe, would be a heart-broken, a weak-minded, a worn-out, unresisting mass, whose self-emancipation would prove as impossible as that of the slaves of Ancient Greece and Rome. We must not forget that strikes and combinations among the serfs were the hot-beds of the mediaeval communes, and that those communes have been in their turn, the source of life of the now ruling bourgeoisie.

I observed in one of my last letters, of what importance the present labor-crisis must turn out to the Chartist movement in England,[a] which anticipation I now find realized by the results obtained in the first two weeks of the reopened campaign by

[a] See this volume, pp. 134-37.—*Ed.*

Ernest Jones, the Chartist leader. The first great open-air meeting was, as you know, to be held on the mountain of Blackstone-Edge. On the 19th ult., the Lancashire and Yorkshire delegates of the respective Chartist localities congregated there, constituting themselves as Delegate-Council. Ernest Jones's petition for the Charter was unanimously adopted as that proposed to emanate from the meetings in the two counties, and the presentation of the Lancashire and Yorkshire petitions was voted to be entrusted to Mr. Apsley Pellatt, M. P. for Southwark, who had agreed to undertake the presentation of all Chartist petitions. As to the general meeting, the most sanguine minds did not anticipate its possibility, the weather being terrific, the storm increasing hourly in violence and the rain pouring without intermission. At first there appeared only a few scattered groups climbing up the hill, but soon larger bodies came into sight, and from an eminence that overlooked the surrounding valleys, thin but steady streams of people could be viewed as far as the eye could carry, through the base pelting of the rain, coming upward along the roads and footpaths leading from the surrounding country. By the time at which the meeting was announced to commence, upward of 3,000 people had met on the spot, far removed from any village or habitation, and during the long speeches, the meeting, notwithstanding the most violent deluge of rain, remained steadfast on the ground.

Mr. Edward Hooson's resolution: "That the social grievances of the working classes of the country are the result of class-legislation, and that the only remedy for such class-legislation is the adoption of the people's Charter," was supported by Mr. Gammage, of the Chartist Executive,[137] and Mr. Ernest Jones, from whose speeches I give some extracts.[a]

"The resolution which has been moved attributed the people's [...] grievances to class-legislation. He thought that no man who had watched the course of events could disagree with that statement. The House of Commons, so called, had turned a deaf ear to all their complaints, and when the wail of misery had arisen from the people, it had been mocked and derided by the men who assumed to be the representatives of the nation, and if by any singular chance the voice of the people found an echo in that House, it was always drowned in the clamor of the murderous majority of our class-legislators. [Loud applause.] The House of Commons not only refused to do justice to the people, but it even refused to inquire into their social condition. They would all recollect that sometime ago, Mr. Slaney had introduced into the House a motion for the appointment of a standing

[a] Here and below Marx quotes from a report entitled "Glorious Revival of Chartism", *The People's Paper*, No. 60, June 25, 1853.—*Ed.*

commission, whose business it should be to inquire into that condition and suggest measures of relief—but such was the determination of the House to evade the question, that on the introduction of the motion, only twenty-six members were present, and the House was counted out. [Loud cries of shame, shame.] And on the reintroduction of that motion, so far from Mr. Slaney being successful, he (Mr. Gammage) believed that out of 656 honorable men, but 19 were present even to enter on a discussion of the question. [...] When he told them what was the actual condition of the people, he thought they would agree with him, that there existed abundant reasons for inquiry. They were told by political economists that the annual production of this country was £820,000,000. Assuming that there were in the United Kingdom 5,000,000 of working families, and that such families received an average income of fifteen shillings per week, which he believed was a very high average compared with what they actually received [cries of "a great deal too high"], supposing them, however, to average this amount, they received out of their enormous annual production a miserable one hundred and ninety-five millions,—[cries of shame],—and all the rest went into the pockets of idle landlords, usurers and the capitalist class generally.... Did they require a proof that these men were robbers? [...] They were not the worst of thieves who were confined within the walls of our prisons; the greatest and cleverest of thieves were those who robbed by the power of laws made by themselves, and these large robberies were the cause of all the smaller ones that were transacted throughout the country.... Mr. Gammage then entered into an analysis of the House of Commons, proving [...] that from the classes to which the members of that House belonged, and the classes which they represented, it was impossible that there should exist the smallest sympathy between them and the working millions. In conclusion, said the speaker, the people must become acquainted with their Social Rights."

Mr. Ernest Jones said:

"To-day we proclaim that the Charter shall be law. [Loud cheers.] I ask you now to reengage in this great movement, because I know that the time has arrived for so doing, and that the game is in your hand, and because I am anxious that you should not let the opportunity go by. Brisk trade and emigration have given you a momentary power, and upon how you use that power depends your future position. If you use it only for the objects of the present, you will break down when the circumstances of the present cease. But if you use it, not only to strengthen your present position, but to secure your future one, you will triumph over all your enemies. If brisk trade and emigration give you power, that power must cease when brisk trade and emigration cease, and unless you secure yourself in the interval, you will be more slaves than ever. [Hear, hear.] But the very sources that cause your strength now will cause your weakness before long. The emigration that makes your labor scarce, will make soon your employment scarcer.... The commercial reaction will set in, and now I ask you, how are you preparing to meet it? [...] You are engaged in a noble labor movement for short time and high wages, and you are practically carrying it through to some extent, [...] but mark! you are not carrying it through Parliament. Mark! the game of the employer is this—amuse them with some concessions, but yield to them no law. Don't pass a Wages bill in Parliament, but concede some of its provisions in the factory. [Hear.] The wages slave will then say, "Never mind a political organization for a Ten Hours bill or a Wages measure—we've got it, ay, ourselves without Parliament." Yes, but can you keep it without Parliament? What gave it you? Brisk trade. What will take it from you? Dull trade. [...] Your employers know this. [...] Therefore, they shorten your hours of work or raise your wages, or remit their stoppages, in hopes that you will forego the political organization for these measures. [Cheers.] They shorten the hours of work, well knowing that soon they will run their mills short time—they raise your wages, well knowing that soon they will give thousands of you no wages at all. But they tell you also—the midland manufacturers—that, even if the laws were passed, this would only force them to seek other means of robbing you—that was the plain meaning of their words. So that in the first place, you can't get the acts passed, because you have not got a People's Parliament. In the second place, if they were passed, they tell you that they would circumvent them. [Loud cries of "hear."] Now, I ask you, how are you preparing for the future? How are you using the vast strength you momentarily possess? [...] That [...] you will be powerless, unless you prepare now—you will lose all you may have gained; and we are here to-day to show you how to keep it and get more. [...] Some people fancy a Chartist organization would interfere with the Labor movement. Good Heaven! it is the very thing to make it successful.... The employed cannot do without the employer, unless he can employ himself. The employed can never employ himself, unless he can command the means of work—land, credit and machinery. He can never command these, unless he breaks down the landed, moneyed and mercantile monopolies, and these he cannot subvert except by wielding sovereign power. Why do you seek a Ten Hours bill? If political power is not necessary to secure labor-freedom why go to Parliament at all? Why not do in the factory at once? Why, because you know, you feel, you by that very act admit tacitly, that political power is needed to obtain social emancipation. [Loud cheers.] Then I point you to the foundation of political power—I point you to the suffrage—I point you to the Charter. [Enthusiastic applause.] ... It may be said: "Why do we not wait till the crisis comes, and the millions rally of their own accord." Because we want not a movement of excitement and danger, but one of calm reason and moral strength. We will not see you led away by excitement, but guided by judgment—and therefore we bid you now reorganize—that you may rule the storm, instead of being tossed by it. Again, continental revolution will accompany commercial reaction—and we need to raise a strong beacon of Chartism to light us through the chaos of tempest. [...] To-day, then, we reinaugurate our movement, and to obtain its official recognition, we go through the medium of Parliament—not that we expect them to grant the petition—but because we use them as the most fitting mouth-piece to announce our resurrection to the world. Yes, the very men that proclaimed our death, shall have the unsought pleasure to proclaim our resurrection, and this petition is merely the baptismal register announcing to the world our second birth." [Loud cheers.]

Mr. Hooson's resolution and the petition to Parliament were here, as well as at the subsequent meetings during the week, enthusiastically accepted by acclamation.

At the meeting of Blackstone-Edge, Ernest Jones had announced the death of Benjamin Ruston, a workingman who seven years before, had presided at the great Chartist meeting held at the same spot[138]; and he proposed that his funeral should be made a great political demonstration, and be connected with the West Riding meeting for the adoption of the Charter, as the noblest obsequies to be given to that expired veteran. Never before in the annals of British Democracy, has such a demonstration been witnessed, as that which attended the revival of Chartism in the West Riding, and the funeral of Benjamin Ruston, on Sunday last,[a] when upward of 200,000 people were assembled at Halifax, a number unprecedented even in the most excited times. To those who know nothing of English society but its dull, apoplectic surface, it should be recommended to assist at these workingmen's meetings and to look into those depths where its destructive elements are at work.

The Coalition has gained the preliminary battle on the Indian question, Lord Stanley's motion for delay of legislation having been rejected by a majority of 182 votes.[b] Pressure of matter obliges me to delay my comments upon that division.

Written on July 1, 1853

First published in the *New-York Daily Tribune*, No. 3819, July 14, 1853; reprinted in the *New-York Semi-Weekly Tribune*, No. 849, July 15, 1853

Signed: *Karl Marx*

Reproduced from the *New-York Daily Tribune*; the title is taken from the *New-York Semi-Weekly Tribune*

[a] June 26, 1853.—*Ed.*
[b] In the House of Commons on June 30, 1853.—*Ed.*

Karl Marx

THE TURKISH WAR QUESTION.— THE *NEW-YORK TRIBUNE* IN THE HOUSE OF COMMONS.—THE GOVERNMENT OF INDIA [139]

London, Tuesday, 5th July, 1853

The courier bearing the rejection of the Russian *ultimatissimum*[a] on the part of Reshid Pasha, reached St. Petersburg on the 24th ult., and, three days later, a messenger was dispatched with orders for Prince Gorchakoff to cross the Pruth, and to occupy the Principalities.

The Austrian Government has sent Count Gyulay on an extraordinary mission to the Czar, no doubt with a view of cautioning him against the danger of revolution lurking behind any general European war. We may infer the answer of the Russian Cabinet in the present instance from that which it returned to similar representations from the same power in 1829. It was as follows:—

"On this occasion the Austrian Cabinet has reproduced all the motives of alarm created by the fermentation which, according to its opinion and the information it possesses, reigns in more than one country, as well as the progress lately made by the revolutionary tendencies. These apprehensions are more particularly betrayed in the letter of the Emperor Francis to Nicholas. [...] We are far from denying the dangers which Austria points out to us. [...] Since [...] by means of foreign influence [...] the resistance of the Porte assumes a character of obstinacy which delays beyond our wishes and our hopes the term of this crisis, and even demands redoubled efforts to new sacrifices on our part, Russia will be found to devote more than ever her whole attention to interests which so immediately affect the power and the welfare of her subjects; from that moment the means which she could oppose to the breaking out of the revolutionary spirit in the rest of Europe must necessarily be paralyzed. No power, then, ought to be more interested than Austria in the conclusion of peace, but of a peace glorious to the Emperor and advantageous to his empire. For if the treaty we should sign did not bear this character, the political consideration and influence of Russia would experience through it a fatal blow, the *prestige* of her strength would

[a] Of June 16, 1853.—*Ed.*

vanish, and the moral support which she might perhaps be called upon to lend in future contingencies to friendly and allied powers would be precarious and inefficacious." (Secret dispatch from Count Nesselrode to M. de Tatistcheff, dated St. Petersburg, 12th February, 1829.)[a]

The Press, of last Saturday,[b] stated that the Czar, in his disappointment at the conduct of England, and more especially of Lord Aberdeen, had instructed M. de Brunnow to communicate no longer with that "good," old man, but to restrict himself to his official intercourse with the Secretary for Foreign Affairs.

The Vienna *Lloyd*, the organ of the Austrian bankocracy, is very determinedly in favor of Austria siding with England and France for the purpose of discountenancing the aggressive policy of Russia.

You will remember that the Coalition Ministry suffered a defeat on the 14th of April, on the occasion of the proposed repeal of the Advertisement Duty.[c] They have now experienced two more defeats, on the 1st inst., on the identical ground. Mr. Gladstone moved on that day to reduce the Advertisement Duty from 1s. 6d. to 6d., and to extend it to advertisements published with any magazine, pamphlet, or other literary work. Mr. Milner Gibson's amendment for the repeal of all duties now payable on advertisements was rejected by 109 against 99 votes. The retainers of Mr. Gladstone thinking that victory had been won, left the House for dinner and a court-ball, when Mr. Bright rose and made a very powerful speech against the taxes on knowledge in general, and the Stamp and Advertisement Duty in particular. From this speech I will quote a few passages[d] which may be of interest to you:

"He (Mr. Bright) held in his hand a newspaper which was the same size as the London daily newspapers without a supplement, and it was as good a newspaper, he undertook to say, as any published in London. It was printed with a finer type than any London daily paper. The paper, the material, was exceedingly good—quite sufficient for all the purposes of a newspaper. The printing could not be possibly surpassed, and it contained more matter for its size than any daily paper printed in London. The first, second and third sides were composed of advertisements. There were a long article upon the American Art-Union investigation, a leading article giving a summary of all the latest news from Europe, a leading article on the Fisheries dispute, and a leading article, with which he entirely concurred, stating that public dinners were public nuisances. [Hear, and a

---

[a] Quoted from *The Portfolio*, 1836, Vol. IV, No. XXVII, pp. 10-12.—*Ed.*
[b] July 2, 1853.—*Ed.*
[c] See this volume, pp. 58 and 69.—*Ed.*
[d] These passages, like the passage from Richard Cobden's speech, are quoted from *The Times*, No. 21470, July 2, 1853.—*Ed.*

laugh.] He had seen articles perhaps written with more style, but never any that had a better tone, or that were more likely to be useful. Then again there were 'Three days later from Europe,' the 'Arrival of the *Asia*,' and a condensation from all the news from Europe. From Great Britain there was an elaborate disquisition upon the Budget[a] of the Rt. Honorable gentleman,[b] which did him justice in some parts, but not in others, and which, so far as the Manchester schools were concerned, certainly did them no justice whatever. [Laughter.] Then there were an account of Mrs. Stowe's visit to Edinburgh, a long article from the London *Times* upon the wrongs of dressmakers, articles from Greece, Spain and other continental countries, the Athlone election, and the returns of Her Majesty's Solicitor General by exactly 189 votes—which would very much surprise an American to read—several columns of ordinary news in paragraphs, and most elaborate mercantile and market tables. It wrote steadily in favor of Temperance and Anti-Slavery, and he [Bright] ventured to say that there was not at this moment in London a better paper than that. The name of that paper was the *New-York Tribune*, and it was laid regularly every morning upon the table of every workingman of that city who chose to buy it at the sum of one penny. [Hear, hear.] What he wanted to ask the Government was this: How comes it, and for what good end, and by what contrivance of fiscal oppression was it that one of our workmen here should pay 5d. for a London morning paper, while his direct competitor in New York could buy a paper for 1d.? We were running a race in the face of all the world with the United States; but if our artisans were to be bound either to have no newspaper at all, or to pay 5d. for it, or were to be driven to the public houses to read it, [...] while the artisan in the United States could procure it for 1d., how was it possible that any fair rivalry could be maintained between the artisans of the two countries? As well say that a merchant in England, if he never saw a price-current, would carry on his business with the same facility as the merchant who had that advantage every day. [Hear, hear.] ... If the Chancellor of the Exchequer should oppose what he had stated, he should tell him at once and without hesitation that it was because he had a latent dread of the liberty of the press; and when the right honorable gentleman spoke about financial difficulties, he said it was but a cloak to conceal his lurking horror lest the people should have a free press and greater means of political information. [Hear.] It was the fear that the press would be free which made them keep the 6d. advertisement duty as the buttress to the stamp."

Mr. Craufurd then moved to substitute in lieu of the figure 6d. the cipher 0d. Mr. Cobden supported the motion, and in reply to Mr. Gladstone's statement, that the Advertisement Duty was no question of much importance with regard to the circulation of cheap newspapers, called his attention to the evidence given by Mr. Horace Greeley, who was examined before the Committee which had sat on this subject in 1851.

"This gentleman was one of the Commissioners of the great exhibition, and he was the proprietor of that very newspaper from which his honorable friend, Mr. Bright, had quoted. He was examined as to what the effect of the advertisement

[a] The reference is to Marx's article, "Riot at Constantinople.—German Table Moving.—The Budget", *New-York Daily Tribune*, No. 3761, May 6, 1853 (see this volume, pp. 67-74). It is this issue that John Bright analyses in his speech.—*Ed.*

[b] William Gladstone.—*Ed.*

duty would be in America, and his reply was that its operation would be to destroy their new papers."

Lord John Russell now got up and said, in rather angry voice, that it was hardly fair to attempt to reverse, in a greatly thinned House, the decisions previously adopted. Of course, Lord John did not recollect that on the very Advertisement Duty his colleagues had been beaten before by a majority of 40, and had only had now a majority of 10. Notwithstanding Lord John's lecture on "constitutional" fairness, the motion of Mr. Gladstone for a duty of 6d. on each advertisement, was negatived by 68 against 63, and Mr. Craufurd's amendment carried by 70 against 61. Mr. Disraeli and his friends voted with the Manchester School.

The House of Commons, in order to do justice to the colossal dimensions of the subject, has been spinning out its Indian debate to an unusual length and breadth, although that debate has failed altogether in depth and greatness of interest. The division leaving Ministers a majority of 322 against 142, is in inverse ratio to the discussion. During the discussion all was thistles for the Ministry, and Sir Charles Wood was the ass officially put to the task of feeding upon them. In the division all is roses, and Sir Charles Wood receives the crown of another *Manu*. The same men who negatived the plan of the Ministry by their arguments, affirmed it by their votes. None of its supporters dared to apologize for the bill itself; on the contrary, all apologized for their supporting the bill, the one because it was an infinitesimal part of a measure in the right direction, the others because it was no measure at all. The former pretend that they will now mend it in Committee; the latter say that they will strip it of all the fancy Reform flowers it parades in.

The Ministry maintained the field by more than one half of the Tory opposition running away, and a great portion of the remainder deserting with Herries and Inglis into the Aberdeen camp, while of the 142 opposite votes 100 belonged to the Disraeli fraction, and 42 to the Manchester School, backed by some Irish discontents and some inexpressibles. The opposition within the opposition has once more saved the Ministry.

Mr. Halliday, one of the officials of the East India Company, when examined before a Committee of Inquiry, stated:

"That the Charter giving a twenty years lease to the East India Company was considered by the natives of India as *farming them out*."[a]

---

[a] Quoted from Richard Cobden's speech in the House of Commons on June 27, 1853, published in *The Times*, No. 21466, June 28, 1853.—*Ed.*

This time at least, the Charter has not been renewed for a definite period, but is revokable at will by Parliament. The Company, therefore, will come down from the respectable situation of hereditary farmers, to the precarious condition of tenants-at-will.[140] This is so much gain for the natives. The Coalition Ministry has succeeded in transforming the Indian Government, like all other questions, into an open question. The House of Commons, on the other hand, has given itself a new testimonial of poverty, in confessing by the same division, its impotency for legislating, and its unwillingness to delay legislating.

Since the days of Aristotle the world has been inundated with a frightful quantity of dissertations, ingenious or absurd, as it might happen, on that question: Who shall be the governing power? But for the first time in the annals of history, the Senate of a people ruling over another people numbering 156 millions of human beings and spreading over a surface of 1,368,113 square miles, have put their heads together in solemn and public congregation, in order to answer the irregular question: Who among us is the actual governing power over that foreign people of 150 millions of souls? There was no Oedipus in the British Senate capable of extricating this riddle. The whole debate exclusively twined around it, as although a division took place, no definition of the Indian Government was arrived at.

That there is in India a permanent financial deficit, a regular over-supply of wars, and no supply at all of public works, an abominable system of taxation, and a no less abominable state of justice and law, that these five items constitute, as it were, the five points of the East Indian Charter, was settled beyond all doubt in the debates of 1853, as it had been in the debates of 1833, and in the debates of 1813, and in all former debates on India. The only thing never found out, was the party responsible for all this.

There exists, unquestionably, a Governor-General of India, holding the supreme power, but that Governor is governed in his turn by a home government. Who is that home government? Is it the Indian Minister, disguised under the modest title of President of the Board of Control, or is it the twenty-four Directors of the East India Company? On the threshold of the Indian religion we find a divine trinity, and thus we find a profane trinity on the threshold of the Indian Government.

Leaving, for a while, the Governor-General altogether one side, the question at issue resolves itself into that of the *double Government*, in which form it is familiar to the English mind. The

Ministers in their bill, and the House in its division, cling to this dualism.

When the Company of English merchant adventurers, who conquered India to make money out of it, began to enlarge their factories into an empire, when their competition with the Dutch and French private merchants assumed the character of national rivalry, then, of course, the British Government commenced meddling with the affairs of the East India Company, and the double Government of India sprung up in fact if not in name. Pitt's act of 1784, by entering into a compromise with the Company, by subjecting it to the superintendence of the Board of Control, and by making the Board of Control an appendage to the Ministry, accepted, regulated and settled that double Government arisen from circumstances in name as well as in fact.

The act of 1833 strengthened the Board of Control, changed the proprietors of the East India Company into mere mortgagees of the East India revenues, ordered the Company to sell off its stock, dissolved its commercial existence, transformed it; as far as it existed politically, into a mere trustee of the Crown, and did thus with the East India Company, what the Company had been in the habit of doing with the East India Princes. After having superseded them, it continued, for a while, still to govern in their name. So far, the East India Company has, since 1833, no longer existed but in name and on sufferance. While thus on one hand, there seems to be no difficulty in getting rid of the Company altogether, it is, on the other hand, very indifferent whether the English nation rules over India under the personal name of Queen Victoria, or under the traditional firm of an anonymous society. The whole question, therefore, appears to turn about a technicality of very questionable importance. Still, the thing is not quite so plain.

It is to be remarked, in the first instance, that the Ministerial Board of Control, residing in Cannon-row, is as much a fiction as the East India Company, supposed to reside in Leadenhall-st. The members composing the Board of Control are a mere cloak for the supreme rule of the President of the Board. The President is himself but a subordinate though independent member of the Imperial Ministry. In India it seems to be assumed that if a man is fit for nothing it is best to make him a Judge, and get rid of him. In Great Britain, when a party comes into office and finds itself encumbered with a tenth-rate "statesman," it is considered best to make him President of the Board of Control, successor of the

Great Mogul, and in that way to get rid of him—*teste Carolo Wood.*[a]

The letter of the law entrusts the Board of Control, which is but another name for its President, with

"full power and authority to superintend, direct, and control all acts, operations and concerns of the East India Company which in any wise relate to or concern the Government or revenues of the Indian territories."[b]

Directors are prohibited

"from issuing any orders, instructions, dispatches, official letters, or communications whatever relating to India, or to the Government thereof, until the same shall have been sanctioned by the Board."

Directors are ordered to

"prepare instructions or orders upon any subject whatever at fourteen days' notice from the Board, or else to transmit the orders of the Board on the subject of India."

The Board is authorized to inspect all correspondence and dispatches to and from India, and the proceedings of the Courts of Proprietors and Directors. Lastly, the Court of Directors has to appoint a Secret Committee, consisting of their Chairman, their Deputy Chairman and their senior member, who are sworn to secrecy, and through whom, in all political and military matters, the President of the Board may transmit his personal orders to India, while the Committee acts as a mere channel of his communications. The orders respecting the Afghan and Burmese wars, and as to the occupation of Scinde were transmitted through this Secret Committee, without the Court of Directors being any more informed of them than the general public or Parliament. So far, therefore, the President of the Board of Control would appear to be the real Mogul, and, under all circumstances, he retains an unlimited power for doing mischief, as, for instance, for causing the most ruinous wars, all the while being hidden under the name of the irresponsible Court of Directors. On the other hand, the Court of Directors is not without real power. As they generally exercise the initiative in administrative measures, as they form, when compared with the Board of Control, a more permanent and steady body, with traditional rules for action and a certain knowledge of details, the whole of the ordinary internal administration necessarily falls to

---

[a] This is demonstrated by Charles Wood.—*Ed.*

[b] Here and below Marx quotes from J. Dickinson's *The Government of India under a Bureaucracy*, p. 8.—*Ed.*

their share. They appoint, too, under sanction of the Crown, the Supreme Government of India, the Governor-General and his Councils; possessing, besides, the unrestricted power to recall the highest servants, and even the Governor-General, as they did under Sir Robert Peel, with Lord Ellenborough. But this is still not their most important privilege. Receiving only £300 per annum, they are really paid in patronage, distributing all the writerships and cadetships, from whose number the Governor-General of India and the Provincial Governors are obliged to fill up all the higher places withheld from the natives. When the number of appointments for the year is ascertained, the whole are divided into 28 equal parts—of which two are allotted to the Chairman and Deputy Chairman, two to the President of the Board of Control, and one to each of the Directors. The annual value of each share of patronage seldom falls short of £14,000.

"All nominations," says Mr. Campbell, "are now, as it were, the private property of individuals, being divided among the Directors, and each disposing of his share as he thinks fit."[a]

Now, it is evident that the spirit of the Court of Directors must pervade the whole of the Indian Upper Administration, trained, as it is, at schools of Addiscombe and Haileybury, and appointed, as it is, by their patronage. It is no less evident that this Court of Directors, who have to distribute, year after year, appointments of the value of nearly £400,000 among the upper classes of Great Britain, will find little or no check from the public opinion directed by those very classes. What the spirit of the Court of Directors is, I will show in a following letter on the actual state of India.[b] For the present it may suffice to say that Mr. Macaulay, in the course of the pending debates, defended the Court by the particular plea, that it was impotent to effect all the evils it might intend, so much so, that all improvements had been effected in opposition to it, and against it by individual Governors who had acted on their own responsibility. Thus with regard to the suppression of the Suttee,[141] the abolition of the abominable transit duties, and the emancipation of the East India press.

The President of the Board of Control accordingly involves India in ruinous wars under cover of the Court of Directors, while

[a] Rendering of a passage from G. Campbell's *Modern India: a Sketch of the System of Civil Government*, pp. 263-64.—*Ed.*

[b] See this volume, pp. 196-200 and 213-16.—*Ed.*

the Court of Directors corrupt the Indian Administration under the cloak of the Board of Control.

On looking deeper into the framework of this anomalous government we find at its bottom a third power, more supreme than either the Board or the Court, more irresponsible, and more concealed from and guarded against the superintendence of public opinion. The transient President of the Board depends on the permanent clerks of his establishment in Cannon-row, and for those clerks India exists not in India, but in Leadenhall-st. Now, who is the master at Leadenhall-st.?

Two thousand persons, elderly ladies and valetudinarian gentlemen, possessing Indian stock, having no other interest in India except to be paid their dividends out of Indian revenue, elect twenty-four Directors, whose only qualification is the holding of £1,000 stock. Merchants, bankers and directors of companies incur great trouble in order to get into the Court for the interest of their private concerns.

> "A banker," said Mr. Bright, "in the City of London commands 300 votes of the East India Company, whose word for the election of Directors is almost absolute law." [a]

Hence the Court of Directors is nothing but *a succursal* to the English moneyocracy. The so-elected Court forms, in its turn, besides the above-mentioned Secret Committee, three other Committees, which are 1. Political and Military. 2. Finance and Home. 3. Revenue, Judicial and Legislative. These Committees are every year appointed by rotation, so that a *financier* is one year on the Judicial and the next year on the Military Committee, and no one has any chance of a continued supervision over a particular department. The mode of election having brought in men utterly unfit for their duties, the system of rotation gives to whatever fitness they might perchance retain, the final blow. Who, then, govern in fact under the name of the Direction? A large stuff of irresponsible secretaries, examiners and clerks at the India House,[b] of whom, as Mr. Campbell observes, in his *Scheme for the Government of India*, only one individual has ever been in India, and he only by accident. Apart from the trade in patronage, it is therefore a mere fiction to speak of the politics, the principles, and the system of the Court of Directors. The real Court of

---

[a] John Bright's speech is quoted from *The Times*, No. 21466, June 28, 1853.—*Ed.*

[b] The East India House was the residence of the Court of Directors of the East India Company in Leadenhall Street in London.—*Ed.*

Directors and the real Home Government, &c., of India are the permanent and irresponsible *bureaucracy*, "the creatures of the desk and the creatures of favor"[a] residing in Leadenhall-st. We have thus a Corporation ruling over an immense Empire, not formed, as in Venice, by eminent patricians, but by old obstinate clerks, and the like odd fellows.

No wonder, then, that there exists no government by which so much is written and so little done, as the Government of India. When the East India Company was only a commercial association, they, of course, requested a most detailed report on every item from the managers of their Indian factories, as is done by every trading concern. When the factories grew into an Empire, the commercial items into ship loads of correspondence and documents, the Leadenhall clerks went on in their system, which made the Directors and the Board their dependents; and they succeeded in transforming the Indian Government into one immense writing-machine. Lord Broughton stated in his evidence before the Official Salaries Committee, that with one single dispatch 45,000 pages of collection were sent.

In order to give you some idea of the time-killing manner in which business is transacted at the India House, I will quote a passage from Mr. Dickinson:

"When a dispatch arrives from India, it is referred, in the first instance, to the Examiners' Department, to which it belongs; after which the Chairs[b] confer with the official in charge of that department, and settle with him the tenor of a reply, and transmit a draught of this reply to the Indian Minister,[c] in what is technically called P.C., i.e. previous communication. [...] The Chairs, [...] in this preliminary state of P.C. depend mainly on the clerks. [...] Such is this dependence that even in a discussion in the Court of Proprietors, after previous notice, it is pitiable [...] to see the chairman referring to a secretary who sits by his side, and keeps on whispering and prompting and chaffing him as if he were a mere puppet, and [...] the Minister at the other end of the system is in the same predicament. [...] In this stage of P.C., if there is a difference of opinion on the draught it is discussed, and almost invariably settled in friendly communication between the Minister and the Chair; finally the draught is returned by the Minister, either adopted or altered; and then it is submitted to the Committee of Directors superintending the department to which it belongs, with all papers bearing on the case, to be considered and discussed, and adopted or altered, and afterward it is exposed to the same process in the aggregate Court, and then goes, for the first time,

[a] These words by E. Burke are quoted from J. Dickinson's *The Government of India under a Bureaucracy*, as also his statement and a passage from the text by the author below (see pp. 15-16).—*Ed.*

[b] The reference is to the Chairman and Vice-Chairman of the Court of Directors of the East India Company.—*Ed.*

[c] Here the reference is to the President of the Board of Control, who was a member of the British Government.—*Ed.*

as an official communication to the Minister," after which it undergoes the same process in the opposite direction.

"When a measure is discussed in India," says Mr. Campbell, "the announcement that it has been referred to the Court of Directors, is [...] regarded as an indefinite postponement."[a]

The close and abject spirit of this bureaucracy deserves to be stigmatised in the celebrated words of Burke:

"This tribe of vulgar politicians are the lowest of our species. There is no trade so vile and mechanical as Government in their hands. Virtue is not their habit. They are out of themselves in any course of conduct recommended only by conscience and glory. A large, liberal and prospective view of the interests of States passes with them for romance; and the principles that recommend it, for the wanderings of a disordered imagination. The calculators compute them out of their senses. The jesters and buffoons shame them out of everything grand and elevated. Littleness in object and in means to them appears soundness and sobriety."

The clerical establishments of Leadenhall-st. and Cannon-row cost the Indian people the trifle of £160,000 annually. The oligarchy involves India in wars, in order to find employment for their younger sons; the moneyocracy consigns it to the highest bidder; and a subordinate Bureaucracy paralyse its administration and perpetuate its abuses as the vital condition of their own perpetuation.

Sir Charles Wood's bill alters nothing in the existing system. It enlarges the power of the Ministry, without adding to its responsibility.

Written on July 5, 1853

First published in the *New-York Daily Tribune,* No. 3824, July 20, 1853; reprinted in the *New-York Semi-Weekly Tribune,* No. 851, July 22, 1853

Signed: *Karl Marx*

Reproduced from the *New-York Daily Tribune*

[a] G. Campbell, *Modern India: a Sketch of the System of Civil Government,* p. 215.—*Ed.*

Karl Marx

[LAYARD'S MOTION.— STRUGGLE OVER THE TEN HOURS' BILL][142]

London, Friday, July 8, 1853

With the actual occupation of the Danubian Principalities and the drawing near of the long-predicted crisis, the English Press has remarkably lowered its warlike language, and little opposition is made to the advice tendered in two consecutive leaders of *The Times*[a] that, "as the Russians could not master their propensity for civilizing barbarian provinces, England had better let them do as they desired, and avoid a disturbance of the peace by vain obstinacy."

The anxiety of the Government to withhold all information on the pending Turkish question betrayed itself in a most ridiculous farce, acted at the same time in both Houses of Parliament. In the House of Commons Mr. Layard, the celebrated restorer of ancient Nineveh,[143] had given notice that he would move this evening that the fullest information with regard to Turkey and Russia should be laid before the House. On this notice having been given, the following scene occurred in the lower House[b]:

Mr. *Layard*—The notice of my motion was given for to-morrow. I received a note yesterday afternoon asking me to put off the motion to Monday, 11th inst. I was not able to return an answer yesterday afternoon—in fact, not till this morning. To my surprise, I find that, without my knowledge, I was in the House yesterday; for I find from the notices of motions printed with the votes, that Mr. Layard postponed his motion from Friday the 8th to Monday 11th! [...] It seems scarcely fair that independent members should be treated in this way.

Mr. *Gladstone*—I do not know by whose direction or authority the notice of postponement was placed on the notes of the House. Of one thing I can assure the hon. member, that whatever was done, was done in perfect *bona fides.*

---

[a] *The Times*, No. 21475, July 8, 1853.—*Ed.*

[b] Rendering of passages from debates in the two Houses on July 7 is according to the report in *The Times*, No. 21475, July 8, 1853.—*Ed.*

Mr. *Layard*—I should like to know who put that notice of postponement in the paper. What reason have you for deferring the motion to Monday?

Mr. *Gladstone*—An indisposition of Lord J. Russell.

Mr. *Layard* then withdrew his motion until Monday.

Mr. *Disraeli*—This appears to me an arrangement of business which requires explanation on the part of the Government—the more so as the India Bill, too, contrary to agreement, is placed on the notes for to-morrow.

After a pause,

Sir *C. Wood* humbly confesses to have been the double sinner, but, availing himself of Mr. Gladstone's suggestion, declared that he had acted with regard to Mr. Layard with the *best intentions in the world.*

The opposite side of the medal was exhibited in the House of Lords, where, at all events, the bodily disposition of poor little Russell had nothing to do with the motion of the Marquis of Clanricarde, similar to that of Mr. Layard, and likewise announced for Friday, after it had already several times been adjourned on the request of Ministers.

Lord *Brougham* rose, with the assurance that he had not communicated with any member of the Ministry, but that he found the motion of Lord Clanricarde, announced for to-morrow, most inconvenient in the present state of affairs. For this he would refer to the Secretary for Foreign Affairs.

Lord *Clarendon* could certainly not say that there would be neither mischief nor inconvenience in a full discussion of the subject at present. Negotiations were going on; but after the various postponements, he felt that he ought not to ask again his noble friend to withdraw his motion. Yet he reserved to himself, in reply to him, to say nothing more than that which his sense of public duty allowed. Nevertheless, he would ask his noble friend whether he would object to at least postponing the motion until Monday next, it being convenient to have this discussion in both Houses at the same time, and Lord J. Russell being extremely unwell?

Earl of *Ellenborough*—The noble Marquis opposite would only exercise a sound discretion if he deferred not only to Monday, but generally, without fixing at present any day for the motion of which he has given notice for to-morrow.

Lord *Derby*—He had been taken by surprise on finding the noble Marquis bringing the question under consideration, and he concurred entirely with the views of the noble Earl (Ellenborough).

Earl *Grey*—After the declaration of Lord Clarendon the propriety of postponing discussion must be obvious to every one.

The Marquis of Clanricarde then withdrew his motion.

Earl *Fitzwilliam*—He would ask whether the Russian manifesto, the declaration of a *holy war* against Turkey, dated June 26, was authentic?

Earl *Clarendon*—He had received that document from Her Majesty's Minister at St. Petersburg.

Earl of *Malmesbury*—It was due to the dignity of their Lordships that they should be assured by Government of its intention to prevent, as far as it could, a similar discussion taking place on Monday in the other House.

Earl of *Aberdeen*—He and his colleagues would exercise any influence they possessed to do their utmost for preventing that discussion.

To resume: The House of Commons is first made to adjourn discussion by a fraud. Then, under the pretense that the House of Commons had adjourned discussion, the House of Lords is made to do the same. Then the "noble" Lords resolve to postpone the motion *ad infinitum*; and lastly, the dignity of the "noblest assembly on the face of the earth" requires that the Commons too should postpone the motion *ad infinitum.*

On an interpellation from Mr. Liddell, Lord Palmerston declared in the same sitting:

> The recent obstruction of the navigation of the Sulina Canal of the Danube, had been caused by the accidental circumstance of the waters of the river having overflowed and spread over the banks, and so far diminished the force of the current as to increase the quantity of mud on the bar. [...] I am bound to say that, for many years past, the Government has had reason to complain of the neglect of the Government of Russia to perform its duties as the possessor of the territory of which the Delta of the Danube is composed, and to maintain the Canal of the Sulina [...] in efficient navigable state, although Russia always admitted that it was her duty to do so, by virtue of the treaty of Adrianople. [...] While these mouths of the Danube formed parts of the Turkish Territory, there was maintained a depth of 16 feet on the bar, whereas, by neglect of the Russian authorities the depth had diminished to 11 feet, and even these 11 feet were reduced to a small and narrow canal from obstructions on the sides, from sand-banks and from vessels wrecked and sunk, and allowed to remain there, so that it was difficult for any vessel to pass except in calm weather and with a skillful pilot. [...] There was rivalship on the part of Odessa, where existed a desire to obstruct the export of produce by the Danube, and to divert it, if possible by way of Odessa.

Probably the English Ministry hope that, in case of the Principalities becoming Russian, the mouths of the Danube will reopen according as the rivalry of Odessa will be shut.

A few months ago I took occasion to remark on the progress of the Ten Hours' agitation in the Factory districts.[a] The movement has been going on all the while, and has at last found an echo in the Legislature. On the 5th inst., Mr. Cobbett, M. P. for Oldham, moved for leave to bring in a bill to restrict factory labor to ten hours on the first five days of the week, and to seven and a half hours on Saturday. Leave was given to bring in the bill. During the preliminary debate, Lord Palmerston, in the warmth of improvisation, allowed a distinct threat to escape him, that, if no other means for protecting the factory women and children existed, he would propose a restriction of the moving power. The sentence had scarcely fallen from his lips, when a general storm of indignation burst forth against the incautious statesman, not only from the direct representatives of millocracy, but particularly from

[a] The reference is to the article "Parliamentary Debates.—The Clergy Against Socialism.—Starvation" (see present edition, Vol. 11, pp. 522-27).—*Ed.*

their and his own Whig friends, such as Sir George Grey, Mr. Labouchere, &c. Lord J. Russell having taken Palmerston aside, and after half an hour's private *pourparler*, had to labor very hard to appease the storm, by assuring them that "it appeared to him that his honorable friend had been entirely misunderstood, and that in expressing himself *for* a restriction of the moving power, his friend had meant to express himself *against* it." Such absurd compromises are the daily bread of the Coalition. At all events *they* have the right to say one thing and to mean another. As to Lord Palmerston himself, be it not forgotten that that old dandy of Liberalism expelled a few years ago some hundred Irish families from his "estates," much in the same way as the Duchess of Sutherland did with the ancient clansmen.[a]

Mr. Cobbett, who moved the bill, is the son of the renowned William Cobbett, and represents the same borough his father did. His politics, like his seat, are the inheritance of his father, and therefore independent indeed, but rather incoherent with the state of present parties. William Cobbett was the most able representative, or, rather, the creator of old English Radicalism. He was the first who revealed the mystery of the hereditary party warfare between Tories and Whigs, stripped the parasitic Whig Oligarchy of their sham liberalism, opposed landlordism in its every form, ridiculed the hypocritical rapacity of the Established Church, and attacked the moneyocracy in its two most eminent incarnations—the "Old Lady of Threadneedle-st." (Bank of England) and Mr. Muckworm & Co. (the national creditors). He proposed to cancel the national debt, to confiscate the Church estates, and to abolish all sorts of paper money. He watched step for step the encroachments of political centralization on local self-government, and denounced it as an infringement on the privileges and liberties of the English subject. He did not understand its being the necessary result of industrial centralization. He proclaimed all the political demands which have afterward been combined in the national charter; yet with him they were rather the political charter of the petty industrial middle class than of the industrial proletarian. A plebeian by instinct and by sympathy, his intellect rarely broke through the boundaries of middle-class reform. It was not until 1834, shortly before his death, after the establishment of the new Poor Law,[144] that William Cobbett began to suspect the existence of a millocracy as hostile to the mass of the

---

[a] See Marx's article "Elections.—Financial Clouds.—The Duchess of Sutherland and Slavery" (present edition, Vol. 11, pp. 486-94).—*Ed.*

people, as landlords, banklords, public creditors, and the clergymen of the Established Church. If William Cobbett was thus, on one hand, an anticipated modern Chartist, he was, on the other hand, and much more, an inveterate John Bull. He was at once the most conservative and the most destructive man of Great Britain—the purest incarnation of Old England and the most audacious initiator of Young England. He dated the decline of England from the period of the Reformation, and the ulterior prostration of the English people from the so-called glorious Revolution of 1688. With him, therefore, revolution was not innovation, but restoration; not the creation of a new age, but the rehabilitation of the "good old times." What he did not see, was that the epoch of the pretended decline of the English people coincided exactly with the beginning ascendancy of the middle class, with the development of modern commerce and industry, and that, at the same pace as the latter grew up, the material situation of the people declined, and local self-government disappeared before political centralization. The great changes attending the decomposition of the old English Society since the eighteenth century struck his eyes and made his heart bleed. But if he saw the effects, he did not understand the causes; the new social agencies at work. He did not see the modern *bourgeoisie*, but only that fraction of the aristocracy which held the hereditary monopoly of office, and which sanctioned by law all the changes necessitated by the new wants and pretensions of the middle class. He saw the machine, but not the hidden motive power. In his eyes, therefore, the Whigs were responsible for all the changes supervening since 1688. They were the prime motors of the decline of England and the degradation of its people. Hence his fanatical hatred against, and his ever recurring denunciation of the Whig oligarchy. Hence the curious phenomenon, that William Cobbett, who represented by instinct the mass of the people against the encroachments of the middle class, passed in the eyes of the world and in his own conviction for the representative of the industrial middle class against the hereditary aristocracy. As a writer he has not been surpassed.

The present Mr. Cobbett, by continuing under altered circumstances the politics of his father, has necessarily sunk into the class of liberal Tories.

The Times, anxious to make good for its humble attitude against the Russian Czar[a] by increased insolence against the English

[a] Nicholas I.—*Ed.*

workingmen, brings a leader on Mr. Cobbett's motion that aims to be monstrous, but happens to turn out plainly absurd. It cannot deny that the restriction of the moving power is the only means for enforcing upon the factory lords a submission to the existing laws with regard to the hours of factory labor. But it fails to understand how any man of common sense who aims at attaining an end can propose the only adequate means to it. The existing *Ten-and-a-half-hours* act,[145] like all other factory laws, is but a fictitious concession made by the ruling classes to the working-people; and the workingmen, not satisfied with the mere appearance of a concession, dare insist upon its reality. *The Times* has never heard of a thing more ridiculous or more extravagant. If a master should be prevented by Parliament from working his hands during 12, 16, or any other number of hours, then, says *The Times*, "England is no longer a place for a freeman to live in."[a] Thus the South Carolina gentleman who was placed before and condemned by a London Magistrate for having publicly whipped the Negro he had brought with him from the other side of the Atlantic, exclaimed in a most exasperated state of mind, "You don't call this a free country where a man is forbidden to whip his own nigger?" If a man becomes a factory hand, and enters into contract with a master, in virtue of which he sells himself for sixteen or eighteen hours, instead of taking his sleep as better-circumstanced mortals can do, you have to explain that, says *The Times*,

> "by that natural impulse which perpetually adjusts the supply to the demand, and directs people to the occupation *most agreeable and most suited to themselves*."

Legislation, of course, must not interfere with this *travail attrayant*.[b] If you restrict the moving power of machinery to a definite portion of the day, say from 6 o'clock, A. M. to 6 P. M., then, says *The Times*, you might as well suppress machinery altogether. If you stop the gas-light in the public thoroughfares as soon as the sun rises, you must stop it also during the night. *The Times* forbids legislative interference with private concerns, and therefore, perhaps, it defends the duty on paper, on advertisements, and the newspaper-stamp, in order to keep down the private concerns of its competitors, asking the Legislature to relieve its own concern of the supplement duty. It professes an utter abhorrence of parliamentary interference with the sacred

[a] Here and below Marx quotes the second editorial of *The Times*, No. 21474, July 7, 1853.—*Ed.*

[b] Attractive labour.—*Ed.*

interest of mill-lords, where the lives and the morals of whole generations are at stake, while it has croaked its most determined interference with cabmen and hackney-coach proprietors, where nothing was at stake except the conveniences of some fat city-men, and perhaps the gentlemen of Printing-house-square.[a] Till now the middle-class economists have told us that the principal use of machinery was its shortening and superseding bodily labor and drudgery. Now *The Times* confesses that, under present class-arrangements machinery does not shorten but prolong the hours of labor—that it firstly bereaves the individual labor of its quality, and then forces the laborer to make up for the loss in quality by quantity—thus adding hour to hour, night labor to day labor, in a process which only stops at the intervals of industrial crises, when the man is refused any labor at all—when the factory is shut before his nose, and when he may enjoy holidays or hang himself if he pleases.

Written on July 8, 1853

First published in the *New-York Daily Tribune*, No. 3826, and the *New-York Semi-Weekly Tribune*, No. 851, July 22, 1853

Reproduced from the *New-York Daily Tribune*

Signed: *Karl Marx*

[a] The square in London where *The Times* had its main offices.—*Ed.*

Karl Marx

THE RUSSO-TURKISH DIFFICULTY.— DUCKING AND DODGING OF THE BRITISH CABINET.—NESSELRODE'S LAST NOTE.— THE EAST INDIA QUESTION[146]

London, Tuesday, July 12, 1853

The Parliamentary farce of Thursday last was continued and brought to a close in the sitting of Friday, 8th inst. Lord Palmerston requested Mr. Layard not only to put off his motion to Monday, but never to make any mention of it again. "Monday was now to go the way of Friday." Mr. Bright took the opportunity of congratulating Lord Aberdeen on his cautious policy, and generally to assure him of his entire confidence.

"Were the Peace Society[147] itself the Cabinet," says *The Morning Advertiser,* "it could not have done more to encourage Russia, to discourage France, to endanger Turkey, and discredit England, than the very good Aberdeen. [...] Mr. Bright's speech was meant as a sort of Manchester manifesto in favor of the tremblers of the Cabinet."[a]

The Ministerial efforts for burking the intended question of Mr. Layard originated in a well-founded fear that the internal dissensions in the Cabinet could have no longer been kept a secret to the public. Turkey must fall to pieces, that the Coalition may keep together. Next to Lord Aberdeen, the Ministers most favorable to the tricks of Russia, are the following: The Duke of Argyll, Lord Clarendon, Lord Granville, Mr. Sidney Herbert, Mr. Cardwell, and the "Radical" Sir William Molesworth. Lord Aberdeen is said to have threatened at one time to offer his resignation. The "vigorous" Palmerston (civis Romanus sum[148]) party, of course, was but wanting such a pretext for yielding. They resolved that a common representation should be addressed

---

[a] "The 'Interpellations' on 'Monday'", *The Morning Advertiser,* July 11, 1853.—*Ed.*

to the Courts of St. Petersburg and Constantinople, recommending that the "privileges demanded by the Czar for the Greek Christians should be secured to Christians of all denominations in the Turkish dominions, under a treaty of guaranty, to which the great powers should be parties." This identical proposition was, however, already made to Prince Menchikoff, on the eve of his departure from Constantinople, and was made, as everybody knows, to no purpose. It is, therefore, utterly ridiculous to expect any result from its repetition, the more so, as it is now a matter beyond all doubt that what Russia insists upon having is exactly a treaty which the great powers, viz.: Austria and Prussia, now no longer resist. Count Buol, the Austrian Premier, is brother-in-law to Count Pouilly Meyendorff, the Russian Minister, and acts in perfect agreement with Russia. On the same day on which the two Coalition parties, the slumbering and the "vigorous," came to the above resolution, the *Patrie* published the following:

"The new Internuncio of Austria, at Constantinople, M. de Bruck, commenced by calling upon the Porte to pay 5,000,000 piasters as an indemnity, and to consent to the delivery of the ports of Kleck and Suttorina. This demand was considered as a support given to Russia."[a]

This is not the only support given by Austria to the Russian interests at Constantinople. In 1848, it will be remembered, that whenever the Princes wanted to shoot their people, they provided a "misunderstanding." The same stratagem is now being employed against Turkey. The Austrian Consul at Smyrna causes the kidnapping of a Hungarian[b] from an English coffee house on board an Austrian vessel, and after the refugees have answered this attempt by the killing of an Austrian officer and the wounding [of] another one, M. de Bruck demands satisfaction from the Porte within 24 hours.[149] Simultaneously with this news, *The Morning Post* of Saturday reports a rumor that the Austrians had entered Bosnia. The Coalition, questioned as to the authenticity of this rumor, in yesterday's sitting of both Houses of Parliament, had, of course, received "no information;" Russell alone venturing the suggestion[c] that the rumor had probably no other foundation than the fact that the Austrians collected troops at Peterwardein. Thus is fulfilled the prediction of M. de Tatistcheff, in 1828, that Austria, when things were come to a decisive turn, would eagerly make ready for sharing in the spoil.

---

[a] *La Patrie*, No. 190, July 9, 1853.—*Ed.*

[b] M. Koszta (arrested by order of Consul Weckbecker).—*Ed.*

[c] In his House of Commons speech of July 11, 1853, published in *The Times*, No. 21478, July 12, 1853.—*Ed.*

A dispatch from Constantinople, dated 26th ult., states:

"The Sultan,[a] in consequence of the rumors that the whole Russian fleet has left Sebastopol and is directing its course toward the Bosphorus, has inquired of the Ambassadors of England and France[b] whether, in the event of the Russians making a demonstration before the Bosphorus, the combined fleets are ready to pass the Dardanelles. Both answered in the affirmative. A Turkish steamer, with French and English officers on board, has just been sent from the Bosphorus to the Black Sea, in order to *reconnoitre.*"[c]

The first thing the Russians did after their entry into the Principalities, was to prohibit the publication of the Sultan's firman confirming the privileges of all kinds of Christians, and to suppress a German paper edited at Bucharest, which had dared to publish an article on the Eastern question. At the same time, they pressed from the Turkish Government the first annuity stipulated for their former occupation of Moldavia and Wallachia, in 1848-49. Since 1828 the Protectorate of Russia has cost the Principalities 150,000,000 piasters, beside the immense losses caused through pillage and devastation. England defrayed the expenses of Russia's wars against France, France that of her war against Persia, Persia that of her war against Turkey, Turkey and England that of her war against Poland; Hungary and the Principalities have now to pay her war against Turkey.

The most important event of the day is the new circular note of Count Nesselrode dated St. Petersburg, 20th June, 1853. It declares that the Russian armies will not evacuate the Principalities until the Sultan shall have yielded to all the demands of the Czar,[d] and the French and English fleets shall have left the Turkish waters. The note in question reads like a direct scorn of England and France. Thus it says:

"The position taken by the two maritime Powers is a maritime occupation which gives us a reason for reestablishing the equilibrium of the reciprocal situations by taking up a military position."[e]

Be it remarked, that Besika Bay is at a distance of 150 miles from Constantinople. The Czar claims for himself the right of occupying Turkish territory, while he defies England and France to occupy neutral waters without his special permission. He extols

---

[a] Abdul Mejid.—*Ed.*

[b] Stratford de Redcliffe and Edmond De la Cour.—*Ed.*

[c] Quoted from *The Morning Post,* No. 24821, July 11, 1853. Part of the passage is freely rendered.—*Ed.*

[d] Nicholas I.—*Ed.*

[e] Here and below Marx quotes from *The Times,* No. 21478, July 2, 1853.—*Ed.*

his own magnanimous forbearance in having left the Porte complete mistress of choosing under what form She will abdicate her sovereignty—whether "convention, sened, or other synallagmatic act, or even under the form of signing a simple note." He is persuaded that "impartial Europe" must understand that the treaty of Kainardji, which gives Russia the right of protecting a single Greek chapel at Stamboul,[150] proclaims her *eo ipso* the Rome of the Orient. He regrets that the West is ignorant of the inoffensive character of a Russian religious protectorate in foreign countries. He proves his solicitude for the integrity of the Turkish Empire by historical facts—"the very moderate use he made in 1829 of his victory of Adrianople," when he was only prevented from being immoderate by the miserable condition of his army, and by the threat of the English admiral, that, authorized or not authorized, he would bombard every coast-place along the Black Sea; when all he obtained was due to the "forbearance" of the Western Cabinets, and the perfidious destruction of the Turkish fleet at Navarino.[151]

"In 1833, he alone in Europe saved Turkey from inevitable dismemberment."

In 1833 the Czar concluded, through the famous treaty of Unkiar-Skelessi, *a defensive alliance* with Turkey, by which foreign fleets were forbidden to approach Constantinople,[152] by which Turkey was saved only from dismemberment, in order to be saved entire for Russia.

"In 1839 he took the initiative with the other Powers in the propositions which, executed in common, prevented the Sultan from seeing his throne give place to a new Arabian Empire."

That is to say, in 1839 he made the other Powers take the initiative in the destruction of the Egyptian fleet, and in the reduction to impotence of the only man[a] who might have converted Turkey into a vital danger to Russia, and replaced a "dressed up turban" by a real head.

"The fundamental principle of the policy of our august master has always been to maintain, as long as possible, the *status quo* of the East."

Just so. He has carefully preserved the decomposition of the Turkish State, under the exclusive guardianship of Russia.

It must be granted that a more ironical document the East has never dared to throw in the face of the West. But its author is

[a] Mohammed Ali.—*Ed.*

Nesselrode—a nettle, at once, and a rod.[a] It is a document, indeed, of Europe's degradation under the rod of counter-revolution. Revolutionists may congratulate the Czar on this masterpiece. If Europe withdraws, she withdraws not with a simple defeat, but passes, as it were, under *furcae Caudinae*.[153]

While the English Queen[b] is, at this moment, feasting Russian Princesses; while an enlightened English aristocracy and bourgeoisie lie prostrate before the barbarian autocrat, the English proletariat alone protests against the impotency and degradation of the ruling classes. On the 7th July the Manchester School held a great Peace meeting in the Odd-Fellows Hall, at Halifax. Crossley, M. P. for Halifax, and all the other "great men" of the School had especially flocked to the meeting from "town."[c] The hall was crowded, and many thousands could obtain no admittance. Ernest Jones (whose agitation in the factory districts is gloriously progressing, as you may infer from the number of Charter petitions presented to Parliament, and from the attacks of the middle-class provincial press), was, at the time, at Durham. The Chartists of Halifax, the place where he has twice been nominated and declared by show of hands[154] as a candidate for the House of Commons, summoned him by electric telegraph, and he appeared just in time for the meeting. Already the gentlemen of the Manchester School believed they would carry their resolution, and would be able to bring home the support of the manufacturing districts to their good Aberdeen, when Ernest Jones rose and put an amendment pledging the people to *war*, and declaring that before liberty was established peace was a crime. There ensued a most violent discussion, but the amendment of Ernest Jones was carried by an immense majority.

The clauses of the India Bill are passing one by one, the debate scarcely offering any remarkable features,[d] except the inconsistency of the so-called India Reformers. There is, for instance, my Lord Jocelyn, M. P., who has made a kind of political livelihood by his periodical denunciation of Indian wrongs, and of the maladministration of the East India Company. What do you think his amendment amounted to? To give the East India Company a lease for 10 years. Happily, it compromised no one but himself. There is another professional "Reformer," Mr. Jos. Hume, who,

---

[a] A pun: "Nessel" in German means "nettle" and "rode" reminds of "rod".—*Ed.*

[b] Victoria.—*Ed.*

[c] London.—*Ed.*

[d] The debate in the House of Commons on July 8, 1853.—*Ed.*

during his long Parliamentary life, has succeeded in transforming opposition itself into a particular manner of supporting the ministry. He proposed not to reduce the number of East India Directors from 24 to 18. The only amendment of common sense, yet agreed to, was that of Mr. Bright, exempting Directors nominated by the Government from the qualification in East India Stock, imposed by the Directors elected by the Court of Proprietors. Go through the pamphlets published by the East Indian Reform Association,[155] and you will feel a similar sensation as when, hearing of one great act of accusation against Bonaparte, devised in common by Legitimists, Orleanists, Blue and Red Republicans, and even disappointed Bonapartists. Their only merit until now has been to draw public attention to Indian affairs in general, and further they cannot go in their present form of eclectic opposition. For instance, while they attack the doings of the English aristocracy in India, they protest against the destruction of the Indian aristocracy of native princes.

After the British intruders had once put their feet on India, and made up their mind to hold it, there remained no alternative but to break the power of the native princes by force or by intrigue. Placed with regard to them in similar circumstances as the ancient Romans with regard to their allies, they followed in the track of Roman politics. "It was," says an English writer, "a system of fattening allies, as we fatten oxen, till they were worthy of being devoured." After having won over their allies in the way of ancient Rome, the East India Company executed them in the modern manner of Change-Alley.[156] In order to discharge the engagements they had entered into with the Company, the native princes were forced to borrow enormous sums from Englishmen at usurious interest. When their embarrassment had reached the highest pitch, the creditor got inexorable, "the screw was turned" and the princes were compelled either to concede their territories amicably to the Company, or to begin war; to become pensioners on their usurpers in one case, or to be deposed as traitors in the other. At this moment the native States occupy an area of 699,961 square miles, with a population of 52,941,263 souls, being, however, no longer the allies, but only the dependents of the British Government, upon multifarious conditions, and under the various forms of the subsidiary[157] and of the protective systems. These systems have in common the relinquishment, by the native States of the right of self-defense, of maintaining diplomatic relations, and of settling the disputes among themselves without the interference of the Governor-General. All of them have to pay a tribute, either in hard cash, or in a contingent of armed forces commanded by British officers. The final absorption or annexation of these native States is at present eagerly controverted between the Reformers who denounce it as a crime, and the men of business who excuse it as a necessity.

In my opinion the question itself is altogether improperly put. As to the native *States* they virtually ceased to exist from the moment they became subsidiary to or protected by the Company. If you divide the revenue of a country between two governments, you are sure to cripple the resources of the one and the administration of both. Under the present system the native States succumb under the double incubus of their native Administration and the tributes and inordinate military establishments imposed upon them by the Company. The conditions under which they are allowed to retain their apparent independence are at the same time the conditions of a permanent decay, and of an utter inability of improvement. Organic weakness is the constitutional law of their existence, as of all existences living upon sufferance. It is, therefore, not the native *States*, but the native *Princes* and Courts about whose maintenance the question revolves. Now, is it not a strange thing that the same men who denounce "the barbarous splendors of the Crown and Aristocracy of England" are shedding tears at the downfall of Indian Nabobs, Rajahs, and Jagheerdars,[158] the great majority of whom possess not even the prestige of antiquity, being generally usurpers of very recent date, set up by English intrigue! There exists in the whole world no despotism more ridiculous, absurd and childish than that of those *Schazenans* and *Schariars* of the *Arabian Nights*. The Duke of Wellington, Sir J. Malcolm, Sir Henry Russell, Lord Ellenborough, General Briggs, and other authorities, have pronounced in favor of the *status quo*; but on what grounds? Because the native troops under English rule want employment in the petty warfares with their own countrymen, in order to prevent them from turning their strength against their own European masters. Because the existence of independent States gives occasional employment to the English troops. Because the hereditary princes are the most servile tools of English despotism, and check the rise of those bold military adventurers with whom India has and ever will abound. Because the independent territories afford a refuge to all discontented and enterprising native spirits. Leaving aside all these arguments, which state in so many words that the native princes are the strongholds of the present abominable English system and the greatest obstacles to Indian progress, I come to Sir Thomas

Munro and Lord Elphinstone, who were at least men of superior genius, and of real sympathy for the Indian people. They think that without a native aristocracy there can be no energy in any other class of the community, and that the subversion of that aristocracy will not raise but debase a whole people. They may be right as long as the natives, under direct English rule, are systematically excluded from all superior offices, military and civil. Where there can be no great men by their own exertion, there must be great men by birth, to leave to a conquered people some greatness of their own. That exclusion, however, of the native people from the English territory, has been effected only by the maintenance of the hereditary princes in the so-called independent territories. And one of these two concessions had to be made to the native army, on whose strength all British rule in India depends. I think we may trust the assertion of Mr. Campbell, that the native Indian Aristocracy are the least enabled to fill higher offices; that for all fresh requirements it is necessary to create a fresh class; and that

"from the acuteness and aptness to learn of the inferior classes, this can be done in India as it can be done in no other country."[a]

The native princes themselves are fast disappearing by the extinction of their houses; but, since the commencement of this century, the British Government has observed the policy of allowing them to make *heirs by adoption*, or of filling up their vacant seats with puppets of English creation. The great Governor-General, Lord Dalhousie, was the first to protest openly against this system. Were not the natural course of things artificially resisted, there would be wanted neither wars nor expenses to do away with the native princes.

As to the *pensioned princes*, the £2,468,969 assigned to them by the British Government on the Indian revenue is a most heavy charge upon a people living on rice, and deprived of the first necessaries of life. If they are good for any thing, it is for exhibiting Royalty in its lowest stage of degradation and ridicule. Take, for instance, the Great Mogul,[b] the descendant of Timour Tamerlane[159]: He is allowed £120,000 a year. His authority does not extend beyond the walls of his palace, within which the Royal idiotic race, left to itself, propagates as freely as rabbits. Even the police of Delhi is held by Englishmen above his control. There he

[a] G. Campbell, *Modern India: a Sketch of the System of Civil Government*, p. 64.—*Ed.*

[b] Bahadur Shah II.—*Ed.*

sits on his throne, a little shriveled yellow old man, trimmed in a theatrical dress, embroidered with gold, much like that of the dancing girls of Hindostan. On certain State occasions, the tinsel-covered puppet issues forth to gladden the hearts of the loyal. On his days of reception strangers have to pay a fee, in the form of guineas, as to any other *saltimbanque* exhibiting himself in public; while he, in his turn, presents them with turbans, diamonds, etc. On looking nearer at them, they find that the Royal diamonds are, like so many pieces of ordinary glass, grossly painted and imitating as roughly as possible the precious stones, and jointed so wretchedly, that they break in the hand like gingerbread.

The English money-lenders, combined with the English Aristocracy, understand, we must own, the art of degrading Royalty, reducing it to the nullity of constitutionalism at home, and to the seclusion of etiquette abroad. And now, here are the Radicals, exasperated at this spectacle! [a]

Written on July 12, 1853

First published in the *New-York Daily Tribune*, No. 3828, July 25, 1853; reprinted in the *New-York Semi-Weekly Tribune*, No. 852, July 26, 1853

Signed: *Karl Marx*

Reproduced from the *New-York Daily Tribune*

[a] This sentence was omitted in the *New-York Semi-Weekly Tribune*.—*Ed.*

Karl Marx

WAR IN BURMA.—THE RUSSIAN QUESTION.—CURIOUS DIPLOMATIC CORRESPONDENCE[160]

London, Friday, July 15, 1853

By the latest overland mail from India, intelligence has been received that the Burmese ambassadors have rejected the treaty proposed by General Godwin. The General afforded them 24 hours more for reflection, but the Burmese departed within 10 hours. A third edition of the interminable Burmese war appears to be inevitable.[161]

Of all the warlike expeditions of the British in the East, none have ever been undertaken on less warranted grounds than those against Burma. There was no possible danger of invasion from that side, as there was from the North-West, Bengal being separated from Burma by a range of mountains, across which troops cannot be marched. To go to war with Burma the Indian Government is obliged to go to sea. To speak of maritime aggressions on the part of the Burmese is as ridiculous, as the idea of their coast-junks fronting the Company's war steamers would be preposterous. The pretension that the Yankees had strong annexation propensities applied to Pegu, is borne out by no facts. No argument, therefore, remains behind, but the want of employment for a needy aristocracy, the necessity of creating, as an English writer says, "a regular quality-workhouse, or Hampton Court[a] in the East." The first Burmese war (1824-26), entered into under the Quixotic administration of Lord Amherst, although it lasted little more than two years, added thirteen millions to the Indian debt. The maintenance of the Eastern settlements at

[a] A palace on the Thames near London, the residence of the English kings from the 16th to the 18th centuries; in Marx's time it was the home of royal pensioners.— *Ed.*

Singapore, Penang and Malacca, exclusive of the pay of troops, causes an annual excess of expenditure over income amounting to £100,000. The territory taken from the Burmese in 1826 costs as much more. The territory of Pegu is still more ruinous. Now, why is it that England shrinks from the most necessary war in Europe, as now against Russia, while she tumbles, year after year, into the most reckless wars in Asia? The national debt has made her a trembler in Europe—the charges of the Asiatic wars are thrown on the shoulders of the Hindoos. But we may expect from the now impending extinction of the Opium revenue of Bengal, combined with the expenses of another Burmese war, that they will produce such a crisis in the Indian exchequer, as will cause a more thorough reform of the Indian Empire than all the speeches and tracts of the Parliamentary Reformers in England.

Yesterday, in the House of Commons, Mr. Disraeli asked Ministers, whether, after the latest circular note of the Russian Cabinet, Mr. Layard might not very properly bring in his motion. Lord John Russell answered, that it appeared to him by far the best not to hear Mr. Layard at present, as, since the publication of that note, it was more important than ever to negotiate. "The notion of the honorable member, that negotiations had come now to a deadlock, was an erroneous notion." Lord John, while actually confessing his Aberdeen *credo,* attempted to re-vindicate the dignity of the *civis Romanus sum*[162] party in the following words:

> "I naturally supposed that a person of the experience and sagacity of Count Nesselrode, would not have affixed his signature to a document declaring to all the world that the Russian Government made the removal of the combined fleets the condition of its evacuation of the Principalities."[a]

In the subsequent Indian debate Mr. Bright moved, that from the ninth clause which provides, "that six of the directors not elected by the Crown, shall be persons who have been ten years in India in the service of the Crown or the Company," the words, "in the service of the Crown or the Company," should be expunged. The amendment was agreed to. It is significant, that during the whole Indian debate no amendments are agreed to by the Ministry, and consequently carried by the House, except those of Mr. Bright. The Peace Ministry, at this moment does everything to secure its *entente cordiale*[163] with the Peace party, Manchester School,[164] who are opposed to any kind of warfare, except by cotton bales and price currents.

---

[a] Quoted from *The Times*, No. 21481, July 15, 1853.—*Ed.*

M. Drouyn de Lhuys, the French Minister of Foreign Affairs, once upper clerk at the Foreign Office under M. Guizot, and declared by his *chef*, to possess hardly the necessary qualifications for that place, is now indulging freely in the pleasure of exchanging notes and circulars with Count Nesselrode. The *Moniteur* of yesterday brings his reply to the last (2d) *circulaire* of the Russian Minister,[165] which concludes in the following terms:

"The moderation of France takes from her all responsibility, and gives her the right to hope that all the sacrifices which she has made to secure the tranquillity of the East will not have been in vain; that the Russian Government will at length discover some mode of reconciling its pretensions with the prerogatives of the Sultan's sovereignty; and that an arrangement [...] be devised that shall settle, without a resort to force, a question, on the solution of which so many interests are dependent."[a]

I mentioned in a former letter the propositions once made by M. de Villèle to Russia, for the maintenance of the integrity of the Ottoman Empire, by a treaty of guarantee between all the Great Powers,[b] propositions which called forth this reply from Count Pozzo di Borgo:

"That a general guarantee of the Ottoman Empire, independently of its being unusual and surprising, would wound the rights acquired by Russia and the principles upon which they are founded."[c]

Well, in 1841, Russia nevertheless agreed to become party to such an unusual treaty,[166] and Nesselrode himself, in his note of 20th June (2d July) refers to that treaty. Why did Russia assent to it, in contradiction to its traditional policy? Because that treaty was not one of "guarantee of the Ottoman Empire," but rather of execution against its then only vital element, Egypt, under Mehemet Ali—because it was a coalition against France, at least in its original intention.

The Paris journal *La Presse* gives in its number of to-day, which has just come to my hands, a correspondence never before published between the late General Sébastiani, Ambassador in London, and Mme. Adélaide, sister of Louis Philippe, a correspondence which reflects a remarkable light on the diplomatic transactions of that epoch. It contains clear proofs that the Treaty of 1841, far from having been originated by Russia, as Nesselrode affirms in his note, was, on the contrary, originated by France and England against Russia, and was only afterward turned by Russia

[a] Quoted from *The Morning Post*, No. 24825, July 15, 1853.—*Ed.*
[b] See this volume, pp. 163-64.—*Ed.*
[c] Quoted from *The Portfolio*, Vol. I, No. II, pp. 130-31.—*Ed.*

into a weapon against France. I translate from this important correspondence as much as the pressure of time permits me to do:

I[a]

London, April 21, 1836

In this country all parties are unanimous as to the necessity of closely watching Russia, and I believe that the Tory party is more decided than the Whigs, or at least it seems so, because it is not moderated by office.

II

London, June 12, 1838

I have had to-day a conference of two hours' duration with Lord Palmerston. I have been highly satisfied with him. I was not mistaken in assuring you that he was a friend of King Leopold, and above all a great partisan of the French Alliance. Lord Palmerston has conversed a great deal with me on Oriental affairs. He thinks that the Pasha of Egypt is decided as to his course of action. He wishes that England and France should make fresh efforts, supported by the presence of their fleets, in order to intimidate Mehemet, and that simultaneously our Ambassadors at Constantinople should inform the Sultan[b] that they have received orders from their Courts to assure him of their support against the attempts of the Pasha of Egypt, under the condition that he would not take the initiative in hostilities. I believe this to be a prudent course, and advisable to be followed by England and France. We must maintain the Porte and not suffer the Provinces of Egypt, Syria and Celesyria to become detached from it. Russia only awaits for the moment for marching up her succours to the Sultan, and that *assistance would be the end of the Ottoman Empire.*

III

London, July 6, 1838

People in this country believe in the general understanding of Europe as to the Oriental question. The answer from Paris is impatiently looked for. I think not to have surpassed the line of conduct traced to me by the King in several conversations. As soon as the *entente* shall be established in principle, the manner of action and the position to be taken up by each of the Powers, will be regulated according to contingencies. The part Russia has to play must, of course, be maritime, like that of France and England, and in order to prevent any danger that might result from the action of the fleet in the Black Sea, she must be brought to the understanding that her squadron in the combined fleet is to be drawn from the Baltic.

---

[a] In the *New-York Daily Tribune* this document was published under No. II after the extract from H. Sébastiani's letter of June 12, 1838, which was erroneously datelined June 12, 1835. Here it is published as printed in *La Presse* of July 15, 1853.—*Ed.*

[b] Mahmud II.—*Ed.*

IV

London, October 3, 1839

England has not accepted the Russian propositions,[167] and Lord Palmerston informed me, on the part of the Government, that she had refused, in order to remain true to the French Alliance. Induced by the same feeling she consents that Mehemet Ali shall receive the hereditary possession of Egypt, and of that portion of Syria within a boundary to be demarked, which should go from St. Jean d'Acre, to the lake of Tabariye. We have, not without difficulty, obtained the assent of the English Government to these latter propositions. I do not think that such an arrangement would be rejected by either France or Mehemet Ali. The Oriental question simplifies itself; it will be terminated by the concurrence of the Powers, and under the guaranty of the integrity of the Ottoman Empire. All the principles are maintained. The Sublime Porte is admitted to the law of nations of Europe. *The exclusive protectorate of Russia is annihilated.* I have asked myself why the Republican faction in France showed itself so favorable to Mehemet Ali, and why it has so warmly espoused his cause. I have not been able to find out any other motive, but the revolutionary principle, that of trying to support, to encourage all that is likely to subvert established governments. I believe we ought never to give in to such a snare.

V

London, November 30, 1839

I learn from an authentic source, that Lord Palmerston, in the last council of Ministers, in giving an account of the situation of Oriental affairs, and of the differences existing between the French and English policies, did so with a moderation and a regard for the alliance of both countries, that deserve our gratitude. He has even drawn the attention of his colleagues to a system similar to that mentioned by me. In conclusion he has yielded as to forms, and has renounced a policy of action and of inevitable complication.

VI

London, Dec. 12, 1839

I have seen Lord Palmerston, as I was anxious to know, whether he had to inform me of anything respecting the communication he recently made to me. He has read to me the letter of *M. de Nesselrode* to the Russian *Chargé d'Affaires*, which corresponded exactly to what he had told me. The arrival of *M. de Brunnow* will initiate us into the secret thoughts of the Cabinet of St. Petersburg. Lord Palmerston has been charming in forms and in matter. He views with pleasure the return of good feelings between the French and English Cabinets, and the continuation of the alliance. Believe me, I do not exaggerate in this. I told him with the confidence of truth, that the new situation was exactly such as France had ever wished it to be. He was forced to recognize it himself. The Prince of Esterházy has written to his Chargé d'Affaires that he had been extremely content with the Marshal,[a] and that he was trying at this moment to bring back the French Cabinet to

[a] N. Soult, Prime Minister of France.— *Ed.*

an *entente* with Austria, but that he had found the King *unmanageable.* I can well believe it. The King does not lend his mind to such impracticable divagations. This I write for you alone. Indeed, I believe with your Royal Highness that *Russia will be caught in her own nets*

VII

London, December 18th, 1839

I have received this morning a dispatch, more than usually strange, from the Marshal. It is an answer to the letter in which I reported to him on the communication I made to Lord Palmerston, in regard to the impression evoked at Paris on the announcement of the new mission of M. de Brunnow, and of its aim. I have read to Lord Palmerston *textuellement* the paragraph of the dispatch addressed to me by the Marshal. But in the statement I made to him about it, I made use of such terms as rendered the same ideas without being identical with those of the Marshal. Now the Marshal is kind enough to assure me that there was no difference between my words and his own expression; but he recommends me that I ought to double my circumspection and endeavor to reestablish in our negotiations the textual meaning of his own dispatches. I am much mistaken if this be not a *querelle allemande,*[a] a subtlety worthy of a *Grec du Bas-Empire*[b].... The Marshal is a novice in the career of diplomacy, and I fear that he seeks ability in fineness. He can find it only in sincerity and straightforwardness.

VIII

London, Jan. 3, 1840

Yesterday Lord Palmerston dined with me, in common with the whole *Corps Diplomatique*.... He told me that Ministers were going to ask for a supplementary vote for their naval forces, but he stated that he would propose to his colleagues not to demand it on account of the reinforcements of the French fleet, in order to avoid wounding an ally by the least allusion. Lord Holland and Lord John Russell are admirable in their efforts for maintaining the alliance.

IX

London, Jan. 20, 1840

Lord Palmerston has communicated to me the project of a convention to be submitted to the Great Powers and to the Porte.... It is not a convention of the five Great Powers between themselves, but a convention of those same Powers with the Porte.... *M. de Brunnow objects to that form* (see Nesselrode's note, dated 2d July, inst., about the Russian initiative!).... This convention consists of a preamble and VIII articles: in the former it is stated in a positive manner, and almost textually, that the integrity of the Ottoman Empire being essentially necessary for the maintenance of the peace of Europe, the five Powers are disposed to lend it the requisite support and to make it enter into the international confidence of Europe. The articles regulate that support....

---

[a] Literally: German quarrel; figuratively: groundless quarrel.—*Ed.*
[b] A Byzantine of the Eastern Roman Empire.—*Ed.*

P.S.—I learn, at this moment, that *Brunnow and Neumann are utterly discontented with the convention of Lord Palmerston.*

X

London, January 21, 1840

The project of convention drawn up by Lord Palmerston appears to me to have been rejected by the Russian and Austrian negotiators. *M. de Neumann* distinguished himself by the violence, and, I venture to say, the stupidity of his complaints. He unveils the policy of his Court. Prince Metternich, who intended to sustain in his hands the balance of power, openly avows his hatred of Russia. He flattered himself to see the propositions of Brunnow received without restrictions, and both have been disappointed to find in Lord Palmerston a Minister who desires sincerely an alliance with France, and who is anxious to operate in understanding with her.

XI

London, Jan. 24, 1840

To-day I had a long conversation with Lord Melbourne, who is a thorough partisan of the alliance with our King. He repeatedly called upon me to show him some means by which a combination of the French and English propositions could be effected.

He judges in the same light as we do the intentions of Russia, and he told me, in a conference with regard to the *Vienna Cabinet, that it was not to be trusted, because it ever turned out in the end, to be the devoted partisan of Russia.*

XII

London, January 27, 1840

The turn now being taken by the Oriental affairs is alarming to me.... There is no doubt that Russia is pushing to war, and that Austria supports her with all her forces.... They have succeeded in frightening England with the "projects of France on the Mediterranean." Algiers and Mehemet Ali are the two means employed by them.... I make all possible efforts to obtain the rejection of the Brunnow propositions, and I had narrowly succeeded in it, when they heard of it, and Austria now presents the Brunnow propositions as her own. This is an evident trickery. But the Council has been convoked, in order to deliberate on the Austrian propositions. It is divided. On the one side, there are Lord Melbourne, Lord Holland and Mr. Labouchere; on the other, Lord Palmerston, Lord J. Russell, and Lord Minto. The other members are fluctuating between the two opinions.

XIII

London, January 28, 1840

The Council has hitherto only deliberated on one point of the project of Lord Palmerston. It has decided that the Convention should be contracted between six, and not between five (powers), as proposed by *M. de Brunnow,* who was not wanting in zeal for his particular interests (solicitude for the Ottoman Empire). The Porte would not consent to a Convention discussed and settled without its cooperation. *By signing a Treaty with the five Great Powers she would come in consequence of this fact itself under the European law of nations.*

XIV

London, 28th January, 1840

Are the politics and the interest of the King given up to the caprices of M. Thiers and his newspaper[a]? The system founded with so great pains, with such efforts, and maintained, notwithstanding so many difficulties, for more than ten years, is doomed to destruction.

Written on July 15, 1853

First published in the *New-York Daily Tribune,* No. 3833, July 30, 1853; reprinted in the *New-York Semi-Weekly Tribune,* No. 854, August 2, 1853

Reproduced from the *New-York Daily Tribune*

Signed: *Karl Marx*

[a] *Le Constitutionnel.—Ed.*

Karl Marx

THE WAR QUESTION.— DOINGS OF PARLIAMENT.—INDIA[168]

London, Tuesday, July 19, 1853

The Czar[a] has not only commenced war, he has already terminated his first campaign. The line of operations is no longer behind the Pruth, but along the Danube. Meanwhile, what are the Western Powers about? They counsel, i.e. compel the Sultan[b] to consider the war as peace. Their answers to the acts of the autocrat are not cannons, but notes. The Emperor is assailed, not by the two fleets, but by no less than four projects of negotiation. One emanating from the English Cabinet, the other from the French, the third presented by Austria, and the fourth improvised by the "brother-in-law" of Potsdam.[c] The Czar, it is hoped, will consent to select from this *embarras de richesses* that which is most suitable to his purposes. The (second) reply of M. Drouyn de Lhuys to the (second) note of M. de Nesselrode[169] takes infinite pains to prove that "it was not England and France who made the first demonstration."[d] Russia only throws out so many notes to the western diplomats, like bones to dogs, in order to set them at an innocent amusement, while she reaps the advantage of further gaining time. England and France, of course, catch the bait. As if the receipt of such a note were not a sufficient degradation, it [the note] received a most pacific comment in the *Journal de l'Empire* in an article signed by M. de La Guéronnière, but written from notes given by the Emperor and revised by him. That article "would permit to Russia the caprice of negotiating on the right bank rather

[a] Nicholas I.—*Ed.*
[b] Abdul Mejid.—*Ed.*
[c] Frederick William IV.—*Ed.*
[d] Quoted from *Le Moniteur universel*, No. 198, July 17, 1853.—*Ed.*

than on the left bank of the Pruth." It actually converts the second note of Count Nesselrode into an "attempt at reconciliation." This is done in the following style:

"Count Nesselrode now speaks only of a moral guarantee, and he announces that, for it, is substituted provisionally a material guarantee *thus making a direct appeal to negotiation.* That being the case it is impossible to consider the action of diplomatists exhausted."[a]

The *Assemblée nationale*, the Russian *Moniteur* at Paris, ironically congratulates the *Journal de l'Empire* for its discovery, however late it had come to it, and regrets only that so much noise should have been made to no purpose.[b]

The English press has lost all countenance.

"The Czar cannot comprehend the courtesy which the Western Powers have shown to him.... He is incapable of courteous demeanor in his transactions with other powers."

So says *The Morning Advertiser*.[c] *The Morning Post* is exasperated because the Czar takes so little note of the internal *embarras* of his opponents:

"To have put forward, in the mere wantonness of insolence, a claim that possessed no character of immediate urgency, and to have done so without any reference to the inflammable state of Europe, was an indiscretion almost incredible."[d]

The writer of the Money Market article in *The Economist* finds out

"that men discover now to their cost, how inconvenient it is that all the most secret interests of the world [i.e., of the Exchange], are dependent upon the vagaries of one man."[e]

Yet in 1848 and '49 you could see the bust of the Emperor of Russia side by side with the *veau d'or*[f] itself.

Meanwhile the position of the Sultan is becoming every hour more difficult and complicated. His financial embarrassments increase the more, as he bears all the burdens, without reaping any of the good chances of war. Popular enthusiasm turns round

---

[a] *Le Pays*, No. 197, July 16, 1853.—*Ed.*

[b] See A. Letellier's article in *L'Assemblée nationale*, No. 198, July 17, 1853.—*Ed.*

[c] *The Morning Advertiser*, July 18, 1853.—*Ed.*

[d] "The Question Between Russia and Turkey...", *The Morning Post*, No. 24827, July 18, 1853.—*Ed.*

[e] *The Economist*, No. 516, July 16, 1853.—*Ed.*

[f] Golden calf.—*Ed.*

upon him for want of being directed against the Czar. The fanaticism of the Mussulman threatens him with palace revolutions, while the fanaticism of the Greek menaces him with popular insurrections. The papers of to-day contain reports of a conspiracy directed against the Sultan's life by Mussulman students belonging to the old Turkish party, who wanted to place Abdul Aziz on the throne.[170]

In the House of Lords, yesterday, Lord Clarendon was asked by Lords Beaumont and Malmesbury to state his intentions, now that the Emperor of France had not hesitated to pronounce his. Lord Clarendon, however, beside a brief avowal that England had indorsed the note of M. Drouyn de Lhuys, concealed himself behind his entrenchment of promises that he would certainly very soon give full information to the House. On the question whether it was true that the Russians had also seized the Civil Government and the Post-Offices of the Principalities, which they had placed under military occupation, Lord Clarendon remained "silent," of course! "He would not believe it, after the proclamation of Prince Gorchakoff."[171] Lord Beaumont replied, he seemed to be very sanguine indeed.

To a question concerning the late Smyrna affray,[a] put by Sir J. Walmsley in the House of Commons, Lord John Russell replied that he had heard indeed of the kidnapping of one Hungarian refugee[b] by the Consul of Austria[c]; but as to Austria having demanded the extradition of all Hungarian and Italian refugees, he had certainly heard nothing of that. Lord John manages interpellations in a style altogether pleasant and not without convenience to himself. Official information he never receives; and in the newspapers he never reads anything that you want him, or expect him to have read.

The *Kölnische Zeitung* in a letter dated Vienna, July 11, contains the following report on the Smyrna affair:

"Chekib Effendi has been sent to Smyrna in order to commence an instruction against the authors of the sedition in which M. de Hackelberg perished. Chekib has also received orders to deliver to Austria the refugees of Austrian or Tuscan origin. Mr. Brown, Chargé d'Affaires of the United States, has had communications on this subject with Reshid Pasha, the result of which was not yet known. I hear at this moment that the assassin of Baron Hackelberg has received from the American Consul at Smyrna a passport that places him out of the reach of the Turkish authorities. *This fact proves that the United States intend intervening in European affairs.* It is also sure that three American men-of-war are with the

---

[a] See this volume, p. 193.—*Ed.*
[b] M. Koszta.—*Ed.*
[c] Weckbecker.—*Ed.*

Turkish fleet in the Bosphorus, and further, that the American frigate *Cumberland* has brought 80,000,000 of piasters to the Turkish Government."[a]

Whatever truth there be in this and like reports, they prove one thing, viz.: that American intervention is expected everywhere, and is even looked upon with favor by portions of the English public. The behavior of the American Captain[b] and Consul are loudly praised in popular meetings, and the "Englishman"[c] in *The Advertiser* of yesterday called the Stars and Stripes to appear in the Mediterranean and to shame the "muddy old Union Jack" into activity.

To sum up the Eastern question in a few words: The Czar, vexed and dissatisfied at seeing his immense Empire confined to one sole port of export, and that even situated in a sea innavigable through one half of the year, and assailable by Englishmen through the other half, is pushing the design of his ancestors, to get access to the Mediterranean; he is separating, one after another, the remotest members of the Ottoman Empire from its main body, till at last Constantinople, the heart, must cease to beat. He repeats his periodical invasions as often as he thinks his designs on Turkey endangered by the apparent consolidation of the Turkish Government, or by the more dangerous symptoms of self-emancipation manifest amongst the Slavonians. Counting on the cowardice and apprehensions of the Western Powers, he bullies Europe, and pushes his demands as far as possible, in order to appear magnanimous afterward, by contenting himself with what he immediately wanted.

The Western Powers, on the other hand, inconsistent, pusillanimous, suspecting each other, commence by encouraging the Sultan to resist the Czar, from fear of the encroachments of Russia, and terminate by compelling the former to yield, from fear of a general war giving rise to a general revolution. Too impotent and too timid to undertake the reconstruction of the Ottoman Empire by the establishment of a Greek Empire, or of a Federal Republic of Slavonic States, all they aim at, is to maintain the *status quo*, i.e., the state of putrefaction which forbids the Sultan to emancipate himself from the Czar, and the Slavonians to emancipate themselves from the Sultan.

The revolutionary party can only congratulate itself on this state of things. The humiliation of the reactionary western governments, and their manifest impotency to guard the interests of

[a] *Kölnische Zeitung*, No. 193, July 14, 1853.—*Ed.*
[b] D. N. Ingraham.—*Ed.*
[c] A. Richards.—*Ed.*

European civilization against Russian encroachment cannot fail to work out a wholesome indignation in the people who have suffered themselves, since 1849, to be subjected to the rule of counter-revolution. The approaching industrial crisis, also, is affected and accelerated quite as much by this semi-Eastern complication, as by the completely Eastern complication of China. While the prices of corn are rising, business in general is suspended, at the same time that the rate of Exchange is setting against England, and gold is beginning to flow to the Continent. The stock of bullion in the Bank of France has fallen off between the 9th of June and the 14th of July, the sum of £2,220,000, which is more than the entire augmentation which had taken place during the preceding three months.

The progress of the India bill through the Committee has little interest. It is significant, that all amendments are thrown out now by the Coalition coalescing with the Tories against their own allies of the Manchester School.

The actual state of India may be illustrated by a few facts. The Home Establishment absorbs 3 per cent. of the net revenue, and the annual interest for Home Debt and Dividends 14 per cent.—together 17 per cent. If we deduct these annual remittances from India to England, the *military charges* amount to about two-thirds of the whole expenditure available for India, or to 66 per cent., while the charges for *Public Works* do not amount to more than $2^3/_4$ per cent. of the general revenue, or for Bengal 1 per cent., Agra $7^3/_4$, Punjab $^1/_8$, Madras $^1/_2$, and Bombay 1 per cent. of their respective revenues. These figures are the official ones of the Company itself.

On the other hand nearly three-fifths of the whole net revenue are derived from the *land*, about one-seventh from *opium*, and upward of one-ninth from *salt*. These resources together yield 85 per cent. of the whole receipts.

As to minor items of receipts and charges, it may suffice to state that the *Moturpha* revenue maintained in the Presidency of Madras, and levied on shops, looms, sheep, cattle, sundry professions, &c., yields somewhat about £50,000, while the yearly dinners of the East India House[a] cost about the same sum.

The great bulk of the revenue is derived from the land. As the various kinds of Indian land-tenure have recently been described in so many places, and in popular style, too, I propose to limit my

[a] Residence of the Court of Directors of the East India Company in Leadenhall Street in London.—*Ed.*

observations on the subject to a few general remarks on the Zemindari and Ryotwar systems.[172]

The Zemindari and the Ryotwar were both of them agrarian revolutions, effected by British ukases, and opposed to each other, the one aristocratic, the other democratic; the one a caricature of English landlordism, the other of French peasant-proprietorship; but pernicious, both combining the most contradictory character—both made not for the people, who cultivate the soil, nor for the holder, who owns it, but for the Government that taxes it.

By the Zemindari system, the people of the Presidency of Bengal were depossessed at once of their hereditary claims to the soil, in favor of the native tax gatherers called *Zemindars*. By the Ryotwar system introduced into the Presidencies of Madras and Bombay, the native nobility, with their territorial claims, merassees, jagheers, &c., were reduced with the common people to the holding of minute fields, cultivated by themselves in favor of the Collector of the East India Company.[173] But a curious sort of English landlord was the Zemindar, receiving only one-tenth of the rent, while he had to make over nine-tenths of it to the Government. A curious sort of French peasant was the Ryot, without any permanent title in the soil, and with the taxation changing every year in proportion to his harvest. The original class of Zemindars, notwithstanding their unmitigated and uncontrolled rapacity against the depossessed mass of the ex-hereditary landholders, soon melted away under the pressure of the Company, in order to be replaced by mercantile speculators who now hold all the land of Bengal, with exception of the estates returned under the direct management of the Government. These speculators have introduced a variety of the Zemindari tenure called *patnee*. Not content to be placed with regard to the British Government in the situation of middlemen, they have created in their turn a class of "hereditary" middlemen called *patnetas*, who created again their sub-patnetas, &c., so that a perfect scale of hierarchy of middlemen has sprung up, which presses with its entire weight on the unfortunate cultivator. As to the Ryots in Madras and Bombay, the system soon degenerated into one of forced cultivation, and the land lost all its value.

"The land," says Mr. Campbell, "would be sold for balances by the Collector, as in Bengal, but generally is not, for a very good reason, viz.: that nobody will buy it."[a]

---

[a] G. Campbell, *Modern India: a Sketch of the System of Civil Government*, p. 359.—*Ed.*

Thus, in Bengal, we have a combination of English landlordism, of the Irish middlemen system, of the Austrian system, transforming the landlord into the tax-gatherer, and of the Asiatic system making the State the real landlord. In Madras and Bombay we have a French peasant proprietor who is at the same time a serf, and a *métayer* of the State. The drawbacks of all these various systems accumulate upon him without his enjoying any of their redeeming features. The Ryot is subject, like the French peasant, to the extortion of the private usurer; but he has no hereditary, no permanent title in his land, like the French peasant. Like the serf he is forced to cultivation, but he is not secured against want like the serf. Like the *métayer* he has to divide his produce with the State, but the State is not obliged, with regard to him, to advance the funds and the stock, as it is obliged to do with regard to the *métayer*. In Bengal, as in Madras and Bombay, under the *Zemindari* as under the *Ryotwar*, the Ryots—and they form 11-12ths of the whole Indian population—have been wretchedly pauperized; and if they are, morally speaking, not sunk as low as the Irish cottiers, they owe it to their climate, the men of the South being possessed of less wants, and of more imagination than the men of the North.

Conjointly with the land-tax we have to consider the salt-tax. Notoriously the Company retain the monopoly of that article which they sell at three times its mercantile value—and this in a country where it is furnished by the sea, by the lakes, by the mountains and the earth itself. The practical working of this monopoly was described by the Earl of Albemarle in the following words:

> "A great proportion of the salt for inland consumption throughout the country is purchased from the Company by large wholesale merchants at less than 4 rupees per *maund*[a]; these mix a fixed proportion of sand, chiefly got a few miles to the south-east of Dacca, and send the mixture to a second, or, counting the Government as the first, to a third monopolist at about 5 or 6 rupees. This dealer adds more earth or ashes, and thus passing through more hands, from the large towns to villages, the price is still raised from 8 to 10 rupees and the proportion of adulteration from 25 to 40 per cent. [...] It appears then that the people [...] pay from £21, 17s. 2d. to £27, 6s. 2d. for their salt, or in other words, from 30 to 36 times as much as the wealthy people of Great Britain."[b]

As an instance of English bourgeois morals, I may allege, that Mr. Campbell defends the Opium monopoly because it prevents

---

[a] Asiatic measure of weight of varying value (Indian standard $\approx 82^2/_7$ lb.).—*Ed.*

[b] Marx gives a rendering of George Albemarle's speech in the House of Lords on July 1, 1853, published in *The Times*, No. 21470, July 2, 1853.—*Ed.*

the Chinese from consuming too much of the drug, and that he defends the Brandy monopoly (licenses for spirit-selling in India) because it has wonderfully increased the consumption of Brandy in India.

The Zemindar tenure, the Ryotwar, and the salt tax, combined with the Indian climate, were the hotbeds of the cholera—India's ravages upon the Western World—a striking and severe example of the solidarity of human woes and wrongs.

Written on July 19, 1853

First published in the *New-York Daily Tribune*, No. 3838, August 5, 1853

Signed: *Karl Marx*

Reproduced from the newspaper

Karl Marx

THE FUTURE RESULTS OF BRITISH RULE IN INDIA

London, Friday, July 22, 1853

I propose in this letter to conclude my observations on India.

How came it that English supremacy was established in India? The paramount power of the Great Mogul was broken by the Mogul Viceroys. The power of the Viceroys was broken by the Mahrattas.[174] The power of the Mahrattas was broken by the Afghans, and while all were struggling against all, the Briton rushed in and was enabled to subdue them all. A country not only divided between Mahommedan and Hindoo, but between tribe and tribe, between caste and caste; a society whose framework was based on a sort of equilibrium, resulting from a general repulsion and constitutional exclusiveness between all its members. Such a country and such a society, were they not the predestined prey of conquest? If we knew nothing of the past history of Hindostan, would there not be the one great and incontestable fact, that even at this moment India is held in English thraldom by an Indian army maintained at the cost of India? India, then, could not escape the fate of being conquered, and the whole of her past history, if it be anything, is the history of the successive conquests she has undergone. Indian society has no history at all, at least no known history. What we call its history, is but the history of the successive intruders who founded their empires on the passive basis of that unresisting and unchanging society. The question, therefore, is not whether the English had a right to conquer India, but whether we are to prefer India conquered by the Turk, by the Persian, by the Russian, to India conquered by the Briton.

England has to fulfill a double mission in India: one destructive, the other regenerating—the annihilation of old Asiatic society, and the laying the material foundations of Western society in Asia.

Arabs, Turks, Tartars, Moguls, who had successively overrun India, soon became *Hindooized*, the barbarian conquerors being, by an eternal law of history, conquered themselves by the superior civilization of their subjects. The British were the first conquerors superior, and therefore, inaccessible to Hindoo civilization. They destroyed it by breaking up the native communities, by uprooting the native industry, and by levelling all that was great and elevated in the native society. The historic pages of their rule in India report hardly anything beyond that destruction. The work of regeneration hardly transpires through a heap of ruins. Nevertheless it has begun.

The political unity of India, more consolidated, and extending farther than it ever did under the Great Moguls, was the first condition of its regeneration. That unity, imposed by the British sword, will now be strengthened and perpetuated by the electric telegraph. The native army, organized and trained by the British drill-sergeant, was the *sine qua non* of Indian self-emancipation, and of India ceasing to be the prey of the first foreign intruder. The free press, introduced for the first time into Asiatic society, and managed principally by the common offspring of Hindoos and Europeans, is a new and powerful agent of reconstruction. The Zemindari and Ryotwar[175] themselves, abominable as they are, involve two distinct forms of private property in land—the great desideratum of Asiatic society. From the Indian natives, reluctantly and sparingly educated at Calcutta, under English superintendence, a fresh class is springing up, endowed with the requirements for government and imbued with European science. Steam has brought India into regular and rapid communication with Europe, has connected its chief ports with those of the whole south-eastern ocean, and has revindicated it from the isolated position which was the prime law of its stagnation. The day is not far distant when, by a combination of railways and steam-vessels, the distance between England and India, measured by time, will be shortened to eight days, and when that once fabulous country will thus be actually annexed to the Western world.

The ruling classes of Great Britain have had, till now, but an accidental, transitory and exceptional interest in the progress of India. The aristocracy wanted to conquer it, the moneyocracy to plunder it, and the millocracy to undersell it. But now the tables are turned. The millocracy have discovered that the transformation of India into a reproductive country has become of vital importance to them, and that, to that end, it is necessary, above all, to gift her with means of irrigation and of internal communication. They intend now drawing a net of railroads over India. And they will do it. The results must be inappreciable.

It is notorious that the productive powers of India are paralyzed by the utter want of means for conveying and exchanging its various produce. Nowhere, more than in India, do we meet with social destitution in the midst of natural plenty, for want of the means of exchange. It was proved before a Committee of the British House of Commons, which sat in 1848, that

> "when grain was selling from 6/ to 8/ a quarter at Khandesh, it was sold at 64/ to 70/ at Poona, where the people were dying in the streets of famine, without the possibility of gaining supplies from Khandesh, because the clay-roads were impracticable."[a]

The introduction of railroads may be easily made to subserve agricultural purposes by the formation of tanks, where ground is required for embankment, and by the conveyance of water along the different lines. Thus irrigation, the *sine qua non* of farming in the East, might be greatly extended, and the frequently recurring local famines, arising from the want of water, would be averted. The general importance of railways, viewed under this head, must become evident, when we remember that irrigated lands, even in the districts near Ghauts, pay three times as much in taxes, afford ten or twelve times as much employment, and yield twelve or fifteen times as much profit, as the same area without irrigation.

Railways will afford the means of diminishing the amount and the cost of the military establishments. Col. Warren, Town Major of the Fort St. William, stated before a Select Committee of the House of Commons:

> "The practicability of receiving intelligence from distant parts of the country, in as many hours as at present it requires days and even weeks, and of sending instructions, with troops and stores, in the more brief period, are considerations which cannot be too highly estimated. Troops could be kept at more distant and healthier stations than at present, and much loss of life from sickness would by this means be spared. Stores could not to the same extent be required at the various dépôts, and the loss by decay, and the destruction incidental to the climate, would also be avoided. The number of troops might be diminished in direct proportion to their effectiveness."

We know that the municipal organization and the economical basis of the village communities has been broken up, but their worst feature, the dissolution of society into stereotype and

[a] Quoted from J. Dickinson's *The Government of India under a Bureaucracy*, pp. 81-82.—*Ed.*

disconnected atoms, has survived their vitality. The village isolation produced the absence of roads in India, and the absence of roads perpetuated the village isolation. On this plan a community existed with a given scale of low conveniences, almost without intercourse with other villages, without the desires and efforts indispensable to social advance. The British having broken up this self-sufficient *inertia* of the villages, railways will provide the new want of communication and intercourse. Besides,

> "one of the effects of the railway system will be to bring into every village affected by it such knowledge of the contrivances and appliances of other countries, and such means of obtaining them, as will first put the hereditary and stipendiary village artisanship of India to full proof of its capabilities, and then supply its defects." (Chapman, *The Cotton and Commerce of India* [pp. 95-97].)

I know that the English millocracy intend to endow India with railways with the exclusive view of extracting at diminished expenses the cotton and other raw materials for their manufactures. But when you have once introduced machinery into the locomotion of a country, which possesses iron and coals, you are unable to withhold it from its fabrication. You cannot maintain a net of railways over an immense country without introducing all those industrial processes necessary to meet the immediate and current wants of railway locomotion, and out of which there must grow the application of machinery to those branches of industry not immediately connected with railways. The railway-system will therefore become, in India, truly the forerunner of modern industry. This is the more certain as the Hindoos are allowed by British authorities themselves to possess particular aptitude for accommodating themselves to entirely new labor, and acquiring the requisite knowledge of machinery. Ample proof of this fact is afforded by the capacities and expertness of the native engineers in the Calcutta mint, where they have been for years employed in working the steam machinery, by the natives attached to the several steam engines in the Burdwan[a] coal districts, and by other instances. Mr. Campbell himself, greatly influenced as he is by the prejudices of the East India Company, is obliged to avow

> "that the great mass of the Indian people possesses a great *industrial energy*, is well fitted to accumulate capital, and remarkable for a mathematical clearness of head, and talent for figures and exact sciences." "Their intellects," he says, "are excellent."[b]

---

[a] The *New-York Daily Tribune* erroneously has "Hurdwar".—*Ed.*

[b] G. Campbell, *Modern India: a Sketch of the System of Civil Government*, pp. 59-60.—*Ed.*

Modern industry, resulting from the railway system, will dissolve the hereditary divisions of labor, upon which rest the Indian castes, those decisive impediments to Indian progress and Indian power.

All the English bourgeoisie may be forced to do will neither emancipate nor materially mend the social condition of the mass of the people, depending not only on the development of the productive powers, but on their appropriation by the people. But what they will not fail to do is to lay down the material premises for both. Has the bourgeoisie ever done more? Has it ever effected a progress without dragging individuals and people through blood and dirt, through misery and degradation?

The Indians will not reap the fruits of the new elements of society scattered among them by the British bourgeoisie, till in Great Britain itself the now ruling classes shall have been supplanted by the industrial proletariat, or till the Hindoos themselves shall have grown strong enough to throw off the English yoke altogether. At all events, we may safely expect to see, at a more or less remote period, the regeneration of that great and interesting country, whose gentle natives are, to use the expression of Prince Soltykov, even in the most inferior classes, "*plus fins et plus adroits que les Italiens*,"[a] whose submission even is counterbalanced by a certain calm nobility, who, notwithstanding their natural langor, have astonished the British officers by their bravery, whose country has been the source of our languages, our religions, and who represent the type of the ancient German in the Jat,[176] and the type of the ancient Greek in the Brahmin.[177]

I cannot part with the subject of India without some concluding remarks.

The profound hypocrisy and inherent barbarism of bourgeois civilization lies unveiled before our eyes, turning from its home, where it assumes respectable forms, to the colonies, where it goes naked. They are the defenders of property, but did any revolutionary party ever originate agrarian revolutions like those in Bengal, in Madras, and in Bombay? Did they not, in India, to borrow an expression of that great robber, Lord Clive himself, resort to atrocious extortion, when simple corruption could not keep pace with their rapacity? While they prated in Europe about the inviolable sanctity of the national debt, did they not confiscate in India the dividends of the rajahs,[178] who had invested their

---

[a] "More subtle and adroit than the Italians." See A. D. Soltykov's *Lettres sur l'Inde*, p. 61.—*Ed.*

private savings in the Company's own funds? While they combatted the French revolution under the pretext of defending "our holy religion," did they not forbid, at the same time, Christianity to be propagated in India, and did they not, in order to make money out of the pilgrims streaming to the temples of Orissa and Bengal, take up the trade in the murder and prostitution perpetrated in the temple of Juggernaut[179]? These are the men of "Property, Order, Family, and Religion."

The devastating effects of English industry, when contemplated with regard to India, a country as vast as Europe, and containing 150 millions of acres, are palpable and confounding. But we must not forget that they are only the organic results of the whole system of production as it is now constituted. That production rests on the supreme rule of capital. The centralization of capital is essential to the existence of capital as an independent power. The destructive influence of that centralization upon the markets of the world does but reveal, in the most gigantic dimensions, the inherent organic laws of political economy now at work in every civilized town. The bourgeois period of history has to create the material basis of the new world—on the one hand universal intercourse founded upon the mutual dependency of mankind, and the means of that intercourse; on the other hand the development of the productive powers of man and the transformation of material production into a scientific domination of natural agencies. Bourgeois industry and commerce create these material conditions of a new world in the same way as geological revolutions have created the surface of the earth. When a great social revolution shall have mastered the results of the bourgeois epoch, the market of the world and the modern powers of production, and subjected them to the common control of the most advanced peoples, then only will human progress cease to resemble that hideous, pagan idol, who would not drink the nectar but from the skulls of the slain.

Written on July 22, 1853

First published in the *New-York Daily Tribune*, No. 3840, August 8, 1853; reprinted in the *New-York Semi-Weekly Tribune*, No. 856, August 9, 1853

Signed: *Karl Marx*

Reproduced from the *New-York Daily Tribune*

Karl Marx

FINANCIAL FAILURE OF GOVERNMENT.—CABS.—IRELAND.—THE RUSSIAN QUESTION[180]

London, Friday, July 29, 1853

Mr. Gladstone, in the sitting of the House of Commons of last night, brought forward a resolution that provision should be made out of the Consolidated Fund for paying off the South-Sea-Stock[181] not commuted under his financial scheme. To bring forward such a resolution was to own the complete failure of his commutation plan. Beside this small defeat the Ministry has had to undergo a very heavy one concerning their India Bill. Sir John Pakington moved the insertion of a clause, by virtue of which the salt-monopoly should cease, and enacting that the manufacture and sale of salt in India shall be absolutely free, subject only to excise or other duty. The motion was carried by 117 against 107, notwithstanding the desperate exertions of Sir Charles Wood, Lord John Russell, Sir J. Hogg, Sir H. Maddock, and Mr. Lowe (of *The Times*). The oligarchy having succeeded in raising the salary of the President of the Board of Control to £5,000, propose now to raise the salaries of the immaculate East India Directors from £300 to £1,000, and those of the Chairman and Deputy-Chairman to £1,500. Evidently they suppose India to possess the same miraculous power as is attributed in Hindostan to the leaves of a fabulous tree on the extreme hights of the Himalaya, viz.: that it converts into gold everything that it touches—the only difference being that what the credulous Hindoo expects from the juice of the leaves, the enlightened Englishman expects from the blood of the natives.

The Chinese Sultan of the *Arabian Nights*, who rose one fine morning and went to his window to look at Aladdin's palace, was astonished to behold nothing but an empty place. He called his

Grand Vizier and asked him if he could see the palace. The Grand Vizier could see nothing, and was not less astonished than the Sultan, who flew into a passion and gave orders to his guards to arrest Aladdin. The public of London, when it rose on Wednesday morning, found itself much in the situation of that Chinese Sultan. London looked as if London had gone out-of-town. There were and there continued to be empty places where we were wont to see something. And as the eye was amazed at the emptiness of the places, so the ear was amazed at their tomb-like tranquillity. What was it that had happened to London? A *cab-revolution*; cabmen and cabs have disappeared, as though by miracle, from the streets, from their stands, from the railway stations. The cab-proprietors and the drivers are in rebellion against the new Cab-act, that great and almost "unique" act of the Ministry of all the talents. They have struck.

It has often been observed that the British public is seized with periodical fits of morality, and that once every six or seven years, its virtue becomes outrageous, and must make a stand against vice. The object of this moral and patriotic fit happened for the present to be *poor cabby*. His extortions from unprotected females and fat city men were to be put down, and his fare to be reduced from 1s. to 6d. per mile. The sixpenny morality grew epidemic. The Ministry, by the organ of Mr. Fitzroy, brought in a draconic law against Cabby, prescribing the terms of the contracts he had to fulfil with the public, and subjecting at the same time his fares and his "Hansoms," his horses and his morals to Parliamentary legislation. Cabby, it appears, was to be forcibly transformed into the type of British respectability. The present generation could not do without improvising at least one virtuous and disinterested class of citizens, and Cabby was selected to form it. So anxious was the Ministry of all the talents to perform its masterpiece of legislation, that the Cab-act, hardly carried through the House, was put into operation before any part of the machinery for working it was ready. Instead of authentic copies of the new regulations and tables of fares and distances, the *Cadis* of London having been provided beforehand, the police magistrates were advised to decide any conflict arising between Cabby and the public in the most summary way. Thus, we had during two weeks the various and elevating spectacle of a continuous fight before the magistrates between a real army of 6d. Hampdens[182] and the "atrocious" cabmen, the one fighting for virtue, and the others for money. Day after day was Cabby moralized, sentenced, imprisoned. At last he made sure that he was unable to pay his proprietor the old rent with the new tariff, and proprietor and driver seceded to their *Mons Sacer*,[183] to the National Hall, in Holborn, where they came to the terrible resolution which for three days has produced the cab-desolation of London. Two things they have already effected: firstly, that the Ministry through the organ of Mr. Fitzroy, have amended their own act so much as nearly to annihilate it; and secondly, that the Eastern Question, the Danish *coup d'état*, the bad harvest, and the approaching cholera have all disappeared before that one great struggle of public virtue, which persists in paying only 6d. per mile, and the private interest which persists in asking 12 pence.

"Strike" is the order of the day. During the present week 5,000 miners have struck in the northern coal district; 400 to 500 journeymen cork-cutters in London; about 2,000 laborers employed by the different wharfingers on the Thames; the police force at Hull, similar attempts being made by the City and general Metropolitan Police; and finally the bricklayers employed at St. Stephens, under the very nose of Parliament.

"The world is becoming a very paradise for laborers. Men are becoming valuable," exclaims *The Times*. In the years 1849, '50, '51, '52, while commerce was progressively growing, industry extending to unheard-of dimensions, and profits continually augmenting, wages in general remained stationary, and were in most instances even maintained at the reduced scale occasioned by the crisis of 1847. Emigration having reduced the numbers, and the rise in the prices of the first necessaries having sharpened the appetites of the people, strikes broke out, and wages rose in consequence of those strikes, and lo! the world becomes a paradise for laborers—in the eyes of *The Times*. In order to reduce that paradise to terrestrial dimensions, the mill-lords of Lancashire have formed an association, for mutually assisting and supporting each other against the demands of the people. But not content with opposing combination to combination, the bourgeoisie threaten to appeal to the interference of law—of law dictated by themselves. In what manner this is done may be inferred from the following expectorations of *The Morning Post*, the organ of the liberal and amiable Palmerston.

"If there be a piece of wickedness which preeminently deserves to be *punished with an iron hand*, it is the system of strikes.... What is wanted is some stringent and summary mode of punishing the leaders and chief men of these combinations. [...] It would be no interference with the freedom of the labor market *to treat these fellows to a flogging*.... It is idle to say that this would interfere with the labor market. As long as those who supply the labor market refrain from jeopardizing the interests of the country, *they may be left* to make their own terms with the employers."[a]

Within a certain conventional limit, the laborers shall be allowed to imagine themselves to be free agents of production, and that their contracts with their masters are settled by mutual convention; but that limit passed, labor is to be openly enforced upon them on conditions prescribed by Parliament, that permanent Combination Committee of the ruling classes against the people. The deep and philosophical mind of the Palmerstonian organ is curiously disclosed in its yesterday's discovery, on that "the hardest used of all classes in this country is the *poor of the higher ranks*," the poor aristocrat who is forced to use a cab instead of a "brougham" of his own.[b]

Like the world in general, we are assured, that Ireland in particular is becoming a paradise for the laborer, in consequence of famine[184] and exodus. Why then, if wages really are so high in Ireland, is it that Irish laborers are flocking in such masses over to England to settle permanently on this side of the "pond,"[c] while they formerly used to return after every harvest? If the social amelioration of the Irish people is making such progress, how is it that, on the other hand, insanity has made such terrific progress among them since 1847, and especially since 1851? Look at the following data from "the Sixth Report on the District Criminal and Private Lunatic Asylums in Ireland":

1851—Sum total of admissions in Lunatic Asylums	2,584
(1,301 males and 1,283 females.)	
1852	2,662
(1,276 males and 1,386 females.)	
March, 1853	2,870
(1,447 males and 1,423 females.)	

And this is the same country in which the celebrated Swift, the founder of the first Lunatic Asylum in Ireland,[185] doubted whether 90 madmen could be found.

The Chartist agitation reopened by Ernest Jones, is proceeding vigorously, and on the 30th inst., a great open-air meeting of the Chartists of London will be held on Kennington Common, the place where the great gathering of April 10, 1848, took place.[186]

Mr. Cobbett has withdrawn his Factory Bill, intimating his intention of reintroducing it early in next session.

---

[a] *The Morning Post*, No. 24835, July 27, 1853.—*Ed.*
[b] *The Morning Post*, No. 24836, July 28, 1853.—*Ed.*
[c] The Irish Sea.—*Ed.*

As to the financial and general prospects of England *The Manchester Guardian* of the 27th inst., entirely confirms my own previous predictions in the following passages of a leading article:—

"Seldom perhaps has there been a time when there were floating in our commercial atmosphere so many elements of uncertainty calculated to excite *uneasiness*—we use that mild word advisedly. At any former period before the repeal of the Corn Laws, and the general adaptation of the free trade policy, we should have used the stronger term of *serious alarm*. These elements are firstly the apprehended deficiency of the crops, secondly the continued abstraction of gold from the cellars of the bank, and thirdly the great probability of war."

The last of the Constitutions of 1848, has now been overthrown by the *coup d'état* of the Danish King.[a] A Russian Constitution has been conferred upon the country, which, by the abolition of the *Lex Regia*, was doomed to become a Russian Province.[187] In a subsequent letter I shall give an exposé of the affairs of that country.[b]

"It is our policy to see that nothing new happens during the next four months, and I hope we shall accomplish it, because *men in general prefer waiting*; but the fifth must be fruitful in events."

Thus wrote Count Pozzo di Borgo on the 28th Nov., 1828, to Count Nesselrode,[c] and Count Nesselrode is now acting on the same maxim. While the military assumption of the Principalities was completed by the assumption of their Civil Government by the Russians, while troops after troops are pouring into Bessarabia and the Crimea, a hint has been given to Austria that her mediation might be accepted, and another to Bonaparte that his proposals were likely to be met with a favorable reception by the Czar. The Ministers at Paris and London were comforted with the prospect that Nicholas would condescend to definitively accept their excuses. All the Courts of Europe, transformed into so many Sultanas, were anxiously waiting which of them, the magnanimous commander of the faithful would throw his handkerchief to. Having kept them in this manner for weeks, nay for months, in suspense, Nicholas suddenly makes a declaration that neither England, nor France, nor Austria, nor Prussia, had any business in his quarrel with Turkey, and that with Turkey alone he could negotiate. It was probably in order to facilitate his negotiations with Turkey, that he recalled his embassy from Constantinople. But while

---

[a] Frederick VII.—*Ed.*

[b] See this volume, pp. 237-38.—*Ed.*

[c] Quoted from *The Portfolio*, 1836, Vol. I, p. 473.—*Ed.*

he declares that the Powers are not to meddle in Russia's concerns, we are informed on the other hand that the representatives of France, England, Austria and Prussia kill their time in meeting at Vienna in conference, and in hatching projects for the arrangement of the Eastern Question, neither the Turkish nor Russian Ambassador participating in these mock-conferences. The Sultan[a] had appointed, on the 8th inst. a warlike ministry, in order to escape from his armed suspension, but was compelled by Lord Redcliffe to dismiss it on the same evening. He has now been so much confused that he intends to send an Austrian courier to St. Petersburg with the mission of asking whether the Czar would re-enter into direct negotiations. On the return of that courier and the answer he brings, shall depend, whether Reshid Pasha is himself to go to St. Petersburg. From St. Petersburg he is to send new draft notes to Constantinople; the new draft notes are to be returned to St. Petersburg, and nothing will be settled before the last answer is again returned from St. Petersburg to Constantinople—and then the fifth month will have arrived, and no fleets can enter the Black Sea; and then the Czar will quietly remain during the winter in the Principalities, where he pays with the same promises that still circulate there from his former occupations, and as far back as 1820.

You know that the Serbian Minister Garašanin has been removed at the instance of Russia. Russia insists now, following up that first triumph, on all anti-Russian officers being expelled the service. This measure, in its turn, was intended to be followed by the reigning Prince Alexander being replaced by Prince Michel Obrenović, the absolute tool of Russia and Russian interests. Prince Alexander, to escape from this calamity, and likewise under the pressure of Austria, has struck against the Sultan, and declared his intention of observing a strict neutrality. The Russian intrigues in Serbia are thus described in the *Presse* of Paris:

"Every body knows that the Russian Consulate at Orsova—a miserable village where not a single Russian subject is to be found, but situated in the midst of a Servian population, is only a poor establishment, yet it is made the hotbed of Muscovite propaganda. The hand of Russia was judiciarily seized and established in the affair of Ibraila in 1840, and of John Lutzo in 1850, in the affair of the recent arrest of 14 Russian officers, which arrest became the cause of the resignation of Garašanin's Ministry. It is likewise known that Prince Menchikoff, during his stay at Constantinople, fomented similar intrigues through his agents at Broussa, Smyrna, as in Thessalonica, Albania and Greece."[b]

[a] Abdul Mejid.—*Ed.*

[b] Quoted from J. Paradis' article in *La Presse*, July 26, 1853.—*Ed.*

There is no more striking feature in the politics of Russia than the traditional identity not only of her objects, but of her manner in pursuing them. There is no complication of the present Eastern Question, no transaction, no official note, which does not bear the stamp of quotation from known pages of history.

Russia has now no other pretext to urge against the Sultan, except the treaty of Kainardji,[188] although that treaty gave her, instead of a protectorate over her correligionists, only the right to build a chapel at Stamboul, and to implore the Sultan's clemency for his Christian subjects, as Reshid Pasha justly urged against the Czar in his note of the 14th inst. But already in 1774, when that treaty was signed, Russia intended to interpret it one day or the other in the sense of 1853. The then Austrian Internuncio at the Ottoman Porte, Baron Thugut, wrote in the year 1774 to his Court:

"Henceforth Russia will always be in a situation to effect, whenever she may deem the opportunity favorable, and without much preliminary arrangement, a descent upon Constantinople from her ports on the Black Sea. In that case a conspiracy concerted in advance with the chiefs of the Greek religion, would no doubt burst forth, and it would only remain for the Sultan to quit his palace at the first intelligence of this movement of the Russians, to fly into the depth of Asia, and abandon the throne of European Turkey to a more experienced possessor. When the capital shall have been conquered, terrorism and the faithful assistance of the Greek Christians will indubitably and easily reduce, beneath the scepter of Russia, the whole of the Archipelago, the coast of Asia Minor and all Greece, as far as the shore of the Adriatic. Then the possession of these countries, so much favored by nature, with which no other part of the world can be compared in respect to the fertility and richness of the soil, will elevate Russia to a degree of superiority surpassing all the fabulous wonders which history relates of the grandeurs of the monarchies of ancient times." [Pp. 579-80.][a]

In 1774, as now, Russia was tempting the ambition of Austria with the prospect of Bosnia, Servia and Albania being incorporated with her. The same Baron Thugut writes thus on this subject:

"Such aggrandizement of the Austrian territory would not excite the jealousy of Russia. The reason is that the requisition which Austria would make of Bosnia, Servia, etc., although of great importance under other circumstances, would not be of the least utility to Russia, the moment the remainder of the Ottoman Empire should have fallen into her hands. For these provinces are inhabited almost entirely by Mahommedans and Greek Christians: the former would not be tolerated as residents there; the latter, considering the close vicinity of the Oriental Russian Empire would not hesitate to emigrate thither; or if they remained, their faithlessness to Austria would occasion continuous troubles; and thus an extension of territory, without intrinsic strength, so far from augmenting the power of the Emperor of Austria, would only serve to weaken it."

---

[a] Here and below, the quotations are from Joseph von Hammer's *Geschichte des Osmanischen Reiches*, Vol. 8.—*Ed.*

Politicians are wont to refer to the testament of Peter I,[189] in order to show the traditional policy of Russia in general, and particularly with regard to her views on Constantinople. They might have gone back still further. More than eight centuries ago, Svyatoslav, the yet Pagan Grand Duke of Russia, declared in an assembly of his Boyars, that "not only Bulgaria, but the Greek Empire in Europe, together with Bohemia and Hungary, ought to undergo the rule of Russia." Svyatoslav conquered Silistria and threatened Constantinople, A.D. 968, as Nicholas did in 1828. The Rurik dynasty transferred, soon after the foundation of the Russian Empire, their capital from Novgorod to Kiev, in order to be nearer to Byzantium. In the eleventh century Kiev imitated in all things Constantinople, and was called the *second Constantinople*, thus expressing the everlasting aspirations of Russia. The religion and civilization of Russia are of Byzantine offspring, and that she should have aimed at subduing the Byzantine Empire, then in the same decay as the Ottoman Empire is now in, was more natural than that the German Emperors should have aimed at the conquest of Rome and Italy. The unity, then, in the objects of Russian policy, is given by her historical past, by her geographical conditions, and by her necessity of gaining open sea-ports in the Archipelago as in the Baltic, if she wants to maintain her supremacy in Europe. But the traditional manner in which Russia pursues those objects, is far from meriting that tribute of admiration paid to it by European politicians. If the success of her hereditary policy proves the weakness of the Western Powers, the stereotyped mannerism of that policy proves the intrinsic barbarism of Russia herself. Who would not laugh at the idea of French politics being conducted on the testament of Richelieu, or the capitularies of Charlemagne[190]? Go through the most celebrated documents of Russian diplomacy, and you will find that shrewd, judicious, cunning, subtle as it is in discovering the weak points of European Kings, ministers and courts, its wisdom is at a complete dead-lock as often as the historical movements of the Western peoples themselves are concerned. Prince Lieven judged very accurately of the character of the good Aberdeen when he speculated on his connivance with the Czar, but he was grossly mistaken in his judgment of the English people when he predicted the continuance of Tory rule on the eve of the Reform move of 1831. Count Pozzo di Borgo judged very correctly of Charles X, but he made the greatest blunder with regard to the French people when he induced his "august master" to treat with that King of the partition of Europe on the eve of his expulsion from France. The Russian policy, with its traditional craft, cheats and subterfuges, may impose upon the European Courts which are themselves but traditional things, but it will prove utterly powerless with the revolutionized peoples.

At Beyrut, the Americans have abstracted another Hungarian refugee from the claws of the Austrian eagle. It is cheering to see the American intervention in Europe beginning just with the Eastern Question. Besides the commercial and military importance resulting from the situation of Constantinople, there are other historical considerations, making its possession the hotly-controverted and permanent subject of dispute between the East and the West—and America is the youngest but most vigorous representative of the West.

Constantinople is the eternal city—the Rome of the East. Under the ancient Greek Emperors, Western civilization amalgamated there so far with Eastern barbarism, and under the Turks, Eastern barbarism amalgamated so far with Western civilization, as to make this center of a theocratical Empire the effectual bar against European progress. When the Greek Emperors were turned out by the Sultans of Iconium,[191] the genius of the ancient Byzantine Empire survived this change of dynasties, and if the Sultan were to be supplanted by the Czar, the *Bas-Empire* would be restored to life with more demoralizing influences than under the ancient Emperors, and with more aggressive power than under the Sultan. The Czar would be for Byzantine civilization what Russian adventurers were for centuries to the Emperors of the Lower Empire—the *corps de garde* of their soldiers. The struggle between Western Europe and Russia about the possession of Constantinople involves the question whether Byzantinism is to fall before Western civilization, or whether its antagonism shall revive in a more terrible and conquering form than ever before. Constantinople is the golden bridge thrown between the West and the East, and Western civilization cannot, like the sun, go around the world without passing that bridge; and it cannot pass it without a struggle with Russia. The Sultan holds Constantinople only in trust for the Revolution, and the present nominal dignitaries of Western Europe, themselves finding the last stronghold of their "order" on the shores of the Neva, can do nothing but keep the question in suspense until Russia has to meet her real antagonist, the Revolution. The Revolution which will break the Rome of the West will also overpower the demoniac influences of the Rome of the East.

Those of your readers who, having read my letters on German

Revolution and Counter-Revolution, written for *The Tribune* some two years ago,[a] desire to have an immediate intuition of it, will do well to inspect the picture[b] by Mr. *Hasenclever*, now being exhibited in the New-York Crystal Palace,[192] representing the presentation of a workingmen's petition to the magistrates of Düsseldorf in 1848. What the writer could only analyze, the eminent painter has reproduced in its dramatic vitality.

Written on July 29, 1853

First published in the *New-York Daily Tribune*, No. 3844 and the *New-York Semi-Weekly Tribune*, No. 857, August 12, 1853

Signed: *Karl Marx*

Reproduced from the *New-York Daily Tribune*

---

[a] See present edition, Vol. 11, pp. 3-96. These articles were written by Engels at the request of Marx and appeared under the signature of Karl Marx as official correspondent of the *New-York Daily Tribune*.—*Ed.*

[b] "Arbeiter und Stadtrath" (1849).—*Ed.*

Karl Marx

[IN THE HOUSE OF COMMONS.— THE PRESS ON THE EASTERN QUESTION.— THE CZAR'S MANIFESTO.—DENMARK] [193]

London, Tuesday, Aug. 2, 1853

London has ceased to be cabless. Cabby parted with his system of passive resistance on Saturday last. Meanwhile Parliament continues to break down its great act of the session, removing step by step every *casus belli* between Cabby and the House of Commons.

The India bill has passed on Friday through its last stage, after the Ministerial propositions for raising the Directors' and Chairmen's salaries had been rejected, and the latter reduced to £900 and £1,000 respectively. The Special Court of East India Proprietors which met on Friday last, offered a most lugubrious spectacle, the desponding cries and speeches clearly betraying the apprehensions of the worthy proprietors, that the Indian Empire might *have been* their property for the better time. One right honorable gentleman gave notice of his intention to move resolutions in the House of Commons rejecting the present bill, and on the part of the Proprietors and Directors declining to accept the part assigned to them by the Ministerial measure. A strike of the honorable East India Proprietors and Directors. Very striking, indeed! The Abolition of the Company's Salt-monopoly by the British House of Commons was the first step to bringing the finances of India under its direct management.

The Naval Coast-Volunteers' bill passed through Committee in yesterday's sitting. The object of this measure is to form a body of 10,000 men, to be trained during four weeks annually for the defense of the British Coasts. They are to receive a bounty of £6, as in the case of the militia. Their service is to be limited to five years in times of peace, and to six in time of danger. When called out, they will receive the pay of able seamen, with an additional two-pence per day during the last year. The men are not to be taken more than fifty leagues from the coasts in time of peace, and 100 in time of danger.

The Irish Landlords' and Tenants' bill[194] likewise passed through the third reading yesterday night. One important amendment in favor of the Tenants was added, viz.: the prohibition of Landlords to seize and sell the standing crops of a Tenant.

Mr. Cobden has published a pamphlet on the origin of the Burmese war.

So great are the fears of a deficient harvest in France, that the Government of Louis Bonaparte has treated with the Syndicate of the Paris bakers for a slight reduction in the prices of bread during the first half of August, notwithstanding the steady rise in flour at the *Halle aux blés*.[a] The bakers are to be indemnified by a subsequent augmentation of prices.

"This," says *The Economist*, "is a conspiracy on the part of the French Government to cheat the people into a belief that the crops are not short, when they are."[b]

Day after day the columns of the Press are inundated with conflicting dispatches on the Eastern affairs, manufactured in Vienna and Berlin, partly by Russian agents, in order to deceive the French and British public as to the operations of Russia, and partly on orders sent expressly from Paris, for stockjobbing purposes. A declaration contained in to-day's *Morning Post* would command consideration were it not that the Palmerstonian organ had quite abused such threats, which it only proffered one day in order to take them in again the day after.

"By the 10th of August the whole matter will be terminated peaceably, or the combined fleets will be commanded to proceed to the Bosphorus, or perhaps to the Black Sea. Active measures will succeed patient negotiation, and the dread of danger will no longer prevent the strong means which may ensure safety. [...] If the Czar accept the proposal now made, [...] the first condition will be the *immediate* evacuation of the [...] Principalities."

The Morning Post then asserts, that on the 24th ult. the representatives of England, France, Austria and Prussia[c] convened on the terms of an *ultimatum* immediately forwarded to St. Petersburg.[195] This assertion, however, is contradictory to the late

[a] Corn market in Paris.—*Ed.*

[b] "The Corn Trade Under Protection", *The Economist*, No. 518, July 30, 1853.—*Ed.*

[c] J. Westmorland, F. Bourqueney, K. Buol-Schauenstein and H. Arnim.—*Ed.*

declarations of Lord Clarendon and Lord John Russell, who spoke only of a joint note of France and England, and is altogether ignored by the French Press. Yet, be this as it may, it indicates at least, that the Palmerston party in the Cabinet has handed an ultimatum to the good Aberdeen, which the latter is to answer on the 10th of August.

As though we had not yet enough of conferences at Vienna and Constantinople, we learn from the *National-Zeitung*, that other conferences are now to sit at Berlin too. The Emperor of Russia, to provide these conferences with the required "stuff," has complacently declared, that, with all his willingness, to renounce the occupation of the Principalities as the material guaranty for his religious associations, he would now be obliged to hold them as a guaranty for the indemnification for his present expenses of occupying them. While Prince Gorchakoff announced in his proclamations that Russia pledged herself to abstain from all interference with the constituted authorities of the Principalities, the Czar issues a decree forbidding the Hospodars of Moldavia and Wallachia[a] to pay any tribute to, or to hold any communication with, the Government of Turkey. In consequence of this notification the Hospodar of Wallachia informed the Russian Consul at Bucharest, that he had already sent his tribute money to the Sultan,[b] to which the Consul replied: *c'est de l'argent perdu*,[c] as the Hospodar would have to pay it again to Russia.

The *Patrie* of yesterday communicates the fact that three of the most influential Boyars of Moldavia had left Jassy for Petersburg, with the especial consent of the Hospodar, in order to remonstrate with the Czar on the conduct of the Russian soldiers, who, in violation of the solemn promise given to the Porte, treated the Danubian Provinces as a conquered country, and committed numberless extortions therein. The Russians can certainly not be accused of seeking to make propaganda by making themselves popular in the Principalities.

Russia continues its armaments with the same ostentation as before. The *Hamburger Nachrichten* publishes the following Imperial manifesto, dated Petersburg, 23d July:

"By the Grace of God, we, Nicholas I, by our manifesto of August 1st (13th), 1834, have ordered that every year levies shall take place in certain parts of our Empire: to-day we order:

---

[a] G. Ghica and B. Stirbei.—*Ed.*
[b] Abdul Mejid.—*Ed.*
[c] This is lost money.—*Ed.*

1. For completing our forces, maritime as well as land, the tenth partial *recrutement* shall take place in the Eastern part of our Empire, at the rate of 7 men in every 1,000, the same as the recruitment which took place in 1852 in the Western portion of the Empire.

2. Besides, a levy of 3 in every 1,000 shall take place in the Eastern Provinces of our Empire as completing the proportion of 6 in every 1,000, of which only one half had been levied by the previous recruitment.

3. To the Districts of Pskov, Vitebsk, and Mogilev, which had been exempted in virtue of our manifesto of 31st Oct., 1845, and of 26th Sept., 1846, on account of the bad harvest, the recruitment for 1853 shall be proceeded with at the rate of 3 in every 1,000. With regard to the Jews in the Districts of Vitebsk and Mogilev, the recruitment among them shall take place the same as in the other Districts, at the rate of 10 in every 1,000.

4. The levy shall begin on 1st November and be completed on 1st December.

Given at St. Petersburg. *Nicholas I.*"

The manifesto is followed by two ukases, regulating the details of this new and extraordinary levy. Beside the above-mentioned districts, there shall take place, according to a second ukase, a recruitment among the odnodworzes[196] and inhabitants of towns in the districts of Kiev, Podolia, Volhynia, Minsk, Grodno, Wilno and Kovno.

The *Hamburger* correspondent reports as follows:

"The armaments in the interior of the Empire continue without interruption. The reserve battalions of the 4th infantry corps are being concentrated near Tula. We learn from an order of the day that the guards and grenadiers still occupy their positions in the camps near Krasnoe Selo, and near Pudost, not far from Gatchina. The field-maneuvers of these two corps, amounting to 100,000 men, continue."[a]

The *Post Zeitung* of Stockholm, of July 16, announces that the Emperor of Russia had given orders for the arming and fitting out of the Baltic fleet, composed of 20 vessels of the line, and of 15 frigates. The *Kölnische Zeitung* of 29th July, states:

"The return of the Danish-Swedish fleet before the term fixed for its evolutions has taken place, in consequence of an order received by the commander to immediately repair to the Baltic."[b]

Both the French journals and *The Morning Chronicle*, of to-day, contain a telegraphic dispatch from Vienna of the 3d of July, stating that America had offered the Porte money and active assistance.

---

[a] The *Hamburger Nachrichten* report and the Manifesto of Nicholas I are apparently quoted from *Le Moniteur universel*, No. 214, August 2, 1853.— *Ed.*

[b] A quotation from the correspondence from Berlin of July 29, published in the *Kölnische Zeitung*, July 31, 1853.— *Ed.*

The impression produced on the Continental mind, by the threatening attitude of Russia, combined with the threatening prospect of the harvests, is most significantly reflected in the following words of *The Economist*:

"The Czar has awakened into life and hope the revolutionary spirit of Europe, and we read of plots in Austria, plots in Italy, and plots in France; and there begins to be more alarm lest there should be fresh revolutionary disturbances, than that governments should go to war."[a]

A well informed Danish gentleman, who has very recently arrived here from fear of the cholera now raging in Copenhagen to such an extent that already 4,000 persons have been attacked with it, and that no less than 15,000 applications for passports to leave the Danish capital have been made, informs me that the Royal message concerning the succession was chiefly carried through the abstention from voting of a great number of Eydermen,[197] who had hoped to avoid a crisis by their passive attitude. The crisis which they apprehended, however, has come upon them in the shape of the octroyed Constitution, and that Constitution is aimed especially against the "peasant's friends"[198]—party by whose support the Danish Crown has achieved its previous triumphs in the succession question. As I propose to recur to this subject in a special letter,[b] I will merely observe here, that the Danish Government has laid before the United Diet (the Landsting and the Folketing together), the notes exchanged with the Great Powers on the subject of its propositions.

Of these documents the most interesting pieces are especially at this moment, the note of England and the note of Russia. The "silent" Clarendon not only approves of the Royal message, but distinctly hints to the Danish Government that it could not go on with the old Democratic Constitution, with Universal Suffrage, and with no House of Lords. The silent Clarendon therefore has taken the initiative, for the interests of Russia, to recommend and provoke the Danish coup d'état. The Russian note, addressed by Count Nesselrode to Baron Ungern-Sternberg, after having reviewed the articles of the Treaty of London, dated 8th of May, 1852,[199] concludes as follows:

"The treaty of the 8th of May does not formally prescribe that the Lex Regia[200] should be canceled; because such a disposition would not have been opportune in a treaty concluded between independent States. It would have been contrary to diplomatic usage, and still more to the respect due to the sovereign dignity of the

[a] "The Eastern Question", *The Economist*, No. 518, July 30, 1853.—*Ed.*
[b] See this volume, pp. 241-42.—*Ed.*

Danish crown. But the Powers in giving their assent to a retrocession destined to supplant the arrangements of the Lex Regia, where the necessity of employing it would occur, in promising their support, have naturally been obliged to leave to his Majesty the King of Denmark[a] the choice of the means adequate toward realizing the object by way of legislating. His Majesty, by making use of his Royal prerogative, has manifested his intention of establishing an order of succession, for all the States subject to his rule, by which, in case of the male descendants of Frederick III becoming extinct, all claims arising from Articles 27 and 40 of the Lex Regia should be excluded, and Prince Christian of Glücksburg called upon the throne with a view of securing the Danish crown to him and his male descendants by his marriage with Princess Louise of Hesse. Such are the stipulations of the Royal Message of October 4, 1852. They express the views which, at least on the part of the Imperial Government, have served as the foundation of the present negotiations. They form in the eyes of the Imperial Cabinet, a whole and cannot be retrenched; for, it appears to us that the abrogation of Articles 27 and 40 of the Lex Regia is a necessary consequence and a condition *sine qua* not only of the stipulations which called Prince Christian of Glücksburg and his descendants to the throne, but also of the principle established in the preambulum of the treaty; that a contingency by which the male descendants should be called to the succession of the throne, in the totality of the States now subjected to the sovereignty of Denmark, was the safest means for securing the integrity of that monarchy.... They declare in Article II of the treaty that they recognize in a permanent manner the principle of the integrity of the Danish monarchy.... They have promptly made known their intention of preventing, combinedly, the return of the complications which have signaled in so unfortunate a manner the course of the last year.... The extinction of the male line of Prince Christian of Glücksburg would revive, without contradiction, the eventual claims which His Majesty the Emperor has renounced[b] in favor of that Prince. The initiative, however, expressly reserved to the King of Denmark, as well as the cooperation of the three Great Powers, in the aforesaid contingencies, when they shall happen, offer henceforth a guarantee to the Danish patriots against the ambitious plans and designs existing nowhere except in their own imagination."

Thus Russia gives to understand, that the temporary suppression of the Lex Regia as agreed upon in the protocol of the 8th May must be interpreted as a permanent one, that the permanent resignation of the Emperor of Russia is only a temporary one, but that the Danish patriots may henceforth repose on the protection of their country's integrity by the European Powers. Do they not witness how the integrity of Turkey has been protected since the treaty of 1841?

Written on August 2, 1853

First published in the *New-York Daily Tribune*, No. 3847, August 16, 1853

Signed: *Karl Marx*

Reproduced from the newspaper

---

[a] Frederick VII.—*Ed.*
[b] The *New-York Daily Tribune* has: "reassumed", which seems to be a misprint.—*Ed.*

Karl Marx

ADVERTISEMENT DUTY.— RUSSIAN MOVEMENTS.—DENMARK.— THE UNITED STATES IN EUROPE[201]

London, Friday, Aug. 5, 1853

The act for the repeal of the Advertisement Duty received the Royal assent last night, and comes into operation this day. Several of the morning papers have already published their reduced terms for advertisements of all kinds.

The dock-laborers of London are on the strike. The Company endeavor to get fresh men. A battle between the old and new hands is apprehended.

The Emperor of Russia[a] has discovered new reasons for holding the Principalities. He will hold them no longer as a material guarantee for his spiritual aspirations, or as an indemnity for the costs of occupying them, but he must hold them now on account of "internal disturbances" as provided by the Treaty of Balta-Liman.[202] And, as the Russians have actually put everything in the Principalities topsy-turvy, the existence of such disturbances cannot be denied. Lord Clarendon confirmed, in the sitting of the House of Lords of August 2d, the statement given in my last letter with regard to the Hospodars having been prohibited from transmitting their tribute to Constantinople, and from entertaining further communications with Turkey.[b] Lord Clarendon declared with great gravity of countenance, and a pompous solemnity of manner, that he would

> "instruct, by the messenger who leaves London this night, Sir Hamilton Seymour to demand from the Russian Cabinet the *explanation* which England is entitled to."[c]

---

[a] Nicholas I.—*Ed.*

[b] See this volume, p. 235.—*Ed.*

[c] Here and below the quotations are from House of Commons speeches of M.P.s, published in *The Times*, No. 21497, August 3, 1853.—*Ed.*

While Clarendon sends all the way to St. Petersburg to request *explanations*, the *Patrie* of to-day[a] has intelligence from Jassy of the 20th ultimo, that the Russians are fortifying Bucharest and Jassy; that the Hospodars of Moldavia and Wallachia[b] are placed under a Russian Board of Control composed of three members; that contributions in kind are levied on the people, and that some refractory Boyards have been incorporated in Russian regiments. This is the "explanation" of the manifesto of Prince Gorchakoff, according to which

"his august master had no intention of modifying the institutions which governed the country, and the presence of his troops would impose upon the people neither new contributions nor charges."

In the sitting of the House of Commons of the same day Lord John Russell declared, in answer to a question put by Lord Dudley Stuart, that the four powers had convened at Vienna on a common proposition to be made to the Czar, "acceptable" to Russia and to Turkey, and that it had been forwarded to St. Petersburg. In answer to Mr. Disraeli he stated:

"The proposition was in fact an *Austrian proposition*, though it came originally from the Government of France."

This original Frenchman, naturalized in Austria, looks very suspicious, and the *Neue Preussische Zeitung*[c] gives, in a Vienna letter, the *explanation* that

"the Russian and Austrian Cabinets have fully resolved in common not to allow English influence to predominate in the East."

The Englishman[d] observes, on the *explanations* of the Coalition Ministry:

"They are great in humiliation, strong in imbecility, and most eloquent in taciturnity."

Moldavia and Wallachia once Russified, Galicia, Hungary and Transylvania would be transformed into Russian "*enclaves*."

I have spoken in a former letter of the "hidden treasures" in the Bank of St. Petersburg, forming the metal reserve for a three times larger paper circulation.[e] Now, the Russian Minister of War[f]

---

[a] The reference is to Charles Schiller's report, published in *La Patrie*, No. 216, August 4, 1853.—*Ed.*

[b] G. Ghica and B. Stirbei.—*Ed.*

[c] *Neue Preussische Zeitung*, No. 177, August 2, 1853.—*Ed.*

[d] A. Richards (below Marx quotes his article "The Demand for Explanations" in *The Morning Advertiser*, No. 19382, August 5, 1853.—*Ed.*

[e] See this volume, p. 117.—*Ed.*

[f] V. A. Dolgorukov.—*Ed.*

has just applied for the transfer of a portion of this treasure into the military chest. The Minister of Finance[a] having objected to this step, the Emperor applied himself to the Holy Synod, the depository of the Church-Property, for a loan of 60 millions of rubles. While the Czar is wanting in wealth, his troops are wanting in health. It is stated on very reliable authority, that the troops occupying the Principalities have suffered enormously from heat on their march, that the number of sick is extraordinary, and that many private houses at Bucharest and Jassy have been converted into hospitals.

The Times of yesterday denounced the ambitious plans of Russia on Turkey, but tried, at the same time, to cover her intrigues in Denmark. It does the work of its august master even while ostentatiously quarreling with him.

"We discredit," says *The Times*, "[...] the assertion that the Russian Cabinet has succeeded in establishing its hold upon the Court of Copenhagen, and the statement that the Danish Government have proceeded, under Russian influence, to abrogate or impair the Constitution of 1849, is wholly inaccurate. The Danish Government have caused a bill or draft to be published, containing *some modifications of the Constitution* now in force, but this bill is to be submitted to the discussion and vote of the Chambers when they reassemble, and it has not been promulgated by Royal authority."

The dissolution of a Legislative Assembly into four separate feudal provincial diets, the right of self-assessment canceled, the election by universal suffrage suppressed, the liberty of the press abolished, free competition supplanted by the revival of close guilds, the whole official, i.e. the only intelligent class in Denmark excluded from being eligible except on Royal permission, that you call "some modifications of the Constitution?" As well you might call Slavery a slight modification of Freedom. It is true that the Danish King[b] has not dared to promulgate this new "fundamental law" as law. He has only sent, after the fashion of Oriental Sultans, the silken string to the Chambers with orders to strangle themselves. Such a proposition involves the threat of enforcing it if not voluntarily submitted to. So much for the "some modifications of the Constitution." Now to the "Russian influence."

In what way did the conflict between the Danish King and the Danish Chambers arise? He proposed to abrogate the Lex Regia,[203] viz.: The existing law of succession to the throne of Denmark. Who urged the King to take this step? Russia, as you will have seen from the note of Count Nesselrode, dated 11th

[a] P.F. Brok.—*Ed.*
[b] Frederick VII.—*Ed.*

May, 1853, communicated in my last letter.[a] Who will gain by that abrogation of the Lex Regia? No one but Russia. The Lex Regia enables the female line of the reigning family to succeed to the throne. By its abrogation the agnates would remove from the succession all the claims of the cognates hitherto standing in their way. You know that the kingdom of Denmark comprehends, besides Denmark Proper, viz.: the Isles and Jutland, also the two Duchies of Schleswig and Holstein. The succession to Denmark Proper and Schleswig is regulated by the same Lex Regia, while in the Duchy of Holstein, being a German fee, it devolves to the agnates, according to the Lex Salica.[204] By the abrogation of the Lex Regia the succession to Denmark and Schleswig would be assimilated to that of the German Duchy of Holstein, and Russia, having the next claims on Holstein, as the representative of the house of Holstein-Gottorp, would in the quality of chief agnate, also obtain the next claim on the Danish throne. In 1848-50, Denmark, being assisted by Russian notes and fleets, made war on Germany[b] in order to maintain the Lex Regia, which forbade Schleswig to be united with Holstein, and to be separated from Denmark.[205] After having beaten the German revolution, under the pretext of the Lex Regia, the Czar confiscates democratic Denmark by abrogating the same law. The Scandinavians and the Germans have thus made the experience that they must not found their respective national claims on the feudal laws of Royal succession. They have made the better experience, that, by quarrelling amongst themselves, instead of confederating, Germans and Scandinavians, both of them belonging to the same great race, only prepare his way to their hereditary enemy, the Sclave.

The great event of the day is the appearance of American policy on the European horizon. Saluted by one party, detested by the other, the fact is admitted by all.

> "Austria must look to the dismemberment of the Turkish Empire for indemnification for the loss of her Italian provinces—a contingency not rendered less likely by the quarrel [...] she has had the folly to bring on her with Uncle Sam. An American squadron in the Adriatic would be a very pretty complication of an Italian insurrection, and we may all live to see it, for the Anglo-Saxon spirit is not yet dead in the West."

Thus speaks *The Morning Herald*,[c] the old organ of the English Aristocracy.

---

[a] See this volume, pp. 237-38.—*Ed.*

[b] The *New-York Daily Tribune* has: "made over to Germany", which seems to be a misprint.—*Ed.*

[c] *The Morning Herald*, No. 22228, August 4, 1853.—*Ed.*

"The Koszta affair," says the Paris *Presse*, "is far from being terminated. We are informed that the Vienna Cabinet has asked from the Washington Cabinet a reparation, which it may be quite sure not to receive. Meanwhile, Koszta remains under the safeguard of the French Consul."[a]

"We must go out of the way of the Yankee, who is half of a buccanier and half a backwoodsman, and no gentleman at all," whispers the Vienna *Presse*.

The German papers grumble about the secret treaty pretended to have been concluded between the United States and Turkey, according to which the latter would receive money and maritime support, and the former the harbor of Enos in Rumelia, which would afford a sure and convenient place for a commercial and military station of the American Republic in the Mediterranean.

"In due course of time," says the Brussels *Emancipation*,[b] "the conflict at Smyrna between the American Government and the Austrian one, caused by the capture of the refugee Koszta, will be placed in the first line of events of 1853. Compared with this fact, the occupation of the Danubian Principalities and the movements of the western diplomacy and of the combined navies at Constantinople, may be considered as of second-rate importance. The event of Smyrna is the beginning of a new history, while the accident at Constantinople is only the unraveling of an old question about to expire."

An Italian paper, *Il Parlamento*, has a leader under the title "*La Politica Americana* in Europa," from which I translate the following passages literally:

"It is well known," says the *Parlamento*, "that a long time has elapsed since the United States have tried to get a maritime station in the Mediterranean and in Italy, and more particularly at such epochs when complications arose in the Orient. Thus for instance in 1840, when the great Egyptian question was agitated, and when St. Jean d'Acre was assailed, the Government of the United States asked in vain from the King of the Two Sicilies[c] to temporarily grant it the great harbor of Syracuse. To-day the tendency of American policy for interfering with European affairs cannot be but more lively and more steadfast. There can be no doubt but that the actual Democratic Administration of the Union manifests the most clamorous sympathies with the victims of the Italian and Hungarian revolution, that it cares nothing about an interruption of the diplomatical intercourse with Austria, and that at Smyrna it has supported its system with the threat of the cannon. It would be unjust to grumble at this aspiration of the great transatlantic nation, or to call it inconsistent or ridiculous. The Americans certainly do not intend conquering the Orient and going to have a land war with Russia. But if England and France make the best of their maritime forces, why should not the Americans do so, particularly as soon as they will have obtained a station, a point of retreat and of "approvisionnement" in the Mediterranean? For them there are great interests at stake, the republican element being diametrically opposed to the

[a] Quoted from Nefftzer's report "Bulletin du jour", *La Presse*, August 4, 1853.—*Ed.*

[b] *L'Emancipation*, No. 204, July 23, 1853.—*Ed.*

[c] Ferdinand II.—*Ed.*

Cossack one. Commerce and navigation having multiplied the legitimate relations and contracts between all peoples of the world, none can consider itself a stranger to any sea of the Old or New Continent, or to any great question like that of the destiny of the Ottoman Empire. The American commerce, and the residents who exercise it on the shores of our seas, require the protection of the stars and stripes, and in order to make it permanent and valid in all seasons of the year, they want a port for a military marine that ranks already in the third line among the maritime powers of the world. If England and France interfere directly with all that regards the Isthmus of Panama, if the former of those powers goes as far as to invent a king of the Mosquitoes, in order to oppose territorial rights to the operations of the United States, if they have come to the final understanding, that the passage from the Atlantic to the Pacific shall be opened to all nations, and be possessed by a neutral State, is it not evident then, that the United States must pretend at exercising the same vigilance with regard to the liberty and neutrality of the Isthmus of Suez, holding their eyes closely fixed on the dissolution of the Ottoman Empire, which will be likely to devolve Egypt and Libya wholly or partly to the dominion of some first-rate power? Suez and Panama are the two great doorways of the Orient, which, shut till now, will hereafter compete with each other. The best way to secure their ascendency in the Transatlantic question is to cooperate in the Mediterranean question. We are assured that the American men-of-war in the neighborhood of the Dardanelles do not renounce the pretension to enter them whenever they please, without being subjected to the restrictions convened upon by the Great Powers in 1841, and this for the incontrovertible reason, that the American Government did not participate in that Convention. Europe is amazed at this boldness, because it has been, since the peace of 1783, in the habit of considering the United States as in the condition of the Swiss Cantons after the Westphalian treaty,[206] viz.: as peoples allowed a legitimate existence, but which it would be too arduous to ask to enter into the aristocracy of the primitive Powers, and to give their votes on subjects of general policy. But on the other side of the Ocean the Anglo-Saxon race sprung up to the most exalted degree of wealth, civilization and power, cannot any longer accept the humble position assigned to it in the past. The pressure exercised by the American Union on the Council of Amphictyons of the Five Powers, till now the arbiters of the globe, is a new force that must contribute to the downfall of the exclusive system established by the treaties of Vienna. Till the Republic of the United States succeed in acquiring a positive right and an official seat in the Congresses arbitrating on general political questions, it exercises with an immense grandeur, and with a particular dignity the more humane action of natural rights and of the *jus gentium*.[a] Its banner covers the victims of the civil wars without distinction of parties, and during the immense conflagration of 1848-49 the hospitality of the American Navy never submitted to any humiliation or disgrace."

Written on August 5, 1853

First published in the *New-York Daily Tribune*, No. 3850, and the *New-York Semi-Weekly Tribune*, No. 859, August 19, 1853

Signed: *Karl Marx*

Reproduced from the *New-York Daily Tribune*

[a] International law.— *Ed.*

Karl Marx

THE WAR QUESTION.— BRITISH POPULATION AND TRADE RETURNS.— DOINGS OF PARLIAMENT[207]

London, Friday, Aug. 12, 1853

Bonaparte compensates the French Navy for their humiliating position in Besika Bay by a reduction in the price of tobacco to the sailors, as we are informed by to-day's *Moniteur*.[a] He won his throne by sausages.[208] Why should he not try to hold it by tobacco? At all events, the Eastern complication will have produced the *démonétisation* of Louis Bonaparte in the eyes of the French peasants and the army. They have learned that the loss of liberty at home is not made up by a gain of glory abroad. The "Empire of all the glories" has sunk even lower than the "Cabinet of all the talents."

From the Constantinople journals which have just arrived, we learn that the Sultan's[b] manifesto to his subjects appeared on the 1st August, that the Russian Consul at Adrianople has received orders from St. Petersburg to withdraw from Turkey, that the other Russian Consuls expect similar orders, and that the Constantinople papers have been prohibited in the Principalities. The *Impartial* of Smyrna, of Aug. 1, has the following communication with regard to Persia:

> "The Shah of Persia,[c] after the correspondence exchanged between the Porte and the Russian Cabinet on the occasion of the pending dispute, had been communicated to him on his request, has officially declared that all the right was on the side of the Porte, and that in case of war, he will fairly stand by her. This news had made a great impression on the Russian Ambassador at Teheran, who is said to prepare for demanding his passports."

The contents of the proposition made to Russia, and accepted by the Czar,[d] according to the mysterious Petersburg dispatch,

[a] *Le Moniteur universel*, No. 223, August 11, 1853.—*Ed.*
[b] Abdul Mejid.—*Ed.*
[c] Nasr-ed-Din.—*Ed.*
[d] Nicholas I.—*Ed.*

form the subject of conjecture through the whole European Press. The Palmerstonian *Morning Post* avers:

"On the 25th of July M. de Meyendorff transmitted to his Imperial master, not indeed the formal propositions" (accepted at the Vienna Conference), "but an account of what had passed at the conference of the 24th.... We believe we shall not be far wrong when we confidently affirm that the affair is settled in such a manner as to preserve intact the independence and integrity of the Ottoman Empire. The mode of settlement will be this: Reshid Pasha will address the Count Nesselrode a note, in which he will inclose the firmans in which are accorded to the Greek Christians, subjects of the Sultan, more privileges than even Russia had asked for them. He will say many civil things to the Czar and assure him of the excellent disposition of the Sultan towards his own subjects, to whom he has accorded such and such rights. This note will be presented by a Turkish Ambassador, and the affair will be at an end.... By the 10th of September the last Russian soldier will have crossed the Pruth!"[a]

On the other hand, private letters from Vienna, alluding to the appearance of Russian gun-boats above the confluence of the Pruth and the Danube, confirm the statement given in my last letter, that the propositions sent to St. Petersburg, do not include at all the withdrawal of the Russian armies from the Principalities, that they emanate from the Austrian Cabinet, to whose intervention the British Ambassador at Vienna,[b] "that true lover of harmony," had appealed, after the French and English proposals had been rejected by the Czar; and that they afford Russia the desired opportunity for prolonging negotiations *in infinitum*.[209] According to the semi-official Frankfort *Ober-Postamts-Zeitung*, Russia has only permitted Austria to enlighten Turkey with regard to her own interests.

The lately published Population Returns prove the slow but steady decrease of the population of Great Britain.[c] In the quarter ending June, 1853,

the number of deaths was	107,861
while the number of births was	158,718
Net increase of births as far as the registered districts are concerned	50,857
The excess of births over deaths in the United Kingdom is assumed to be	79,820
Number of emigrants during the quarter	115,959
Excess of emigration over increase of births	36,139

[a] *The Morning Post*, August 11, 1853.—*Ed.*
[b] J. Westmorland.—*Ed.*
[c] The data are quoted from *The Times*, No. 21498, August 4, 1853.—*Ed.*

The last Return showed an excess of emigration over births of only 30,000.

The decrease of population, resulting from emigration, coincides with an unprecedented increase in the powers of production and capital. When we remember Parson Malthus denying emigration any such influence, and imagining he had established, by the most elaborate calculations, that the united navies of the world could never suffice for an emigration of such dimensions as were likely to affect in any way the overstocking of human beings, the whole mystery of modern political economy is unraveled to our eyes. It consists simply in transforming transitory social relations belonging to a determined epoch of history and corresponding with a given state of material production, into eternal, general, never-changing laws, natural laws, as they call them. The thorough transformation of the social relations resulting from the revolutions and evolutions in the process of material production, is viewed by the political economists as a mere Utopia. They see the economical limits of a given epoch, but they do not understand how these limits are limited themselves, and must disappear through the working of history, as they have been created by it.

The accounts relating to Trade and Navigation for the six months ending July 5, 1853, as published by the Board of Trade, show in general a great increase when compared with the exports, imports, and shipping in the corresponding period of the year 1852.[a] The import of oxen, bulls, cows, calves, sheep and lambs has considerably increased.

The total import of grains amounted, in the six months ending July 5th, 1852, to	qrs.	2,604,201
But in the corresponding months of 1853, to	qrs.	3,984,374
The total imports of Flour and Meal amounted, during six months of 1852, to	qrs.	1,931,363
And in the corresponding months, 1853, to	qrs.	2,577,340
Total imports of Coffee, 1852	lbs.	19,397,185
Total imports of Coffee, 1853	lbs.	21,908,954
Total imports of Wine, 1852	gals.	2,850,862
Total imports of Wine, 1853	gals.	4,581,300
Total imports of Eggs, 1852	No.	64,418,591
Total imports of Eggs, 1853	No.	67,631,380
Total imports of Potatoes, 1852	cwts.	189,410

[a] Below the figures are quoted from "Accounts Relating to Trade and Navigation" and other material published in *The Economist*, No. 519, August 6, 1853.—*Ed.*

Total imports of Potatoes, 1853	cwts.	713,941
Total imports of Flax, 1852	cwts.	410,876
Total imports of Flax, 1853	cwts.	627,173
Total imports of Raw Silk, 1852	lbs.	2,354,690
Total imports of Raw Silk, 1853	lbs.	2,909,733
Total imports of Cotton, 1852	cwts.	4,935,317
Total imports of Cotton, 1853	cwts.	5,134,680
Total imports of Wool (sheep and lambs), 1852	lbs.	26,916,002
Total imports of Wool (sheep and lambs), 1853	lbs.	40,189,398
Total imports of Hides (tanned), 1852	lbs.	1,075,207
Total imports of Hides (tanned), 1853	lbs.	3,604,769

A decrease is found in cocoa, guano, unrefined sugar, tea, &c. As to the exports we find:

Those of Cotton Manufactures in 1852	£11,386,491
Those of Cotton Manufactures in 1853	13,155,679

As to cotton yarn—and the same remark applies to linen and silk yarn—we find that the exported *quantity* has decreased, but that the declared *value* had considerably risen.

Linen Manufactures, 1852	£2,006,951
Linen Manufactures, 1853	2,251,260
Silk Manufactures, 1852	467,838
Silk Manufactures, 1853	806,419
Woolen Manufactures, 1852	3,894,506
Woolen Manufactures, 1853	4,941,357
Earthen Ware Manufactures, 1852	590,663
Earthen Ware Manufactures, 1853	627,218
Glass Manufactures, 1852	187,470
Glass Manufactures, 1853	236,797
Haberdashery and Millinery, 1852	884,324
Haberdashery and Millinery, 1853	1,806,007
Hardware and Cutlery, 1852	1,246,639
Hardware and Cutlery, 1853	1,663,302
Machinery, 1852	476,078
Machinery, 1853	760,288
Iron Bars, Bolts and Rods, 1852	1,455,952
Iron Bars, Bolts and Rods, 1853	2,730,479
Wrought Iron, 1852	696,089
Wrought Iron, 1853	1,187,059
Wire, 1852	42,979
Wire, 1853	106,610

With regard to the imports of manufactures, the greatest increase is found in shoes, boots and gloves, and the greatest decrease in glass manufactures, watches, woolen stuffs, and Indian silk manufactures. With regard to exports, the increase is greatest in linen, silks, woolens and metals. As to the importations of articles of consumption, we find that, with the exception of grains and cattle, the increase in nearly all articles bears witness that the home consumption of the higher and middle classes has advanced in a much larger proportion than that of the working classes. While, for instance, the consumption of wine has doubled, the consumption of cocoa, unrefined sugar, and tea has decidedly retrograded.

Out of 260 reports on the wheat crops throughout the United Kingdom, only 25 speak of the crop as fine and abundant, 30 as an average one, and above 200 reports declare it to be bad and deficient. Oats, barley and beans are expected to turn out less unfavorable, as the wet has benefited them; but the potatoes are blighted in all parts of the country. Messrs. J. [and] C. Sturge & Co. remark, in their last circular on the wheat crop:

> "The wheat crop on the aggregate will probably be the least productive of any since 1816, and unless the harvest of 1854 is very early, we may require an importation of all kinds of grain and breadstuffs greater even than that of 1847—probably not less than 15,000,000 quarters—but our present prices are sufficient to induce imports to this extent, unless France should compete with us in the producing markets."

As to a very early crop in 1854, there seems to be no great prospect of that, inasmuch as experience has shown that bad harvests generally follow in succession just as the good ones; and the succession of good harvests since 1848 has already been unusually long. That England will obtain a sufficient supply of corn from foreign countries is, perhaps, pretty sure; but that the exportation of her manufactures will, as Free Traders expect, keep pace with the importations of grains, cannot be presumed. The probable excess of importation over exportation will, besides, be accompanied by a falling off in the home consumption of manufactures. Even now the bullion reserve in the Bank of England is decreasing week after week, and has sunk to £17,739,107.

The House of Lords in its sitting of Friday last rejected the Combination of Workmen Bill, which had passed through the Commons. This bill was but a new interpretation of the old Combination Act of 1825,[210] and intended, by removing its cumbrous and equivocal terminology, to place the workingmen on a more equal footing with their employers, as far as the legality of combination is concerned. The sentimental lords who please themselves in treating the workingmen as their humble clients, feel exasperated whenever that rabble asks for rights instead of sympathies. The so-called Radical papers have, of course, eagerly seized on this opportunity to denounce the Lords to the proletarians as their "hereditary foes." I am far from denying it. But let us now look at these Radicals, the "natural friends" of the workingmen. I told you in a former letter that the Manchester master-spinners and manufacturers were getting up an association for resisting the demands of their "hands."[a] This association calls itself "an association for the purpose of aiding the trade in regulating the excitement among the operatives in the Manchester district." It purports to have been formed for the following purposes:

"1. The establishment of wages for various operations connected with spinning and weaving, similar to those paid in the other districts of the cotton trade.

"2. The mutual protection of its members in the payment of such wages against the resistance offered to them on the part of the operatives employed by them respectively.

"3. The securing to the operatives themselves the advantage of a uniformity of adequate wages, to be paid to them throughout town and neighborhood."[b]

In order to effect these purposes they have resolved to set up a whole organization, by forming local associations of master-spinners and manufacturers, with a central committee.

"They will resist all demands made by *associated bodies* of mill-hands, as any concession to them would be injurious to employers, operatives, and the trade generally."

They will not allow the machinery set up by and for themselves to be counterbalanced by a similar machinery set up by their men. They intend fortifying the monopoly of capital by the monopoly of combination. They will dictate terms as an associated body. But the laborers shall only dispute them in their individual capacity. They will attack in ranged battle, but they will not be resisted, except in single fight. This is "*fair competition*," as understood by the Manchester Radicals and model Free Traders.

In its sitting of Aug. 9, the House of Lords had to decide on the fate of three Ireland Bills, carried through the Commons after ten months' deliberation, viz.: the *Landlord and Tenant Bill*, removing

---

[a] See this volume, pp. 225-26.—*Ed.*

[b] This and the following quotation are from "Manchester.—Meeting of Manufacturers" in *The People's Paper*, No. 63, July 16, 1853.—*Ed.*

the laws concerning mortgages, which form at present an insuperable bar to the effective sale of the smaller estates not falling under the *Encumbered Estates Act*[211]; the *Leasing Powers Bill*, amending and consolidating more than sixty acts of Parliament which prohibit leases to be entered into for 21 years, regulating the tenant's compensation for improvements in all instances where contracts exist, and preventing the system of sub-letting; lastly, the *Tenant's Improvement Compensation Bill*, providing compensation for improvements effected by the tenant in the absence of any contract with the landlord, and containing a clause for the retrospective operation of this provision. The House of Lords could, of course, not object to parliamentary interference between landlord and tenant, as it has laden the statute book from the time of Edward IV to the present day, with acts of legislation of landlord and tenant, and as its very existence is founded on laws meddling with landed property, as for instance the *Law of Entail*. This time, the noble lords sitting as Judges on their own cause, allowed themselves to run into a passion quite surprising in that hospital of invalids.

"Such a bill," exclaimed the Earl of Clanricarde, "as the Tenants' Compensation Bill, such a total violation and disregard of all contracts, was never before, he believed, submitted to Parliament, nor had he ever heard of any government having ventured to propose such a measure as was carried out in the retrospective clauses of the bill."[a]

The Lords went as far as to threaten the Crown with the withdrawal of their feudal allegiance,[212] and to hold out the prospect of a landlord rebellion in Ireland.

"The question," remarked the same nobleman, "touched nearly [...] the *whole question of the loyalty* and confidence of the landed proprietors in Ireland in the Government of this country.[...] If they saw landed property in Ireland treated in such a way, he would like to know what was to *secure their attachment to the Crown, and their obedience to its supremacy*?"

Gently, my lord, gently! What was to secure their obedience to the supremacy of the Crown? One magistrate and two constables. A landlord rebellion in Great Britain! Has there ever been uttered a more monstrous anachronism? But for a long time the poor Lords have only lived upon anachronisms. They naturally encourage themselves to resist the House of Commons and public opinion.

---

[a] M.P.s' speeches in the House of Lords are quoted from *The Times*, No. 21503, August 10, 1853.—*Ed.*

"Let not their lordships," said old Lord St. Leonards, "for the sake of preventing what was called a *collision* with the other House, or for the sake of popularity, or on account of a pressure from without, pass imperfect measures like these." "I do not belong to any party," exclaimed the Earl of Roden, "but I am highly interested in the welfare of Ireland."

That is to say, his lordship supposes Ireland to be highly interested in the welfare of the Earl of Roden. "This is no party question, but a Lords' question," was the unanimous shout of the House; and so it was. But between both parties, Whig Lords and Tory Lords, Coalition Lords and Opposition Lords, there has existed from the beginning a secret understanding to throw the bills out, and the whole impassioned discussion was a mere farce, performed for the benefit of the newspaper reporters.

This will be evident when we remember that the bills which formed the subject of so hot a controversy were originated, not by the Coalition Cabinet, but by Mr. Napier, the Irish Attorney-General under the Derby Ministry, and that the Tories at the last elections in Ireland appealed to the testimony of these bills introduced by them. The only substantial change made by the House of Commons in the measures introduced by the Tory Government was the excluding of the growing crops from being distrained upon. "The bills are not the same," exclaimed the Earl of Malmesbury, asking the Duke of Newcastle whether he did not believe him. "Certainly not," replied the Duke. "But whose assertion would you then believe?" "That of Mr. Napier," answered the Duke. "Now," said the Earl, "here is a letter of Mr. Napier, stating that the bills are not the same." "There," said the Duke, "is another letter of Mr. Napier, stating that they are."

If the Tories had remained in, the Coalition Lords would have opposed the Ireland Bills. The Coalition being in, on the Tories fell the task of opposing their own measures. The Coalition having inherited these bills from the Tories and having introduced the Irish party into their own cabinet, could, of course, not oppose the bills in the House of Commons; but they were sure of their being burked in the House of Lords. The Duke of Newcastle made a faint resistance, but Lord Aberdeen declared himself contented with the bills passing formally through a second reading, and being really thrown out for the session. This accordingly was done. Lord Derby, the chief of the late Ministry, and Lord Lansdowne, the nominal President of the present Ministry, yet at the same time one of the largest proprietors of land in Ireland, managed, wisely, to be absent from indisposition.

On the same day the House of Commons carried the *Hackney Carriages Duties Bill* through the third reading, renewing the official price-regulations of the 14th century, and accepting the clause proposed by Mr. F. Scully, which subjects cab proprietors' strikes to legal penalties. We have not now to settle the question of state interference with private concerns. We have only to state that this passed in a free-trade House. But, they say, that in the cab trade there exists monopoly and not free competition. This is a curious sort of logic. First they subject a particular trade to a duty, called license, and to special police regulations, and then they affirm that, in virtue of these very burdens imposed upon it, the trade loses its free-trade character and becomes transformed into a state monopoly.

The *Transportation Bill* has also passed through Committee. Except a small number of convicts who will continue to be transported to Western Australia, the penalty of transportation is abolished by this bill. After a certain period of preliminary imprisonment the offenders will receive tickets of leave in Great Britain, liable to be revoked, and then they will be employed on the public works at wages to be determined by Government. The philanthropic object of the latter clause is the erection of an artificial surplus in the labor market, by drawing forced convict-labor into competition with free labor; the same philanthropists forbidding the workhouse paupers all sort of productive labor from fear of creating competition with private capital.

The London *Press*, a weekly journal, inspired by Mr. Disraeli, and certainly the best informed paper as far as ministerial mysteries are concerned, made, on Saturday last, and accordingly before the arrival of the Petersburg dispatch, the following curious statement:

"We are informed, that in their private and confidential circles, the ministers declare that there is not only now no danger of war, but that the peril, if it ever existed, has long been averted. It seems that the proposition formally forwarded to St. Petersburg, [...] had been previously approved by the Emperor; and while the British Government assume in public countenance a tone which is exercising a deleterious influence on the trade of the country, in private they treat the panic as a hoax, scoff off any idea of war having ever been seriously contemplated by any power, and speak of the misunderstanding in question 'as a thing that has been settled these three weeks.' What does all this mean, what is the mystery of all this conduct? ... The propositions now at St. Petersburg, and which were approved by the Emperor before they were transmitted to St. Petersburg, involve a complete concession by Turkey to Russia of all those demands, a resistance to which brought about the present war between these two countries. Those demands were resisted by the Porte under the counsel and at the special instigation of England and France. By the advice and special instigation of England and France, those demands, according to this project, are now to be complied with. [...] There is some change of form, [...] but there is nothing material in that change. [...] The Emperor of Russia, in virtually establishing the Protectorate over the great bulk of the population of European Turkey, is to declare, that in so doing he has no wish to impugn the sovereign rights of the Sultan. Magnanimous admission!"[a]

Royalty in Great Britain is supposed to be only a nominal power, an assumption which accounts for the peace all parties keep with it. If you were to ask a Radical why his party abstained from attacking the prerogatives of the Crown, he would answer you: It is a mere State decoration which we don't care about. He would tell you that Queen Victoria has only once dared to have a will of her own, at the time of the famous bed chambermaid's catastrophe, when she insisted upon retaining her female Whig *entourage*, but was forced to yield to Sir Robert Peel, and dismiss it. Various circumstances, however, connected with the Oriental question—the inexplicable policy of the Ministry, the denunciations of foreign journals, and the successive arrival of Russian princes and princesses, at a moment when England was supposed to be on the eve of a war with the Autocrat—have accredited the rumor that there existed, during the whole epoch of the Eastern crisis, a Court conspiracy with Russia, sustaining the good old Aberdeen in office, paralyzing the showy alliance with France, and counteracting the official resistance to Russian encroachments. The Portuguese counter-revolution is hinted at, which was enforced by an English fleet, for the sole interest of the Coburg family.[213] It is iterated that Lord Palmerston, too, had been dismissed from the Foreign Office in consequence of Court intrigues. The notorious friendship between the Queen and the Duchess of Orleans is alluded to. It is remembered that the Royal Consort is a Coburg,[b] that the Queen's uncle is another Coburg,[c] highly interested as King of Belgium and as the son-in-law of Louis Philippe, in the fall of Bonaparte, and officially received into the circle of the Holy Alliance, by the marriage of his son[d] with an Austrian Archduchess.[e] Lastly, the reception which the Russian guests meet with, is contrasted with the imprisonment and chicanery English travelers lately met with in Russia.

The Paris *Siècle* some weeks ago denounced the English Court. A German paper dwelt on the Coburg-Orleans conspiracy, which, for the sake of family interests, had, through the medium of King

---

[a] *The Press*, No. 14, August 6, 1853.—*Ed.*
[b] Prince Albert.—*Ed.*
[c] Leopold I.—*Ed.*
[d] Léopold Louis Philippe Marie Victor.—*Ed.*
[e] Marie Henriette.—*Ed.*

Leopold and Prince Albert, enforced upon the English Ministry a line of policy dangerous to the Western nations, and fostering the secret intentions of Russia. The Brussels *Nation* had a long report of a Cabinet Council held at London, in which the Queen had formally declared that Bonaparte, by his pretensions to the Holy Shrines, had been the only cause of the present complications, that the Emperor of Russia wished less to humiliate Turkey than his French rival, and that she would never give her Royal assent to any war against Russia for the interest of a Bonaparte.

These rumors have been delicately alluded to by *The Morning Advertiser*, and have found a loud echo in the public, and a cautious one in the weekly press.

"Without desiring," says *The Leader*,[a] "to put constructions too wide, let us simply observe facts. The Princess Olga has come to England with her husband,[b] and her sister,[c] the Duchess of Leuchtenberg, the Emperor's most diplomatic daughter. She has been received by Baron Brunnow, and [...] she is at once welcomed *at Court*, and surrounded by the representatives of good society in England, Lord Aberdeen being among that [...] number."

Even *The Examiner*, the first of the first-rate London weekly papers, announces the arrival of these guests under the laconic rubric "*More Russians.*" In one of its leaders we find the remark,

"No earthly reason now exists why the Peace Society should not reappear before the world, in the most approved form, *under the patronage of His Royal Highness, Prince Albert.*"[d]

A more direct allusion is not allowable in a journal of the standing of *The Examiner*. It concludes the article from which I quote by contrasting the English Monarchy with the Transatlantic Republic:

"If the Americans should be ambitious to seize the place we once held in Europe, that is no affair of ours. Let them reap the present honor and ultimate advantage of enforcing the law of nations, and of being reverenced as the protectors of the feeble against the [...] strong. England is content, provided only Consols be at par, and her own coasts [...] secure against any immediate attack of a foreign army."

On a vote of £5,820, to defray the charge of works, repairs, furniture, etc., at the residence of the British Ambassador at Paris,

---

[a] *The Leader*, No. 176, August 6, 1853.—*Ed.*

[b] Charles Frederick Alexander.—*Ed.*

[c] Maria Nikolayevna.—*Ed.*

[d] Here and below Marx quotes from "Triumph of the Peace Party" in *The Examiner*, No. 2375, August 6, 1853.—*Ed.*

for the year ending 31st March, 1854, being proposed, Mr. Wise asked what had become of the £1,100 a year, voted for the last thirty years, in order to keep in repair the residence of the British Ambassador at Paris. Sir William Molesworth was compelled to own that the public money had been misapplied, and that, according to the architect Albano, sent by Government to Paris, the residence of the British Ambassador was in a most dilapidated state. The verandah around the house had fallen in; the walls were in a state of decay; the house had not been painted for several years; the staircases were unsafe; the cesspools were exhaling a most offensive effluvium; the rooms were full of vermin, which were running over the tables, and maggots were in every place on the furniture and on the curtains, while the carpets were stained by the dirt of dogs and cats.

Lord Palmerston's *Smoke Nuisance Suppression Bill* has passed a second reading. This measure once carried, the metropolis will assume a new aspect, and there will remain no dirty houses in London, except the House of Lords and the House of Commons.

Written on August 12, 1853

First published in the *New-York Daily Tribune*, No. 3854, August 24, 1853 and in abridged form in German in *Die Reform*, No. 43, August 27, 1853

Signed: *Karl Marx*

Reproduced from the *New-York Daily Tribune*

Karl Marx

URQUHART.—BEM.— THE TURKISH QUESTION IN THE HOUSE OF LORDS[214]

London, Tuesday, August 16, 1853

David Urquhart has published four letters on the Oriental question,[a] purporting to expose four delusions—firstly, that regarding the identity of the Oriental and Russian Churches; secondly, of there being a diplomatical contest between England and Russia; thirdly, of there being a possibility of war between England and Russia; and lastly, the delusion of union between England and France. As I intend to recur another time more fully to these letters,[215] I confine myself for the present to communicating to you the following letter addressed by Bem to Reshid Pasha, a letter published for the first time by Mr. Urquhart.

"Monseigneur! Not seeing the order arrive to command my presence at Constantinople, I conceive it to be my duty to address to your Highness some considerations which appear to me to be urgent. I commence by declaring that the Turkish troops which I have seen, cavalry, infantry, and field artillery—are excellent. In bearing, instruction, and military spirit, there can be no better. The horses surpass those of any European cavalry. That which is inappreciable is the desire felt by all the officers and all the soldiers to fight against Russia. With such troops I would willingly engage to attack a Russian force double their number, and I should be victorious. And as the Ottoman Empire can march against the Russians more troops than that Power can oppose to them, it is evident that the Sultan[b] may have the satisfaction to see restored to his sceptre all the Provinces treacherously withdrawn from his ancestors by the Czars of Moscow....

Bem."[c]

---

[a] D. Urquhart, "What Means Protection of the Greek Church", "Time in Diplomacy.—The European Recognition", "The Relative Power of Russia and Great Britain", "War between England and France", *The Morning Advertiser*, August 11, 12, 15, 16, 1853.—*Ed.*

[b] Abdul Mejid.—*Ed.*

[c] *The Morning Advertiser*, August 15, 1853.—*Ed.*

The Austrian Minister of Foreign Affairs[a] has sent to all the European Courts a note relative to the conduct of the American frigate *St. Louis*, in the Koszta affair, denouncing the American policy in general. Austria contends that she has the right to kidnap foreigners from the territory of a neutral power, while the United States have no right to commence hostilities in order to defend them.

On Friday, in the House of Lords, the Earl of Malmesbury did not inquire into the mystery of the Vienna Conference, or of the propositions forwarded by it to the Czar,[b] nor did he inquire as to the present state of transactions. His curiosity was rather of a retrospective and antiquarian character. What he moved for was "simple translations" of the two manifestos addressed by the Emperor, in May and June, to his diplomatical agents, and published in the *St. Petersburg Gazette*,[216] and also "for any answer which Her Majesty's Government might have sent to the statements therein contained." The Earl of Malmesbury is no ancient Roman. Nothing could be more repulsive to his feelings than the Roman manner of openly examining foreign Ambassadors amid the *patres conscripti*.

> The two Russian circulars he stated himself to "have been published openly to all Europe by the Emperor of Russia [...] in his own language, and [...] have also appeared in the English and French languages in the public prints."[c]

What possible good, then, could result from translating them again from the language of the writers of the public prints into the language of the clerks of the Foreign Office?

> "The French Government did answer the circulars immediately and ably.... The English reply, as we are told, was made soon after that of the French Government."

The Earl of Malmesbury was anxious to know how the indifferent prose of M. Drouyn de Lhuys might look when translated into the noble prose of the Earl of Clarendon.

He felt himself bound to remind "his noble friend opposite," that John Bull, after thirty years of peace, of commercial habits, and of industrial pursuits, had become "somewhat nervous" with regard to *war*, and that this nervosity had, since the month of

---

[a] *K. Buol-Schauenstein.—Ed.*

[b] *Nicholas I.—Ed.*

[c] Here and below passages from Malmesbury's speech and from those of other speakers in the House of Lords on August 12, 1853, are quoted from *The Times*, No. 21506, August 13, 1853.—*Ed.*

March last, "increased from the continued and lengthened mystery which the Government have drawn over their operations and negotiations." In the interest of peace, therefore, Lord Malmesbury interpellates, but in the same interest of peace the Government keeps silence.

The first signs of aggression of Russia on European Turkey no one was more annoyed at than the noble Earl himself. He had never suspected such a thing as Russian designs upon Turkey. He would not believe in what he saw. There was above all "the honor of the Emperor of Russia." But did the aggrandizement of his Empire ever damage the honor of an Emperor? There was "his conservative policy [...] which he had emphatically proved during the revolutions of 1848." Indeed, the Autocrat did not join in the wickedness of those revolutions. Especially, in 1852, when the noble Earl held the Foreign Office

"it was impossible for any Sovereign to give more repeated assurances, or to show a more sincere interest in the maintenance of the treaties by which Europe is bound, and the maintenance of the territorial arrangements which have existed for the happiness of Europe for so many years."

Certainly, when Baron Brunnow induced the Earl of Malmesbury to sign the treaty of 8th May, 1852, with regard to the succession of the Danish throne, he caught him with repeated assurances as to the foible of his august master for existing treaties; and when he persuaded him, at the time the Earl hailed the usurpation of Bonaparte, to enter into a secret alliance with Russia, Prussia, and Austria against this same Bonaparte, he made a great show of his sincere interest in the maintenance of the existing territorial arrangements.

In order to account for the sudden and unexpected change which has overcome the Emperor of Russia, the Earl of Malmesbury then enters into a psychological analysis "of the new impressions made on the *Emperor of Russia's mind*." The "feelings" of the Emperor, he ventures to affirm, "were irritated at the conduct of the French Government in regard to the Holy Shrines in Palestine." Bonaparte, it is true, in order to allay those irritated feelings, dispatched M. De la Cour to Constantinople, "a man of singularly mild and conciliatory conduct." But says the Earl, "it appears that in the Emperor of Russia's mind, what had passed had not been effaced," and that there remained a residue of bitter feeling with regard to France. M. De la Cour, it must be confessed, settled the question finally and satisfactorily, before Prince Menchikoff's arrival at Constantinople. "Still the impression on the mind of the Russian Emperor remained unaltered." So strong was this impression, and the mental aberration resulting from it, "that the Emperor still suspected the Turkish Government of wishing to impose upon Russia conditions which she had no right to impose." The Earl of Malmesbury owns that it is "impossible" not only for "any human being," but even for an English Lord, to "read the human mind;" nevertheless, "he cannot help thinking that he can account for those strange impressions effected upon the Emperor of Russia's mind." The moment, he says, had arrived, which the Russian population had been taught for many generations to look forward to as the "predestinated epoch of their obtaining Constantinople, and restoring the Byzantine Empire." Now he supposes "these feelings" to have been shared by "the present Emperor." Originally, the sagacious Earl intended to explain the Emperor's obstinate suspicion, that the Turkish Government wanted to hurt him in his rights, and now he informs us that he suspected Turkey, because he thought the proper moment to have arrived of swallowing her. Arrived at this point the noble Earl had necessarily to change the course of his deductions. Instead of accounting for the new impressions on the Emperor of Russia's mind which altered the old circumstances, he accounts now for the circumstances, which restrained for some time the ambitious mind and the old traditional feeling of the Czar from "giving way to temptation." These circumstances resolve themselves in the one great fact, that at one period the Earl of Malmesbury was "in," and that at the other period he was "out."

When "in" he was the first, not only to acknowledge Boustrapa,[a] but also to apologize for his perjury, his murders, and his usurpation. But, then,

> "the newspapers of the day continually found fault with what they called a subservient and cringing policy to the French Emperor."

The Coalition Ministry came, and with it Sir J. Graham and Sir Charles Wood,

> "condemning at public meetings the policy and character of the French Emperor, and condemning the French people, too, for the choice of this prince as their sovereign."

---

[a] A nickname of Louis Bonaparte, composed from the first syllables of the towns Boulogne and Strasbourg, where Bonapartist putsches were organised in 1836 and 1840, and of Paris, where a coup d'état was staged on December 2, 1851.—*Ed.*

Then followed the Montenegro affair,[217] and the Coalition

"allowing Austria to insist on the Sultan giving up any further coercion of the rebellious Montenegrins, and not even securing to the Turkish army a safe and peaceable retreat, thus causing Turkey a loss of from 1,500 to 2,000 men."[a]

At a later period the recall of Col. Rose from Constantinople, the refusal of the British Government to order simultaneously with France their fleet to Besika Bay or Smyrna—all these circumstances together, produced the impression on the Emperor of Russia's mind that the people and the Government of England were hostile to the French Emperor, and that no true alliance was possible between the two countries.

Having thus traced with a delicacy worthy of a romance-writer, who analyzes the undulating feelings of his heroine, the succession of circumstances belaboring the Emperor of Russia's impressionable mind and seducing him from the path of virtue, the Earl of Malmesbury flatters himself to have broken through the prejudices and antipathies which had alienated for centuries the French from the English people by his close alliance with the oppressor of the French people, he congratulates the present Government upon having inherited from him the intimate alliance with the Western Czar, and upon having reaped where the Tories had sown. He forgets that it is exactly this intimate alliance under the auspices of which the Sultan has been sacrificed to Russia, the Coalition being backed by the French Emperor, while the French Soulouque eagerly seizes the opportunity of slipping on the shoulders of the Mussulman into a sort of Vienna Congress and becoming respectable. In the same breath in which he congratulates the Ministry on their close alliance with Bonaparte, he denounces the very policy which has been the fruit of that *mésalliance.*

We shall not follow the Earl in his expectorations on the importance of Turkish integrity, in his denial of her decay, in his repudiation of the Russian religious Protectorate, nor in his reproaches to the Government for not having declared the invasion of the Principalities a *casus belli,* and for not having answered the crossing of the Pruth by sending out their fleet. He has nothing new except the following letter, "perfectly unsurpassed for insolence," addressed by Prince Menchikoff to Reshid Pasha on the eve of his departure from Constantinople:

---

[a] Here Marx quotes not from Malmesbury's speech, as below and above, but from Clarendon's speech in the House of Lords on August 12, 1853.—*Ed.*

"Buyukdere, May 9, [21st]

"At the moment of departure from Constantinople, the undersigned Ambassador of Russia, has learnt that the Sublime Porte manifested its intention to proclaim a guaranty for the exercise of the spiritual rights vested in the clergy of the Eastern Church, which, in fact, renders doubtful the maintenance of the other privileges which that Church enjoys. Whatever may be the motive of this determination, the undersigned is under the necessity of informing his Highness, the Minister of Foreign Affairs, that a declaration or any other act, which, although it may preserve the integrity of the purely spiritual rights of the orthodox Eastern Church, tends to invalidate the other rights, privileges and immunities accorded to her religion and clergy, from the most ancient times, and which they enjoy at the present moment, will be considered by the Imperial Cabinet as an act of hostility to Russia and to her religion.

"The undersigned begs, &c.

"Menchikoff."

The Earl of Malmesbury "could hardly believe that the Russian Emperor countenanced the conduct of Prince Menchikoff, or the manner in which he acted," a doubt confirmed by Nesselrode's notes following Menchikoff's departure, and the Russian army following Nesselrode' notes.

The "silent" Clarendon, "painful as it was to him," was obliged "to give the same answer over and over again," viz.: to give no answer at all. He felt it "his public duty not to say a word" which he had not already said, of "not laying any communication before them, and of not producing any separate dispatch." The noble Earl accordingly gave not one iota of information which we did not know before. His principal aim was to establish that, during the whole time that the Austrian and Russian Cabinets were making their encroachments, he was in "constant communication" with them. Thus he was in constant communication with the Austrian Government when it sent Prince Leiningen to Constantinople and its troops to the frontier, "because," at least this, says the innocent Clarendon, was the "reason given"—"because it apprehended an outbreak of its own subjects on the frontier." After the Sultan had yielded to Austria, by withdrawing his force, the energetic Clarendon "was again in communication with Austria, in order to insure the full execution of the treaty."

"I *believe*," continues the credulous Lord, "it was carried out, *for* the Austrian Government *assured* us that such was the case."

Very good, my Lord! As to the *entente cordiale* with France, it had ever existed since 1815! As to the part the French and English Governments took "with respect to the sending of their respective fleets," there "was not a shade of difference." Bonaparte ordered his fleet to proceed to Salamis,

"believing that danger was imminent," and, "although he" (Clarendon) "told him the danger was not so imminent, and that for the moment it was not necessary for the French fleet to leave the French ports," he ordered the French fleet to leave them; but this circumstance did not make the *slightest difference because* it was much more handy and more advantageous to have one fleet at Salamis and the other at Malta, than to have one at Malta and the other at Toulon."

Lord Clarendon further states that throughout the insolent pressure of Prince Menchikoff on the Porte

"it was a matter of satisfaction that the fleet was not ordered out because no one could say that the Turkish Government acted under their dictation."

After what has passed, it is indeed probable, that, had the fleet then been ordered out, the Sultan would have been forced to draw in. As to Menchikoff's "valedictory letter," Clarendon owned it to be correct, "but such language in diplomatic negotiations with governments was, fortunately, rare, and he hoped would long remain so." As to the invasion of the Principalities, the English and French Governments

"advised the Sultan to waive his undoubted right of treating the occupation of the Principalities as a *casus belli*."

As to the negotiations yet pending, all he would say was that,

"an official communication had been received this morning from Sir Hamilton Seymour, that the propositions agreed upon by the Ambassadors at Vienna, *if slightly modified*, would be received at St. Petersburg."

As to the terms of the settlement, he would rather die than let them slip out.

The noble Lord was responded to by Lord Beaumont, the Earl of Hardwicke, the Marquis of Clanricarde, and the Earl of Ellenborough. There was not one single voice to felicitate Her Majesty's Government on the course pursued in these negotiations. There were very great apprehensions on all sides that the ministerial policy had been the wrong way; that they had acted as mediators in behalf of Russia, instead of as defenders of Turkey, and that an early display of firmness on the part of England and France, would have placed them in a better position than that which they now hold. The old obstinate Aberdeen answered them, that "it was easy to speculate on what would have been the case, after the event had occurred; to say what might have been the case, had they followed a different course." However, his most startling and important statement was the following:

> "Their Lordships must be aware that they were not bound by any treaty. He denied that this country was bound by the stipulations of any treaty to take part in any hostilities in support of the Turkish Empire."

The Emperor of Russia, when England and France first showed their disposition to meddle with the pending Turkish affair, utterly repudiated the binding force of the treaty of 1841 upon his own dealings with the Porte, and the right of interposition resulting therefrom on the part of the Western Cabinets. At the same time he insisted upon the exclusion of the ships of war of the other Powers from the Dardanelles, in virtue of the same treaty of 1841. Now, Lord Aberdeen, in open and solemn assembly of Parliament, endorses this arrogant interpretation of a treaty which is only respected by the Autocrat when it excludes Great Britain from the Euxine.[a]

Written on August 16, 1853

First published in the *New-York Daily Tribune*, No. 3862 and the *New-York Semi-Weekly Tribune*, No. 863, September 2, 1853

Signed: *Karl Marx*

Reproduced from the *New-York Daily Tribune*

[a] Ancient name of the Black Sea.—*Ed.*

Karl Marx

THE TURKISH QUESTION IN THE COMMONS[218]

London, Friday, Aug. 19,[a] 1853

Lord John Russell having postponed his explanations on the Turkish question again and again, till at last, the last week of the Parliamentary session had happily arrived, came suddenly forward on Monday last, and gave notice that he would make his long deferred statement on Tuesday. The noble lord had ascertained that Mr. Disraeli had left London on Monday morning. In the same manner Sir Charles Wood, when he knew Sir J. Pakington and his partisans to be out of the House, suddenly brought in his India Bill, as amended by the House of Lords, and carried, in a thin house, without division, the re-enactment of the Salt-Monopoly. Such mean and petty tricks are the nerves and sinews of Whig Parliamentary tactics.

The Eastern question in the House of Commons, was a most interesting spectacle. Lord J. Russell opened the performances in a tone quite conformed to the part he had to play. This diminutive earthman, supposed to be the last representative of the once powerful Whig tribe, spoke in a dull, low, dry, monotonous, and barren-spirited manner—not like a Minister, but like a police reporter, who mitigates the horrors of his tale by the trivial, commonplace, and business-like style in which he relates it. He offered no "apology," but he made a confession. If there was any redeeming feature in his speech, it was its stiffness itself, which seemed intended to conceal some painful impressions laboring in

[a] The article is dated "August 18" in the *New-York Daily Tribune.* This is evidently a slip of the pen because Friday was on August 19, which was also put down in Marx's notebook as the date of sending the article to New York.—*Ed.*

the little man. Even the inevitable phrase of "the independence and integrity of the Ottoman Empire," sounded like an old reminiscence, recurring, by some inadvertence, in a funeral oration over that same Empire. The impression produced by this speech, which purported to announce the settlement of the Eastern complication, may be judged from the fact that, as soon as transmitted by telegraph to Paris, the funds fell immediately.

Lord John was right in stating that he had not to defend the Government, the Government not having been attacked; on the contrary, every disposition had been shown on the part of the House to leave negotiations in the hands of the Executive. Indeed no motion has been put by any member of Parliament to force discussion upon Ministers and there has not been held any meeting out of the House to force such a motion upon members of Parliament. If the ministerial policy has been one of secrecy and mystification, it was so with the silent consent of Parliament and of the public. As to the withholding of documents while negotiations were pending, Lord John asserted it to be an eternal law established by parliamentary tradition. It would be tedious to follow him in the narration of events familiar to everybody, and infused with no new life by his manner of rather enumerating than reciting them. There are, however, some important points Lord John was the first officially to confirm.

Before Prince Menchikoff's arrival at Constantinople the Russian Ambassador[a] informed Lord John that the Czar[b] intended to send a special mission to Constantinople with propositions relating exclusively to the Holy Cross and the immunities of the Greek Church connected with them. The British Ambassador at St. Petersburg,[c] and the British Government at home suspected no other intention on the part of Russia. It was not until the beginning of March, when the Turkish Minister informed Lord Stratford (Mr. Layard, however, affirms that Colonel Rose and many other persons at Constantinople were already initiated in the secret) that Prince Menchikoff had proposed a secret treaty[219] incompatible with Turkish independence, and that he had declared it to be the intention of Russia to consider any communication of the fact to either France or England as an act of direct hostility against Russia. It was known at the same time, not

---

[a] F. I. Brunnow.—*Ed.*
[b] Nicholas I.—*Ed.*
[c] G. H. Seymour.—*Ed.*

from mere rumor, but from authentic reports that Russia was accumulating great masses of troops on the frontiers of Turkey and at Odessa.

As to the note forwarded by the Vienna Conference to the Czar, and agreed upon by him, it had been prepared at Paris by M. Drouyn de Lhuys, who took the reply of Reshid Pasha to the last Russian note[220] for his basis. It was afterward taken up, in an altered form, by Austria, as her own proposition, on the 24th July, and received its final touch on the 31st of July. The Austrian Minister[a] having previously communicated it to the Russian Ambassador at Vienna,[b] it was already, on the 24th, conveyed to St. Petersburg before it was finally arranged, and it was not sent to Constantinople till the 2d of August, when the Czar had already agreed to it. Thus, after all, it is a Russian note addressed through the means of the four Powers to the Sultan, instead of a note of the Four Powers addressed to Russia and Turkey. Lord John Russell states that this note has "not the *exact form of Prince Menchikoff's note*," owning thereby that it has its exact contents. To leave no doubt behind, he adds:

"*The Emperor considers that his objects will be attained.*"[c]

The draft contains not even an allusion to the evacuation of the Principalities.

"Supposing that note," says Lord John, "to be finally agreed upon [...] by Russia and [...] Turkey, *there will still remain the great question of the evacuation of the Principalities.*"

He adds at the same time, that the British Government "considers this evacuation to be essential," but upon the mode by which this object is to be obtained he asks permission to say nothing. He gives us, however, sufficiently to understand that the fleets of England and France may have to leave Besika Bay before the Cossacks shall have left the Principalities.

"We ought not to consent to any arrangement by which it may be stipulated that the advance of the fleets to the neighborhood of the Dardanelles should be considered as equivalent to an actual invasion of the Turkish Territories. But, of course, if the matter is settled, if peace is secured, Besika Bay is not a station which would be of any advantage either to England or France."

---

[a] K. Buol-Schauenstein.—*Ed.*

[b] P. K. Meyendorff.—*Ed.*

[c] Russell's speech and those of other speakers in the House of Commons on August 16, 1853, are quoted from *The Times*, No. 21509, August 17, 1853.—*Ed.*

Now, as no man in his senses has ever supposed the French and English fleets are to remain for all time at Besika Bay, or France and England to enter into a formal stipulation forbidding them to advance to the neutral neighborhood of the Dardanelles, these ambiguous and cumbrous phrases, if they have any meaning at all, mean that the fleets will retire, after the note shall have been accepted by the Sultan and the Cossack promised to evacuate the Principalities.

> "When the Russian Government," says Lord John, "had occupied the Principalities, Austria [...] declared that, in conformity with the spirit of the Treaty of 1841, it was absolutely necessary that the representatives of the Powers should meet in conference, and should endeavor to obtain some amicable solution of a difficulty which might otherwise threaten the peace of Europe."

Lord Aberdeen, on the contrary, declared some days ago[a] in the House of Lords, and also, as we are informed from other sources, in a formal note communicated to the Cabinets of St. Petersburg and Constantinople in the course of last June, that

> "the Treaty of 1841 did not in any way impose upon the Powers who signed it the obligation of actual assistance in behalf of the Porte [but of a temporary abstention from entering the Dardanelles!] and that the Government of Her British Majesty[b] held themselves perfectly free to act or not to act, according to its own interests."

Lord Aberdeen only repudiates all obligations toward Turkey, in order not to possess any right against Russia.

Lord John Russell concludes with "*a fair aspect*" of the negotiations approaching their crowning result. This seems a very sanguine view of the matter, at the moment when the Russian note, arranged at Vienna and to be presented by Turkey to the Czar, has not yet been accepted by the Sultan, and when the *sine qua non* of the Western Powers, viz.: the evacuation of the Principalities, has not yet been pressed upon the Czar.

Mr. Layard, the first speaker who rose in response to Lord John, made by far the best and most powerful speech—bold, concise, substantial, filled with facts, and proving the illustrious scholar to be as intimately acquainted with Nicholas as with Sardanapalus, and with the actual intrigues in the Orient as well as with the mysterious traditions of its past.

Mr. Layard regretted that Lord Aberdeen had "on several occasions, and in several places, declared that his policy is essentially a policy based on peace." If England shrank from

[a] On August 12, 1853.—*Ed.*
[b] Victoria.—*Ed.*

maintaining her honor and interests by war, she encouraged on the part of a lawless Power like Russia, pretensions which must inevitably lead sooner or later to war. The present conduct of Russia must not be considered as a mere casual and temporary occurrence, but as part and parcel of a great scheme of policy.

As to the "concessions" made to France and the "intrigues" of M. de Lavalette, they could not even afford a pretext to Russia, because

> "a draught of the firman making those concessions, of which Russia complains, was delivered by the Porte to M. de Titoff some days, if not weeks, before it was issued, and [...] no objection whatever was made to the terms of that firman."

Russia's designs with regard to Serbia, Moldo-Wallachia and the Christian population of Turkey were not to be misunderstood. Immediately after his public entry at Constantinople, Prince Menchikoff demanded the dismissal of M. Garašanin, from his post of Serbian Minister. That demand was complied with, although the Serbian Synod protested. M. Garašanin was one of the men brought forward by the insurrection of 1842, that national movement against Russian influence which expelled the then reigning Prince Michel from Serbia,[221] he and his family being mere tools in the hands of Russia. In 1843 the Russian Government claimed the right of interference in Serbia. Completely unauthorized by any treaty, she was authorized by *Lord Aberdeen,* then Minister of Foreign Affairs, who declared, "*that Russia had the right to place her own construction on her own treaties.*"

> "By her success in that transaction," says Mr. Layard, "Russia showed that she was mistress of Serbia and could check any rising independent nationality."

As to the Danubian Principalities, Russia first took advantage of the national movement of 1848 in those provinces, compelling the Porte to expel from them every man of liberal and independent opinions. Then, she forced upon the Sultan the treaty of Balta-Liman,[222] by which she established her right to interfere in all the internal affairs of the Principalities,

> "and her present occupation of them has proved that Moldavia and Wallachia are to all intents and purposes Russian provinces."

There remained the Greeks of Turkey and the Slavonians of Bulgaria professing the Christian religion.

> "The spirit of inquiry and independence has sprung up among the Greeks, and this together with their commercial intercourse with the free States of Europe, has

greatly alarmed the Russian Government. There was another cause, viz., the spread of the Protestant faith among the Christians of the East, [...] mainly through the influence and teachings of American missionaries, scarcely a considerable town exists in Turkey, in which there is not a nucleus of a Protestant community. [Another motive for American intervention.] The Greek clergy backed by the Russian mission have done all in their power to check this movement, and, when persecution was no longer available, Prince Menchikoff appeared at Constantinople. [...] The great end of Russia has been to crush the spirit of religious and political independence, which has manifested itself of late years among the Christian subjects of the Porte."

As to the establishment of a so-called *Greek Empire at Constantinople,* Mr. Layard, meaning of course the Greeks in contradistinction to the Slavonians, stated that the Greeks amount hardly to 1,750,000; that the Slavonians and Bulgarians have been struggling for years to throw off all connection with them, by refusing to accept for their clergy and bishops the priests of the Greek nation; that the Serbians have created a Patriarch of their own in lieu of that at Constantinople; and that establishing the Greeks at Constantinople would be playing the whole of Turkey into the hands of Russia.

To the members of the House, who declared that it would signify little whether Constantinople was in the hands of Russia or not, Mr. Layard replied that, Constantinople being broken, all the great Provinces which constitute Turkey, as, for instance, Asia Minor, Syria and Mesopotamia, would fall into a state of confusion and anarchy. The power into whose hands they were to fall, would command India. The power which held Constantinople, would ever be looked upon in the East as the dominant power of the world.

Russia, however, was aware that no European State would permit her to take possession of Constantinople at this time. Meanwhile,

"her object is to render all independent nationalities in that country impossible—to weaken the Turkish power gradually, but surely; and to show to those who would oppose her designs, that any such opposition is not only useless, but would entail upon them her vengeance; in fact, to render any other government but her own impossible in Turkey. *In those designs she has entirely succeeded on this occasion.*"

Mr. Layard represented that the Government, after the demand of a secret treaty by Prince Menchikoff, and the great Russian armaments on the frontier and at Odessa, were satisfied with the explanations and assurances given at St. Petersburg, and failed to declare that England and France would consider the passing of the Pruth as a *casus belli*, and that they had not interdicted Russia from entering into any treaties or engagements with Turkey without their participation.

> "If we had taken that step Russia would never have dared to cross the Pruth."

Mr. Layard then exposed how the Principalities, independent, united with Bessarabia and leaning on Hungary, would ultimately be the only means of preserving Constantinople from the Russians and of cutting the great Sclav race in two. He thinks that Russia *will* evacuate the Principalities.

> "It would not be worth the while of Russia to engage in a war with the Great Powers of Europe on account of those provinces, which are already, to all intents and purposes, her own. [...] Russia has gained, without firing a shot, what is worth to her a bloody and expensive campaign; she has established her power in the East; she has humiliated Turkey; she has compelled her to go to all the expense of a war, and has exhausted her resources; but, what is more, she has humiliated this country and France in the eyes of her own subjects and of the populations of the East."

The note drawn up by the Vienna Conference will have the result that,

> "if the Porte declines to adhere to it, Russia will have turned the tables completely upon us, and made us her ally against Turkey in compelling her to accept an unjust proposal. If she accept, England has directly sanctioned the right of Russia to interfere in behalf of twelve millions of Christians, the subjects of the Porte.... Look at the question as we will; it is clear that we have taken the place of a second-rate Power in it, and conceded that of a first-rate Power to Russia alone.... We had an opportunity which, perhaps, will never occur again of settling on a proper basis this great Eastern question.... Russia has been enabled to strike a blow from which Turkey will never recover.... The result of the policy which this country has pursued will not end here. Sweden, Denmark, every weak State of Europe, which has placed dependence on the character of this country, [...] will see that it is useless any more to struggle against the encroachments of Russia."

Sir John Pakington next made some remarks, which were important as declaratory of the views of the Tory opposition. He regretted that Lord John Russell could not make a statement more satisfactory to the House and to the country. He assured the Government that its determination to consider the evacuation of the Principalities as a *sine qua non*, will "be supported not only by the opinion of this House, but by the almost unanimous opinion of the people of this country." Till the papers should have been produced, he must reserve his judgment on the policy of advising Turkey not to consider the occupation of the Principalities as a *casus belli*, of not following a more vigorous and decisive policy at an earlier period, of injuring and holding in suspense the interests of Turkey and of Great Britain, and their commerce, by transactions protracted for six months.

Lord Dudley Stuart indulged in one of his habitual good-natured Democratic declamations, which are certainly more gratifying to the man who spouts them than to anybody else. If you compress inflated balloons or blown up phrases, there remains nothing in your hands, not even the wind that made them appear like something. Dudley Stuart repeated the often repeated statements on the improvements going on in Turkey, and on the greater liberality of the Sultan's rule, whether in regard to religion or commerce, when compared with that of Russia. He remarked, justly, that it was useless to boast of peace, while the unhappy inhabitants of the Danubian Principalities actually endured the horrors of war. He claimed for the inhabitants of these provinces the protection of Europe against the terrible oppression to which they were now subjected. He showed, by facts from Parliamentary history, that the members of the House had the right of speechifying, even while negotiations were going on. He forgot hardly anything, which must be familiar to a true and constant reader of *The Daily News*. There were two "points" in his speech:

> "Although the explanation of the noble lord" (J. Russell) "had not been very full, for he told the House nothing but what it knew before, still, from its very omissions, he was afraid that they must come to the conclusion, *that the noble lord had been doing something of which he ought to be ashamed.*"

As to the Earl of Aberdeen,

> "he had told them that peace had been preserved for thirty years, with great advantage to the prosperity and liberty of Europe, but he" (Dudley Stuart) "denied that the liberty of Europe had been benefited by the peace. Where, he would ask, was Poland? where Italy? where Hungary?—nay, where Germany?"

Borne along by the power of fluency, that fatal gift of third-rate orators, the Democratic lord cannot stop, till he arrives, from the despots of the Continent, to his native monarch, "who rules in the hearts of her subjects."

Mr. M. Milnes, one of those ministerial retainers, on whose brow you read:

> "Do not talk of him
> But as a property,"[a]

[a] Shakespeare, *Julius Caesar*, Act IV, Scene 1.—*Ed.*

did not dare to make a decidedly ministerial speech. He made an alternative speech. On the one side he found that Ministers, by withholding the papers from the table of the House, "acted with very great prudence and judgment," but, on the other hand, he gave them to understand that they would have acted "more strongly and firmly" the other way. On the one hand he thought the Government might have been right in submitting to the demands of Russia, but, on the other hand, it seemed questionable to him whether they had not, in some degree, encouraged Turkey to pursue a line of policy which they were not prepared to support, etc., etc. On the whole, he made out that "the more he reflected on those subjects, the more extreme were the difficulties which they presented to his mind"—the less he understood those subjects, the better he understood the temporizing policy of the Government.

After the alternative juggle and perplexed mind of Mr. Monckton Milnes we are refreshed by the rough straightforwardness of Mr. Muntz, M.P. for Birmingham, and one of the matadors of the Reform-House of 1831.

> "When the Dutch Ambassador made to Charles II some very objectionable proposition, the King replied: 'God bless me! you never made such a proposition to Oliver Cromwell.' 'No,' said the Ambassador, 'you are a very different man from Oliver Cromwell.' If this country had had now such a man as Oliver Cromwell, we should have had a different Minister, and a very different Government, and Russia would never have marched into the Danubian Provinces. [...] The Emperor of Russia knew, that nothing would make this country go to war: witness Poland, witness Hungary. This country was now reaping the benefit of its own conduct in those instances. [...] He considered the state of this country in relation to its foreign affairs was a very objectionable and a very unsatisfactory one. And he believed that the people of England felt that their character had been degraded, and that all sense of honor on the part of the Government was absorbed in consideration of mere pounds, shillings and pence. The only questions mooted by the Government now were simply what would be the expense, and would war be agreeable to the different tradesmen of the nation?"

Birmingham happening to be the center of an armament-manufacturing and musket-selling population, the men of that town naturally scoff at the Manchester Cotton-Peace-Fraternity.

Mr. Blackett, the member for Newcastle-upon-Tyne, did not believe that the Russians would evacuate the Principalities. He warned the Government

> "*not to be swayed by any dynastic sympathies or antipathies.*"

Assailed on all sides, from all shades of opinion, the Ministers sat there mournful, depressed, inanimate, broken down; when

Richard Cobden suddenly rose, congratulating them for having adopted his peace doctrines and applying that doctrine to the given case, with all the sharp ingenuity and fair sincerity of the *monomaniac,* with all the contradictions of the *idéologue,* and with all the calculating cowardice of the shop-keeper. He preached what the ministry had openly acted, what the Parliament had silently approved, and what the ruling classes had enabled the ministry to do and the Parliament to accept. From fear of war he attained for the first time to something like historical ideas. He betrayed the mystery of middle-class policy, and therefore he was repudiated as a traitor. He forced middle-class England to see herself as in a mirror, and as the image was by no means a flattering one, he was ignominiously hissed. He was inconsistent, but his inconsistency itself was consistent. Was it his fault if the traditional fierce phrases of the aristocratic past did not harmonize with the pusillanimous facts of the stockjobbing present?

He commenced by declaring that there was no difference of opinion on the question:

> "Still, there was apparently very great uneasiness on the subject of Turkey."

Why was this? Within the last twenty years there had been a growing conviction that the Turks in Europe were intruders in Europe; that they were not domiciled there; that their home was Asia; that Mohammedanism could not exist in civilized States; that we could not maintain the independence of any country, if she could not maintain it for herself; that it was now known that there were three Christians to every Turk in European Turkey.

> "We could not take a course which would insure Turkey in Europe as an independent power against Russia, unless the great bulk of the population were with us in our desire to prevent another power from taking possession of that country.... As to sending our fleets up to Besika Bay, and keeping out the Russians, no doubt we could do that, because Russia would not come into collision with a maritime power; but we were keeping up these enormous armaments, and were not settling the Eastern Question.... The question was, what were they going to do with Turkey, and with the Christian population of Turkey. Mohammedanism could not be maintained; and we should be sorry to see this country fighting for Mohammedanism in Europe."

Lord Dudley Stuart had talked about maintaining Turkey on account of commerce. He (Cobden) never would fight for a tariff. He had too much faith in free trade principles to think that they needed fighting for. The exports to Turkey had been overrated. Very little of it was consumed in the countries under the dominions of the Turks.

"All the commerce which we had in the Black Sea, was owing to the encroachments of Russia upon the Turkish coast. Our grain and flax we did not now get from Turkey, but from Russia. And would not Russia be as glad to send us her tallow, hemp and corn, whatever aggressions she might make on Turkey? [...] We had a trade with Russia in the Baltic.... What prospect had we of a trade with Turkey? It was a country without a road. [...] Russia was the more commercial people. Let us look at St. Petersburg, at her quays and wharves, and warehouses.... What natural alliance then could we have with such a country as Turkey?... Something had been said about the balance of power. That was a political view of the question.... A great deal had been said about the power of Russia, and the danger to England in consequence of her occupying those countries on the Bosphorus. [...] Why, what an absurdity it was to talk of Russia coming to invade England! Russia could not move an army across her own frontiers, without coming to Western Europe for a loan.... A country [...] so poor, [...] a mere aggregate of villages without capital and without resources, as compared with England, never could come and injure us, or America, or France.... England was ten times more powerful than she had ever been, and far more able to resist the aggressions of a country like Russia."

And now Cobden passed to the incomparably greater dangers of war to England in her present condition than at former epochs. The manufacturing population had greatly increased. They were far more dependent on the export of their produce and on the import of raw materials. They possessed no longer the monopoly of manufacture. The repeal of the Navigation Laws[223] had thrown England open to the competition of the world in shipping as well as in everything else.

"He begged [...] Mr. Blackett to consider that no port would suffer more than that which he represented. [...] The Government had done wisely in disregarding the cry of thoughtless men.... Their taking up a position for maintaining the integrity of the Turkish Empire he did not blame, as that was a traditional policy handed down to them.... The Government of the day would obtain credit for having been as peaceable as the people would allow them to be."

Richard Cobden was the true hero of the drama, and shared the fate of all true heroes—a tragical one. But then came the sham hero; the fosterer of all delusions, the man of fashionable lies and of courtly promises; the mouthpiece of all brave words that may be said in the act of running away; Lord Palmerston came. This old, experienced and crafty debater saw at once that the criminal might escape sentence by disavowing his advocate. He saw that the Ministry, attacked on all sides, might turn the tables by a brilliant diatribe against the only man who dared to defend it, and by refuting the only grounds on which its policy possibly might have been excused. There was nothing easier than to show the contradictions of Mr. Cobden. He had stated his perfect concurrence with the precedent orators, and ended by differing from them on every point. He had defended the integrity of Turkey, and did everything to show that she was worth no defence. He, the preacher of peace, had advocated the aggressions of Russia. Russia was weak, but a war with Russia would be inevitable ruin to England. Russia was a conglomerate of mere villages, but St. Petersburg being a finer city than Constantinople, Russia was entitled to possess them both. He was a Free Trader, but he preferred the protective system of Russia to the free-trade system of Turkey. Whether Turkey consumed herself, or was a canal through which passed articles of consumption to other parts of Asia, was it indifferent to England that she should remain a free passage? Mr. Cobden was a great advocate for the principle of non-intervention, and now he would dispose, by parliamentary enactments, of the destinies of the Mohammedans, Greeks, Slavonians, and other races inhabiting the Turkish Empire. Lord Palmerston exalted the progress Turkey had made, and the forces she now commanded. "Turkey, it is certain, has no Poland and no Siberia."[a] Because Turkey possessed so much strength, Lord Palmerston would, of course, compel her to suffer a few provinces to be invaded by the Russians. A strong empire can suffer anything. Lord Palmerston proved to Richard Cobden that there existed not one sound reason for adopting the course adopted by Lord Palmerston and his colleagues, and, interrupted at each sentence by enthusiastic cheers, the old histrion contrived to sit down, with the impudent and self-contradictory phrase:

> "I am satisfied that Turkey has within itself the elements of life and prosperity, and I believe that the course adopted by Her Majesty's Government is a sound policy, deserving the approbation of the country, and which it will be the duty of every English Government to pursue." (Cheers.)

Palmerston was great in "*fearful bravery*," as Shakespeare calls it.[b] He showed, as Sidney said, "a fearful boldness, daring to do that which he knew that he knew not how to do."

Written on August 19, 1853

First published in the *New-York Daily Tribune*, No. 3862 and the *New-York Semi-Weekly Tribune*, No. 863, September 2, 1853

Signed: *Karl Marx*

Reproduced from the *New-York Daily Tribune*

---

[a] The *Hansard's Parliamentary Debates*, 3rd Ser., Vol. CXXIX, p. 1809, gives "Circassia" instead of "Siberia" as cited in the report of *The Times*.—*Ed.*

[b] Shakespeare, *Julius Caesar*, Act V, Scene 1.—*Ed.*

Karl Marx

AFFAIRS CONTINENTAL AND ENGLISH[224]

London, Tuesday, Aug. 23, 1853

The German and Belgian papers affirm, on the authority of the telegraphic dispatches from Constantinople, of the 13th inst., that the Porte has acceded to the proposals of the Vienna Conference. The French papers, however, having received dispatches from Constantinople of the same date, state merely that the Divan had shown a willingness to receive those proposals. The definitive answer could hardly reach Vienna before the 20th inst. The pending question, and a very serious one, is, whether the Porte will send its Ambassador to St. Petersburg before or after the withdrawal of the Russian troops from the Principalities.

The last accounts from the Black Sea announce that the north-east winds had begun to disturb the navigation. Several ships anchored at Penderekli and other places on the coast, had been compelled to quit their anchorage to avoid being cast ashore.

You know that after the events in Moldavia and Wallachia, the Sultan[a] had ordered the Hospodars[b] to leave the Principalities for Constantinople, and that the Hospodars refused to comply with their sovereign's demands. The Sultan has now deposed the Hospodar of Wallachia on account of his favorable reception of the Russian troops and the support he gave them. On the 9th inst. this firman was read to the Assembly of Boyards, who resolved to petition the Hospodar not to abandon the Government in the present critical circumstances. The Prince acted accordingly. Mano, the Secretary of State, and Ioanidis, the Director of the Ministry of the Interior, have also been summoned to Constan-

[a] Abdul Mejid.— *Ed.*
[b] G. Ghica (Moldavia) and B. Stirbei (Wallachia).— *Ed.*

tinople; they, however, refused to go, on the pretext that public order might be disturbed. The French and British Consuls, upon this, suspended immediately all relations with the rebel Government.

Affairs in Serbia are taking a complicated turn. The Paris *Constitutionnel* of last Friday had the following Constantinople intelligence.[a] Austria, taking advantage of the Sultan's difficulties, had pressed certain demands upon him.

An Austrian Consul-General, having lately made a tour of inspection through Bosnia and Serbia, declared to Alexander, the Prince of Serbia, that Austria was prepared to occupy Serbia with her troops in order to suppress any dangerous movement among the population. The Prince, having refused the offer of the Consul-General, at once dispatched a special messenger to Constantinople with an account of this Austrian overture, and Reshid Pasha referred to Baron de Bruck for explanations. The latter said that the Consul-General had previously communicated with the Prince, alleging the fear Austria was in, lest her subjects, on the borders of Serbia, should become involved in any disturbances arising in that province. The reply of Reshid Pasha was to the effect that any occupation of Serbia by Austrian troops would be considered an act of hostility by the Porte, which would itself be answerable for the tranquility of that province; moreover, the Pasha promised that a special Commissioner should be at once sent to see and report on the state of affairs in Serbia.

The day after, several London papers announced the entrance into Serbia of the Austrian troops, an announcement which, however, has turned out to be unfounded. Yesterday the same papers communicated the outbreak of a counter-revolution in Serbia, yet this news likewise rested on no better foundation than a false translation of the German word, *Auflauf*,[b] the fact being that only a small riot had taken place. To-day the German papers publish news from Constantinople of the 9th inst. According to them, several divans had been held on Serbian affairs. The conduct of Prince Alexander was much approved of, and the decision arrived at that, if Austrian troops should attempt to occupy that province, they should, if necessary, be expelled by force. A division of troops has actually been directed towards the frontiers of Bosnia. Private letters received at Constantinople on the 8th inst.,

[a] The reference is to the report in *Le Constitutionnel*, No. 231, August 19, 1853.—*Ed.*

[b] Unlawful assembly, riot, tumult.—*Ed.*

conveyed thither the news of Prince Alexander having, in consequence of his conflict with the Austrian Consul, appealed to the decision of the Consuls of France and England, and absented himself momentarily from Belgrade. It is said that he went to Nissa, there to wait for orders from the Porte.

Mr. D. Urquhart, in a letter[a] addressed to *The Morning Advertiser* of this day, remarks, with regard to the Serbian complication:

"War with Turkey is not [...] at present contemplated by Russia; for, by the cooperation of Austria, she would lose her 'Greek' allies, but she involves Austria in a preparatory collision, which will bring Serbia into a condition parallel to that of the Principalities. Thus will be introduced a religious warfare between Latins and Greeks.... Russia, by a sudden shifting of decorations, may render her own occupation of the Principalities acceptable to Turkey, as a protection against the Austrian occupation of Serbia, and thus mutually engage Austria and Turkey in projects of dismemberment, and support them therein."

The Hospodar of Moldavia proposes to contract a loan with Russian bankers in order to meet the extraordinary expenses of the occupation.

The want of provisions is so great in the fortresses of Bulgaria that the strictest economy has to be observed, and the garrisons are suffering severely.

The *Journal de Constantinople* reports from Aleppo:

"A discovery has recently been made of a gang of evil-disposed Turks about to rise, as in 1850, against the Christian population of that town. But thanks to the extreme vigilance of the Governor Pasha,[b] and of Ali Asmi Pasha, the Commander-in-Chief of the troops at Aleppo, their attempts have been suppressed and public order has been preserved. On this occasion Demetrius, the Patriarch of the Greek Catholic creed, and Basilius, the Patriarch of the Armenian creed, have addressed in the name of their respective communities a collective letter of gratitude to Reshid Pasha, for the protection afforded to the Christians by the Sultan's Government."

The German *St. Petersburg Gazette* has the following in a leader on Oriental affairs:

"What the friends of peace could only hope for at the commencement of July, has become a certainty in the latter days. The work of mediation between Russia and Turkey is now definitively placed in the hands of Austria. At Vienna there will be devised a solution of the Eastern question, which in these latter times has kept in suspense all the action between the Black Sea and the Ocean, and which alone has prevented European Diplomacy from taking its habitual holidays."

---

[a] "The Kaiser and the Czar."—*Ed.*

[b] Osman Pasha.—*Ed.*

Observe the studious affectation with which, in lieu of the four Powers, Austria alone is constituted mediator, and which places the suspense of nations, in the true Russian style, only on a scale with the interrupted holidays of diplomacy.

The Berlin *National Zeitung* publishes[a] a letter from Georgia, dated 15th July, stating that Russia intends a new campaign against the people of the Caucasus at the end of the present month, and that a fleet in the Sea of Azov is fitted out in order to support the operations of the land army.

The session of 1853 was brought to a close on Saturday last—Parliament being prorogued until October 27. A very indifferent and meager speech, purporting to be the Queen's[b] message, was read by commission. In answer to Mr. Milnes Lord Palmerston assured Parliament that it could safely disband, as far as the evacuation of the Principalities was concerned, giving, however, no pledge of any kind but "his confidence in the honor and the character of the Russian Emperor," which would move him to withdraw his troops *voluntarily* from the Principalities.[c] The Coalition Cabinet thus revenged itself for his speech against Mr. Cobden,[d] by forcing him to record solemnly his "confidence in the character and the honor" of the Czar. The same Palmerston received on the same day a deputation from the aristocratic fraction of the Polish Emigration at Paris and its collateral branch at London,[225] presenting his lordship with an address and medallions in gold, silver and bronze of Prince Adam Czartoryski, in testimony of their gratitude to his lordship for allowing the sequestration of Cracow in 1846, and for otherwise exhibiting sympathy with the cause of Poland. The inevitable Lord Dudley Stuart, the patron of the London branch of the Paris society, was of course the master of ceremonies. Lord Palmerston assured these simple-minded men "of his deep interest in the history of Poland, which was a very painful history."[e] The noble lord omitted not to remind them that he spoke not as a member of the Cabinet, but received them only as a private amateur.

The first half of the long protracted session of 1853 was filled up with the death-struggle of the Derby Ministry, with the

---

[a] *National-Zeitung*, No. 384, August 19, 1853.—*Ed.*

[b] Victoria.—*Ed.*

[c] Quoted according to *The Times*, No. 21513, August 22, 1853.—*Ed.*

[d] See this volume, pp. 275-76.—*Ed.*

[e] Quoted from "Lord Palmerston and the Poles" published in *The Times*, No. 21513, August 22, 1853.—*Ed.*

formation and final victory of the Coalition Cabinet, and with the Easter recess of Parliament. As to the real session, its most remarkable features were the dissolution of all the old political parties, the corruption of the members of Parliament, and the petrifaction of the privileged constituencies revealing the curious working of the Government, embracing all the shades of opinion, and all the talents of the official world, proclaiming postponement the solution of all questions, shifting all difficulties by half-and-half measures, feeding upon promises, declaring "performance as a kind of will or testament which argues a great weakness in his judgment that makes it," retracting, modifying, unsettling its own legislative acts as quickly as it brought them in, living upon the inheritance of predecessors whom it had fiercely denounced, leaving the initiative of its own measures to the house which it presumed to lead, and reaping failure as the inevitable fate of the few acts, the uncontroverted authorship of which it holds. Thus parliamentary reform, national education reform, and law reform (a few trifles apart) have been postponed. The Transportation bill, the Navigation bill, etc., were inherited from the Derby Cabinet. The Canada Clergy Reserves[226] bill was dreadfully mutilated by the Government a few days after having introduced it. As to the budget, the Succession act was proposed by the Chancellor of the Exchequer only after he had voted against it. The Advertisement act was undergone by him only when his opposition to it had twice been voted down. The new regulation of the licensing system was finally abandoned, after it had suffered various transformations. Introduced by Mr. Gladstone with pretensions to a great scheme, a thing worth the budget as a whole, it came out of the House as a miserable patch-work, as a mere conglomerate of fortuitous, incoherent and contradictory little items. The only great feature of the India bill, the non-renewal of the Company's charter, was introduced by the Ministry after they had announced its renewal for 20 years more. The two acts truly and exclusively belonging to the Ministry of all the talents: the Cab act and the Conversion of the Public Debt, had scarcely passed the threshold of the House, when they were publicly hissed as failures. The foreign policy of the "strongest Government England ever saw," is owned by its own partisans to have been the *nec plus ultra* of helpless, vacillating weakness. The Chesham Place Treaty, however, contracted between the Peelite bureaucrats, the Whig oligarchs and the sham-Radicals,[227] has been linked the more strongly by the threatening aspect of things abroad and by the even more imminent symptoms of popular discontent at home—manifested through the unprecedented intensity and generality of strikes, and the renewal of the Chartist agitation. In judging the external policy of the ruling classes and of the Cabinet, we must not lose sight of a war with Russia training behind it a general revolutionary conflagration of the Continent, and at this time likely to meet with a fatal echo from the masses of Great Britain.

As to the House of Lords, its doings admit of a very short *résumé*. It has exhibited its bigotry by the rejection of the Jewish Emancipation bill,[228] its hostility to the working classes by burking the Workingmen's Combination bill, its interested hatred of the Irish people by shelving the Irish Land bills, and its stupid predilection for Indian abuses by re-establishing the Salt monopoly. It has acted throughout in secret understanding with the Government that whatever progressive measures might by chance pass the Commons, should be canceled by the enlightened Lords.

Among the papers laid on the table of Parliament before its prorogation, there is a voluminous correspondence carried on between the British and Russian Governments with regard to the obstructions to navigation in the Sulina mouth of the Danube. The correspondence begins on Feb. 9, 1849, and concludes in July, 1853, having concluded nothing whatever. Things have now arrived at such a point that even the Austrian Government is forced to announce that the mouth of the Danube has become impassable for navigation, and that its own mails to Constantinople will be henceforth forwarded by Trieste. The whole difficulty is the fruit of British connivance at Muscovite encroachments. In 1836 the English Government acquiesced in the usurpation of the mouth of the Danube by Russia, after having instructed a commercial firm to resist the interference of the officers of the Russian Government.

The so-called peace concluded with Burma, announced with a proclamation of the Governor-General of India,[a] dated June 30, 1853, and upon which the Queen is made to congratulate Parliament, is nothing but a simple truce. The King of Ava,[b] starved into submission, expressed his desire for the cessation of war, set the British prisoners at liberty, asked for the raising of the river blockade, and forbade his troops to attack the territories of Mecadeay and Toungu, where the British Government had placed garrisons—in the same manner as the Turkish Government has forbidden its troops to attack the Russians stationed in the

[a] J. Dalhousie.—*Ed.*
[b] Mindon.—*Ed.*

Principalities. But he does not recognize the claims of England to Pegu or to any other portion of the Burmese Empire. All that England has got by this struggle is a dangerous and controverted frontier instead of a secure and acknowledged one. She has been driven out of the ethnographical, geographical and political circumscription of her Indian dominions, and the Celestial Empire itself no longer forms any natural barrier to her conquering force. She has lost her point of gravitation in Asia and pushed into the indefinite. She is no longer mistress of her own movements, there being no stopping but where the land falls into the sea. England seems thus to be destined to open the remotest Orient to Western intercourse, but not to enjoy nor to hold it.

The great colliers' strikes in South Wales not only continue, but out of them have arisen new strikes among the men employed at the iron mines. A general strike among the British sailors is anticipated for the moment when the Merchant Shipping bill will come into operation, the foreigners being, as they say, admitted only for the purpose of lowering their wages. The importance of the present strikes, to which I have repeatedly called the attention of your readers, begins now to be understood even by the London middle-class press. Thus, the *Weekly Times* of last Saturday remarks:

> "The relations between employer and employed have been violently disturbed. Labor throughout the length and breadth of the land has bearded capital, and it may safely be asserted that the quarrel thus evoked has only just commenced. The working classes have been putting forth strong feelers to try their position. [...] The agitation at present is limited to a series of independent skirmishes, but there are indications that the period is not very distant when this desultory warfare will be turned into a systematic and universal combination against capital ...."[a]

Written on August 23,1853

First published in the *New-York Daily Tribune,* No. 3864, September 5, 1853; reprinted in the *New-York Semi-Weekly Tribune,* No. 864, September 6, 1853

Signed: *Karl Marx*

Reproduced from the *New-York Daily Tribune*

[a] Quoted from "The Parliamentary Doings of '53" in the *Weekly Times,*No. 345, August 21, 1853.—*Ed.*

Karl Marx

MICHAEL BAKUNIN[229]

TO THE EDITOR OF *THE MORNING ADVERTISER*

Sir,—Messrs. Herzen and Golovine have chosen to connect the *New Rhenish Gazette*, edited by me in 1848 and 1849, with the polemics going on between them and "F.M.,"[a] with regard to Bakunin. They tell the English public that the calumny against Bakunin took origin in that paper, which had even ventured to appeal to the testimony of George Sand. Now, I care nothing about the insinuations of Messrs. Herzen and Golovine. But, as it may contribute to the settlement of the question raised about Michael Bakunin, permit me to state the real facts of the case:

On July 5th, 1848, the *New Rhenish Gazette* received two letters from Paris—the one being the authographic correspondence of the Havas-Bureau, and the other a private correspondence, emanating from a Polish refugee,[b] quite unconnected with that concern—both stating that George Sand was in possession of papers compromising Bakunin as having lately entered into relations with the Russian Government.

The *New Rhenish Gazette*, on July 6th, published the letter of its Paris correspondent.

Bakunin, on his part, declared in the *Neue Oder-Zeitung*[c] (a Breslau[d] paper), that, *before the appearance* of the Paris correspondence in the *New Rhenish Gazette*, similar rumours had been secretly colported at Breslau, that they emanated from the Russian embassies, and that he could not better answer them than by

[a] Francis Marx.—*Ed.*
[b] A. Ewerbeck, who is referred to below as the Paris correspondent.—*Ed.*
[c] In 1846-49 known as *Allgemeine Oder-Zeitung*.—*Ed.*
[d] Wrocław.—*Ed.*

appealing to George Sand. His letter to George Sand was published simultaneously with his declaration. Both the declaration and the letter were reprinted immediately by the *New Rhenish Gazette*, (vide *New Rhenish Gazette*, July 16, 1848). On August 3, 1848, the *New Rhenish Gazette* received from Bakunin, through the means of M. Kościelski, a letter addressed by George Sand to its editor, which was published on the same day, with the following introductory remarks:—

"In number 36, of this paper, we communicated a rumour circulating in Paris, according to which George Sand was stated to be possessed of papers which placed the Russian refugee, Bakunin, in the position of an agent of the Emperor Nicholas. We gave publicity to this statement, because it was communicated to us simultaneously by two correspondents wholly unconnected with each other. By so doing, we only accomplished the duty of the public press, which has severely to watch public characters. And, at the same time we gave to Mr. Bakunin an opportunity of silencing suspicions thrown upon him in certain Paris circles. We reprinted also from the *Neue Oder-Zeitung* Mr. Bakunin's declaration, and his letter addressed to George Sand, without waiting for his request. We publish now a literal translation of a letter addressed to the Editor of the *New Rhenish Gazette* by George Sand, which perfectly settles this affair."—(Vide *New Rhenish Gazette*, Aug. 3, 1848.)[a]

In the latter part of August, 1848, I passed through Berlin, saw Bakunin there, and renewed with him the intimate friendship which united us before the outbreak of the revolution of February.

In its number of October 13, 1848, the *New Rhenish Gazette* attacked the Prussian ministry for having expelled Bakunin, and for having threatened him with being delivered up to Russia if he dared to re-enter the Prussian States.

In its number of February 15, 1849, the *New Rhenish Gazette* brought out a leading article on Bakunin's pamphlet—*Aufruf an die Slaven*, which article commenced with these words—"*Bakunin is our friend.* This shall not prevent us from subjecting his pamphlet to a severe criticism."[b]

In my letters, addressed to the *New-York Daily Tribune* on "Revolution and Contre-revolution in Germany," I was, as far as I know, the first German writer who paid to Bakunin the tribute due to him for his participation in our movements, and, especially

---

[a] See present edition, Vol. 7, p. 315.—*Ed.*

[b] See Frederick Engels, "Democratic Panslavism" (present edition, Vol. 8, p. 363).—*Ed.*

in the Dresden insurrection,[230] denouncing, at the same time, the German press and the German people for the most cowardly manner in which they surrendered him to his and their enemies.[a]

As to "F.M." proceeding, as he does, from the fixed idea, that continental revolutions are fostering the secret plans of Russia, he must, if he pretend to anything like consistency, condemn not only Bakunin, but every continental revolutionist as a Russian agent. In his eyes revolution itself is a Russian agent. Why not Bakunin?

London, August 30, 1853.

Reproduced from the newspaper

First published in *The Morning Advertiser*, September 2, 1853

Signed: *Karl Marx*

---

[a] The articles, written by Engels, were published in the *New-York Daily Tribune* under the signature of Marx as its official correspondent. For the relevant passage on Bakunin see present edition, Vol. 11, p. 90.—*Ed.*

Karl Marx

RISE IN THE PRICE OF CORN.—CHOLERA.—STRIKES.—SAILORS' MOVEMENT[231]

London, Tuesday, Aug. 30, 1853

The Breslau *Gazette* states that the exportation of corn from Wallachia is definitively prohibited.

There is at this moment a somewhat greater question at issue than the Eastern one, viz.: the question of subsistence. Prices of corn have risen at Königsberg, Stettin, Dantzic, Rostock, Cologne, Hamburg, Rotterdam, and Antwerp, and of course at all importing markets. At the principal provincial markets in England wheat has advanced from 4 to 6s. per qr. The constantly increasing prices of wheat and rye in Belgium and France, and the consequent dearness of bread, create much anxiety. The French Government is buying up grain in England at Odessa, and in the Baltic. The conclusive report of the crops in England will not be out before next week. The potatoe disease is more general here than in Ireland. The export of grain has been prohibited by all Italian Governments, including that of Lombardy.

Some cases of decided Asiatic cholera occurred in London during the last week. We also hear that the cholera has now reached Berlin.

The battle between labor and capital, between wages and profits, continues. There have been new strikes in London on the part of the coal-heavers, of the barbers, of the tailors, ladies' boot and shoe makers, umbrella and parasol coverers, shirtmakers and makers of underclothing generally, and of other working people employed by slopsellers and wholesale export-houses. Yesterday, a strike was announced from several bricklayers, and from the Thames lightermen, employed in the transit of goods between the wharfs and ships in the river. The strikes of the colliers and iron-workers in South Wales continues, and a new strike of colliers in Resolven has to be added to the list, etc., etc.

It would be tedious to go on enumerating, letter after letter, the different strikes which come to my knowledge week after week. I shall therefore merely dwell occasionally on such as offer peculiar features of interest, among which, though not yet exactly a strike, the pending conflict between the police-constables and their chief, Sir Richard Mayne, deserves to be mentioned. Sir Richard Mayne, in his circular addressed to the several divisions of the metropolitan police force, has prohibited policemen from holding meetings, or combining, while he professed himself willing to attend to individual complaints. The policemen respond to him that they consider the right of meeting to be inalienable from Englishmen. He reminds them that their scale of wages was struck at a time when provisions were much dearer than they are at present. The men reply that "their claim is not grounded on the price of provisions only, but that it rests on the assurance that flesh and blood are not so cheap as they have been."

The most important incident in this history of strikes is the declaration of the "Seamen's United Friendly Association," calling itself the Anglo-Saxon Sailor's Bill of Rights. This declaration refers to the Merchant Shipping Bill, which repeals the clause of the Navigation Act,[232] rendering it imperative on British owners to carry at least three-fourths of British subjects on board their ships; which bill now throws open the coasting trade to foreign seamen even where foreign ships are excluded. The men declare this bill to be, not a Seamen's bill but an Owners bill. Nobody had been consulted but the ship-owner. The manning clause had acted as a check on the conduct of masters in the treatment and retention of crews. The new law would place seamen completely in the power of any bad officer. The new law proceeded upon the principle "that the 17,000 masters were all men of kind disposition, overflowing with generosity, benevolence and amiability; and that all seamen were untractable, unreasonable and naturally bad." They declare that while the owner may take his ships wherever he pleases, their labor is restricted to their own country, as the Government had repealed the Navigation law without first procuring reciprocal employment for them in the ships of other nations.

"Parliament having offered up the seamen as a holocaust to the owners, we as a class are constrained to combine and take measures for our own protection."

These measures consist chiefly in the intention of the seamen to uphold on their part the *manning clause*, it being declared at the same time

"that the seamen of the United States of America be considered as British; that an appeal be made to them for aiding their union; and that, as there would be no advantage to sail as an Englishman after the first of October, when the above law will be passed; as on the contrary freedom from impressment or service in Her Majesty's Navy during war might be secured by serving as foreigners in British ships during peace, and as there would be more protection during peace by possessing the freedom of America, [...] the seamen [...] will procure certificates of the United States citizenship, on arrival at any port of that Republic."[233]

Written on August 30, 1853

First published in the *New-York Daily Tribune*, No. 3873, September 15, 1853; reprinted in the *New-York Semi-Weekly Tribune*, No. 867, September 16 and the *New-York Weekly Tribune*, No. 627, September 17; published simultaneously in abridged form in German in *Die Reform*, No. 49, September 17, 1853

Signed: *Karl Marx*

Reproduced from the *New-York Daily Tribune*

Karl Marx

TO THE EDITOR OF *THE PEOPLE'S PAPER*[234]

Dear Sir,—*The Morning Advertiser*, of the 3rd inst., published the subjoined article, "How to write History.—By a Foreign Correspondent," while he refused to insert my answer to the "Foreign Correspondent." You will oblige me by inserting into *The People's Paper* both, the Russian letter and my reply to it.

Yours truly,

Dr. *Karl Marx*.

London, September 7th.

HOW TO WRITE HISTORY.— BY A FOREIGN CORRESPONDENT

"Bakunin is a Russian agent—Bakunin is not a Russian agent. Bakunin died in the prison of Schlisselburg, after having endured much ill-treatment—Bakunin is not dead: he still lives. He is made a soldier and sent to the Caucasus—no, he is not made a soldier: he remains detained in the Citadel of St. Peter and St. Paul. Such are the contradictory news which the press has given us in turn concerning Michael Bakunin.

"In these days of extensive publicity, we only arrive at the true by affirming the false, but, has it at least been proved that Bakunin has not been in the military pay of Russia?

"There are people who do not know that humanity makes men mutually responsible—that in extricating Germany from the influence which Russia exercises on it, we react upon the latter country, and plunge it anew into its despotism, until it becomes vulnerable to revolution. Such people it would be idle to attempt to persuade that Bakunin is one of the purest and most generous representatives of progressive cosmopolitism.

"'Calumniate, calumniate,' says a French proverb, [and] 'something will always remain.' The calumny against Bakunin, countenanced in 1848 by one of his friends, has been reproduced in 1853 by an unknown person.

"'One is never betrayed but by one's own connexion,' says another proverb; 'and it is better to deal with a wise enemy than with a stupid friend.' The conservative journals have not become the organ of the calumny insinuated against Bakunin. A friendly journal undertook that care.

"Revolutionary feeling must be but slightly developed, when it can be forgotten for a moment, as Mr. Marx has forgotten, that Bakunin is not of the stuff of which police spies are made. Why, at least, did he not do, as is the custom of the English papers—why did he not simply publish the letter of the Polish refugee, which denounced Bakunin? He would have retained the regret of seeing his name associated with a false accusation!"

THE FOREIGN CORRESPONDENT IN SATURDAY'S
MORNING ADVERTISER

"'It is better to deal with a wise enemy than a stupid friend.' Exactly so.

"Is he not a 'stupid friend' who is astonished at the discovery, that a controversy involves antagonistic opinions, and that historical truth cannot be extricated but from contradictory statements?

"Is he not a 'stupid friend' who thinks necessary to find fault with explanations in 1853, with which Bakunin himself was satisfied in 1848, to 'plunge Russia anew in its despotism,' from which she has never emerged, and to call French a trite Latin proverb?

"Is he not a 'stupid friend' who assures a paper to have 'countenanced' a statement made by its Foreign Correspondent and unmarked by its editor?

"Is he not a 'stupid friend' who sets up 'conservative journals' as models for 'revolutionary feeling' at its highest pitch, invented the *lois des suspects*,[235] and suspected the 'stuff' of a traitor even in the Dantons, the Camille Desmoulins, and the Anacharsis Clootses, who dares attack third persons in the name of Bakunin, and dares not defend him in his own name?

"In conclusion, let me tell the friend of proverbial commonplace that I have now done with him and with all such-like friends of Bakunin."

"Karl Marx.

"London, September 4th."

First published in *The People's Paper*, No. 71, September 10, 1853

Reproduced from the newspaper

Karl Marx

[THE VIENNA NOTE.— THE UNITED STATES AND EUROPE.—LETTERS FROM SHUMLA.—PEEL'S BANK ACT][236]

London, Friday, Sept. 9, 1853

When I told you in my letter of August 30, that the Vienna Note was "rejected" by the Porte, inasmuch as the alterations demanded by it and the condition of immediate and previous evacuation[a] cannot be considered otherwise than as a refusal of Russia's pretensions, I found myself in contradiction with the whole Press, which assured us that the alterations were insignificant, not worth speaking of, and that the whole affair might be regarded as settled.[237] Some days later, *The Morning Chronicle*[b] startled the confiding stockjobbers with the announcement that the alterations proposed by the Porte were of a very serious character, and by no means easy to be dealt with. At this moment there exists only one opinion, namely, that the whole Eastern question has come back to its point of issue, an impression in no way impaired by the complete publication in yesterday's papers of the official Note addressed by Reshid Pasha to the Representatives of Austria, France, Great Britain, and Prussia, dated August 19, 1853.

That the Russian Emperor will reject the Turkish "alterations" there is not the slightest doubt. Already, we are informed by the *Assemblée nationale*, the Paris *Moniteur* of the Emperor of Russia, that,

"according to correspondences received to-day at Paris, the first impressions produced on the Cabinet of St. Petersburg were by no means favorable to the modifications proposed by the Porte. [...] Whatever may be the resolution of that Cabinet we must prepare ourselves beforehand to take it coolly and to repress our

---

[a] Of the Danubian Principalities.— *Ed.*

[b] Of September 3, 1853.— *Ed.*

fears. We have to consider that even were the Russian Cabinet to refuse the proposed change of the note, there would remain the resources of fresh negotiation at Constantinople."[a]

The intimation contained in this last hint, that Russia will attempt to gain another delay of the decision of the dispute, is confirmed by the Berlin *Lithographic Correspondence*:

"The Austrian Government has presented a memorial to the Emperor Nicholas containing new propositions of modification, and it has undertaken to terminate the crisis in a manner quite different from all previous attempts."

In a letter published by the Vienna *Wanderer* from Odessa dated 26th Aug. the solution of the Oriental question is stated "to be not so near at hand as was expected by some people. The armaments have not been suspended for one day, and the army in the Principalities continually receives reinforcements."[b] The Kronstadt *Satellite* positively announces that the Russian troops will take up their winter quarters in the Principalities.

A note issued from Washington could scarcely have produced a greater sensation in Europe than your editorial remarks on Capt. Ingraham.[c] They have found their way, with and without commentaries, into almost the whole weekly press of London, into many French papers, the Brussels *Nation*, the Turin *Parlamento*, the *Basle Gazette*, and every liberal newspaper of Germany. Your article on the Swiss-American alliance having simultaneously been reprinted in a number of German journals, you may consider the following passage from an article of the Berlin *Lithographic Correspondence* as partly addressed to you:

"Some time since the press has had various occasions to pronounce itself on the United States theory with regard to intervention. Very recently the Koszta affair at Smyrna has renewed the discussion, and this affair is not yet terminated, when already foreign and native journals hold out the prospect of an intervention on the part of the United States in favor of Switzerland, if it should be threatened by an attack. To-day we are informed that several Powers have the intention of making a collective declaration against the doctrine of international right put forth by the United States, and that we may hope to see those Cabinets arrive at a perfect understanding. If the American intervention theories were not *refuted* in a peremptory manner, *the extirpation of the revolutionary spirit in Europe would meet with an insuperable obstacle.* We may add, as an important fact, that France is among the Powers ready to participate in this remonstrance."

---

[a] *L'Assemblée nationale*, No. 251, September 8, 1853.—*Ed.*

[b] *Der Wanderer*, September 4, 1853.—*Ed.*

[c] The reference is to the editorial "Peace or War" in the *New-York Daily Tribune*, No. 3839, August 6, 1853.—*Ed.*

On this last point, the *Constitutionnel* of Tuesday last takes good care not to leave any doubt, when it says:

"It is necessary to be candid in all things. It is not as a citizen of the United States that Koszta is defended against Austria by the agents of the American Republic, but as a revolutionist. But none of the European Powers will ever admit as a principle of public law that the Government of the United States has the right to protect revolution in Europe by force of arms. On no grounds would it be permitted to throw obstacles in the way of the exercise of the jurisdiction of a government, under the ridiculous pretense that the offenders have renounced their allegiance, and from the real motive that they are in revolt against the political constitution of their country. The Navy of the American Union might not always have such an easy triumph, and such headstrong conduct as that pursued by the Captain of the *St. Louis* might on another occasion be attended with very disastrous consequences."[a]

The *Impartial* of Smyrna, received to-day, publishes the following interesting letters from Shumla:

"Shumla, Aug. 8, 1853

"The Commander-in-Chief, Omer Pasha, has so ably distributed his troops, that on the first emergency, he may within 24 hours concentrate at any point on the Danube, a mass of 65,000 men, infantry and cavalry, and 180 pieces of cannon. A letter I received from Wallachia, states that typhus is making frightful havoc in the Russian army, and that it has lost not less than 13,000 men since its entry into campaign. Care is taken to bury the dead during the night. The mortality is also very high among the horses. Our army enjoys perfect health. Russian detachments, composed of 30 to 60 soldiers, and dressed in Moldavian uniform, appear from time to time on the opposite bank of the Danube. Our general is informed of all their movements. Yesterday 1,000 Roman Catholic Albanians arrived. They form the vanguard of a corps of 13,000 men expected without delay. They are sharpshooters. Yesterday there arrived also 3,000 horse, all of them old soldiers, perfectly armed and equipped. The number of our troops is increasing every day. Ahmet Pasha started yesterday for Varna. He will wait there for the Egyptian forces, in order to direct them to the points they are to occupy.

"Shumla, Friday, Aug. 12, 1853

"On the 9th inst. two regiments of infantry and one battery of light artillery, belonging to the guards of the Sultan, started for Rasgrad. On the 10th we got news that 5,600 Russians had encamped themselves on the bank of the Danube near the port of Turtukai, in consequence of which the outposts of the two armies are only at the distance of a rifle-shot from each other. The gallant Colonel Skander-Bey has left for that post, with several officers. Omer Pasha has established telegraphs, with a view of having communicated to the headquarters at every time of day or night the events passing on every point of the river.

"We have had continual rains for some days past, but the works of fortification have none the less been continued with great activity. A salute of cannon is fired

[a] Quoted from Boniface's article in *Le Constitutionnel* of September 5, 1853.—*Ed.*

twice a day, at sunrise and sunset. We hear nothing of this sort from the opposite side of the river.

"The Egyptian troops, after having undergone their quarantine at Constantinople, will embark for Varna, whence they are to be directed to Babadegh. The Brigadier Izzet Pasha expects them there In the district of Dobrudja-Ovassi 20,000 Tartars have assembled, in order to participate in the war against the Russians. They are for the greater part ancient emigrants, who left the Crimea at the time of its conquest by Russia. The Ottoman army, whose strength augments every day by the arrival of troops, both regular and irregular, is tired of passiveness, and burns with the desire of going to war. It is to be feared that we shall have one of these days a transit across the Danube without superior orders, especially now that the presence of the Russians, who show themselves on the opposite bank, adds to the excitement. Several physicians, Mussulmans and Christians, left some days ago, in order to establish military hospitals on the European plan at Plevna, at Rasgrad, at Widin, and at Silistra. On the 11th there arrived from Varna two superior English officers. They have had a long audience with Omer Pasha, and have visited the fortifications, attended by several Turkish officers. They have found them in a perfect state of defense, provided with ample magazines, baking-stoves, fountains of fresh water, etc. All these fortifications are constructed with the greatest solidity. The most severe discipline prevails among our troops.

"Shumla, Monday, Aug. 15, 1853

"On the 13th, the English General O'Donnell arrived from Constantinople. He had an interview of two hours' duration with Omer Pasha, and left on the following day, attended by an aide-de-camp of the Commander-in-Chief, for the purpose of inspecting the fortifications. Yesterday three batteries and an immense train of ammunition arrived from Varna. To-morrow a reinforcement of one battery, two battalions of infantry, and 1,000 horse, will leave for the port of Rahova.[a] The engineers at this place are busily engaged in restoring the fortifications destroyed by the Russians in 1828. Turkey may have unbroken confidence in her army."

The Earl of Fitzwilliam addressed a letter on Thursday last to the meeting of Sheffield cutlers, in which he protests against the monstrous assumption with which Parliament was closed by the heroic Palmerston, that "reliance was to be placed on the honor and character of the Emperor of Russia."

Mr. Disraeli has summoned his constituents to meet him at Aylesbury on the 14th inst. *The Daily News* of yesterday attempted, in a long and dull article, to combat what Mr. Disraeli is supposed by it to be likely to tell his electors. Such a performance I think *The Daily News* might have left with greater propriety to its venerable grandsire, the London *Punch*.

It is now the fourth time since January, that the rate of interest has been raised by the Bank of England. On Sept. 4, it was fixed at 4 per cent.

---

[a] Orekhovo.—*Ed.*

"Another attempt has been made *to reduce the circulating medium of the country*—another effort to arrest the tide of national prosperity,"

exclaims the London *Sun*.[a] On the other hand, it comforts itself with the consideration that the Bank of England has lost much of its mischievous power in consequence of the Peel Act of 1844.[238]

The Sun is mistaken in what it fears, and in what it hopes. The Bank of England has as little as any other bank either the power of expanding or of contracting the currency of the country. The really mischievous powers possessed by it are by no means restricted, but on the contrary strengthened by the Peel Act of 1844.

As the Bank Act of 1844 is generally misunderstood, and as its working will become, in the approaching crisis, of paramount importance not only to England but to the whole commercial world, I propose briefly to explain the tendency of the act.

Peel's Bank Act of 1844 proceeds on the assumption that the metallic circulation is the normal one; that the amount of the currency regulates prices; that in the case of a purely metallic circulation, the currency would expand with a favorable exchange and with an influx of bullion, while it would be contracted by an adverse exchange and a drain of bullion; that a circulation of bank notes has exactly to imitate the metallic circulation; that accordingly there had to be a degree of correspondence between the variations in the amount of bullion in the vaults of the Bank of England and the variations in the quantity of its notes circulating among the public; that the issue of notes must be expanded with a favorable, and contracted with an unfavorable exchange; lastly, that the Bank of England had the control over the amount of its notes in circulation.

Now there is not one of these premises which is not utterly fallacious and contradictory to facts. Suppose even a purely metallic circulation, the amount of currency could not determine prices, no more than it could determine the amount of commercial and industrial transactions; but prices on the contrary would determine the amount of currency in circulation. Unfavorable exchanges, and a drain of bullion, would not contract even a purely metallic circulation, as they would not affect the amount of currency in circulation, but the amount of currency in reserve, sleeping in the banks as deposits, or in private hoards. On the other hand, a favorable exchange and a concomitant influx of bullion, would augment, not the currency in circulation, but the

---

[a] *The Sun*, September 3, 1853.—*Ed.*

currency deposited with bankers or hoarded by private individuals. The Peel Act, therefore, starting upon a false conception of a purely metallic circulation, naturally arrives at a false imitation of it by a paper circulation. The idea itself, that a bank of issue has a control over the amount of its outstanding notes, is utterly preposterous. A bank issuing convertible notes or advancing notes generally on commercial securities, has neither the power of augmenting the natural level of circulation nor the power to cripple it by one single note. A bank may certainly issue notes to any amount its customers will accept; but, if not wanted for circulation, the notes will be returned to it in the form of deposits, or in payment for debts, or in exchange for metal. On the other hand, if a bank intend to forcibly contract its issues, its deposits would be withdrawn to the amount needed for filling up the *vacuum* created in the circulation. Thus a bank has no power whatever over the quantity of circulation, whatever may be its power for the abuse of other people's capital. Although in Scotland banking was practically unrestricted before 1845, and the number of banks had considerably increased since 1825, the circulation declined, and there was only £1 (of paper) per head of population, while there was in England £2 per head, notwithstanding that the whole circulation below £5 was metallic in England and paper in Scotland.

It is an illusion that the amount of circulation must correspond to the amount of bullion. If the bullion increases in the vaults of a bank, that bank certainly tries by all means to extend its circulation, but, as experience teaches, to no purpose. From 1841-'43, the bullion in the Bank of England rose from £3,965,000 to £11,054,000, but its total circulation declined from £35,660,000 to £34,094,000. Thus the Bank of France had, on March 25, 1845, an outstanding circulation of 256,000,000 f., with a bullion reserve of 234,000,000 f.; but on March 25, 1846, its circulation was 249,404,000 f., with a bullion reserve of only 9,535,000 f.

It is an assumption no less incorrect, that the internal circulation must diminish in the case of a drain of bullion. At this moment, for instance, while the efflux of bullion is going on, $3,000,000 have been brought to the mint and added to the circulation of the country.

But the main fallacy rests on the supposition that demand for pecuniary accommodation, i.e. loan of capital, must converge with demand for additional means of circulation; as if the greater amount of commercial transactions were not effected by bills, checks, book-credits, clearing-houses, and other forms of credit quite unconnected with the so-called circulation. There can exist no better mode of verifying the facility of bank-accommodations than the market rate of interest, and no more efficient means for ascertaining the amount of business actually done by a bank than the return of bills under discount. Let us proceed on this two-fold scale of measurement. Between March and September, 1845, when with the speculation mania the fictitious capital reached its utmost height and the country was inundated with all possible enterprises on an immense scale, the rate of interest being nearly 2½ per cent., the circulation of bank notes remained nearly stationary, while at a later period in 1847, the rate of interest being 4½ per cent., the price of shares having sunk to the lowest ebb, and discredit spreading in all directions, the circulation of bank notes reached its maximum.

The note circulation of the Bank of England was £21,152,853 on the 17th April; £19,998,227 on the 15th of May; and £18,943,079 on the 21st of August, 1847. But while this falling off in the circulation occurred, the market rate of interest had declined from 7 and 8 to 5 per cent. From the 21st Aug., 1847, the circulation increased from £18,943,079 to £21,265,188 on Oct. 23. At the same time the market rate of interest rose from 5 to 8 per cent. On the 30th of October the circulation was £21,764,085, the interest paid in Lombard-st. amounting to 10 per cent. Take another instance:

	Bank of England Bills under Discount	Notes in Circulation
Sept. 18, 1846	£12,323,816	£20,922,232
April 5, 1847	18,627,116	20,815,234

So that the banking accommodation in April, 1847, greater by 6,000,000 than that of Sept., 1846, was carried on with a less amount of circulation.

Having exposed the general principles of Peel's Bank Act, I come now to its practical details. It assumes that £14,000,000 of bank notes form the necessary minimum amount of circulation. All notes issued by the Bank of England beyond that amount shall be represented by bullion. Sir Robert Peel imagined he had discovered a self-acting principle for the issue of notes, which would determine with mechanical accuracy the amount of the circulation, and which would increase or diminish [it] in the precise degree in which the bullion increased or decreased. In order to put this principle into practice, the Bank was divided into two departments, the Issue Department and the Banking Department, the former a mere fabric of notes, the latter the true Bank, receiving the deposits of the State and of the public, paying the dividends, discounting bills, advancing loans, and performing in general the business with the public, on the principles of every other banking concern. The Issue Department makes over its notes to the Banking Department to the amount of £14,000,000, plus the amount of bullion in the vaults of the Bank. The Banking Department negotiates those notes with the public. The amount of bullion necessary to cover the notes beyond £14,000,000, remains in the Issue Department, the rest being surrendered to the Banking Department. If the amount of bullion diminish beneath the circulation exceeding £14,000,000, the notes returning to the Banking Department in discharge of its advances, or under the form of deposits, are not reissued nor replaced, but annihilated. If there were a circulation of £20,000,000, with a metallic reserve of £7,000,000, and if the Bank were further drained by an efflux of £1,000,000, all the bullion would be requested by the Issue Department, and there would not remain one sovereign in the Banking Department.

Now everybody will understand that this entire machinery is illusory on the one hand, and of the most pernicious character on the other hand.

Take, for instance, the Bank returns in last Friday's *Gazette*.[a] There you find, under the head of the Issue Department, the amount of notes in circulation stated to be £30,531,650, i.e., £14,000,000+£16,962,918—the latter sum corresponding to the bullion reserve of last week. But, turning to the head of Banking Department, you will find £7,755,345 in notes in its assets. This is the portion of the £30,531,650 not accepted by the public. Thus the self-acting principle determines only the £30,531,650 in notes to be transported from the Issue Department to the Banking Department. But there they remain. As soon as the Banking Department comes into contact with the public, the amount of circulation is regulated, not by Peel's Act, but by the wants of business. The self-acting principle, accordingly, extends its operation not beyond the vaults of the Bank premises.

On the other hand, there occur moments, when the Bank of England, by her exceptional position, exercises a real influence, not only on English commerce, but on the commerce of the world.

[a] *The Economist*, No 523, September 3, 1853.—*Ed.*

This happens in moments of general discredit. In such moments the Bank may, by raising in accordance with the Peel Act its minimum rate of interest, correspondingly with the efflux of bullion, and by refusing her accommodation, depreciate the public securities, lower the prices of all commodities, and enormously aggravate the disasters of a commercial crisis. It may, in order to stop the efflux of bullion and to turn the exchanges, transform every commercial stagnation into a monetary peril. And in this manner the Bank of England has acted and was forced to act by the Peel Act in 1847.

This, however, is not all. In every banking concern, the heaviest liabilities are not the amount of notes in circulation, but the amounts of notes and metals in deposit. The banks of Holland, for instance, had, as Mr. Anderson stated before a Committee of the House of Commons, before 1845, £30,000,000 in deposit, and £3,000,000 only in circulation.

> "In all commercial crises," says Mr. Alex. Baring, "for instance, in 1825, the claims of the depositors were the most formidable, not those of the holders of notes."

Now, while the Act of Peel regulates the amount of bullion to be held in reserve for the convertibility of notes, it leaves Directors the power to do with the deposits as they please. Yea, more. The very regulations of this act, as I have shown, may force the Banking Department to stop the payment of the deposits and of the dividends, while bullion to any amount may lie in the vaults of the Issue Department. This happened, indeed, in 1847. The Issue Department being yet possessed of £61,000,000 of bullion, the Banking Department was not saved from bankruptcy but by the interference of Government suspending, on their responsibility, the Peel Act, on 25th Oct., 1847.

Thus the result of the Peel Act has been that the Bank of England changed its rate of interest thirteen times during the crisis of 1847, having changed it only twice during the crisis of 1825; that it created amid the real crisis a series of money panics in April and October, 1847; and that the Banking Department would have been obliged to stop but for the stoppage of the act itself. There can, therefore, exist no doubt that the Peel Act will aggravate the incidents and severity of the approaching crisis.

Written on September 9, 1853

First published in the *New-York Daily Tribune*, No. 3881, September 24, 1853

Reproduced from the newspaper

Karl Marx

POLITICAL MOVEMENTS.— SCARCITY OF BREAD IN EUROPE

London, Tuesday, Sept. 13, 1853

The *Sunday Times* published in its last number a dispatch from Lord Clarendon to Sir H. Seymour, in answer to the note of Count Nesselrode of June 20. This dispatch bears date July 16. It is a mere "doublière" of the reply of M. Drouyn de Lhuys.[a] A correspondent of *The Leader* on Saturday last, expresses himself in the following spirited manner on the "antagonism" between Lords Aberdeen and Palmerston[b]:

"Lord Aberdeen [...] could never understand Lord Palmerston's affectations—never seeing that, consequent upon these affectations, *Lord Palmerston was always able to promote unmolested the Russian system, even better than Lord Aberdeen himself*.... Lord Palmerston [...] disguises cynicism in *Compromise*.... Lord Aberdeen did, as Lord Palmerston did not, express his convictions.... Lord Palmerston sees the expediency, and Lord Aberdeen does not see the expediency of talking intervention, while acting non-intervention.... Lord Aberdeen knowing, from his acquaintance with the governing classes, how seats are got, and voters bought, does not think the British Constitution the most perfect of human institutions; and, calculating that the people of Continental Europe are not more amiable or more honest than the people of Great Britain, he abstains from urging on continental governments the desirability of abolishing paternal despotism in favor of self-government by governing classes.... Lord Aberdeen [...] perceives that Great Britain is a power made up of conquests over nationalities, and scorns a foreign policy affecting to befriend struggling nationalities. Lord Aberdeen does not see why England, which has conquered and plundered India, and keeps India down for India's good, should set up for a hater of Czar Nicholas, who [...] a good despot in Russia, and keeps Poland down for Poland's obvious good. Lord Aberdeen does not see why England, which has crushed several rebellions in Ireland, should be fanatically angry with Austria for keeping down Hungary; and knowing that England

---

[a] See this volume, pp. 203-09.—*Ed.*

[b] Below is quoted the second article of the series "The Governing Classes", dealing with Aberdeen's surrender (*The Leader*, No. 181, September 10, 1853).—*Ed.*

forces an alien Church on Ireland, he understands the eagerness of the Pope[a] to plant Cardinal Wiseman in Westminster. He knows that we have had Kaffir wars, and does not think Nicholas a ruffian for thinning his army among the Caucasians; he knows that we send off periodically, rebellious Mitchells and O'Briens to Van Diemen's Land[b] and does not feel horror because Louis Napoleon institutes a Cayenne. Whenever he has to write to the Neapolitan Government about Sicilian affairs, he does not plunge into ecstatic liberalism, because he bears in mind that Great Britain has a proconsul at Corfu.... It is a happy arrangement, a Coalition Government, which includes, with Lord Aberdeen *acting* the Russian, Lord Palmerston, to *talk* the Bermondsey *policy*."[239]

As a proof that I have not undervalued the heroism of Switzerland,[c] I may allege a letter addressed by its Federal Council to the Ticinese Government, contending that

"the affair of the Capuchins[240] is purely a Cantonal question, and that consequently it is for the Canton of Ticino to consider whether it is better for it to resist, and continue subject to the rigorous measures of Austria, or to make to the Government offers of renewal of negociations."[d]

Thus it appears that the Swiss Federal Council tries to bring down its dispute with Austria within the proportions of a simple Cantonal affair. The same Council has just ordered the expulsion of the Italians, Clementi, Cassola and Grillenzoni, after the Jury at Chur had acquitted them from the charge of having abetted the Milan insurrection[241] by the forwarding of arms across the Ticinese frontier.

The British support to Juggernaut appears not yet to have been altogether done away with. On the 5th of May, 1852, the following dispatch was addressed by the Court of Directors to the Governor of India:

"We continue to be of opinion that it is desirable finally to dissever the British Government from all connection with the temple, and we therefore authorize to make arrangements for accomplishing this object by the discontinuance of any periodical allowance to it, in lieu of which some final payment may be made in the way of compensation to any persons who may appear upon a liberal construction of past engagements or understandings to be entitled to such indemnifications."

On the 11th April, 1853, however, nothing had been done by the Indian Government, the subject being still under consideration at that date.

A week has been consumed in a government inquiry into the cruelties practised upon the prisoners in Birmingham jail, cruelties which have induced several of them to commit and others to

---

[a] Pius IX.—*Ed.*
[b] Tasmania.—*Ed.*
[c] See this volume, pp. 107-08.—*Ed.*
[d] *The Leader*, No. 181, September 10, 1853.—*Ed.*

attempt suicide. Startled on one side by an exposition of atrocities not surpassed by any committed in an Austrian or Neapolitan *carcere duro*,[a] we are on the other side surprised at the tame acquiescence of the visiting magistrates in the representations which were made to them by interested parties, and at their utter want of sympathy with the victims. Their solicitude for the barbarous gaoler was so great that they regularly forewarned him of their approaching visits. The chief culprit, Lieutenant Austin, is one of those persons whom Carlyle designated in his *Model Prisons*[242] as the true officers of the pauper and criminal.

One of the topics of the day is *Railway morality*. The Yorkshire and Lancashire Board of Directors particularly announce on their tickets that

> "whatever accident may happen, whatever injury may be inflicted through their own negligence or that of their servants, they would hold themselves absolved from all legal responsibility."[b]

At the same time the Directors of the Birmingham and Shrewsbury line appeared before the Vice-Chancellor's Court on Saturday for having cheated their own shareholders. There exists a rivalry between the Great Western and the North-Western lines as to which of the two should absorb the above line in question. The majority of the shareholders being in favor of amalgamation with the North-Western, and the Directors of absorption into the Great Western, it occurred to the latter to turn a number of shares held by them in trust for the Company to account, for the manufacture of fictitious voters. For this purpose the shares were transferred to a number of nominal holders—in some instances it would seem without the concurrence of the parties whose names were used, and in one instance to a child of nine years of age—who paid no consideration for the shares, but executed re-transfers of them into the hands of the Directors, and supplied them, in virtue of their nominal ownership, with a given number of proxies, to insure a majority in favor of the union with the Great Western. The learned Judge remarked that "anything more flagrant or more gross could scarcely be conceived, and the way in which the plan had been carried out was still more gross." With this reflection he dismissed the guilty parties, as is usual among the bourgeoisie, while a poor devil of a proletarian would have been sure to be transported for a theft beyond five pounds.

---

[a] Punishment cell.—*Ed.*

[b] This and the following quotation are from "Vice-Chancellor's Court, Saturday, Sept. 3", *The Times*, No. 21525, September 5, 1853.—*Ed.*

It is curious to observe the British public in its fluctuating indignation now against the morality of mill lords, and now against the pit-owners, now against the little dealers in adulterated drugs, and then against the railwaymen who have supplanted the obsolete highwaymen; in short, against the morality of every particular class of capitalists. Taking the whole, it would seem that capital possesses a peculiar morality of its own, a kind of superior law of *a raison d'état*, while ordinary morals are a thing supposed to be good for the poor people.

Manchester Parliamentary Reformers seem to be in a pretty fix. The election revelations of the last session concerned almost exclusively boroughs, and even the great ones, as Hull, Liverpool, Cambridge and Canterbury. The liberal election-broker, Mr. Coppock, confessed in a fit of veracity: "What St. Albans was all other boroughs are." Now the oligarchy meditate turning these exposures to recount in effecting a reform in favor of counties and at the cost of boroughs. The Manchester Reformers, who desire no general extension of the suffrage, but only one within the borough-limits, are, of course, dumb under such a proposition. It is pitiful to see how their organ, *The Daily News*, struggles to get out of this difficulty.

On January 14, 1846, the Bank rate of interest was raised to 3 $^1/_2$ per cent.; on Jan. 21, 1846, to 4 per cent.; and it was not until April, 1847, that the rate rose to 5 per cent.; but it is known that in the last three weeks of April, 1847, almost all operations of credit were at a deadlock. In 1853, the upward movement of the Bank rate of interest was by far more rapid. From 2 per cent., at which it was on 24th April, 1852, it rose to $2^1/_2$ per cent. on Jan. 8, 1853; to 3 per cent. on the 22d of the same month, to $3^1/_2$ per cent. on the 4th June, to 4 per cent. on the 1st of September, and already the rumor runs through the city that it will shortly rise to 5 per cent. In Nov. 1846, the average price of wheat was 56/9 per qr.; in the latter weeks of August, 1853, it had reached 65/ to 66/. About this period last year the Bank of England

held in its cellars	£21,852,000
It now holds only	£16,500,068
Being a difference of	£5,351,932

The bullion decreased during last week but one by £208,875, and in last week by £462,852. The effect upon prices at the Stock Exchange has been immediate, every description of security declining. We read in the Money article of last Wednesday's *Times*:

"Notwithstanding the depression in the Stock-market, Exchequer bills remained at 2 per cent. discount to 1 per cent. premium, but an impression is entertained that the Chancellor of the Exchequer, in order to sustain the price, causes them to be purchased on Government account, in the absence of any funds immediately available for that purpose, by the sales of 3 per cent. Stocks held on account of savings-banks."[a]

This would be a masterpiece on the part of Mr. Gladstone: selling Consols at a low figure and purchasing Exchequer bills at a high one, causing a loss of half the income of the 3 per cent. stocks by converting them into Exchequer bills bearing little more than $1^1/_2$ per cent. interest.

How can we reconcile an unfavorable exchange or drain of bullion with the unprecedented increase of British exports, which at the end of the year will surpass by £16,000,000 even the exports of 1852?

"As we give credit [...] to all the world in the case of our exports, and pay ready money in the case of our imports, a large expansion of our trade at any moment must necessarily lead to a considerable balance in the payments against us at the time, but which must all be returned when the credit upon our exports has expired, and remittances ought to be made for them."

So says *The Economist*.[b] According to this theory, if the exports of 1854 were to surpass again those of 1853, the exchange must continue to be against England, and a commercial crisis would be the only means of adjustment. *The Economist* thinks that disasters like those of 1847 are out of the question, because no considerable portion of capital has been fixed now as then, in railways, etc. He forgets that it has been converted into factories, machinery, ships, etc. On the other hand, *The Observer* laments the

"foolish investments in *foreign railways*, and other companies of very doubtful and suspicious character."[c]

The Economist thinks that the extended commercial operations, so far as Europe is concerned, may receive a *wholesome check* from the high price of corn, but that *America and Australia*, etc., are *sure*. *The Times* at the same time asserts that the tightness of the New-York money market will put a *wholesome check* on American operations.

"We must not calculate on the same extent of orders from the United States that we have hitherto experienced," exclaims *The Leader*.[d]

---

[a] *The Times*, No. 21527, September 7, 1853.—*Ed.*

[b] In "As Applied to Interest on Capital", *The Economist*, No. 524, September 10, 1853.—*Ed.*

[c] *The Observer*, September 11, 1853. The passages rendered below are from the issue of September 4, 1853.—*Ed.*

[d] "The Threatened Stop in the Rise of Wages", *The Leader*, No. 180, September 3, 1853.—*Ed.*

Australia remains. Here steps in *The Observer*:

"Exports have been pushed injudiciously forward. [...] From the 74,000 tons of shipping now entered in London for the southern colonies, the condemnatory notices we gave from Adelaide, Melbourne, etc., will receive their justification. It is not to be denied that present prospects are not promising."

As to the Chinese market all reports are unanimous on the point that there exists a great alacrity to sell, but as great a reluctance to buy, the precious metals being hoarded, and any alteration of this state of things remains out of question as long as the revolutionary movement in the monster Empire has not accomplished its end.

And the home market?

"Large numbers of the power-loom weavers in Manchester and its neighborhood have followed the example of Stockport in striking for an advance of 10 per cent. on their wages.... The factory heads will probably find, before the end of the winter, that the question is not whether an increase of 10 per cent. will be conceded, but whether the manufacturers will allow work to be resumed at the present rate of wages."

In these terms, not to be misunderstood, *The Morning Chronicle*[a] alludes to the imminent decline of the domestic market.

I have repeatedly dwelt on the immense enlargement of the old factories, and the unparalleled erection of new ones. I reported to you upon some new-built mills which form, as it were, whole manufacturing towns. I stated that at no former epoch had such a proportion of the floating capital accumulated during the period of prosperity, been directly sunk for manufacturing purposes[b]. Now, take these facts on the one hand, and on the other the symptoms of overstocked markets at home and abroad; remember also, that an unfavorable exchange is the surest means to precipitate over-exports into foreign markets.

But it is the bad harvest which, above all, will drive the long-accumulated elements of a great commercial and industrial crisis to eruption. Every other sort of produce, when enhanced, checks its own demand; but Corn, as it becomes appreciated, is only the more eagerly sought for, drawing depreciation on all other commodities. The most civilized nation, like the most brutal

[a] On September 7, 1853.—*Ed.*

[b] See Marx's articles "Pauperism and Free Trade.—The Approaching Commercial Crisis" and "Political Prospects.—Commercial Prosperity.—Case of Starvation" (present edition, Vol. 11, pp. 357-63, 477-85).—*Ed.*

savage, must procure its food before it can think of procuring anything else, and the progress of wealth and civilization is generally in the same proportion, in which the labor and cost of producing food diminish.—A general bad harvest is in itself a general contraction of markets, at home and abroad. Now the present harvest is at least as deficient in the southern part of Europe, in Italy, France, Belgium, Rhenish Prussia, as it was in 1846-47. It is by no means promising in the north-west and north-east. As to England, *The Mark Lane Express*, that *Moniteur* of the London Corn Exchange, states in its number of yesterday week[a]:

"That the produce of wheat in the United Kingdom will be the smallest gathered for many years, does not admit of question. [...] The average yield will fall materially short in almost all parts of the kingdom, [...] independent of which it must be borne in mind that the breadth of land sown was, owing to the unpropitious weather during the seeding time, at least one-fourth less than usual."

This situation will not be alleviated by the delusion of commercial convulsions, industrial over-production, and bad harvests having been simultaneously done away with by *free trade*. On the contrary.

"Holders," remarks the same *Mark Lane Express*, "cannot yet realize the idea of scarcity under Free Trade. Hence few are disposed to hold heavy stocks. [...] If our necessities should drive us hereafter to import largely, the chances are, that we shall have to pay *dearly* for supplies."

The Mark Lane Express of yesterday adds:

"There is still so large a proportion of the crops abroad that the character of the weather for some weeks to come will have great influence on trade. [...] The quality of the grain exposed in the fields has already suffered from the last rains, [...] and a continuance of wet might be productive of an immense amount of mischief.... The ultimate result of the harvest threatens to be [...] less satisfactory than appeared likely a week or two ago.... The accounts which have reached us the last few days with regard to *potatoes*, are less favorable than those previously received.... Notwithstanding the enormously large supplies from abroad during last week (88,833 qrs.), the reaction on prices has been only small, the fall from the highest point not having exceeded 1s. to 2s. per quarter.... The probable result of the harvest in the Baltic is on the whole of an unsatisfactory character.... According to the latest advices, wheat was at 60s. f. o. b. at Dantzic, at 56s. 3d.at Königsberg, 54s. at Stettin, 58s. at Rostock."

The consequences of the dearth are already appearing, as in 1847, on the political horizon. At Naples the town authorities are without means to employ the laborers on public works, and the Exchequer is unable to pay the State officers. In the Papal States,

---

[a] Of September 5, 1853.—*Ed.*

at Tolentino, Terni, Ravenna and Trastevere, there have been bread riots by no means mitigated by the recent arrests, the invasion of the Austrians, and the threat of the bastinado. In Lombardy the political consequences of dearth and industrial stagnation will not be avoided by Count Strassoldo's imposing an additional tax of $6^1/_2$ kreuzen per florin, payable on the 20th Sept. and 10th Oct., this year, and to be levied on all payers of direct taxes, including the income tax and the tax upon salaries. The general distress in Austria is betrayed by her lingering after a new loan, introduced on the market as usual by the assertion that she wants the money only to reduce her army. The feverish anxiety of the French Government may be inferred from its false harvest accounts, its false assize of bread at Paris, and its immense purchases of corn on all markets. The provinces are disaffected, because Bonaparte feeds Paris at their expense; the bourgeoisie are disaffected because he interferes with commerce in behalf of the proletarians; the proletarians are disaffected because he gives wheat bread instead of brown to the soldiers, at the moment when peasants and workmen are menaced with the prospect of no bread at all; lastly, the soldiers are disaffected because of the humble anti-national attitude of France in the Eastern question. In Belgium several food riots have echoed the foolish festivities lavished by the Coburgs on the Austrian Archduchess.[a] In Prussia the fear of the Government is so great that several corn-brokers have been arrested by way of show, and the rest summoned before the Police President, who "requested" them to sell at "honest" prices.

I conclude by again recording my opinion, that neither the declamation of the demagogues, nor the twaddle of the diplomats will drive matters to a crisis, but that there are approaching economical disasters and social convulsions which must be the sure forerunners of European revolution. Since 1849 commercial and industrial prosperity has stretched the lounge on which the counter-revolution has slept in safety.

Written on September 13, 1853

First published in the *New-York Daily Tribune*, No. 3886 and the *New-York Semi-Weekly Tribune*, No. 871, September 30, 1853

Signed: *Karl Marx*

Reproduced from the *New-York Daily Tribune*

---

[a] Marie Henriette.—*Ed.*

Karl Marx

[THE WESTERN POWERS AND TURKEY.— IMMINENT ECONOMIC CRISIS.— RAILWAY CONSTRUCTION IN INDIA[243]]

London, Tuesday, Sept. 20, 1853

In my letter of July 19, I said:

"The Western Powers [...] *commence* by encouraging the Sultan[a] to resist the Czar, from fear of the encroachments of Russia, and *terminate by compelling the former to yield*, from fear of a general war giving rise to a general revolution."[b]

Now, at this moment the strength of the combined fleets is intended to be used *for Russia against Turkey*. If the Anglo-French fleet enter the Dardanelles at all, it will be done not to bombard Sebastopol, but to reduce to terms the Mussulmans who might prevent the Sultan from accepting *without conditions* the Vienna Note.

"On the 13th of September," says D. Urquhart, "[...] the four Foreign Secretaries[c] quietly assembled in Downing-st., and decided to send orders to Constantinople to enforce upon the Porte the withdrawal of the modifications which the European Conference had accepted. Not content with this, and in case the Sultan should find himself unable to resist the exasperation of his people, they send orders for the squadron to advance into the waters of the Bosphorus to support him against his subjects. Nor content with this, they also dispatched orders to Omer Pasha to forbid him from passing from one province to another in his Sovereign's Dominions.

"They have consequently contemplated the rebellion as the result of their dispatch, and provided means for putting it down, these means being the allied squadron."[d]

---

[a] Abdul Mejid.— *Ed.*

[b] See this volume, p. 212.— *Ed.*

[c] Clarendon, the Foreign Secretary at the time, and the former Foreign Secretaries Aberdeen, Palmerston and Russell.— *Ed.*

[d] [D. Urquhart,] "The Political Malefactors", *The Morning Advertiser*, September 20, 1853. Below on pp. 315-16 Marx quotes from the same article.— *Ed.*

It was from Sunday's *Journal des Débats* that the English public became aquainted with this news. The *Journal des Débats* stated that Mr. Reeve, having left London on the 13th inst., with dispatches for Lord Stratford de Redcliffe, arrived in Paris on the morning and left it on the evening of the 14th, after he had communicated to the French Government the tenor of his instructions, ordering the English Ambassador to demand the entire adhesion of the Porte to the Vienna proposals, the retraction of its modifications of the 19th August, threatening it with the withdrawal of the support of the four Powers in the event of a war arising from its refusal to yield, and offering it the assistance of the French and English fleets for putting down any insurrection that might break out in Constantinople if the Porte were to comply with the Vienna Note, and against Omer Pasha, if he dared to act in disobedience to the orders of the Porte. Before the arrival of the *Journal des Débats*, we were informed that the Vienna Conference, on receipt of the Emperor's[a] refusal, sent proposals to the Sultan that he should recall his words, that he should sign the note he had refused to sign, and be content with an assurance that the Conference would put any interpretation on the note agreeable to the Sultan himself. *The Times* avoids speaking of the compromising revelations made by the *Journal des Débats*. So does *The Morning Chronicle*, *The Morning Post*, and the whole of the governmental London press. In the meantime *The Morning Post* denounces the fanaticism of the Constantinople mob, *The Morning Chronicle* is exciting its dull readers by romantic descriptions of the fierce and undisciplined Asiatic hordes inundating European Turkey, and swelling Omer Pasha's army; the gallant *Globe* publishes day after day carefully selected extracts from the peace-mongering press of the Manchester school, and, in due time, the respectable classes of England will be prepared "*to annihilate Paganism,*" and to shout with Prince Gorchakoff, "Long life to the Czar! Long life to *the God of the Russians!*"

In its to-day's number *The Times* discovers that "*the Turkish question has plainly become a question of words*;" the inference to be drawn from its premises being, that the Sultan who intends exposing the peace of the world for mere words, must be forcibly brought to reason by the more sober-minded Palmerstons and Aberdeens. The Czar, we are told by *The Times*, having preferred unjust demands upon the Sultan, the Sultan rejected them, the Czar seized the Danubian Principalities, England and France dispatched their fleets

[a] Nicholas I.—*Ed.*

to Besika Bay, and the representatives of these Powers met those of Austria and Prussia in Vienna.

Why did they meet them in Vienna? *In favor of Turkey*, says *The Times*.

"Not only could there be *no desire of coercing the Ottoman Government*, but there was *no occasion for such an action*."

If, then, there is now a desire on the part of the four Powers for *coercing* the Ottoman Government, "it is simply because there is now" an *occasion* for "such an action." Would it then be wrong to suppose that the sole and principal aim of the Vienna Conference and of the interference of Palmerston and Aberdeen has been the affording such an occasion, that they made only a show of resistance to Russia, in order to gain a pretext for coercing Turkey into submission to her?

"The demands of Russia," continues *The Times*, were "thought unjustifiable by the other Great Powers, [...] incompatible with the sovereign rights of the Sultan," and therefore, the Great Powers drew up a Note to be presented by the Sultan to the Czar, ratifying all the demands of the Czar and something more.

"The terms of this document," says *The Times*, "were *liable to misconstruction*, [...] but two points were unimpeachably clear—first, that the four Powers intended to maintain the territorial and administrative rights of the Porte; and, next, that in the event of dispute *they would have been bound by this intention*."

Why should the Sultan not subscribe a note derogatory of his sovereign rights and surrendering the protectorate of twelve millions of his subjects to the control of the autocrat, while he feels himself backed by the good "*intentions*" of the four Powers and by their being *bound* by hidden "good *intentions*" in the case of a dispute? As the Sultan has had occasion to learn, the four Powers feel themselves not bound either by the law of nations, or by explicit treaties, to defend him in the event of a dispute with Russia; why should he not trust to their valor in the event of a dispute arising from a note which endows Russia with open claims and Turkey with "hidden intentions?"

"Let us take," says *The Times*, "the extreme case of supposing that, after the acceptance [...] *pure et simple* of the original Vienna Note, the Czar should [...] have availed himself of those opportunities with which the note [...] is thought to have provided him."

What then?

"*The Sultan would have protested*, and the case would have arisen for the application of the adjustment of 1853."

As if there had arisen no case for the application of the adjustment of 1840 and 1841, of the treaty of Balta-Liman,[244] and of the violation of the law of nations, characterized by Lord Clarendon himself as "an act of piracy!"

"The ambiguity," says *The Times*, "[...] would merely have misled the Emperor of Russia."

Exactly so, as the treaty of 1841 has "misled" him to keep the united fleets out of the Dardanelles while he himself entered the Principalities.

The Sultan, however, is stiff-necked. He has refused compliance with a note which was able to express its good intentions for Turkey only by delivering her up to Russia. He proposed certain modifications in this note, and "the four Powers," says *The Times*, "showed by their approval of the Turkish modifications, that they believed them to coincide with their own proposals." But, as the Emperor of Russia is of a contrary opinion, and as *The Times* thinks it most undoubtedly true, that the Czar's "proceedings in this dispute deserve *no consideration whatever*," *The Times* comes to the conclusion that, as Russia will not yield to the reasonable [...] conditions of Turkey, Turkey must yield to the unreasonable conditions of Russia, and that

"a state which [...] is yet so impotent as to require European protection at every menace of aggression from without or insurrection from within, *must at least so far pay the penalty of its weakness as to receive aid indispensable to its existence on the terms least onerous to its supporters.*"

The four Powers, of course, must join Russia against Turkey, because Turkey is supposed to want their aid in order to resist Russia.—Turkey must "pay the penalty for its weakness," in having had recourse to the four Great Powers she is obliged by treaties to appeal to.

"There is no alternative. Either the laws of England have to be exercised in their penal rigour[a] upon the persons of four traitors" (Aberdeen, Clarendon, Palmerston, and Russell), "or the Czar of Russia commands the world."

Such declamation as this uttered in *The Morning Advertiser* by D. Urquhart, is good for nothing. Who is to judge the four traitors? Parliament. Who forms that Parliament? The representatives of the Stockjobbers, the Millocrats, and the Aristocrats. And what foreign policy do these representatives represent? That of the *paix*

[a] *The Morning Advertiser* has "vigour".—*Ed.*

partout et toujours.[a] And who execute their ideas of foreign policy? The identical four men to be condemned by them as traitors, according to the simple-minded *Morning Advertiser.* One thing must be evident at least, that it is the Stockjobbers, and the Peacemongering Bourgeoisie, represented in the Government by the Oligarchy, who surrender Europe to Russia, and that in order to resist the encroachments of the Czar, we must, above all, overthrow the inglorious Empire of those mean, cringing and infamous adorers of the *veau d'or.*[b]

Immediately after the arrival of the Vienna Note at Constantinople, the Ottoman Porte called 80,000 men of the Redifs[c] under arms. According to a telegraphic dispatch dated Constantinople, Sept. 5, the Turkish Ministry had resolved, after a conference held at the house of the Grand Vizier,[d] to maintain their last note at the hazard of war. The enthusiasm of the Mussulman population has reached its highest pitch. The Sultan, having reviewed the Egyptian troops, and being received with deafening acclamations, was, after the review, lifted from his horse by the multitude and carried in triumph through the streets of Stambul. He has reiterated to the Hospodars of Moldavia and Wallachia[e] his order to quiet the Principalities. As the Russian subjects resident at Constantinople have been convicted of intriguing against the Turkish Government, Reshid Pasha has given a warning to the Russian Consul on their behalf. A Constantinople journal states that the Israelite community at Constantinople has offered to the Sultan a million of piasters in order to contribute to the expenses occasioned by the military preparations of the Empire. The Smyrna Israelites are said to have come to a similar resolution. A letter in the Vienna *Presse* informs us that several boyards have been arrested at Galatz because they had entered into a secret correspondence with Omer Pasha informing him of all details with regard to the state of the Russian army in the Principalities. A letter of Omer Pasha has been found inviting these boyards to enlist as many foreigners as possible.

Prince Menchikoff had arrived at Vienna on the 13th instant, accompanied by a Secretary, and as the bearer of a new manifesto of the Emperor Nicholas, addressed to the European Powers, and

---

[a] Peace at all costs.—*Ed.*
[b] The golden calf.—*Ed.*
[c] Reserve troops in the Ottoman Empire.—*Ed.*
[d] Mustafa Pasha.—*Ed.*
[e] Ghica and Stirbei.—*Ed.*

explaining his reasons for rejecting the Turkish modifications. The Emperor himself will arrive at Olmütz on the 21st instant, accompanied by Count Nesselrode and by Baron de Meyendorff. The King of Prussia[a] whom he had summoned by Prince de Lieven to the Olmütz Conference, has refused to make his appearance on the ground that, under existing circumstances, such a step on his part would have too much *éclat.* A Russian corps d'armée 30,000 strong is stationed now at Krajova on the frontiers of Bulgaria. Until now there have existed only eight army commissariats in the Russian Empire. A regular ninth commissariat has just been established at Bucharest—a sure indication that the Russians do not think of evacuating the Principalities.

On the 15th of Sept. the Bank of England raised its rates of interest to $4^1/_2$ per cent. The Money article in to-day's *Times* tells us that "The measure is regarded with general satisfaction." In the same article, however, we find it stated that,

> "at about 2 p.m. business at the Stock Exchange was in fact almost wholly suspended, and when the announcement was made, shortly afterward, of the advance to $4^1/_2$ per cent., prices declined to 95 for money and $95^1/_8$ to $^1/_4$ for the 13th of Oct. A general opinion prevailed, that if the advance had been to 5 instead of $4^1/_2$ per cent., the effect on the market would possibly have been less unfavorable, since the public would then have considered the probability of any further action to have ceased.... In the Railway market [...] a severe relapse occurred after the breaking up of the Bank Court, and prices of all kinds left off with a very unsettled appearance."[b]

The writer in *The Times* congratulates the Bank Directors on their following up the policy of the Peel Act.

> "In proportion as the circulation diminished from the drain of gold, the Directors have asked a higher price for the use of what remained, and have thus allowed the Bank Charter Act of Sir R. Peel that *free course,* by which alone its soundness can be demonstrated, and which was prevented by the infatuated proceedings of the Directors in 1847."

Now I have shown in a former letter that the infatuation of the Directors in 1847 consisted precisely in their close adherence to the Peel Act, the "free course" of which had to be interrupted by Government, in order to save the Banking Department from the necessity of stopping payment.[c] We read in *The Globe*:

---

[a] Frederick William IV.—*Ed.*

[b] This and the following quotation are from *The Times,* No. 21535, September 16, 1853.—*Ed.*

[c] See this volume, pp. 300-01.—*Ed.*

"It is highly improbable that the causes which have produced our present prosperity will continue to operate in the same proportion. Unhealthy results have already appeared in Manchester, where some of the largest firms have been compelled to limit their amount of production.... All departments of the Stock Exchange continue in a very depressed state. The Railway market is in a complete state of panic.... The efflux of gold to the Continent continues, and nearly half a million of money goes over to St. Petersburg in a day or two by steamer.... One object of its" (the Bank's) "husbanding its resources of specie is probably a desire to assist the Chancellor of the Exchequer with the seven or eight millions which he will require to pay off the South Sea stockholders and other dissentients."[a]

The Morning Post of the 14th inst. reports from Manchester:

"The market for cloth and yarn is dull, and the prices of all descriptions of manufactures are barely supported. The absence of demand from almost every foreign market and the anticipated money pressure at home, have mainly contributed to a state of things which is most anomalous, when contrasted with the accounts of prosperity generally current."

The same journal, of the 15th inst., winds up a leading article on the collecting elements of the approaching crisis in the following terms:

"We warn the commercial world that we are at a phase in which care and steady consideration are eminently requisite in the conception and conduct of enterprise. Our financial position, besides, is one which, in our view, is full of dangers even more serious and more difficult of avoidance than our commercial."

From the combined statements of *The Globe* and *Morning Post*, it follows that while the demand is declining on the one hand, the supply, on the other, has been overdone. Manufacturers will attempt to cover their retreat by falling back on the quarrel existing with their workmen. The trade reporter in yesterday's *Morning Chronicle* writes from Manchester:

"Manufactures are becoming greatly indifferent about entering into engagements, from the persuasion that an extensive, if not *universal stoppage of mills* must take place before any settlement of the wages question can be effected. On this subject there have been conferences among employers in various parts of the districts within the last few days; and it is evident that the exorbitant clamors set up by the operatives, together with the wild attempts at dictation, are forcing the millowners into a general combination for self-defense."

We read in the money article of *The Times*:

"Masters are forming Unions for self-defense in all the districts. At Ashton, Stalybridge, Hyde, and Glossop, nearly 100 firms have placed their names to a

[a] *The Globe*, September 13, 1853.—*Ed.*

deed of Union within the last few days. At Preston the masters have entered into heavy bonds to each other to resist the operatives by closing their mills for three months."[a]

A telegraphic dispatch from Marseilles reports that wheat has again advanced by 2 frs. 25 cent. per hectolitre.

"The augmentation of the interest on treasury bonds, announced in the *Moniteur*, produced a most unfavorable impression at the Bourse, that measure being generally considered as a sign that the Government is in want of money. [...] A loan was spoken of which the Government would be obliged to contract. [...] The Minister of Finance[b] has sent a circular to a vast number of landed proprietors, asking them to pay six months' taxes in advance, as a mark of gratitude for the great benefits which the present Government had conferred on them, and for the additional value which it had imparted to property." "This," remarks *The Observer*, "is the beginning of the end."[c]

Having dwelt in a former letter on the vital importance of railways for India,[d] I think fit to give now the latest news which has been published with regard to the progress and prospects of the intended network. The first Indian railway was the line now in operation between Bombay and Thane. Another line is now to be carried from Calcutta to Russnehael on the Ganges, a distance of 180 miles, and then to proceed along the right bank of the river to Patna, Benares and Allahabad. From Allahabad it will be conducted across the Doab to Agra and thence to Delhi, traversing in this manner a space of 1,100 miles. It is contemplated to establish steam ferry-boats across the Soane and Tunona,[e] and that the Calcutta line will finally proceed from Delhi to Lahore. In Madras a railway is to be commenced forthwith, which, running 70 miles due west, will branch off into two arms—one pursuing the Ghats and terminating at Calicut, the other being carried on by Bellary and Poona to Bombay. This skeleton of the chain of railways will be completed by the Bombay, Baroda and Central India Railway, the preliminary surveys for which are now proceeding under the sanction of the Court of Directors. This line will pass from Bombay by Baroda to Agra, where it will meet the great trunk railway from Calcutta to Delhi, and by its means Bombay, the Capital of Western India and the best port of communication with Europe, for all Hindostan, will be put in

[a] *The Times*, No. 21537, September 19, 1853.—*Ed.*
[b] J. M. Bineau.—*Ed.*
[c] *The Observer*, September 19, 1853.—*Ed.*
[d] See this volume, pp. 218-21.—*Ed.*
[e] Jumna.—*Ed.*

communication with Calcutta on the one hand, and with the Punjab and the north-western provinces on the other. The promoters of this scheme intend also to throw out branches into the great cotton district of the interior. In the meantime, measures are in progress for extending the electric telegraph throughout the whole of the peninsula of India.

Written on September 20, 1853

First published in the *New-York Daily Tribune*, No. 3889, and the *New-York Semi-Weekly Tribune*, No. 872, October 4, 1853; reprinted in the *New-York Weekly Tribune*, No. 630, October 8, 1853

Signed: *Karl Marx*

Reproduced from the *New-York Daily Tribune*

Karl Marx

[THE WESTERN POWERS AND TURKEY.— SYMPTOMS OF ECONOMIC CRISIS][245]

London, Friday, Sept. 23, 1853

The Globe, in its number of Sept. 20, denies the authenticity of the statement of the *Journal des Débats* with regard to the mission of Mr. Reeve, and *The Times* of Wednesday reprints the article of *The Globe* under the head of *gobemoucherie,* accusing the French press of trading in *canards.* But did not the leading article of *The Times* I analyzed in my last letter[a] wholly confirm the statement of the *Journal des Débats*? Has there appeared any refutation in the Paris *Moniteur*? Did not, on the same day that *The Globe* gave the lie to the *Débats,* the *Assemblée nationale* reiterate that

> "Lord Redcliffe was to notify to the Sultan that, if he refused to withdraw his modification, the English fleet would enter the Dardanelles, and the French fleet would not be slow to follow?"[b]

Did not *The Times,* on the same day on which it reproduced the denial of *The Globe,* explicitly declare that

> "England and France have no business to interfere between Russia and Turkey, except on the terms proposed by the four allied Powers, and accepted by Russia, whether these terms were *agreeable* to the haughty spirit of Turkey or not?"

Were we not told by *The Morning Post,* before the *Journal des Débats* had arrived at London, that

> "on the receipt of the Emperor of Russia's[c] answer to the proposal for the modifications of the Vienna Note, the Conference of the Representatives of the Great Powers had immediately assembled, and on the 4th inst. dispatched a courier

---

[a] See this volume, pp. 310-12.—*Ed.*

[b] Quoted from Am. Pellier's article in *L'Assemblée nationale,* No. 263, September 20, 1853.—*Ed.*

[c] Nicholas I.—*Ed.*

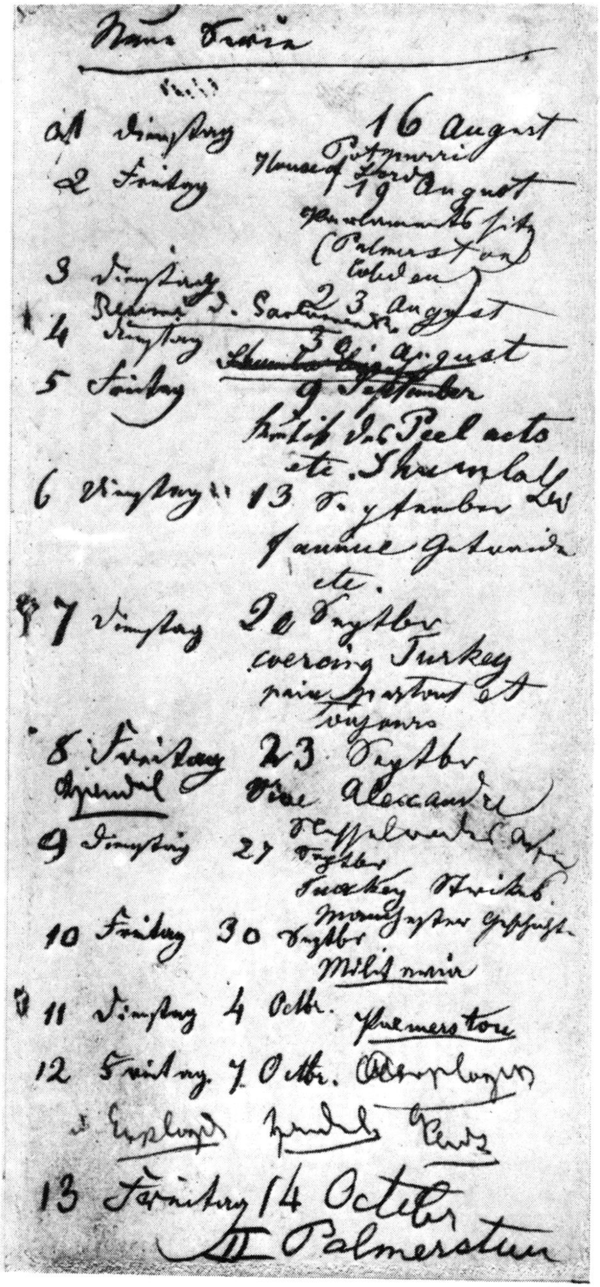

A page from Marx's notebook with notes on the mailing of articles to the *New-York Daily Tribune*

to Constantinople with *certain communications* from the Conference to the Divan, which it was hoped would *induce* the Porte to accept the Vienna Note!"[a]

Finally, we read in a morning paper of to-day that

"Mr. Reeve is going to Constantinople, that he is the bearer of dispatches from Lord Clarendon to Lord Stratford de Redcliffe, and that a connection of the most intimate kind exists between him and the Foreign Office, he having been the channel of communication between Downing-st. and Printing-house Square."

The truth is, that since the last revelations made by the French Press, the Eastern question has again assumed quite a new aspect, and the ignominious resolutions the English Ministry had decided upon are likely to be frustrated by events contrary to all their calculations and expectations.

Austria has seceded from the joint action with her pretended allies; the Vienna Conference has been broken off, at least for a moment. Russia has pulled off the mask she thinks no longer of any avail, and the English Ministry is driven out of its last entrenchments.

"Lord Aberdeen," as the *Liverpool Courier*[b] justly remarks, "recommended that the Sultan[c] should have recourse to a transparent and contemptible fraud; that the parties to the Vienna Conference should exercise a *mental reservation* with regard to the note, and that the Sultan should read it in an *unnatural sense*, i.e., the terms of the note being clear and precise, and the Emperor of Russia having refused point-blank to adopt the Sultan's modifications, the Powers should hold themselves prepared, hereafter, to act *as if those modifications had been received.*"

M. Drouyn de Lhuys suggested to the Vienna Conference an explanatory note conceived in that hypocritical sense, and to be communicated to the Porte, but Count Buol rejected this proposition, declaring that it

"was too friendly to the Porte, that the time was gone by for collective action, and that each power was free to act as it pleased."

Thus the English Ministry has lost the resource of covering itself with the *common* arbitration of the *European* Areopagus, that joint-stock company disappearing before one word of the Austrian Minister, as it had been conjured up by him. In the beginning Austria wanted no conference at all till Russia had crossed the Pruth. Russia having advanced to the Danube, Austria does want the conference no more, at least no more on its primitive

[a] *The Morning Post*, No. 24881, September 19, 1853.—*Ed.*
[b] Of September 21, 1853.—*Ed.*
[c] Abdul Mejid.—*Ed.*

conditions. On the other hand Count de Nesselrode has published two circulars, which do not any longer allow backing the original Vienna Note by hidden "good intentions" or interpreting it in any other sense than its literal one.

The modifications proposed by the Porte have reduced the whole question to "a mere question of words,"[a] shouted the whole ministerial press.

By no means, says Nesselrode. The Czar puts the same interpretation upon the original text as the Sultan did. The original note is nothing and has never been intended to be anything but a second edition of Menchikoff's note, and we do abide by the text, the whole text, and nothing but the text. The ministerial *Globe* is of course amazed at the discovery that both the Czar and the Sultan, regard the original note "as implying recognition of those demands which Russia had preferred, which Turkey had refused, and which the four Powers did not" (?) "intend to indorse,"[b] and that "Russia insists upon an *absolute* recognition of the claims which she first advanced." And why should she not? If she was bold enough to advance those claims four months ago, why should she desist now after having won the first campaign?

The same *Globe* which pretended some days ago the Turkish modifications to be scholastic *quibbles, superfluous* subtilities, is now obliged to own that "the Russian interpretation shows that they were *necessary.*"

The *first* dispatch of Nesselrode is not yet made public, but *The Morning Post* assures us that it declares "the Vienna Note to be neither more nor less than the equivalent of Prince Menchikoff's note," and the evening *Globe* adds, that according to it,

> "The Emperor regarded [...] the Vienna Note as securing for him that recognition on Turkey, and that hold upon her Government, which the Porte, with the support of the four Powers, had refused, and which it was the object of the mediation to prevent. [...] That the Emperor [...] never ceased to reserve to himself the right of dealing directly with Turkey alone, setting aside the mediators whom he affected to acknowledge."

At no time did he affect to acknowledge them as mediators. He permitted three of them to march in the rear of Austria, while he allowed Austria herself to come an humble supplicant to him.

---

[a] *The Times*, No. 21538, September 20, 1853. See also this volume, p. 310.—*Ed.*

[b] Here and below the quotations are from the leader in *The Globe*, September 22, 1853.—*Ed.*

As to the *second* dispatch, dated St. Petersburg, 7th, published by the Berlin *Zeit* on the 18th inst., and addressed to Baron Meyendorff at Vienna, Nesselrode is perfectly right in stating that the original note was described to him as an "*ultimatum*" by the Austrian Envoy, which Russia obliged herself to give her consent to upon the express condition of its being accepted by the Porte *without any alteration whatever.* "Will any one refuse to hear this testimony to the *loyauté* of the Emperor?"[a] It is true that he has committed a little act of "piracy" on the Principalities; that he has overrun them, seized them, taxed them, governed them, plundered them, appropriated them, eaten them up, notwithstanding the proclamations of Gorchakoff; but never mind. Did he not, on the other hand, "on the receipt of a first draft of a note, notify his accession to it by telegraph, *without waiting to learn if it had been approved in London or in Paris*?" Could he be expected to do more than to notify by telegraph, that a note, dictated by a Russian Minister at Vienna, would not be rejected by a Russian Minister at St. Petersburg? Could he do more for Paris and London than not even to wait for their approval? But he did more, indeed. The draft, whose acceptance he condescended to notify by telegraph, was "*altered*" at Paris and London, and "did he retract his consent, or raise the smallest difficulty?" It is true, that according to his own statement, the note in its "final form" is "neither more nor less than an *equivalent* of Prince Menchikoff's note;" but an equivalent note remains, at all instances, "*different*" from the original one; and had he "not stipulated the acceptance of the Menchikoff note without *any* alteration?" Might he not, "on this ground alone, have refused to take it into consideration?" He did not do so. "Could a more conciliatory spirit be shown?" The *ultimatum* of the Vienna Conference is no business of his; it is their own property. "It is *their affair* to consider the *delays* which will result" from the Sultan not yielding. He, for his part, does not care about staying some months longer in the Principalities, where his troops are clothed and fed for nothing.

Odessa does not suffer from the mouth of the Danube being blocked, and, if the occupation of the Principalities contributes to raise the price of wheat at Mark-lane,[b] the profane Imperials will find the quicker their way back to the Holy Russia. It is, therefore, for Austria and the Powers to

[a] Nesselrode's dispatch is quoted from and presented according to *The Times*, No. 21540, September 22, 1853.—*Ed.*

[b] The Corn Exchange.—*Ed.*

"declare to the Porte, frankly and firmly, that they, after having in vain opened up to it the only road that could lead to an immediate restoration of its relations with us, henceforth leave *the task for itself alone*."

They did enough for the Sultan by having opened the road to the Danube to the Czar and closed the road to the Black Sea to the Allied Squadron. Nesselrode's "august master" denounces then, "the *warlike* inspiration which seems at present to influence the Sultan and the majority of his Ministers." He, on his part, would certainly prefer the Sultan taking it coolly, opposing peace tracts to gunboats, and compliments to Cossacks. "He has exhausted the measure of concessions, without the Porte having yet made a single one. His Majesty can go no further." Certainly not, he *can go no further*, without crossing the Danube. Nesselrode compresses his whole argument into a masterly dilemma not to be escaped from. Either the alterations proposed by the Porte mean nothing, or they mean something. If they mean nothing, why should the Porte insist upon them? If they mean something, "it is very simple that we refuse to accede to them."

"The evacuation of the Principalities," said Lord Clarendon, "is a *sine qua non, preliminary* to any settlement."[a] Quite the contrary, answers Nesselrode. "The settlement," i.e., the arrival of the Turkish Ambassador bearing the Austrian note without *alterations* "is a *sine qua non* preliminary to the evacuation of the Principalities."

In one word, the magnanimous Czar is ready to part with the Vienna Conference humbug, as it is no longer wanted for terminating his first campaign; but he will hold the closer the Principalities, as they are the indispensable condition for commencing the second one.

If it be true, as we are informed to-day by telegraphic dispatch, that the Conference has resumed business, the Powers will repeat to Nicholas the song Alexander was received with by the Paris mob:

Vive Alexandre,
Vive le roi des rois,
Sans rien prétendre
Il nous donne des lois.[b]

---

[a] Quoted from Clarendon's House of Lords speech on August 8, 1853 in *The Times*. No. 21502, August 9, 1853.—*Ed.*

[b] Long live Alexander,
King of Kings.
He grants us laws
And asks for nothing in return.—*Ed.*

The Czar himself, however, holds no longer his former control over the Eastern complication. The Sultan has been forced to conjure up the old fanatic spirit, to cause a new invasion of Europe by the rude warlike tribes of Asia, not to be soothed down with diplomatic notes and conventional lies, and there seems transpiring, even through the insolent note of the Muscovite, something like an apprehension at the "warlike spirit" domineering over Stambul. The manifesto, addressed by the Sultan to the Mussulmans, declines any other concession to Russia, and a deputation of the Ulemas[246] is said to have called upon the Sultan to abdicate or to declare war without further delay. The division in the Divan is extreme, and the pacific influence of Reshid Pasha and Mustafa Pasha is giving way to that of Mehemet Ali, the Seraskier.[a]

The infatuation of the so-called *radical* London press is quite incredible. After having told us some days ago, that "the laws of England have to be exercised in their *penal rigor*[b] *upon the persons of four traitors*"[c] (Aberdeen, Clarendon, Palmerston and Russell), *The Morning Advertiser*, of yesterday, concludes one of its leaders as follows:

> "Lord Aberdeen must, therefore, make way for a successor. Need we say who that successor must be? There is but one man to whom the country points at this important junction, as fit to be entrusted with the helm of affairs. *That man is Lord Palmerston.*"

The Morning Advertiser being unable to read events and facts, should at least be able to read the articles of Mr. Urquhart, published day after day in its own columns.

On Tuesday evening a meeting of the inhabitants of Sheffield was called, by requisition to the Mayor, "to take into consideration the present unsettled and unsatisfactory state of the Eastern question and the propriety of memorializing government on the subject." A similar meeting is to be held at Stafford and many other attempts are afloat at getting up public demonstrations against Russia and the ministry of "all the talents." But, generally, public attention is absorbed by the rate of discount, corn prices, strikes and commercial apprehensions, and more yet by the *cholera* ravaging Newcastle and being met with explanatory notes by the

---

[a] War Minister.—*Ed.*

[b] *The Morning Advertiser* has "vigour".—*Ed.*

[c] Quoted from Urquhart's article in *The Morning Advertiser*, September 20, 1853. Marx quotes this statement more fully in his article of September 20, 1853 (see this volume, pp. 312-13).—*Ed.*

London Board of Health. An order in council has been issued, putting in force the provisions of the *Epidemic Disease Act* for the next six months throughout the Islands; and hasty preparations for the due reception of the scourge are making in London and other great towns. If I shared the opinions of Mr. Urquhart, I should say, that the Czar had dispatched the Cholera morbus to England with the "*secret mission*" to break down the last remnant of what is called the Anglo-Saxon spirit.

A wonderful change has come over the manufacturing districts during the last four weeks. In July and the beginning of August there was nothing to be seen but bright prosperity, only slightly overshadowed by the distant cloud of the "Eastern Question," and more so, perhaps, by the fear that a shortness of hands would prevent our cotton-lords to explore to the dregs that immense mine of profitable business which they saw before them. The Eastern dispute seemed settled, the crop might certainly turn out a little short, but there was free trade to keep prices down with the never-failing supplies of America, of the Black Sea and the Baltic. Day after day the demand for manufactured goods went on increasing. California ,and Australia poured forth their golden treasures into the lap of British industry. *The Times*, forgetting Malthus and all its own former rhapsodies about overpopulation, seriously discussed the question whether the shortness of the supply of working-hands, and consequent rise of wages, would not, by raising the cost of production of British manufactures in a proportionate manner, put a stop to this flourishing trade, unless the Continent sent a colony of workmen. The working classes were, as their employers said, only *too well off*, so much so, that their demands knew no bounds, and their "impudence" was daily becoming more intolerable. But that was in itself a proof of the immense, unheard-of prosperity which the country was enjoying; and what could be the cause of this prosperity but Free Trade? And what was worth more than all this, was the certitude that the enormous trade done was *sound*, that there were no stocks, no wild speculation. Thus the manufacturers, one and all, were wont to express themselves, and they acted upon these views; they built factories by the hundred, they ordered steam-engines of thousands of horse-power, thousands of power-looms, hundreds of thousands of spindles. Never was engineering and machine-making a more profitable trade than in 1853. Establishments broken down in the whole of their internal organization by the great strike of 1851,[247] now regained their position, and even improved it; and I could name more than one first-rate and celebrated machine-making firm who, but for this unprecedented business, would have succumbed under the consequence of the blow inflicted by the mechanics during the great turn-out.

The fact is that the bright sunshine of prosperity is for the moment hidden by gloomy clouds. No doubt the altered aspect of the Eastern dispute has contributed a good deal; but that affects the home American and Colonial trade very little. The raising of the rate of discount is less a cause than a symptom of "something being rotten in the state of Denmark."[a] The shortness of the crop and increase in the price of provisions are no doubt causes which have counteracted and will counteract still more the demand for manufactured goods from those markets which are exposed to the operation of these causes, and among these the home market, the mainstay of British industry, stands in the first rank. But the rise in the price of provisions is at this moment, in most districts of England and Scotland, very nearly or altogether compensated by the rise of wages, so that the purchasing power of the consumer can hardly be said to have been *already* lessened much. Then the rise in wages has raised the cost of production in those branches of industry in which manual labor prevails; but the price of nearly all manufactured goods was, up to August, pushed a good deal ahead of the cost of production by the large demand. All these causes have cooperated to deaden business; but, after all, they are not sufficient to account for the general anxiety that pervades the commercial classes of the manufacturing districts.

The fact is, that the spell of the Free Trade delusions is vanishing away, and the bold industrial adventurers begin to have a glimmering that economical revulsions, commercial crises and recurrence of over-production are yet not quite so impossible in a Free Trade country as they dreamt. And over-production there has been, there is, there must be, for even those bugbears of *The Manchester Guardian*, the "*Stocks*," are there; aye, and increasing too. The demand for goods is decidedly falling off, while the supply increases every day. The largest and most numerous of the new industrial constructions are only *now gradually coming into operation*. The shortness of hands, the strikes of the building trades, the impossibility of supplying the enormous quantities of machinery on order, have caused many an unforeseen delay and postponed, for a time, the eruption of those symptoms of industrial plethora which otherwise would have shown themselves sooner. Thus the largest mill in the world, Mr. T. Salt's, near

[a] Shakespeare, *Hamlet*, Act I, Scene 4.—*Ed.*

Bradford, was only to be opened this week, and it will take some time yet, ere the whole of the productive power employed there can be brought fully to bear on the market. Thus plenty of the larger new concerns in Lancashire will not be fit for work before winter, *while it will be spring, and perhaps later, before the market will feel the full effect of this new and stupendous accession of productive power.* According to the last news from Melbourne and Sydney, import markets were becoming much duller, and many shipments will now be indefinitely postponed. As to *over-speculation,* we shall hear of that by and by, when accounts come to be closed. Speculation has been distributed over such a variety of articles that it shows less this time than before, although there is plenty of it.

Written on September 23, 1853

First published in the *New-York Daily Tribune,* No. 3892 and the *New-York Semi-Weekly Tribune,* No. 873, October 7, 1853

Signed: *Karl Marx*

Reproduced from the *New-York Daily Tribune*

Karl Marx

[PANIC ON THE LONDON STOCK EXCHANGE.— STRIKES][248]

London, Tuesday, Sept. 27,[a] 1853

The intelligence that the combined fleets had passed up the Dardanelles, concurrent with rumors of a change in the Ministry and of commercial difficulties, produced a real panic at the Stock Exchange on Saturday:

> "To describe the state of the English funds, or the scene that has prevailed in the Stock Exchange, would be a task of no small difficulty. It is rare that such excitement is witnessed, and it is well that it is infrequent.... It is perhaps no inflation to assert that the *Bearing* at the present time equals almost what took place during the French Revolution.... Funds have this week been done at $91^1/_2$ [...] and [...] have not been so low since 1849.... In the railway market there has been an incessant fall."

Thus says *The Ministerial Observer.*[b] All the leading railway shares were about 68 s. to 80 scp. under the prices of the previous week. As to the sudden pressure of stock upon the market, it would not signify much, as the mere time-dealers are able, at a given moment, to turn the market and intimidate the *bona fide* stockholders. But, coinciding, as it does, with general symptoms of a commercial crisis, the great fluctuation of funds, even if it be of a mere speculative character, will prove fatal in its consequences. At all events, this consternation in the Money market is condemnatory of any State loans looming in the future, and particularly so of the Austrian ones. Moreover, capitalists are reminded that Austria did pay, in 1811, a dividend 1s. 7d.

---

[a] In the *New-York Daily Tribune* the article was datelined: "Thursday, Sept. 29". Here it is corrected on the basis of a note in Karl Marx's notebook.— *Ed.*

[b] Here and below the quotations are from *The Observer*, September 26, 1853.— *Ed.*

farthing in the pound on their promissory notes; that, notwithstanding her revenue having been screwed up from £12,000,000 to £18,000,000 sterling, by means of a greatly increased pressure of taxation exerted on Hungary and Lombardy since 1849, her annual deficit amounts, on an average, to more than one-quarter of her whole revenue; that about £50,000,000 have been added to her national debt since 1846; and that she only has been prevented from a new bankruptcy by the interested forbearance of the children of Israel, who still hope to rid their tills of heaps of Austrian paper accumulated in them.

"Trade has been pushed on somewhat beyond its proper limits, and our commercial liabilities have partially outstripped our means," says *The Observer*. "It is useless," exclaims *The Morning Post*, "to evade the question, for although there are [...] some favorable features in the pending crisis which did not exist in 1847, it must be perceptible to every intelligent observer of passing events that, to say the least of it, a very trying condition of affairs has arrived."[a]

The bullion reserve in the Bank of England has again decreased by £338,954, and its reserve of notes—i.e., the fund available for discounts,—amounts but to seven millions, a sum fully required by the Chancellor of the Exchequer[b] for paying off the dissentient holders of South Sea stock. As to the state of the Corn market, we learn the following from yesterday's *Mark Lane Express*[c]:

"With average crops we have for [...] years consumed some millions of quarters of foreign wheat per annum. What, then, are our requirements likely to be under existing circumstances? The produce of wheat at the utmost cannot be estimated at more than three-quarters of an average, and there is [...] no excess in the yield of any other crop. Potatoes are seriously affected by disease, and have been forced into consumption so rapidly, owing to their unfitness for storing, that this article of food must very shortly become scarce. So enormous has been our consumption that with an importation of 3,304,025 qrs. of wheat and 3,337,206 cwts. of flour during the eight months ending the 5th inst., the stocks in granary are by no means excessive.... We are anxious not to exaggerate the difficulties the country may be placed in, but *that difficulties exist it would be folly to deny*.... The reports as to the yield of wheat are *very unsatisfactory*; in many cases where the produce has been tested by thrashing, the quantity turned out little more than half of what had been calculated upon."

While thus the bright sunshine of commercial and industrial prosperity is hidden by gloomy prospects, *strikes* are still forming, and will for some time yet form, an important feature of our industrial condition; only they are beginning to change their

---

[a] *The Morning Post*, No. 24887, September 26, 1853.—*Ed.*
[b] Gladstone.—*Ed.*
[c] Of September 26, 1853.—*Ed.*

character contemporary with the change that is now going on in the general condition of the country.

At Bury a new advance of 2d. per 1,000 hanks has been asked on the part of the spinners. Masters refusing, they left work, and the weavers will do so as soon as they have worked up the yarn on hand. At Preston, while the weavers still demand an advance of 10 per cent., being supported by the operatives of the surrounding districts, six masters have already locked up their mills and the others are likely to follow them. Two thousand operatives have thus been thrown out of work. At Blackburn the mechanics of Mr. Dickinson, iron-founder, still remain out. At Wigan the capreelers of one mill have struck for an advance of 1d. per score, and the throstle-spinners of another mill refused to commence work until their wages were advanced. The mills were closed. At the same place the coal-miners' strike, embracing about 5,000 hands, is going on. The Earl of Crawford, and other extensive coal-miners in the neighborhood, dismissed their hands on Wednesday evening. A numerous meeting of the colliers was then held in Scales' Orchard. At Manchester 5,000 looms stand still, besides the minor strikes going forward, such as that of the fustian-dyers, the skein-dyers, felt-hat makers, etc. At Bolton, meetings of the operative cotton-spinners are being held for an advance of wages. There are shoemakers' strikes at Trenton, Bridgewater, etc.; cab-drivers' strikes at Glasgow; masons' strikes at Kilmarnock; threatened turn-outs of the police at Oldham, etc. At Birmingham, nailers demand an advance of 10 per cent.; at Wolverhampton, the carpenters one of 6d. per day; the London carpenters ditto, and so on. While through the principal manufacturing towns of Lancashire, Cheshire, Derbyshire, etc., the operatives are holding public meetings, to decide upon measures for the support of their suffering brethren, the masters on the other hand are resolved to close their establishments for an indefinite period, with the design of starving their hands into subjection.

"We find," says the *Sunday Times*, "that, generally speaking, the demand for an advance of wages has not exceeded 6d. a day; and, looking at the present price of provisions, [...] it can hardly be said [...] that the demand is an unreasonable one. We know it has been said that one aim of the present strikers is to obtain a sort of *communistic share* of the real or supposed profits of the manufacturer; but the comparison between the *increased demand for wages* and the *enhanced value of the prime necessaries of life*, furnishes an ample refutation of the charge."[a]

---

[a] "The Wages Movement,—'The Strikes'", *Sunday Times*, No. 1616, September 25, 1853.—*Ed.*

When the working people ask for more than "the prime necessaries of life," when they pretend "to share" in the profits resulting from their own industry, then they are accused of *communistic* tendencies. What has the price of provisions to do with the "eternal and supreme law of supply and demand?" In 1839, 1840, 1841, and 1842, while there was a continued rise in the price of provisions, wages were sinking until they reached the starvation point. "Wages," said then the same manufacturers, "don't depend upon the price of provisions, but upon the eternal law of supply and demand."

"The demands of the working people," says the *Sunday Times*, "may be submitted to when urged in a *respectful* manner."

What has *respect* to do with the "eternal law of supply and demand?" Has any one ever heard of the price of coffee rising at Mincing-lane[a] when "urged in a *respectful* manner?" The trade in human flesh and blood being carried on in the same manner as that of any other commodity, give it at least the chances of any other.

The wages-movement has been going on now for a period of six months. Let us judge it by the test acknowledged on the part of the masters themselves, by the "eternal laws of supply and demand," or are we, perhaps, to understand, that the eternal laws of political economy must be interpreted in the same manner as the eternal peace treaties Russia has concluded with Turkey?

Six months ago the work-people, had they even found their position not strengthened by the great demand for their labor, by constant and enormous emigration to the gold fields and to America, must have inferred the enhancement of industrial profits from the general prosperity-cry uttered by the middle-class press exulting at the blessings of Free Trade. The workmen, of course, demanded their share of that so loudly proclaimed prosperity, but the masters fought hard against them. Then, the workmen combine, threaten to strike, enforce their demands in a more or less amicable manner. Wherever a strike occurs, the whole of the masters and their organs in pulpit, platform and press, break out into immoderate vituperation of the "impudence and stupidity" "of such *attempts at dictation*." Now, what did the strikes prove, if not that the workmen preferred applying a mode of their own of testing the proportion of the supply to the demand rather than to

---

[a] A London street, centre of trade in spices and other goods brought from the colonies.— *Ed.*

trust to the interested assurances of their employers? Under certain circumstances, there is for the workman no other means of ascertaining whether he is or not paid to the actual market value of his labor,[249] but to strike or to threaten to do so. In 1852, on an average, the margin between the cost of the raw material and the price of the finished goods—for instance, the margin between the cost of raw cotton and that of yarn, between the price of yarn and that of cotton goods, was greater, consequently the profit of the spinner and the manufacturer was undoubtedly larger than it has been in 1853. Neither yarn nor goods have, until very lately, risen in the same proportion as cotton. Why, then, did the manufacturers not advance wages at once in 1852? There was no cause, they say, in the relative position of supply and demand justifying such a rise of wages in 1852. Indeed? Hands were not quite as short a year ago as they are now, but the difference is out of proportion to the sudden and repeated rise of wages forced out of the manufacturers since then, by virtue of the law of supply and demand, as expounded by turn-outs. There are, certainly, more factories at work than last year, and more able-bodied workmen have emigrated since then, but at the same time never has there been such a supply of factory labor poured into our "hives of industry" from agricultural and other pursuits, as during the last twelve months.

The fact is that the "hands," as usual, perceived only too late, that the value of their labor had risen 30 per cent. many a month ago, and then, in the summer of this year—only then—they began to strike, first for 10 per cent., then for another 10 per cent., and so on, for as much, of course, as they could get. The constant success of these strikes, while it generalized them all over the country, was the best proof of their legitimacy, and their rapid succession in the same branch of trade, by the same "hands" claiming fresh advances, fully proved that according to supply and demand the work-people had long been entitled to a rise of wages, which was merely kept from them on account of their being ignorant of the state of the labor market. When they at last became acquainted with it, the manufacturers, who had all the while preached "the eternal law of supply and demand," fell back on the doctrine of "enlightened despotism," claiming the right to do as they liked with their own, and propounding as their angry *ultimatum* that the work-people don't know what is good for them.

The change in the general commercial prospects must change the relative position of the work-people and their employers. Sudden as it came on, it found many strikes begun, still more in preparation. No doubt, there will be more, in spite of the depression, and, also, for a rise of wages, for as to the argument of the manufacturer, that he cannot afford to advance, the workmen will reply, that provisions are dearer; both arguments being equally powerful. However, should, as I suppose, the depression prove lasting, the work-people will soon get the worst of it, and have to struggle—very unsuccessfully—against *reduction.* But then their activity will soon be carried over to the *political field,* and the *new organization of trades, gained in the strikes, will be of immense value to them.*

Written on September 27, 1853

First published in the *New-York Daily Tribune,* No. 3900, October 17, 1853; reprinted in the *New-York Semi-Weekly Tribune,* No. 876, October 18; published simultaneously in abridged form in German in *Die Reform,* No. 60, October 19, 1853

Signed: *Karl Marx*

Reproduced from the *New-York Daily Tribune*

Frederick Engels

THE RUSSIANS IN TURKEY[250]

The certainty of war, and the probability that each steamer that now arrives from Europe will report the maneuvers of armies and the results of battles, render it more than ever necessary accurately to understand the respective positions and forces of the combatants, and the various facts which will govern the movements of the campaign. This necessity we propose to meet by a succinct analysis of the elements of offense and defense on both sides, and of the leading strategic considerations which are likely to have weight on the minds of the opposing commanders.

The Russian troops occupying the Danubian Principalities consisted, at the beginning, of two infantry corps and the usual amount of reserve cavalry and artillery. An infantry corps in Russia, counts three divisions, or six brigades of infantry, several regiments of light cavalry, and a brigade of artillery, which, altogether, should amount to about 55,000 men, with about a hundred guns. To every two infantry corps there is a "reserve cavalry corps" and some reserve artillery, including heavy siege artillery. Thus, the original army of occupation amounts, upon paper, to something like 125,000 men. A third infantry corps has since begun to cross the Pruth, and we may, therefore, after all due deductions, consider the Russian forces concentrated on the Danube to number from 140,000 to 150,000 fighting men. How many, in a given moment, may be able to rally around the standards, depends upon the sanitary condition of the district, the greater or less efficiency of the Russian commissariat, and other circumstances of a similar nature which it is impossible correctly to estimate at a distance.

From all the information at our command, the Turkish army opposed to the Russians on the Danube, may be estimated at the very outside, at 110,000 to 120,000 men. Before the arrival of the Egyptian contingent, it was generally asserted not to surpass 90,000 men. There is, then, as far as we can judge, an evident inferiority of numbers on the part of the Turks. And as to the intrinsic value and quality of either army, an equal superiority on the part of the Russians must be admitted. It is true that the Turkish artillery, formed by excellent French and Prussian officers, enjoys a high reputation, while the Russian gunners are notoriously poor marksmen; but in spite of all recent improvements, the Turkish infantry cannot be compared to Russian grenadiers, and Turkish horsemen still lack that discipline and steadiness in battle which will allow of a second and a third charge after the first has been repulsed.

The Generals, on both sides, are comparatively new men. The military merits of Prince Gorchakoff, the Russian commander, and the reasons why the Emperor appointed him to that post, we have already had occasion to state to our readers.[251] An honest man, and a zealous partisan of Russia's "manifest destiny," it yet remains to be seen whether he can conduct a campaign of such magnitude as that now opening. Omer Pasha, the Turkish Generalissimo, is better known, and what we know of him is generally favorable. His expeditions against Kurdistan and Montenegro were, the first successful under difficult circumstances; the second, exceedingly well planned, and certain of almost bloodless success, but for the interference of diplomacy.[252] The chief superiority, then, which can be found on the side of the Turks is, perhaps, that of generalship; in most other respects the Russians have the advantage.

Though the Turks have declared war, and are perhaps, more vehement in their disposition to come to blows than the Russians, it seems evident, that as the weaker party, they will find the greater advantage in defensive, and the Russians in offensive action. This of course excludes the chances which may arise from glaring mistakes in the arrangements of either General. If the Turks were strong enough for the offensive, their tactics would be plain. They would then have to deceive the Russians by false maneuvers on the upper Danube, concentrate their forces rapidly between Silistra and Orsova, cross the lower Danube, fall upon the enemy where his position is weakest, namely, at the narrow strip of land forming the frontier between Wallachia and Moldavia; and then separating the Russian troops in both

Principalities from each other, repel with concentrated forces the corps in Moldavia, and crush that which would find itself isolated and cut off in Wallachia. But as all the chances of an offensive movement are against the Turks, they could reasonably undertake a similar operation in consequence only of egregious blunders on the part of the Russian General.

If the Russians seize the opportunity for offensive action, they have two natural obstacles to pass before they penetrate to the heart of the Turkish Empire; first the Danube and then the Balkan. The passage of a large river, even in presence of a hostile army, is a military feat so often performed during the revolutionary and Napoleonic wars, that every lieutenant now-a-days can tell how it is to be done. A few feigned movements, a well-appointed pontoon train, some batteries to cover the bridges, good measures for securing the retreat, and a brave vanguard, are about all the conditions required. But the crossing of a great mountain range, and especially one provided with so few passes and practicable roads as the Balkan, is a more serious operation. And when this mountain range runs parallel to the river, at a distance of no more than forty or sixty miles, as the Balkan does to the Danube, the matter becomes more serious still, as a corps defeated on the hills may, by active pursuit, be cut off from its bridges and thrown into the river before succor can arrive; an army, thus defeated in a great battle, would be inevitably lost. It is this proximity and parallel direction of the Danube and the Balkan which forms the natural military strength of Turkey. The Balkan, from the Macedo-Servian frontier to the Black Sea, that is the Balkan proper, "Veliki Balkan," has five passes, two of which are high roads, such as high roads are in Turkey. These two are the passes of Ikhtiman, on the road from Belgrade, through Sofia, Philippopolis and Adrianople to Constantinople, and of Dobrol, on the road from Silistra and Shumla. The other three, of which two are between the above and the third towards the Black Sea, may be considered as impracticable for a large army, with the impediments of war. They may give passage to smaller corps, perhaps even to light field artillery, but they cannot be made the lines of operation and of communication for the main body of the invaders.

In 1828 and 1829, the Russian forces operated upon the line from Silistra by Dobrol to Adrianople, Ainadjik, this route being the shortest and most direct from the Russian frontier to the Turkish Capital, offers itself as the most natural to any Russian army which comes from the north, is supported by a fleet in undisputed possession of the Black Sea, and whose object is to bring matters to a speedy decision by a victorious march upon Constantinople. In order to pass by this road, a Russian army, after having passed the Danube, has to force a strong position flanked by the two fortresses of Shumla and Varna, to blockade or to take both of these fortresses, and then to pass the Balkan. In 1828, the Turks risked their main strength in this position. They were defeated at Kulevcha[253]; Varna and Shumla were taken, the defense of the Balkan was but feeble, and the Russians arrived at Adrianople, very much enfeebled, it is true, but yet having encountered no resistance, as the Turkish army was completely dissolved and not a brigade at hand for the defense of Constantinople. The Turks committed, on that occasion, a great mistake. A range of mountains, as every officer understands, must not be defended by a defensive position in front of it, nor by dividing the defending armies so as to block up all the passes; but by taking up a central position behind it, by observing all the passes, and when the enemy's intentions are clearly developed, by falling with concentrated forces upon the heads of his columns as they emerge from the various ravines of the mountain range. The strong position across the Russian line of operations between Varna and Shumla led the Turks to make that decisive stand there, which, with more concentrated strength and against an enemy necessarily weakened by sickness and detachments, they ought to have made in the plain of Adrianople.

Thus we see that in the defense of the line from Silistra to Adrianople the passage of the Danube ought to be defended without risking a decisive action. The second stand should be made *behind*, not *between*, Shumla and Varna, and no decisive action risked unless the chances of victory are *very great*. Retreat across the Balkan is the next step leaving the passes defended by detachments, capable of as much resistance as may appear advisable without bringing on a decisive engagement. In the meantime the Russians will weaken themselves by blockading the fortresses, and, if they follow their anterior practice, they will again take these fortresses by storm, and lose a great many men by the operation; for it is a curious fact, and characteristic of the Russian army, that up to the present time it has, unaided, *never been able to lay a regular siege*. The want of skilful engineers and artillerists, the impossibility of creating in a barbarous country large magazines of war, material for sieges, or even to carry across immense tracts of country whatever material may exist, have always driven the Russians to the necessity of carrying every fortified place by assault after a short, violent, but seldom very effective cannonade. Thus Suwaroff took Ismail and Otchakov[254]; thus, in 1828 and 1829, the Turkish fortresses in Europe and Asia were stormed; and thus they carried Warsaw in 1831.[255] In either case the Russian army will arrive at the passes of the Balkan in a weakened condition, while the Turks have had time to concentrate their detachments from all sides. If the invaders are not repelled while attempting to cross the Balkan, by a dash of the whole Turkish army, the decisive battle may be fought under the walls of Adrianople, and then, if the Turks are defeated, they will at least have exhausted all the chances left them.

But a Russian victory at Adrianople can, under present circumstances, decide very little. The British and French fleets are at Constantinople, and in their teeth no Russian General can march upon that capital. The Russians, arrested at Adrianople, unable to rely on the support of their fleet, which itself would be menaced, would soon fall victims by thousands to disease, and have to retrace their steps beyond the Balkan. Thus, even in victory, they would be defeated as regards their great object in the war. There is, however, another line of operations which they may, perhaps, more advantageously take. It is indicated by the route which leads from Widin and Nikopolis, by way of Sofia, to Adrianople. Apart from political considerations, it would never enter the head of any sensible Russian General to follow this route. But so long as Russia can depend on Austria—so long as the approach of a Russian army to the Serbian frontier, combined with Russian intrigues in Serbia, may excite insurrectionary movements in that country, in Montenegro, and among the predominant Greco-Slavic population of Bosnia, Macedonia, and Bulgaria—so long as the crowning operation of a strictly military campaign, the taking of Constantinople, is out of the question, from the presence of a European fleet—so long this plan of campaign will be the only one which the Russians can adopt with much chance of success, and without forcing England and France to determined hostile action by too direct a march upon Constantinople.

It appears, indeed, from the present position of the Russian army, that something of this sort is projected. Its right wing has been extended to Krajova, near the western frontier of Wallachia, and a general shifting of its array toward the upper Danube has taken place. As this maneuver is entirely out of the line of operations by Silistra and Shumla, it can only have for its object to put the Russians in communication with Servia, the center of

Slavic nationality and Greek Catholicism in Turkey. A defensive position on the lower Danube, combined with an advance across the upper Danube toward Sofia, would be perfectly safe if supported by Austria, combined with a movement of the Turkish Slavonians in favor of national independence; and such a movement could not be more forcibly provoked than by a march of the Russian army into the very heart of the Slavonian population of Turkey. Thus, the Czar[a] will obtain far more easily and in a far less offensive manner what he has claimed throughout the controversy. This is the organization of all the Turkish Slavonians in distinct principalities, such as Moldavia, Wallachia and Servia now are. With Bulgaria, Montenegro and Macedonia under the nominal sovereignty of the Sultan[b] and the real protection of the Czar, Turkey in Europe would be confined to the environs of Constantinople and deprived of its nursery of soldiers, Albania. This would be a far better result for Russia than a decisive victory at Adrianople, followed by a dead stand of her armies. It is a result which appearances indicate that she is about to try for. Whether she is not mistaken in relying on the Slavonians of Turkey is a doubtful question, though there will be no cause of astonishment should they all declare against her.

Written on September 29, 1853

First published in the *New-York Daily Tribune*, No. 3900, October 17, 1853, as a leader; reprinted in the *New-York Weekly Tribune*, No. 632, October 22, 1853

Reproduced from the *New-York Daily Tribune*

[a] Nicholas I.—*Ed.*
[b] Abdul Mejid.—*Ed.*

KARL MARX

LORD PALMERSTON[256]

Written in October-beginning of December, 1853

First published in *The People's Paper* Nos. 77, 78, 79, 80, 81, 84, 85 and 86, October 22 and 29, November 5, 12 and 19, December 10, 17 and 24, 1853, signed by Dr. Marx; in incomplete form published as leaders in the *New-York Daily Tribune*, Nos. 3902, 3916, 3930 and 3973, October 19, November 4 and 21, 1853, January 11, 1854, and in the *New-York Weekly Tribune*, Nos, 632, 635, 638, October 22, November 12, December 3, 1853, and also as pamphlets in London, in 1853-54

Reproduced from *The People's Paper*, checked with the text in the *New-York Daily Tribune* and of the pamphlets

LORD PALMERSTON.

Written for the "New York Tribune," by Dr. MARX, and communicated by him to us.

FIRST ARTICLE.

RUGGIERO is again and again fascinated by the false charms of Alcine, which he knows to disguise an old witch—

Sans teeth, sans eyes, sans taste, sans everything

and the knight-errant cannot withstand falling in love with her anew whom he knows to have transmuted all her former adorers into asses and other beasts. The English public is another Ruggiero, and Palmerston is another Alcine. Although a septuagenarian, and since 1847 occupying the public stage, almost without interruption, he contrives to remain a novelty, and to evoke all the hopes that used to centre on an untried and promising youth. With one foot in the grave, he is supposed not yet to have begun his true career. If he were to die to-morrow, all England would be surprised at learning that he has been a Secretary of State half this century.

If not a good statesman of all work, he is at least a good actor of all work. He succeeds in the comic as in the heroic—in pathos as in familiarity—in the tragedy as in the farce: although the latter may be more congenial to his feelings. He is no first class orator, but he is an accomplished debater. Possessed of a wonderful memory, of great experience, of a consummate tact, of a never-failing *presence d'esprit*, of a gentlemanlike versatility, of the most minute knowledge of parliamentary tricks, intrigues, parties, and men, he handles difficult cases in an admirable manner and with a pleasant volubility, sticking to the prejudices and susceptibilities of his public, secured from any surprise by his cynic impudence, from any self-confession by his selfish dexterity, from running into a passion by his profound frivolity, his perfect indifference, and his aristocratic contempt. Being an exceedingly happy joker, he ingratiates himself wtih everybody. Never losing his temper, he imposes on an impassioned antagonist. When unable to master a subject, he knows how to play with it. If wanting of general views, he is always ready to tissue elegant generalities.

Endowed with a restless and indefatigable spicit, he abhors inactivity, and pines for agitation, if not for action. A country like England allows him, of course, to busy himself in every corner of the earth. What he aims at is not the substance, but the mere appearance of success.

If he can do nothing, he will devise anything. Where he dares not interfere, he intermeddles. Not able to vie with a strong enemy, he improvises a weak one.

Being no man of deep designs, pondering on no combinations of long standing, pursuing no great object, he embarks in difficulties with a view to disentangle himself in a showy manner. He wants complications to feed his activity, and when he finds them not ready, he will create them. He exults in show-conflicts, show-battles, show enemies, diplomatical notes to be exchanged, ships to be ordered to sail, the whole movement ending for him in violent parliamentary debates, which are sure to prepare him an ephemeral success, the constant and the only object of all his exertions. He manages internal conflicts like an artist, driving matters to a certain point, retreating when they threaten to become serious, but having got, at all events, the dramatic excitement he wants. In his eyes, the movement of history itself is nothing but a pastime, expressly invented for the private satisfaction of the noble Viscount Palmerston of Palmerston.

Yielding to foreign influence in facts, he opposes it inwards. Having inherited from Canning England's mission to propagate Constitutionalism on the Continent, he i never in the act of piracy, while admitting that Denmark had evidenced no hostility whatever towards Great Britain, he contended that they were right in bombarding its capital and stea'ing its fleet, because they had to prevent Dan sh neutrality from being, perhaps, converted into open hostility by the compulsion of France. Ths was the new law of nations, proclaimed by ny lord Palmerston.

When again speechifying, we find that English minister *par excellence*, engaged in the defence of foreign troops, called over from the continent to England, with the express mission of maintaining forcibly the oligarchic rule, to establish which William had, in 1688, come over from Holland, with his Dutch troops. Palmerston answered to the well-founded "apprehensions for the liberties of the country," originating from the presence of the King's German Legion, in a very flippant manner. Why should we not have 16,000 of those foreigners at home; while you know, that we employ "a far larger proportion of foreigners abroad." (House of Commons, March 10, 1812.)

When similar apprehensions for the constitution arose from the large standing army, maintained since 1815, he found "a sufficient protection of the constitution in the very constitution of our army," a large proportion of its officers being "men of property and connexions." (House of Commons, March 8, 1816.)

When the large standing army was attacked from a financial point of view, he made the curious discovery that "much of our financial embarrassments had bem caused by our former low peace establishmen." (House of Commons, March 8, 1816.)

When the "burders of the country," and the "misery of the peole" were contrasted with the lavish military expenditure, he reminded parliament that these burdens and that misery "were the price which we (viz., the English oligarchy) agreed to pay for our freedom and independence." House of Commons, May 16, 1828.)

In his eyes, military despotism was not to be apprehended from the exertions of "those self-called, but misled Reformers, who demand that sort of reform in the country which, according to every first principle of government, must end, if it were acceded to, in a military despotism." (House of Commons, June 14, 1820.)

While large standing armies were thus his panacea for maintaining the constitution of the country, flogging was his panacea for maintaining the constitution of the army. He defended it in the debates on the Mutiny Bill, on the 5th of March, 1824, he declared it to be "absolutely indispensable" on March 11, 1825, he recommended it again on March 10, 1828; he sto d by it in the debates of April, 1833, and he proved an amateur of flogging on every subsequent occasion.

There existed no abuse in the army, he did not find plausible reasons for, if it happened to foster the interests of aristocratic parasites. Thus, for instance, in the debates on the Sale of Commission. (House of Commons, March 12, 1828.)

Lord Palmerston likes to parade his constant exertions for the establishment of religious liberty. Now, he voted against Lord Russell's motion for the Repeal of Test and Corporation Acts. Why? Because he was "a warm and zealous friend to religious liberty," and could, therefore, not allow the Dissenters to be relieved from "imaginary grievances, while real afflictions pressed upon the Catholics." (House of Commons, Feb. 26, 1828.)

In proof of his zeal for religious liberty he informs us of his "regret to see the increasing numbers of the Dissenters. It is my wish that the Established Church should be the predomi-

Part of a page of *The People's Paper* with the first article of Marx's series *Lord Palmerston*

FIRST ARTICLE[a]

[*The People's Paper,* No. 77, October 22, 1853]

Ruggiero is again and again fascinated by the false charms of Alcina, which he knows to disguise an old witch—

> Sans teeth, sans eyes, sans taste, sans everything,[b]

and the knight-errant cannot withstand falling in love with her anew whom he knows to have transmuted all her former adorers into asses and other beasts. The English public is another Ruggiero, and Palmerston is another Alcina. Although a septuagenarian, and since 1807 occupying the public stage, almost without interruption, he contrives to remain a novelty, and to evoke all the hopes that used to centre on an untried and promising youth. With one foot in the grave, he is supposed not yet to have begun his true career. If he were to die to-morrow, all England would be surprised at learning that he has been a Secretary of State half this century.

If not a good statesman of all work, he is at least a good actor of all

---

[a] The article published in the *New-York Daily Tribune* on October 19, 1853 began as follows: "The Eastern complications have worked a great change in England, if not as to parties, at least as to the men at the head of parties. Lord Palmerston has again become a popular favorite. He is in everybody's mouth, he is the only man to save England, he is confidently announced as the indispensable Premier of any modified Cabinet, extolled alike by the Tories, the Whigs, the self-styled patriots, the press, and public opinion in general.

"So extraordinary a phenomenon is the Palmerston mania that one is tempted to suppose it to be of a merely fictitious character, got up not for home consumption, but as an article of export, destined for foreign use. This, however, would be a mistake."—*Ed.*

[b] Shakespeare, *As You Like It,* Act II, Scene 7. Ruggiero and Alcina are characters from Ariosto's poem *L'Orlando furioso.—Ed.*

work. He succeeds in the comic as in the heroic—in pathos as in familiarity—in the tragedy as in the farce: although the latter may be more congenial to his feelings. He is no first class orator, but he is an accomplished debater. Possessed of a wonderful memory, of great experience, of a consummate tact, of a never-failing *présence d'esprit*,[a] of a gentlemanlike versatility,[b] of the most minute knowledge of parliamentary tricks, intrigues, parties, and men, he handles difficult cases in an admirable manner and with a pleasant volubility, sticking to the prejudices and susceptibilities of his public, secured from any surprise by his cynic impudence, from any self-confession by his selfish dexterity, from running into a passion by his profound frivolity, his perfect indifference, and his aristocratic contempt. Being an exceedingly happy joker, he ingratiates himself with everybody. Never losing his temper, he imposes on an impassioned antagonist. When unable to master a subject, he knows how to play with it. If wanting of general views, he is always ready to tissue elegant generalities.

Endowed with a restless and indefatigable spirit, he abhors inactivity, and pines for agitation, if not for action. A country like England allows him, of course, to busy himself in every corner of the earth. What he aims at is not the substance, but the mere appearance of success.

If he can do nothing, he will devise anything. Where he dares not interfere, he intermeddles. Not able to vie with a strong enemy, he improvises a weak one.

Being no man of deep designs, pondering on no combinations of long standing, persuing no great object, he embarks in difficulties with a view to disentangle himself in a showy manner. He wants complications to feed his activity, and when he finds them not ready, he will create them. He exults in show-conflicts, show-battles, show-enemies, diplomatical notes to be exchanged, ships to be ordered to sail, the whole movement ending for him in violent parliamentary debates, which are sure to prepare him an ephemeral success, the constant and the only object of all his exertions. He manages internal[c] conflicts like an artist, driving matters to a certain point, retreating when they threaten to become serious, but having got, at all events, the dramatic excitement he wants. In his eyes, the movement of history itself is nothing but a pastime, expressly

[a] Presence of mind.—*Ed.*

[b] The *New-York Daily Tribune* has "variety of talent" instead of "versatility".—*Ed.*

[c] The *New-York Daily Tribune* has "international".—*Ed.*

invented for the private satisfaction of the noble Viscount Palmerston of Palmerston.[a]

Yielding to foreign influence in facts, he opposes it in words. Having inherited from Canning England's mission to propagate Constitutionalism on the Continent, he is never in need of a theme to pique the national prejudices, and to counteract revolution abroad, and, at the same time, to hold awake the suspicious jealousy of foreign powers. Having succeeded in this easy manner to become the *bête noire* of the continental courts, he could not fail in being set up as the truly English minister at home. Although a Tory by origin, he has contrived to introduce into the management of foreign affairs all the shams and contradictions that form the essence of Whiggism. He knows how to conciliate a democratic phraseology with oligarchic views,[b] how to cover the peacemongering policy of the middle classes with the haughty language of England's aristocratic past—how to appear as the aggressor where he connives, and as the defender where he betrays—how to manage an apparent enemy, and how to exasperate a pretendant ally—how to find himself, at the opportune moment of the dispute, on the side of the stronger against the weak, and how to utter brave words in the act of running away.

Accused by the one party of being in the pay of Russia, he is suspected by the other of Carbonarism.[257] If, in 1848, he had to defend himself against the motion of impeachment for having acted as the minister of Nicholas, he had, in 1850, the satisfaction of being persecuted by a conspiracy of foreign ambassadors, which was successful in the House of Lords, but baffled in the House of Commons.[258] If he betrayed foreign peoples, he did it with great politeness—politeness being the small coin of the devil, which he gives in change for the life-blood of his dupes. If the oppressors were always sure of his active support, the oppressed did never want a great ostentation of his rhetorical generosity. Poles, Italians, Hungarians, Germans, found him in office, whenever they were crushed, but their despots always suspected him of secret conspiracy

---

[a] In the *New-York Daily Tribune* the phrase "the private satisfaction of" is omitted and this sentence is followed by the text: "He is a great sample of that species designated by Thomas Carlyle as the sham captains of the world."—*Ed.*

[b] In the *New-York Daily Tribune*: "He knows how to conciliate a large phraseology with narrow views."—*Ed.*

with the victims they had allowed him to make. Till now, in all instances, it was a probable chance of success to have him for one's adversary, and a sure chance of ruin to have him for one's friend. But, if this art of diplomacy does not shine in the actual results of his foreign negotiations, it shines the more brilliantly in the construction he induced the English people to lay upon them, by accepting phrases for facts, phantasies for realities, and high-sounding pretexts for shabby motives.

Henry John Temple, Viscount Palmerston, deriving his title from a peerage of Ireland, was nominated Lord of the Admiralty in 1807, on the formation of the Duke of Portland's Administration. In 1809, he became Secretary of War, and he continued to hold this office till May, 1828. In 1830 he went over, very skilfully too, to the Whigs, who made him their permanent Secretary for Foreign Affairs. Excepting the intervals of Tory administration, from November 1834 to April 1835, and from 1841 to 1846, he is responsible for the whole foreign policy England has pursued from the revolution of 1830 to December 1851.

Is it not a very curious thing to find, at first view, that Quixote of "free institutions," and that Pindarus of the "glories of the constitutional system," a permanent and an eminent member of the Tory administrations of Mr. Perceval, the Earl of Liverpool, Mr. Canning, Lord Goderich, and the Duke of Wellington, during the long epoch of the Anti-Jacobin war carried on, the monster-debt contracted, the Corn Laws promulgated,[259] foreign mercenaries stationed on the English soil,[260] the people—to borrow an expression from his colleague, Lord Sidmouth,[a]—"bled," from time to time, the press gagged, meetings suppressed, the mass of the nation disarmed, individual liberty suspended together with regular jurisdiction, the whole country placed as it were in a state of siege—in one word, during the most infamous and most reactionary epoch of English history?

His *debut* in parliamentary life is a characteristic one. On February 3, 1808, he rose to defend—what?—secrecy in the working of diplomacy, and the most disgraceful act ever committed by one nation against another nation, viz., the bombardment of Copenhagen, and the capture of the Danish fleet, at the time when England professed to be in profound peace with Denmark.[261] As to the former point, he stated that,

---

[a] The phrase "to borrow an expression from his colleague, Lord Sidmouth" is omitted in the *New-York Daily Tribune.—Ed.*

"In this particular case, his Majesty's Ministers are pledged" (by whom?) "to secrecy;" but he went farther[a]: "I also object generally to making public the working of diplomacy, because it is the tendency of disclosures in that department to shut up future sources of information."

Vidocq would have defended the identical cause in the identical terms. As to the act of piracy, while admitting that Denmark had evidenced no hostility whatever towards Great Britain, he contended that they were right in bombarding its capital and stealing its fleet, because they had to prevent Danish neutrality from being, perhaps, converted into open hostility by the compulsion of France. This was the new law of nations, proclaimed by my lord Palmerston.

When again speechifying, we find that English minister *par excellence*, engaged in the defence of foreign troops, called over from the Continent to England, with the express mission of maintaining forcibly the oligarchic rule, to establish which William had, in 1688, come over from Holland with his Dutch troops. Palmerston answered to the well-founded "apprehensions for the liberties of the country," originating from the presence of the King's German Legion, in a very flippant manner. Why should we not have 16,000 of those foreigners at home; while you know, that we employ "a far larger proportion of foreigners abroad." (House of Commons, March 10, 1812.)

When similar apprehensions for the constitution[b] arose from the large standing army, maintained since 1815, he found "a sufficient protection of the constitution in the very constitution of our army," a large proportion of its officers being "men of property and connexions." (House of Commons, March 8, 1816.)

When the large standing army was attacked from a financial point of view, he made the curious discovery that "much of our financial embarrassments had been caused by our former low peace establishment." (House of Commons, April 25, 1816.)

When the "burdens of the country," and the "misery of the people" were contrasted with the lavish military expenditure, he reminded Parliament that those burdens and that misery "were the price which we" (viz., the English oligarchy) "agreed to pay

---

[a] In the *New-York Daily Tribune* the end of the quotation and the following sentence are given as follows: "...his Majesty's Ministers 'are pledged to security,' but he improved on this statement".— *Ed.*

[b] The phrase "for the constitution" is omitted in the *New-York Daily Tribune.*— *Ed.*

[c] In the *New-York Daily Tribune* in this article on Palmerston and in the following articles, there are, as a rule, no references to the House sittings.— *Ed.*

for our freedom and independence." (House of Commons, May 16, 1820.)

In his eyes, military despotism was not to be apprehended from the exertions of

"those self-called, but misled Reformers, who demand that sort of reform in the country which, according to every first principle of government, must end, if it were acceded to, in a military despotism." (House of Commons, June 14, 1820.)

While large standing armies were thus his panacea for maintaining the constitution of the country, flogging[a] was his panacea for maintaining the constitution of the army. He defended it in the debates on the Mutiny Bill,[262] on the 5th of March, 1824, he declared it to be "absolutely indispensable" on March 11, 1825, he recommended it again on March 10, 1828; he stood by it in the debates of April, 1833, and he proved an amateur of flogging on every subsequent occasion.

There existed no abuse in the army, he did not find plausible reasons for, if it happened to foster the interests of aristocratic parasites. Thus, for instance, in the debates on the Sale of Commission. (House of Commons, March 12, 1828.)

Lord Palmerston likes to parade his constant exertions for the establishment of religious liberty. Now, he voted against Lord Russell's motion for the Repeal of Test and Corporation Acts.[263] Why? Because he was "a warm and zealous friend to religious liberty," and could, therefore, not allow the Dissenters[264] to be relieved from "imaginary grievances, while real afflictions pressed upon the Catholics." (House of Commons, Feb. 26, 1828.)

In proof of his zeal for religious liberty he informs us of his "regret to see the increasing numbers of the Dissenters. It is my wish that the Established Church should be the predominant Church in this country," and it is his wish "that the Established Church should be fed at the expense of the misbelievers." His jocose lordship accuses the rich Dissenters of affording churches for the poor ones,[b] while

"with the Church of England it is the poor alone who feel the want of Church accommodation.... It would be preposterous to say, that the poor ought to subscribe for churches out of their small earnings." (House of Commons, April 9, 1824.)

It would be, of course, more preposterous yet to say, that the rich members of the Established Church ought to subscribe for the church out of their large earnings.

---

[a] In the *New-York Daily Tribune*: "corporal punishment and flogging".— *Ed.*

[b] In the *New-York Daily Tribune*: "of satisfying the ecclesiastical wants of the poorer ones".— *Ed.*

Let us now look at his exertions for Catholic Emancipation,[265] one of his great "claims" on the gratitude of the Irish people. I shall not dwell upon the circumstances, that, having declared himself for Catholic Emancipation, when a member of the Canning Ministry, he entered, nevertheless, the Wellington Ministry, avowedly hostile to that emancipation. Perhaps Lord Palmerston considered religious liberty as one of the Rights of Man, not to be intermeddled with by Legislature. He may answer for himself,

"Although I wish the Catholic claims to be considered, I never will admit those claims to stand upon the ground of right.... If I thought the Catholics were asking for their right, I, for one, would not go into the committee." (House of Commons, March 1, 1813.)

And why is he opposed to their asking their right?

"Because the Legislature of a country has the right to impose such political disabilities upon any class of the community, as it may deem necessary for the safety and the welfare of the whole.... This belongs to the fundamental principles on which civilised government is founded." (House of Commons, March 1, 1813.)

There you have the most cynic confession ever made, that the mass of the people have no rights at all, but that they may be allowed that amount of immunities, the Legislature—or, in other words, the ruling class—may deem fit to grant them. Accordingly, Lord Palmerston declared in plain words, "Catholic Emancipation to be a measure of grace and favour." (House of Commons, Feb. 10, 1829.)

It was then entirely upon the ground of expediency that he condescended to discontinue the Catholic disabilities. And what was lurking behind this expediency?

Being himself one of the great Irish proprietors, he wanted to entertain the delusion, that other remedies for Irish evils than Catholic Emancipation are impossible, that it would cure absenteeism,[266] and prove a substitute for Poor Laws.—(House of Commons, March 18, 1829.)

The great philanthropist, who afterwards cleared his Irish estates of their Irish natives, could not allow Irish misery to darken, even for a moment, with its inauspicious clouds, the bright sky of the landlords and moneylords.[a]

"It is true," he said, "that the peasantry of Ireland do not enjoy all the comforts which are enjoyed by all the peasantry of England" (only think of all the

[a] In the *New-York Daily Tribune*: "the bright sky over the Parliament of landlords and moneylords."—*Ed.*

comforts enjoyed by a family at the rate of 7s. a week). Still, he continues, "still however, the Irish peasant has his comforts.... He is well supplied with fuel, and is seldom" (only four days out of six), "at a loss for food."

What a comfort![a] But this is not all the comfort he has—"he has a greater cheerfulness of mind than his English fellow sufferer!"—(House of Commons, May 7, 1829.)

As to the extortions of Irish landlords, he deals with them in as pleasant a way as with the comforts of the Irish peasantry.

It is said that the Irish landlord insists on the highest possible rent that can be extorted. Why Sir, I believe that is not a singular circumstance; certainly in England the landlord does the same thing.—(House of Commons, May 7, 1829.)

Are we then to be surprised that the man, so deeply interested in the mysteries of the "glories of the English constitution," and the "comforts of her free institutions," should aspire at spreading them all over the Continent?

SECOND ARTICLE

[*The People's Paper*, No. 78, October 29, 1853]

When the Reform Movement[267] had grown irresistible, Lord Palmerston deserted the Tories, and slipped into the Whiggery camp. Although he had apprehended the danger of military despotism springing up, not from the presence of the King's German legion on the English soil, nor from keeping large standing armies, but only from the "self-called Reformers," he patronised, nevertheless,[b] already in 1828, the extension of the franchise to such large industrial places as Birmingham, Leeds, and Manchester. But why?

"Not because I am a friend to Reform in principle, but because I am its decided enemy."

He had persuaded himself that some timely concessions made to the overgrown manufacturing interest[c] might be the surest means

---

[a] In the *New-York Daily Tribune* this sentence is omitted.—*Ed.*

[b] The *New-York Daily Tribune* of October 19, 1853 has the beginning of this passage as follows: "It is known that, when the Reform-movement had grown irresistible, Lord Palmerston deserted the camp of the Tories, and skilfully effected his junction with the Whigs. We have seen that he once apprehended danger of military despotism from the demands of the self-called Reformers. Nevertheless...."—*Ed.*

[c] The *New-York Daily Tribune* gives "factory-kings" instead of "manufacturing interest".—*Ed.*

of escaping "the introduction of general reform." (House of Commons, June 27th, 1828.) Once allied with the Whigs, he did not even pretend that the Reform Bill aimed at breaking through the narrow trammels of the Venetian Constitution; but, on the contrary, at the increase of its strength and solidity, by disjoining the middle classes from the people's opposition.

"The feelings of the middle classes will be changed, and their dissatisfaction will be converted into that attachment to the constitution, which will give to it a vast increase of strength and solidity."

He consoled the peers with the prospect of the Reform Bill not really endangering the "influence of the House of Lords," and their "interfering in elections." He told the aristocracy that the constitution was not to lose its feudal character, "the landed interest being the great foundation upon which rests the fabric of society, and the institutions of the country." He allayed their fears by throwing out the ironical hint that "we have been charged with not being in earnest or sincere in our desire to give to the people a real representation," that "it was said, we only proposed to give a different kind of influence to the aristocracy and the landed interest." He went even as far as to own that, besides the inevitable concession to be made to the middle classes, "disfranchisement," viz., the disfranchisement of the old Tory rotten boroughs for the benefit of new Whig boroughs, "was the chief and leading principle of the Reform Bill."[a] (House of Commons, March 24th, 1831, and May 14, 1832.)

It is now time to return to the performances of the noble lord in the foreign branch of policy[b]:

In 1823, when, consequent on the resolutions of the Congress of Verona,[268] a French army was marched into Spain, in order to overturn the constitution of that country, and to deliver it up to the merciless revenge of the Bourbon idiot[c] and his suite of bigot monks, Lord Palmerston disclaimed any "Quixotic crusades for abstract principles," any intervention in "favour of the people," whose heroic resistance had saved England from the sway of Napoleon. The words he addressed on that occasion to his Whig

[a] The *New-York Daily Tribune*, instead of "viz., the disfranchisement of the old Tory rotten boroughs for the benefit of new Whig boroughs", has: "that is to say, a new kind of distribution of rotten boroughs between the Tory Aristocrats and the Whig Aristocrats was the chief and leading principle of the Reform Bill".—*Ed.*

[b] In the *New-York Daily Tribune* this sentence ends as follows: "during the Tory period of his life".—*Ed.*

[c] Ferdinand VII.—*Ed.*

adversaries are a lively and true picture of his own foreign policy, after he had turned himself into the permanent Minister of Foreign Affairs for those who then were his opponents. He said,

"Some would have had us use threats in negotiation, without being prepared to go to war, if negotiation failed.[...] To have talked of war, and to have meant neutrality; to have threatened an army, and to have retreated behind a state paper; to have brandished the sword of defiance in the hour of deliberation, and to have ended in a penful of protests on the day of battle, would have been the conduct of a cowardly bully, and would have made us the object of contempt, and the laughing-stock of Europe."—(House of Commons, April 30, 1823.)

At last, we arrive at the Greco-Turkish debates, affording to Lord Palmerston the first opportunity for displaying his unrivalled talents, as the unflinching and persevering advocate of Russian interests, in the Cabinet and in the House of Commons. One by one, he re-echoed all the watch-words given out by Russia of Turkish cruelty, Greek civilisation, religious liberty, Christianity, and so forth. At first, we meet him repudiating, in his ministerial capacity,[a] any intention of passing "a censure" upon the meritorious conduct "of Admiral Codrington," which had caused the destruction of the Turkish fleet at Navarino,[269] although he admits that "this battle took place against a power with which we are not at war," and that it was "an untoward event."—(House of Commons, January 31, 1828.)

Then, having retired from office, he opens the long series of his attacks upon Aberdeen, by reproaching him with having been too slow in executing the orders of Russia.[b]

"Has there been much more energy and promptitude in fulfilling our engagements to Greece? [...] July, 1829, is coming fast upon us, and the treaty of July, 1827,[270] is still unexecuted.... The Morea, indeed, has been cleared of the Turks.... But why were the arms of France checked at the Isthmus of Corinth?... The narrow policy of England stepped in, and arrested her progress.... But why do not the allies deal with the country north of the Isthmus, as they have done with that of the south, and occupy at once all that which must be assigned to Greece? I should have thought that the allies had had enough of negotiating with Turkey about Greece."—(House of Commons, June 1, 1829.)

Prince Metternich was, as is generally known, at that time opposing the encroachments of Russia, and accordingly her diplomatic agents—I remind you of the despatches of Pozzo di Borgo and Prince Lieven—had been advised to represent Austria as the great enemy of Grecian emancipation and of European civilisation, the

---

[a] The *New-York Daily Tribune* has: "as the Minister of War".—*Ed.*

[b] The *New-York Daily Tribune* has: "the Czar's orders".—*Ed.*

furtherance of which was the exclusive object of Russian diplomacy.[a] The noble lord follows, of course, in the beaten track.

"By the narrowness of her views, the unfortunate prejudices of her policy, Austria almost reduced herself to the level of a second-rate power;" and consequent on the temporising policy of Aberdeen, England is represented as "the key-stone of that arch of which Miguel, Spain, Austria, and Mahmud are the component parts.... People see in the delay in executing the treaty of July not so much fear of Turkish resistance as inevitable[b] repugnance to Grecian freedom."—(House of Commons, June 1, 1829.)

Again he assails Aberdeen because of his anti-Russian diplomacy[c]:

"I, for one, shall not be satisfied with a number of despatches from the government of England, which will no doubt read well and smooth enough, urging, in general terms, the propriety of conciliating Russia, but accompanied, perhaps, by strong expressions of the regard which England bore to Turkey, which, when read by an interested party, might easily appear to mean more than was really intended.... I should like to see that, whilst England adopted a firm resolution—almost the only course she could adopt—upon no consideration and in no event to take part with Turkey in that war—that that decision was fairly and frankly communicated to Turkey.... There are three most merciless things—time, fire, and the Sultan."—(House of Commons, Feb. 16, 1830.)

Arrived at this point, I must recall to memory some few historical facts, in order to leave no doubt about the meaning of the noble Lord's philo-Hellenic feelings.[d]

Russia, having seized upon Gokcha, a strip of land bordering on the Lake of Sevan, which was an indisputed possession of Persia, demanded as the price of its evacuation the abandonment of Persia's claims to another portion of her own territory, the lands of Kapan. Persia not yielding, she was overrun, vanquished, and forced to subscribe to the treaty of Turkmanchai,[271] in February, 1828. According to this treaty Persia had to pay an indemnity of

---

[a] In the *New-York Daily Tribune* this sentence ends as follows: "to denounce Austria, as the stupid ally of the Sultan".—*Ed.*

[b] "Invincible" according to G. H. Francis' *Opinions and Policy of the Right Honourable Viscount Palmerston*, London, 1852.—*Ed.*

[c] Instead of "Again he assails Aberdeen because of his anti-Russian diplomacy", the *New-York Daily Tribune* has: "For half a century one phrase has stood as a barrier between Russia and Constantinople—the phrase of the integrity of the Turkish Empire being necessary to the balance of power. 'I object,' exclaims Palmerston on Feb. 5, 1830, 'to the policy of making the integrity of the Turkish dominion in Europe an object essentially necessary to the interests of Christian and civilized Europe.' Again he returns to attack Aberdeen."—*Ed.*

[d] The end of the sentence beginning with "in order to leave no doubt" is omitted in the *New-York Daily Tribune.*—*Ed.*

two millions sterling to Russia, to cede the provinces of Erivan and Nakhichevan, including the fortresses of Erivan and Abbasabad, the exclusive purpose of this arrangement being, as Nicholas stated, to define the common frontier by the Araxes, the only means, he said, of preventing any future dispute of the two empires, although he refused simultaneously to give back Talish and Moghau, which are situated on the Persian bank of the Araxes. Finally, Persia pledged herself to maintaining no navy on the Caspian Sea. Such were the origin and the results of the Russo-Persian war.

As to the religion and the liberty of Greece, Russia cared at that epoch as much about them as the god of the Russians cares now about the key of the "Holy Sepulchre" and the famous "Cupola."[272] It was the traditionary policy of Russia, to excite the Greeks to revolt, and, then, to abandon them to the revenge of the Sultan. So deep was her sympathy for the regeneration of Hellas, that she treated them as rebels at the congress of Verona, acknowledging the right of the Sultan to exclude all foreign intervention between himself and his Christian subjects. Yea, the Czar[a] offered "to aid the Porte in suppressing the rebellion;" a proposition which was, of course, rejected. Having failed in that attempt, he turned round upon the Great Powers with the opposite proposition, "To march an army into Turkey, for the purpose of dictating peace under the walls of the Seraglio." In order to hold his hands bound by a sort of common action, the other Great Powers concluded a treaty with him at London, July 6, 1827, by which they mutually engaged in enforcing, if need be, by arms, the adjustment of the differences between the Sultan and the Greeks. A few months before she had signed that treaty, Russia concluded another treaty with Turkey, the treaty of Akerman,[273] by which she bound herself to renounce all interference with Grecian affairs. This treaty was brought about, after Russia had induced the crown prince of Persia to invade the Ottoman dominions, and after she had inflicted the greatest injuries on the Porte, in order to drive her to a rupture. After all this had passed, the resolutions of the London treaty of July 6, 1827, were presented to the Porte by the English Ambassador,[b] or in the name of Russia and the other Powers. By virtue of the complications resulting from these frauds and lies, Russia found at last the pretext for beginning the war of 1828 and 1829. That war

[a] Nicholas I.—*Ed.*
[b] Stratford de Redcliffe.—*Ed.*

terminated with the treaty of Adrianople,[274] whose contents are resumed in the following quotations from McNeill's celebrated pamphlet on the *Progress of Russia in the East*:

"By the treaty of Adrianople the Czar acquired Anapa and Poti with a considerable extent of coast on the Black Sea, a portion of the Pashalik of Akhalzikh, with the fortresses of Akhalkalaki and Akhalzikh, the islands formed by the mouths of the Danube, the stipulated destruction of the Turkish fortress of Giurgevo, and the abandonment by Turkey of the right bank of the Danube to the distance of several miles from the river.... Partly by force, and partly by the influence of the priesthood, many thousand families of the Armenians were removed from the Turkish provinces in Asia to the Czar's territories.... He established for his own subjects in Turkey an exception from all responsibility to the national authorities, and burdened the Porte with an immense debt, under the name of expenses for the war and for commercial losses—and, finally, retained Moldavia, Wallachia, and Silistra, in pledge for the payment.... Having by this treaty imposed upon Turkey the acceptance of the protocol of March 22, which secured the suzerainty of Greece, and a yearly tribute from that country, Russia used all her influence to procure the independence of Greece, which was erected into an independent state, of which Count Capo d'Istria, who had been a Russian Minister, was named President." (Pp. 105-07.)

Such are the facts. Now look at the picture drawn of them by Lord Palmerston's hand[a]:

"It is perfectly true that the war between Russia and Turkey arose out of aggressions made by Turkey on the commerce and rights of Russia, and violations of treaties."—(House of Commons, Feb. 16, 1830.)

When the Whig-incarnation of the office of Foreign Affairs, he improved on this statement:

"The honourable and gallant member" (Col. Evans) "has represented the conduct of Russia as one of unvarying aggression upon other States from 1815 to the present time. He adverted more particularly to the wars of Russia with Persia and Turkey. Russia was the aggressor in neither of them, and although the result of the Persian war was an aggrandisement of her power, it was not the result of her own seeking.... Again, in the Turkish war, Russia was not the aggressor. It would be fatiguing to the house to detail all the provocations Turkey offered to Russia; but I believe there cannot be a doubt that she expelled Russian subjects from her territory, detained Russian ships, and violated all the provisions of the treaty of Akerman, and then, upon complaint being made, denied redress—so that, if there ever was a just ground for going to war, Russia had it for going to war with Turkey. She did not, however, on any occasion, acquire any increase of territory, at least in Europe. I know there was a continued occupation of certain points" [Moldavia and Wallachia are only points, and the mouths of the Danube are mere zeros] "and some additional acquisitions on the Euxine in Asia; but she

[a] The *New-York Daily Tribune* erroneously adds: "in a speech in the House of Commons on Aug. 7, 1832".—*Ed.*

had an agreement with the other European powers that success in that war should not lead to any aggrandisement in Europe."—(House of Commons, Aug. 7, 1832.)

Your readers will now understand Sir Robert Peel's telling the noble lord, in a public session of the house,[a] that "he did not know whose representative he was."[275]

THIRD ARTICLE[b]

[*The People's Paper*, No. 79, November 5, 1853]

The noble viscount is generally known as the chivalrous protector of the Poles, and never fails to give vent to his painful feelings with regard to Poland before the deputations that wait upon him once every year by "dear, dully, deadly" Dudley Stuart,[c]

> "a worthy who makes speeches, passes resolutions, votes addresses, goes up with deputations, has at all times the necessary quantity of confidence in the necessary individual, and can, also, if necessary, give three cheers for the Queen."

The Poles had been in arms for about a month when the noble lord came into office, in November, 1830. As early as August 8th, 1831, Mr. Hunt presents to the House of Commons a petition from the Westminster Union, in favour of the Poles, and "for the dismissal of Lord Palmerston from his Majesty's councils." Mr. Hume stated on the same day he concluded from the silence of the noble lord that the government "intended to do nothing for the Poles, but allow them to remain at the mercy of Russia." Lord Palmerston replied that, "whatever obligations existing treaties

---

[a] On February 16, 1830.—*Ed.*

[b] In the *New-York Daily Tribune* of November 4, 1853, and also in the pamphlet *Palmerston and Russia*, published on the basis of the newspaper text in London in 1853, the article begins as follows: "At a recent meeting in London, to protest against the action of the British Ministry, in the present controversy between Russia and Turkey, a gentleman who presumed to find special fault with Lord *Palmerston*, was saluted and silenced by a storm of indignant hisses. The meeting evidently thought that if Russia had a friend in the Ministry it was not the noble Viscount, and would no doubt have rent the air with cheers, had some one been able to announce that his Lordship had become Prime Minister. This astonishing confidence in a man so false and hollow, is another proof of the ease with which people may be imposed on by brilliant abilities, and a new evidence of the necessity of taking off the mask from this wily enemy to the progress of human freedom. Accordingly, with the history of the last twenty-five years, and the debates of Parliament for guides, we proceed with the task of exposing the real part which this accomplished actor has performed in the drama of modern Europe."—*Ed.*

[c] The *New-York Daily Tribune* adds: "who has been described by one, not too friendly or too just to his Lordship, as 'a worthy...'".—*Ed.*

imposed, would at all times receive the attention of the government." Now, what sort of obligation was there imposed in his opinion upon England by existing treaties?

"The claims of Russia," he tells us himself, "to the possession of Poland bear the date of the treaty of Vienna."—(House of Commons, July 9, 1833.)

And that treaty makes this possession dependent upon the observance of the Polish constitution by the Czar, but

"the mere fact of this country being a party to the treaty of Vienna, was not synonymous with our guaranteeing that there would be no infraction of that treaty by Russia."—(House of Commons, March 25, 1834.)

If you guarantee a treaty, you do by no means guarantee the observance of the treaty. Thus answered the Milanese to the Emperor Barbarossa: "You have had our oath, but remember we did not swear to keep it."[276]

For one thing, however, the treaty of Vienna is good. It gives to the British government, as one of the contracting parties,

"a right to entertain and express an opinion on any act which [...] tends to a violation of that treaty.... The contracting parties to the treaties of Vienna had a right to require that the constitution of Poland should not be touched, and this was an opinion which I have not concealed from the Russian government. I communicated it *by anticipation* to that government previous to the taking of Warsaw, and before the result of hostilities was known. I communicated it again when Warsaw fell. [...] The Russian government, however, took a different view of the question."—(House of Commons, July 9, 1833.)

He is quietly anticipating the downfall of Poland, and watches this opportunity for expressing and entertaining an opinion on certain articles of the treaty of Vienna, persuaded as he is that the magnanimous Czar waits only for having crushed the Polish people by armed force, in order to honour a constitution trampled upon when they were yet possessed of unbounded means of resistance. Simultaneously the noble lord charges the Poles with having "taken the uncalled for, and, in his opinion, *unjustifiable* steps of the [...] dethronement of the Emperor."—(House of Commons, July 9, 1833).

"He could also say that the Poles were the aggressors, for they commenced the contest."—(House of Commons, August 7, 1832.)

When the apprehensions for the extinction of Poland became troublesome, he declared that

"to exterminate Poland, either *morally or politically*, is so perfectly impracticable that I think there need be no apprehension of its being attempted."—(House of Commons, June 28, 1832.)

When reminded afterwards of the wayward expectations thus held out, he assures that he had been misunderstood, that he had said so not in the political but in the Pickwickian sense of the word, meaning that the Emperor of Russia was unable

"to exterminate *nominally or physically* so many millions of men as the Polish kingdom in its divided state contained."—(House of Commons, April 20, 1836.)

When the house makes a pretence of interfering during the struggle of the Poles,[a] he appeals to his ministerial responsibility. When the thing is done, he coolly tells them that

"no vote of this house would have the slightest effect in reversing the decision of Russia."—(House of Commons, July 9, 1833.)

When the atrocities committed by the Russians, after the fall of Warsaw, are denounced, he recommends to the house great tenderness towards the Emperor of Russia, declaring that

"no person could regret more than he did—the expressions which had been uttered" (House of Commons, June 28, 1832), that "the present Emperor of Russia was a man of high and generous feelings"—that "where cases of undue severity on the part of the Russian government to the Poles have occurred, we may set this down as a proof that the power of the Emperor of Russia is practically omitted, and we may take it for granted that the Emperor has, in those instances, yielded to the influence of others, rather than follow the dictates of his spontaneous feelings."—(House of Commons, July 9, 1833.)

When the doom of Poland was sealed on the one hand, and on the other the dissolution of the Turkish Empire became imminent, from the rebellion of Mehemet Ali,[b] he assured the house that "affairs in general were proceeding in a satisfactory train."—(House of Commons, January 26, 1832.)

A resolution for granting subsidies to the Polish refugees having been moved, it is

"exceedingly painful to him to oppose the grant of any money to those individuals which the natural and spontaneous feelings of every generous man would lead him to acquiesce in; [...] but, [...] it is [...] not consistent with his duty [...] to propose any grant of money to those unfortunate persons."—(House of Commons, March 25, 1834.)

The same tender-hearted man had defrayed, as we shall see by and by, the cost of Poland's fall, to a great extent, out of the pockets of the British people.

---

[a] In the *New-York Daily Tribune* this sentence begins as follows: "When the house threatened to interfere during the struggle in favor of the Poles...."—*Ed.*

[b] In the *New-York Daily Tribune* this sentence begins as follows: "When on the one side the utter ruin of Poland was secured, and on the other the dissolution of the Turkish Empire became imminent from the progress of Ibrahim Pasha...."—*Ed.*

The noble lord has taken good care to withhold all state papers on the Polish catastrophe from the parliament. But statements made in the House of Commons, which he did never as much as attempt to controvert, leave no doubt as to the game he played at that fatal epoch.

After the Polish revolution had broken out, the Consul of Austria did not quit Warsaw, and the Austrian government went so far as to send a Polish agent, M. Walewski, to Paris, with the missions of negotiating with the governments of France and England about the re-establishment of a Polish kingdom. The Court of the Tuileries declared "it was ready to join England in case of her consenting to the project." Lord Palmerston rejected the offer. In 1831 M. de Talleyrand, the Ambassador of France, at the Court of St. James, proposed a plan of combined action on the part of France and England, but met with a distinct refusal, and with a note from the noble lord, stating that

"an amicable intermediation on the Polish question would be declined by Russia. The powers had just declined a similar offer on the part of France; the intervention of the two Courts of France and England could only be by force in case of a refusal on the part of Russia, and the amicable and satisfactory relations between the Cabinet of St. James and the Cabinet of St. Petersburg, would not allow his British Majesty[a] to undertake such an interference. The time was *not yet* come to undertake such a play with success against the will of a sovereign, whose *rights were indisputable.*"

This was not all.[b] On February 23, 1848, Mr. Anstey made the following declaration in the House of Commons:

"Sweden was arming her fleet for the purpose of making diversion in favour of Poland, and of regaining to herself the provinces in the Baltic, which have been so unjustly wrested from her in the last war. The noble lord instructed our ambassador at the Court of Stockholm, in a contrary sense, and Sweden discontinued her armaments. The Persian Court [...] had, with similar purpose, despatched an army three days on its march towards the Russian frontier, under the [...] command of the Persian Crown prince. [...] The Secretary of Legation at the Court of Teheran, Sir John McNeill followed the prince, at a distance of three days' march from his headquarters, overtook him, and there, under instructions from the noble lord, and in the name of England, threatened Persia with war if the prince advanced another step towards the Russian frontier. Similar inducements were used by the noble lord to prevent Turkey from renewing war on her side."

---

[a] William IV.—*Ed.*

[b] The text beginning with the words "This was not all", and ending with the quotation from Knight's speech in the House of Commons on July 13, 1840, is omitted in the *New-York Daily Tribune.*—*Ed.*

To Colonel Evans asking for the production of papers with regard to Prussia's violation of her pretended neutrality in the Russo-Polish war, the noble lord objected,

"that the ministers of this country could not have witnessed that contest without the deepest regret, and [...] it would be most satisfactory for them to see it terminated."—(House of Commons, August 16, 1831.)

Certainly he wished to see it terminated as soon as possible, and Prussia shared in his feelings.

On a subsequent occasion, Mr. H. Gally Knight thus resumed the whole proceedings of the noble lord with regard to the Polish insurrection—

"There is something *curiously inconsistent* in the proceedings of the noble lord when Russia is concerned.... On the subject of Poland, the noble lord has disappointed us again and again. Remember when the noble lord was pressed to exert himself in favour of Poland, then he admitted the justice of the cause—the justice of our complaints; but he said, 'Only restrain yourselves at present, there is an ambassador fast setting out of known liberal sentiments, you may be sure we will do all that is right; you will only embarrass his negotiation, if you incense the power with whom he has to deal. So, take my advice, be quiet at present, and be assured that a great deal will be effected.' We trusted to those assurances; the liberal ambassador went; whether he ever approached the subject or not, was never known, but all we got were the fine words of the noble lord, and no results."—(House of Commons, July 13, 1840.)

The so-called kingdom of Poland having disappeared from the map of Europe, there remained still, in the free town of Cracow, a fantastic remnant of Polish nationality. The Czar Alexander had, during the general anarchy resulting from the fall of the French empire, not conquered the Duchy of Warsaw, but simply seized it, and wished, of course, to keep it, together with Cracow, incorporated with the Duchy by Bonaparte. Austria, once possessed of Cracow, wished to have it back. The Czar being unable to obtain it himself and unwilling to concede it to Austria, proposed to constitute it as a free town. Accordingly the treaty of Vienna stipulated in article VI,[a]

"that the town of Cracow with the territory is to be for ever a free, independent, and strictly neutral city, under the protection of Austria, Russia, and Prussia," and in its article IX "that the Courts of Russia, Austria, and Prussia engage to respect, and to cause to be always respected, the neutrality of the free town of Cracow and its territory. *No armed force shall be introduced upon any pretence whatever.*"

Immediately after the close of the Polish insurrection of 1830-31, the Russian troops suddenly entered Cracow, the

[a] Here and below the *New-York Daily Tribune* has no references to numbers of articles in the 1815 Treaty of Vienna.—*Ed.*

occupation of which lasted two months.[a] This, however, was considered as a transitory necessity of war, and in the turmoil of that time was soon forgotten.

In 1836, Cracow was again occupied by the troops of Austria, Russia, and Prussia, on the pretext of forcing the authorities of Cracow to deliver up the individuals concerned in the Polish revolution five years before. The constitution of Cracow was abrogated, the three consular residencers assumed the highest authority—the police was entrusted to Austrian spies—the senate was overthrown—the tribunals were destroyed—the university of Cracow put down in consequence of the prohibitions to the neighbouring provinces—and the commerce of the free city with the surrounding countries destroyed.[b]

On March 18th, 1836, when interpellated on the occupation of Cracow, the noble viscount declared that occupation to be of a merely transitory character. Of so palliative and apologetic a kind was the construction he put on the doings of his three northern allies, that he felt himself obliged suddenly to stop and to interrupt the even course of his speech by the solemn declaration.

> "I stand not up here to defend the measure, which, on the contrary, I *must* censure and condemn. I have merely stated those circumstances which, though they do not excuse the forcible occupation of Cracow, might yet afford a justification, &c...."

He admits that the treaty of Vienna bound the three Powers to abstain from any step without the previous consent of England, but,

> "they may be justly said to have paid an *involuntary* homage to the justice and plain dealing of this country, by supposing that we would never give our assent to such a proceeding."

Mr. Patrick Stewart[c] having, however, found out that there existed better means for the preservation of Cracow than the

---

[a] Instead of this sentence the *New-York Daily Tribune* has: "In 1831, Cracow was temporarily occupied by Russian troops."—*Ed.*

[b] Instead of this passage the *New-York Daily Tribune* has: "In 1836, Cracow was again occupied by the troops of Russia, Austria and Prussia, on the pretext of their being obliged to accomplish, in that way, the expulsion of some Polish refugees from the town and its territory. On this occasion the noble Lord abstained from all remonstrance on the ground, as he stated, in 1836 and in 1840, 'that it was difficult to give effect to our remonstrances.'—As soon, however, as Cracow was definitively confiscated by Austria, a simple remonstrance appeared to him to be 'the only effectual means'."—*Ed.*

[c] Here and below the *New-York Daily Tribune* erroneously has: "Sir Stratford Canning".—*Ed.*

"abstention from remonstrance," moved on April 20, 1836, that the government should be ordered to send a representation to the free town of Cracow as consul, there being three consuls there from the three Northern Powers. The joint arrival of an English and French consul at Cracow would prove an event.[a] The noble viscount seeing that the majority of the house was for the motion induced Mr. Stewart to withdraw it by solemnly pledging himself that the government "intended to send a consular agent to Cracow." On March 22, 1837, being reminded by Lord Dudley Stuart of his promise, the noble lord answered that "he had altered his intention, and had not sent a consular agent to Cracow, and it was not at present his intention to do so." Lord D. Stuart having given notice that he should move for papers elucidatory of this singular declaration, the noble viscount succeeded in defeating the motion by the simple process of being absent and of causing the house to be counted out.[b]

In 1840, the "temporary" occupation continued, and the people of Cracow had addressed a memorandum to the governments of France and England, which says, amongst other things:

> "The misfortunes which overwhelm the free city of Cracow and its inhabitants, are such that the undersigned see no further hope for themselves and their fellow citizens than in the powerful and enlightened protection of the governments of France and England. The situation in which they find themselves placed, gives them a right to invoke the intervention of every power that subscribed to the treaty of Vienna."[c]

Being interrogated on July 13th, 1840, about this petition from Cracow, the noble viscount declared

> "that between Austria and the British government the question of the evacuation of Cracow remained only a question of time."

As to the violation of the treaty of Vienna

> "there were no means of enforcing the opinions of England, supposing that this country was disposed to do so by arms, [...] because Cracow was evidently a place where no English action could possibly take place."

---

[a] After these words the *New-York Daily Tribune* has: "and must, in any case, have prevented the noble lord from afterward declaring himself unaware of the intrigues pursued at Cracow by the Austrians, Russians and Prussians".— *Ed.*

[b] The *New-York Daily Tribune* has after this: "He never stated why or wherefore he had not fulfilled his pledge, and withstood all attempts to squeeze out of him any papers on the subject." The following text beginning with: "In 1840, the 'temporary' occupation continued" and ending with the quotation from Palmerston's statement on August 17, 1846, is omitted in the *Tribune.*— *Ed.*

[c] Quoted from Canning's speech in the House of Commons on July 13, 1840.— *Ed.*

Be it remarked that two days after this declaration the noble lord concluded a treaty with Russia, Austria, and Prussia for closing the Black Sea[277] to the English navy, probably in order that no English action could take place in those quarters. It was at the very same time that the noble lord renewed a Holy Alliance with those Powers against France. As to the commercial loss sustained by England, consequent upon the occupation of Cracow, the noble lord demonstrated that "the amount of general exports to *Germany* had not fallen off," which, as Sir Robert Peel justly remarked, had nothing to do with Cracow. As to his intentions on the subject and to the consular agent to be sent to Cracow,

> "he thought that his experience of the manner in which his unfortunate assertion" (made by the noble lord in 1836, in order to escape from the censure of a hostile house) "of an intention to appoint a British Consul at Cracow, had been taken up by honourable gentlemen opposite, justified him in positively refusing to give any answer to such a question, which might expose him to similar [...] unjustifiable attacks."

On August 17, 1846, he stated that

> "whether the treaty of Vienna is, or is not executed and fulfilled by the Great Powers of Europe, depends not upon the presence of a consular agent at Cracow."

On January 28, 1847, when again asked[a] for the production of papers relative to the *non-appointment* of a British Consul at Cracow, he declared that

> "the subject had *no necessary* connexion with the discussion on the incorporation of Cracow, and he saw no advantage in reviving an angry discussion on a subject which had *only a passing interest*."

He proved true to his opinion in the production of state papers, pronounced on March 17, 1837:

> "If the papers bear upon questions now under consideration, their production would be dangerous; if they refer to questions that are gone by, they can obviously be of no use."

The British government was very exactly informed of the importance of Cracow, not only from a political but also from a commercial point of view, their own Consul at Warsaw, Colonel Duplat having reported to them that[b]

---

[a] In the *New-York Daily Tribune* this sentence begins as follows: "Ten years afterward, when Cracow was doomed, and when the noble Lord was again asked ..."—*Ed.*

[b] The *New-York Daily Tribune* has: "The Consul at Warsaw, Col. Duplat, having reported in detail thereupon...." The following quotation from this report is omitted.—*Ed.*

"Cracow, since its elevation into an independent state, has always been the depot of very considerable quantities of English merchandise sent thither by the Black Sea, Moldavia, and Galicia, and even *via* Trieste; and which afterwards find their way to the surrounding countries. In the course of years it came into railway communication with the great lines of Bohemia, Prussia, and Austria.... It is also the central point of the important line of railway communication between the Adriatic and the Baltic. It will come in direct communication of the same description with Warsaw.... Looking, therefore, to the almost certainty of every great point of the Levant, and even of India and China, finding its way up the Adriatic, it cannot be denied that it must be of the greatest commercial importance, even to England, to have such a station as Cracow, in the centre of the great net of railways connecting the Western and Eastern Continent."[a]

Lord Palmerston himself was obliged to confess to the house that the Cracow insurrection of 1846[278] had been intentionally provoked by the Three Powers.

"I believe the original entrance of the Austrian troops into the territory of Cracow was in consequence of an application from the government. But, then, those Austrian troops retired. *Why* they retired has never yet been explained. With them retired the government and the authorities of Cracow; the *immediate*, at least, the early, consequence of that retirement, was the establishment of a provisional government at Cracow. (House of Commons, Aug. 17, 1846.)

On the 22nd of February, 1846, the army of Austria, and afterwards of Russia and Prussia, took possession of Cracow. On the 26th of the same month the Prefect of Tarnów issued his proclamation calling upon the peasants to murder their proprietors, and promising them "a sufficient recompense, in money,"[b] which proclamation was followed by the Galician atrocities, and the massacre of about 2,000 proprietors. On March the 12th appeared the Austrian proclamation to the "faithful Galicians having aroused themselves for the maintenance of order and law, and destroyed the enemies of order." In the official *Gazette*[c] of April 28th, Prince Frederick of Schwarzenberg stated that "the acts that had taken place had been *authorised* by the Austrian government," which, of course, acted on a common plan with Russia and with Prussia, the footman of the Czar.[d] Now, after all

---

[a] Marx gives this passage from Duplat's report to Aberdeen of March 10, 1846 as quoted in the speech of Stuart Wortley in the House of Commons on March 16, 1847.—*Ed.*

[b] This and the following documents are cited according to Milnes' speech in the House of Commons on August 17, 1846.—*Ed.*

[c] *Oesterreichisch Kaiserliche Wiener Zeitung.*—*Ed.*

[d] The phrase "the footman of the Czar" is omitted in the *New-York Daily Tribune.*—*Ed.*

these abominations had passed, Lord Palmerston thought fit to declare in the house,

"I have too high an opinion of the sense of justice and of right that must animate the governments of Austria, Russia, and Prussia, to believe that they can feel any disposition or intention to deal with Cracow otherwise than Cracow is entitled by treaty-engagements to be dealt with." (House of Commons, Aug. 17th, 1846.)

For the noble lord the only business in hand was to get rid of parliament, the session drawing to a close. He assured the Commons that "on the part of the British government everything shall be done to ensure a due respect being paid to the provisions of the treaty of Vienna." Mr. Hume, giving vent to his doubts about Lord Palmerston's "*intention* to cause the Austro-Russian troops to retire from Cracow," the noble lord begged of the house not to give credence to the statements made by Mr. Hume, as he was in possession of better information, and was convinced that the occupation of Cracow was only a "*temporary*" one. The parliament of 1846 having been got rid of, in the same manner as that of 1853, out came the Austrian proclamation of November 11th, 1846, incorporating Cracow into the Austrian dominions. When parliament re-assembled on January 19th, 1847, it was informed by the Queen's[a] Speech that Cracow was gone, but that there remained in its place a protest on the part of the brave Palmerston. To deprive this protest of even the appearance of a meaning, the noble lord contrived at that very epoch to engage, on the occasion of the Spanish marriages,[279] England in a quarrel with France, very near setting the two countries by the ears, as he was twitted in the teeth by Mr. Smith O'Brien. The French government having applied to him for his co-operation in a joint protest against the incorporation of Cracow, Lord Normanby, under instructions from the noble viscount, answered that the outrage of which Austria had been guilty in annexing Cracow was not greater than that of France in effecting a marriage between the Duke of Montpensier and the Spanish Infanta—the one act being a violation of the treaty of Vienna, and the other of the treaty of Utrecht.[280] Now, the treaty of Utrecht, renewed in 1782, was definitively abrogated by the Anti-Jacobin war; and that, therefore, ever since 1792 ceased to exist. There was no man in the house better informed of this circumstance than the noble lord, as he had stated himself on the occasion of the blockades of Mexico and Buenos Ayres,[281] that

[a] Queen Victoria.—*Ed.*

"the provisions of the treaty of Utrecht have long lapsed in the variations of war, with the exception of the single clause relating to the boundaries of Brazil and French Guiana, because that clause had been expressly incorporated in the treaty of Vienna."[a]

We have not yet done with the exertions of the noble lord for resisting the encroachments of Russia on Poland.[b]

There existed a curious convention between England, Holland, and Russia—the so-called *Russian-Dutch loan.* During the Anti-Jacobin war the Czar Alexander had contracted a loan with Messrs. Hope and Co., at Amsterdam; and after the fall of Bonaparte, the King of the Netherlands[c] "desired to make a suitable return to the Allied Powers for having delivered his territories," and for having annexed to his own Belgium, upon which he had no claim whatever, and engaged himself—the other Powers waiving their common pretensions in favour of Russia, then in great need of money—to execute a convention with Russia for paying her by successive instalments the twenty-five millions of florins she owed to Messrs. Hope and Co. England, in order to cover the robbery she committed on Holland, of her colonies at the Cape of Good Hope, Demerara, Essequibo, and Berbice, became a party to that convention, and bound herself to pay a certain proportion of the subsidies granted to Russia. This stipulation became part of the treaty of Vienna, but upon the *express condition* "that the payment should cease if the union between Holland and Belgium were broken prior to the liquidation of the debt." When Belgium separated itself by revolution[d] from Holland, she of course refused to pay her portion[e] to Russia. On the other hand, there remained, Mr. Herries stated, "not the smallest iota of a claim on the part of Russia for the continuance of debt by England." (House of Commons, Jan. 26, 1832.)

Lord Palmerston, however, found it quite natural that,

"at one time Russia is paid for supporting the union of Belgium with Holland, and that at another time she is paid for the separation of these countries." (House of Commons, July 16th, 1832.)

---

[a] Quoted from Palmerston's speech on March 19, 1839.—*Ed.*

[b] The *New-York Daily Tribune* has "upon Europe" instead of "on Poland".—*Ed.*

[c] William I.—*Ed.*

[d] This refers to the revolution of 1830-31.—*Ed.*

[e] After the words "to pay her portion" the *New-York Daily Tribune* has: "on the ground that the loan had been contracted to continue her in the undivided possession of the Belgian provinces, and that she no longer had the sovereignty of that country".—*Ed.*

He appealed in a very tragical manner to the faithful observance of treaties—and above all, of the treaty of Vienna; and he contrived to carry a new convention with Russia, dated 16th November, 1831, in the preamble of which it is expressly stated that it is contracted "in consideration of the general arrangements of the Congress of Vienna which remain in full force."

When the convention relating to the Russo-Dutch loan, had been inserted in the treaty of Vienna, the Duke of Wellington exclaimed,

> "This is a master-stroke of diplomacy on the part of Lord Castlereagh; for Russia has been tied down to the observance of the Vienna treaty by a pecuniary obligation."

When Russia, therefore, withdrew her observance of the Vienna treaty by the Cracow confiscation, Mr. Hume moved to stop any further payment[a] to Russia from the British Treasury. The noble viscount, however, thought that although Russia had a right to violate the treaty of Vienna with regard to Poland, England remained tied to the treaty with regard to Russia.

But this is not the most extraordinary incident of the noble lord's proceedings. After the Belgian revolution had broken out, and before parliament had sanctioned the new loan to Russia, the noble lord defrayed the costs of the Russian war against Poland, under the false pretext of paying off the old debt contracted by England in 1815, although we may state, on the authority of the greatest English lawyer, Sir E. Sugden, now Lord St. Leonards, that

> "there was not a single debatable point in that question, [...] and [...] the government had no power whatever to pay a shilling of the money." (House of Commons, January 26, 1832.)

And on the authority of Sir Robert Peel that "the noble lord was *not warrantable by law* in advancing the money." (House of Commons, July 12, 1832.)

Now we understand why the noble lord is reiterating on every occasion that "nothing can be more painful to men of proper feeling than discussions upon the subject of Poland."[b]

---

[a] The *New-York Daily Tribune* has: "any further annual payment".—*Ed.*

[b] In the *New-York Daily Tribune* this passage ends as follows: "They can also appreciate the degree of earnestness he is now likely to exhibit in resisting the encroachments of the power he has so uniformly served."—*Ed.*

FOURTH ARTICLE[a]

[*The People's Paper*, No. 80, November 12, 1853]

The great and eternal themes of the noble viscount's self-glorification are the services he has rendered to the cause of constitutional liberty all over the continent. The world owes him, indeed, the invention of the "constitutional" kingdoms of Portugal, Spain, and Greece,—three political phantoms, only to be compared with the *homunculus* of *Faust's* Wagner.[b] Portugal, under the yoke of that huge hill of flesh, Donna Maria da Gloria, backed by a Coburg,[c]

"must be looked upon as one of the *substantive* powers of Europe." (House of Commons, March 10, 1837.)

At the very time the noble viscount uttered these words, six British ships-of-the-line anchored at Lisbon, in order to defend the "substantive" daughter of Don Pedro from the Portuguese people, and to help her to destroy the constitution she had sworn to defend. Spain, at the disposition of another Maria,[d] who, although a notorious sinner, has never found a Magdalene,

"holds out to us a fair, [...] a flourishing, and even a formidable power among the European kingdoms." (Speech of Lord Palmerston, H. of C., March 10, 1837.)[e]

---

[a] In the *New-York Daily Tribune* of November 21, 1853, the article begins as follows: "There are those who expect that in the war between Turkey and Russia, which has now begun, the British Government will at last abandon its system of half-way measures and fruitless negotiations to act with energy and effect in repelling the Muscovite invader back from his prey and from the universal dominion he dreams of. Such an expectation may not be without some ground of abstract probability and policy to justify it, but how little real reason there is for it will appear to whoever ponders the facts below set forth with regard to the past conduct of that English Minister who is thought to be most hostile to the advance of Russian despotism in Europe. Indeed, most people in England who are dissatisfied with the policy of the Government in the contest between Turkey and Russia, fondly believe that matters would be in a very different state if Lord *Palmerston* had the control of them. Such persons, in recalling the noble Viscount's history, must leave blank the whole eventful period from 1832 to 1847—a blank which we will fill up for their instruction."—*Ed.*

[b] The *New-York Daily Tribune* has: "the constitutional model-kingdoms"; the end of this sentence, beginning with the words "three political phantoms", is omitted.—*Ed.*

[c] Ferdinand August.—*Ed.*

[d] Maria Cristina.—*Ed.*

[e] The *New-York Daily Tribune* has instead of this sentence: "Spain, crushed beneath the yoke of another Maria—the she-wolf of Naples, 'holds out to us,' according to his sanguine view of the case, 'a fair and legitimate hope that she may yet become what she has proved in former times—a flourishing and even a formidable power among the European Kingdoms'."—*Ed.*

Formidable, indeed, to the holders of Spanish bonds. The noble lord has even his reasons ready for having delivered the native country of the Pericles and the Sophocles to the nominal sway of an idiot Bavarian boy.

"King Otto belongs to a country where there exists a free Constitution." (H. of C., August 8, 1832.)

A free constitution in Bavaria, the German Bastia![a] This passes the *licentia poetica*[b] of rhetorical flourish, the "legitimate hopes" held out by Spain, and the "substantive" power of Portugal. As to Belgium, all Lord Palmerston did for it was burdening it with a part of the Dutch debt, reducing it by the Province of Luxemburg, and adding to it a Coburg dynasty. As to the *entente cordiale* with France, waning from the moment he pretended to give it the finish by the Quadruple Alliance[282] of 1834, we have already seen how far the noble lord understood to manage it in the instance of Poland, and we shall hear, by and by, what became of it in his hands.[c]

One of those facts, hardly adverted to by contemporaries, but broadly marking the boundaries of historical epochs, was the military occupation of Constantinople by the Russians, in 1833.

The eternal dream of Russia was at last realised. The barbarian from the icy banks of the Neva held in his grasp luxurious Byzantium, and the sunlit shores of the Bosphorus. The self-styled heir to the Greek Emperors occupied, however temporarily, the Rome of the East.[d]

"The occupation of Constantinople by Russian troops [...] sealed the fate of Turkey as an independent power. [...] The fact of Russia having occupied Constantinople even for the purpose" (?) "of saving it, was as decisive a blow to Turkish independence as if the flag of Russia now waved on the Seraglio." (Speech of Sir Robert Peel, H. of C., March 17, 1834.)

In consequence of the unfortunate war of 1828-29,[e] the Porte had lost her prestige in the eyes of her own subjects. As usual with Oriental empires, when the paramount power is weakened, successful revolts of Pashas broke out. As early as October, 1831,

---

[a] A town in Corsica; the *New-York Daily Tribune* has: "the German Boeotia!"; both these towns symbolise provincial backwardness.—*Ed.*

[b] Poetical liberty.—*Ed.*

[c] The *New-York Daily Tribune* has instead of the last sentence: "But let us come to the Turks and Russians."—*Ed.*

[d] This sentence is omitted in the *New-York Daily Tribune*.—*Ed.*

[e] The *New-York Daily Tribune* has further: "and the treaty of Adrianople".—*Ed.*

commenced the conflict between the Sultan[a] [and] Mehemet Ali, the Pasha of Egypt, who had supported the Porte during the Greek insurrection. In the spring of 1832, Ibrahim Pasha, his son, marched his army into Syria, conquered that province, by the Battle of Homs, crossed the Taurus, annihilated the last Turkish army at the battle of Konia, and moved on the way to Stambul. The Sultan was forced to apply to St. Petersburg, on February 2, 1833. On February 17, the French Admiral Roussin arrived at Constantinople, remonstrated with the Porte two days afterwards, and engaged for the retreat of the Pasha on certain terms, including the refusal of Russian assistance; but, unassisted as he was, he was, of course, unable to cope with Russia. "You have asked for me, and you shall have me."[b] On February 20, a Russian squadron sailed from Sebastopol, and disembarked a large force of Russian troops on the shores of the Bosphorus, and laid siege to the capital. So eager was Russia for the protection of Turkey, that a Russian officer was simultaneously dispatched to the Pashas of Erzerum and Trebizond, to inform them that, in the event of Ibrahim's army marching towards Erzerum, both that place and Trebizond should be immediately protected by a Russian army. At the end of May, 1833, Count Orloff arrived from St. Petersburg, and intimated to the Sultan that he had brought with him a little bit of paper, which the Sultan was to subscribe to, without the concurrence of any minister, and without the diplomatic agent, at the Porte. In this manner the famous treaty of Unkiar-Skelessi was brought about and concluded for eight years to come. By virtue of it the Porte entered into an alliance, offensive and defensive, with Russia, resigned the right of entering into any new treaties with other powers, except with the concurrence of Russia, and confirmed the former Russo-Turkish treaties, especially that of Adrianople.[c] By a secret article, appended to the treaty, the Porte obliged herself,

> "in favour of the Imperial Court of Russia, to close the Straits of the Dardanelles—viz., not to allow any foreign man-of-war to enter it under any pretext whatever."[d]

Whom was the Czar indebted to for occupying Constantinople by his troops, and for transferring, by virtue of the treaty of

---

[a] Mahmud II.—*Ed.*

[b] Quoted from Mozart's opera *Don Giovanni.*—*Ed.*

[c] The phrase "especially that of Adrianople" is omitted in the *New-York Daily Tribune.*—*Ed.*

[d] Martens, *Recueil de traités.* T. II, p. 659.—*Ed.*

Unkiar-Skelessi, the supreme seat of the Ottoman empire from Constantinople to St. Petersburg? To nobody else but to the Right Honourable Henry John Viscount Palmerston, Baron Temple, a Peer of Ireland, a Member of His Majesty's Most Honourable Privy Council, Knight of the Great Cross of the Most Honourable Order of the Bath, a Member of Parliament, and His Majesty's Principal Secretary of State for Foreign Affairs.

The treaty of Unkiar-Skelessi was concluded on July 8th, 1833. On July 11th, 1833, Mr. H. L. Bulwer, moved for the production of papers with respect to the Turko-Syrian affairs. The noble lord opposed the motion,

"because the *transactions* to which the papers called for referred, were *incomplete*, and the character of the whole transaction would depend upon its termination. [...] As the results were not yet known, [...] the motion was premature."—(H. of C., July 11, 1833.)

Accused by Mr. Bulwer of not having interfered for the defence of the Sultan against Mehemet Ali, and not having thus prevented the advance of the Russian army, he began that curious system of defence and of confession, developed on later occasions, the *membra disjecta*[a] of which I shall now gather together.

"He was not *prepared* to deny, that the latter part of last year an application was made on the part of the Sultan to this country for assistance."—(H. of C., July 11, 1833.)

The Porte made formal application for assistance in the course of August—(H. of C., August 24, 1833.)

No, not in August.

"The request of the Porte for naval assistance has been made in the month of October, 1832."—(H. of C., August 28, 1833.)

No, it was not in October.[b]

"Its assistance was asked by the Porte in November 1832."—(H. of C., March 17, 1834.)

The noble lord is as uncertain of the day when the Porte implored his aid, as Falstaff was of the number of rogues in buckram suits, who came at his back, in Kendal green.[c] He is not

---

[a] Scattered parts, disjointed quotations.—*Ed.*

[b] The *New-York Daily Tribune* has after this: "as we learn from a speech made a year later".—*Ed.*

[c] Shakespeare, *Henry IV*, Part I, Act II, Scene 4.—*Ed.*

prepared, however, to deny that the armed assistance offered by Russia was rejected by the Porte, and that he was applied to. He refused to comply with her demands. The Porte did again apply to the noble lord. First she sent M. Maurogeni to London; then she sent Namick Pasha, who entreated the assistance of a naval squadron on the condition of the Sultan undertaking to defray all the expenses of that squadron, and promising in future requital for that succour, the grant of new *commercial* privileges, and advantages to British subjects in Turkey. So sure was Russia of the noble lord's refusal, that she joined the Turkish Envoy in praying his lordship for the affording of the demanded succour. He tells us himself,

"it was but justice that he should state, that so far from Russia having expressed any jealousy as to this government granting this assistance, the Russian Ambassador[a] officially communicated to him, [...] while the request was still under the consideration, that he had learned that such an application had been made, and that, from the interest taken by Russia in the maintenance and preservation of the Turkish empire, it would afford satisfaction if ministers could find themselves able to comply with that request."—(H. of C., August 28, 1833.)

The noble lord remained, however, inexorable to the demands of the Porte, although backed by disinterested Russia herself. Then, of course, the Porte knew what she was about. She understood that she was doomed to make the wolf shepherd. Still she hesitated, and did not accept the Russian assistance till three months later.[b]

"Great Britain," says the noble lord, "never complained of Russia granting that assistance, but, on the contrary, was glad that Turkey had been able to obtain effectual relief from any quarter."—(H. of C., March 17, 1834.)

At whatever epoch the Porte may have implored the aid of Lord Palmerston, he cannot but own,

"No doubt if England had *thought fit* to interfere, the progress of the invading army would have been stopped, *and the Russian troops would not have been called in.*"—(H. of C., July 11, 1833.)

Why then did he not "*think fit*" to interfere and to keep the Russians out?

---

[a] K. Lieven.—*Ed.*

[b] Instead of the three last sentences the *New-York Daily Tribune* has: "Then, of course, the Porte knew what it was about, and comprehended that it was doomed to accept the Russian assistance."—*Ed.*

First he pleads *want of time.* According to his own statement the conflict between the Porte and Mehemet Ali arose as early as October 1831, while the decisive battle of Konia was not fought till December 21st 1832. Could he find no time during all this period? A great battle was won by Ibrahim Pasha in July 1832,[283] and again he could find no time from July to December. But he was all that time waiting for a *formal* application, which, according to his last version, was not made till the 3rd of November.

"Was he then," asks Sir Robert Peel, "so ignorant of what was passing in the Levant, that he must wait for a formal application?"—(H. of C., March 17, 1834.)

And from November, when the formal application was made, to the latter part of February, there elapsed again four long months, and Russia did not arrive until February 20, 1833. Why did not he?

But he has better reasons in reserve.

The Pasha of Egypt was but a rebellious subject, and the Sultan was the Suzerain.

"As it was a war against the sovereign by a subject, and that sovereign was in alliance with the King of England, it would have been inconsistent with good faith to have had *any communication* with the Pasha." (H. of C., August 28, 1833.)

Etiquette prevented the noble lord from stopping Ibrahim's armies. *Etiquette* forbade him giving instructions to his Consul at Alexandria to use his influence with Mehemet Ali.[a] Like the Spanish Grandee, the noble lord would rather let the Queen burn to ashes than infringe on *etiquette* and interfere with her petticoats. Perchance it so appears that the noble lord had already in 1832 accredited consuls and diplomatic agents to the "subject" of the Sultan without the consent of the Sultan, that he entered into treaties with Mehemet altering existing regulations and arrangements touching matters of trade and revenue and establishing other ones in their room; that he did so without the consent of the Porte beforehand, or caring for its approbation afterwards.[b]—(H. of C., February 23, 1848.)

Accordingly, we are told by Earl Grey, the then chief of the noble viscount, that

---

[a] These two sentences are omitted in the *New-York Daily Tribune.*—*Ed.*

[b] In the *New-York Daily Tribune* the end of this sentence is given as follows: "that he had entered into treaties with Mehemet Ali altering existing regulations and arrangement touching matters of trade and revenue; that he did not ask the consent of the Porte beforehand, not even care for its approbation afterward: and that he had thus treated 'the rebellious subject' as an independent power".—*Ed.*

"They had at the moment extensive commercial relations with Mehemet Ali which it would not have been their interest to disturb."—(House of Lords, February 4, 1834.)

What commercial relations with the "rebellious subject."[a]

But the noble viscount's fleets were occupied in the Duero, and the Tagus, and blockading the Schelde, and doing the service of the midwife at the birth of the constitutional empires of Portugal, Spain, and Belgium, and he was, therefore, not in a situation to spare one single ship.—(H. of C., July 11, 1833, and March 17, 1834.)

But what the Sultan insisted on was precisely naval assistance. For argument's sake we will grant the noble lord to have been unable to dispose of one single vessel.[b] But there are great authorities assuring us that what was wanted was not a single *vessel*, but only a single *word*[c] on the part of the noble lord. There is Admiral Codrington, the destroyer of the Turkish fleet at Navarino.

"Mehemet Ali," he states, "had of old felt the strength of our representations on the subject of the evacuation of the Morea. He had then received orders from the Porte to resist all applications to induce him to evacuate it at the risk of his head, and he did resist accordingly, but at last prudently yielded and evacuated the Morea."—(H. of C., April 20, 1836.)

There is the Duke of Wellington.

"If, in the session of 1832 or 1833, they had plainly told Mehemet Ali, that he should not carry on his contest in Syria and Asia Minor, they would have put an end to the war without the risk of allowing the Emperor of Russia to send a fleet and an army to Constantinople."—(House of Lords, February 4, 1834.)

But there are better authorities. There is the noble lord himself.

"Although," he says, "his Majesty's government did not comply with the demand of the Sultan for naval assistance, yet the moral assistance of England was afforded; and the communications made by the British government to the Pasha of Egypt, and to Ibrahim Pasha, commanding in Asia Minor, did materially contribute to bring about that arrangement" (of Kutaiah) "between the Sultan and the Pasha, by which that war was *terminated*."—(H. of C., March 17, 1834.)

---

[a] This sentence is omitted in the *New-York Daily Tribune*.—*Ed.*

[b] The *New-York Daily Tribune* has after this: "for such trifles as preventing Russia from occupying Constantinople, or Mehemet Ali from endangering the *status quo* of the world".—*Ed.*

[c] The *New-York Daily Tribune* has further: "in order to check the ambition of Mehemet Ali and the armies of Ibrahim Pasha. Lord Mahon tells us this, and when he made his statement he had just been employed at the Foreign Office under Sir Robert Peel".—*Ed.*

There is Lord Derby, then Mr. Stanley and a member of the Palmerston Cabinet, who

> "boldly asserts that what stopped the progress of Mehemet Ali, was the distinct declaration of France and England that they would not permit the occupation of Constantinople by his troops."—(H. of C., March 17, 1834.)

Thus then, according to Lord Derby and to Lord Palmerston himself,[a] it was not the Russian squadron and army at Constantinople, but it was a *distinct declaration* on the part of the British consular agent at Alexandria, that stopped Ibrahim's victorious march upon Constantinople, and brought about the arrangement of Kutaiah, by virtue of which Mehemet Ali obtained, besides Egypt, the Pashalik of Syria, of Adana and other places, added as appendage. But the noble lord thought fit not to allow his consul at Alexandria to make this distinct declaration till after the Turkish army was annihilated—Constantinople overrun by the Cossacks, the treaty of Unkiar-Skelessi signed by the Sultan, and pocketed by the Czar.

If want of time and want of fleets, forbade the noble lord to assist the Sultan, and a superfluity of *etiquette* to check the Pasha, did he at least employ his ambassador at Constantinople to guard against excessive influence on the part of Russia, and to keep her influence confined to narrow bounds? Quite the contrary. In order not to clog the movements of Russia, the noble lord took good care to have no ambassador at all at Constantinople during the most fatal period of the crisis.

> "If ever there was a country in which the weight and station of an ambassador were useful—or a period in which that weight and station might be advantageously exerted—that country was Turkey, during the six months before the 8th of July."—(Speech of Lord Mahon, H. of C., April 20, 1836.)

Lord Palmerston tells us, that the British Ambassador, Sir Stratford Canning, left Constantinople in September, 1832—that Lord Ponsonby, then at Naples, was appointed in his place in November, and that "difficulties experienced in making the necessary arrangements for his conveyance,"—although a man-of-war was in waiting for him—"and the unfavourable state of the weather, did prevent his getting to Constantinople until the end of May, 1833."—(H. of C., March 17, 1834.)

The Russian was not yet in, and Lord Ponsonby was accordingly

[a] The *New-York Daily Tribune* has after this: "—and this is the most curious feature of these curious transactions". —*Ed.*

ordered to require seven months for sailing from Naples to Constantinople.[a]

But why should the noble lord prevent the Russians from occupying Constantinople?

"He for his part had great doubts that *any* intention to partition the Ottoman Empire *at all* entered into the policy of the Russian government."—(H. of C., July 11, 1833.)

Certainly not. Russia wants not to partition the empire but to keep the whole of it. Besides the security Lord Palmerston possessed in this *doubt* he had another security "in the *doubt*, whether it enters into the policy of Russia *at present* to accomplish the object," and a third "security" in the third "*doubt*"

"whether the *Russian nation*" (just think of a Russian *nation*!)[b] "would be prepared for that transference of power, of residence, and authority to the southern provinces which would be the necessary consequence of the conquest by Russia of Constantinople."—(H. of C., July 11, 1833.)

Besides these negative arguments the noble lord had an affirmative one:

"if they had quietly beheld the temporary occupation of the Turkish capital by the forces of Russia, it was because they had full confidence in the honour and good faith of Russia.... The Russian government in granting its aid to the Sultan had pledged its honour, and in that pledge *he* reposed the most implicit confidence."[c]—(H. of C., July 11, 1833.)

So inaccessible, indestructible, integral, imperishable, inexpungable, incalculable, incommensurable, and irremediable; so boundless, dauntless, and matchless was the noble lord's confidence, that still on March 17, 1834, when the treaty of Unkiar-Skelessi had become a *fait accompli*, he went on declaring that, "in their *confidence* ministers were not deceived." Not his is the fault if nature has developed his protuberance of confidence to altogether anomalous dimensions.

---

[a] Instead of the sentence beginning with the words: "The Russian was not yet in", the *New-York Daily Tribune* has: "Sir Stratford Canning is recalled in September and Lord Ponsonby appointed in November. But Ibrahim Pasha had not yet crossed the Taurus, not yet fought the battle of Konia and the Russians had not yet seized upon Czarigrad. Accordingly Lord Ponsonby is ordered to employ seven months in sailing from Naples to Constantinople."—*Ed.*

[b] The phrase in brackets is omitted in the *New-York Daily Tribune*.—*Ed.*

[c] The *New-York Daily Tribune* has after the quotation: "With the same confidence he had relied upon Russia not abolishing the Polish Constitution and Nationality. Meanwhile the Czar had abolished both by the Organic Statute of 1832[284]—but the most implicit confidence of the noble lord remained unshaken."—*Ed.*

ARTICLE FIFTH

[*The People's Paper,* No. 81, November 19, 1853]

The contents of the treaty of Unkiar-Skelessi were published by *The Morning Herald,* on Aug. 21, 1833.[a] On August 24, Sir Robert Inglis asked Lord Palmerston in the House of Commons,

"whether there really had been concluded a treaty, offensive and defensive, between Russia and Turkey? [...] He hoped that the noble lord would be prepared, before the prorogation of parliament to lay before the house, not only the treaties that had been made, but all communications connected with the formation of those treaties between Turkey and Russia."

Lord Palmerston answered that

"when they were *sure* that such a treaty as that alluded to really did exist; and when they were in possession of that treaty, it would *then* be for them to determine what was the course of policy they ought to pursue.... It could be no blame to him if the newspapers were sometimes beforehand with the government." (House of Commons, August 24, 1833.)

Seven months afterwards he assures that

"it was perfectly impossible that the treaty of Unkiar-Skelessi, not to be ratified at Constantinople until the month of September, should have been officially known to him in August." (H. of C., March 17, 1834.)

He did know the treaty, but not officially.[b]

"The British government was surprised to find that when the Russian troops quitted the Bosphorus, they carried that treaty [...] with them." (Speech of Lord Palmerston, H. of C., March 1, 1848).

Yea, the noble lord was in possession of the treaty *before* it had been concluded.

"No sooner had the Porte received it" (viz., the draft of the treaty of Unkiar-Skelessi), "than the treaty was communicated by them to the British Embassy at Constantinople, with the prayer for our protection against Ibrahim Pasha, and [...] against Nicholas. [...] The application was rejected,—but that was not all. With an atrocious perfidiousness, the fact was made known to the Russian Minister. Next day the very copy of the treaty which the Porte had lodged with the British Embassy, was returned to the Porte by the Russian Ambassador,[c] who ironically

[a] Instead of "by *The Morning Herald*" the *New-York Daily Tribune* of November 21, 1853, has: "by the journals of London".—*Ed.*

[b] The *New-York Daily Tribune* has: "Now, was the noble lord really not sure in August that such a treaty 'really' existed? Was he at that time not yet in possession of that treaty? At a later epoch, in March, 1850 [there is a mistake in the date: it should be 1848.—*Ed.*], he himself stated that..."—*Ed.*

[c] K. Lieven.—*Ed.*

advised the Porte—'to choose better another time its confidents.'" (H. of C., Feb. 8, 1848.)[a]

But the noble viscount had obtained all he cared for. He was interrogated with respect to the treaty of Unkiar-Skelessi, of whose existence he was not sure on August 24, 1833. On August 29 parliament was prorogued, receiving from the throne the consolatory assertion that

"the hostilities which had disturbed the peace of Turkey had been terminated, and they might be assured that the king's[b] attention would be carefully directed to any events which might affect the present state or the future independence of that empire."

Here we have the key to the famous Russian treaties of July. In July they are concluded; in August, something about them is transpiring through the public press. Lord Palmerston is interrogated in the Commons. He, of course, is aware of nothing. Parliament is prorogued—and, when it reassembles, the treaty has grown old, or, in 1841, has already been executed, in spite of public opinion.[c]

Parliament was prorogued on August 29, 1833, and it reassembled on Feb. 5, 1834. The interval between the prorogation and its reassembling was marked by two incidents intimately interwoven with each other. On the one hand, the united French and English fleets proceeded to the Dardanelles, displayed there the tricoloured, and the national flag of England, sailed their way to Smyrna, and returned from thence to Malta. On the other hand, a new treaty was concluded between the Porte and Russia, on January 29, 1834, the treaty of St. Petersburg.[285] This treaty was hardly signed when the united fleet was withdrawn.

This combined manoeuvre was intended to stultify the British people and Europe into the belief that the hostile demonstration on the Turkish seas and coasts, directed against the Porte, for having concluded the treaty of Unkiar-Skelessi, had enforced upon Russia the new treaty of St. Petersburg. This treaty, by promising the evacuation of the Principalities,[d] and reducing the Turkish payments to one-third of the stipulated amount, appar-

---

[a] From the speech of M.P. Th. Ch. Anstey.—*Ed.*

[b] William IV.—*Ed.*

[c] The *New-York Daily Tribune* has: "in spite of Parliament and public opinion".—*Ed.*

[d] The *New-York Daily Tribune* has after that: "with the exception of Silistra".—*Ed.*

ently relieved the Porte from some engagements enforced on her by the treaty of Adrianople. In all other instances it was a ratification of the treaty of Adrianople, not at all relating to the treaty of Unkiar-Skelessi, nor dropping a word about the passage of the Dardanelles. On the contrary, the alleviations it granted to Turkey, were the purchase-money for the exclusion of Europe, by the treaty of Unkiar-Skelessi, from the Dardanelles.

"The very day on which the demonstration" (of the British fleet) "was being made, an assurance was given by the noble lord to the Russian Ambassador[a] at this court, that this combined movement of the [...] squadrons was not intended in any sense hostile to Russia, nor to be taken as a hostile demonstration against her; but, that, in fact, it meant nothing at all. I say this on the authority of Lord Ponsonby, the noble lord's own colleague, the Ambassador at Constantinople."—(Speech of Mr. Anstey, H. of C., Feb. 23, 1848.)

After the treaty of St. Petersburg had been ratified, the noble lord expressed his satisfaction with the moderation of the terms imposed by Russia.[b]

When Parliament had reassembled, there appeared in *The Globe*, the organ of the Foreign Office, a paragraph stating that

"The treaty of St. Petersburg was a proof either of the moderation or good sense of Russia, or of the influence which the union of England and France, and the firm and concerted language of those two powers had acquired in the councils of St. Petersburg."—(*Globe*, Feb. 24, 1834.)

Thus public attention was to be diverted from the treaty of Unkiar-Skelessi, and the animosity it had aroused in Europe against Russia, to be soothed down.[c]

Artful as the dodging was, it would not do. On March 17, 1834, Mr. Sheil brought in a motion for

"the copies of the treaties between Turkey and Russia, [...] and of any correspondence between the English, Russian, and Turkish Governments, respecting those treaties, to be laid before the house."

The noble lord resisted this resolution to his utmost, and succeeded in baffling it by assuring the house that "peace [...]

---

[a] K. Lieven.—*Ed.*

[b] This sentence is omitted in the *New-York Daily Tribune*.—*Ed.*

[c] In the pamphlet *Palmerston and the Treaty of Unkiar Skelessi*, published in 1854, this paragraph was given as follows: "Thus, on the one hand, the Treaty of Adrianople, protested against by Lord Aberdeen and the Duke of Wellington, was surreptitiously to be recognised on the part of England by Lord Palmerston officially expressing his satisfaction with the convention of St. Petersburg, which was but a ratification of that Treaty. On the other hand, public attention was to be diverted from the Treaty of Unkiar-Skelessi, and the animosity it had aroused in Europe against Russia, to be soothed down."—*Ed.*

could be preserved only by the house reposing confidence in the government," and refusing to accede to the motion.[a] So grossly inapt were the reasons he stated to prevent him from producing the papers, that Sir Robert Peel called him, in his parliamentary language "a very unconclusive reasoner," and his own Colonel Evans could not help exclaiming:

"The speech of the noble lord appeared to him the most unsatisfactory he had ever heard from him."

Lord Palmerston strived to convince the house that,[b] according to the *assurances* of Russia, the treaty of Unkiar-Skelessi was to be looked upon "as one of reciprocity," that reciprocity being, that if the Dardanelles should be closed against England in the event of war they should be closed against Russia also. The statement was altogether false, but if true, this certainly would have been Irish reciprocity, for it was all on one side. To cross the Dardanelles is for Russia not the means to get at the Black Sea, but on the contrary, to leave it.

So far from refuting Mr. Sheil's statement, "the consequence of the treatv of Unkiar-Skelessi was [...] the same as if the Porte surrendered to Russia the possession of the Dardanelles," Lord Palmerston owned that the treaty closed the Dardanelles to British men-of-war, and that "under its provisions even *merchant vessels* might, [...] in effect, be practically excluded from the Black Sea," in the case of a war between England and Russia. But if the government acted with a "temper," if it "showed no unnecessary distrust," that is to say, if it quietly submitted to all further encroachments of Russia, he was

"inclined to think that the case might not arise in which that treaty would be called into operation; and that therefore it would, in practice, remain a dead letter."—(H. of C., March 17, 1834.)

Besides, "the assurance and explanations" which the British government had received from the contradictory parties to that treaty greatly tended to remove its objections to it. Thus then it was not the articles of the treaty of Unkiar-Skelessi, but the assurances Russia gave with respect to them, not the acts of Russia,

---

[a] In the *New-York Daily Tribune* this phrase was given as follows: "He enjoined the House not to press upon him, as 'peace could be preserved only by the House reposing confidence in the Government,' which, if let alone, would certainly protect the interests of England from encroachment."—*Ed.*

[b] The *New-York Daily Tribune* has: "In order to mystify the House, he dropped some words to the effect...." —*Ed.*

but her language, he had in his opinion to look upon. Yet, as on the same day his attention was called to the protest of the French chargé d'affaires, M. Lagrené, against the treaty of Unkiar-Skelessi, and the offensive and contumacious language of Count Nesselrode, answering in the *St. Petersburg Gazette*[a] that "the Emperor of Russia would act as if the declaration contained in the note of M. Lagrené had no existence," then the noble lord, eating up his own words, propounded the opposite doctrine that

> "it was on all occasions the *duty* of the English government to look rather to the acts of foreign power, than to the language which the power might hold on any particular subject on any occasion."[b]

One moment he appealed from the acts of Russia to her language, and the other from her language to her act.

Still in 1837 he assured that

> "the treaty of Unkiar-Skelessi was a treaty between two independent powers."—(H. of C., December 14, 1837.)[c]

Ten years later, the treaty having long since elapsed, and the noble lord being just about acting the play of the Truly English Minister and the "*civis Romanus sum,*"[286] he told the house plainly,

> "the treaty of Unkiar-Skelessi [...] was no doubt to a certain degree forced upon Turkey by Count Orloff, the Russian Envoy, under circumstances"—created by the noble lord himself—"which rendered it difficult for Turkey to refuse acceeding to it.... It gave practically to the Russian government a power of interference and dictation in Turkey, not consistent with the independence of that state."—(H. of C., March 1, 1848.)

During the whole course of the debates about the treaty of Unkiar-Skelessi, the noble lord, like the clown in the comedy, had an answer of most monstrous size, that must fit all demands and serve all questions—the Anglo-French alliance. When his conniv-

---

[a] This newspaper is not mentioned in the *New-York Daily Tribune*.—*Ed.*

[b] Quoted from Palmerston's speech in the House of Commons on March 17, 1834.—*Ed.*

[c] In the *New-York Daily Tribune* this sentence was given as follows: "Three years later [in 1837.—*Ed.*], in a thin House, composed almost entirely of his retainers, he came roundly out and told Mr. Thomas Attwood very coolly that 'the treaty of Unkiar-Skelessi was a matter which had gone by,' and that it had never been 'the intention of the Government to have recourse to hostile measures to compel Russia and Turkey—two independent powers—to cancel the treaty made between them." This sentence was given in a different place.—*Ed.*

ance with Russia was pointed at, in sneers, he gravely retorted[a]:

"If the present relations established between this country and France, were pointed at in these sneers, he would only say, that he should look [...] with feelings of pride and satisfaction at the part he had acted in bringing about that good understanding."—(H. of C., July 11, 1833.)

When the production of the papers relating to the treaty of Unkiar-Skelessi was demanded, he answered that

"England and France had now cemented a friendship [...] which had only grown stronger."—(H. of C., March 17, 1834.)

"He could but remark," exclaimed Sir Robert Peel, "that whenever the noble lord was thrown into a difficulty as to any part of our European policy, he at once found a ready means of escape, by congratulating the House upon the close alliance [...] between this country and France," simultaneously the noble lord was strengthening the suspicions of his Tory opponents that "England was compelled to connive [...] at an aggression upon Turkey, which *France* had directly encouraged."[b]

At that time, then, the ostensible alliance with France was to cover the secret infeoffment to Russia, as, in 1840, the clamorous rupture with France was to cover the official alliance with Russia.

While the noble lord fatigued the world with ponderous folios of printed negotiations on the affairs of the constitutional empire of Belgium and with ample explanations, verbal and documentary, with regard to the "substantive power" of Portugal, to this moment it has proved quite impossible to wrest out of him any document whatever relating to the first Syro-Turkish war, and to the treaty of Unkiar-Skelessi. When the production of the papers was first demanded, on July 11th, 1833, "The motion was premature, the transactions incomplete, and the results not yet known." On August 24th, 1833, "the treaty was not officially signed, and he was not in possession of it." On March 17th, 1834, "Communications were still carrying on ... the discussions, if he might so call them, were not yet completed." Still, in 1848, when Mr. Anstey told him that, in asking for the papers, he did ask for the

[a] In the *New-York Daily Tribune* this passage reads as follows: "The great triumphant argument which, during the whole transactions with respect to the treaty of Unkiar-Skelessi, the noble lord had ready to oppose to all the attacks upon his connivance with Russia, was that of his intimate alliance with France. Like the clown in the comedy, he had an answer of most monstrous size, that must meet all demands and serve all questions, namely: The Anglo-French Alliance. When he was pointed at with sneers because he had allowed the Russian occupation of Constantinople, he retorted that...." —*Ed.*

[b] Quoted from Peel's speech in the House of Commons on March 17, 1834.—*Ed.*

proof of the noble lord's collusion with the Czar, the chivalrous minister preferred killing time by a five hours' speech to killing suspicion by self-speaking documents. Notwithstanding all this, he had the cynic impudence to assure Mr. T. Attwood, on December 14th, 1837,[a] that "the papers connected with that treaty, viz., the treaty of Unkiar-Skelessi, were laid before the house three years ago," that is to say in 1834, when "peace could be preserved only" by withholding the papers from the house. On the same day he told Mr. Attwood that

> "this treaty was a matter which had gone by, that it was entered into for a limited period, [...] and that period having expired, [...] its introduction by the honourable member was wholly unnecessary and uncalled for."

According to the original stipulation, the treaty of Unkiar-Skelessi was to expire on July 8th, 1841. Lord Palmerston tells Mr. Attwood that it had already expired on December 14th, 1837.[b]

> "What trick, what devise, what starting hole, can'st thou now find to hide thee from this open and apparent shame? Come let's hear, Jack—what trick hast thou now?"[c]

ARTICLE SIXTH

[*The People's Paper*, No. 84, December 10, 1853]

There is no such word in the Russian vocabulary as "honour." As to the thing itself, it is considered to be a French delusion.

---

[a] In the *New-York Daily Tribune* this sentence begins as follows: "His system of fictions, pretexts, contradictions, traps and incredible statements reached its climax, when, on December 14, 1837, he objected to a resolution of Mr. T. Attwood for the production of the papers connected with the treaty of Unkiar-Skelessi, on the ground that...."—*Ed.*

[b] The *New-York Daily Tribune* has: "The noble Viscount knew as well that the papers were not laid before the House in 1834, or at any other period, as that the treaty of Unkiar-Skelessi, far from having expired on December 14, 1837, continued to remain in full vigor till July 8, 1841."—*Ed.*

[c] W. Shakespeare, *Henry IV*, Part I, Act II, Scene 4.—*Ed.*

In the *New-York Daily Tribune* the article ends as follows: "Such a gross system of fraud formed the last refuge of an English Minister, who had opened Constantinople to a Russian army, and closed the Dardanelles to the English navy, and who had helped the Czar to get possession of Constantinople for months and the control of Turkey for years. How absurd then to suppose that he is now likely to turn about and oppose a friend he has so long and so faithfully served."—*Ed.*

"Schto takoi honneur? Eto Fransusski chimere," is a Russian proverb. For the invention of Russian honour the world is exclusively indebted to my Lord Palmerston, who, during a quarter of a century, used, at every critical moment, to pledge himself, in the most emphatical manner, for the "honour" of the Czar.[a] So he did at the close of the Session of 1853, as at the close of the Session of 1833.

Now it happens that the noble lord, while he expressed "his most implicit confidence in the honour and good faith" of the Czar, had just got into possession of documents, concealed from the rest of the world, and leaving no doubt, if any existed, about the nature of Russian honour and good faith. He had not even to scratch the Muscovite in order to find the Tartar. He had caught the Tartar in his naked hideousness. He found himself possessed of the self-confessions of the leading Russian ministers and diplomatists, throwing off their cloaks, opening out their most secret thoughts, unfolding, without constraint, their plans of conquest and subjugation, scornfully railing at the imbecile credulity of European Courts and Ministers, mocking the Villèles, the Metternichs, the Aberdeens, the Cannings, and the Wellingtons; and devising, in common, with the savage cynicism of the barbarian, mitigated by the cruel irony of the courtier, how to sow distrust against England at Paris, and against Austria at London, and against London at Vienna, how to set them all by the ears, and how to make all of them the mere tools of Russia.

At the time of the insurrection of Warsaw, the vice-royal archives kept in the palace of Prince Constantine, and containing the secret correspondence of Russian ministers and ambassadors from the beginning of the century down to 1830, fell into the hands of the victorious Poles. Polish Refugees brought these papers over first to France, and, at a later period, Count Zamoyski, the nephew of Prince Czartoryski, placed them in the hands of Lord Palmerston, who buried them in Christian oblivion. With these papers in his pockets, the noble viscount was the more eager to proclaim in the British Senate and to the world "his most implicit confidence in the honour and good faith of the Emperor of Russia."[b]

Not the fault of the noble viscount, that those startling papers were at length published at the end of 1835, through the famous

---

[a] Nicholas I.—*Ed.*

[b] Quoted from Palmerston's speech in the House of Commons on August 20, 1853.—*Ed.*

Portfolio. King William IV, whatever he was in other respects, was a most decided enemy of Russia. His private secretary, Sir Herbert Taylor, was intimately connected with David Urquhart, introducing this gentleman to the King himself, and from that moment royalty was conspiring with those two friends against the policy of the "truly English" minister.

"William IV [...] ordered the above-mentioned papers to be given up by the noble lord. They were given up and examined at the time at Windsor Castle, and it was found desirable to print and publish them. [...] In spite of the great opposition of the noble lord, the king compelled him to lend the authority of the Foreign Office to their publication, [...] so [...] that the editor, who took the charge of revising them for the press, published not a single word which had not the signature or initials attached. I, myself, have seen the noble lord's initial attached to one of those documents, although the noble lord has denied these facts. Lord Palmerston was compelled to place the documents in the hands of Mr. Urquhart for publication. Mr. Urquhart was the real editor of *The Portfolio*." (Speech of Mr. Anstey, House of Commons, February 23rd, 1848.)

After the death of the king, Lord Palmerston refused to pay the printer of *The Portfolio*, and disclaimed, publicly and solemnly, all connexion on the part of the Foreign Office, and induced, in what manner is not known, Mr. Backhouse, his under-secretary, to set his name to those denials.[a] We read in *The Times* of January 26th, 1839:

"It is not for us to understand how Lord Palmerston may feel, but we are sure there is no misapprehending how *any other person* in the station of a gentleman, and in the position of a minister, *would feel*, after the notoriety given to the correspondence between Mr. Urquhart, whom Lord Palmerston dismissed from office, and Mr. Backhouse, whom the noble viscount has retained in office, by *The Times* of yesterday. There never was a fact apparently better established through this correspondence than that the series of official documents contained in the well-known publication, called *The Portfolio*, were printed and circulated by Lord Palmerston's authority, and that his lordship is responsible for the publication of them, both as a statesman to the political world here and abroad, and as an employer of the printers and publishers, for the pecuniary charge accompanying it."[b]

In consequence of her financial distress, resulting from the exhaustion of the treasury by the unfortunate war of 1828-29, and the debt to Russia stipulated by the treaty of Adrianople, Turkey found herself compelled to extend that obnoxious system of monopolies by which the sale of almost all articles was granted only to those who had paid government licenses. Thus a few

[a] Published in *The Times*, No. 16948, January 25, 1839.—*Ed.*
[b] Marx apparently quotes from *The Portfolio*, 1843, Vol. II, No. VI.—*Ed.*

usurers were enabled to seize upon the entire commerce of the country. Mr. Urquhart proposed to King William IV, a commercial treaty to be concluded with the Sultan,[a] which treaty, while guaranteeing great advantages to British commerce, intended at the same time to develop the productive resources of Turkey, to restore her Exchequer to health, and thus to emancipate her from the Russian yoke. The curious history of this treaty cannot be better related than in the words of Mr. Anstey:

"The whole of the contest between Lord Palmerston on the one hand, and Mr. Urquhart on the other, was directed to this treaty of commerce. On the third of October, 1835, Mr. Urquhart obtained his commission as Secretary of Legation at Constantinople, given him for the one purpose of securing the adoption there of the Turkish commercial treaty. He delayed his departure however till June or July, 1836. Lord Palmerston pressed him to go. The applications to him urging his departure were numerous, but his answer invariably was: I will not go until I have this commercial treaty settled with the Board of Trade and the Foreign Office; and then I will accompany it, and procure its acceptance at the Porte.... Finally, Lord Palmerston gave his approbation to the treaty, and it was forwarded to Lord Ponsonby, the Ambassador at Constantinople." (In the meantime the latter had been instructed by Lord Palmerston to take the negotiations entirely out of the hands of Mr. Urquhart into his own, contrary to the engagement entered into with Mr. Urquhart.) "As soon as the removal of Mr. Urquhart from Constantinople had been effected through the intrigues of the noble lord, the treaty was immediately thrown overboard. Two years later the noble lord resumed it, giving Mr. Urquhart before Parliament the compliment of being the author of it, and disclaiming for himself all merits in it. But the noble lord had destroyed the treaty, falsified it in every part, and converted it to the ruin of commerce. The original treaty of Mr. Urquhart placed the subjects of Great Britain in Turkey, upon the footing of the most favoured nation"—viz., the Russians. "As altered by Lord Palmerston, it placed the subjects of Great Britain upon the footing of the taxed and oppressed subjects of the Porte. Mr. Urquhart's treaty stipulated for the removal of all transit duties, monopolies, taxes, and duties of whatever character, others than those stipulated by the treaty itself. As falsified by Lord Palmerston, it contained a clause, declaring the perfect right of the Sublime Porte to impose whatever regulations and restrictions it pleased, with regard to commerce. Mr. Urquhart's treaty left importation subject only to the old duty of three shillings; that of the noble lord raised the duty from three shillings to five shillings. Mr. Urquhart's treaty stipulated for an *ad valorem* duty in this manner, that if any article of commerce was so exclusively the production of Turkey, as to insure it a ready sale, at the prices usually received under the monopoly in foreign ports, then the export duty to be assessed by two commissioners appointed on the part of England and Turkey, might be a high one, so as to be remunerative and productive of revenue, but that, in the case of commodities produced elsewhere than in Turkey, and not being of sufficient value in foreign ports to bear a high duty, a lower duty should be assessed. Lord Palmerston's treaty stipulated a fixed duty of twelve shillings *ad valorem* upon every article whether it would bear the duty or not. [...] The original treaty extended the benefit of Free Trade to Turkish ships and produce; [...] the

[a] Mahmud II.—*Ed.*

substituted treaty contained no stipulation whatever on the subject.... I charge these falsifications, I charge also the concealment of them, upon the noble lord, and further—I charge the noble lord with having falsely stated to the house that his treaty was that which had been arranged by Mr. Urquhart."—(Speech of Mr. Anstey, H. of C., February 23rd, 1848.)

So favourable to Russia, and so obnoxious to Great Britain, was the treaty as altered by the noble lord, that some English merchants in the Levant resolved to trade henceforth under the protection of Russian firms, and others, as Mr. Urquhart states, were only prevented from so doing by a sort of national pride.

With regard to the secret relations between the noble lord and William IV, Mr. Anstey stated to the house,

"The king forced the question of the progress of Russian encroachment in Turkey, upon the attention of the noble lord.... I can [...] prove that the noble lord was obliged to take the directions in this matter from the late King's private secretary, and that his existence in office depended upon his compliance with the wishes of the monarch.... The noble lord did on one or two occasions, as far as he dared, resist, but his resistance was [...] invariably followed by *abject* expressions of *contrition* and *compliance*. I will not take upon myself to assert that, on one occasion, the noble lord was actually out of office for a day or two, [...] but I am able to say that the noble lord was [...] in danger of a most unceremonious expulsion from office on that occasion. I refer to the discovery which the late king had made, that the noble lord consulted the feelings of the Russian government as to the choice of an English ambassador at the Court of St. Petersburg, and that Sir Stratford Canning, originally destined for the embassy, was set aside to make room for the late Earl of Durham, an ambassador more agreeable to the Czar."—(H. of C., Feb. 23, 1848.)

It is one of the most astonishing facts that, while the king was vainly struggling against the Russian policy of the noble lord—the noble lord and his Whig-allies succeeded in keeping alive the public suspicion that the king—who was known as a Tory—was paralysing the anti-Russian efforts of the "truly English" minister. The pretended Tory predilection of the monarch for the despotic principles of the Russian Court, was of course made to explain the otherwise inexplicable policy of Lord Palmerston. The Whig Oligarchs smiled mysteriously when H. L. Bulwer informed the house, that

"no longer ago than last Christmas Count Apponyi, the Austrian ambassador of Paris, stated, in speaking of the affairs of the East, that this Court had a greater apprehension of French principles than of Russian ambition."—(H. of C., July 11, 1833.)

They smiled again, when Mr. T. Attwood interrogated the noble lord "what reception Count Orloff, having been sent over to England after the treaty of Unkiar-Skelessi, had met with at his Majesty's Court."—(H. of C., August 28, 1833.)

The papers entrusted by the dying king and his Secretary, the late Sir Herbert Taylor, to Mr. Urquhart "for the purpose of vindicating, upon the fitting opportunity, the memory of William IV"—will, when published, throw a new light upon the past career of the noble lord and the Whig Oligarchy, of which the public generally know little more than the history of their pretensions, their phrases, and their so-called principles—in a word, the theatrical and fictitious part,—the mask.

This is a fitting occasion to give his due to Mr. David Urquhart, the indefatigable antagonist for twenty years of Lord Palmerston, who has proved his only adversary—one not to be intimidated into silence, bribed into connivance, charmed into suitorship, while, what with cajoleries, what with seductions, Alcina Palmerston contrived to change all other foes into fools. We have just heard the fierce denunciation of his lordship by Mr. Anstey.

"A circumstance most significant is that the accused minister sought the member"—viz., Mr. Anstey—"[...] and was content to accept his [...] co-operation and private friendship without the forms of recantation or apology. [...] Mr. Anstey's recent legal appointment by the present government speaks for itself." (D. Urquhart's *Progress of Russia.*)

On February 8, 1848, the same Mr. Anstey had compared the noble viscount with

"the *infamous* Marquis of Carmarthen, Secretary of State to William III, [...] whom, during his visit to his court, the Czar, Peter I, found means to corrupt to his interests with the gold of British merchants."—(H. of C., February 8, 1848.)

Who defended Lord Palmerston on that occasion against the accusations of Mr. Anstey? Mr. Sheil; the same Mr. Sheil which had, on the conclusion of the treaty of Unkiar-Skelessi, in 1833, acted the same part of accuser against his lordship as Mr. Anstey in 1848. Mr. Roebuck, once his strong antagonist, procured him the vote of confidence in 1850. Sir Stratford Canning, having denounced during a decennium the noble lord's connivance with the Czar, was content to be got rid of as Ambassador at Constantinople. The noble lord's own dear Dudley Stuart was intrigued out of Parliament for some years for having opposed the noble lord. When returned back to it, he had become the *âme damnée* of the truly English minister. Kossuth, who might have known from the Blue Books[a] that Hungary had been betrayed by the noble viscount, called him "the dear friend of his bosom" when landing at Southampton.

SEVENTH ARTICLE[287]

[*The People's Paper,* No. 85, December 17, 1853]

One glance at the map of Europe will show you on the Western littoral of the Black Sea the outlets of the Danube, the only river which, springing up in the very heart of Europe, may be said to form a natural highway to Asia. Strictly opposite, on the Eastern side, to the south of the river Kuban, begins the mountain-range of the Caucasus, stretching from the Black Sea to the Caspian in a south-easterly direction for some seven hundred miles and separating Europe from Asia.

If you hold the outlets of the Danube, you hold the Danube, and with it the highway to Asia, and a great part of the commerce of Switzerland, Germany, Hungary, Turkey, and above all of Moldo-Wallachia. If you hold the Caucasus too, the Black Sea becomes your property,[b] and to shut up its door, you only want Constantinople and the Dardanelles. The possession of the Caucasus mountains makes you at once master of Trebizond, and through their domineering the Caspian Sea, of the northern seaboard of Persia.

The greedy eyes of Russia embraced at once the outlets of the Danube and the mountain-range of the Caucasus. There, the business in hand was to conquer supremacy, here to maintain it. The chain of the Caucasus separates Southern Russia from the luxurious provinces of Georgia, Mingrelia, Imeretia, and Guria, wrested by the Muscovite from the Mussulman. Thus the foot of the monster empire is cut off from its main body. The only military road deserving to be called such winds from Mozdok to Tiflis, through the *Engpass* of Dariel, fortified by a continuous line of entrenched places, but exposed on both sides to the never-ceasing attacks from the Caucasian tribes. The union of those

---

[a] "Correspondence Relative to the Affairs of Hungary. 1847-1849. *Presented to both Houses of Parliament by command of Her Majesty.* August 15, 1850."—*Ed.*

[b] In the *New-York Daily Tribune* of January 11, 1854, this sentence begins as follows: "But give the same power the Caucasus in addition, and the Black Sea will exclusively belong to it as a *mare clausum* [closed sea]...."—*Ed.*

tribes under one military chief might even endanger the bordering country of the Cossacks. "The thought of the dreadful consequences which a union of the hostile Circassians under one head would produce in the south of Russia fills one with terror"—exclaims M. Kupffer, a German, who presided over the scientific commission, which, in 1829, accompanied the expedition of General Emmanuel to Elbruz.[a]

At this very moment our attention is directed with equal anxiety to the banks of the Danube, where Russia has seized the two corn-magazines of Europe, and to the Caucasus, whence she is menaced in the possession of Georgia.[b] It was the treaty of Adrianople, that prepared Russia's usurpation of Moldo-Wallachia, and recognised her claims to the Caucasus.

Article IV of that treaty stipulates,

> "All the countries situated north and east of the line of demarcation between the two empires" (Russia and Turkey), "towards Georgia, Imeretia, and the Guria, as well as all the littoral of the Black Sea, from the mouth of the Kuban, as far as the port of St. Nicholas inclusively, shall remain under the domination of Russia."

With regard to the Danube the same treaty stipulates,

> "The frontier line will follow the course of the Danube to the mouth of St. George, leaving all the islands formed by the different branches in the possession of Russia. The right bank will remain as formerly in the possession of the Ottoman Porte. It is however agreed that that right bank from the point where the arm of St. George departs from that of Sulina, still remain uninhabited to a distance of two hours" (six miles) "from the river, and that no kind of structure shall be raised there, and in like manner, on the islands which still remain in the possession of the Court of Russia. With the exception of quarantines which will be there established, it will not be permitted to make any other establishment or fortification."

Both these paragraphs, inasmuch as they secure to Russia an "extension of territory and exclusive commercial advantages," openly infringed upon the protocol of April 4, 1826, drawn up by the Duke of Wellington at St. Petersburg, and on the treaty of July 6, 1827, concluded between Russia and the other Great Powers at London.[288] The English Government, therefore, refused to recognise the treaty of Adrianople. The Duke of Wellington protested against it. (Speech of Lord Dudley Stuart, H. of C., March 17, 1837.)

Lord Aberdeen protested.

---

[a] Kupffer, *Voyage dans les environs du Mont Elbrouz dans le Caucase, entrepris par ordre de la sa Majesté l'Empereur en 1829*, p. 4.—*Ed.*

[b] In the *New-York Daily Tribune* this sentence is followed by: "Her movements in both these regions have a common origin."—*Ed.*

"In a dispatch to Lord Heytesbury dated October 31st, 1829, he commented with no small dissatisfaction on many parts of the Treaty of Adrianople, and especially notices [...] the stipulations respecting the islands of the Danube. He denies that that peace" (the Treaty of Adrianople), "has respected the territorial rights of the Sovereignty of the Porte, and the condition and the interests of all maritime states in the Mediterranean."—(Speech of Lord Mahon, H. of C., April 20, 1836.)

He declared that

"the independence of the Porte would be sacrificed, and the peace of Europe endangered by this treaty being agreed to."—(Speech of Earl Grey, H. of L., Feb. 4th, 1834.)

Lord Palmerston himself informs us,

"As far as the extension of the Russian frontier is concerned [...] in the South of the Caucasus, and the shores of the Black Sea, it is certainly not consistent with the solemn declaration made by Russia in the face of Europe, previous to the commencement of the Turkish war." (H. of C., March 17th, 1837.)

The Eastern littoral of the Black Sea, by blockading of which and cutting off supplies of arms and gunpowder to the north-western districts of the Caucasus, Russia could alone hope to realise her nominal claim to those countries—this littoral of the Black Sea and the outlets of the Danube are certainly no places "where an English action could possibly take place,"[a] as was lamented by the noble lord in the case of Cracow. By what mysterious contrivance, then, has the Muscovite succeeded in blockading the Danube, in blocking up the littoral of the Euxine, and in forcing Great Britain to submit, not only to the Treaty of Adrianople, but at the same [time] to the violation by Russia herself of that identical treaty?

These questions were put to the noble viscount in the House of Commons, on April 20th, 1836, numerous petitions having poured in from the merchants of London, of Glasgow, and other commercial towns, against the fiscal regulations of Russia in the Black Sea, and her enactments and restrictions tending to intercept English commerce on the Danube. There had appeared, on February 7th, 1836, a Russian ukase, which, by virtue of the Treaty of Adrianople, established a quarantine on one of the islands formed by the mouths of the Danube. In order to execute that quarantine, Russia claimed a right of boarding and search, of levying fees, and seizing and marching off to Odessa refractory ships, proceeding on their voyage up the Danube. Before the quarantine was established, or rather before a custom-house and

---

[a] Marx quotes from Palmerston's speech in the House of Commons on July 13, 1840.—*Ed.*

fort were erected, under the false pretence of a quarantine, the Russian authorities threw out their feelers, to ascertain the risk they might run with the British government. Lord Durham, acting upon instructions received from England, remonstrated with the Russian Cabinet, for the hindrance which had been given to British trade.

"He was referred to Count Nesselrode, Count Nesselrode [...] referred him to the Governor of South Russia, and the Governor of South Russia again referred him to the Consul at Galatz, who communicated with the British Consul at Brăila, who was instructed to send down the captains from whom toll had been exacted, to [...] the Danube, the scene of their injuries, in order that inquiry might be made on the subject, it being well known that the captains thus referred to were then in England."—(H. of C., April 20, 1836 [Speech of Mr. Patrick Stewart].)

The formal ukase of the 7th Feb., 1836, aroused, however, the general attention of British commerce.

"Many ships had sailed, and others were going out, to whose captains strict orders had been given, not to submit to the right of boarding and search, which Russia [...] claimed. [...] The fate of these ships must be inevitable, unless some expression of opinion were made on the part of that house. [...] Unless that were done, British shipping, to the amount of not less than 5,000 tons, would [...] be seized and marched off to Odessa, until the insolent commands of Russia were complied with." (Speech of Mr. Patrick M. Stewart, H. of C., April 20, 1836.)

Russia required the marshy islands of the Danube, by virtue of a clause of the Treaty of Adrianople, which clause itself was a violation of the treaty she had previously contracted with England and the other powers in 1827. The bristling [of] the gates of the Danube with fortifications, and these fortifications with guns, was a violation of the Treaty of Adrianople itself, which expressly prohibits any fortification to be erected within six miles of the river. The exaction of tolls, and the obstruction of the navigation, was a violation of the Treaty of Vienna, declaring that the navigation of rivers along their whole course, from the point where each of them becomes navigable to its mouth, shall be entirely free, that "the amount of the duties shall in no case exceed those now" (1815) "paid;" and that "no increase shall take place, except with the common consent of the states bordering on the river." Thus, then, all the argument on which Russia could plead not guilty was the treaty of 1827, violated by the Treaty of Adrianople, the Treaty of Adrianople violated by herself, the whole backed by a violation of the Treaty of Vienna.

It proved quite impossible to wring out of the noble lord any declaration, whether he did or did not recognise the treaty of Adrianople. As to the violation of the Treaty of Vienna, he had "received no official information that anything has occurred which is not warranted by the treaty. [...] When such a statement is made by the parties concerned, it shall be dealt with [...] in such manner as the law-advisers of the Crown shall deem consistent with the rights of the subjects of this country." (Speech of Lord Palmerston, H. of C., April 20, 1836.)

By the treaty of Adrianople, Art. 5, Russia guarantees the "prosperity" of the Danubian Principalities and full "liberty of trade" for them. Now, Mr. Stewart proved that the Principalities of Moldavia and Wallachia were objects of deadly jealousy to Russia, as their trade had taken a sudden development since 1834, as they vied with Russia's own stable production, as Galatz was becoming the great depot of all the grain of the Danube, and driving Odessa out of the market. If, answered the noble lord,

"if my honourable friend had been able to show that whereas some years ago we had had a large and important commerce with Turkey, [...] and that that commerce had, by the aggression of other countries, or by the neglect of the government of this, dwindled down to an inconsiderable trade, then there might have been ground to call upon parliament." In lieu of such an occurrence, "my honourable friend has shown that during the last few years the trade" with Turkey "has risen from next to nothing to a very considerable amount."

Russia obstructs the Danube navigation, because the trade of the Principalities is growing important, says Mr. Stewart. But she did not so when that trade was next to nothing, retorts Lord Palmerston. You neglect to oppose the recent encroachments of Russia on the Danube, says Mr. Stewart. We did not so at the epoch these encroachments were not yet ventured upon, replies the noble lord. What "circumstances" have, *therefore*, "occurred against which the Government [...] are [...] not likely to guard, unless driven thereto by the direct interference of this House?"[a] He prevented the Commons from passing a resolution by assuring them that,

"there is no disposition of his Majesty's[b] government to submit to aggressions on the part of any power, be that power what it may, and be it more or less strong," and by warning them that, "we should also cautiously abstain from anything which might be construed by other powers, and *reasonably* so, as being a provocation on our part."

A week after these debates had taken place in the House of Commons, a British merchant[c] addressed a letter to the Foreign Office with regard to the Russian Ukase.

---

[a] This sentence is omitted in the *New-York Daily Tribune*.—*Ed.*
[b] William IV.—*Ed.*
[c] James Bell.—*Ed.*

"I am directed by Viscount Palmerston," answered the Under-Secretary[a] at the Foreign Office, "to acquaint you that his lordship has called upon the law-adviser for the Crown for his opinion as to the regulations promulgated by the Russian Ukase of Feb. 7, 1836; but in the meantime Lord Palmerston directs me to acquaint you, with respect to the latter part of your letter, that it is the opinion of his Majesty's government, that no toll is justly demanded by the Russian authorities at the mouth of the Danube, and that you have acted properly in directing your agents to *refuse* to pay it."[b]

The merchant acted according to this letter. He is abandoned to Russia by the noble lord; a Russian toll is, as Mr. Urquhart states, now exacted in London and Liverpool by Russian Consuls on every English ship sailing for the Turkish ports of the Danube; and "the quarantine still stands on the Island of Leti."

Russia did not limit her invasion on the Danube to a quarantine established, to fortifications erected, and to tolls exacted. The only mouth of the Danube remaining still navigable, the Sulina mouth, was acquired by her through the treaty of Adrianople. As long as possessed by the Turks, there was kept a depth of water in the channel of from fourteen to sixteen feet. Since, in the possession of Russia, the water became reduced to eight feet, a depth wholly inadequate to the conveyance of the vessels employed in the corn trade. Now Russia is a party to the treaty of Vienna, and that treaty stipulates in Art. 113, that

"each state shall be at the expense of keeping in good repair the Towing Paths, and shall maintain the necessary work in order that no obstruction shall be experienced by the navigation."

For keeping the channel in a navigable state, Russia found no better means than gradually reducing the depth of the water,[c] paving it with wrecks, and choking up its bar with an accumulation of sand and mud. To this systematic and protracted infraction of the treaty of Vienna she added another violation of the treaty of Adrianople, which forbids any establishment at the mouth of the Sulina, except for quarantine and light-house purposes, while, at her dictation, a small Russian fort has there sprung up, living from the extortions upon the vessels, the occasion for which is afforded by the delays and expenses for lighterage, consequent upon the obstruction of the channel.

---

[a] John Backhouse.— *Ed.*

[b] This quotation and those following, including passages from the Vienna Treaty of 1815, are given according to D. Urquhart, *Progress of Russia in the West, North, and South.*— *Ed.*

[c] The phrase "gradually reducing the depth of the water" is omitted in the *New-York Daily Tribune.*— *Ed.*

> *Cum principia negante non est disputandum,*[a] of what use is it to dwell upon abstract principles with despotic governments, who are accused of measuring right by power, and of ruling their conduct by expediency, and not by justice.—(Speech of Lord Palmerston, April 30, 1823.)

According to his own maxim the noble viscount was contented to dwell upon abstract principles with the despotic government of Russia; but he went farther. While he assured the house on July 6, 1840, that the freedom of the Danube navigation was "guaranteed by the treaty of Vienna"—while he lamented on July 13, 1840, that the occupation of Cracow being a violation of the treaty of Vienna, "there were no means of enforcing the opinions of England, because Cracow was evidently a place where no English action could possibly take place;" two days later he concluded a Russian treaty, closing the Dardanelles to England[b] "during times of peace with Turkey," and thus depriving England of the only means of "enforcing" the treaty of Vienna, and transforming the Euxine into a place where no English action could possibly take place.

This point once obtained, he contrived to give a sham satisfaction to public opinion by firing off a whole battery of papers, reminding the "despotic government, which measures right by power, and rules its conduct by expediency, and not by justice," in a sententious and sentimental manner, that

> "Russia, when she compelled Turkey to cede to her the outlet of a great European river, which forms the commercial highway for the mutual intercourse of many nations, undertook duties and responsibilities to other states which she should take a pride in making good."

To this dwelling upon abstract principles Count Nesselrode was giving the inevitable answer that, "the subject should be carefully examined," and expressing from time to time "a feeling of soreness on the part of the imperial government at the mistrust manifested as to their intentions."

Thus, through the management of the noble lord, in 1853 things arrived at the point where the navigation of the Danube was declared impossible, and corn rotting at the mouth of the Sulina, while famine threatened to invade England, France, and the South of Europe. Thus Russia was not only adding, as *The Times* says, "to her other important possessions, that of an iron

---

[a] There can be no dispute with him who denies principles. This phrase is omitted in the *New-York Daily Tribune.—Ed.*

[b] The *New-York Daily Tribune* has: "to English men-of-war".—*Ed.*

gate between the Danube and the Euxine,"[a] she possessed herself of the key to the Danube, of a bread-screw, which she can put on, whenever the policy of Western Europe becomes obnoxious to punishment.[b]

EIGHTH ARTICLE

[*The People's Paper*, No. 86, December 24, 1853]

The petitions presented to the House of Commons, on April 20th, 1836, and the resolution moved by Mr. Patrick M'Stewart in reference to them, did not only refer to the Danube, but to Circassia too, the rumour having spread through the commercial world that the Russian government, on the plea of blockading the coast of Circassia, pretended to exclude English ships from landing goods and merchandise in certain ports of the Eastern littoral of the Black Sea. On that occasion Lord Palmerston solemnly declared:

"If parliament will place their confidence in us—if they will leave it to us to manage the foreign relations of the country [...] we shall be able to protect the interests, and to uphold the honour of the country, without being obliged to have recourse to war."—(House of Commons, April 20th, 1836.)

Some months afterwards, on October 29th, 1836, the *Vixen*, a trading vessel belonging to Mr. George Bell, and laden with a cargo of salt, set out from London on a direct voyage for Circassia. On November 25th, she was seized in the Circassian Bay of Soudjouk-Kale by a Russian man-of-war, for "having been employed on a blockaded coast." (Letter of the Russian Admiral Lazareff to the English Captain, Mr. Childs, December 24th, 1836.[c]) The vessel, her cargo, and her crew were sent to the port

---

[a] This statement from *The Times*, No. 16062, March 28, 1836, is quoted according to D. Urquhart, *Progress of Russia in the West, North, and South*.—*Ed.*

[b] In the *New-York Daily Tribune* the article ends as follows: "The mystery, however, of Lord Palmerston's transactions with Russia as to her schemes on the Danube was not revealed till during the course of the debates on Circassia. Then it was proved by Mr. Anstey on February 23, 1848, that 'the noble Viscount's first act on coming into office'" (as the Minister of Foreign Affairs) "'was to accept the treaty of Adrianople,'—the same treaty against which the Duke of Wellington and Lord Aberdeen had protested.

"How this was done and how Circassia was delivered by Lord Palmerston to Russia, as far as he had the power to deliver it, may perhaps, form the subject of another article."[289]—*Ed.*

[c] D. Urquhart, *Progress of Russia in the West, North, and South*, p. 320.—*Ed.*

of Sebastopol, where the condemnatory decision of the Russians was received on January 27th, 1837. This time, however, no mention was made of a "blockade," but the *Vixen* was simply declared a lawful prize, because "it was guilty of smuggling;" the importation of salt being prohibited, and the Bay of Soudjouk-Kale, a Russian port, not provided with a custom-house. The condemnation was executed in an exquisitely ignominious and insulting manner. The Russians, who effected the seizure, were publicly rewarded with decorations. The British flag was hoisted, then hauled down, and the Russian flag hoisted in its stead. The master and crew, put as captives on board the *Ajax*—the captor—were despatched from Sebastopol to Odessa, and from Odessa to Constantinople, whence they were allowed to return to England. As to the vessel itself, a German traveller, who visited Sebastopol a few years after this event, wrote, in a letter addressed to the *Augsburg Gazette*:

"After all the Russian ships-of-the-line which I visited, no vessel excited my curiosity more than the *Soudjouk-Kale*, formerly the *Vixen*, [...] under Russian colours, she has now quite changed her appearance. [...] This little vessel is now the best sailer in the Russian fleet, and is generally employed as transport between Sebastopol and the coast of Circassia."[a]

The capture of the *Vixen* certainly afforded Lord Palmerston a great occasion for fulfilling his promise "to protect the interests, and to uphold the honour of the country." Besides the honour of the British flag and the interests of British commerce there was another question at stake—*the independence of Circassia*. At first Russia justified the seizure of the *Vixen* on the plea of an infraction of the blockade proclaimed by her; but the ship was condemned on the opposite plea of a contravention against her custom-house regulations. By proclaiming a blockade, Russia declared Circassia a hostile foreign country, and the question was whether the British government had ever recognised that blockade? By the establishment of custom-house regulations, Circassia was, on the contrary, treated as a Russian dependency, and the question was whether the British government had ever recognised the Russian claims to Circassia?

Before proceeding, let it be remembered that Russia was at that epoch yet far from having completed her fortifications of Sebastopol.

Any Russian claim to the possession of Circassia could only be derived from the treaty of Adrianople, as explained in a previous

---

[a] Quoted from *The Portfolio*, 1844, Vol. II, No. VIII, p. 533.—*Ed.*

article. But the treaty of July 6th, 1827, bound Russia to not attempting any territorial aggrandisement, nor securing any exclusive commercial advantage from her war with Turkey. Any extension, therefore, of the Russian frontier, attendant on the treaty of Adrianople, openly infringed the treaty of 1827, and was, as shown by the protest of Wellington and Aberdeen, not to be recognised on the part of Great Britain. Russia, then, had no right to receive Circassia from Turkey. On the other hand, Turkey could not cede to Russia what she never possessed, and Circassia had always remained so independent of the Porte that, at the time when a Turkish Pasha yet resided at Anapa, Russia herself had concluded several conventions with the Circassian chieftains as to the coast-trade, the Turkish trade being exclusively and legally restricted to the port of Anapa. Circassia being an independent country, the municipal, sanitary, or customs' regulations with which the Muscovite might think fit to provide her were as binding as his regulations for the port of Tampico.

On the other hand, if Circassia was a foreign country hostile to Russia, the latter had only a right to blockade, if that blockade was no paper blockade—if Russia had the naval squadron present to enforce it, and really domineered the coast. Now, on a coast extending 200 miles, Russia possessed but three isolated forts, all the rest of Circassia remaining in the hands of the Circassian tribes. There existed no Russian fort in the bay of Soudjouk-Kale. There was in fact no blockade, because no maritime force was employed. There was the offer of the distinct testimony of the crew of two British vessels who had visited the bay—the one in September, 1834—the other, that of the *Vixen* itself—confirmed subsequently by the public statements of two British travellers who visited the harbour in the years 1837 and 1838, that there was no Russian occupation whatever of the coast.—(*Portfolio,*VIII, March l, 1844.)

When the *Vixen* entered the harbour of Soudjouk-Kale,

> "there were no Russian ships of war in sight nor in the offing.... A Russian vessel of war came into the harbour 36 hours after the *Vixen* had cast anchor, and at the moment when the owner and some of the officers were on shore [...] in fixing the dues demanded by the Circassian authorities, and payable on the value of the goods.... The man-of-war came not coastwise, but from the open sea."—(Speech of Mr. Anstey, H. of C., Feb. 23, 1848.)

But need we give further proofs than the St. Petersburg Cabinet itself seizing the *Vixen en pretext* of blockade, and confiscating it *en pretext* of custom-house regulations?

The Circassians thus appeared the more favoured by accident, as the question of their independence coincided with the question of the free navigation of the Black Sea—the protection of British commerce, and an insolent act of piracy committed by Russia on a British merchant ship. Their chance of obtaining protection from the mistress of the seas seemed less doubtful as

"the Circassian declaration of independence had a short time ago been published after mature deliberation and several weeks' correspondence with different branches of the government, in a periodical" (*The Portfolio*) "connected with the foreign department, and as Circassia was marked out as an independent country in a map revised by Lord Palmerston himself."—(Speech of Lord Stanley, H. of C., June 21, 1838.)

Will it then be believed that the noble and chivalrous Viscount knew how to handle the case so masterly, that the very act of piracy committed by Russia against British property afforded him the long sought-for occasion of formally recognising the treaty of Adrianople, and the extinction of Circassian independence?

On March 17, 1837, Mr. Roebuck moved, with reference to the confiscation of the *Vixen*, for

"a copy of all correspondence between the government of this country and the governments of Russia and Turkey [...] relating to the treaty of Adrianople, as well as [...] all transactions or negotiations connected with the ports and territories on the shores of the Black Sea by Russia since the Treaty of Adrianople."

Mr. Roebuck, from fear of being suspected of humanitarian tendencies, and of defending Circassia on the ground of abstract principles, plainly declared:

"Russia may endeavour to obtain possession of all the world, and I regard her efforts with indifference; but the moment she interferes with our commerce, I call upon the government of this country" (which country exists in appearance somewhere beyond the limits of all the world), "to punish the aggression."

Accordingly he wanted to know "if the British government had acknowledged the treaty of Adrianople?"

The noble lord, although pressed very hard, had ingenuity enough to make a long speech, and

"to sit down without telling the house [...] who was in actual possession of the Circassian coast at the present moment [...] whether it really belonged to Russia, and whether it was by right of a violation of fiscal regulations, or in consequence of an existing blockade, that the *Vixen* had been seized, and whether or not he recognised the Treaty of Adrianople." (Speech of Mr. Hume, H. of C., March 17th, 1837.)

Mr. Roebuck stated that, before allowing the *Vixen* to proceed to Circassia, Mr. Bell had applied to the noble lord, in order to ascertain whether there was any impropriety or danger to be apprehended of a vessel landing goods in any part of Circassia, and that the Foreign Office answered in the negative. Thus, Lord Palmerston found himself obliged to read to the house the correspondence exchanged between himself and Mr. Bell. Reading these letters, one would fancy he was reading a Spanish comedy of the cloak and the sword, rather than an official correspondence between a minister and a merchant. When he heard the noble lord read the letters respecting the seizure of the *Vixen*, Daniel O'Connell exclaimed, "He could not help calling to his mind the expression of Talleyrand that language had been invented to conceal thoughts."

For instance, Mr. Bell asks, "whether there were any restrictions on [...] trade recognised by His Majesty's government—as, if not, he intended to send thither a vessel with a cargo of salt?" "You ask me," answers Lord Palmerston, "whether it would be for your advantage to engage in a speculation in salt," and informs him "that it is for commercial firms to judge for themselves whether they shall enter or decline a speculation." "By no means," replies Mr. Bell. "All I want to know is, whether or not His Majesty's government recognise the Russian blockade on [...] the Black Sea to the South of the river Kuban?" "You must look at the London *Gazette*," retorts the noble lord, "in which all the notifications, such as those alluded to by you, are made." The London *Gazette* was, indeed, the quarter to which a British merchant had to refer for such information, instead of the ukases of the Emperor of Russia. Mr. Bell, finding no indication whatever in the *Gazette* of the acknowledgement of the blockade or of other restrictions, despatched his vessel. The result was, that some time after he was himself placed in the *Gazette*.

> "I referred Mr. Bell," says Lord Palmerston, "to the *Gazette*, where he would find that no blockade had been [...] communicated or declared to this country by the Russian government—consequently, none was acknowledged."

By referring Mr. Bell to the *Gazette*, Lord Palmerston did not only deny the acknowledgement on the part of Great Britain of the Russian blockade, but simultaneously affirmed that, in his opinion, the coast of Circassia formed *no part* of the Russian territory, because blockades of their own territories by foreign states—as for instance against revolted subjects—are *not* to be notified in the *Gazette*. Circassia forming no part of the Russian territory could not, of course, be included in Russian custom-house regulations. Thus, according to his own statement, Lord Palmerston denied, in his letters to Mr. Bell, Russia's right to blockade the Circassian coast, or to subject it to commercial restrictions. It is true that, through his speech, transpired the desire to induce the house to infer that Russia had possession of Circassia. But, on the other hand, he stated plainly,

"As far as the extension of the Russian frontier is concerned [...] on the South of the Caucasus and the shores of the Black Sea, [...] it is certainly not consistent with the solemn declaration made by Russia in the face of Europe, previous to the commencement of the Turkish war."

When he sat down, pledging himself ever "to protect the interests and to uphold the honour of the country," he seemed to labour beneath the accumulated miseries of his past policy, rather than hatching treacherous designs for the future. On that day he met with the following cruel apostrophe:

"The want of vigour and alacrity to defend the honour of the country which the noble lord had displayed was most culpable; [...] the conduct of no former minister had ever been so vacillating, so hesitating, so uncertain, so cowardly, when insult had been offered to British subjects. [...] How much longer [...] did the noble lord propose to allow Russia thus to insult Great Britain, and thus to injure British commerce? [...] The noble lord was *degrading* England by holding her out in the character of a bully—haughty and tyrannical to the weak, humble and abject to the strong."

Who was it that thus mercilessly branded the truly English Minister? Nobody else than Lord Dudley Stuart.

On November 25th, 1836, the *Vixen* was confiscated. The stormy debates of the House of Commons, just quoted, took place on March 17th, 1837. It was not till April 19th, 1837, that the noble lord requested the Russian government

"to state the reasons on account of which it had thought itself warranted to seize, [...] in time of peace, a merchant vessel belonging to British subjects."

On May 17th, 1837, the noble lord received the following despatch from the Earl of Durham, the British Ambassador at St. Petersburg[a]:

"My Lord,—With respect to the military *de facto* occupation of Soudjouk-Kale, I have to state to your lordship that there is a fortress in the bay which bears the

[a] Passages from Palmerston's correspondence with Durham, the English Ambassador to Russia, are quoted from "Letters from the Black Sea and the Caucasus.—The *Vixen* again", *The Portfolio*, 1844, Vol. II, No. VIII.—*Ed.*

name of the Empress (Alexandrinski), and that it has always been occupied by a Russian garrison.

"I have &c.

"*Durham.*"

It need hardly be remarked that the fort Alexandrinski had not even the reality of the pasteboard towns exhibited by Potemkin, before the Empress Catherine II, on her visit to the Crimea.[290] Five days after the receipt of this despatch, Lord Palmerston returns the following answer to St. Petersburg:

"His Majesty's government, considering in the first place that Soudjouk-Kale which was acknowledged by Russia in the Treaty of 1783 as a Turkish possession, now belongs to Russia, as stated by Lord Nesselrode, by virtue of the Treaty of Adrianople, [...] see no sufficient reason to question the right of Russia to seize and confiscate the *Vixen.*"[a]

There are some very curious circumstances connected with the negotiation. Lord Palmerston requires six months of premeditation for opening, and hardly one to close it. His last despatch, of May 23d, 1837, suddenly and abruptly cuts off any further transactions. It quotes the date before the Treaty of Kutshuk-Kainardji, not after the Gregorian, but after the Greek chronology. Besides, "between April 19th, and May 23d," as Sir Robert Peel said,

"a remarkable change from official declaration to satisfaction, occurred [...] apparently induced by the *assurance* received from Count Nesselrode, that Turkey had ceded the coast in question to Russia by the Treaty of Adrianople. [...] Why did he not protest against this ukase?" (H. of C., June 21st, 1838.)

Why all this? The reason is very simple. King William IV had secretly instigated Mr. Bell to despatch the *Vixen* to the coast of Circassia. When the noble lord delayed negotiation, the King was still in full health. When he suddenly closed the negotiations, William IV was in the agonies of death, and Lord Palmerston disposed as absolutely of the Foreign Office, as if he was himself the Autocrat of Great Britain. Was it not a master-stroke on the part of his jocose lordship to formally acknowledge by one dash of the pen the Treaty of Adrianople, Russia's possession of Circassia, and the confiscation of the *Vixen*, in the name of the dying king, who had despatched that saucy *Vixen*, with the express view to mortify the Czar,[b] to disregard the Treaty of Adrianople, and to affirm the independence of Circassia?

---

[a] Quoted from D. Urquhart, *Progress of Russia in the West, North, and South*, p. 320.—*Ed.*

[b] Nicholas I.—*Ed.*

Mr. Bell, as we stated, went into the *Cazette*, and Mr. Urquhart, then the first secretary of the Embassy at Constantinople, was recalled, because of "having persuaded Mr. Bell to carry his *Vixen* expedition into execution."

As long as King William IV was alive, Lord Palmerston dared not openly countermand the *Vixen* expedition, as is proved by the Circassian declaration of independence, published in *The Portfolio*, by the Circassian map—revised by his lordship—by his uncertain correspondence with Mr. Bell, by his vague declarations in the house, by the supercargo of the *Vixen*, Mr. Bell's brother receiving, when setting out, despatches from the Foreign Office, for the Embassy at Constantinople, and direct encouragement from Lord Ponsonby, the British Ambassador to the Sublime Porte.

In the earlier times of Queen Victoria, the Whig ascendancy seemed to be safer than ever, and accordingly the language of the chivalrous viscount suddenly changed. From deference and cajolery, it became at once haughty and contemptuous. Interrogated by Mr. T. Attwood, on December 14, 1837, with regard to the *Vixen* and Circassia—

"As to the *Vixen*, Russia had given such explanations of her conduct as ought to satisfy the government of this country. That ship was not taken during a blockade. It was captured because those who had the management of it contravened the municipal and customs' regulations of Russia."

As to Mr. Attwood's apprehension of Russian encroachment—

"I say that Russia gives to the world quite as much security for the preservation of peace as England." (Speech of Lord Palmerston, H. of C., Dec. 14, 1837.)

At the close of the session the noble lord laid before the house the correspondence with the Russian government, the two most important parts of which we have already quoted.

In 1838 party aspects had again changed, and the Tories recovered an influence. On June 21st they gave Lord Palmerston a round charge, Sir Stratford Canning, the present Ambassador at Constantinople, moving for a Select Committee to inquire into the allegations made by Mr. George Bell against the noble lord, and into his claims of indemnification. At first his lordship was highly astonished that Sir Stratford's motion should be of "so trifling a character."

"You," exclaimed Sir Robert Peel, "are the first English minister who dares to call trifles the protection of the British property and commerce."

"No individual merchant," said Lord Palmerston, "was entitled to ask Her Majesty's government to give an opinion on questions of that sort, as the right of

Russia to the sovereignty of Circassia, [...] or to establish those customs and sanitary regulations she was enforcing by the power of her arms."

"If that be not your duty, what is the use of the Foreign Office at all?" asked Mr. Peel.

"It is said," resumed the noble lord, "that Mr. Bell, this innocent Mr. Bell, was led into a trap by me by the answers I gave him. [...] The trap, if there was one, was laid not for Mr. Bell, but by Mr. Bell," namely, by the questions he put to innocent Lord Palmerston.

In the course of these debates (June 21st, 1838), out came at length the great secret. Had he been willing to resist in 1836 the claims of Russia, the noble lord had been unable to do so from the very simple reason that, already in 1831 his first act on coming into office was to acknowledge the Russian usurpation of the Caucasus, and thus, in a surreptitious way, the treaty of Adrianople. Lord Stanley (now Lord Derby) stated that, on August 8th, 1831, the Russian Cabinet informed its representative at Constantinople of its intention

"to subject to sanitary regulations the communications which freely exist between the inhabitants of the Caucasus and the neighbouring Turkish provinces," and that he was "to communicate the above-mentioned regulations to the foreign missions at Constantinople as well as to the Ottoman Government."

By allowing Russia the establishment of so-called sanitary and custom-house regulations on the coast of Circassia, although existing nowhere except in the above letter, Russian claims to the Caucasus were acknowledged, and consequently the treaty of Adrianople, on which they were grounded.

"Those instructions," said Lord Stanley, "had been communicated in the most formal manner to Mr. Mandeville" (Secretary to the Embassy), "at Constantinople, expressly for the information of the British merchants, and transmitted to the noble Lord Palmerston."

Neither did he, nor dared he, "according to the practice of former governments, communicate to the committee at Lloyd's[291] the fact of such a notification having been received." The noble lord made himself guilty of "a six years' concealment," exclaimed Sir Robert Peel.

On that day his jocose lordship escaped from condemnation by a majority of sixteen; 184 votes being against, and 200 for him. Those sixteen votes will neither out-voice history nor silence the mountaineers,[292] the clashing of whose arms proves to the world that the Caucasus does not "now belong to Russia, as stated by Count Nesselrode," and as echoed by Lord Palmerston!

Karl Marx

THE WAR QUESTION.—FINANCIAL MATTERS.—STRIKES[293]

London, Friday, Oct. 7, 1853

On Friday last, *The Morning Chronicle*, in its fourth edition, communicated a telegraphic despatch, according to which the Sultan[a] had declared war against Russia. The Paris *Patrie* of yesterday evening announces, in a semi-official note, that the intelligence received from the East, does not confirm the statement of *The Morning Chronicle*. According to another Ministerial paper, the *Constitutionnel*, it was on the reiterated representations of Mr. de Bruck, the Austrian Internuncio, that the Divan assembled on the 25th, with the view to deliberate on the Vienna note, when it declared it would abide by the last note of Reshid Pasha.[294] A Grand Council was convoked on the following day. This Council consisting of 120 of the principal Ministers, Councillors, Pashas and religious dignitaries, resolved that

> "it would be contrary to the dignity, and subversive of the sovereign authority of the Sultan to sign the Vienna note without the modifications suggested by the Divan, and that, inasmuch as the Czar[b] had declared those modifications to be totally inadmissible, and refused to abandon his demand for an engagement destructive of the independence of the Ottoman Empire, it only remained for the Council to advise the Sultan to proceed at once to adopt the measures necessary for the preservation of his Empire, and to free his dominions from the presence of the invader."[c]

As to the *formal* declaration of war, it has not yet been confirmed by any authentic dispatch. This time, at least, the Porte

---

[a] Abdul Mejid.—*Ed.*
[b] Nicholas I.—*Ed.*
[c] Quoted according to the article published in *The Morning Post*, October 5, 1853 and reprinted in *Le Constitutionnel*, No. 279, October 6, 1853.—*Ed.*

has caught the Western diplomats. The English and French Governments, not daring to call their fleets home, unable to hold any longer their ridiculous position at Besika Bay, unwilling to pass the straits in open defiance to the Czar, wanted the Porte to send for ships from Besika Bay on the pretext that danger to the Christians at Constantinople was to be apprehended during the *fêtes* of the Bairam. The Porte refused, observing that there was no danger; that if there was, it would protect the Christians without foreign aid, and that it did not wish to summon the ships until after the *fêtes*. But the vanguard of the united fleets had hardly crossed the straits, when the Porte, having now put its vacillating and treacherous allies into a fix, declared for war. As to the war itself, it commenced three months ago, when the Russian forces crossed the Pruth. The first campaign was even brought to a close when the Russian legions reached the banks of the Danube. The only change that can now take place will be that the war will cease to be a one-sided one.

Not only the Bey of Tunis,[a] but the Shah of Persia,[b] notwithstanding the intrigues of Russia, has placed at the disposal of the Sultan a corps of 60,000 of his best troops. The Turkish army, then, may truly be said to be a mustering of all the available forces of Mohammedanism in Europe, Africa, and Western Asia. The hosts of the two religions which have long struggled for supremacy in the East, the Russo-Greek and the Mohammedan are now fronting each other, the one summoned by the arbitrary will of a single man—the other by the fatal force of circumstances, according to their mutual creeds, as the Russo-Greek Church rejects the dogma of predestination, while Mohammedanism centers upon fatalism.

To-day two meetings are to be held, the one in Downing-st.—the other at the London Tavern; the one by the Ministers—the other against them; the one in favor of the Czar—the other in favor of the Sultan.

From the leaders of *The Times* and *Morning Chronicle*, we might infer, if there could exist any doubt about the intention of the Coalition, that it will try to the utmost to prevent war, to resume negotiations, to kill time, to paralyze the Sultan's army, and to support the Czar in the Principalities.

"The Czar has declared for peace," *The Times* is happy to

---

[a] Ahmed.—*Ed.*
[b] Nasr-ed-Din.—*Ed.*

state,[a] upon undoubted authority. The Czar has expressed "pacific sentiments at Olmütz[295] *by his own lips.*" He will not accept the modifications the Porte has proposed; he will abide by the original Vienna note, but he will allow the Vienna conference to interpret the note in a *preternatural sense,* contradictory to his own Nesselrode's interpretation. He will allow them to occupy themselves with conferences, provided they allow him, meanwhile, to occupy the Principalities.

The Times, in its peace paroxysm, compares the two Emperors of Russia and Austria to a couple of savage chiefs in the interior of Africa, in order to arrive at the conclusion:

"After all, what does the world care for the Emperor of Russia, *that it should go to war out of deference to his political mistakes?*"

The banks of Turin, Paris, Berlin and Warsaw have raised their rate of discount. In the bank returns of last week, the bullion reserve of the Bank of England was stated to have again decreased by £181,615, its total amount now being only £15,680,783. The active circulation of notes has decreased to the extent of nearly £500,000, while the discount of bills has increased by £400,000,[b] a coincidence which confirms the statement I made in my letter on the Peel Act, that the amount of bank notes in circulation does not rise and fall in proportion to the amount of banking business which is done.[c]

Mr. Dornbush concludes his monthly commercial circular as follows:

"Political events during the last week have greatly added to the agitation in the Corn trade, caused by the increasing reports of a deficient wheat crop, the spreading of the potato disease and the scarcity of ship-room. Town flour has advanced to 70 shillings per 280 pounds, new wheat to 80 shillings, with a rising discount approaching 5 per ct. A great excitement now pervades the corn trade—the probability of a war in the East, the prohibition of exporting grain from Egypt, the confirmed deficiency in the wheat crop in England, the spreading of the potato disease, the falling off in the foreign arrivals (especially from the South of Europe), the continued demand for France, Belgium and Holland—these were the principal exciting causes that again drove up prices of wheat variously from one shilling to six shillings per quarter in the leading provincial markets held last week.... Generally, immediately after harvest, the tendency of prices is and remains

[a] Here and below Marx quotes from the leaders in *The Times,* No. 21552, October 6, 1853.—*Ed.*

[b] Based on an account of September 24, 1853 in *The Economist,* No. 527, October 1, 1853.—*Ed.*

[c] See this volume, pp. 295-300.—*Ed.*

downward till Christmas. This year the movement has been the reverse.... Prices have been rising for some months past. At this moment there is no actual want of corn in any part of this quarter of the globe; many granaries, barns and rick-yards are full to repletion, and in some sea ports store-room is wanting. The late rise in price, therefore, has not been caused by a present, but by a prospective scarcity of corn, founded on the presumption of a deficiency in the crops, the effects of which are expected to be felt as the season advances. The coming winter is likely to prove one of great hardship and privation.... The prevailing opinion is still in favor of a further advance in prices; and while the bulk of speculators continue 'buying and storing,' the tendency is likely to remain upward, probably till next spring.... The presumable high range of prices during the next winter is likely to become, in the following spring, a great attraction to the importation of corn from distant regions, which, in ordinary seasons, cannot be reached on account of the distance and high cost of carriage; next spring an accumulation of arrivals from all accessible parts of the world is not improbable; and the very cause which now contributes to raise the price by the withdrawal of stocks from sale, will, with the setting in of the downward tide of prices, tend to depress the value of corn with a force commensurate to the then eagerness of holders to dispose of their stocks. Now the rule is to buy; then the watchword will be to sell. *Next year may prove as dangerous and disastrous as* 1847."

The general depression in the Manchester market continues. In proportion as the news from Australia and China, as well as that regarding the Eastern complication, are taking a more gloomy character, the minds of cotton-spinners, manufacturers and merchants, become more unsettled. The fall in prices may now be considered in ordinary qualities and Nos. of yarn to be from $^7/_8$ to 1d. per lb., from the highest point two months ago, which is very near twice as much as the fall in the corresponding quality of cotton, amounting to no more than $^1/_2$ to $^5/_8$ d. And even at the extreme reduction of 1d., people find it difficult to sell, and stocks, the bugbears of our sympathetic school of political economists, go on accumulating. Of course it must not be expected that this accumulation of stocks will increase very rapidly; at the present moment both merchants and manufacturers, on finding several markets overstocked, have yet the outlet of sending their goods, on consignment, to other markets, and this faculty they *very largely use just now.* But to throw the entire exportable produce of British industry, large enough to swamp, at regular intervals, the whole world, upon a few more or less confined markets, will necessarily excite the same state of plethora, and the revulsions consequent upon it, in those very markets which are as yet stated to be healthy. Thus it is that the slightly improved news from India, according to which there still is no chance of profitable exportation to that country, but merely a chance of diminishing loss upon fresh exports, has induced a rather considerable business to that country, partly on account of the regular India houses, partly on account of the Manchester spinners and manufacturers themselves, who, rather than submit to the loss incumbent upon sales in a declining market, prefer taking whatever slight chance of a better sale there may result from a speculative export to India. And here I may add, that it has been ever since 1847 a regular practice with the Manchester spinners and manufacturers to send out for their own account large shipments to India, etc., and to have the returns in Colonial produce, sold equally for their own account either in British North America or Continental harbors. These speculations do not, certainly, belong to the legitimate trading sphere of the manufacturer, who is necessarily not half as well informed of the state of the markets as the sea-port merchant, but they please the British cotton-spinner who, while directing such distant operations, believes that favorite illusion realized, in which he imagines himself the supreme director, the ruling mind, as it were, of the world's trade and commercial destinies. And if it were not for these speculations which hold fast for a year or eighteen months a considerable portion of the industrial surplus capital, there is no doubt that the extension of manufactures in England would for the last five years have gone on at a still more rapid rate.

In the dry goods market, domestics are the articles suffering under the greatest depression; stocks continue to accumulate although a great number of looms have been stopped. Yet it cannot be said that there is anything doing in other sorts of goods.

A similar stagnation prevails at Leeds and Bradford, at Leicester and Nottingham. At the latter place the hours of work have been reduced to ten and even eight in the lace trade; hosiery has been depressed ever since June last, when the production was at once reduced in Nottingham by one-third of its amount. The only trade that appears to go on in uninterrupted prosperity for the present, is the hardware trade of Birmingham and its vicinity.

At London, bankruptcy begins to spread among the small shop-keepers.

In my letter of August 12, I stated that the master spinners and manufacturers were getting up "An Association for the purpose of aiding the trade in regulating the excitement among the operatives in the Manchester District," that that Association was to consist of local Associations, with a Central Committee, and that it intended "resisting all demands made by *associated bodies* of mill-hands, fortifying the monopoly of capital by the monopoly of combination, and dictating terms as an Associated body."[a]

Now, is it not a very curious fact, that this scheme, of which I informed you about two months ago, has, to this very moment, never been alluded to by the London papers, although silently carried out in the meantime, and already doing its work at Preston, Bolton and Manchester? The London press, it appears, was anxious to withhold the fact from the eyes of the world, that the Factory Lords were systematically arraying their class against the class of Labor, and that the successive steps taken by them, instead of being the spontaneous result of circumstances, are the premeditated effects of a deep-laid conspiracy of an organized Anti-Labor League! This English Capitalist League of the nineteenth century is yet to find its historian, as the French Catholic League did in the authors of the *Satyre Menippée*, at the end of the sixteenth century.[296]

The work-people, in order to succeed in their demands, must naturally try to keep the one party *in* till the strike of the others has proved victorious. Where this plan is acted upon, the millowners combine to close *all* their mills, and, thus, to drive their hands to extremities. The Preston manufacturers,[297] as you know,[b] were to begin the game. Thirteen mills are already closed, and, at the expiration of another week, every mill is to be shut up, throwing out of work more than 24,000 men. The weavers have addressed a memorial to the masters, soliciting an interview, or offering to refer the matters in dispute to arbitration, but their request was rejected. As the Preston weavers are assisted by penny collections from the operatives of the surrounding districts, from Stalybridge, Oldham, Stockport, Bury, Withnell, Blackburn, Church-Parish, Acton, Irwell-Vale, Enfield, Burnley, Colne, Bacup, &c.; the men having discovered that the only means of resisting the undue influence of capital, was by union among themselves; the Preston factory-lords, on their part, have sent out secret emissaries to undermine the means of succor for the men on strike, and to induce the millowners of Burnley, Colne, Bacup, &c., to close their establishments, and to cause a general cessation of labor. In certain places, as at Enfield, the overlookers have been induced to inform their masters, who had taken a part in forwarding the movement, and accordingly a number of penny collectors have been discharged. While the Preston men are

[a] See this volume, p. 250.—*Ed.*
[b] See this volume, p. 316.—*Ed.*

exhorted by the work-people of the surrounding districts to remain firm and united, the Preston masters meet with an immense applause from the other manufacturers, being extolled as the true heroes of the age.

At Bury, matters are taking a similar turn as at Preston. At Bolton, the bedquilt makers having lots cast to decide which of them were to begin striking, the masters of the whole trade at once closed their mills.

Besides the simultaneous closing of mills, other means of combination are resorted to. At Keighley, for instance, the weavers of Mr. Lund struck for an advance of wages, the principal cause of their turn-out being his giving less than was received by the weavers of Mr. Anderton, at Bingley. A deputation of the weavers having asked for an interview with Mr. Lund, and proceeded to his lodgings, they had the door politely shut in their faces. But, a week afterward, Mr. Anderton's work-people were informed by notice that a reduction would be made in the wages of his weavers of 3d. per piece, and of his woolcombers of one farthing per pound, Mr. Lund and Mr. Anderton having, in the meantime, concluded an alliance offensive and defensive, with a view to fight the weavers of the one by pulling down the wages of the other. Thus, it is supposed, Mr. Lund's weavers will be driven to submission or Mr. Anderton's weavers to a turn-out, and the additional weight of another turn-out doing away with all chance of support, both sets will bend to a general reduction.

In other instances the masters try to enlist the shop-keepers against the working men. Thus Mr. Horsfall, the coal king of Derby main pit, when, in consequence of a reduction of wages, his hands struck, went to all the butchers, bakers and provision dealers of the neighborhood the colliers trade with, to prevail on them not to let his men have anything on credit.

In all localities where the Association for "regulating the excitement among the operatives" exists, the associated masters have pledged themselves to heavy fines, in case of any individual member violating the status of their League, or yielding to the demands of the "hands." At Manchester these fines amount to £5,000, at Preston to £3,000, at Bolton to £2,000, etc.

There is one feature which, above all, distinguishes the present conflict from past ones. At former periods—as in 1832, 1839, 1840, 1842—a *general holiday*, as it was called, viz.: a general and simultaneous stopping of labor throughout the whole kingdom, was a favorite idea with the operatives, and the great object they aimed at. This time, it is capital which threatens a general withdrawal. It is the masters who endeavor to bring about a general closing of mills. Do you not think that, if successful, it may prove a very dangerous experiment? Is it their intention to drive the English people to an insurrection of June,[298] in order to break their rising spirit, and to lay them prostrate for a series of years to come?

At all events, we cannot too closely watch the symptoms of the civil war preparing in England, especially as the London press intentionally shuts its eyes to great facts, while it diverts its readers with descriptions of such trifles as the banquet given by Mr. Titus Salt, one of the factory princes of Yorkshire, at the opening of his palace-mill, where not only the local aristocracy were regaled, but his hands, too. "Prosperity, health, and happiness to the working class," was the toast proposed by him, as the public is told by the Metropolitan press, but it is not told, that, some days afterwards, his moreen weavers received notice of *another reduction* in their wages from 2/3 to 2/1. "If this means either health or prosperity to the moreen weavers," writes one of his victims to *The People's Paper*, "I, for one, do not want it."[a]

You will perhaps have seen from *The Times* that a Mrs. MacDonnell, of Knoydart, Glengarry, has, in imitation of the Duchess of Sutherland, undertaken to clear her estates, in order to replace men by sheep.[b] *The People's Paper*, informed by a correspondent on the spot, gives the following graphic description of this Malthusian operation!

"This lady had a number of cottagers on her domains, many of whom were unable to pay their rents—some being considerably in arrears, *as we are told.* She, therefore, ordered them all off, and drove them to take refuge in the woods and caves, where they have since been lurking, or rather dying, while Mrs. MacDonnell's horses have been warmly bedded in secure and comfortable dwellings. She at the same time offered them a free passage to Canada, passage money being cheaper than poor rolls, and permission to sell 'their little stocks,' they having no stock whatever to sell, except the clothes they stand in, a broken table, or a rheumatic cat. Finally, she forgave them the arrears—she could not get. This is called '*noble generosity.*'"

---

[a] Quoted from the postscript to the article of Ernest Jones "The Highland Lady.—The Yorkshire Factory Prince" in *The People's Paper*, No. 74, October 1, 1853. The quotation below is from the same article.—*Ed.*

[b] See K. Marx, "Elections.—Financial Clouds.—The Duchess of Sutherland and Slavery" (present edition, Vol. 11, pp. 486-94).—*Ed.*

Such ejections appear to be again the order of the day, throughout the Highlands. Thus, at least, we are informed by Sir Charles Forbes, a Highland laird, writing to *The Times*,

> "that sheep-farms are now becoming so valuable, that it will pay our English sheep-farmers to hire sheep at any time, and to pay for the removal of all who stand in their way." [a]

Written on October 7, 1853

First published in the *New-York Daily Tribune*, No. 3904, October 21, 1853; reprinted in the *New-York Semi-Weekly Tribune*, No. 878, October 25; published simultaneously in abridged form in German in *Die Reform*, Nos. 64 and 65, October 24 and 25, 1853

Signed: *Karl Marx*

Reproduced from the *New-York Daily Tribune*

---

[a] *The Times*, No. 21544, September 27, 1853.—*Ed.*

Karl Marx

[THE TURKISH MANIFESTO.— FRANCE'S ECONOMIC POSITION][299]

London, Tuesday, October 18, 1853

The Turkish manifesto addressed on the 4th of October to the four Great Powers as a justification of the Sultan's[a] declaration of war against the Czar,[b] is, in every respect, superior to the huge mass of state papers, which Europe has been inundated with since May, 1853.

The Sultan, it states, has given no motive for quarrel. There remained not even a pretext for it, after the question of the Holy Shrines had been settled. On the part of Russia all treaties were infringed; on the part of Turkey all means of conciliation exhausted. According to the Powers themselves, the Sultan was not to subscribe to Prince Menchikoff's note. How, then, could he be expected to adopt the Vienna note, which, as a whole, was not different from that of Prince Menchikoff's? The explanatory epistle of the Vienna conference could not change the condition of affairs. The *clear* and *precise* paragraph of the treaty of Kainardji being misconstrued by Russia, what would not be the risk of "placing in her hands *vague* and *obscure* paragraphs affording her a solid pretext for her pretentions to a religious Protectorate?" Moreover, the modifications proposed by the Sultan have been fully justified by the subsequent explanations published by Nesselrode. The occupation of the Principalities had, at first sight, constituted a *casus belli*, and the Porte is now decided to proclaim it a *casus belli*. Prince Gorchakoff has, accordingly, been summoned to evacuate the Danubian provinces. If fifteen days after

[a] Abdul Mejid.—*Ed.*
[b] Nicholas I.—*Ed.*

the arrival of that notification he should answer in the negative, Omer Pasha is to commence hostilities, the Russian agents are to quit the Ottoman states, and the commercial relations of the two countries to be broken off. No embargo, however, will be laid upon Russian merchant vessels, but they will receive orders to leave the Turkish ports. The straits will remain open to the mercantile navy of friendly Powers.

Such is the substance of the Sultan's manifesto.

The Turkish ultimatum was intimated to Prince Gorchakoff on the 9th inst. Accordingly, the term for evacuating the Principalities expires on the 25th inst. The threat, however, of commencing hostilities cannot be understood in a literal sense, as Omer Pasha is certain not to abandon his strong positions, with a view to attacking the Russians.

In *The Morning Herald* of yesterday you will find confirmed my observations on the westward movement of the Russian army, and the secret understanding with Austria which this movement indicates.[a]

Russia, true to the old Asiatic system of cheating and petty tricks, now plays upon the credulity of the Western World by spreading the rumor that the Czar had "*just* sent a courier in *all* haste to Vienna to declare that he accepted freely and completely the whole of the conditions proposed by the mediating powers," when, unfortunately, "he became informed of the declaration of war on the side of the Porte." Then, of course, the God of the Russians retracted at once *all the concessions* he had ever made, and exclaimed that "nothing remained but war, and war to the knife," (guerre à l'outrance). Thus the Czar, it appears, has been forced into war by the Sultan.

Mr. de Bruck, the Austrian Internuncio, is said to have interrogated the Porte whether it intended to appeal to the political refugees in order to form a foreign legion. Reshid Pasha replied that, notwithstanding the propositions incessantly made to the Porte, he had not yet come to any decision; but that in the case of Turkey being abandoned by her allies, she would believe herself perfectly justified in making use of all means for her proper defense, and in employing the services of the political refugees disseminated throughout the several countries of Europe.

We read in the *Constitutionnel*[b]:

---

[a] See this volume, pp. 339-40.—*Ed.*
[b] Of October 15, 1853.—*Ed.*

"We have reason to believe that there has arrived at this moment at Paris and London an official demand for the succor of France and England on the part of the Sublime Porte."

You will read in the newspapers that the Emperor of Austria[a] has reduced his army by about 100,000 men. The truth is that this number have been dismissed on furlough, but are revocable at any moment. The financial pressure on the one side, and the hope of thus catching the money-lenders on the other, have induced the Vienna Cabinet to take this step.

The following extract from a London commercial circular, concerning the corn trade of France, will, I suppose, be read with interest:

"From a very extensive correspondence [...] taking every possible trouble to ascertain the real state of the case, we believe the crop of wheat in France to be on an average fully one-third short, varying according to locality, the greatest deficiency being in the south. It is true that journals under the influence of the Government have endeavored to persuade the public that such is not the case, but the very acts of the Government are a sufficient contradiction to such assertions. It first relaxed the Navigation Laws in favor of this country; it then repealed them altogether; next it anticipated the reduction of the duty, which the sliding-scale would of itself have secured, by fixing it at the minimum (without reference to the sections into which France is divided at various rates of duty) and opened the ports to foreign vessels free of tonnage dues. Since then it has opened all the rivers and canals free to corn vessels, and invited the railways to carry the food at reduced rates; it has opened Algeria free, and allowed it to ship to France by any tonnage; it has prohibited the export of potatoes and vegetables, and has not hesitated to interfere arbitrarily in many markets between buyers and sellers. Surely all this confirms a short crop, or are very unnecessary precautions. The trade in France has, however, been in a state of suspense for some time: not that the merchants throughout the kingdom have any doubt as to the result of the harvest, but the false step which the Government adopted with regard to fixing the price of bread has so perplexed them that they have been afraid to act, and it is notorious that as soon as the decree was issued, telegraphs were sent off in all directions, cancelling the orders given for corn; and it is impossible to estimate the ultimate consequence this measure may have upon prices. The average production of wheat in France is estimated at 80 millions of hectolitres (about 28 millions qrs.), the highest production during the last 25 years having been 97 millions in 1847, and the lowest 52 millions in 1830. The growth of wheat has increased very much of late years, much faster in proportion than the population; and the fact that stocks are completely exhausted at the present time, shows that the population have been much better fed and in a more prosperous condition than they used to be.

"The following table will show the progress of the population and production during the last 25 years:

[a] Francis Joseph I.—*Ed.*

	Population		Average production of Wheat in five years. Hectolitres
1831	32,569,223	from 1827 to 1831	57,821,336
1836	33,540,910	from 1832 to 1836	68,684,919
1841	34,240,178	from 1837 to 1841	71,512,258
1846	35,400,486	from 1842 to 1846	72,015,564
1851	35,781,821	from 1847 to 1851	86,121,123

"The increase of consumption, in proportion to the increase of population, will cause the effect of a bad harvest to be more severely felt, as there are no old stocks left to fall back upon, and of course no stocks of foreign grain in warehouse."[a]

The sinister intentions of the governing classes of England, with regard to Turkey, may be inferred from the sermons of Messrs. Bright and Cobden at Edinburgh, from the Gladstone speeches at Manchester, and from the hint thrown out by several papers, that, in the case of a Russo-Turkish war, Lord Aberdeen will be replaced by Lord Palmerston, the chivalrous antagonist of Russia.

Jail Inquiries are now a constant feature in the reports of the press. From what has been disclosed it appears that prison discipline in Birmingham consists of collars and mural torture; in Leicestershire of cranks,[300] and in Hampshire of the less artificial method of starvation. And "you call this a free country!"

I stated, in a former letter, that the so-called peace concluded with Burma, was but an armistice, and that the new acquisitions would prove an endless source of new troubles to the British conquerors.[b] The last overland mail informs us, indeed, that the war party in Burma is increasing in strength; that the new territories are literally overrun by large bands of robbers, instigated by the Government of Ava and requiring a considerable increase of military force at Prome, and that

"the British troops are sick and disgusted, healthy sites for barracks having not yet been discovered."[c]

The shameful neglect of all means of irrigation on the part of the Indo-British rulers, is again producing, in the district of Patna, its regular quota of cholera and famine, consequent on the long continued drouth.

---

[a] Quoted from *The Economist*, No. 529, October 15, 1853.—*Ed.*
[b] See this volume, pp. 201-02 and 282-83.—*Ed.*
[c] *The Times*, No. 21560, October 15, 1853.—*Ed.*

From a return just issued I abstract the following statistics of wrecks of British and foreign vessels on the coasts of the United Kingdom[a]:

Year	Total wrecks	Sunk by leaks or collisions	Strand-ed	Lives lost	Total sum of wrecks
1850	277	84	304	784	681
1851	358	—	348	750	701
1852	—	—	—	about 900	1,100
Sum total of wrecks during the 3 years					2,482
And of lives lost					2,434

Written on October 18, 1853

First published in the *New-York Daily Tribune,* No. 3912, October 31, 1853; reprinted in the *New-York Semi-Weekly Tribune,* No. 880, November 1, and the *New-York Weekly Tribune,* No. 634, November 5, 1853

Signed: *Karl Marx*

Reproduced from the *New-York Daily Tribune*

[a] "Wreck Chart of the British Isles" (a fourth report) issued by the Department of the Admiralty.— *Ed.*

Karl Marx

[ARREST OF DELESCLUZE.—DENMARK.— AUSTRIA.—*THE TIMES* ON THE PROSPECTS OF WAR AGAINST RUSSIA][301]

London, Friday, Oct. 21, 1853

Among the arrests recently made at Paris, the most important is that of M. Delescluze, private Secretary to M. Ledru-Rollin. He had been sent to Paris on a secret mission, and compromising papers, as is stated, have been seized upon him. One cannot understand M. Ledru-Rollin's trusting to a man who has never cleared himself from the suspicion of having betrayed in 1848 the Belgian Legion in the famous affair of Risquons-Tout.[302]

At Copenhagen the consummation of the coup d'état seems imminent, as the Ministry will not yield, and as the *Folketing* has pronounced against the abolition of the existing Constitution, unless the Government submit to them its own project of a Constitution for the whole Danish monarchy. The two separate projects for the Duchies of Schleswig and Holstein have appeared.[303] They are poor imitations of the constitutions of the old Prussian Provincial Diets, distributing the representation among the several "orders," making the right of election dependent on the holding of landed property, and limiting its exercise by the condition of "domicile" in the respective electoral districts. The most remarkable paragraphs in these constitutions are two, one of which deprives the courts of law of their ancient right of canceling administrative decrees, and the other excluding all individuals from the right of voting who compromised themselves in the revolutionary struggle from 1848-50, whether they have since been amnestied or not.

I told you in my last letter that the Austrian decree reducing the army was intended merely to entrap the money-lenders[a]; and now

---

[a] See this volume, p. 418.—*Ed.*

that all chance of obtaining a loan has vanished—now that the Government declare they never intended to contract any loan—now that they have entered upon a fresh emission of paper, we are informed that

"no arrangements are being made for carrying into execution the Imperial decree relative to the reduction of the army, and that, on the contrary, the generals who command in Lombardy, Hungary, and Croatia, have, all of them, demanded reenforcements on account of the state of the public mind in those countries."[a]

A Paris correspondent writes as follows to *The Morning Post* with reference to the proceedings of the Emperor of Russia during his late visits to Olmütz and Berlin:

"The Czar's[b] chief object was to make a new alliance between the Northern Powers.... To overcome the resistance of Prussia he used every argument—I may say every bribe; for he offered, in the event of his advancing into and holding Turkish territory, to yield the occupation of Warsaw and the military dominion of Poland to Prussia."[c]

As to the reported successes of the Russians over Shamyl, letters have arrived at Paris which show them to be nothing but inventions, no engagement of any description having taken place in the Caucasus since the month of May, when the victory at Mendoh was gained by Shamyl, and the Russians were driven back from their attempts upon Malka.

"We quite understand the popularity of a war with Russia on behalf of the Poles or the Hungarians, even if there was no ground of our interference except political sympathy.... We do not understand a war on behalf of the Turk."

Thus wrote *The Times* on Oct. 12. A week later we are told by the same paper:

"The first collision between British and Russian armies would be a signal of revolution all over the Continent, and we think it by no means unlikely, nor, indeed, altogether objectionable, that such a consideration may have occasionally passed through the minds of our aristocratic, plutocratic, [...] despotic, and anything but democratic rulers.... We are deliberately to go to war with Russia, in defense of the Turkish *nominal* sovereignty over certain really independent provinces, because by so doing we shall provoke a rebellion in the Austrian Empire."[d]

---

[a] Judging by Marx's notebook, this is quoted from the letter from Vienna published in the *Frankfurter Journal* as reprinted in *The Morning Post*, October 21, 1853.—*Ed.*

[b] Nicholas I.—*Ed.*

[c] *The Morning Post*, October 19, 1853.—*Ed.*

[d] *The Times*, No. 21563, October 19, 1853.—*Ed.*

One day England is not to go to war with Russia, because by so doing it would defend the Turks, instead of the Poles and Hungarians; and the next day because any war in behalf of Turkey would be simultaneously a war in behalf of the Poles and the Hungarians.

The Vienna *Presse* states that Abd-el-Kader has been asked by the Sultan to accept a military command in the case of a war with Russia. The negotiations were managed by the Sheikh-ul-Islam,[a] and the Emir declared his willingness to enter the service of Turkey on the condition that the advice of Bonaparte was previously asked. The command destined for him was that of the Asiatic army.

Written on October 21, 1853

First published in the *New-York Daily Tribune*, No. 3917, November 5, 1853; reprinted in the *New-York Semi-Weekly Tribune*, No. 882, November 8, 1853

Signed: *Karl Marx*

Reproduced from the *New-York Daily Tribune*

[a] Arif Hikmet Bey.—*Ed.*

Frederick Engels

MOVEMENTS OF THE ARMIES IN TURKEY

Several important military movements have recently taken place in the seat of war in Turkey, which more clearly define the positions and plans of the respective parties. The Russians—to whom we first advert because they are the attacking party, and as such must be regarded as taking the initiative—have continued to extend their line of operations toward the West. Brigade after brigade has been sent in the direction of Widin, on the upper Danube; and now the front of the Russian army may be said to extend from Kalafat, opposite Widin, to Orasch, opposite Orsova, in a direction which equally menaces the road to Constantinople, and that to Servia and Macedonia. The first movement toward Kalafat was sufficient to establish the certainty of a Russian diversion toward the centers of the Slavonic and Greek population of Turkey. It made it probable, at the same time, that the plan of the campaign would be defensive action and mere demonstrations on the direct road to Constantinople, with energetic offensive action on the road to Sofia, in Servia and Macedonia. However, when these movements were made, the Turks had not declared war. This event has since taken place, and appears to have irritated the Czar[a] to such a degree that he is likely to impart a far more energetic impulse to his troops than was previously to be expected. Not only is Prince Paskiewich called to the command of the Russian forces, but he is also said to bring with him 40,000 soldiers from the army in Poland, who next to the guards and grenadiers, are considered the best troops in the Russian pay. Such reenforcements would establish a superiority for the Russian

[a] Nicholas I.—*Ed.*

arms which might justify offensive action, both on the Upper and Lower Danube, while at the same time they might be considered as a counterpoise against any French and British forces, that, according to rumor, are likely to be sent to the support of Turkey. At all events, these Russian reenforcements cannot arrive on the Danube in time for operations this season. From Warsaw to Bucharest, by way of Dubno, Chotin and Jassy, the distance is eight hundred miles across a country in which an army cannot move more than eight or ten miles a day. It will then be three months or till the beginning of January before these fresh troops can take up their positions; and considering the season of the year, it is even probable that it will take them longer. These troops, then, must remain entirely in the background until the beginning of the spring campaign.

The Russian forces, now in the Principalities, have been estimated at from 130,000 to 150,000 men. Supposing they have lost by sickness and desertion from 20,000 to 30,000, they still maintain a numerical superiority over the Turks opposed to them. For if we know but little more of the actual strength of the Russians than what may be concluded from the number of divisions and brigades marched into Turkey, and from the effective numbers they ought to show on their rolls, the numbers of the Turkish forces on the Danube are very well known through the reports of British, French and Piedmontese officers sent there by their respective Governments. Now, all these reports agree in this fact, that even after the arrival of the Egyptian contingent, the Turkish active army, under Omer Pasha, did not number more than 110,000 combatants, of whom only 80,000 were regulars. Behind them, at Adrianople, an army of reserve was being formed which was to consist of 80,000 Redifs (old soldiers called in again), but of the state of this reserve we have no positive information. The fact, then, is this, that on the day when the first shot will be fired, Omer Pasha will command an army numerically inferior to that of his opponent, and that nothing but blunders on the part of his enemy, or capital generalship on his own part, will save him from defeat.

We have equally good information as to the position and the defensive preparations of the Turks. Three lines have been fortified: first, the Danube, to prevent its being passed by the enemy; second, that from Varna to Shumla; third, that a few leagues in the rear of the second, on the river Kamčiya, where is the fort which guards the passes of the Balkan. These fortifications are described by the foreign officers as formidable, and likely to frustrate any attempt of an enemy to carry them. Now, with all respect for the important art of field fortification, and for the judgment of the officers who give this report, we may be allowed to say that such opinions must be received with great caution. How many field-works considered to be impregnable have been carried, after a few rounds of grape-shot, on the first assault; and who does not know that the most celebrated field-works ever constructed, the lines of Torres Vedras,[304] were strong, not by their passive capacity of resistance but because Wellington had 100,000 men to defend them, while Masséna could only bring 30,000 men to the attack? Single, detached field-works, as in mountain passes for instance, have often done great service; but never in modern times has a superior army, commanded by an able General, been defeated in a general action on account of the passive resistance offered by field-works. And then the manner in which field-works are defended is almost everything; but half-disciplined troops, or soldiers without any discipline, are of little avail behind breastworks when a vigorous shower of grape is directed upon them.

But let us look at the three lines of defense the Turks have fortified. The first is that of the Danube. Now, to fortify the line of the Danube can only mean to erect such works as will prevent the Russians from crossing that river. The course of the Danube, from Orsova to the sea, is nearly 600 miles long; to fortify such a line effectually and to garrison the fortifications, would require six times as many men as the Turkish General can command, and if he had them he would commit the greatest blunder should he put them to such a use. We conclude then that this first line of fortifications must be confined to works between Rustchuk and Orsova, by which the passage of the river is molested, but not effectually prevented.

The second position from Shumla to Varna is exactly the same in which the Turks were routed in 1829, and in which they are again sure to be annihilated if they there accept a decisive battle. The position appears to possess striking advantages for defense, and to be susceptible of great additional strength by art; and the position on the Kamčiya, to the rear of Varna and Shumla, appears to be still stronger, and has the advantage of forcing the enemy to leave troops behind to blockade those fortresses. But both have this disadvantage, that they have a narrow pass in their rear as the only means of retreat, which outweighs, for an inferior army, all other advantages, and which would make it an egregious mistake to accept a battle unless the inferior army were as sure as the British were at Waterloo that at the decisive moment an allied army would fall upon the flanks of the attacking enemy.[305]

As to Omer Pasha we have no means of judging to what use he really intends turning these fortifications. We cannot doubt but he knows very well that his part in the war will be chiefly defensive; and he is, therefore, perfectly justified in strengthening his defensive position by all the means which the art of fortification places at his disposal. We do not know, whether he intends these fortifications to frighten the Russians from passing the Danube at those points by which Constantinople is most directly menaced or whether he proposes to accept a decisive battle in them. It is said that he has disposed his army in such a manner that at whatever point toward Shumla the Russians shall cross the river, he will be prepared to fall upon the head of their main column and beat it before support can arrive. In that case, the second line of fortifications would form a secure retreat if the operation should be frustrated. But the truth is that a great defensive battle on any of the three lines would be a mistake; for either the Russians will concentrate all their forces for the attack, and then Omer Pasha will stand but a poor chance; or they will divide themselves, and then he ought to leave his fortified lines in order to fall upon one of their columns. The best use to which he could turn these fortifications, and the only one consistent with the modern system of warfare, would be to use them as a provisional base for offensive operations against detached Russian columns, on their passing the Danube; to check the Russian advance by a more or less obstinate defense of each line; and to hold, by means of the third line, the most important passes of the Balkan as long as this can be done without a general engagement. At the same time it cannot be denied that any army, and particularly the Turkish army, would be exceedingly demoralized by the abandonment without a battle, of these fortifications; for if they cannot hold out behind ditches and bulwarks, how are they to beat the Russians in the open field? This is the way the private soldier always reasons, especially if only half-disciplined; and therefore, if the fortifications in question actually have the importance ascribed to them, we cannot but consider them more dangerous to the Turks themselves than to the Russians.

But the Russians have fortified themselves, too, in Wallachia? Certainly, and their case is different. They are the attacking party; their fortifications merely serve to cover retreat and check pursuit in case of disaster; and they have four lines of rivers, one behind the other, crossing their line of retreat, and forming as many lines of defense. These lines are, the Danube, the Arges, the Buzeu and the Sereth. Here is a fair case for precautionary fortifications; here are natural lines of defense which form, to a European army, no obstacle for retreat, while with a little artificial improvement they may become serious obstacles to pursuit; and above all, here is no intention of accepting a general battle with only one line of retreat in the rear. The Russian fortifications, as far as we can judge, belong decidedly to the European system of warfare, while the Asiatic spirit predominates in those of the Turks. This same unreflecting character is the ruling feature of the general position of the latter. They defend Constantinople by placing themselves across the nearest road which leads to it, while the Russians appear to direct their first attack, not upon that city, but upon the central parts of the peninsula, where Turkish dominion is most vulnerable, and where, after all, for a Russian army lies the shortest way to the capital.

There is, however, one thing which we must not forget. The Russian army is, and ever has been, slow and cautious in its movements. It will most probably not act during the winter season. A few skirmishes may take place in order to secure this or that island of the Danube to either party. But unless the Czar commands extraordinary activity—which command would most likely be frustrated by the passive pedantry of his generals—there is very little chance of decisive maneuvers before spring. The Danube might be passed but the Balkan cannot be traversed, and between the two, the position of the Russian army would be most dangerous.

In the meantime, the Turks have sent their fleet to Varna. Admiral Slade, an Englishman, who commands it, appears to be in high spirits. But that movement, too, is full of risk. The Russian fleet, indeed, appears inferior to the Turkish in everything but numbers; but as long as the Russians have two guns and two ships of the line to one of the Turks, the latter cannot venture an action out of the reach of their strand batteries. And in that case, the fleet would be safer and better placed in the Bosphorus, where it is not likely the Russians will blockade it. Once at Varna, the Turkish fleet is exposed to be deprived of all possibility of movement; while in the Bosphorus, it retains its freedom of action, and might be used for expeditions to Trebizond, to the Caucasian coast, or against detached positions of the Russian fleet.

In every respect, then, we are unwillingly compelled to believe the Russians to be superior to the Turks. Whether Omer Pasha, who is really an able soldier, will succeed by his personal qualities in changing the balance, remains to be seen. Old Paskiewich, however, although a slow, is an experienced general, and will not easily be caught.

Written about October 21, 1853

First published in the *New-York Daily Tribune*, No. 3919, November 8, 1853, as a leader; reprinted in the *New-York Weekly Tribune*, No. 635, November 12, 1853

Reproduced from the *New-York Daily Tribune*

Frederick Engels

THE HOLY WAR[306]

The war has at last opened on the Danube,—a war of religious fanaticism on both sides, of traditional ambition with the Russians, of life and death with the Turks. As was to have been expected, Omer Pasha has been the first to begin positive hostilities; it was in the line of his duty to make some demonstration toward the forcible expulsion of the invaders from the Ottoman territory; but it is by no means certain that he has thrown from thirty to fifty thousand men across the Danube, as is rumored from Vienna, and there is reason to fear that if he has done so he has committed a fatal blunder. On the shore he leaves, he has ample resources of defense and a good position; on the shore he seeks he has inferior power of attack and no retreat in case of disaster. The report of his crossing with such numbers must therefore be doubted till more positive advices.

While the struggle in Europe is commenced under disadvantageous circumstances for the Turks, the case is otherwise in Asia. There, the frontier territories of Russia and Turkey divide themselves, in a military point of view, into two quite distinct theaters of operation. It is the high ridge, or rather concatenation of ridges, connecting the Caucasus with the table-land of Central Armenia, and dividing the waters that run toward the Black Sea from those which the Araxes leads to the Caspian Sea, or the Euphrates to the Persian Gulf; it is this ridge which formerly parted Armenia from Pontus that now forms the partition of the two distinct districts where the war is to be waged. This range of abrupt and generally barren rocks, is traversed by very few roads—the two principal of which are those from Trebizond and Batum to Erzerum. Thus for all military purposes, the hills in question may be considered as nearly impassable, forcing both parties to have distinct corps on either side, operating more or less independently of each other.

The country on the shore of the Black Sea is intersected by a number of rivers and mountain torrents, which form as many military positions for defense. Both the Russians and the Turks have fortified posts on important points. In this generally broken country (the valley of the river Rioni is the only one which forms anything like a plain), a defensive war might be carried on with great success against a superior army (as very few positions are liable to be turned on the land side, on account of the mountains), were it not for the cooperation of the respective fleets. By advancing, and, in case of need, landing troops upon the flank of the enemy, while the army engages him in front, a fleet might turn all these strong positions, one by one, and neutralize, if not destroy, fortifications which, on neither side of the frontier, are very respectable. Thus the possession of the Black Sea coast belongs to him who is master of the Sea; or, in other words, unless the allied fleets cooperate actively with the Turks, it will in all likelihood belong to the Russians.

The country in the interior, on the inland side of the mountains, comprises the territory in which the Euphrates, the Araxes and the Kura (Cyrus) take their rise; the Turkish province of Armenia is on the one, the Russian province of Georgia on the other side of the frontier. This country, too, is extremely mountainous and generally impassable to armies. Erzerum on the part of the Turks, Tiflis on the part of the Russians, may be said to be the two immediate bases of operations, with the loss of which the possession of the whole neighboring country would be inevitably lost. Thus the storming of Erzerum by the Russians decided the Asiatic campaign of 1829.

But what is the immediate *basis* of operation for one party, will be the direct *object* of operations to the other. Thus the roads connecting Tiflis and Erzerum will be the lines of operations for both. There are three roads; one by the upper Kura and Akhalzikh, the other by the upper Araxes and Erivan, the third in the midst between these two, across the mountains by way of Kars. All these roads are guarded on either side by fortified towns and posts, and it would be difficult to say which would be for Turks or Russians the most eligible. Suffice it to say that the road by Akhalzikh is the one which would lead a Turkish army most directly upon the insurgent districts of the Caucasus, but that very advance of the Turks would be turned by a Russian corps advancing from Batum up the valley of the Chorokh by Olti upon Erzerum; the road from Batum joins that from Tiflis only about 15 miles from Erzerum, which would enable a Russian corps advancing in the direction alluded to, to cut off the communication of the Turks, and, if strong enough, to take possession even of Erzerum, the fortifications of which are of a merely Asiatic character and not capable of serious resistance.

The key to the theater of war in Asia, and on either side of the hills, then, is Batum, and considering this, as well as its commercial importance, we need not wonder at the efforts the Czar[a] has always been making to get hold of it. And Batum is the key of the theater of war, nay, of all Turkey in Asia, because it commands the only passable road from the coast to the interior—a road which turns all the Turkish positions in advance of Erzerum. And whichever of the two fleets in the Black Sea drives the other back into its harbors, that fleet commands Batum.

The Russians are perfectly aware of the importance of this post. They have sent, by land and by water, reinforcements to the Transcaucasian coast. A short time ago it might have been believed that the Turks, if weaker in Europe, enjoyed a decided superiority in Asia. Abdi Pasha, who commands the Asiatic army, was said to have collected 60,000 or 80,000, nay 120,000 men, and swarms of Bedouins, Kurds and other warlike irregulars were reported to flock daily to his standard. Arms and ammunitions were said to be in store for the Caucasian insurgents, and as soon as war was declared, an advance was to be made into the very heart of these centres of resistances to Russia. It may, however, be as well to observe that Abdi Pasha cannot possibly have more than about 30,000 regular troops, and that before the Caucasus is reached, with these, and with these alone, he will have to encounter the stubborn resistance of Russian battalions. His Bedouins and Kurdish horsemen may be capital for mountain warfare, for forcing the Russians to detach largely and to weaken their main body; they may do a great deal of damage to the Georgian and Colonist villages in the Russian territory, and even open some sort of an underhand communication with the Caucasian mountaineers. But unless Abdi Pasha's regulars are capable of blocking up the road from Batum to Erzerum, and can defeat whatever nucleus of an active army the Russians may be enabled to bring together, the success of the irregulars will be of a very ephemeral nature. The support of a regular army is

[a] Nicholas I.—*Ed.*

now-a-days necessary to the progress of all insurrectionary or irregular warfare against a powerful regular army. The position of the Turks on this frontier would be similar to that of Wellington in Spain, and it remains to be seen whether Abdi Pasha will know to husband his resources as well as the British general did, against an enemy decidedly his superior in regular warfare and the means of carrying it on. In 1829 the Russian forces in Asia, amounted, before Erzerum, to 18,000 men only, and considering the improvements that have since then taken place in the Turkish army (although that of Asia has least participated in them), we should say the Russians would have a fair chance of success if they could unite 30,000 men in a body before the same place now.

Whether they will be able to do so or not, who can decide at the present time, when there is even less of real facts known, and more idle rumors spread as to the Russian army in Asia than as to that in Europe? The Caucasian army is officially computed at 200,000 men, at its full complement; 21,000 Cossacks of the Black Sea have been marched toward the Turkish frontier; several divisions are said to have been embarked from Odessa for Redut Kale, on the South Caucasian coast. But everybody knows that the Caucasian army does not count half its official complement, that the reenforcement sent beyond the Caucasus cannot, from obvious causes, have the strength reported by Russian papers, and from the conflicting evidence we receive, we are absolutely at a loss to make anything like an estimate of the Russian forces on the Asiatic frontier. But that we may say, that in all probability the forces of both parties (an immediate general insurrection of the Caucasians left out of the question), the forces will be pretty nearly balanced, that the Turks may, perhaps, be a little stronger than the Russians, and therefore will be, on this theater of war, justly entitled to undertake *offensive* operations.

The chances for the Turks are, indeed, far more encouraging in Asia than in Europe. In Asia they have but one important post to guard, Batum; and an advance, be it from Batum, or from Erzerum toward the Caucasus, opens to them in case of success a direct communication with their allies, the mountaineers, and may at once cut off the communication, at least by land, of the Russian army south of the Caucasus with Russia; a result which may lead to the entire destruction of that army. On the other hand, if defeated, the Turks risk losing Batum, Trebizond and Erzerum; but even if that be the case, the Russians will then not be strong enough to advance any further. The advantages are far superior to the loss to be undergone in case of defeat; and it is therefore, for sound and satisfactory reasons, that the Turks appear to have decided upon offensive warfare in those regions.

Written about October 27, 1853

First published in the *New-York Daily Tribune*, No. 3925, November 15, 1853, as a leader; reprinted in the *New-York Weekly Tribune*, No. 636, November 19, 1853

Reproduced from the *New-York Daily Tribune*

Karl Marx

WAR.—STRIKES.—DEARTH[307]

London, Tuesday, Nov. 1, 1853

The news of the cannonade of Isakchea[308] had hardly reached London, when the intelligence was telegraphed from Vienna to London and Paris, that the Porte, at the request of the representatives of the four Powers, had issued orders for the adjournment of the hostilities, if they should not have already commenced, till the 1st November. Is the exchange of cannon-shots at Isakchea to be or not to be considered as a commencement of hostilities? That is the question now stirring the Stock Exchange and the press. In my opinion it is a very indifferent one, as in any event the *armistice* would have elapsed to-day.

It is rumored that the Turkish army had crossed the Danube at Widin and Matchin, viz.: at the north-eastern and north-western frontiers of Bulgaria. The accuracy of this dispatch appears very doubtful. According to the Paris *Presse* of to-day, it was resolved by a military council held in the Seraskirat[a] on the 15th or 16th Oct., that as soon as the refusal of Prince Gorchakoff to evacuate the Principalities would be officially known, the hostilities were to commence in Asia, on two different points: against the fortress of Poti, at the Black Sea, and on the frontier of Georgia. The same paper informs us, that Gen. Baraguay d'Hilliers, the newly appointed French Ambassador at Constantinople, has set out accompanied by a staff composed of officers of the *génie* and of the *artillerie.* Mr. Baraguay is known as a bad General and a good intriguer. I remind you of his exploits at the famous Club of the Rue de Poitiers.[309]

[a] War Ministry of the Ottoman Empire.—*Ed.*

While the first cannon bullets have been exchanged in the war of the Russians against Europe, the first blood has been spilt in the war now raging in the manufacturing districts, of capital against labor. On Friday night a riot took place at Wigan, arising out of the contest between the colliers and the coal kings; on Saturday the town was stated to be perfectly quiet, but to-day we are informed by electric telegraph that at the colliery of Lord Crawford or of the Earl Balcarres, an attack was made by the colliers; that the armed force was called out; that the soldiers fired, and that one of the workmen was killed.[310] As I am to receive private information from the spot, I adjourn my report on this event,[a] only warning your readers against the reports of *The Daily News* and *The Times*, the former of these papers being in the direct pay of the Manchester School, and the latter being, as *The Morning Herald* justly remarks, "the bitter, unforgiving, relentless enemy of the working classes."

In 1842, when the Manchester School, under the banner of free trade, enticed the industrial proletariat into insurrectionary movements, and, in the time of peril,[311] treacherously abandoned them, as Sir Robert Peel plainly told the Cobdens in the House of Commons—at that epoch their watchword was: *Cheap food and dear wages.* The Corn Laws having been abrogated and free trade, as they do understand it, realized, their battle-cry has been changed into: *Cheap wages and dear food.* With the adoption of the Manchester commercial system by Government, the millocracy had imposed upon themselves a problem impossible to be resolved under their régime: the securing of an uninterrupted continuance of brisk trade and commercial prosperity. For the hour of adversity, they had cut off any position to fall back upon. There was no more deluding the masses with Parliamentary reform, as in 1831; the legislative influence, conquered by that movement for the middle classes, having been exclusively employed against the working classes; and the latter having, in the meantime, got up a political movement of their own—Chartism. There is no more charging the aristocratic protectionists with all the anomalies of the industrial system and the deadly conflicts springing up from its very bowels, as free trade has worked for about eight years under wonderfully fortunate circumstances with a California and an Australia—two worlds of gold, extemporized, as it were, by the imaginative powers of the modern *demiurge.* Thus, one by one, step by step, the industrial bourgeoisie have removed, with their

---

[a] See this volume, pp. 446-47.—*Ed.*

own hands, all the carefully propagated delusions that could be conjured up at the hour of danger, in order to deturn the indignation of the working classes from their real antagonist, and to direct it against the antagonists of the millocracy, against the landed aristocracy. In 1853, there have waned away the false pretenses on the part of the masters and the silly illusions on the part of the men. The war between those two classes has become unmitigated, undisguised, openly avowed and plainly understood. "The question," exclaim the masters themselves in one of their recent manifestoes—"is no longer one of *wages* but one of *mastership*."[a] The Manchester liberals, then, have at last thrown off the lion's skin. What they pretend at—is mastership for capital and slavery for labor.

Lock-out vs. *Turn-out*, is the great lawsuit now pending in the industrial districts, and bayonets are likely to give judgment in the case. A whole industrial army, more than 70,000 working-men are disbanded and cast upon the streets. To the mills closed at Preston and Wigan there have been added those of the district of Bacup, which includes the townships of Bacup, Newchurch, Rawtenstall, Sharnford, and Stanford. At Burnley the mills stopped last Friday; at Padiham on Saturday; at Accrington the masters are contemplating a lock-out; at Bury, where about 1,000 men are already out of work, the masters have given notice to their hands of a "lock-out unless they discontinued their contributions to those out of work in their own town and at Preston;" and at Kindley, three large mills were closed on Saturday afternoon, and more than a thousand additional persons thrown out of employment.

While the hypocritical, phrase-mongering, squint-eyed set of Manchester humbugs spoke peace to the Czar[312] at Edinburgh, they acted war with their own countrymen at Manchester. While they preached *arbitration* between Russia and Europe, they were rejecting scornfully all appeals to arbitration from their own fellow-citizens. The workmen of Preston had carried in an open air meeting the resolution

> "that the delegates of the factory operatives recommend the Mayor to call a public meeting of the manufacturers and the operatives to agree to an amicable settlement of the dispute now pending."[b]

---

[a] Here and below Marx quotes from the article "As They've Made Their Bed Se They Must Lie", published in *The People's Paper*, No. 78, October 29, 1853.—*Ed.*

[b] *The People's Paper*, No. 78, October 29, 1853; *The Times*, No. 21568, October 25, 1853.—*Ed.*

But the masters do not want *arbitration.* What they pretend at is *dictation.* While, at the very moment of a European struggle, those Russian propagandists cry for reduction of the army, they are at the same time augmenting the army of civil war, the police force, in Lancashire and Yorkshire. To the workmen we can only say with *The People's Paper.*

"If they close all the mills of Lancashire do you send delegates to Yorkshire and enlist the support of the gallant men of the West Riding. If the mills of the West Riding are closed, appeal to Nottingham and Derby, to Birmingham and Leicester, to Bristol and Norwich, to Glasgow and Kidderminster, to Edinburgh and Ipswich. Further and further, wider and wider, extend your appeals and rally your class through every town and trade. If the employers choose to array all their order against you, do you array your entire class against them. If they will have the vast class struggle, *let them have it,* and we will abide the issue of that tremendous trial."

While, on the one hand, we have the struggle of masters and men, we have, on the other, the struggle of commerce with overstocked markets, and of human industry with the shortcomings of nature.

At a very early period of the Chinese revolution, I drew the attention of your readers to the disastrous influences it was likely to exercise on the social condition of Great Britain.[a]

"The Chinese insurrection," we are now told by *The Examiner,*[b] "is rampant in the tea districts, the result of which is that teas are *looking up* in the market of London, and calicos are *looking down* in the market of Shanghai." "At Shanghai," we read in the circular of Messrs. Bushby & Co., a Liverpool house, "the tea market has opened at prices about 40 to 50 per cent. above last season. Stocks were light, and supplies coming [...] slowly."[c]

The last advices from Canton state that the

"insurgents are [...] generally spreading themselves throughout the country *to the entire ruin of trade,* that manufactures, almost without exception, have given way in price; in some instances, the fall is very serious. Stocks are large and fast accumulating, and we fear the prospect of amendment is rather remote. At Amoy the trade in imports, beyond a few chests of opium, appears at an end for the present."

The following is described as the state of the markets at Shanghai:

---

[a] See this volume, pp. 93-100.—*Ed.*

[b] Of October 29, 1853.—*Ed.*

[c] Here and below quotations from accounts of various firms are given according to *The Economist,* No. 531, October 29, 1853.—*Ed.*

"Both black teas and raw silks have been offering freely, but the conditions imposed by holders have been such as greatly to restrict operations; *no desire appeared to take manufactures*, and transactions have been chiefly effected by means of opium at very low prices, and bullion from Canton. Large amounts of treasure have been removed from that place, but the supply is rapidly being exhausted, and we must look to other quarters for silver bullion and coin, without which we shall soon be unable to purchase produce, unless a great improvement should take place in the import market. Business in the latter has been very limited, and chiefly confined to sales of damaged goods at auction."

In the commercial circular from Messrs. Gibson & Co., dated Manchester, Oct. 21, we find noticed, as a most prominent cause of the actual depression,

"not only present bad advices from our great Chinese market, [...] but the prospect of such continuing to arrive in that absence of confidence in monetary transactions there, which must so inevitably be the result, and for a protracted period, of the complete and radical changes which appear likely to be effected in the government and institutions of that vast Empire."

As to the Australian markets, *The Melbourne Commercial Circular* states, that

"where goods purchased only about a month ago [...] have been sold, if then delivered, at a profit of no less than 100 @ 150 per cent., [...] now [...] they would not realize enough to cover the expenses."[a]

Private letters from Port Philip, received last week, are also extremely unfavorable with regard to the state of the markets. Goods continue to pour in from all parts of the world, and the prices they could command were so low, that rather than submit to immediate sacrifices, ships were being purchased in numbers, to be used for storage.

We can then not be surprised at the commercial circulars continuing to record dullness and declining prices in the markets of the industrial districts. Thus we read in the circulars of Messrs. Fraser, Son & Co., dated Manchester, Oct. 21:

"The extent of operations, whether for the home trade, or for foreign parts, has been on an exceedingly limited scale, and prices have suffered throughout to a greater or lesser extent. The further decline in $^7/_8$ prints and madapolams may be stated at $1^1/_2$d. to 3d. per piece; in 56 to 66 reed 34 in. to 36 in. shirtings $4^1/_2$d. to 6d. per piece; in 36-72 reed shirtings, 3d. per piece; in 39 in. shirtings, of low quality, weighing $5^1/_4$ to 6 lbs., about $4^1/_2$d. per piece; in 39 in. 60 to 64 reed shirtings 3d. per piece; in 45 to 54 in. shirtings $4^1/_2$d. to $7^1/_2$d. per piece; in low 5 to 8 jaconets $1^1/_2$d.,

[a] Quoted from a letter from Australia published in *The Times*, No. 21568, October 25, 1853, p. 7.—*Ed.*

and in 14 to 16 square jaconets 3d. per piece; in T cloths $1^1/_2$d., in long cloths 3d. per piece and in domestic of certain classes about 1-16d. per yard. In yarns, watered twist has declined the most for common and middling qualities, which may be considered as $^1/_4$d. to $^1/_2$d. per lb. below last month's quotations. Mule yarns have been most affected in No. 40's, which have been selling at a reduction of fully 1d. per lb. from the highest point of the year. [...] Other yarns at 20s. below 60 have been similarly affected."

As to the food market, the London *Weekly Dispatch*[a] states:

"In so far as wheat is concerned, the opinions of farmers, as they proceed to thrash their grain and count their stocks, is that the crop will be shorter still than they anticipated. Indeed they call it [...] *a half-crop.*"

The wetness of the weather since about a fortnight, highly unfavorable for wheat-sowing and seeding in the ground, evokes, too, serious apprehensions for the harvest of 1854.

From Oxfordshire it is reported as follows:

"As to the wheat crop, as a whole it is a miserable failure; farms that usually produce from 40 to 44 bushels per acre are this year yielding from 15 to 20 bushels; and some well cultivated wheat and bean lands are yielding but from 8 to 10 bushels per acre. [...] Potatoes sadly diseased, are an insignificant yield."

A Yorkshire report informs us that:

"The wet has caused a complete cessation of all active out-door operations; and the remains of the latter harvest, we are sorry to say—all the beans, the bulk of spring wheat, and some oats, are, by being exposed to the action of the weather, rendered so soft as to prevent the hope that it can ever be fit to thrash after the drying winds of spring. It is, moreover, sadly sprouted, and a sad waste of this last resource will doubtless inevitably take place. We give a faint idea of the extent of the loss to which we now refer. Commencing at the Tees, and from thence to Catterick, at Stokesley, and embracing the lowlands of Cleveland, and eastward of Thirsk to the sea, westward of Harrogate and from the Humber to the sea, [...] vast quantities of corn are abroad and spoiled by the wet, with a rainy sky overhead; a full fifty per cent. of the potatoes irrevocably diseased, and a new demand for seed has sprung up, with small stocks of old corn. *It is certain that the whole of the wheat-growing districts of the country are deficient and spoiled beyond any former period within our recollection.*"

A Hertfordshire report states:

"It is very extraordinary at this period of the year *not to have concluded the harvest in this country.* Such, however, is the fact, as there are many fields of oats not yet carted, and a considerable portion of the spring-sown beans, with an occasional field of barley; indeed, there are some fields of lent-corn not yet cut."

---

[a] No. 2707, October 30, 1853.—*Ed.*

The Economist of last Saturday publishes the following table, showing the quantities of wheat and grains of all kinds, and of meal and flour of all kinds imported into the United Kingdom during the period from Jan. 5 to Oct. 10, 1853:

Countries from which exp't'd	Wheat, qrs.	Wheat, meal, or flour, cwts.	Corn [...] of all kinds, qrs.	Agg. of meal and fl'r of all kinds, cwts.
Russia, viz.:				
Northern Ports	69,101	64	307,976	65
Ports within Black Sea	704,406	—	1,029,168	—
Sweden	3,386	13	3,809	13
Norway	—	1	561	1
Denmark	220,728	5,291	733,801	5,291
Prussia	872,170	3,521	899,900	3,521
M'kl'nbg-Schwerin	114,200	—	123,022	—
Hanover	19,187	—	146,601	—
Oldenburg	2,056	—	19,461	—
Hanseatic Towns	176,614	53,037	231,287	53,066
Holland	58,034	306	132,255	308
Belgium	15,155	353	20,829	353
Channel Islds. (foreign produce)	526	4,034	629	4,034
France	96,652	857,916	470,281	858,053
Portugal	4,217	4	21,657	4
Azores	630	—	14,053	1
Spain	13,939	177,963	48,763	177,985
Gibraltar	—	9	4,368	9
Italy, viz.: Sardinian Territories	7,155	2,263	8,355	2,263
Tuscany	48,174	67,598	45,597	67,598
Papal Territories	39,988	—	41,488	—
Naples and Sicily	8,618	2	11,977	2
Austrian Territories	44,164	370	106,796	370
Malta	28,569	—	56,281	—
Ionian Islands	82	—	16,220	—
Greece	1,417	—	10,221	—
Wall'hia and Moldavia	209,048	—	601,481	—
Syria	21,043	—	24,686	—
Egypt	297,980	—	543,934	—

Countries from which exp't'd	Wheat, qrs.	Wheat, meal, or flour, cwts.	Corn [...] of all kinds, qrs.	Agg. of meal and fl'r of all kinds, cwts.
Othr. Turk'h Dom'n	218,407	7,370	689,703	7,340
Algeria	—	—	21,661	—
Morocco	3	3	13,451	—
British East India	—	205	—	205
British N. America	45,587	232,216	62,626	232,493
U.S. of America	434,684	2,388,056	630,324	2,389,283
Brazil	—	3	237	320
Other Parts	1	148	8	148
Total	3,770,921	3,800,746	7,093,458	3,802,743

The total of wheat is	qrs. 3,770,921
The equivalent of 3,802,743 cwts. of meal and flour is	qrs. 1,086,522
Total of grain, flour and meal	qrs. 8,179,980

The Economist, in order to allay the apprehensions of the city merchants, draws the following conclusions from the foregoing table:

"In 1847, notwithstanding the extraordinary stimulus of high prices, we imported of wheat and flour, in the whole year, only 4,464,000 quarters. In the first nine months of the present year we have imported, without any such stimulus, except during the last two months, 4,856,848 quarters. [...] Now, *one of two things must be true* with regard to these large imports as they affect our own home supply—either they have to a great extent been consumed, and have thereby saved in the same proportion our own home production, or they are *warehoused*, and they will be available hereafter."

Now, this dilemma is utterly inadmissible. Consequent on the prohibitions or the threatened prohibitions of the export of corn from the continent, the corn merchants thought it fit to warehouse their stores meanwhile in England, where they will be only available hereafter in case of the corn prices ranging higher in England than on the continent. Besides, in contradistinction to 1847, the supply of the countries likely to be affected by a Russo-Turkish war amounts to 2,438,139 quarters of grain and 43,727 cwt. of flour. From Egypt, too, exportation will be prohibited after 30th November next. Finally, England has this year to look only to the usual *annual* surplus of other nations, while, before the abrogation of the Corn Laws, it had at its disposition, in seasons of want, the foreign stocks accumulated during the favorable seasons.

The Weekly Times, from its point of view, sums up the situation in the following terms:

> "The quartern loaf is a shilling—the weather is worse than it has been for half a century at this season of the year—the operative classes are in the delirium of strikes—Asiatic cholera is raging among us once more, and we have got a war mania. We only want war taxes and famine to make up the orthodox number of the plagues of England."[a]

Written on November 1, 1853

First published in the *New-York Daily Tribune*, No. 3925, November 15, 1853

Signed: *Karl Marx*

Reproduced from the newspaper

---

[a] *The Weekly Times*, No. 355, October 30, 1853.—*Ed.*

Karl Marx

[PERSIAN EXPEDITION IN AFGHANISTAN AND RUSSIAN EXPEDITION IN CENTRAL ASIA.— DENMARK.—THE FIGHTING ON THE DANUBE [AND IN ASIA.—WIGAN COLLIERS][313]

London, Friday, Nov. 4, 1853

Shafi Khan, the Persian Ambassador at the Court of St. James, has been suddenly recalled from England by the Shah. This recall coincides strangely with the operations of Persia in Afghanistan, where it was said to have taken Herat, and with the Russian expedition upon Khiva, the capital of the Khanate of Khiva.[314] The Persian expedition and the Russian one may be considered as two movements, the one from the west, the other from the north, centered on the Punjab, the northern outpost of the British dominions in the East. The Russian expedition is commanded by Gen. Perowski, the same whose Khiva expedition in 1839-40 proved abortive. The Russians having organized, of late years, a flotilla in the Aral Sea, are now able to ascend the river Amu-Darya.

A large Russian fleet is cruising in the Baltic, where it recently took an opportunity to inspect the fortifications of Slite, and the harbor of the Swedish Island of Gothland, of which Russia is covetous, in the manner she got possession of the Island of Aland, close to the coast of Sweden, and strongly fortified by Russia in 1836. From Gothland the Russian fleet proceeded to the Cattegat and the Sound, with a view to support the King of Denmark's[a] intended *coup d'état* in the very probable case of the Copenhagen Diet not quietly accepting the so-called Whole-State Constitution (*Gesammt-Staats-Verfassung*) octroyed by the magnanimous Czar. The state of affairs at Copenhagen is this: the Danish Government has succeeded in carrying the abolition of the *Lex Regia*,[315] and introducing the new law of royal succession, by the support they

---

[a] Frederick VII.—*Ed.*

received from the Peasant-leaguers.[316] This party, under the leadership of Col. Tscherning, aims principally at the transformation of the *Feste Gut*, a sort of feudal peasant-tenure, into free property; and the introduction of municipal laws favorable to the interests and the development of the peasantry. The properly called national and liberal party—the party of the Eyderdanes, who formed the Casino Ministry[317] in 1848, forced the Constitution of 1849 upon the King, and carried the war against Schleswig-Holstein—consisting chiefly of professional gentlemen, had neglected, like the rest of the liberal party all over the Continent, to consult the interests of the mass of the people, formed in Denmark by the peasantry. Thus their influence on the people was lost, and the Government has succeeded in excluding them almost altogether from the present Folketing, where they can hardly be said to muster more than ten men. The Government, however, having got rid of the obnoxious opposition of the Eyderdanes by the aid of the Peasant-leaguers, threw off the mask, called Mr. Oersted, who was odious to both parties, to the Ministry; and so far from any longer cajoling the peasant party, a royal veto prevented the publication of the new Municipal law, originally introduced by the Government itself in order to catch the peasants. The Peasant-leaguers, duped and abused by the Government, have entered into a coalition with the Eyderdanes, and appointed Monrad, a clergyman and one of the leaders of the Eyderdanes, as Vice-President of the Committee sitting on the Constitutional question. This coalition has baffled all hope of overthrowing the Constitution in a constitutional way, and accordingly the whole plan having been formed by and for the Muscovites, a Russian fleet appears in the Danish waters at the very moment of the crisis.

All the journals of Vienna and Berlin confirm the intelligence of the passage of the Danube by strong divisions of the Turkish army. According to the *Oesterreichische Correspondenz* the Turks have been repulsed by the Russians in Lesser Wallachia. A telegraphic dispatch states that a serious engagement took place on the 21st ult. between the two armies in Asia. We must wait for more ample and authentic information to account for the circumstances which may have induced the Turkish Commander-in-Chief to cross the Danube at Widin, a maneuver which, at first view, must be regarded as a gross blunder. The *Kölnische Zeitung* announces that Prince Gorchakoff has seized upon all the treasure-chests (it is not said whether governmental or other) of Wallachia; and, according to another German paper, the same

General has removed to the interior all deposits of corn on the Danube designed to be exported to foreign countries.

The news of advantages gained by Shamyl over Prince Woronzoff, are confirmed by the French papers of to-day. We read in the *Agram Gazette*, that an important letter has been received by Prince Danilo from Russia, and the Prince after having received it, gave orders to have all the corn which had been gathered in from the Montenegrin territory removed to Zabljak. Cartridges are being made and bullets cast. It is said that Russia has informed the Vladika that a collision between the Turks and Russians was imminent, and that the war had a patriotic and sacred character; and that the Montenegrins ought to watch their frontiers narrowly, in order that neighboring provinces should not furnish aid to the Porte.

The *Wanderer* of Vienna, of the 27th ult., says that a letter from St. Petersburg states, that the Emperor Nicholas has ordered the formation of an army of reserve, the headquarters of which are to be in Volhynia.

On last Tuesday a riot occurred at Blackburn on occasion of the election of councillors at St. Peter's Ward, and the soldiery was forced to interfere.

With regard to the Wigan riots, Mr. Cowell, the leader of the laborers at Preston, has declared in a public meeting that—

> "he very much regretted what had occurred in Wigan. He was sorry the people of Wigan had no more sense than to have recourse to a system of leveling. There was no sense in working people collecting together and destroying the property they had produced. The property itself never did them any injury—it was the men that held the property that were the tyrants. Let them respect property and life, and by proceeding in a peaceable, orderly and quiet manner, they might rely on the struggle terminating in their favor."[a]

Now I am far from defending the aimless acts of violence committed by the Wigan colliers, who have paid for them with the blood of seven men. But, on the other hand, I understand that there is a great difficulty, especially for the inferior elements of the working classes, to which the colliers undoubtedly belong, in proceeding "peaceably, orderly and quietly," when they are driven to acts of frenzy by utter destitution and by the cool insolence of their masters. The riots are provoked by the latter in order to enable themselves to appeal to the armed force and to put down, as they have done in Wigan, all meetings of the workingmen by

[a] Quoted according to "The Operatives of Preston" in *The People's Paper*, No. 79, November 5, 1853.—*Ed.*

order of the magistrates. The riot which occurred in the town of Wigan, on Friday afternoon, was occasioned by the coal kings of the district meeting in large numbers at Whiteside's Royal Hotel, in order to deliberate on the demands of the colliers, and by their coming to the resolution to repudiate all compromise with the men. The attack on the saw-mills at Haigh, near Wigan, which occurred on Monday, was directed against the foreign colliers, brought over from Wales by Mr. Peace, the Agent for the Earl of Balcarres, in order to replace the turnouts of the coal pits.

The colliers were certainly not right in preventing their fellow-laborers, by violence, from doing the work they had abandoned themselves. But when we see the masters pledging each other by heavy fines, with a view to enforce their *lock-out*, can we be astonished at the more rude and less hypocritical manner in which the men attempt to enforce their *turn-out*? Mr. Joseph Hume himself says, in a letter addressed to the operatives at Preston:

> "I see on the list of advocates for arbitration to settle the disputes of nations, instead of having recourse to war, many master-manufacturers who are at this moment in strife against their men."[a]

The Manufacturers' Association at Preston have published a manifesto in order to justify the general lock-out.[b] Their sincerity may be inferred from the fact, that the masters' secret league, the programme of which I communicated to your readers about two months ago,[c] is not mentioned in a single word, thus giving the hue of a necessity, which the masters were unable to escape, to the deliberate result of conspiracy. They reproach the workingmen with asking for 10 per cent. neither more or less. They do not tell the public that, when the masters took off 10 per cent. in 1847, they promised to restore it as soon as trade had revived, and that the men have been informed again and again of the revival of trade by the glowing descriptions of Messrs. Bright, Cobden & Co., by the declamations of the whole middle-class press, and by the royal speech on the opening of Parliament. They do not tell us that bread is more than 40 per cent. dearer, coals 15 to 20 per cent., meat, candles, potatoes, and all other articles, largely entering in the consumption of the working classes, about 20 per

[a] "The Wages Movement.—Preston, Oct. 29", *The Times*, No. 21573, October 31, 1853.—*Ed.*

[b] *The Times*, No. 21576, November 3, 1853.—*Ed.*

[c] See this volume, p. 250.—*Ed.*

cent. dearer than before, and that the manufacturers vanquished their antagonists under the banner of: *Cheap bread and dear labor!* They reproach the men with continuing to enforce an equalization of wages in the same town for the mills of the same description. Why, does not the whole doctrine of their masters, of Ricardo and Malthus, proceed from supposing such an equalization to exist throughout the whole country? The men, they say, are acting under the orders of a Committee. They are instigated by "strangers," "intruders," "traders in agitation." Just the same thing was contended on the part of the protectionists reproaching, at the time of the Corn Law League,[318] the same manufacturers with being directed by Messrs. Bright and Cobden, "two professional traders in agitation," and with blindly acting under the orders of the Revolutionary Committee at Manchester, levying taxes, commanding an army of lecturers and missionaries, inundating the country with small and large prints and forming a state in the state. The most curious fact is that while the masters accuse the men of "acting under the orders of a Committee," they call themselves the "United Manufacturers' Association," publishing their very manifesto through a *Committee* and plotting with the "strangers" of Manchester, Bolton, Bury, etc. The "strangers" of whom the masters' manifesto speaks, are merely the men of the neighboring industrial localities.

I am far, however, from supposing that the workmen will obtain the immediate end their strikes aim at. On the contrary, I have stated in a former letter, that at no distant period they will have to strike against a *reduction* instead of for an *advance* of wages.[a] Already reductions of wages are growing numerous, and producing their correspondent quota of strikes. The true result of this whole movement will be, as I stated on a previous occasion, that "the activity of the working classes will soon be carried over to the political field, when the new organization of trades, gained in the strikes, will prove of immense value to them." Ernest Jones and the other Chartist leaders, are again in the field; and at the great meeting at Manchester, on last Sunday, the following resolution was passed:

"That after witnessing the united exertions of the master class against the trades of this country, by opposing a fair day's wages for a fair day's work, this meeting is of opinion that the present struggle of labor cannot be carried to a successful issue, except by [...] subverting the monopolies of the master class, through the representation of the laboring classes in the Commons's House of

[a] See this volume, pp. 333-34.—*Ed.*

Parliament by the enactment of the People's Charter, when alone they will be enabled to make laws in their own interest, to repeal those that are injurious, and to obtain the command of means of work, high wages, cheap food, steady trade, and independent self-employment."[a]

Written on November 4, 1853

First published in the *New-York Daily Tribune*, No. 3928 and the *New-York Semi-Weekly Tribune*, No. 885, November 18, 1853; reprinted in the *New-York Weekly Tribune*, No. 637, November 26; published simultaneously in abridged form in German in *Die Reform*, No. 87, November 19, 1853

Signed: *Karl Marx*

Reproduced from the *New-York Daily Tribune*

[a] *The People's Paper*, No. 79, November 5, 1853.—*Ed.*

Frederick Engels

THE PROGRESS OF THE TURKISH WAR

There is no longer a doubt that military operations have begun on the Danube. Omer Pasha has crossed that river at Widin, occupied Kalafat, a village on the opposite side, and marched his advanced guard upon Krajova, while another attack of the Turks, from Rustchuk, has been made upon the opposite town of Giurgevo, and a third and fourth attack in the direction of Braila and Turnu are spoken of. At the same time another engagement, in which the Russians were the attacking party, has taken place at Oltenitza. This last affair is reported by one of our dispatches to have lasted three hours and to have ended in the repulse of the Russians; while another dispatch, received from Vienna on the evening of the 8th inst., states that the battle lasted twenty-eight hours, and that even the result was not ascertained. The former account seems more likely to be true.

The results of the other rencontres are also variously stated. That at Giurgevo appears by all accounts to have been fruitless; of the effects of those near Braila and Turnu, we are ignorant; as to the advance from Kalafat, some telegraphs report advantages gained by the Turks and a repulse of the Russians—others, the Turks to have been checked at once, and driven back upon Kalafat. The probabilities remain in favor of the first report.

What is certain, on the whole, is this: Omer Pasha, from reasons hereafter to be considered, has abandoned what we have before this declared to be the natural position of the Turks on this frontier, namely, the defensive.[a] He has taken offensive steps, and profiting by the withdrawal of the Russians from Lesser Wallachia,

[a] See this volume, pp. 336 and 427.—*Ed.*

he crossed the Danube at the extreme left of his own position, at Widin, on the 28th of October; with what force, we are utterly at a loss to make out. However, as since then we have only heard of simulated or partial attacks of the Turks on other points, and as it would be a gratuitous madness to pass a river like the Danube in the face of a powerful enemy, with a force of no consequence, we may take it for granted that Omer Pasha has with him the main portion of his disposable active army. For, unless convinced by undoubtable intelligence, we will not believe that he has committed himself, so far as some dispatches maintain, by crossing the Danube with 7,000 men, and having no nearer supports or reserves than 8,000 men at Sofia, 150 miles off. Yet, as the main body of the Turkish army has but very lately been concentrated at Varna, Shumla and Rustchuk, we find it equally difficult to explain how Omer Pasha should all at once succeed in concentrating the gross of his army at Widin, 250 miles, on an average, distant from the above places.

The most probable solution is, that on seeing the advance of the Russians toward Widin, Omer Pasha has shifted the position of his army in a considerable degree to the left; leaving the defense of the direct road to Constantinople to the garrisons of Rustchuk, Silistra, Varna and Shumla, he has taken Rustchuk for the support of his right, Widin for that of his left wing, Nicopolis for the rallying point of his center. In this position, extending from Rustchuk to Widin, some 200 miles, he has rallied to his left wing whatever troops he could collect with him, and passed the Danube, thus apparently turning the right wing of the Russians. He expected to fall upon their advance corps and to force them to retreat behind the river Shil, the passage of which he might either force in front, or by sending near Rahova another corps across the Danube, which would thus turn the Shil. The river Aluta, the second tributary of the Danube which runs across the road from Widin to Bucharest, might be forced in the same way, by throwing another portion of the Turkish center across the Danube at Nicopolis and Turnu, below the junction of this river with the Aluta. Finally, simulated attacks lower down, at Giurgevo and Braila, might contribute to lead the Russians into error as to the real points at which the Turks were arriving.

There can be hardly a doubt that, leaving political motives for a moment out of the question, such must have been the plans of Omer Pasha. The London *Times*[a] speaks of an *actual passage* of the

[a] No. 21579, November 7, 1853.—*Ed.*

Turks at Giurgevo; but this is an evident falsehood. There is not an ensign in any disciplined army who would commit such a blunder as to cross the greatest river in Europe—where it is broadest and most difficult, too—with two corps, at two different points, 250 miles asunder, in the presence of a respectable and concentrated enemy.

What, then, does Omer Pasha's maneuver amount to? It is an attempt to turn the flank of the enemy, and to roll up by simultaneous flank and front attacks his whole line of battle. Such a maneuver is perfectly justified when you can bring, unawares, your own main strength upon the enemy's flank; when your front is safe from attack; when your retreat, in case of a check, is secured; and when, by rolling up, from one flank to the other, the enemy's position, you cut off his communications with his base of operations. Now, in the present instance, the latter conviction is not fulfilled. On the contrary, while Omer Pasha's retreat may be menaced by the right wing of his corps in Wallachia being outflanked, and the road to Kalafat thus cut off (in which case his only retreat would be into Austria), the attack from Kalafat toward Bucharest does not at all interfere with the Russian line of retreat. It will be recollected that, upon that ground, we stated some time ago, the only useful line of attack for the Turks to be that from the Danube toward the Sereth, or the narrow strip of land which divides Bessarabia from the Austrian frontier.[a] Instead of the movement which would at once have menaced, if not interrupted the Russian line of communications, the Turks attack at the opposite end where, even in case of victory, no decisive success is to be expected. As to the Turkish front being safe from attack, that may be the case, insofar as the main operations taking place between Widin and Krajova or Slatina, the Russians are not likely to cross the Danube lower down—unless they were bolder in their strategy than we know them to be. But at the same time, the Turkish front from Widin to Rustchuk is equally impeded by the large river which separates it from the enemy, and there must be comparative inaction in that quarter.

The main condition, however, is not fulfilled in this instance.

We have a splendid historical example of this sort of maneuver in the battle of Jena.[319] Napoleon succeeded in bringing the mass of his forces unawares upon the left flank of the Prussians, and in eight hours rolled them up so completely, that the Prussian army

[a] See this volume, pp. 336-37.—*Ed.*

was cut off from its retreat, and annihilated, and has never been heard of since as an army. But that took place on a ground twenty miles square and within twenty hours. Here we have a territory two hundred miles by fifty, with no roads, and the duration of every movement corresponding thereto. The surprise, the vigor and impetuosity of attack, to which Napoleon at Jena owed his complete success, must here, after a few efforts, literally stick fast in the mud. This will be more apparent if we look at the map. The Turks, from Kalafat, have to march upon Krajova. Here they meet with the first of those rivers, which descending from the Transylvanian Alps to the Danube, traverse Wallachia from north to south, and form as many lines of defense to be forced by an attacking army. The country is exactly similar in this respect to Lombardy, and the two rivers here in question, the Shil and Aluta, may be compared to the Mincio and Adige, whose military importance has so often been conspicuous.

Supposing the Turks force the passage of the Shil, which they may perhaps do, they will meet the first serious resistance on the Aluta, near Slatina. The Aluta is a much more formidable barrier by its width and depth; besides, with a little alacrity, the Russians may there concentrate an army capable not only of repelling all Turkish attacks, but of following up the victory at once. Indeed, a Russian victory at Krajova, unless very strongly defined, would not be of much importance, as in three forced marches the Turks could reach Kalafat and the Danube, and thus escape pursuit. But a Turkish defeat at Slatina, besides being more decisive from the greater mass of Russian troops collected there, would give the Russians five or six days of pursuit; and everybody knows that the fruits of a victory are not collected on the field of battle, but during the pursuit, which may bring about a total disorganization of the discomfited army. It is, then, not likely that Omer Pasha, if Gorchakoff wishes to oppose him there, will ever be able to cross the Aluta; for taking every chance in favor of the Turks, Omer Pasha cannot bring more than 25,000 men to the banks of that river, while Gorchakoff may easily collect 35,000 in good time. As to the flank attacks of the Turks from the southern shore of the Danube, they are tolerably harmless, if the attacking force does not dispose of a prodigious quantity of pontoons and other materials very rarely met with among the Turks. But supposing that even the Aluta were forced, and even the Arges, another important river further east, who will imagine that Omer Pasha can succeed in forcing the Russian retrenchments at Bucharest, and in putting to flight, in a pitched battle, an army which must certainly outnumber by about one-third the troops he could bring against it?

If the war, then, is conducted upon anything like military principles on the Russian side, Omer Pasha's defeat appears certain; but if it is carried on not according to military but to *diplomatic* principles, the result may be different.

The voluntary retreat of the Russians from the important military position of Kalafat, after so many troops had been sent there to menace Servia; the unresisted passage of the Danube by Omer Pasha; his comparatively unmolested and very slow movements in Lesser Wallachia (the country west of the Aluta); the insignificance, as far as we can judge, of the Turkish attacks on all other points; lastly, the strategical errors implied in the advance from Widin, and which nobody can for a moment suppose Omer Pasha to have overlooked—all these facts seem to give some ground for a conclusion which has been adopted by some competent judges, but which appears rather fanciful. It is, that there is a sort of tacit understanding between the two opposing generals, by which Lesser Wallachia is to be ceded by the Russians to the Turks. The Aluta, say those who entertain this opinion, forms a very comfortable natural barrier, across which the two armies may look at each other the whole dreary winter long, while the diplomatists again busy themselves to find out a solution. The Russians, by receding so far, would not only show their generosity and peaceable feelings, but they would at the same time get a sort of right upon the usurped territory, as a *joint occupation* of the Principalities by Russians and Turks is a thing exceedingly in harmony with existing treaties. They would, by this apparent generosity in Europe, escape real dangers in Asia, where they appear to be worse off than ever, and above all, they would at any moment be strong enough to drive the Turks out of the strip of territory allowed to them on the left bank of the Danube. Curious but by no means satisfactory evidence in favor of this theory may be found in the fact that it is openly propounded by Vienna journals enjoying the confidence of the Court. A few days will show whether this view of the question is correct, or whether actual war, in good earnest, is to be carried on. We shall be disappointed if the latter does not prove to be the case.

In Asia we begin to find out that both parties are a good deal weaker than was supposed. According to the *Journal de Constantinople*, the Turks had, on the 9th October, in Erzerum 10,000 men, as a reserve; in Batum, 4,000 regulars and 20,000 irregulars, intended, evidently, for an active army; in Bayazid, on the Persian frontier, 3,000 men; in Kars and Ardahan, the two most important points on the Russian frontier (next to Batum), advanced guards of, together, 16,000 men.[a] These were to be reenforced in a few days by 10,000 or 12,000 fresh troops from Syria. This certainly is a very considerable reduction from what other reports led us to suppose; they are 65,000 instead of 100,000! But on the other hand, if the news by way of Constantinople is to be trusted, the main pass of the Caucasus, connecting Tiflis and Georgia with Russia, is in the hands of the mountaineers; Shamyl has driven the Russians back to within nine miles of Tiflis; and Gen. Woronzoff, commander in Georgia, has declared that in case of a Turkish war he could not hold that province unless reenforced by 50,000 men. How far these accounts may be correct we cannot judge; but the reenforcements sent in great haste by sea to Jerkum Kale, Redut Kale and other points on the Transcaucasian coast prove that the star of Russia does not shine very brilliantly in that quarter. As to the strength of these reenforcements, reports differ; it was first said 24,000 men had been sent, but where were the Russians to get ships for such an army? It now turns out that the 13th Division, the first of the 5th corps (General Lüders) has been sent thither; that would be some 14,000 men, which is more than likely. As to the story of the Cossacks of the Black Sea having rounded by land the western point of the Caucasus, and succeeded in passing undisturbed along the rocky and narrow shore toward Redut Kale, to the strength of 24,000 men (this seems to be a favorite number with the Russians), the longer we looked at it, the more incredible it seems. The Tchornomorski[b] Cossacks have plenty to do to guard the line of the Kuban and the Terek, and as to cavalry passing, single-handed and unattacked, in such force, a defile of one hundred and fifty miles, through a hostile population, where a few men might stop them or cut their column in two—these things are only heard of in Russia, where up to the present day it is affirmed that Suwaroff beat Masséna at Zurich.[320]

Here, then, is the best ground for the Turks to act. Rapid, concentrated attacks of the regulars on one main road to Tiflis—along shore, if the Turks can hold out at sea; by Kars or

[a] The figures are evidently taken from the report in *The Times*, No. 21578, November 5, 1853, which refers to the *Journal de Constantinople* of October 19, 1853. Instead of "on the 9th October" this sentence should read "on the 19th October"; this is evidently a misprint in the newspaper.—*Ed.*

[b] Tchornoye morye is the Russian for the Black Sea.—*Ed.*

Ardahan, in the interior, if they cannot—accompanied by an indefatigable, energetic, sudden warfare, according to their own fashion, by the irregulars, would soon put Woronzoff in an inextricable position, open a communication with Shamyl, and ensure a general insurrection of the whole Caucasus. But here more than on the Danube boldness, rapidity, and *ensemble* of action is required. It remains to be seen whether these qualities belong to the Turkish commanders in that region.

Written about November 8, 1853

First published in the *New-York Daily Tribune*, No. 3934, November 25, 1853, as a leader

Reproduced from the newspaper

Frederick Engels

THE RUSSIAN DEFEATS[321]

We have carefully examined the European journals brought by the *Canada* in order to gather all possible light as to the fighting which has taken place between the Turks and the Russians in Wallachia, and are able to add some important facts to those reported by the *Washington*, which we commented upon on Friday last.[a] We knew then that several engagements had taken place, and with regard to their details we know little more now. Our reports are still incoherent, contradictory and scanty, and so will probably remain till we receive the official dispatches of the Turkish Generals. So much is, however, clear, namely, that the Turks have been maneuvered with a degree of skill and have fought with a steady enthusiasm sufficient to justify the laudations of their warmest admirers,—laudations that by the mass of cool and impartial men have been regarded as exaggerated. The result is a general surprise. Of Omer Pashá's talents as a commander, all persons were prepared to receive very brilliant proofs, but the merit of his army has not been recognized by western journalists or statesmen at its true value. It is true its ranks are filled by Turks, but they are a very different sort of soldiers from those Diebich drove before him in 1829. They have beaten the Russians with heavy odds and under unfavorable circumstances. We trust this may prove but the augury and beginning of far more conclusive defeats.

We now learn for the first time that the Council of War at Constantinople had concentrated at Sofia an army of some 25,000 men in order to operate in Servia in case of need. Of this force

[a] See this volume, pp. 450-56.—*Ed.*

and its destination, strange to say, no previous information seems to have reached Western Europe, but it is clear that Omer Pasha has made the best use of it. Its disposition at Sofia was a blunder since if the Servians should not revolt and make common cause with the Russians,—which under the reigning prince[a] they are not likely to do,—there is no occasion for an army in that quarter; while in case of a revolt the Turks must either march into the country and suppress it, for which, with the Russians in Wallachia, 25,000 men would not suffice, or else they must occupy the passes of the frontier and confine the Servians at home, for which a quarter of that force would be ample. Omer Pasha evidently viewed the matter in this light, for he has marched the corps straight to Widin, and added it to the force he had there previously. This reenforcement has, no doubt, essentially contributed to the victory he has now gained over the right wing of the Russians under General Dannenberg, a victory of which we have no particulars beyond the number of Russian officers killed and captured; but which must have been quite complete, and will prove morally even more beneficial to the Turks than it was materially.

We now learn, also, that the Turkish force which crossed from Turtukai (a point between Rustchuk and Silistra), to Oltenitza, was led by *Ismail Pasha* or [by] General Guyon (he has not renounced Christianity though he holds a high rank in the Sultan's army), whose gallantry in the Hungarian war gave him a high reputation as a bold, energetic and rapid executive officer. Without remarkable strategic talent, there are few men who will carry out orders with such effect, as he has proved on the present occasion, where he repelled his assailant with the bayonet. The defeat of Gen. Pawloff at Oltenitza, must substantially open the country behind the Aluta, and clear the way to Bucharest, since it is proved that Prince Gorchakoff has not advanced to Slatina, as was reported, but remains at the Capital of the Principalities, wisely preferring not to divide his forces, which is again an indication that he does not think himself entirely secure. No doubt a decisive battle has been fought long ere this in the vicinity of that place. If Gorchakoff is not a humbug, and if he can concentrate there from seventy to eighty thousand men—a number which all reasonable deductions from the official force of the Russians still leave to him,—the advantage is decidedly on his side. But seeing how false and exaggerated are the figures reported from the Russian camp;

[a] Alexander Karageorge.—*Ed.*

seeing how much more powerful and effective is Omer Pasha's army than has been supposed, the conditions of the campaign become more equal than has been imagined, and the defeat of Gorchakoff comes within the probabilities of the case. Certainly, if the Turkish Generalissimo can concentrate for the decisive struggle fifty or sixty thousand troops already flushed with victory—and we now see nothing to prevent it—his chance of success is decidedly favorable. In saying this we desire to speak with moderation, for there is no use in making the Turks seem better off than they are because our sympathies are with them.

It is impossible to study the geographical structure of Wallachia, especially in a military point of view, without being reminded of Lombardy. In the one the Danube and in the other the Po and its confluents form the southern and western boundaries. The Turks have also adopted a similar plan of action with that pursued by the Piedmontese in the campaign of 1849, ending in the disastrous battle of Novara.[322] If the Turks prove victorious, the greater will be their claim on our admiration, and the more palpable the bullying incapacity of the Muscovite. At all events Gorchakoff is no Radetzky and Omer Pasha no Ramorino.

Written about November 11, 1853

First published in the *New-York Daily Tribune*, No. 3936, November 28, 1853, as a leader

Reproduced from the newspaper

Karl Marx

THE LABOR QUESTION[323]

London, Friday, Nov. 11, 1853

Golden opportunities, and the use made of them, is the title of one of the most tragi-comical effusions of the grave and profound *Economist.*[a] The "golden opportunities" were, of course, afforded by free trade, and the "use" or rather "abuse" made of them refers to the working classes.

"The working classes, for the first time, had their future in their own hands! The population of the United Kingdom began actually to *diminish,* the emigration carrying off more than its natural increase. How have the workingmen used their opportunity? What have they done? Just what they used to do formerly, on every recurrence of temporary sunshine, married and multiplied as fast as possible. [...] At this rate of increase it will not be long before emigration is effectually counterbalanced, and the golden opportunity thrown away."

The golden opportunity of *not* marrying and *not* multiplying, except at the orthodox rate allowed by Malthus and his disciples! Golden morality this! But, till now, according to *The Economist* itself, population has diminished, and has not yet counterbalanced emigration. Overpopulation, then, will not account for the disasters of the times.

"The next use the laboring classes should have made of their rare occasion ought to have been to accumulate savings and become capitalists. [...] In scarcely one instance do they seem to have [...] risen, or begun to rise, into the rank of capitalists. [...] They have thrown away their opportunity."

The opportunity of becoming capitalists! At the same time *The Economist* tells the workingmen that, after they had at last obtained ten per cent. on their former earnings, they were able to pocket

---

[a] *The Economist,* No. 532, November 5, 1853.—*Ed.*

16s. 6d. a week instead of 15s. Now, the mean wages are too highly calculated at 15s. per week. But never mind. How to become a capitalist out of 15 shillings a week! That is a problem worthy of study. The workingmen had the false idea that in order to ameliorate their situation they must try to ameliorate their incomes. "They have struck," says *The Economist*, "for more than would have done them any service." With 15 shillings a week they had the very opportunity of becoming *capitalists*, but with 16s. 6d. this opportunity would be gone. On the one hand workingmen must keep hands scarce and capital abundant, in order to be able to force on the capitalists a rise of wages. But if capital turns out to be abundant and labor to be scarce, they must by no means avail themselves of that power for the acquisition of which they were to stop marrying and multiplying. "They have lived more luxuriously." Under the Corn Laws, we are told by the same *Economist*, they were but half-fed, half-clothed, and more or less starved. If they were then to live at all, how could they contrive to live less luxuriously than before? The tables of importation were again and again unfolded by *The Economist*, to prove the growing prosperity of the people and the soundness of the business done. What was thus proclaimed as a test of the unspeakable blessings of free trade, is now denounced as a proof of the foolish extravagance of the working classes. We remain, however, at a loss to understand how importation can go on increasing with a decreasing population and a declining consumption; how exportation can continue to rise with diminishing importation, and how industry and commerce can expand themselves with imports and exports contracted.

"The third use made of the golden opportunity should have been to procure the best possible education for themselves and their children, so as to fit themselves for the improvement in their circumstances, and to learn how to turn it to the best account. Unhappily, we are obliged to state that [...] schools have seldom been so ill attended, or school fees so ill paid."

Is there anything marvellous in this fact? Brisk trade was synonymous with enlarged factories, with increased application of machinery, with more adult laborers being replaced by women and children, with prolonged hours of work. The more the mill was attended by the mother and the child, the less could the school be frequented. And, after all, of what sort of education would you have given the opportunity to the parents and their children? The opportunity of learning how to keep population at the pace described by Malthus, says *The Economist*. Education, says

Mr. Cobden, would show the men that filthy, badly ventilated, overstocked lodgings, are not the best means of conserving health and vigor. As well might you save a man from starving by telling him that the laws of Nature demand a perpetual supply of food for the human body. Education, says *The Daily News*, would have informed our working classes how to extract nutritive substance out of dry bones—how to make tea cakes of starch, and how to boil soup with devil's dust.

If we sum up then the golden opportunities which have thus been thrown away by the working classes, they consist of the golden opportunity of *not* marrying, of the opportunity of living *less* luxuriously, of not asking for higher wages, of becoming capitalists at 15 shillings a week, and of learning how to keep the body together with coarser food, and how to degrade the soul with the pestiferous doctrines of Malthus.

On Friday last Ernest Jones visited the town of Preston to address the factory-hands locked out of the mills, on the labor question. By the appointed time at least 15,000 persons (the *Preston Pilot* estimates the number at 12,000) had assembled on the ground, and Mr. Jones, on proceeding to the spot, was received with an enthusiastic welcome.[a] I give some extracts from his speech:

> "Why have these struggles been? Why are they now? Why will they return? Because the fountains of your life are sealed by the hand of Capital, that quaffs its golden goblet to the lees and gives the dregs to you. Why are you locked out of life when you are locked out of the factory? Because you have no other factory to go to—no other means of working for your bread. [...] What gives the capitalist this tremendous power? That he holds all the means of employment.... The means of work is, therefore, the hinge on which the future of the people turns.... It is a mass movement of all trades, a national movement of the working classes, that can alone achieve a triumphant result.... Sectionalize and localize your struggle and you may fail—nationalize it and you are sure to win."

Mr. George Cowell in very complimentary terms moved, and Mr. John Matthews seconded, a vote of thanks to Ernest Jones for his visit to Preston and the services he was rendering to the cause of labor.

Great exertions had been made on the part of the manufacturers to prevent Ernest Jones visiting the town; no hall could be had for the purpose, and bills were accordingly printed in Manchester

---

[a] When describing Jones and other speakers at the meeting in Preston on November 4, 1853, Marx closely followed the article "Immense Demonstration at Preston" published in *The People's Paper*, No. 80. The quotation from Jones' speech is given according to that article.—*Ed.*

convening an open-air meeting. The report had been industriously circulated by some self-interested parties, that Mr. Jones was going to oppose the strike, and sow division among the men, and letters had been sent that it would not be personally safe for him to visit Preston.

Written on November 11-12, 1853

First published in the *New-York Daily Tribune,* No. 3936, November 28, 1853; reprinted in the *New-York Semi-Weekly Tribune,* No. 888, November 29, 1853

Signed: *Karl Marx*

Reproduced from the *New-York Daily Tribune*

Karl Marx

PROSPERITY.—THE LABOR QUESTION

London, Tuesday, Nov. 15, 1853

"The Trade Returns and the Money Market" is the title under which *The Economist* publishes an article intended to prove the general prosperity and the fair prospects of trade, although we are told in the same number that

"provisions are high and are still rising in price," that "a quarter of wheat will sell at 80 shillings," and that "the state of the Cotton trade [...] is not such as to make the millowners at all anxious to recommence work."[a] "There is much of instruction," says *The Economist*, speaking of the tables of importations, "conveyed in these long columns of figures—so much that goes to confirm great principles which have been the subject of strong political contest—so much that explains the recent events, with regard to the Money Market, and [...] casts light upon the future—so much that is highly instructive to the statesman, the financier, the banker, and the trader, in enabling them to take an accurate view of the state of things at present, and to make a just estimate of their position hereafter—that we feel we cannot perform a better service than to call attention to some of the main facts developed by these returns, and trace their connection with other most important features of the time."

Let us then sit down at the feet of this prophet and hearken to his very circumlocutory oracles. This time the tables of importation are referred to in order to prove, not the lavish expenditure of the working classes, but the unspeakable blessings these very classes are reaping from free trade. These tables are as follows:

[a] "Faults and Follies of Wages Movement", *The Economist*, No. 533, November 12, 1853. The tables and quotations below are cited from the above-mentioned article published in the same issue of *The Economist*.—*Ed.*

TABLE I

Consumed from Jan. 5 to Oct. 10

		1852	1853
Cocoa	lb.	2,668,822	3,162,233
Coffee	lb.	25,123,946	28,607,613
Tea	lb.	42,746,193	45,496,957
Sugar	cwt.	5,358,967	5,683,228
Tobacco	lb.	21,312,459	22,296,398
Wine	gals.	4,986,242	5,569,560

One glance over this table shows us the fallacy of *The Economist.* All we know of the enumerated commodities is, not that they have been *consumed,* as is stated, but that they have been *entered* for consumption, which is quite a different thing. There is no shop-keeper so ignorant as not to be able to distinguish between the stock of commodities that may have entered his premises, and the stock that has been really sold and consumed by the public.

"This list may be regarded as including the chief articles of luxury of the operative classes," and down *The Economist* puts it to the account of these classes. Now, one of these articles, viz., coffee, enters but sparingly into the consumption of the English operative, and wine does not enter it at all. Or does *The Economist* think the operative classes must be better off because their masters are consuming more wine and coffee in 1853 than in 1852? As to tea, it is generally known that, consequent upon the Chinese revolution and the commercial disturbances connected with it, a speculative demand has sprung up based on the apprehensions for the future, but not on the wants of the present. As to sugar, the whole difference between October, 1852 and 1853, amounts but to 324,261 cwt.; and I don't pretend to the omniscience of *The Economist,* which knows, of course, that not one cwt. out of these 324,261 has entered the stocks of the shop-keeper or the sweetmeats of the upper classes, but that all of them must have inevitably found their way to the tea of the operative. Bread being dear, he will have fed his children upon sugar, as Marie Antoinette, during the famine of 1788, told the French people to live upon macaroons. As to the rise in the import of tobacco, the demand for this article on the part of the operatives regularly increases in the same proportion as they are thrown out of work, and their regular course of living is interrupted.

Above all, we must not forget that the amount of commodities imported in October, 1853, was determined not by the actual demand of that month, but by a conjectural demand calculated on an altogether different state of the home market. So much for the first table and its "connection with other most important features of the time."

TABLE II

Imported from Jan. 5 to Oct. 10

		1852	1853
Bacon	cwt.	62,506	173,729
Beef salted	cwt.	101,531	160,371
Pork salted	cwt.	77,788	130,142
Hams salted	cwt.	6,766	14,123
Lard	cwt.	14,511	102,612
Total		263,102	580,977
Rice	cwt.	633,814	1,027,910
Potatoes	cwt.	238,739	820,524
Grain and Flour	qrs.	5,583,082	8,179,956
Cheese	cwt.	218,846	294,053
Butter	cwt.	205,229	296,342
Eggs	qrs.	89,433,728	103,074,129

To *The Economist* the glorious discovery was certainly reserved that, in years of dearth and imminent famine, the relative excess of imports above those of common years, of provisions, rather proves the sudden development of consumption than the unusual falling off of production. The sudden rise in the price of an article is no doubt a premium on its importation. But has any one ever contended that the dearer an article the more eagerly it will be consumed? We come now to a third class of importations, constituting the *raw materials* of manufactures:

TABLE III

Imported from Jan. 5 to Oct. 10

		1852	1853
Flax	cwt.	971,738	1,245,384
Hemp	cwt.	798,057	788,911

		1852	1853
Silk, Raw	lbs.	3,797,757	4,355,865
Silk, Thrown	lbs.	267,884	577,884
Cotton	cwt.	6,486,873	7,091,999
Wool	lbs.	63,390,956	83,863,475

As the production of 1853 has largely surpassed that of 1852, more raw materials were wanted, imported, and worked up. *The Economist,* however, does not pretend that the surplus of manufactures produced in 1853 has entered the home consumption. He puts it to the account of *exports.*

"The most important fact is the enormous increase in our exports. The increase upon the single months ending the 10th October is no less than £1,446,708, completing an aggregate increase [in the nine months] of £12,596,291; the amount being £66,987,729 in the present year, against £54,391,438 in the corresponding period of 1852.... Taking only our exports of British produce, the increase is no less than 23 per cent. in the year."

But how does it stand with these additional £12,596,291. "A large portion of these exports are only on the way to their ultimate markets," where they will arrive just at the proper moment to completely undo them. "A considerable part of the increase is to Australia," which is glutted; "to the United States," which are overdone; "to India," which is depressed; "to South America," which is altogether unable to absorb the over-imports repelled from the other markets.

"The enormous increase of articles imported and consumed, is already paid by this country, or [...] the bills thrown for [...] them are running and will be paid in a very short period.... *When* shall we be paid for the exports? In six months, nine months, twelve months, and for some in eighteen months or two years' time."

It "is but a *question* of time," says *The Economist.* What an error! If you throw this enormous surplus of manufactures upon markets already inundated by your exports, the time you wait for, may *never* arrive. What appears in your tables as an enormous list of imaginary wealth, may turn out an enormous list of real losses, a list of bankruptcies on a world-wide scale. What then do table No. III and the boasted figures of exports prove? What all of us were long since aware of, that the industrial production of Great Britain has enormously increased in 1853, that it has overshot the mark, and that its movement of expansion is becoming accelerated at the very moment when markets are contracting.

The Economist arrives, of course, at an opposite result.

"The pressure on the Money Market, and the rise in the rate of interest," he tells us, "are but the transitory consequence of the large imports being immediately paid, while the enormous surplus of exports is advanced on credit."

In his eyes, then, the tightness of the Money Market is but the result of the additional amount of exports. But we may as justly say that in these latter months the increase of exports has been but the necessary result of the pressure on the Money Market. That pressure was attended by an influx of bullion and an adverse exchange—but is an adverse exchange not a premium on bills drawn on foreign countries, or in other words, a premium on exportation? It is precisely by virtue of this law that England, in times of pressure on her own Money Market, deranges all the other markets of the world, and periodically destroys the industry of foreign countries, by bombarding them with British manufactures at reduced prices.

The Economist has now found out the "two points" in which the workingmen are decidedly wrong, decidedly blameable and foolish.

"In the first place they are at issue, in most cases, on the merest fraction of a coin."

Why is this? Let *The Economist* answer himself:

"The dispute has been changed from being a question of contract to being a struggle for power." "Secondly, [...] the operatives have not managed their own business, but have submitted to the dictation of irresponsible, if not self-styled leaders.... They have acted in combination, and through [...] a body of insolent clubs.... We do not fear the political opinions [...] of the working classes themselves; but we do fear and deprecate those of the men whom they allow to prey upon them and speak for them."

To the class organization of their masters the operatives have responded by a class organization of their own; and *The Economist* tells them that he will discontinue "to fear" them, if they dismiss their generals and their officers and resolve to fight single-handed. Thus the mouth-pieces of the allied despots of the north assured the world again and again, during the period of the first struggles of the French revolution, that they did "not fear" the French people itself, but only the political opinions and the political actions of the savage *Comité du Salut Public*,[324] the insolent clubs, and the troublesome generals.

In my last letter I told *The Economist* that it was not to be wondered at if the working classes had not used the period of prosperity to educate their children and themselves. I am now enabled to forward you the following statement, the names and particulars of which have been given me, and are about to be sent to Parliament: In the last week of September, 1852, in the township of ... four miles from ..., at a bleaching and finishing establishment called..., belonging to ..., Esq., the undermentioned parties attended their work *sixty hours* consecutively, with the exception of *three hours for rest!*

Girls	Age	Girls	Age
M.S.	22	H.O.	15
A.B.	20	M.L.	13
M.B.	20	B.B.	13
A.H.	18	M.O.	13
C.N.	18	A.T.	12
B.S.	16	C.O.	12
T.T.	16	S.B.	10!
A.T.	15	Ann B.	9!
M.G.	15		
Boys		Boys	
W.G.	9	J.K.	11

Boys of nine and ten working 60 hours consecutively, with the exception of three hours' rest! Let the masters say nothing about neglecting education now. One of the above, Ann B., a little girl only nine years of age, fell on the floor asleep with exhaustion, during the 60 hours; she *was roused and cried, but was forced to resume work!!*

The factory operatives seem resolved to take the education movement out of the hands of the Manchester humbugs. At a meeting held[a] in the Orchard by the unemployed operatives at Preston, as we hear:

"Mrs. Margaret Fletcher addressed the assembly on the impropriety of married females working in factories and neglecting their children and household duties. Every man was entitled to a fair day's wages for a fair day's work, by which she meant, that he ought to have such remuneration for his labor as would afford him the means of maintaining himself and family in comfort; of keeping his wife at home to attend to domestic duties, and of educating his children. [Cheers.] The speaker concluded by moving the annexed resolution:

"*Resolved*, that the married portion of the females in this town do not intend to go to work again until their husbands are fairly and fully remunerated for their labor.

"Mrs. Ann Fletcher (sister of the last speaker) seconded the resolution, and it was carried unanimously.

[a] On November 7, 1853.—*Ed.*

"The Chairman announced that when the 10 per cent. question was settled, there would be such an agitation raised respecting the employment of married women in factories as the millowners of the country little expected."[a]

Ernest Jones, in his tour through the manufacturing districts, is agitating for a "Parliament of Labor."[325] He proposes that

"a delegation from all trades shall assemble in the center of action, in Lancashire, in Manchester, and remain sitting until the victory is obtained. This would be an expression of opinion so authoritative and comprehensive as would fill the world with its voice, and divide with St. Stephen's[b] the columns of the press.... At a crisis like this the ear of the world would hang more on the words of the humblest of those delegates than on those of the coroneted senators of the loftiest House."[c]

The organ of Lord Palmerston is of a quite different opinion:

"Among ourselves [...]," exclaims *The Morning Post*,[d] "the boasted *progress* has been effectually checked, and since the wretched failure of the 10th of April[326] no further attempt has been made to convert laborers into legislators, or tailors into tribunes of the people."

Written on November 15, 1853

First published in the *New-York Daily Tribune*, No. 3938, November 30, 1853

Signed: *Karl Marx*

Reproduced from the newspaper

---

[a] Quoted from "The Operatives of Preston" in *The People's Paper*, No. 79, November 5, 1853.—*Ed.*

[b] The British Parliament.—*Ed.*

[c] Ernest Jones, "A Parliament of Labour. To the Trades and Working Men in General", *The People's Paper*, No. 80, November 12, 1853.—*Ed.*

[d] Of November 14, 1853.—*Ed.*

Frederick Engels

PROGRESS OF THE TURKISH WAR

The news from the seat of war, brought by the steamer *Humboldt*, confirms the report previously received by the *Europa* that the Turks, after having again and again made good their position at Oltenitza, against heavy odds, and with hard fighting, finally retired across the river about the 14th ult. and took up their position in their former entrenchments at Turtukai. We presume that when we receive our letters and journals this will be explained, but at present we do not altogether understand the reason for the movement. It is stated in the dispatch that it was accomplished without molestation, which precludes the supposition that it was the result of any decided advantage gained by Prince Gorchakoff, unless indeed we are to believe that the Russian commander had succeeded in mustering for his second attack on that place twice the force that he had brought against it on the first. But the truth is, that he had no such corps of 45,000 men for such a purpose, as will appear on a careful review of all the facts in our possession. It is also stated that the Turks return to Turtukai, in order not to expose themselves to the danger of a surprize at Oltenitza in winter, when retreat across the river would be difficult; but this statement contradicts the fact that they are acting on the offensive without a check hitherto and with undeniable preponderance of forces. Besides, their left wing is not only maintained at Widin, on the Wallachian side of the Danube, but is even strengthened, which indicates anything but a general retrograde movement on their part. And, taking the hypothesis of a projected movement, with a large force, across the river at Braila or Galatz, which is probably true, we are at a loss to understand why *Omer Pasha* should withdraw his troops from the strong position at Oltenitza simply because he was about, with another body of men, to move decisively against the Russian left flank. But the perplexities of the case will be better understood by referring to the events of the campaign since its beginning.

It is certain first of all that the Turks were allowed to cross the river without serious opposition, both at Widin and Turtukai. There was nothing surprising in this, as military experience has established the impossibility of preventing an active enemy from crossing a river, however large; and also, that it is always most advantageous to attack him after he has got part of his troops across—thus falling upon them with a superior force, and while they have only one line of retreat and that encumbered. But that the Turks should establish themselves upon the left bank of the Danube; that in every action fought they should come off victorious; that they should keep possession of Oltenitza, not more than forty miles from Bucharest, for ten days without the Russians being able to dislodge them from that important position; and that they should finally retire from it unmolested and of their own accord—all this shows that the proportionate strength of the Turkish and Russian forces opposed to each other in that quarter has been greatly mistaken.

We know pretty accurately what forces the Turks had to dispose of; but as to the forces of the Russians, we have always been obliged to grope in the dark. Two army Corps, it was stated, had crossed the Pruth, and part of a third followed them shortly afterward. Supposing this to be correct, the Russians could not have less than 150,000 men in the Principalities. Now, however, when events have already shown that there is no such Russian force in Wallachia—now at last we receive an authentic account, by way of Vienna, of what they really have there.[a] Their forces consist of:

1. The Fourth Army Corps, under Gen. Dannenberg, consisting of the following 3 divisions of infantry:	
A The 10th Division (Gen. Simonoff)	16,000 men
B The 11th Division (Gen. Pawloff)	16,000 men
C The 12th Division (Gen. Liprandi)	16,000 men
D One battalion of riflemen	1,000 men
2. One brigade of the 14th Division, belonging to the Fifth Army Corps, and commanded by Gen. Engelhardt	8,000 men
Total, Infantry	57,000 men

[a] Below Engels makes use of the data from the report of the Vienna correspondent of *The Times* and the editorial in its No. 21587, November 16, 1853.—*Ed.*

3. Two divisions of light horse, commanded by Gen. Nirod and Gen. Fischbach, together 8,000 men, and 10 regiments of Cossacks. 6,000 men, making in all .... 14,000 men
4. One division of artillery, of about one battery (12 guns) for every infantry regiment, or altogether 170 to 180 guns.

It also appears, that the Fifth Army Corps, that of Gen. Lüders, is not even concentrated at Odessa, but has part of its troops at Sebastopol, and part in the Caucasus; that the Third Army Corps under Gen. Osten-Sacken, is still in Volhynia, or at least has but just crossed the Pruth, and cannot be brought down to the theater of war in less than three or four weeks; and that the Russian cavalry of reserve—mostly heavy horse—are behind the Dnieper, and will require five or six weeks to march to the place where they are wanted. This information is no doubt correct; and if it had been before us six weeks ago we should have said that Omer Pasha ought to pass the Danube, no matter where or how, but the sooner the better.

There is, in fact, nothing which can rationally explain the foolhardiness of the Russians. To march with something like 80,000 men into a *cul-de-sac* like Wallachia, to stop there a couple of months, to have, as the Russians themselves have confessed, about 15,000 men sick in hospital, and to trust to good luck, without getting further reenforcements, is a thing that has never been done, and that nobody had any right to suspect in people like the Russians, who are generally so very cautious, and always take care to be on the safe side. Why, this whole available army in Wallachia, after deducting detachments, would only come to some 46,000 men, who might, besides, be wanted at different points!

But such is the fact, and we can only explain it by an absolute confidence on the part of the Russians in the diplomatic intrigues of their friends in the British Government, by an unwarranted contempt for their opponents, and by the difficulties which the Russians must find in concentrating large bodies of troops and large masses of stores at a point so remote from the center of their Empire.

The Turks, on the other hand, are 25,000 strong at Kalafat, in Lesser Wallachia, and are strengthening that force. As to the ulterior movements of this corps we know little. They seem not to have advanced even as far as Krajova, and indeed, to have done nothing more than occupy the neighboring villages. The reason for this is also doubtful, and we can only suppose that Omer Pasha is in some way controlled in his movements by the Council at Constantinople, which originally stationed those 25,000 men at

Sofia. At any rate, as far as it is possible to judge at this distance, this corps is quite useless where it is, and its presence there is a mistake, since even for hypothetical and improbable use against the Servians, it is, as we have shown on a former occasion, either too large or too small.[a] It would apparently have been far better to move it lower down the Danube, for it crossed on Oct. 28, and up to Nov. 15 it had not advanced much, or in any way operated actively. These fifteen days might have been better employed in moving it 150 miles lower down the Danube, as far as Sistova, where it would have been in immediate connection with the left wing of the Turkish grand army, and a couple of marches more would have brought it down upon Rustchuk, the headquarters of the Turkish left. That these 24,000 men united with the main body would have been worth twice their number at Kalafat nobody can doubt; and events support this opinion, for, as before stated, we have not yet heard that during the nineteen days since they crossed the Danube, they have given any active support to *Omer Pasha.*

The attacks of the Turks at Nicopolis and Rustchuk were mere feints. They appear to have been well executed, with no more troops than was necessary, and yet with that vigor which is apt to lead an enemy into error as to the ulterior objects of the attacking party. The main attack was at Oltenitza. What force they brought there is even now uncertain. Some reports say that as early as the 11th the Turks had 24,000 men at Oltenitza, and the Russians 35,000 to oppose them. But this is evidently false. If the Russians were stronger than the Turks in the proportion of three to two, they would have very soon sent them back to the other side of the Danube, when the fact is that the 11th saw a Russian defeat.

It would seem now as much as ever that nothing but exceedingly bad generalship can prevent the Turks from driving Gorchakoff out of Wallachia. It is certain, however, that there have been some singular specimens of generalship on both sides. On the 2d of November the Turks crossed at Oltenitza—evidently their main point of passage. On the 3d, 4th and 5th they successfully repulsed the attacks of the Russians, thereby establishing their superiority upon the left bank of the Danube. During these three days their reenforcements ought to have arrived, and they ought to have been at once in a position to march upon Bucharest. This was the way Napoleon acted, and every general

[a] See this volume, pp. 457-58.—*Ed.*

since his time has known that rapidity of movement can in itself make up for deficiency of strength, inasmuch as you fall upon your opponent before he has time to concentrate his forces. Thus, as men say in trade, Time is money; so we may say in war, Time is troops. But here in Wallachia, this maxim is neglected. The Turks quietly keep possession of Oltenitza during nine days, from the 6th to the 15th, and excepting petty skirmishes, nothing at all is done, so that the Russians have time to concentrate their forces, to dispose them as maturely as possible, and if their line of retreat is menaced, to restore and secure it. Or are we to suppose that Omer Pasha intended merely to keep the Russians near Oltenitza till his main army had crossed lower down and entirely intercepted their retreat? Possibly, though this is an operation which, with 24,000 men at Kalafat and 24,000 at Oltenitza, presupposes some 50,000 more lower down toward Orsova. Now, if he had such a force there, as very possibly he may, they might have passed the time much better than in all these artificial and subtle maneuvers. In that case, why not throw 70,000 or 80,000 men in one mass across the Danube at Braila, and cut the Russians in Wallachia off at once from their communications? As we have said, it is probable that this movement is now to be made, but why this long delay, and why these complicated preliminaries, does not appear. With so great a preponderance of force all ready on the line of operations, there was no particular advantage to be gained by deceiving Prince Gorchakoff. He should rather have been cut off and crushed at once.

As to the Turkish soldiers themselves, in the few engagements where they have acted, they have so far come out in capital style. The artillery has everywhere proved that the Emperor Nicholas did not exaggerate when he pronounced it among the best in Europe. A battalion of riflemen, organized only ten weeks before the beginning of hostilities, and armed with Minié rifles, then just arrived from France, has, during this short time, gained high proficiency in the skirmishing service, and furnished first-rate marksmen, who well know how to use that formidable weapon; at Oltenitza they had an opportunity of showing this by picking off almost all the superior officers of the Russians. The infantry in general must be quite capable of the ordinary line and column movements, and besides, must have attacked at Oltenitza with great courage and steadiness, as at least on two days out of three, the charge of the Turkish infantry decided the battle, and that at close quarters; and with the bayonet, the Russian infantry, it is well-known, are no contemptible opponents.

The news from Asia is even more decisively in favor of the Turks than that from Europe. It appears certain that there has been a general and combined rising of the Circassian tribes against the Russians; that they hold the Gates of the Caucasus, and that Prince Woronzoff has his communications cut off in the rear, while he is pressed by the Turkish forces in front. Thus the war everywhere opens with disasters for the Czar. Let us hope that such may be its history to the end, and that the Russian Government and people may be taught by it to restrain their ambition and arrogance, and mind their own business hereafter.

Written about November 18, 1853

First published in the *New-York Daily Tribune*, No. 3944, December 7, 1853, as a leader

Reproduced from the newspaper

Karl Marx

DAVID URQUHART[327]

In one of the English newspapers to arrive here recently by steamer we discover to our amazement that Mr. D. Urquhart, often mentioned lately as an agitator for the anti-Russian meetings in England, is described as a *tool in the service of Russia.*[a] We can only put this absurdity down to intrigues on the part of "free Slavdom", for the whole of Europe has so far known Urquhart only as a dyed-in-the-wool, almost maniacal Russophobe and Turkophile. When he was Secretary to the embassy in Constantinople the Russians had even demonstrably tried to poison him. Therefore a few remarks about a man whose name is on everyone's lips but whose actual significance hardly anyone can account for.

Urquhart systematically rides a fixed idea. For 20 years he has been *unsuccessfully* denouncing Palmerston and the Russian tricks and dodges, and was, therefore, naturally bound to go half-crazy, as would anybody who had a *particular* idea that was right, but of which he could not convince the world. The fact that Palmerston has been able to hold on until today with his diplomacy, he puts down to the quarrel between the Whigs and Tories, which is partly, but of course only partly, correct. For the English Parliament of today, which judges every issue not on its own merits but solely according to whether a party is "*in office*" or "*out of office*", he, who is basically conservative, sees no other salvation but strengthening the royal prerogative, on the one hand, and *local, municipal self-government*, on the other. To put up a front

[a] The reference is to the article "A Russian Movement in England", in *The People's Paper*, No. 80, November 12, 1853.—*Ed.*

against Russia he wants the West to form as compact and uniform a mass as the Russian. He, therefore, *will not hear of parties* and is a bitter enemy of all efforts to bring about centralisation. As all the revolutions since 1848 have temporarily been favourable to Russia's progress, he foolishly attributes this outcome to Russian diplomacy, seeing it as Russia's *original motive.* Russia's agents are, therefore, according to Urquhart, the secret commanders of the revolutions. As *Austria* is the direct counter-force to Russia within the old conservative system, he shows a preference for Austria and a dislike of anything that could imperil its international power. In contrast to the Russian way of levelling things out, on the one hand, and to the revolutionary way of doing so, on the other, he clings to the individuality and particular characteristics of peoples. In his eyes, therefore, the Jews, the Gypsies, the Spaniards and the Mohammedans, including the Circassians, are the four finest peoples, as they have not been tainted by the vulgarism of Paris and London. From all this it is clear that his conception of history had necessarily to assume a very subjective character. History to him is more or less exclusively the work of diplomacy. As far as the objective, material conception of history is concerned, he thinks it is like making crimes into general laws instead of bringing them to trial.

"He is an honest, obstinate, truth-loving, enthusiastic, totally illogical old man, tormenting himself with his deep-seated prejudices", as one of his critics says of him.

However, as he has but *one* cause in life, his campaign against Russia, which he conducts with monomaniacal acumen and a great deal of expert knowledge, none of this does any harm. The knight with *one* cause in life is bound once more to be "the noble knight of the woeful countenance", nor is there any lack of Sancho Panzas, here or in Europe. A modified example of this species appears in the guise of "A.P.C.",[a] the London A-B-C scholar from the *Tribune.*[328]

Written about November 20, 1853

First published in *Die Reform*, No. 112, December 19, 1853

Printed according to the newspaper

Translated from the German

Published in English for the first time

[a] F. Pulszky.— *Ed.*

KARL MARX

THE KNIGHT OF THE NOBLE CONSCIOUSNESS[329]

Written about November 21-28, 1853

First published as a pamphlet in New-York, January 1854

Signed: *Karl Marx*

Printed according to the pamphlet
Translated from the German
Published in English for the first time

The man of small-scale war (see Decker's *Theorie des kleinen Kriegs*) does not need to be a man at all noble, but must have a *noble* consciousness. According to Hegel, the consciousness that is noble becomes transmuted necessarily into a consciousness that is *base*.[a] I shall elucidate this transmutation from the effusions of Herr Willich—who is Peter the Hermit and Walther Havenought in one person. I shall confine myself to the *cavaliere della ventura*[b]; the *cavalieri del dente*[c] standing behind him I leave to their mission.

To make it clear from the outset that the man of the noble consciousness is wont to express truth in the "higher" sense by lies in the "ordinary" sense, Herr Willich begins his reply to my *Revelations*[330] with the words:

> "Dr. Karl Marx published a report on the Cologne Communist trial in the *Neue-England-Zeitung* and the *Criminal-Zeitung*."[d]

I have never reported on the Cologne Communist trial in the *Criminal-Zeitung*. It is common knowledge that I published the *Revelations* in the *Neue-England-Zeitung* and Herr Willich published Hirsch's confessions[e] in the *Criminal-Zeitung*.

---

[a] G.W.F. Hegel, *Phänomenologie des Geistes*, section "Die Bildung und ihr Reich der Wirklichkeit".—*Ed.*

[b] Knight of fortune, adventurer.—*Ed.*

[c] Parasites.—*Ed.*

[d] A. Willich, "Doctor Karl Marx und seine Enthüllungen", *Belletristisches Journal und New-Yorker Criminal-Zeitung*, October 28, 1853. Below Marx quotes this issue of the newspaper.—*Ed.*

[e] W. Hirsch, "Die Opfer der Moucharderie, Rechtfertigungsschrift", *Belletristisches Journal und New-Yorker Criminal-Zeitung*, April 1, 8, 15, 22, 1853 (see this volume, pp. 40-43).—*Ed.*

17-2346

On p. 11 of the *Revelations* it is stated: "From the list of documents stolen from the Willich-Schapper party and from the dates of these documents it follows that although the party had been warned by Reuter's burglary, it still constantly found ways and means of having its documents stolen and allowing them to fall into the hands of the Prussian police." On p. 64 this passage is repeated.[a]

"Herr Marx," replied Herr Willich, "knows very well that these documents were themselves mostly falsified, and in part invented."

Mostly falsified, therefore not *wholly* falsified. *In part* invented, therefore not wholly invented. Herr Willich, therefore, admits: both before and after Reuter's burglary, documents belonging to his faction found their way to the police. Just as I assert.

So the noble-mindedness of Herr Willich consists in detecting a *false consciousness* behind a *correct fact*. "Herr Marx *knows*." How does Herr Willich know what Herr Marx knows? I know of some of the documents in question that they are genuine. About none of them do I know that during the proceedings at the trial it was shown to be falsified or invented. But I *ought* to have known "more", since "a certain Blum, who was among Willich's closest associates", was "Marx's informant". Blum, therefore, flourished[b] in Willich's immediate neighbourhood. So much the more distant did he keep himself from me. All that I know about Blum, to whom I have never spoken, not even metaphorically,[c] is that he is said to be a Russian by birth and a shoemaker by trade, that he also plays the part of Morison, swears by Willich's Morison pills, and now probably lives in Australia.[331] About the activity of the Willich-Kinkel missionaries, I received information from Magdeburg, not London. Hence the man of the noble consciousness could have spared himself the certainly painful operation of publicly vilifying one of his sons in the faith on the basis of mere suspicion.

At first the noble-minded one tells a lie attributing a non-existent informant to me, then he tells a lie denying the existence of an existing letter. He quotes: "Page 69 of the *Revelations*, note A[d] *from* the *alleged* letter of Becker's."

---

[a] See present edition, Vol. 11, p. 406.—*Ed.*
[b] A pun in German: "Blume" means "flower".—*Ed.*
[c] A pun on words: "durch die Blume sprechen" means "to speak metaphorically".—*Ed.*
[d] See present edition, Vol. 11, p. 452.—*Ed.*

Der Ritter

vom

edelmüthigen Bewußtsein,

von

Karl Marx.

Title page of the first edition of Marx's pamphlet *The Knight of the Noble Consciousness*

Herr Willich is too noble-minded to assume that "a man of intellect and character" like Becker could fail to see the intellect and character of a man like Willich. Hence, he converts Becker's letter into an alleged one and me into a forger. He does so, of course, out of nobility of mind. The alleged letter is still in the possession of defence counsel Schneider II. I sent it to Cologne for the defence at the time of the trial, because it refutes that Becker had any part in Willich's stupidities. Not only was the letter written by Becker, but the Cologne and London postmarks testify to the date of despatch and receipt.

"Previously, however, Frau Kinkel wrote a fairly long, informative letter to me" (Willich); "Becker in Cologne undertook its despatch. He told her that the letter had been mailed—I have never seen it. Has *Herr Marx*, Becker, or the post, *kept* it?"

Not the post, Willich asserted. Perhaps Becker? As long as he was in freedom, no Willich had asked him about it. Therefore, "Herr Marx". In his quiet way, Herr Willich contrives to make out that I publish letters which Becker did *not* write to me and that I suppress letters which Becker entrusted to me for despatch. Unfortunately, Becker was so kind as *never* to trouble me with any mailing of letters, whether from Frau Johann or from Herr Johann Gottfried.[a] Neither the prison nor the Black Bureau[332] stands in the way of approaching Becker with inquiries of such a neutral content. Herr Willich lyingly perpetrates a foul insinuation out of a pure intention to promote virtue and to depict the elective affinity between the good, between the Kinkels and Willichs, as victorious over all divisive arts of the wicked.

"The party situation within the proletariat is that between the Marx party and the Willich-Schapper party, according to *Herr Marx's designation, not mine.*"

The man of the noble consciousness has to prove his own modesty by the overweening conceit of others. Therefore, he converts the "*designation of the Cologne bill of indictment*" (see p. 6 of the *Revelations*[b]) into "*Herr Marx's designations*". Similarly, out of modesty he converts the party situation within a particular German secret society,[333] about which I speak (see loc. cit.), into the "party situation within *the* proletariat".

"When in the autumn of 1850 Techow came to London—Marx *contrived* to have Dronke write to him that Techow had made *highly contemptuous statements* about me; the letter was read out. Techow arrived, we spoke to each other as man to man, the information given in the letter had been invented!!"

---

[a] An allusion to Gottfried Kinkel and his wife, Johanna Kinkel.—*Ed.*
[b] See present edition, Vol. 11, p. 402.—*Ed.*

When Techow came to London, I *had* Dronke write to me, I received the letter, I read it aloud, and *then* Techow came. The false consecutio temporum reflects the embarrassment of the noble-minded one, who is trying to create a false causal connection between me, Dronke's letter and Techow's coming. In Dronke's letter, which incidentally is addressed to Engels and not to me, the incriminating passage reads word for word as follows:

"Today I caused Techow to change his opinion somewhat, although in doing so I became involved in a heated dispute with him and Schily"—*Schily is at this moment in London*—"and he repeatedly declared the attacks on Sigel to be a personal whim of Willich's, to whom he incidentally denies even the *slightest* military talent."

Dronke, therefore, speaks not of Techow's highly contemptuous statements in general, but of Techow's contemptuous utterances about Herr Willich's military talent. Hence, if Techow did declare anything to have been *invented*, it was not the information in Dronke's letter, but the information by the noble-minded one about Dronke's information. In London, Techow did not modify the view he held in Switzerland about Herr Willich's military talent, although perhaps he did modify other views he had held about the false ascetic. My connection with Dronke's letter and Techow's coming is, therefore, confined to the fact that I read out Dronke's letter, just as I as President of the Central Authority[a] had to read out all letters. Thus, among others, a letter from Karl Bruhn, in which he, too, made merry over Willich's military talent. At the time, Herr Willich was convinced that I *had let* Bruhn write this letter. But since Bruhn, unlike Techow, has not yet gone to Australia, Herr Willich prudently suppresses "this sample of my tactics". Similarly, I had to read out a letter in which Rothacker writes:

"I will join any other community,—but *this one*" (viz. Willich's) "*never*".

He relates how, owing to simple opposition to Willich's views on "the striking arming of Prussia", he incurred the fate of having one of Willich's henchmen

"demand his immediate expulsion from the League, while another wanted to have a commission appointed to investigate how this Rothacker had come into the League, which he considered *suspicious*".

Herr Willich was convinced that I *had* Rothacker write this letter. But since instead of digging for gold in Melbourne,

[a] Of the Communist League.—*Ed.*

Rothacker is putting out a newspaper in Cincinnati, Herr Willich has again found it convenient to deprive the world of this further "sample of my tactics".

In accordance with his nature, the noble-minded one wants to evoke delight whenever he goes, and to receive homage everywhere. If, therefore, he finds his good opinion of himself contradicted, if Techow denies him military talent or Rothacker denies him political competence, or if Becker goes so far as to call him "*stupid*", then these unnatural experiences are accounted for by pragmatic reference to the tactical opposition between Ahriman—Marx and Engels—and Ormuzd—Willich; accordingly, his nobility of mind finds expression in the extremely base occupation of detecting, inventing, and lying about the secrets of this imagined tactic. We see, says Hegel, how this consciousness is concerned not with what is highest, but with what is lowest, namely with itself.

"Here," exclaims Herr Willich triumphantly, "are some samples of the tactics of Herr Marx."

> "The first contradiction between Marx, Engels and myself showed itself when the invitation to a meeting was sent to us from the men of the revolution living in London who possessed a greater or lesser sphere of influence. I wanted to accept it; I demanded that our party line and organisation should be safeguarded, but that the *scandal of internal dissensions among the émigrés* should not be spread *outside*. I was voted down, the invitation was refused, *and from that day date the disgusting dissensions among the London émigrés*, the consequences of which are still *present* today, although now they have certainly lost all significance for public opinion."

Herr Willich, as a "partisan" in the war, finds that in peace also it accords with his mission to go from one party to another,[a] and it is fully in accord with the truth that his noble-minded desires for a coalition were voted down. The admission is all the more naive since Herr Willich later tried to spread the word that the émigrés had expelled us from their guild organisation. Here he admits that we had expelled the émigrés' guild from our midst. So much for the facts. Now for their *transfiguration*. The noble-minded one has to prove that it was only due to Ahriman that he was prevented from the noble work of obviating all the evil that had befallen the émigrés. To this end he had once again to resort to lying with an evangelist-like distortion of secular chronology (see Bruno Bauer's *Synoptiker*[b]).[334] Ahriman—Marx and Engels—announced their

---

[a] A pun on the word *Parteigänger* (partisan) the second component of which is derived from an old German word meaning "to go", "to walk".—*Ed.*

[b] B. Bauer, *Kritik der evangelischen Geschichte der Synoptiker.*—*Ed.*

withdrawal from the Workers' Society of Great Windmill Street[335] and their split away from Willich in the meeting of the Central Authority on September 15, 1850.[a] From that day they withdrew from all public organisations, demonstrations, and manifestations. It was, therefore, since September 15, 1850. On July 14, 1851 "the notable men of all factions" were invited to Citizen Fickler, on July 20, 1851 the "Agitation Union" was founded, and on July 27, 1851 the German "Émigré Club".[336] "From *that* day", when the secret desires of the noble-minded one were fulfilled, "date the disgusting dissensions" among the "London émigrés", and the struggle on both sides of the ocean between the "Émigrés" and the "Agitators", the great war between frogs and mice.[b]

Now who will give me words and who the tongue,
To sing of such brave deeds in sonorous sounds!
For ne'er was strife upon this earth begun
More proudly fought on bloodier battle grounds;
Compared to this all other wars are roses.
To tell of it my lyric art confounds
For on this earth there ne'er was seen such glory
Or noble valour bright as in this story.

(After Boiardo, *Orlando Innamorato*, Canto 27)

The "significance of these disgusting dissensions" never existed in "public opinion", but only in the private opinion of the frog-and-mouse warriors. But "the consequences *are* still *present*". Even the stay of Herr Willich in America is a consequence. The money which found its way from America to Europe in the shape of a loan[337] made the journey from Europe back to America in the shape of Willich. One of his first occupations there was the formation of a secret committee in ..., to safeguard the Holy Grail,[338] the democratic gold, for Gottfried of Bouillon and Peter the Hermit[c] against Arnold Winkelried-Ruge and Melanchthon-Ronge.

Although the "noble ones" were left to themselves and, according to the expression of Eduard Meyen, were *all* united "up to and including Bucher", the process of scission proceeded so famously, not only among the main armies but also within each camp, that the Agitation Union was soon reduced to a half-complete pleiad, while the Émigré Club, in spite of the cohesive power of the

[a] See present edition, Vol. 10, p. 483.—*Ed.*
[b] An allusion to *Batrachomyomachia—The Battle of the Frogs and the Mice,* a mock-heroic Greek poem, which parodies Homer's *Iliad.—Ed.*
[c] An allusion to Gottfried Kinkel and August Willich.—*Ed.*

man of the noble consciousness, was reduced to the trinity of Willich, Kinkel, and the innkeeper Schärttner. Even the trinitarian loan-regency—so attractive was the noble consciousness—degenerated into something which cannot even be called a duality, namely, Kinkel-Willich. Herr Reichenbach was too respectable to remain as the third in such an alliance for long. He learned to know the "personal character" of the noble-minded one from practical experience.

Among the samples which the noble-minded one gives of the "tactics of Marx", are included also his experiences with Engels. At this point I insert a letter from Engels himself:

"*Manchester*, November 23, 1853. I, too, have the honour to figure in the novel which Herr August Willich published to justify himself in the *New-Yorker Criminal-Zeitung* (dated October 28 and November 4). I am compelled to put on record a few words on this matter, insofar as it concerns me.

"That friend Willich, who confuses pure idleness with *pure* activity and, therefore, is exclusively concerned with friend Willich, possessed an excellent memory in everything that touches on his person, and that he kept a kind of register of every remark made about him even in beer-drinking company, long ago ceased to be a secret to those who had the pleasure of his acquaintance. Friend Willich, however, for a long time past has known how to make very good use of his memory and his register. On each occasion when trifles of this sort came to be spoken of again, a slight distortion, a few apparently unintentional omissions, made him the hero of the dramatic event, the focal point of a group, of a living picture. In the details of Willich's novel as in its entirety, the struggle always and everywhere turns on the artless and therefore persecuted Willich. In each separate episode we find at the end honest Willich making a speech and the infamous opponents defeated, broken, crushed and knuckling under in the consciousness of their nullity. *Et cependant on vous connaît, ô chevaliers sans peur et sans reproche!*[a]

"In Willich's novel, therefore, the era of suffering, during which the noble-minded one had to suffer so much iniquity at the hands of Marx, Engels and the other impious ones, is at the same time an era of triumph, in which he always victoriously crushes his opponents, and each new triumph surpasses all the previous ones. Friend Willich depicts himself, on the one hand, as the suffering

---

[a] And nevertheless one knows you, o you knights without fear and without reproach!—*Ed.*

Christ, who took on himself the sins of Marx, Engels and Co., but on the other hand, as the Christ who came to judge the living and the dead. It was left for friend Willich to unite two such contradictory roles *simultaneously* in *one* person. One who represents these two aspects simultaneously, must indeed be believed.

"For us, who have long known by heart these self-indulgent fantasies with which an elderly bachelor fills his sleepless nights, for us the only surprising thing is that all these idiosyncrasies still crop up today in the same unaltered form as in 1850. Now for the details.

"Friend Willich, who converts Herr Stieber and Co. into agents of a German 'federal police', which has not existed since the long past affair of the demagogues,[339] and who relates a quantity of equally wondrous 'facts', asserts with his usual accuracy that I wrote a 'pamphlet' on the Baden campaign of 1849. Friend Willich, who has studied with rare thoroughness that part of my work in which he is mentioned, knows very well that I never issued any such 'pamphlet'. What I wrote was a series of articles on the campaign for an Imperial Constitution in the *Neue Rheinische Zeitung. Revue*, Hamburg and New York, 1850, in one of which I published an account of my experiences during the Palatinate-Baden campaign.[a] In this article, of course, friend Willich also figures and, he says, this article was 'very appreciative' of him, but immediately brought him into conflict with his habitual modesty by making him, as it were, a 'competitor of so many other great statesmen, dictators and generals'.

"And what was the nature of this great 'appreciation' on my part which so rejoices the noble heart of Herr Willich? It consists in the fact that I 'appreciated' Herr Willich as, in certain circumstances, a thoroughly useful battalion commander, who in twenty years, when a Prussian lieutenant, had acquired the requisite knowledge; who was not without aptitude for a small war, particularly a guerilla war, with, finally, the advantage that he was the right man at the right place as leader of a volunteer corps of 600-700 men, whereas the majority of the superior officers in that campaign were persons who either had had no military training at all or one wholly unsuitable for their position. To say that Herr Willich could lead 700 men better than a student, non-commissioned officer, schoolmaster or shoemaker, taken at

[a] The reference is to the fourth article, "To Die for the Republic!" of Engels' "The Campaign for the German Imperial Constitution" (see present edition, Vol. 10, pp. 203-39).—*Ed.*

random, is of course 'very appreciative' in the case of a Prussian lieutenant who had had twenty years to prepare himself! *Dans le royaume des aveugles le borgne est roi.*[a] And it goes without saying that in his subordinate position he bore less responsibility, hence could make fewer mistakes than his 'competitors' who were divisional or top-ranking generals. Who knows whether Sigel, who was out of place as an "Obergeneral", would not also have achieved something as a simple battalion commander?

"And now for the doleful lament of modest Willich, who meanwhile, by virtue of seniority, has been promoted by some American newspapers to the rank of 'general', probably through my fault,—that my 'appreciation' had exposed him to the danger of also becoming a general in partibus, and not merely a general, but commander of an army, a *statesman*, indeed—a *dictator*! Friend Willich must have developed some peculiar notions of the brilliant rewards which the Communist Party holds in store for a moderately good battalion or volunteer-corps commander who joins it.

"In the above-mentioned article I spoke of Willich only as of a soldier, for he could be of public interest only in that capacity, since it was but later that he became a '*statesman*'. If I had possessed the malice towards him that he ascribes to me and my friends, if I had been interested in giving a picture of his personal character, what stories could have been told! If I were to have confined myself even to merely the amusing aspect, how could I have left out the story of the apple tree under which he and his Besançons[340] had sworn an oath to die while singing a song rather than once again forsake German soil. How could I have failed to relate the comedy at the frontier, when friend Willich behaved as if this oath was now going to be fulfilled; when some honest fellows came to me in full earnest to induce me to make brave Willich abandon his resolve; when finally Willich asked the assembled corps whether they would not rather die on German soil than go back into exile, and after a long general silence a single death-defying Besançon cried out: 'stay here!', and when in conclusion the whole company with great satisfaction and with their weapons and baggage crossed into Switzerland. Would not the subsequent history of the baggage itself have made quite an episode, not without value today as Willich himself invites half the world to speak out about his 'character'. Anyone who should desire further details about this and other adventures need only

---

[a] In the kingdom of the blind the one-eyed man is king.—*Ed.*

turn to one of his 300 Spartans, who had at that time searched in vain for their Thermopylae.[341] They were always ready to relate behind Willich's back the greatest scandals about his personal character. Of this I have plenty of witnesses.

"I am not going to waste any words on the story about my 'courage'. To my surprise at the time, I discovered in Baden that courage is one of the commonest of all qualities, and not worth speaking about; that crude courage alone, however, is of no more value than mere *goodwill*, and that, therefore, it often happens that each individual is a hero as regards courage, and yet the whole battalion takes to its heels as one man. We have an example of this in the expedition of Willich's corps to Karlsdorf, which is described at some length in my account of the campaign for an Imperial Constitution.[a]

"On this occasion, namely, on New Year's Eve 1850, Willich claims to have preached me a victorious moral sermon. Since I am not accustomed to keep a record of how I spend the transition from one year to the next, I cannot vouch for the date. At any rate, Willich never delivered the sermon in the shape in which he has had it printed.

"In the Refugee Committee,[342] he says, I and several others behaved in an 'unworthy' manner towards the great man. Shocking![b] But where then were the victorious moral arguments at the time when Willich, pulveriser of the impious, suddenly found himself powerless against mere 'unworthy behaviour'. No one will demand that I should pay serious attention to such silly remarks.

"In the meeting of the Central Authority,[c] when it came to a challenge to a duel between Schramm and Willich, I am supposed to have committed the crime of having 'left the room' together with Schramm shortly before the scene took place, and, therefore, of having prepared the whole scene in advance.

"Previously it was Marx who was alleged to have 'egged on' Schramm, now for a change I am supposed to have done so. A duel between a Prussian lieutenant, an old hand at pistol shooting, and a *commerçant*, who perhaps had never had a pistol in his hand, was truly a remarkable means to 'get rid' of the lieutenant. Yet friend Willich maintained everywhere, orally and in writing, that we had wanted to get him shot.

---

[a] See present edition, Vol. 10, pp. 215-18.—*Ed.*
[b] Engels uses the English word.—*Ed.*
[c] In late August 1850.—*Ed.*

"It is quite possible—I do not keep a record of when certain needs cause me to leave the room—that I left the room at the same time as Schramm; but it is not likely, since from the minutes of that meeting of the Central Authority deposited with me I see that on that evening Schramm and I took turns in recording the minutes. Simply, Schramm was furious at Willich's shameless behaviour, and to the great astonishment of us all he challenged him to a duel. A few minutes before, Schramm himself had no inkling that it would come to this. Never was an action more spontaneous. Here again Willich relates that he made a speech, saying: 'You, Schramm, leave the room!' Actually, Willich appealed to the Central Authority to expel Schramm. The Central Authority ignored his request and Schramm departed only after being personally addressed by Marx, who wanted to avoid any further scandal. On my side there is the minute book, on that of Herr Willich is his personal character.

"Frederick Engels"

Herr Willich relates further that in the Workers' Society he gave an account of the "unworthy behaviour" of the Refugee Committee, and that he made it the basis for a motion.

"When the indignation against Marx and his clique rose to a climax," the noble-minded one reports, "*I voted* for the matter to be dealt with by the *Central Authority. This* took place."

What took place? Willich's voting or the Central Authority's dealing with the matter? What magnanimity! His imperious vote rescues his enemies from the popular indignation that had risen to a climax. Herr Willich forgets the fact that the Central Authority was the *secret* committee of a *secret* society, whereas the Workers' Society was a *public*, open society. He forgets that treatment of the matter by the Central Authority could not therefore be made the subject of a vote in the Workers' Society, and so the Samaritan scene in which he figures as the hero could not have happened. Friend Schapper will help him to refresh his memory.

From the public Workers' Society, Herr Willich leads us into the secret Central Authority, and from the Central Authority to Antwerp, to the duel, to his duel with Schramm[a]:

"Schramm came to Ostend in the company of a *former Russian officer*, who according to *his own account* went over to the Hungarians in the Hungarian revolution, and who *vanished without trace* after the duel."

---

[a] The duel was fixed for September 11, 1850.—*Ed.*

This "former Russian officer" is no other than *Henryk Ludvic Miskowsky.*

"This is to testify," states one of the certificates of the *former Russian officer,* "that the bearer Henri Lewis Miskowsky, a *Polish* gentleman, has served *during the late Hungarian war* 1848-1849 as officer in the 46th battalion of the Hungarian *Honveds,* and that he behaved as such *praiseworthy* and *gallantly.*

"*London, November* 12, 1853. *L. Kossuth,* late Governor of Hungary."[a]

Mendacious man of noble consciousness! But the intention is *noble.* The opposition of good and evil must be presented in striking contrast as a living picture. What an artistic grouping! On one side the noble-minded one, surrounded

"by Techow, now in Australia, Vidil, French captain of Hussars, then in exile and now a prisoner in Algiers, and Barthélemy, owing to French newspapers known as one of the most resolute revolutionaries".

In short, on one side is Willich in person, surrounded by the élite of two revolutions. On the other side is Schramm, the depraved, deserted except for a "former Russian officer", whose participation in the Hungarian revolution is not a matter of fact, but only occurred "according to his own account", and who even "vanished without trace after the duel", and is, therefore, in the final analysis, the devil himself. In a picturesque description, virtue puts up at the "best hotel" in Ostend, where a "Prussian prince" is lodged, whereas depravity, together with the Russian officer, "lived in a private house". The Russian officer does not seem to have entirely "vanished after the duel", since, according to Herr Willich's further account, "Schramm remained behind at the stream with the Russian officer". Moreover, the Russian officer has not vanished from the world as the noble-minded one hopes, which is proved by the statement reproduced below:

"London, Nov. 24, 1853

"Under the date October 28, in the *Criminal-Zeitung* there is an article by Herr Willich in which, among other things, he describes the duel he fought with Schramm in Antwerp in 1850. I regret to say that not all points of the description give the public a truthful account. The article says: 'The duel was arranged, etc.; Schramm came accompanied by a former Russian officer, etc., who, etc., vanished.' This is an untruth. I was never in the service of Russia, and all the other *Polish* officers in the Hungarian war of liberation could, just as much as myself, be called *Russian.* I served in Hungary from the beginning of the war in 1848 until 1849 when the end came at Villagos. Furthermore, I have not vanished without trace. After Schramm's shot, which he fired at Willich at half a pace from the initial position, had missed, Willich fired at Schramm from where he stood and his bullet

[a] This text is in English in the original.—*Ed.*

wounded Schramm slightly in the head. I remained with Schramm *because we had no doctor*" (Herr Willich had arranged the duel), "washed and bandaged his wound, paying no attention to the seven persons who were haymaking nearby, who had witnessed the duel, and who could have become dangerous for me. Willich and his named companions left the scene in haste, while Schramm and I remained where we were, watching them go. Soon they were out of sight. I must point out, furthermore, that Willich and his companions were already at the scene of the duel when we arrived, and that they had marked out the duelling ground, on which Willich took up a position that placed him in the shade. I pointed this out to Schramm, who said: let it be. Schramm was in good spirits, fearless and quite unperturbed. That I was *compelled* to remain behind in Belgium was not unknown to the persons concerned. I do not wish to dwell on the other circumstances of this in form so peculiar duel.

"Henryk Ludvic Miskowsky"

The wheel-work of the noble-minded one is wound up. He conjured up a Russian officer only to make him vanish without trace. In his place I must now necessarily make my appearance on the battlefield as Samiel, albeit in incorporeal form.

"Early next morning" (after Herr Willich's arrival in Ostend), "he" (a friendly French citizen) "showed us the *Précurseur de Bruxelles*, in which newspaper there was a private correspondent's report containing the following passage: '*A number of German refugees have arrived in Brighton.* A message from this town informs us: in the next few days Ledru-Rollin and the French refugees from London will hold a congress in Ostend together with Belgian democrats.' Who can claim the honour of calling this idea his own? It did not come from a *Frenchman*, it was too à propos for that. This honour belongs exclusively to Herr Marx, *for although* one of his friends *may* have undertaken it—the brain is the source of ideas and not the hand."

"A friendly French citizen" showed Herr Willich and Co. the *Précurseur de Bruxelles*. He *showed* them something that does not exist. There is, of course, a *Précurseur d'Anvers*. Systematic falsification and distortion in regard to topography and chronology is an essential function of the noble consciousness. Ideal time and ideal space are the appropriate framework for its ideal productions.

In order to prove that this idea, namely the article in the *Précurseur de Bruxelles* "came from" Marx, Herr Willich assures us that "it did not come from a Frenchman". *This* idea did not *come from*! "It was too à propos for that." Mon dieu, an idea which Herr Willich himself can only describe in French could not come from a Frenchman? But how does the Frenchman appear on the scene at all, noble-minded one? What has the Frenchman to do with Willich and Schramm and the former Russian officer and the *Précurseur de Bruxelles*?

The spokesman of the noble-minded one's thoughts gives tongue out of season and betrays the fact that he finds it à propos to conjure away an essential intermediate link.

Before Schramm had challenged Herr Willich to a duel, the Frenchman Barthélemy had agreed to fight a duel with the Frenchman Songeon, and this was to take place in Belgium. Barthélemy chose Willich and Vidil as seconds. Songeon travelled to Belgium. The incident with Schramm came in between. Both duels were then to take place on the same day. Songeon did *not* turn up. On his return to London, Barthélemy asserted *publicly*: Songeon was responsible for the article in the *Précurseur d'Anvers*.

The noble-minded one hesitated for a long time before he finally applied the idea concerning Barthélemy to his own person and the idea about Songeon to me. Originally, as Techow himself told Engels and me after his return to London, the noble-minded one was firmly convinced that through Schramm I aimed at his removal from this world, and he put this idea in writing everywhere. On closer reflection, however, he found it impossible that a diabolical tactician could hit on the idea of getting rid of Herr Willich by means of a duel with Schramm. Hence, he seized on the idea "which did not come from a Frenchman".

Thesis: "This honour belongs exclusively to Herr Marx." *Proof*: "*For although* one of his friends *may* have undertaken" (to *undertake* an idea!) "*it*" (for the pure-minded one an *idea* is not feminine[a] but sexless),—"the brain is the source of ideas and not the hand." *"For although!"* A significant *"although"*! To prove that Marx had *invented* "it", Herr Willich imputes that a friend of Marx's had *undertaken* "it", or rather "may have undertaken it". *Quod erat demonstrandum.*

> "*If*," says the noble-minded one, "if it is established that Szemere, Marx's friend, betrayed the crown of Hungary to the Austrian Government, that *would* be a convincing proof, etc."

However, precisely the opposite is true. But that has no bearing on the matter. If Szemere had committed treason, then for Herr Willich that *would* be a "convincing" proof that Marx had undertaken the article in the *Précurseur de Bruxelles. Although,* however, the premise is *not* an established fact, the conclusion remains valid, and it is established that if Szemere betrayed holy Stephen's crown, Marx betrayed holy Stephen himself.

---

[a] In German "Idee" is of feminine gender.—*Ed.*

After the Russian officer vanished without trace, Herr Willich reappeared, and this in the "Workers' Society in London", where

> "the workers unanimously condemned Herr Marx" and "on the day after his resignation from the Society in a general meeting of the London District unanimously expelled him from the League".

Previously, however,

> "Marx with the majority of the Central Authority adopted a resolution to transfer the Central Authority from London"

and, despite Schapper's well-meant remonstrances, resolved to form a section for themselves. According to the statutes of the secret society the majority had the right to transfer the Central Authority to Cologne and provisionally to expel the entire Willich group, which was *not entitled to pass resolutions* in regard to it. The striking fact remains that on this occasion the noble-minded one, with his predilection for petty dramatics, in which Herr Willich plays a great rhetorical role, allowed the catastrophe itself, the scene in which the split occurred, to pass without taking advantage of it. The temptation was great, but unfortunately the dry text of the minutes exists and it proves that the triumphant Christ sat for hours silent and embarrassed in face of the accusations of the evil ones, then finally made off, left friend Schapper in the lurch, and did not recover his speech until he was in the "circle" of the believers. En passant: whereas Herr W. in America proclaims the glories of the "Workers' Society linked with him by respect and confidence", even Herr Schapper has considered it necessary for the time being to resign from Herr Willich's Society.

For a moment the man of the noble consciousness rises from the sphere of "tactical" procedure characteristic of him to the sphere of theory. Or so it seems. In actual fact he continues to furnish "samples of the tactics of Herr Marx". On p. 8 of the *Revelations* it says: "The Schapper-Willich party" (Herr Willich quotes it as Willich-Schapper) "have never laid claim to the dignity of having their own ideas. Their own contribution is the peculiar misunderstanding of other people's ideas".[a] In order to show the public how well provided he is with ideas of *his own,* Herr W. reports as his latest discovery, and indeed as a refutation of the views of Engels and myself, "what *institutions*" the petty bourgeoisie would "adopt" if it came to power. In a circular letter[b] drawn up by Engels and myself, which the police of Saxony

[a] See present edition, Vol. 11, p. 403.—*Ed.*
[b] Karl Marx and Frederick Engels, "Address of the Central Authority to the Communist League" (see present edition, Vol. 10, pp. 277-87).—*Ed.*

found on Bürgers, and which was published in the most widely-read German newspapers and forms the basis of the Cologne bill of indictment, there is a rather lengthy account of the pious wishes of the German petty bourgeoisie. This provides the text for Willich's sermon. The reader should compare the original and the copy. How human of virtue to copy vice, even if with a "peculiar misunderstanding"! The improved sentiments compensate for the inferior style.

On p. 64 of the *Revelations* it says that in my view the Communist League "aims at forming not the *government party of the future* but the *opposition party of the future*".[a] Herr Willich is so noble that he craftily omits the first part of the sentence, "not the *government party*", in order firmly to seize on the latter part, "the opposition party of the future". By this ingenious halving of the sentence he proves that the Party of *office-seekers* is the true Party of the revolution.

The other idea of "his own" which Herr Willich produces is that the practical opposition between the noble consciousness and its opponents can be also *theoretically* expressed as "a division of mankind into two species", the Willichs and the anti-Willichs, the noble species and the ignoble species. Concerning the former, we learn that its main characteristic lies in the fact "*that they recognise one another*". To be boring is the privilege of the noble-minded one when he ceases to amuse by his samples of tactics.

We have seen how the man of the noble consciousness distorts or adapts facts by means of lies, or accords ludicrous hypotheses the rank of serious theses,—all in order to show that the opposite to himself is *in fact* the ignoble, the base. We have seen how in consequence his whole activity consists exclusively in discovering the base. The reverse aspect of this activity is that the actual complications with the world into which he himself gets entangled, however compromising they may appear to be, are transformed into proofs of his own noble-mindedness. To the pure, all is pure, and an opponent who fails to see the nobility of his deeds proves by that very fact that he is impure. The noble-minded one, therefore, does not have to *justify* himself, but has merely to express his moral indignation and astonishment at an opponent who compels him to provide justification. Hence the episode in which Herr Willich pretends to *justify* himself could just as well have been omitted altogether, as anyone can see by comparing my *Revelations*, Hirsch's confessions and

[a] See present edition, Vol. 11, p. 449.—*Ed.*

Herr Willich's reply. Hence, I shall give only a few examples to characterise the *men* of the noble consciousness.

Herr Willich was less compromised by my *Revelations* than by Hirsch's confessions, although the latter were originally intended to glorify him as the deliverer of his own enemies. Hence, he is careful to avoid dealing with Hirsch's confessions. He avoids even any mention of them. Hirsch is the notorious tool of the Prussian police against the party to which I belong. In contrast to this fact, Herr Willich puts forward the suggestion that *really* Hirsch was chosen by me to "smash" the Willich party.

> "Very soon he" (Hirsch) "intrigued with some followers of Marx, in particular a certain Lochner, in order to smash the Society. *As a result of this* he was put under observation. He was found out, etc. On a motion from me, he was expelled; Lochner stood up for him and was likewise expelled.... Hirsch *then* intrigued particularly against O. Dietz.... This intrigue was again immediately discovered."

That Hirsch was expelled as a spy from the Workers' Society of Great Windmill Street on a motion from Herr Willich, I myself reported in the *Revelations*, p. 67.[a] This expulsion carried no weight with me, since I ascertained what Herr Willich himself now confirms, namely, that it took place not on the basis of proven facts, but on the suspicion of imaginary intrigues between Hirsch and me. I knew Hirsch to be innocent of this crime. As for Lochner, he demanded proof of Hirsch's guilt. Herr Willich replied that Hirsch's sources of subsistence were unknown. But what about the sources of subsistence of Herr Willich? asked Lochner. On account of this "unworthy" utterance, Lochner was brought before a *court of honour* and since he refused to repent his sin in spite of all spiritual admonition, he was "expelled". After Hirsch had been expelled, and Lochner had been sent off after him, Hirsch

> "*then* intrigued particularly against O. Dietz with a very suspicious former police agent, who denounced Dietz to us".

Stechan, who had escaped from a Hanover prison, came to London, joined Willich's Workers' Society and denounced O. Dietz. Stechan was neither "suspicious" nor a "former Saxon police agent". What led him to denounce O. Dietz was the fact that the examining magistrate in Hanover had shown him a number of letters sent by him to London addressed to Dietz, the secretary of Willich's Committee.[343] At approximately the same

---

[a] See present edition, Vol. 11, p. 451.—*Ed.*

time as Stechan, Lochner appeared on the scene, also Eccarius II,[a] who had just been released from prison in Hanover and deported, Gimpel, for whose arrest a warrant had been issued on account of his participation in the Schleswig-Holstein affairs, and Hirsch, who had been imprisoned in Hamburg in 1848 because of a revolutionary poem, and who asserted that he was again being hunted by the police. Together with Stechan, they formed a kind of opposition and committed the sin against the Holy Ghost of contesting Herr Willich's articles of faith in the public discussions of the Society. All of them were struck by the fact that Stechan's denunciation of Dietz was answered by the expulsion of Hirsch by Willich. Soon all of them resigned from the Workers' Society and for a period formed with Stechan a society of their own.[344] They did not come into contact with me until *after* their resignation from Herr Willich's Society. The noble-minded one betrays his lie by distorting the time-sequence and omitting Stechan, the essential but irksome intermediate link.

On p. 66 of the *Revelations* I say: "Not long before the court action in Cologne, Kinkel and Willich sent a journeyman tailor[b] as emissary to Germany, etc."[c]

"Why," exclaims the noble-minded one indignantly, "why does Herr Marx lay stress on the *journeyman tailor*?"

I do not "lay stress" on the journeyman tailor in the way that, for example, the noble-minded one lays stress on Pieper, "the private tutor with Rothschild", although as a result of the Cologne Communist trial Pieper lost his job with Rothschild and instead won a place on the editorial board of the organ of the English Chartists.[d] I call the journeyman tailor a journeyman tailor. Why? Because I must not mention his name and yet prove to the Herren Kinkel-Willich that I was well acquainted with the personality of their emissary. The noble-minded one, therefore, accuses me of high treason against all journeyman tailors and tries to secure their votes by a Pindaric ode to journeyman tailors. In order to spare the good reputation of journeyman tailors, he magnanimously omits to say that Eccarius, whom he calls one of the expelled he-goats, is a journeyman tailor, which so far has not prevented Eccarius from being one of the greatest thinkers of the German

[a] Johann Friedrich Eccarius.— *Ed.*
[b] August Gebert.— *Ed.*
[c] See present edition. Vol. 11, p. 450.— *Ed.*
[d] *The People's Paper*.— *Ed.*

proletariat and from gaining a position of prestige among the Chartists themselves by his English articles in *The Red Republican*, the *Notes to the People*, and *The People's Paper*. This is how Herr Willich *refutes* my revelations of the activity of the journeyman tailor whom he and Kinkel sent to Germany.

We now come to the case of *Hentze*. The man of the noble consciousness tries to cover up his own position by an attack on me.

> "*Among other things, he*" (Hentze) "*lent Marx 300 talers.*"

In May 1849 I gave Herr Rempel an account of the financial difficulties of the *Neue Rheinische Zeitung*, which increased as the number of subscribers grew larger since expenses were in cash but receipts were to come in later. More, considerable losses were caused by the desertion of almost all the shareholders as a result of the articles in favour of the Paris June insurgents and against the Frankfurt parliamentarians, the Berlin agreement-seekers, and the members of the March Associations.[345] Herr Rempel referred me to Hentze, and Hentze advanced the *Neue Rheinische Zeitung* 300 talers against my written undertaking. Hentze, who at the time was himself being harried by the police, found it necessary to leave Hamm and travelled with me to Cologne, where I was greeted by the news of my expulsion from Prussia. The 300 talers borrowed from Hentze, the 1,500 talers for subscriptions which I received through the Prussian post, and the rapid printing-press, etc., belonging to me, were all used to cover the debts of the *Neue Rheinische Zeitung* to compositors, printers, paper merchants, office workers, correspondents, editorial personnel, etc. No one knows this better than Herr Hentze, since he himself lent my wife a travelling case in which to pack her silver in order to take it to a pawnshop in Frankfurt and thus obtain the means to meet our private needs. The account books of the *Neue Rheinische Zeitung* are in Cologne in the care of the merchant Stephan Naut, and I authorise the noble-minded one to have an officially certified extract from them made for him there.

After this digression, let us return to the matter in hand.

The *Revelations* does not find it at all unclear that Herr Willich was Hentze's friend and received support from him. What it finds unclear (p. 65[a]) is that Hentze, whose house had been searched and whose documents were seized, who was proved to have sheltered Schimmelpfennig on a secret mission in Berlin, and who,

---

[a] See present edition, Vol. 11, p. 450.—*Ed.*

on his own "admission", was an accomplice of the League, that this Hentze at the period when the Cologne trial was approaching a decision, when the attention of the Prussian police was strained to the utmost and every half-suspected German in Germany or England was being kept under the strictest surveillance, that this Hentze received permission from the authorities to travel to London and to consort freely there with Willich, and then came to Cologne in order to give "false evidence" against Becker. The specific time gives the relationship between Herr Hentze and Herr Willich its specific character, and the circumstances mentioned must have appeared strange to Willich himself, although he did not know that Hentze communicated with the Prussian police by telegraph from London. It is a question of the specific time. Herr Willich correctly feels that this is so, and therefore declares in his noble manner:

"He" (Hentze) "came to London before the trial" (this I, too, maintain), "not to me, but to the *Great Exhibition.*"

The noble-minded one has his own Great Exhibition just as he has his own *Précurseur de Bruxelles.* The real Great Exhibition in London closed in October 1851; Herr Willich makes Hentze travel "to *it*" in August *1852.* This circumstance can be testified to by Schily, Heise, and the other guarantors of the Kinkel-Willich loan, on each of whom Herr Hentze danced attendance in order to gain their votes for the transference of the American money from London to Berlin.

Long before Herr Hentze stayed with Herr Willich he had been invited to appear at the Cologne court trial as a witness, not for the defence but for the prosecution. As soon as we learned that Herr Willich had instructed Hentze to testify *against* Becker, "the man of intellect and character" (p. 68 of the *Revelations*[a]), the necessary information was sent at once to lawyer Schneider II, Becker's defence counsel. The letter arrived on the day when Hentze was being heard as a witness; the nature of his testimony agreed with our prediction. *For that reason,* Becker and Schneider cross-examined him publicly about his relation to Willich. The letter is to be found in the dossiers of the defence in Cologne, and the report on the cross-examination of Hentze in the *Kölnische Zeitung.*

I do not put forward the argument: *If* it is established that Herr Hentze did this or that, that *would* be a striking proof of the

[a] See present edition, Vol. 11, p. 452.—*Ed.*

activity of Herr Willich; "for although" friend Hentze "may have undertaken it—the brain is the source of ideas and not the hand". I leave this dialectic to the man of the noble consciousness.

Let us return to Herr Willich's proper domain:

"*A few more samples* of the *tactics*" (pursued by Marx) "for their full appreciation."

At the time of passive resistance in Hesse, of the mobilisation of the *Landwehr*[a] in Prussia, and of the simulated conflict between Prussia and Austria,[346] the noble-minded one was on the point of achieving a military insurrection in Germany, to be brought about by sending "to some persons in Prussia a short draft plan for forming committees of the *Landwehr*", and by the *willingness* of Herr Willich "***himself*** to go to Prussia".

"It was Herr Marx, who having been informed by one of his agents, made my *intended departure* more widely known and subsequently boasted of having hoaxed me with *false letters from Germany*."

Indeed![b] Becker sent me with comical marginal notes the lunatic letters with which Willich favoured the public in Cologne. I was not so cruel as to deprive my friends of the enjoyment of reading them. Schramm and Pieper took delight in hoaxing Herr Willich with replies, not "*from Germany*" but through the *London post*. The noble-minded one will take care not to produce the postmarks of the letters. He asserts that he "received *one* letter in an imitated handwriting and recognised it as false". This is impossible. These letters were all written by the same hand. While, therefore, Herr Willich "boasts" of having discovered a non-existent imitated handwriting, and of having discovered *one* that was false among a number of letters each of which was in its way as genuine as any of the others, he was much too noble-minded to recognise the hoax from the glorification of his person couched in Asiatic hyperbolae, the crudely comic account of his fixed ideas, and the romantic exaggeration of his presumptions. Even if Herr Willich had seriously intended his departure, it was frustrated not by my "making it more widely known to third persons", but by what was made known to Herr Willich himself. For the last letter which he received tore away the transparent veil. Until the present moment his vanity has compelled him to declare the letter which undeceived him to be *false*, and the letters which *made a fool* of

---

[a] Army reserve.—*Ed.*
[b] Marx uses the English word.—*Ed.*

him to be genuine. Does the noble-minded one, because he is virtuous, believe that there shall indeed be sect and cakes[a] but no humour in the world? It was ignoble of the noble-minded one to withhold from the public the enjoyment of these letters.

"As regards the correspondence with Becker mentioned by Marx, what is said about it is *false.*"

As regards this false correspondence and Herr Willich's *intention* to travel to Prussia in person, and my making it more widely known to third persons, I found it appropriate to send a copy of the *Criminal-Zeitung* to ex-Lieutenant Steffen. Steffen was a witness for the defence on behalf of Becker, who had entrusted all his documents to him for safe-keeping. Compelled by the police to leave Cologne, he is now a teacher in Chester, for he belongs to the ignoble species of human beings who have to *earn* their living, even in exile. The man of the noble consciousness, true to his ethereal nature, does not live from capital, which he does not possess, nor from work, which he does not perform. He lives from the manna of public opinion, from the *respect* of other people. Hence he fights for this as his sole capital.

Steffen writes to me:

"Chester, November 22, 1853

"Willich is very angry at your giving me fragments from a letter of Becker's. He describes the letter, and therefore also the passages quoted from it, as *fictitious.* To this clumsy assertion I counterpose the facts in order to provide documentary evidence for Becker's view of Willich. One evening, with a hearty laugh, Becker gave me two letters and told me to read them when I was in low spirits; the contents would be the more effective in cheering me up, because I would be in a position to judge them from a military standpoint in view of my earlier circumstances. In fact, on reading those letters sent by August Willich to Becker, I found they contained extremely comic and remarkable *orders of the day to the troops* (to make use of an appropriate royal Prussian expression), in which the great Field-Marshal and social Messiah sends out from England the order to capture Cologne, to confiscate private property, to establish an artificially contrived military dictatorship, to introduce a military-social code of laws, to ban all newspapers except *one,* which would have to publish daily orders about the prescribed mode of thought and behaviour, and a quantity of further details. Willich was kind enough to promise that *when* this job in Cologne and the Prussian Rhine province was *done,* he *himself* would come to separate the sheep from the goats and to pass judgment on the living and the dead. Willich claims that his 'short draft plan would be easy to put into effect *if* some persons took the initiative', and 'that it would have *highly important* consequences' (for whom?). For my edification I should very much like to know who were the deep-thinking '*Landwehr* officers' who 'later explained' this to Willich, and whether these gentlemen, who made a pretence of believing in 'the

[a] Marx uses the English phrase "sect and cakes".—*Ed.*

highly important consequences of the short draft plan', stayed in England during the mobilisation of the Prussian *Landwehr* or in Prussia, where the child of the world was to be brought into being. It was very good of Willich to have sent the birth announcement and the description of the child to 'some' persons. None of these persons, however, seem to have been more inclined to act as godfather at the baptism than Becker, 'the man of intellect and character'. On one occasion, Willich sent over an adjutant named....[a] This man did me the honour of having me summoned and was very firmly convinced that he could judge the whole situation in advance better than anyone confronted by the facts day by day. Hence he came to have a very low opinion of me when I informed him that the officers of the Prussian army would not consider themselves lucky to fight under his and Willich's banner, and were not at all inclined to proclaim a Willichian republic at the earliest possible moment. He was still more angry when he found that no one was stupid enough to want to multigraph the Appeal, which he had brought with him ready-made, inviting the officers to declare themselves immediately and openly in favour of 'that' which he called democracy. Full of rage, he left 'the Cologne enslaved by Marx' (as he wrote to me) and arranged for his nonsense to be multigraphed elsewhere, sent it to a great many officers, and *thus* it came about that the chaste secret of this cunning method of turning Prussian officers into republicans was prostituted by the 'Spectator' of the *Kreuzzeitung*.

"Willich says he is absolutely incapable of believing that persons of 'Becker's character and intellect' could laugh at his plan. He declares the utterance of this fact a clumsy lie. If he had read the *Cologne Trial*, and after all he has every reason to do so, he would have found that both Becker and I *openly* expressed the judgment on his plan contained in the letter published by you. If Willich would like to have a correct *military* description of the then existing situation, which he depicts according to his fantasy, I can oblige him.

"I regret that it is not only in Weydemeyer and Techow that Willich finds former comrades who deny him the wished-for admiration of his military genius and practical understanding of the situation.

"*W. Steffen*"

Now for the final "sample of the tactics of Marx".

Herr Willich gives a fantastic description of a February banquet in 1851 organised by Louis Blanc as a counter-demonstration to Ledru-Rollin's banquet and against the influence of Blanqui.

"Herr Marx, of course, was not invited."

Of course not. Anyone could get in for two shillings, and a few days later Louis Blanc asked Marx with great emphasis why he had not been present at it.

"Thereupon" (where? at the banquet?) "an *undelivered toast* of Blanqui's, with an introduction reviling the celebration and calling Schapper and Willich misleaders of the people, was distributed as a leaflet among the workers in Germany."

The "undelivered toast of Blanqui's"[347] forms an essential part of the story recounted by the noble-minded one, who, believing in

[a] Marx also quotes this passage in his pamphlet *Herr Vogt* (see present edition, Vol. 17). There the name Schimmelpfennig is given instead of dots.—*Ed.*

his words in the *higher* sense, is accustomed to state emphatically: "*I never lie.*"

Some days after the banquet the Paris *Patrie* published a toast which Blanqui had sent from Belle-Île to the organisers of the celebration at their request, and in which in his customary pregnant manner he scourged the entire Provisional Government of 1848 and particularly the father of the banquet, M. Louis Blanc. The *Patrie* said it was surprised that this toast had been suppressed at the banquet. Louis Blanc immediately declared in the London *Times* that Blanqui *was* an abominable intriguer and had never sent any such toast to the banquet committee. On behalf of the banquet committee, MM. Louis Blanc, Landolphe, Barthélemy, Vidil, Schapper, and *Willich himself*, stated in the *Patrie* that they had *never* received the toast in question. Before printing this statement, however, the *Patrie* made enquiries of M. Antoine, Blanqui's brother-in-law, who had sent the toast for publication. *Below* the statement of the gentlemen mentioned above, the newspaper printed Antoine's reply, which was to the effect that he had certainly sent the toast to Barthélemy and had received from him an acknowledgement of its receipt. "Thereupon", M. Barthélemy declared that it was true he had received the toast but had put it aside as unsuitable without notifying the committee about it. Unfortunately, however, ex-Captain Vidil, who was one of the signatories, had already written to the *Patrie* that his military sense of honour and his instinct for truth compelled him to confess that he himself, Louis Blanc, Willich and all the others had lied in their first statement. The committee, he said, did not consist of the six persons named but had thirteen members. Blanqui's toast had been submitted to all of them, it had been discussed by all of them, and after a fairly lengthy debate it was decided by a majority of seven to six to suppress it. He himself was among the six who had voted *in favour* of its being read out.

One can understand the jubilation of the *Patrie* when, after Vidil's letter, it received M. Barthélemy's declaration, which it published with the following "preface".

"We have often asked ourselves, and it is a difficult question to answer, whether the demagogues are notable more for their boastfulness or their stupidity. A fourth letter from London has increased our perplexity. There they are, we do not know how many poor wretches, who are so tormented by the longing to write and to see their names published in the *reactionary* press that they are undeterred even by the prospect of infinite humiliation and mortification. What do they care for the laughter and the indignation of the public—the *Journal des Débats*, the *Assemblée nationale* and the *Patrie* will publish their stylistic exercises; to achieve this no cost to the cause of cosmopolitan democracy can be too high.... In the name of literary commiseration we therefore include the following letter from 'citizen' Barthélemy—it is a novel, and, we hope, the last proof of the authencity of Blanqui's famous toast whose existence they first all denied and now fight among themselves for the right to acknowledge."[a]

So much for the history of Blanqui's toast. As a result of "Blanqui's undelivered toast", the *Société des proscrits démocrates [et] socialistes* broke off its agreement with Herr Willich's Society.

Simultaneously with the split in the German Workers' Society and the German Communist Society, a split took place in the *Société des proscrits démocrates [et] socialistes.* A number of members suspected of gravitating towards *bourgeois* democracy, towards *Ledru-Rollinism,* handed in their resignations and were subsequently expelled. Ought then the man of the noble consciousness to tell this society what he now says to the bourgeois democrats, that Engels and Marx had prevented him from sinking into the arms of bourgeois democracy, from remaining "united by bonds of sympathy with *all* companions of the revolution", or ought he to tell them that "in the split the various views about revolutionary development played *no* part"? *On the contrary,* the noble-minded one said that in both societies the split occurred as a result *of the same* diametrically opposed principles, that Engels, Marx, etc., represented the *bourgeois element* in the German Society just as Madier and Co. did in the French one. The noble-minded one is even afraid that mere contact with this bourgeois element could endanger the "true faith" and therefore with calm nobility moved that the bourgeois element should not be admitted to the Société des proscrits, "not even as *visitors*".

Invented! False! exclaims the noble-minded one in his staunch monosyllables. "Samples of tactics" on my part! Voyons!

"*Présidence du citoyen Adam. Séance du 30 Sept. 1850.*

"Trois délégués de la société démocratique allemande de Windmill-Street sont introduits. Ils donnent connaissance de leur mission qui consiste dans la communication d'une lettre dont il est fait lecture." (In this letter the reasons for the split are allegedly set out.) "*Le citoyen Adam* fait remarquer *l'analogie* qui existe entre les événements qui viennent de s'accomplir dans les deux sociétés de chaque côté *l'élément bourgeois* et *le parti prolétaire* ont fait scission dans les circonstances *identiques* etc. etc. *Le citoyen Willich* demande que les membres démissionaires" (he then corrects himself, as the minutes state, and says: "expulsés") "de la société

[a] P. Mayer [Editorial Preface to Barthélemy's letter], *La Patrie,* No. 71, March 12, 1851.—*Ed.*

allemande, ne puissent être reçus même comme *visiteurs* dans la société française." (Extraits conformes au texte original des procès verbaux).

"*L'archiviste de la société des proscrits démocrates [et] socialistes.*

J. Clédat"[a]

Herewith ends the mellifluous, singular, grandiloquent, unprecedented, truthful, and adventurous story of the world-renowned *knight of the noble consciousness.*

"An honest mind and plain; he must speak truth,
And they will take it so; if not, he's plain.
These kind of knaves I know."[b]

Karl Marx

London, November 28, 1853.

---

[a] "*Meeting of 30 Sept. 1850, citizen Adam in the chair.*

"Three delegates from the German Democratic Society of Windmill Street are introduced. They make known their mission, which is to deliver a letter that is read out." (In this letter the reasons for the split are allegedly set out.) "*Citizen Adam* calls attention to the *analogy* between the events which have taken place in the two societies, in both of them the *bourgeois element* and the *proletarian party* have separated from each other under *identical* circumstances, etc., etc. *Citizen Willich* moves that the members who have resigned" (he then corrects himself, as the minutes state, and says "who have been excluded") "from the German Society should not be admitted to the French Society, even as visitors." (Extracts conform to the original text of the minutes).

"*Recorder of the Society of Exiled Democrats and Socialists*

J. Clédat."

[b] Quoted by Marx in English from Shakespeare's *King Lear*, Act 2, Scene 2.—*Ed.*

Karl Marx

[MANTEUFFEL'S SPEECH.— RELIGIOUS MOVEMENT IN PRUSSIA.— MAZZINI'S ADDRESS.—LONDON CORPORATION.— RUSSELL'S REFORM.—LABOR PARLIAMENT]

London, Tuesday, Nov. 29, 1853

Yesterday morning the Prussian Chambers[a] were opened by a speech of the Prime Minister, Mr. Manteuffel. The passage relative to the eastern complication, as communicated to us by electric telegraph, is couched in terms clearly intended to allay the suspicions afloat with respect to a conspiracy between the courts of St. Petersburg, Berlin, and Vienna. It is the more remarkable as it is generally known that Frederick William IV, by the organ of the same Manteuffel, has condescended at various previous occasions, to solemnly communicate to his loyal people, that the Chambers have no call to intermeddle with matters of foreign policy, since the external relations of the state fall as much under the exclusive control of the crown, as the king's own demesne lands. The above-mentioned passage, involving as it does, something like an appeal to the people, betrays the extreme difficulties the Prussian Government finds itself placed in, menaced on the one hand by Russia and France, and on the other by its own subjects, at the same time that it is stimulated by the high price of provisions, a deeply depressed commerce, and the remembrance of an atrocious breach of faith still to be expiated.[348] The Prussian Government itself has cast off the refuge of working on public opinion through the means of the Chambers, which are deliberately constituted by the king as a mere sham, intentionally treated by the ministers as a mere sham, and accepted by the people as a mere sham, in a manner not to be misunderstood. It will not do to tell them now

[a] "Opening of the Prussian Chambers", *The Times*, No. 21598, November 29, 1853.—*Ed.*

that these mock institutions are, all of a sudden, to be looked upon as the bulwarks of "Fatherland."

"The Prussians," says *The Times* of to-day, "have hardly shown the sense and sagacity for which they once had credit, by the undeserved contempt into which they have allowed the Chambers elected under the present constitution to fall."

On the contrary, the Prussians have fully shown their good sense, by allowing the men who betrayed the revolution in the hope of reaping its fruits, to enjoy not even the *appearance* of influence, and to prove to the government that they are not the dupes of its juggle, and that the Chambers, in their opinion, if they are anything at all, are but a new bureaucratic institution, added to the old bureaucratic institutions of the country.

Every one not thoroughly acquainted with the past history of Germany will be at a loss to understand the religious quarrels again and again troubling the otherwise dull surface of German society. There are the remnants of the so-called German Church,[349] persecuted now, as eagerly as in 1847, by the established governments. There is the question of marriages between Catholics and Protestants, setting the Catholic clergy and the Prussian Government by the ears, as in 1847.[350] There is, above all, the fierce combat between the Archbishop of Freiburg,[a] excommunicating the Baden Government, and having his letter publicly read from the pulpits, and the Grand Duke[b] ordering the recreant churches to be closed, and the parish priests to be arrested; and there are the peasants assembling and arming themselves, protecting their priests and driving back the gendarmes, which they have done at Bischofsheim, Königshofen, Grünsfeld, Gerlachsheim, where the Mayor of the village was forced to fly, and at many other villages. It would be a mistake to consider the religious conflict in Baden as possessed of a purely local character. Baden is only the battleground the Catholic party has deliberately chosen for attacking the Protestant princes. The Archbishop of Friburg represents in this conflict the whole Catholic clergy of Germany, as the Grand Duke of Baden represents all the great and small potentates confessing the reformed creed. What then are we to think of a country renowned on the one hand for the profound, bold and unparalleled criticism to which it has subjected all religious traditions, and surprising, on the other, all Europe, at periodically recurring epochs, with the

[a] Hermann Vicari.—*Ed.*
[b] Frederick I.—*Ed.*

resurrection of the religious quarrels of the 17th century? The secret is simply this, that all popular commotions, lurking in the background, are forced by the governments to assume at first the mystical and almost uncontrollable form of religious movements. The clergy, on their part, allow themselves to be deceived by appearances, and, while they fancy they direct the popular passions for the exclusive benefit of their corporation, against the government, they are, in truth, the unconscious and unwilling tools of the revolution itself.

The daily London press exhibits a great show of horror and moral indignation at an address issued by Mazzini, and found in the possession of Felice Orsini, leader of the National Band No. 2, destined to rise in the province of Lugagnano, which contains portions of Modena, Parma, and the Kingdom of Piedmont. In this address the people are exhorted to "act *by surprise,* as the people of Milan tried to do, and will again."[a] The address then says: "The *dagger,* if it strikes unexpectedly, does good service and supplies the place of muskets." This the London press represents as an open appeal to "*secret, cowardly assassination.*" Now I want only to know how, in a country like Italy, where public means of resistance are nowhere, and police spies are everywhere, an insurrectionary movement could expect any chance of success if *surprise* be not resorted to? I want to know, if the people of Italy are to fight with the troops of Austria at all, with what kind of weapons they are to fight except with those left to them—with the *daggers* Austria has not succeeded in taking away? Mazzini is far from telling them to use the dagger for cowardly assassination of the *unarmed* foe—exhorts them to use it "by surprise," it is true, but in the broad light [of] day, as *at Milan,* where a few patriots, armed only with knives, rushed on the guard-houses of the armed Austrian garrisons.

> But, says *The Times,* "constitutional Piedmont is to undergo the same fate as Rome, Naples, and Lombardy!"

Why not? Was it not the King of Sardinia[b] who betrayed the Italian revolution in 1848 and in 1849, and can Italy be transformed into a Republic with a King of Piedmont[c] any more than Germany with a King of Prussia? So much as to the morality of Mazzini's address. As to its political value, it is quite another

---

[a] Here and below Marx quotes from the second editorial in *The Times,* No. 21592, November 22, 1853.—*Ed.*

[b] Charles Albert.—*Ed.*

[c] Victor Emmanuel.—*Ed.*

question. I, for my part, think Mazzini to be mistaken, both in his opinions about the Piedmontese people and in his dreams of an Italian revolution, which he supposes is not to be effected by the favorable chances of European complications, but by the private action of Italian conspirators acting by surprise.

You will have seen by the London papers that Government has appointed a commission for inquiring into the corrupt practices and the whole organization of that most venerable body known as the Corporation of the City. The following are some of the facts contained in the reports of the commission, whose labors are still far from having arrived at a close:

The revenue of the Corporation of London is estimated at £400,000, without taking all items into account, and the gross amount paid away in salaries reaches the very considerable sum of £107,000, or more than 25 per cent. of the whole income. The legal salaries are set down at £14,700, of which the Recorder receives £3,000, the Common Sergeant, £1,500, and the Judge of the Sheriff's Court, £1,200. The Town Clerk receives £1,892; the Secretary, £1,249, and the Remembrancer, £1,765. The Chief Clerks at the Mansion-House and Guildhall[a] receive between them £1,250, a year. The Mace-bearer receives £550, and the Sword-bearer £550; the Upper Marshal £450 or £500, the Under Marshal £200 or £300. These Bumbles draw besides, £70 for uniforms, £14 for boots, and £20 for cocked hats. Mr. Bennoch stated in his evidence that

> "the whole expense of the establishments in the Corporation of London is much greater than the whole expense of the Federal Government of the United States, or, what is perhars a more startling statement, its expenditure upon itself, in administering the funds of the Corporation, is larger than the whole amount of revenue from rents, tolls and fees from brokers which it receives."[b]

The great secret of the Reform pills Lord John Russell intends to administer to the British public has at last come out. He proposes: 1, a repeal of the property qualification for members of Parliament, a qualification which has long since become a nominal one; 2, a readjustment of the constituencies by doing away with some small boroughs and adding more large ones; 3, a reduction of the county constituencies from the £20 to the £10 borough qualification. A fourth proposition to lower the franchise to £5 has been abandoned, as by this means, says *The Times*,

---

[a] Residence of Lord Mayor and the City Hall.—*Ed.*

[b] "City Corporation Commission", *The Times*, No. 21593, November 23, 1853.—*Ed.*

"the present electors would be virtually disenfranchised, because the class to be admitted will greatly outnumber all others put together, and has only to be unanimous to be supreme."

In other words, enfranchising the majority even of the small trading class would disenfranchise the minority. A very ingenious argument this. The most important feature of the Reform bill looming in the future is, however, not this point, or all its points taken together. This important feature is the general and absolute indifference its announcement meets with. Every police report attracts a great deal more of public attention than the "*great measure*," the new Reform bill, the common work of the "Ministry of all the talents."

Ernest Jones was quite right in anticipating that the first note sounded of the mass movement of the people and a national organization headed by a Labor Parliament would strike alarm into the moneyed classes, and force the London class papers to take notice of it. *The Times* has immediately seen the importance of this new movement, and has given for the first time a report of the Chartist meeting held in the People's Institute at Manchester.[a] All its contemporaries are filled with leading articles on the labor movement and the Labor Parliament proposed by the Chartists, who were long since supposed to have died of exhaustion. *The Economist* has no less than four articles on the question. The reports, however, of the highly important meeting at Manchester cannot be said to afford any idea of its character or the business there transacted. I think fit, therefore, to give a report of my own. The following resolutions were proposed and adopted:

"1. That this meeting, after witnessing the futility of sectional struggles on the part of isolated bodies of workingmen to maintain a just standard of wages and to achieve the emancipation of labor, is of the opinion that the time has now arrived when a united and mass movement of the working classes, based on a national organization, and guided by one directing body, can alone insure adequate support to the men now locked out of employment and on strike, and enable workingmen in the future to emancipate labor from the thraldom of capital. The mass movement of the people and national organization be not intended to, and shall not, interfere with the present Trade Unions and combinations of workingmen, but that its action be to centralize, concentrate and confederate the strength of all, and of the entire body of workingmen. [...]

"2. That to carry the foregoing resolution it will be imperatively necessary that a Labor Parliament should meet as soon as possible; that Parliament to consist of delegates elected by the workingmen of each town in public meeting assembled. That the duties of that Parliament shall be to organize machinery whereby support may be rendered to the people now out on strike, or locked out by the manufacturers, by raising a national subscription of the most extensive character to

[a] "The Strikes", *The Times*, No. 21593, November 23, 1853.—*Ed.*

lay down a specific plan of action for the guidance of the working classes in their contest with the employers, and to propound the means by which labor may be emancipated from the undue influence of capital and become independent, self-employing and remunerative, without the necessity of strikes.

"3. That this meeting elect a Committee to correspond for the above purpose with the various towns and districts to make all necessary arrangements for the calling of the Labor Parliament, and to arrange and publish the necessary details for the sitting of the delegates, as well as a programme of the business to be brought before the delegation."[a]

By far the most remarkable speech was that of Mr. Jones, of which I give some extracts:

"The employer says, in The London *Times*, you have nothing to do with his profits. You must only count your own heads, not his profits. If there are many heads, although you want more, you will get less. And that he calls the law of supply and demand. That alone, he says, should regulate your wages. But does it? [...] No! If you've no business to claim a rise of wages when his profits are high, he should not pull you down when his profits become low. But then he'll tell you, though not one hand less may be employed—'trade's bad, times are hard, my profits have grown smaller—I can't afford to pay you the same wages.' It is not the law of supply and demand, then, but the law of dear cotton and small profits that regulates your labor. [...] The law of supply may be true, but the law of life is truer. The law of demand may be strong, but the law of starvation will be stronger still! We say, if the one capital, money, has a right to profits, so has the other capital, labor, too; and labor has the greater right, because labor made money, and not money labor. What is profit? The capital that remains after deduction of all working charges. The wages you have hitherto received are merely a portion of the working charges. That which only keeps soul and body together is no reward for toil. It is merely the necessary cost of keeping the human machine in working order. [...] You must have a surplus over and above the working cost of feeding and housing the machine of flesh and blood. You must have food for heart and brain, as well as for the mouth and belly. [...] The employer dreads your getting more wages; not because he can't afford to pay them, for his capital has increased more than 100 per cent, in the last seven years, and you asked for only 10 on your wage out of his 100 on your work. He dreads it, because higher wages would lead to independence; he dreads it, because higher wages would lead to education; he dreads it, because an enlightened people will not be slaves; he dreads it, because he knows you would then no more submit to work so many hours; he dreads it, because you would then not allow your wives to slave in the factory hell; he dreads it, because you would then send your children to school instead of the mill; he dreads it, because he knows if the wife was at the fireside, the child at the school and short time at the factory, the surplus hands that now beat wages down would flee from his control and labor would become a priceless pearl, gemming the diadem of human freedom. But the question has once more changed its aspect; it is not merely one of obtaining a share in the employer's profits, or a rise of 10 per cent.; it is one of preventing a fall of 20. [...] Good trade or bad trade makes little change to them; in the one they plunder the world abroad—in the other they

[a] Passages from the resolutions adopted at the Chartist meeting on November 20, 1853 and Jones' speech are quoted from the report by J. Benson: "Highly Important Meeting At Manchester" in *The People's Paper*, No. 82, November 26, 1853.—*Ed.*

plunder the world at home. [...] The question is rapidly changing for you, not into one of lower or higher wages, but into one of starvation or existence; of life in the factory hell or death at the factory door. The capitalists, those Cossacks of the West, first crossed the Danube of labor's rights; they have proclaimed their martial law of gold, and hurl starvation into our ranks from the batteries of monopoly. Town after town is placed in a state of siege. Non-employment digs the trenches, hunger scales the citadel of labor, the artillery of famine plays on the lines of toil. Every day their great confederation spreads; every day their movement becomes more national. [...] How are you prepared to confront them? Your movement is running into chaos and confusion. [...] As the lock-outs spread and your isolated action continues, you will be poaching in each other's preserves; the collectors of the one place will meet those of the others on the same ground—you will stand as foes where you should shake hands as allies—you will weaken each other's help where you should help each other's weakness. [...] The Wigan colliers were close to Preston, to Stockport, to Manchester, to Oldham, and they were left to fall unaided. [...] The factory operatives are on strike at Wigan too. And what do they say to the defeat of their brother workingmen the miners? They consider it a happy riddance. [...] They cannot help it—because they stand in each other's way. But why do they so stand? [...] Because you hedge your movement within the narrow limits of one trade, one district and one interest. [...] The movement of your employers is becoming national, and national must be your resistance also. As it is you are running into anarchy and ruin. Do not suppose that I impugn the wisdom, conduct or integrity of the Trades Unions. [...]

"But the leading strings that support the child become impediments that clog the man. [...] That isolation which worked well in the infancy of the labor movement becomes ruin in its manhood. [...] Let all the trades be represented whose support you seek. [...] Place the cause of labor not in the hands of one mill, or one town, or even one district, but place it in the hands of a laborers' Parliament."

Written on November 29, 1853

First published in the *New-York Daily Tribune*, No. 3948, December 12, 1853; reprinted in the *New-York Semi-Weekly Tribune*, No. 892, December 13, and the *New-York Weekly Tribune*, No. 640, December 17, 1853

Signed: *Karl Marx*

Reproduced from the *New-York Daily Tribune*

Frederick Engels

THE WAR ON THE DANUBE[351]

As we have already observed, the retreat of the Turks from Oltenitza appears to indicate the conclusion of the first epoch of the Turko-Russian war; with it at least a first and distinct series of operations, beginning with the passage at Kalafat, seems to be concluded, to make room either for the tranquility of winter quarters, or for the execution of new plans not yet developed. The moment seems opportune for a review of the campaign up to that epoch, the more so as the official and non-official reports of the only action of consequence fought on the Danube, the Russian attack upon the Turkish tête-du-pont[a] at Oltenitza, are just come to hand.

On the 28th of October the Turks crossed from Widin to Kalafat. They were hardly disturbed in their occupation of this point, except by reconnoitering skirmishes; for when the Russians were on the point of concentrating an effective force at Krajova for the attack on Kalafat, they were disturbed by the news of a second and more dangerous advance of the Turks, who, on the 2d of November, had crossed the Danube at Oltenitza, whence they seriously menaced the Russian communications. Simulated and secondary attacks were at the same time made by the Turks on the whole line of the Danube from Widin to Oltenitza, but these either found the Russians well prepared, or were not undertaken with a sufficient force to deceive the enemy and lead him into any serious error.

The corps at Kalafat therefore, remained unmolested and gradually received reinforcements, which are said to have swelled

[a] Bridge-head.—*Ed.*

it to something like 24,000 men. But as this corps has neither advanced or suffered a repulse, we may for the present leave it out of consideration.

The passage at Oltenitza took place according to Omer Pasha's report[a] in the following way. Oltenitza is a village situated near the confluence of the Arges River and the Danube. Opposite the mouth of the Arges there is an island in the Danube; on the southern bank of this river the village and fort of Turtukai are situated, on a steep bank rising to some 600 or 700 feet, on the top of which elevation the fort of Turtukai is constructed. The guns of Turtukai, therefore, form a most effective support to any corps crossing the river at this point. On the lst Nov. the Turks crossed over to the island and there threw up solid entrenchments during the night. On the 2d they crossed from this island to the Wallachian shore, east of the Arges. Two battalions, with 100 horsemen and two guns passed in boats to the Wallachian side; a few gun-shots from Turtukai drove the Russian outposts from a lazaretto building situated near the riverside, and this building, which was immediately taken possession of by the Turks, proved a great advantage to them. It was massively constructed, with vaulted chambers, thereby offering, with hardly any additional labor, all the advantages of that great desideratum in field fortification, a *réduit*. Consequently the Turks at once began throwing up entrenchments from the Arges to the Danube; four hundred men were kept constantly employed, galianes and fascines having been prepared beforehand. From all the reports we receive, we can only conclude that these entrenchments were continuous lines, cutting off entirely every communication from the Russian positions to the Turkish points of landing. Fortification by continuous entrenched lines has been long since generally condemned and found ineffective; but the special destination of this entrenchment as a bridge-head, the fact that a capital *réduit* was found ready-made, the want of engineers among the Turks, and other circumstances peculiar to the Turkish army, may have rendered it, after all, more advisable to employ this antiquated system. In the Arges the Turks found a number of boats which were at once employed, together with what they had before, in the construction of a bridge across the Danube. All these works were nearly completed by the morning of Nov. 4.

At Oltenitza, then, the Turks had a mere bridge-head on the left bank of the Danube; the Turkish army had not crossed the river,

[a] Published in *The Times*, No. 21600, December 1, 1853.—*Ed.*

nor has it done so since; but it had a safe *débouché* on the left bank, which might be turned to account the very moment when a sufficient force was concentrated at Turtukai. They had the means, beside, of taking either the right or the left of the Arges; and, finally, all their operations in the vicinity of the river were protected by ten heavy guns in the fort on the hights of Turtukai, whose range, consequent upon this elevated position and the narrowness of the river at that point, extended at least half a mile beyond the bridge-head.

The bridge-head was occupied by three battalions of the line (2,400 men), two companies of guards (160 men), two of sharp shooters (200 men), 100 cavalry and some artillery, who attended to the 12 heavy guns placed in the Lazaretto. The right wing of the entrenchment was enfiladed and flanked by the guns of Turtukai, which besides could sweep the whole of the plain in front of the center of the bridge-head. The left wing, resting on the River Arges, was flanked by the battery on the island, but part of this ground was thickly studded with brush-wood, so as to offer considerable shelter to the Russians in approaching.

When on Nov. 4, the Russians attacked the Turkish lines they had, according to Omer Pasha, 20 battalions, 4 regiments of cavalry and 32 guns, altogether about 24,000 men. It appears they formed in the following order: twelve battalions and 14 guns opposite the center of the bridge-head; two battalions and two guns in the wood to the left (Russian right) on the river Arges, six battalions, *en échélon*, with four guns against the Turkish right, toward the Danube, their line being prolongated and outflanked by the cavalry. The center first formed a column of attack, after the fire of the Russian guns had been kept up for a time; the two wings followed; then the artillery, which had first fired at a distance of some 1,200 yards from the parapets came up to effective grape range (600 to 700 yards), and the columns of attack were hurried forward. As may be anticipated, the column of the Russian left (nearest the Danube) was shattered by the fire of the Turtukai guns; that of the center very soon shared the same fate; that of the right (on the Arges) was crushed by the fire from the island, and appears to have been far too weak to do any good. The attack was once or twice repeated, but without the *ensemble* of the first assault, and then the Russians had enough of it. They had marched resolutely up to the brink of the ditch (which must not be too literally understood), but the Turkish fire proved overwhelming before they came to a hand-to-hand fight.

During the fight Omer Pasha sent a battalion of regulars across the river to act as reserve. Thus the Turks engaged may be estimated at 3,600 infantry, with 44 heavy guns.

The forces of the Russians are less easily ascertained. While Omer Pasha speaks of twenty battalions, two British officers in his camp agree in reducing the force actually engaged to some 8,000 men. These two statements are not exactly contradictory. The Russians might have some twenty battalions in order of battle, and yet from the nature of the ground, or from contempt of their opponents, the actual mass of the attacking columns might not exceed eight battalions at a time; and a circumstance which the British officers do not mention, but which Omer Pasha reports, shows that the Russians had ample reserves. It is this, that every fresh attack was headed by a fresh battalion drawn from the reserves for the purpose. Besides, the reports of the two "officers of her Majesty's guards" bear in every line the stamp of that ignorant and inexperienced self-sufficiency which belongs to subalterns of the privileged corps of all armies.

Upon the whole, therefore, we think Omer Pasha's statement entitled to credit. There may have been eighteen or twenty Russian battalions present during the action, of which ten or twelve may successively have been brought to act, although from six to eight thousand may be the number of those who at a given time advanced simultaneously and ineffectually upon the Turkish entrenchments. The loss of the Russians, which must have amounted at least to 1,500 or 2,000, also proves what numbers they must have brought into the field. They were finally repulsed, leaving 500 muskets, plenty of baggage and ammunition, and 800 killed and wounded in the hands of the Turks, and retreated partially in disorder.

If we look at the tactics of this conflict on either side, we are surprised to find a gross blunder committed by the Russians, which was deservedly expiated by their signal defeat. They showed a contempt of their adversaries which has been seldom equaled. They had to attack pretty strong lines, with a capital *réduit* flanked by ten heavy guns on the island, commanded by twenty-two guns at Turtukai, which also commanded the ground in front of the lines; altogether, forty-four, or at least thirty-eight guns, all or mostly of heavy metal. Now every officer knows that in attacking a field fortification, you have first by your artillery to silence its guns and the batteries that may support it; then to destroy, as much as possible, the parapets, palisades and other defenses; then, by approaching your batteries still closer to the attacked works, to sweep the parapets with a continued hail-storm of grape-shot, until at last you can risk launching your columns of attack upon the half-demolished work and its demoralized defenders. In order to do all this, you must have a decided superiority in the number and caliber of your artillery. But what do we see the Russian attempt? To storm a bridge-head, defended by artillery superior to their own in number, superior in caliber, and still more superior in practice, after a short cannonade from twelve 12-pounders and twenty 6-pounders! This Russian cannonade can only be considered as a mere formality, a sort of civility offered to the Turks, for it could have no serious purpose; and if, as all reports agree, the Russian batteries advanced up to within 650 yards of the bridge-head, it is a wonder that we do not hear of a number of dismounted guns. At the same time we must acknowledge the bravery of the Russian troops, who were very likely for the first time exposed to fire and that under such adverse circumstances, yet advanced to within fifty yards of the Turkish lines before they were crushed by the superior fire poured in upon them.

As to the Turks, we cannot say much in favor of their tactics either. It was very well that Omer Pasha during the assaults did not crowd together more troops in the bridge-head than were necessary for its defense. But how is it that he did not concentrate a reserve, especially of cavalry, on the Turtukai end of the bridge and on the island? that, as soon as the repulse of the Russians was becoming manifest, he did not launch his cavalry on the beaten foe? and that, after all, he was satisfied with the moral effect of the victory and neglected to gather all its fruits, by which he might have decided the campaign? We can only find two excuses: firstly, that the system of continuous lines in field fortification does not easily admit of any vigorous offensive action after the repulse of the enemy, as the uninterrupted lines do not offer any wide space for sudden and energetic sallies of masses of troops; and secondly, that Omer Pasha either distrusted the capacity of his troops for fighting in the open field, or that he had not troops enough at hand to follow up the victory.

This leads us to the strategic questions connected with this action. If Omer Pasha had had at Oltenitza the troops who were lounging without anything to do at Kalafat, would he not have acted with more decision? How was it that a corps of 12,000 men, with a reserve of equal force, was directed upon Kalafat, to menace that point of the Russian position, where of all points it must have been most desirable to the Russians to be attacked?

How came it that on the point where the Turks could gain decisive advantages these 24,000 men were not present?

But this is only one point. The Russians, it is now ascertained beyond doubt, could not muster more than 50,000 or 55,000 combatants in Wallachia at the end of October. Taking into consideration the want of roads, the intersected nature of the country, detachments not to be avoided, the regular wear and tear of an active army, the Russians, it is certain, could on no point muster more than 30,000 men in a single mass. Forty thousand Turks collected upon any given spot of Wallachia were sure to beat them, and there is no doubt that the Turks, if they had been so minded and taken proper steps in proper time, could have collected that body, or even twice as many, with comparative ease. But the interference of European diplomacy, irresolution in the Divan, vacillation in the Turkish policy towards Servia, and other similar considerations, appear to have produced a series of half-measures, which placed Omer Pasha in a very singular position when hostilities broke out. He knew the weakness of the Russians; he himself had a far superior army, eager to go to war; but his army was spread upon an extent of country three hundred and fifty miles long, and fifty to one hundred miles wide. The lameness of his operations in the first half of November was the necessary consequence of this. The passage at Kalafat, otherwise a mistake, thus became a sort of necessity, Widin being the natural point of concentration of some twenty thousand men, who without that passage would have been entirely inactive, being too far distant from the main army. This passage enabled them at least to paralyze a portion of the Russian forces, and to create a moral impression in favor of the Turks.

The passage at Oltenitza—which was intended evidently as the main attack by which Bucharest was to be taken, and the Russians allured westward by the Kalafat operation, to be cut off from their retreat—had no effect whatever, because the necessary forces for a march on Bucharest appear not to have been forthcoming. The moral effect of the combat at Oltenitza was certainly a great gain, but the inactivity after the victory—an inactivity which lasted *nine days*, and ended in the voluntary retreat of the Turks behind the Danube, in consequence of the rains setting in—this inactivity and retreat may not destroy the flush of victory on the cheek of the Turkish soldier, but it undermines the reputation of the Turkish General, most probably more than he deserves. But here, if the original fault lies with the Divan, there must be some fault with Omer Pasha. To pass twelve days on the left bank of the Danube, to possess a bridge and a bridge-head strong enough to repel the united force of the Russians, to have behind him an army numerous and eager to fight and not to find means to carry 30,000 or 40,000 men across—why, all this cannot have been done without some negligence on the part of the General. The Russians may be thankful for their escape. Never did a Russian army get out of a scrape half as bad as this with so little material damage. They deserved to be cut to pieces, and they are all safe. Whether they will ever be taken at such advantage again may well be doubted.

Written about December 2, 1853

First published in the *New-York Daily Tribune,* No. 3952, December 16, 1853, as a leader; reprinted in the *New-York Weekly Tribune,* No. 641, December 24, 1853

Reproduced from the newspaper

Karl Marx

THE TURKISH WAR.—INDUSTRIAL DISTRESS[352]

London, Friday, Dec, 2, 1853

No more fighting of any account has taken place in Turkey since my last letter, but Russian diplomacy, more dangerous than Russian generalship, is again at work, and the revival of the famous London Conferences of 1840 and 1841, which terminated with sanctioning the treaty of Unkiar-Skelessi, under a slightly altered form, is more or less clearly announced through the medium of the ministerial papers on both sides of the Channel. *The Times* even hints at *"vigorous measures of pacification,"* viz.: a sort of *armed pacification* directed *against* Turkey by her self-styled protectors. There is one great diplomatic fact not to be misunderstood, namely, the last Note sent by the English Cabinet to Constantinople, presented by the British Ambassador to the Porte, rejected by the Divan on the 14th Nov., and turning out to be but a second edition of Reshid Pasha's answer to Prince Menchikoff's ultimatum in the month of May last.[353] This is the manner in which the Palmerstons and Aberdeens give the Sultan[a] to understand that, however the face of things may have otherwise changed, the relative situations of Turkey and Russia have undergone no change whatever since the month of May last, Turkey having won nothing nor Russia lost anything in the eyes of Western diplomacy.

As Prince Alexander of Servia forbids the Turkish troops to cross his territory, asks for the return of the Russian Consul-General, and treats, in his declaration to the Sultan, Turkey and Russia as the two protecting powers placed on the same footing with regard to the Principality, serious conflicts with Servia may be

[a] Abdul Mejid.—*Ed.*

apprehended, which, fatal as they might have proved to Turkey at any other moment, are at present perhaps the only means of saving her from the claws of Western diplomacy. Every new incident adding to the present complication, driving bankrupt Austria out of her dangerous neutrality, augmenting the chances of an European war, and enforcing upon Turkey the alliance with the revolutionary party, must turn out favorable to her, at least in her conflict with Russia. The constitutional causes of her decay will, of course, continue to do their work, if not counteracted by thorough transformation of the Turkish rule in Europe.

From the war carried on in the Principalities between Russians and Turks, let us return for one moment to the war raging in the manufacturing districts of England between masters and men. You will remember the epoch when the masters fiercely opposed and denounced the short-time movement on the part of the men. Now the tables are turned, and, as I predicted at the time, the system of short time is *enforced* by the masters on the men.[a] The lock-out exhibits its true meaning as a *financial measure* on the part of the masters, as a sort of antidote to an industrial over-production unparalleled in the "history of prices."[b] Since Monday last the mills have resumed work, but only for four days per week, in the Rochdale district—Burnley, Bacup, Newchurch—at Bury in the Ashton district—Ashton, Stalybridge, Glossop, Hyde, Newton. Bolton will soon be obliged to follow. Manchester is deliberating the question not *whether*, but *when*, to give way. In two or three weeks short time will be general, save in some few favored branches of industry. This, of course, must be followed by a stoppage of the supplies to the Preston resistants. But even four days' work still overruns the demand. Just think that not three weeks ago the Preston masters had on hand a stock equal to twenty weeks' production, which proved almost unsalable. The industrial crisis has no longer to begin; it has fairly set in.

"The reduction of time," says *The Times*, "is accompanied by a reduction of wages to the standard [...] before the recent advances were obtained by the hands."[c] "A pauper cannot dictate conditions—he must take what is offered him," says *The Economist*, in a fit of sincerity.[d]

---

[a] See this volume, pp. 410-14.—*Ed.*

[b] An allusion to Th. Tooke's works: *A History of Prices, and of the State of the Circulation, from 1793 to 1837*, Vol. I-II, *A History of Prices, and of the State of the Circulation, in 1838 and 1839* and *A History of Prices, and of the State of the Circulation, from 1839 to 1847 inclusive.—Ed.*

[c] "Short Time Movement by the Employers", *The Times*, No. 21599, November 30, 1853.—*Ed.*

[d] "The Turn-outs and the Poor Law", *The Economist*, No. 535, November 26, 1853.—*Ed.*

I have repeatedly stated that the turn-outs of the men, by beginning at too late an epoch, when the opportunities afforded by unprecedented prosperity were already vanishing away, could not prove successful in an economical point of view, or as far as their immediate end was concerned. But they have done their work. They have revolutionized the industrial proletariat, and, stirred up by dear food and cheap labor, the political consequences will show themselves in due time. Already the idea of a Parliament of Labor which, in fact, means nothing but a general reassembling of the workingmen under the banners of Chartism, evokes the fears of the middle-class press.

"Mr. Ernest Jones [...]," says *The Economist*, "the editor of *The People's Paper*, is described as the successor of Mr. Feargus O'Connor, as Mr. O'Connor was the successor of Mr. Hunt.... From following Hunt and O'Connor, the workingmen got nothing but hard knocks and great losses; nevertheless, they place equal confidence in the successor of these great kings, and now look to be saved by Jones."[a]

From the following quotations you will see that the English class papers, if stimulated by party motives, as is the case with *The Morning Herald*, or if inspired, as *The Morning Post*, by a cynical but keen observer like Palmerston, know how to judge the present state of affairs, and how to deal with the vulgarism of Prosperity-Robinson[b]:

"To hear them now, you would suppose that the authority of millowners was nothing less than divine, and that the safety of the empire depended on their being allowed to exercise powers little short of those of the French Emperor[c].... Some 60,000 of the workingmen of Lancashire are at this moment living on fare which barely suffices to keep soul and body together, without so much as a thought of a plunder or violence, although in towns which manufacturing economy has left wholly unguarded by police. Right or wrong these men have stood by their opinions and their leaders manfully, and it would not be easy to find another instance of a movement at once so peacefully and so effectually carried out."

(*Morning Herald*)

"Our economists boasted of the overwhelming blessings which would flow, past all our dreams, as the result of free trade; yet there we are with the winter before us, and the pestilence only waiting the return of spring, and just when our poor are most in need of more than usual food and clothing to raise their physical system up to the point most capable of resisting disease—just at this time, they are actually crushed by the unprecedented high prices of all the necessaries of life. Not a sign is visible of the milk and honey that were to enrich the land; while all that

---

[a] "The Labour Parliament", *The Economist*, No. 535, November 26, 1853.—*Ed.*

[b] A nickname of the Chancellor of Exchequer F. J. Robinson, who predicted prosperity on the eve of the crisis in 1825.—*Ed.*

[c] Napoleon III.—*Ed.*

was predicated of the perpetuity of cheapness and plenty seems in a fair way of being classed among the other thousand popular delusions by which society has been gulled.... English society is a filthy, pestilent, immoral, ignorant, cruel, blundering, discontented, and uncommonly hard up community."

Such is the language of *The Morning Post*,[a] the drawing-room print, and the official organ of my Lord Palmerston.

Written on December 2, 1853

First published in the *New-York Daily Tribune*, No. 3952 and the *New-York Semi-Weekly Tribune*, No. 893, December 16, 1853

Signed: *Karl Marx*

Reproduced from the *New-York Daily Tribune*

[a] *The Morning Post*, November 17, 1853.—*Ed.*

Karl Marx

THE QUADRUPLE CONVENTION.— ENGLAND AND THE WAR[354]

London, Friday, Dec. 9, 1853

Your readers have followed, step by step, the diplomatic movements of the Coalition Cabinet, and they will not be surprised at any new attempt, on the part of the Palmerstons and the Aberdeens, to back the Czar[a] under the pretext of protecting Turkey and securing the peace of Europe. Even the resurrection of a Vienna Conference[355] or of a London Congress they are fully prepared for. The Metropolitan Stock Exchange was first informed by *The Morning Chronicle*,[b] on Friday last, of England having succeeded in inducing Austria and Prussia to support the Western Powers in their attempt at a new mediation between the belligerent parties. Then came *The Morning Post* with the news of "this attempt" and with the consolatory announcement that

"in this attempt the cooperation of Prussia and Austria has been sought and obtained, and the four Powers have signed a protocol, engaging them, implicitly, to maintain the *present territorial distribution of Europe*, and inviting the belligerent Powers to come to an amicable adjustment of their differences by means of an European conference. The first step that will be taken, in consequence of this proceeding of the four Powers, will be to ascertain the views of Turkey on the bases upon which she will allow negotiations for an arrangement of the Eastern dispute to be conducted. This clearly ascertained, the four Powers will then invite Russia to state her views in regard to the [...] bases of the proposed arrangement, and then both Powers will be requested to send plenipotentiaries to a conference of the Great Powers, [...] at some time and place to be hereafter determined upon.... *The Czar's dignity* might be preserved while the interests of Turkey would be fully upheld, in the first place *by a treaty between Turkey and Russia of amity and peace and of commerce*, stipulating for a due protection of the subjects of either state within the territories of the other, and, in the second place, by a treaty between the

[a] Nicholas I.— *Ed.*
[b] Of December 2, 1853.— *Ed.*

Sultan[a] and the five Powers, *such a treaty as that of the Dardanelles of 1841*, in which the Sultan should undertake to respect the *existing constitutions and privileges of the Danubian Principalities and of Servia*, and in which he should bind himself *as in the treaty [of] Kainardji*, but this time to Europe, and not to Russia—specially to protect the Christian religion within his dominions."[b]

At last came the thunderer of Printing House-square, announcing in a first edition[c] that the alliance between the four Powers had been definitively concluded, and that they had laid down conditions which Russia and the Porte would, if necessary, "be *forced* to accept." Instantly the funds rose; but the satisfaction of the stockjobbers proved short-lived, as the same *Times* announced in its second edition that the four Powers had indeed drawn up a protocol and presented the draft of a collective note, without having, however, bound themselves to *enforce* its acceptance. Down went the funds again. At last the "startling news" was reduced to the old story of the resurrection of the dead body of the late Vienna Conference—it would be preposterous to speak of its ghost—and a telegraphic dispatch confirmed the report that

"the Conference of the four Powers at Vienna had on the 6th forwarded to Constantinople another proposal for the arrangement of the pending differences founded on a new project, and that negotiations for peace will continue, even though hostilities should not be suspended."

On the very eve of war the Vienna Conference, that retrospective Pythia, had just proposed to Turkey to accept Prince Menchikoff's ultimatum. After the first defeat Russia had undergone, England and France took up Reshid Pasha's answer to Prince Menchikoff's ultimatum. What phase of the past transactions they will now have arrived at in their retrograde movement, it is impossible to predict. The *Augsburger Zeitung* states that the *new* propositions of the Conference express the desire of the four Powers to "prevent war."[d] A startling novelty this!

Insipid, as all this diplomatic gossip may appear at a moment, when the *status quo* has been supplanted by a *status belli*, we must not forget that the hidden intentions of the British Cabinet transpire through these fantastical projects of conferences and congresses; that the ministerial papers throw out their feelers to ascertain how far the Ministry may venture to go; and that the

---

[a] Abdul Mejid.—*Ed.*

[b] Quoted, with slight digressions, from *The Morning Post*, December 6, 1853.—*Ed.*

[c] Of December 6, 1853.—*Ed.*

[d] *Allgemeine Zeitung*, No. 337, December 3, 1853.—*Ed.*

unfounded rumors of to-day more than once have foreshadowed the events of to-morrow. So much is sure, that if not accepted by Austria, the quadruple alliance *has* been proposed by England with a view to enforce upon Turkey the resolutions to be agreed upon by the four Powers. If no alliance has been concluded, a "protocol" has at least been signed by the four Powers, establishing the principles upon which to conduct the transactions. It is no less sure that the Vienna Conference, which prevented Turkey from moving till the Russian army had occupied the Principalities and reached the frontiers of Bulgaria, has again resumed its work and already dispatched a new note to the Sultan. That the step from a Vienna Conference to a European Congress, at London, is by no means a great one, was proved in 1839 at the epoch of Mehemet Ali's insurrection. The Congress pursuing its work of "pacification," while Russia pursued her war against Turkey, would be but a repetition of the London Congress of 1827-29, resulting in the destruction of the Turkish fleet, at Navarino, and the loss of Turkish independence, by the treaty of Adrianople. The bases upon which the British Cabinet have proposed, and the other Powers agreed to conduct negotiations, are clearly indicated by the ministerial papers. Maintenance of the "present territorial distribution of Europe." It would be a great mistake to consider this proposition as a simple return to the provisions of the peace of Vienna. The extinction of the Kingdom of Poland, the possession of the mouths of the Danube by Russia, the incorporation of Cracow, the transformation of Hungary into an Austrian province—all these "territorial arrangements" have never been sanctioned by any European Congress. A sanction, then, of the present "territorial distribution of Europe" would be, instead of a simple admission of Turkey to the treaty of Vienna, as is pretended, rather a sanction of all the violations of that treaty by Russia and Austria, since 1830. "A treaty of amity, and peace, and commerce between Russia and Turkey"—such are the identical terms in the preamble of the treaties of Kainardji, Adrianople and Unkiar-Skelessi. "A treaty as that of the Dardanelles of 1841," says the Palmerstonian paper.[a] Exactly so. A treaty like that which excluded Europe from the Dardanelles and transformed the Euxine into a Russian lake. But, says *The Times*, why should we not stipulate for the free entrance of the Dardanelles for men-of-war, and the free navigation of the Danube. But read the letter addressed by Lord Palmerston in

[a] *The Morning Post.—Ed.*

September, 1839, to Mr. Bulwer,[356] the then Envoy at Paris, and we shall find that similar hopes were held out at that epoch.

"The Sultan, bound to respect the existing constitutions of the Principalities and Servia." But these existing constitutions distribute the sovereignty over the provinces between the Czar and the Sultan, and they have, till now, never been acknowledged by any European Congress. The new Congress then, would add to the *de facto* protectorate of Russia over Turkish provinces, the sanction of Europe. The Sultan would then be bound not to the Czar, but to Europe, to protect "the Christian religion within his dominions." That is to say, the right of interference between the Sultan and his Christian subjects by foreign powers, would become a paragraph of European international law, and, in case of any new conflicts occurring, Europe would be bound by treaty to back the pretentions of Russia, who, as a party to the treaty, would have a right to interpret in her sense the protection to be asked for by the Christians in the Sultan's dominions. The new treaty, then, as projected by the Coalition Cabinet, and as explained by its own organs, is the most comprehensive plan of European surrender to Russia ever conceived, and a wholesale sanction of all the changes brought about by the counter-revolutions since 1830. There is, therefore, no occasion for throwing up caps and being astonished at the change of the policy of Austria, a change, as *The Morning Post* feigns to believe, "effected suddenly within the last ten days." As to Bonaparte, whatever his ulterior designs may be, for the moment the Parvenu Emperor is content enough to climb up into the heaven of the old legitimate powers, with Turkey as his ladder.

The views of the Coalition Cabinet are clearly expressed by *The Guardian*, the ministerial weekly paper:

"To treat Russia as a beaten enemy and fancy we have her by the throat because Russian troops have been foiled at the trenches of Oltenitza and some forts captured on the Black Sea, is simply ridiculous; these petty losses would in themselves but exasperate her pride and indispose her to treat till she could do so on better terms. But sovereigns, like other men, are governed by mixed motives. The Czar is a proud and passionate, but he is also a prudent man. He is engaged in a quarrel in which he may lose and cannot gain. His policy is that of his predecessors, who have throughout gained more by threatening than by waging war, and whose steady and undeviating system of encroachment had in it a vein of elastic pliability, which enabled them to avoid great disasters and even to *turn minor reverses to profitable account.* The preliminary resolution of the four Powers, that no change shall be made or permitted in the territorial arrangements of Europe, appears to be based on *this rational* view of his position and policy. It will disappoint those who see in imagination the feet of England on his neck, or who suffer themselves to be misled by the chimerical nonsense of the *Protectionist* papers. But the business in hand *is not the humiliation of Russia* but the pacification of Europe" (in a Russian sense of course), "the establishment, as far as possible, of that durable peace for which the French Soldier-Envoy[a] pledges his master's honor to the Sultan. And the *coming treaty*, we may be sure, [...] will not be a mere restoration of the *status quo*, but will attempt at least to settle on some permanent footing the relations of Turkey with Europe and of the Turkish Government with its Christian subjects, attempt—for, settle it so durably as we may, *any arrangement which leaves a Turkish Empire in Europe will always be provisional* at bottom. Such a *provisional* arrangement, however, is the thing now practicable and needful."[b]

The ultimate object, then, the powers aim at, is to help the Czar "to turn minor reverses to profitable account," and "to leave no Turkish Empire in Europe." The provisional arrangement will, of course, prepare that ultimate consummation as far as "the thing is now practicable."

Some circumstances, however, have singularly confounded the calculations of the Coalition politicians. There is intelligence of new victories gained by Turkey on the shores of the Black Sea and on the frontiers of Georgia. There is, on the other hand, a peremptory assertion representing the whole army in Poland as under orders for the Pruth, while we are informed from the frontiers of Poland that "in the night from the 23d and 24th ult., the brinka, or levy of men for the army, took place, and in places, where formerly one or two men were taken, eight or ten have now been drawn." This, at least, proves little confidence on the part of the Czar in the pacifying genius of the four Powers. The official declaration on the part of Austria, "that no alliance had been concluded between the four Courts," proves on her part that, willing as she is to enforce conditions upon Turkey, she dares not assume even the appearance of coercing the Czar to submit to conditions projected in his own interest. Lastly, the Sultan's reply to the French Ambassador that "at present an amicable arrangement is quite unacceptable without the complete abandonment by Russia of the pretensions which she has raised and without the immediate evacuation of the Principalities," has struck the Congress-mongers like a thunderbolt, and the organ of the crafty and experienced Palmerston now frankly tells the other fellows of the brotherhood the following piece of truth:

"To the immediate evacuation of the Principalities and the total abandonment of all her claims, [...] Russia cannot submit without a loss of [...] dignity and influence which it is foolish to suppose a power of her magnitude will endure

[a] A. Baraguay d'Hilliers.—*Ed.*

[b] *The Guardian*, No. 418, December 7, 1853.—*Ed.*

without a desperate struggle. For this present attempt at negotiation we are sorry, therefore, that we can only prognosticate failure."[a]

Defeated Russia can accept no negotiations at all. The business in hand is, therefore, to turn the balance of war. But how to effect this, but by enabling Russia to gain time? The only thing she wants is procrastination, time to levy new troops, to distribute them throughout the empire—to concentrate them, and to stop the war with Turkey till she has done with the mountaineers of Caucasus. In this way the chances of Russia may improve, and the attempt at negotiation "may be successful when Russia proves victorious instead of defeated." Accordingly, as stated by the Vienna *Ost-Deutsche Post*, and the ministerial *Morning Chronicle*, England has urged on Turkey the propriety of consenting to a three months' armistice.[b] Lord Redcliffe had a five hours' interview with the Sultan, for the purpose of obtaining from His Highness that consent to the suggested armistice which his Ministers had refused, and the result was, that an extraordinary council of Ministers was convened to take the matter into consideration. The Porte definitively refused to accede to the proposed armistice, and could not accede to it without openly betraying the Ottoman people.

"In the present state of feeling," remarks the to-day's *Times*, "it will not be easy to bring the pretentions of the Porte within the bounds of moderation."

The Porte is immoderate enough to understand that it is perfectly irreconcilable with the dignity of the Czar to be defeated, and that it must therefore grant him a three months' armistice in order to frustrate its own success, and to help him to become again victorious and "magnanimous." All hope of bringing about the three months' armistice has not yet been parted with.

"Possibly," says *The Times*, "an armistice recommended by the four Powers may fare better."

The good-natured *Morning Advertiser* is

"unwilling to assume that these representations are correct," because "a more direct attempt to betray the Ottoman cause into the hands of the Czar, or one better adapted to answer that purpose, could not have been devised by the most ingenious mind."[c]

---

[a] *The Morning Post*, December 8, 1853.—*Ed.*
[b] *The Morning Chronicle*, December 7, 1853.—*Ed.*
[c] *The Morning Advertiser*, December 8, 1853.—*Ed.*

The confidence of the radical *Morning Advertiser* in "the honor and the good faith" of Palmerston, and its ignorance of the history of England's diplomatic past, seem equally incommensurable. This paper being the property of the Licensed Victuallers' Association, I suspect, that those very victuallers themselves write from time to time the editorial articles.

While England is thus occupied at Constantinople and Vienna, the outpost of Russia, let us see how on the other hand, the Russians manage affairs in England.

I have already, in a previous letter, informed your readers that at this very epoch, when the Coalition feigns to threaten Russia in the Black Sea, Russian men-of-war, the two frigates *Aurora* and *Navarino*,[357] are fitting out in the Queen's dockyards at Portsmouth. On Saturday last[a] we were informed by *The Morning Herald* and *The Daily News*, that six sailors had escaped from the Russian frigate *Aurora*, and nearly reached Guildford, when they were overtaken by an officer of the Russian frigate *Aurora* and an English inspector of police, brought back to Portsmouth, placed on board the *Victorious*—an English ship occupied by the crew of the *Aurora*, while out-fitting—subjected to cruel, corporeal punishment and placed in irons. When this became known in London, some gentlemen obtained, through the instrumentality of Mr. Charles Ronalds, solicitor, a writ of habeas corpus, directed to Rear-Admiral Martin, some other English officers of the navy, and to the Russian captain, commander of the frigate *Aurora*, ordering them to bring the six sailors before the Lord Chief Justice of England. The English dockyard authorities declined to obey the writ, the English captain appealing to the Vice-Admiral and the Vice-Admiral to the Admiral, and the Admiral feeling himself obliged to communicate with the Lord of the Admiralty, the famous Sir James Graham, who, ten years before, in the case of the Bandieras, placed the British Post Office at the service of Metternich.[358] As to the Russian captain, although the Queen's[b] writ was served on him on board the English ship the *Victorious*, and though he was fully informed of its nature by an interpreter, he threw it contemptuously from the vessel, and when thrust through a port-hole, it was thrown out again. "If," said the Russian captain, "it came from Her Majesty in reality, it would be sent to his Ambassador or Consul." The Consul being absent, the Vice-Consul refused to interfere. On Dec. 6, fresh writs were

[a] I.e., on December 3.—*Ed.*
[b] Victoria.—*Ed.*

served on the naval authorities at Portsmouth, commanding them in the Queen's name to produce not only the six men in question before the Lord Chief Justice, but the Russian captain also. Instead of the writ being complied with, the Admiralty used every effort to tow the ship out of the harbor and to get her to sea, and the other day, the *Aurora*, Capt. Isylmetieff, was seen, by daylight, sailing for the Pacific, defying the writ of the habeas corpus. In the meantime, as we are informed, by yesterday's *Daily News*,

> "the Russian corvette, *Navarino*, is still in dock, undergoing a thorough re-caulking and repair. A number of dockyard men are engaged on her."

Now mark in what manner this "startling" case has been dealt with by the Ministerial Press.

The Morning Chronicle, the Peelite organ, chose to remain silent, its own Graham being the most compromised man in the whole affair. The Palmerstonian *Morning Post* was the first to break silence, as its Lord could not let escape such an occasion of proving his mastership in making pleasant apparently difficult cases. The whole case, it stated, was greatly exaggerated and overrated. The six deserters, it stated on the authority of the Russian captain, who ordered them to be cruelly flogged and hulked,

> "these seamen say that they did not desert from their own inclination, but were inveigled away by persons who introduced themselves to them in the streets,"[a]

these seamen having also contrived against their inclination and against the orders of the Russian captain to get ashore at Portsmouth,

> "made them intoxicated and then took them away in a carriage, up the country," and then deserted the deserters, "giving them directions how to get to London, with the address of some persons, to whom to go to there."

The absurd story is invented by the Palmerstonian organ with a view to induce the public to believe, that the "deserters gave themselves up to the Police," a lie too gross to be reechoed by *The Times* itself. The whole affair, insinuates *The Post*, with a great show of moral indignation, was got up by some Polish refugees, who, probably, intended wounding the feelings of Lord Palmerston, its magnanimous master.

Another ministerial organ, *The Globe*,[b] states that

---

[a] Here and below Marx quotes from "The Russians at Portsmouth.—Singular Affair", *The Morning Post*, December 6, 1853.—*Ed.*

[b] Of December 7, 1853.—*Ed.*

"the plea that a foreigner is only bound to recognize processes coming to him from the Minister of his own country is manifestly untenable; otherwise, any foreigners in a British seaport could break our law and could be brought under no responsibility, except by the intervention of an Ambassador."

The Globe arrives therefore at the moderate conclusion that the reply of the Russian captain to the clerk who served on him the writ of habeas corpus "is not perfectly satisfactory." But in human matters it would be idle to aspire to anything like perfection.

"If the Russian captain had hanged them" (viz., the six recaptured sailors) "all at the yard-arm of his frigate the next morning, he would have been altogether [...] *beyond* the control of the English law," exclaims *The Times*.[a]

And why this? Because in the treaty of navigation concluded between Russia and Great Britain in 1840 (under the direction of Lord Palmerston) there is a provision to this effect:

"The Consuls, Vice-Consuls, and commercial agents [...] of the [...] high contracting parties, residing in the dominions of the other, shall receive from the local authorities such assistance as can by law be given them, for the recovery of deserters from the ships of war or merchant vessels of their respective countries."

But, good *Times*, the question is exactly what assistance the English authorities were warranted by law to give the Russian captain. As to the Russian authorities themselves, "sending their vessels to England to be repaired at this crisis in political affairs," it appears to *The Times*, "to be an act of great indelicacy and bad taste," and it thinks, "the position, in which the officers of these vessels have been placed here, is that of spies." But, it says, "the British Government could no more forcibly express its contempt for such politics" than by admitting the Russian spies into the Queen's own dockyards "even at some public inconvenience," by placing at their disposal British men-of-war, employing the dockyard men, paid out of the pockets of the British people, in their service and firing parting salutes to them, when they run away after having insulted the laws of England.

Written on December 9, 1853

First published in the *New-York Daily Tribune*, No. 3960, December 26, 1853; reprinted in the *New-York Semi-Weekly Tribune*, No. 896, December 27, 1853

Signed: *Karl Marx*

Reproduced from the *New-York Daily Tribune*

[a] *The Times*, No. 21605, December 7, 1853.—*Ed.*

Karl Marx

THE RUSSIAN VICTORY.— POSITION OF ENGLAND AND FRANCE[359]

London, Tuesday, Dec. 13, 1853

"With the fleets of France and England in the Black Sea, the astonished Sultan of Turkey is already surprised that one of his ships is captured with impunity by a Russian vessel. The spring will bring him further wonders."

Thus we were informed by last Saturday's *Press.*[a] The following Monday brought the "further wonders," not expected until spring. Defeat of a Turkish squadron by a Russian fleet in the Black Sea, off Sinope[360]—such were the contents of a Russian dispatch from Odessa, dated 5th inst., confirmed afterward by the French *Moniteur*[b]. Although we are not yet in possession of the exact details of this occurrence, so much is clear that the Russian report greatly exaggerates the case; that the whole matter in question is to be reduced to the surprise of some Turkish frigates and a certain number of transports, which had on board troops, provisions, ammunition and arms, destined for Batum; that the Russian force was largely superior in number to the Turkish one, and that, nevertheless, the latter only surrendered after a desperate engagement, lasting an hour.

"Our fleet," says the *Englishman,*[c] "at all events, is *not* there to prevent the Russians from attacking Turkey. The fleet is *not* there to interfere with Russian convoys of men and arms to the Caucasus. The fleet is *not* there to see that the

[a] Of December 10, 1853.—*Ed.*

[b] The reference is to the reports published on December 12, 1853 in *The Times,* No. 21609, and in *Le Moniteur universel,* No. 346.—*Ed.*

[c] A. Richards, "The New Battle of Navarino", *The Morning Advertiser,* December 13, 1853.—*Ed.*

Black Sea is not a Russian lake. The fleet is *not* there to help our ally, nor to save him from destruction. The fleet is *not* there to avert a Navarino, after the memorable pattern.... Russian Admirals may maneuver, we suppose, within gun-shot of Constantinople, and the screws of England will continue as impassive as the prime screw of Lord Aberdeen himself. Will these costly farces be tolerated by the people?"

The coalition is exasperated at the Czar having beaten the Turks at sea instead of on the *terra firma*. A victory of the latter sort they wanted. Russian successes at sea may endanger their places, just at the moment when Count Buol has assured the Sultan[a] of the Czar's strictly *defensive* intentions, and when Lord Redcliffe was urging on him a three months' armistice. It is very amusing to observe how the business of soothing down the public has been distributed between the several organs of the Coalition Ministry.

The Times, as the representative of the whole of the Cabinet, expresses its *general* indignation at the ingratitude of the Czar, and ventures even upon some menaces.

The Morning Post, of course, is still more warlike, and gives its readers to understand that the "untoward" event at Sinope could never have occurred if Lord Palmerston were the Premier, or at least the Minister for Foreign Affairs.

"It is at least evident," says *The Post*,[b] "that a Russian naval force, dispatched to act on the Turkish coast, has been able to strike a sudden and heavy blow at the resources of the Porte, precisely in the quarter where the Divan had the best reason to expect that if there were anything substantial, anything beyond mere ostentation, in the professed services of her allies, the value and operation of such services might now be expected to become available. It will hardly be urged, we suppose, that the Black Sea is an appropriate stage for another scene of the diplomatic comedy which has been played in the Principalities under the name of the 'Material Guarantee.'[361] [...] The Russians, therefore, may be taken to have abandoned the hypocrisy of their *defensive attitude*. [...] It must be a subject of deep regret, that the extent to which *our*" (read Aberdeen's) "suiting policy has gone, has brought heavy damage on our ally and a shadow of reproach on ourselves. It would be a matter of lasting blame and scandal, should a second such disaster be suffered to occur for want of that protection which our fleets were expressly dispatched to afford."

The philosophical *Morning Chronicle*, the special organ of the Peelites, thinks

---

[a] Abdul Mejid.—*Ed.*

[b] Of December 13, 1853.—*Ed.*

"it not improbable that the power which has disturbed the peace of the world may *now* be disposed to acquiesce in the termination of the war." [a]

The Emperor Nicholas, on the plea that "he does not wish to oppose the *expression of the free will*" of the Hospodars Stirbei and Ghica to withdraw from the government of Moldavia and Wallachia, has, by rescript of Nov. 8, entrusted their functions to General von Budberg, placed, however, under the superior control of Prince Gorchakoff.

The fact of England urging upon Turkey an armistice at a moment when it cannot but assist the Czar in gaining time to concentrate his troops and to work at the decomposition of the ostensible alliance between France and England; the simultaneous intrigues of Nicholas to upset Bonaparte and to replace him by Henry V; the loudly boasted-of "fusion" of the two Bourbon branches negotiated in common by King Leopold, Prince Albert and the Princes of Orléans—such are the circumstances which induce the public to direct anew their attention to Windsor Castle, and to suspect it of a secret conspiracy with the courts of Brussels, Vienna and St. Petersburg.

"The present race of Englishmen," says the aristocratic *Morning Herald*, "should see that the policy of this country be not made subordinate to Orleanistic dreams of restoration, Belgian terrors of annexation, and infinitesimal German interests."

"There are," insinuates *Lloyd's Weekly Newspaper*, "conspirators not watched by the Home Office [...], conspirators whose names, like stars upon a frosty night—glitter in *The Court Circular*. They do not live in St. John's Wood, neither dwell they in Chelsea. No. They enjoy a somewhat larger accommodation in the Halls of Claremont.[362] One of those conspirators—the frequent guest of our gracious Queen—called by compliment the Duke of Nemours, went fresh from his English home to Frohsdorf to make that bridge—that is, to bridge the abyss for the Bourbons back to France. And doubtless he will return and again eat his venison at Buckingham Palace or Windsor Castle.[b]

"Your ministers," writes the Paris correspondent of *The Leader*, "are doing what Victoria tells them to do. Queen Victoria wishes all that King Leopold wishes. King Leopold desires all that Emperor Nicholas desires, so that *Nicholas is de facto the present King of England*." [c]

The position of Bonaparte is at this moment more critical than ever before, although, at first view, his chances of fortune never

---

[a] *The Morning Chronicle*, December 13, 1853.—*Ed.*

[b] "Our Foreign Conspirators", *Lloyd's Weekly London Newspaper*, No. 577, December 11, 1853.—*Ed.*

[c] "Letters from Paris. Letter CII", *The Leader*, No. 194, December 10, 1853.—*Ed.*

seemed more promising. He has succeeded in slipping into the circle of European royalty. The character Nicholas has lost, he has won. For the first time in his life he has become "respectable." The power which, combined with Russia, tumbled down his uncle[a] from his gigantic throne, England, has been forced into an apparent alliance with himself against Russia. Circumstances have almost constituted him the arbiter of Europe. The prospect of a European war, dragging along with it insurrectionary movements in Italy, Hungary, and Poland—countries where the people looking almost exclusively to the recovery of their national independence, are by no means too scrupulous as to the quarter from which to receive assistance—these eventualities seem to allow the man of the 2d of December to lead the dance of the peoples, if he should fail to play the pacificator with the kings. The enormous blunders committed by his predecessors have given his policy even the appearance of national vigor, as he, at least, evokes apprehensions on the part of the powers, while they, from the Provisional Government down to the *Burgraves* of the Assemblée Legislative,[363] had assumed only the power to tremble at everything and everybody.

But now let us look at the opposite side of the medal. The fusion between the two branches of the Bourbon dynasty, whatever may be its intrinsic value, has taken place under the auspices of the Courts of London and Vienna, and at the dictation of the Emperor Nicholas. It is, therefore, to be considered as the first act of a Holy Alliance directed against Bonaparte. On the other hand it has, for the moment, conciliated the different parties of the French *Bourgeoisie*, whose very divisions prevented them in 1848-51 from opposing the usurpation of the hero of Strasbourg and Boulogne.[b] The blue Republicans themselves, meeting at the house of Mr. Carnot, have decided, almost unanimously, that they would lend their aid to the Legitimists in any attempt to overthrow Bonaparte. These gentlemen seem fully resolved to run again through the traditionary cycles of restoration, Bourgeois-monarchy and Republic. For them the Republic meant never anything but, "*Ote-toi de là, que je m'y mette*,"[c] and if they cannot take themselves the place of their rival, they will at least inflict upon him the greatest punishment they are aware of—the loss of place. The

[a] Napoleon I.—*Ed.*

[b] An allusion to the abortive Bonapartist putches in Strasbourg on September 30, 1836, and in Boulogne on August 8, 1840.—*Ed.*

[c] Go so that I can take your place.—*Ed.*

parts to be acted have already been distributed. The generals, the ministers, all the principal functionaries are already nominated. The danger threatening Bonaparte from this side is a military insurrection which, if it do not lead to the restoration of the Bourbons, may afford the occasion for a general outbreak. But after all this Malet conspiracy,[364] dependent on the support of the Cossacks, is no more dangerous than the Ledru-Rollin conspiracy, dependent on the support of the Turks. Let me remark, *en passant*, that if the whole French emigration at London and Jersey were to meet, Ledru would hardly venture to present himself. The great majority of the French refugees belonging to different fractions of the socialist party, have joined together in the Société des proscrits démocrates et socialistes, avowedly hostile to the pretensions of Ledru. He is said to possess still some influence with the French peasantry, but power must be conquered, not in the departments, but at Paris, and at Paris he will meet with a resistance he is not the man to overcome.

The serious dangers to be apprehended on the part of Bonaparte rise from quite a different quarter, viz.: from the high prices of provisions, the stagnation of trade, and the utter dilapidation and exhaustion of the Imperial exchequer. It was the peasantry who, in their superstitious faith in the magic powers of the name of "Napoleon," and in the golden promises held out by the hero of Strasbourg, first imposed him on France. For them the restoration of the Bonaparte dynasty was the restoration of their own supremacy, after they had been abused by the restoration, speculated upon by the monarchy of July, and made by the Republic to pay the expenses of the revolution of February. They are now disabused, not only by dragonnades but by famine too. Incendiarism spreads, at this moment, through France at an unparalleled pace. As to the middle classes, they were foolish enough to suspect the Assemblée Nationale of having caused, by the disputes and intrigues going on among its different fractions, and by their common opposition to the executive power, the transitory commercial stagnation of 1851. They deserted not only their own representatives, but they provoked intentionally the *coup d'état* with a view to restore what they called "a regular Government," and above all, "sound business." They have now discovered that industrial crises are neither to be prevented by military despotism nor alleviated by its stretching public credit to its utmost limits, exhausting it by the most lavish expenditure, and making a financial crisis the inevitable partner of a commercial one. The middle class pine, therefore, for a new change of power, to afford them at last "a regular Government" and "sound business." As to the proletarians, they accepted Bonaparte from the first moment only as a transitory necessity, as the destroyer of the *république cosaque*,[a] and their avenger on the *party of order*.[365] Weakened as they were by successive defeats before the 2d of December, and fully occupied as they were during the years 1852 and 1853, they have had time to watch the occasion when general causes and the universal discontent of all other classes would enable them to resume their revolutionary work anew.

The following Paris commercial report will throw some light on the social state of France:

"The state of commercial affairs in Paris during the last week is not satisfactory. Except the manufacturers who are preparing New Year's presents for the shop-keepers, and those employed in dress-making, trade appears to be at a complete standstill. One great cause of this is the dearness of provisions in the provinces, which prevents the mass of the population from making their usual purchases. The wheat crop, the chestnuts, and the vintage failed simultaneously in the central departments of France, and the peasants, being compelled to make sacrifices in order to buy bread, deprive themselves of everything but articles of first necessity. The provincial letters state that the principal portion of the cotton goods offered for sale at the late fairs found no buyers, which easily accounts for the stagnation in trade apparent at Rouen. All exportation is confined at present to the South American States. The markets of New-York and New Orleans are represented as glutted with French produce, and consequently no orders are expected from those quarters. The houses which fabricate generally for Belgium and Germany have almost all suspended their works, all orders from their correspondents abroad having ceased. [...] Business must be dull in Paris when the Bank of France finds, as it does at present, the commercial bills offered for discount decrease considerably in amount. The corn market, which was dull ten days since, with declining prices, has become animated, and the holders of wheat are more firm in their banks.[b] The bakers have shown a greater inclination to purchase flour, and several buyers from the eastern departments have definitively arrested the downward tendency of prices. The corn factors in Paris not being able to execute all the orders received on Wednesday last, the buyers proceeded to Havre, where a decline of 2f. a barrel had previously been announced. Flour immediately on the arrival of the buyers rose from 44f. to 47f. the barrel, and wheat from 83f. to 86f. the measure of 200 kilogrammes. A similar rise took place in the markets through the department of the North. The corn market at Strasbourg has been well supplied, and wheat has declined 1f. the hectolitre; at Lyons the market was quiet, but without a fall. Rye has again risen in Paris; [...] sales 12,000 quintals of oats at 22f. 9c. the 100 kilogrammes. A letter from Marseilles of the 2d inst., states that 341 ships, bearing 804,270 hectolitres of wheat

---

[a] A paraphrase of Napoleon's statement: "In fifty years Europe will be republican or Cossack" (cf. Karl Marx, *The Eighteenth Brumaire of Louis Bonaparte*, present edition, Vol. 11, p. 182).—*Ed.*

[b] The Economist has "... in their demands".—*Ed.*

entered that port between the 1st and 30th of November. These arrivals make 2,102,467 hectolitres of wheat imported into Marseilles by 714 ships, within the last 4 months."[a]

Written on December 13, 1853

First published in the *New-York Daily Tribune*, No. 3961, December 21, 1853; reprinted in the *New-York Semi-Weekly Tribune*, No. 897, December 30 and in abridged form in the *New-York Weekly Tribune* No. 642, December 31, 1853

Signed: *Karl Marx*

Reproduced from the *New-York Daily Tribune*

[a] "France", *The Economist*, No. 537, December 10, 1853.—*Ed.*

Karl Marx

PALMERSTON'S RESIGNATION[366]

The most interesting and important piece of intelligence brought by the steamer *Africa* is the resignation of *Lord Palmerston* as a member of the Coalition Ministry under Lord Aberdeen.[367] This is a master-stroke of that unscrupulous and consummate tactician. Those journals at London which speak for the Ministry, carefully inform the public that the event does not grow out of the Eastern difficulty, but that his conscientious Lordship, like a true guardian of the British Constitution, quits office because he cannot give his consent to a measure of Parliamentary Reform, even of the pigmy dimensions natural to such a Whig as Lord John Russell. Such is, indeed, the official motive of resignation he has condescended to communicate to his colleagues of the Coalition. But he has taken good care that the public shall have a different impression, and in spite of all the declarations of the official organs, it is generally believed that while the Reform Bill is the pretext, the Russian policy of the Cabinet is the real cause. Such has been for some time, and especially since the close of the last session of Parliament, the tenor of all the journals in his interest. On various keys, and in multiform styles, they have played a single tune, representing Lord Palmerston as vainly struggling against the influence of the Premier, and revolting at the ignominious part forced upon him in the Eastern drama. Rumors have been incessantly circulated concerning the division of the Ministry into two great parties, and nothing has been omitted to prepare the British public for an exhibition of characteristic energy from the chivalrous Viscount. The comedy having been thus introduced, the *mise en scene* arranged, the noble Lord, placed behind the curtain, has chosen, with astonishing sagacity, the exact moment when his appearance on the stage would be most startling and effective.

Lord Palmerston secedes from his friends of the Coalition just as Austria has eagerly seized the proposition for new conferences; just as the Czar[a] is spreading wider his nets of intrigue and war, effecting an armed collision between the Servians and Bosnians, and threatening the reigning prince of Servia[b] with deposition should he persist in remaining neutral in the conflict; just as the Turks, relying on the presence of the British and French fleets, have suffered the destruction of a flotilla and the slaughter of 5,000 men by a Russian fleet three times as powerful; when Russian captains are allowed to defy the British law in British ports, and on board of British vessels; when the dynastic intrigues of the "spotless Queen" and her "German Consort"[c] have become matters of public notoriety; and, lastly, when the dull British people, injured in their national pride abroad, and tortured by strikes, famine, and commercial stagnation at home, begin to assume a threatening attitude, and have nobody upon whom to avenge themselves but their own pitiful Government. By retiring at such a moment, Lord Palmerston throws off all responsibility from his own shoulders upon those of his late partners. His act becomes a great national event. He is transformed at once into the representative of the people against the Government from which he secedes. He not only saves his own popularity, but he gives the last finish to the unpopularity of his colleagues. The inevitable downfall of the present Ministry appearing to be his work, he becomes a necessary element of any that may succeed it. He not only deserts a doomed Cabinet, but he imposes himself on its successor.

Besides saving his popularity and securing a prominent place in the new administration, Lord Palmerston directly benefits the cause of Russia by withdrawing at the present momentous crisis. The Coalition Cabinet, at whose procrastinating ingenuity Russian diplomacy has mocked, whose Orleanist and Coburg predilections have ever been suspected by Bonaparte, whose treacherous and pusillanimous weakness begins even to be understood at Constantinople—this Ministry will now lose what little influence it may have retained in the councils of the world. An administration disunited, unpopular, not relied upon by its friends, nor respected

[a] Nicholas I.—*Ed.*
[b] Alexander Karageorgević.—*Ed.*
[c] Queen Victoria and Prince Albert.—*Ed.*

by its foes; considered as merely provisional, and on the eve of dissolution; whose very existence has become a matter of doubt—such an administration is the least adapted to make the weight of Great Britain felt in the balance of the European powers. Lord Palmerston's withdrawal reduces the Coalition, and with it England herself, to a nullity as far as foreign policy is concerned; and never has there existed an epoch when the disappearance of England from the public stage, even for a week or a fortnight, could do so much for the Autocrat. The pacific element has triumphed over the warlike one in the councils of Great Britain. Such is the interpretation that must be given at the courts of Berlin, Paris and Vienna to Lord Palmerston's resignation; and this interpretation they will press upon the Divan, already shaken in its self-confidence by the last success of Russia, and consulting under the guns of the united fleets.

It should not be forgotten that since Lord Palmerston became a member of the Coalition Ministry, his public acts, as far as foreign policy is concerned, have been limited to the famous gunpowder plot,[a] and the avowed employment of the British police as spies against the political refugees; to a speech wherein he jocosely treated the obstruction by Russia of the navigation of the Danube as of no account[b]; and, lastly, to the oration with which he dismissed Parliament,[c] assuring the Commons that all the Government had done in the Eastern complication had been right—that they might quietly disband since the Ministers remained at their posts, and pledging himself "for the honor and good faith of the Emperor of Russia."

Besides the general causes we have enumerated, Lord Palmerston has had a special reason for surprising the world with this last act of self-sacrificing patriotism. He has been found out. His prestige has begun to wane, his past career to be known to the public. The people of England, who had not been undeceived by his avowed participation in the conspiracy of the 2d of December, which overthrew the French Republic,[368] and by his gunpowder comedy, have been aroused by the revelations of Mr. *David Urquhart*, who has vigorously taken his Lordship in hand. This gentleman, by a recently published work called the *Progress of Russia*, by articles in the English journals, and especially by speeches at the anti-Russian meetings held throughout the

[a] See this volume, pp. 82-84.—*Ed.*
[b] July 7, 1853 (see this volume, p. 187).—*Ed.*
[c] On August 20, 1853.—*Ed.*

Kingdom, has struck a blow at the political reputation of Lord Palmerston which future history will but confirm. Our own labors in the cause of historical justice have also had a share, which we were far from counting upon, in the formation of a new opinion in England with regard to this busy and wily statesman. We learn from London, quite unexpectedly, that Mr. Tucker has reprinted there and gratuitously circulated fifty thousand copies of an elaborate article in which, some two months since, we exposed his Lordship's true character and dragged the mask from his public career.[a] The change in a public feeling is not a pleasing one for its subject, and he thinks perhaps, to escape from the rising tide of reprehension, or to suppress it by his present *coup.* We predict that it will not succeed, and that his lengthened career of official life will ere long come to a barren and unhappy end.

Written on December 16, 1853

First published in the *New-York Daily Tribune*, No. 3965, December 31, 1853, as a leader; reprinted in the *New-York Weekly Tribune*, No. 643, January 7, 1854

Reproduced from the *New-York Daily Tribune*

---

[a] [K. Marx,] *Palmerston and Russia*, reprinted from the *New-York Daily Tribune*, where it was published as the third article in the series "Lord Palmerston" (see this volume, pp. 358-69).—*Ed.*

Frederick Engels

PROGRESS OF THE TURKISH WAR[369]

After a long delay we are at last in possession of official documents in relation to the two victories which Russia so loudly boasts of and so liberally rewards.[a] We allude, of course, to the destruction of the Turkish squadron at Sinope and the engagement near Akhalzikh,[370] in Asia. These documents are the Russian bulletins; but the fact that the Turkish official organ has maintained a profound silence on the subject, when its communications, if it had any to make, should have reached us before those from St. Petersburg, makes it certain that the Porte has nothing agreeable to publish. Accordingly we proceed, on the information we have, to analyse the events in question, in order to make our readers acquainted with the real state of the case.

The battle of Sinope was the result of such an unparalleled series of blunders on the part of the Turks that the whole affair can only be explained by the mischievous interference of Western diplomacy or by collusion with the Russians of some parties in Constantinople connected with the French and English Embassies. In November, the whole Turkish and Egyptian fleet proceeded to the Black Sea, in order to draw the attention of the Russian Admirals from an expedition sent to the coast of the Caucasus in order to land supplies of arms and ammunition for the insurgent mountaineers. The fleet remained eighteen days at sea without meeting with a single Russian man-of-war; some say the Russian squadron never left Sebastopol during all that time, whereby the

[a] The reference is to the publication of news, with comments, from Russian newspapers of December 23, 1853 in the English press, notably *The Times*, No. 21619 and *The Morning Herald*, No. 22349.—*Ed.*

expedition to the Caucasus was enabled to effect its object; others report that, being well informed of the plans of the Turks, it withdrew eastward, and merely watched the vessels conveying stores, which, in consequence, never reached the Caucasian shore, and had to return to Sinope, while the main fleet reentered the Bosphorus. The great amount of powder on board the Sinope squadron, which caused the explosion of several of them at a comparatively early period of the engagement, appears to be a proof that the latter version is correct.

Thus seven Turkish frigates, two steamers, three sloops, and one or two smaller ships, together with some transports, were abandoned in the harbor of Sinope, which is little better than an open roadstead, formed by a bay open towards the sea, and protected by a few neglected and ill-constructed batteries, the best of which was a castle constructed at the time of the Greek Emperors, and most likely before artillery was known in Europe. How it happened that a squadron of some three hundred guns, mostly of inferior caliber, was thus abandoned to the tender mercies of a fleet of three times its force and weight of metal, at that point of the Turkish shore, which from its proximity to Sebastopol is most exposed to a Russian attack, while the main fleet was enjoying the tranquil ripple of the Bosphorus, we have yet to learn. We know that the dangerous position of this squadron was well appreciated and warmly debated at headquarters; that the discordant voices of Turkish, French and British admirals, were loudly heard in the councils of war, and that the ever-meddling ambassadors were there also, in order to speak their minds upon the matter, but nothing was done.

In the meantime it appears, according to one statement, that an Austrian steamer reported at Sebastopol the position of the squadron. The Russian official report maintains on the contrary, that Nachimoff while cruising off the coast of Asia, descried the squadron, and took measures to attack it. But, if the Russians descried the Turks at Sinope, the Turks from the tower and minarets of the town must necessarily have descried the Russians long before. How then came it to pass that the Turkish batteries were in such bad trim, when a couple of days' labor might have done a great deal toward their repair? How happened it that the Turkish vessels were at anchor in places where they obstructed the fire of the batteries, and were not shifted to moorings more fit to meet the threatened danger? There was time enough for all this; for Admiral Nachimoff states that he first sent to Sebastopol for three three-deckers before he ventured the attack. Six days, from

November 24 to November 30, would not have been allowed to elapse without some effort on the part of the Turks: but indeed, the report of the Turkish steamer *Taïf*, which escaped to Constantinople, amply proves that the Turks were taken by surprise.[a] So far, then, the Russian report cannot be correct.

Admiral Nachimoff had under his command three ships-of-the-line, one of them a three-decker, six frigates, several steamers, and six or eight smaller vessels, a force of at least twice the weight of metal of the Turkish squadron. Yet he did not attack until he got three more three-deckers, which, by themselves, should have been quite sufficient to perform the exploit. With this disproportionate superiority he proceeded to the assault. A fog, or as some say, the use of the British flag, enabled him to approach unmolested to a distance of 500 yards. Then the fight began. The Russians, not liking to stand under canvas on a lee shore, dropped their anchors. Then the firing from the two moored fleets, without any naval maneuvers, and having rather the character of a cannonade on shore, went on for four hours. The possibility of doing away with all naval tactics, with all movements, was very favorable to the Russians, whose Black Sea fleet, manned almost exclusively with "land-lubbers," and especially with Polish Jews, might have had very poor success if opposed to the well-manned Turkish ships in deep water. Four hours were required by the Russians before they could silence the feeble ships of their opponents. They had, besides, this advantage, that any stray shot on their part would do harm either in the batteries or in the town, and what a number of misses, in comparison to the hits, they must have made, appears from the almost total destruction of the place, accomplished long before the hostile fleet was silenced. The Russian report says only the Turkish quarter was burnt down, and that the Greek quarter escaped as if by miracle. This is, however, contradicted by better authority, which states that the whole town is in ruins.

Three Turkish frigates were burnt during the action, four were run ashore and burnt afterwards, along with one steamer and the smaller vessels. The steamer *Taïf*, however, cut her cables, boldly steamed through the Russian lines, and escaped to Constantinople, although chased by Admiral Korniloff with three Russian steamers. Considering the clumsiness of Russian naval maneuvers, the bad position of the Turkish fleet in front, and in the line of fire, of their own batteries, and above all the *absolute certainty of destruction*, it would have perhaps been better if the whole Turkish

[a] Published in *Le Moniteur universel*, No. 356, December 22, 1853.—*Ed.*

squadron had got under weigh and borne down as far as the wind permitted upon the enemy. The ruin of some, which could by no means be avoided, might have saved at least a portion of the squadron. Of course the direction of the wind must have decided as to such a maneuver, but it seems doubtful whether Osman Pasha ever thought of such a step at all.

The victory of Sinope has no glory for the Russians, while the Turks fought with almost unheard of bravery; not a single ship having struck its flag during the whole action. And this loss of a valuable portion of their naval force, the momentary conquest of the Black Sea, and the dejecting moral consequences of such an event upon the Turkish population, army and navy, is entirely due to the "good offices" of Western diplomacy, which prevented the Turkish fleet from standing out and protecting or fetching home the Sinope squadron. And it is equally due to the secret information given to the Russians enabling them to strike the blow with certainty and safety.

The second victory of which the Russians boast, came off at Akhalzikh, in Armenia. The Turks have for some time past been checked in the offensive movements which they had effected on the Georgian frontier. Since the taking of Shefkatil, or St. Nicholas, not a place of any importance has been taken, nor any victory gained of more than ephemeral effect. And this in a country where the Russians must fight under all imaginable disadvantages, where their land communications with Russia are reduced to two roads infested by insurgent Circassians, where their sea communications might very easily be cut off or endangered, and where the Transcaucasian country occupied by them, with Tiflis for its centre, might be considered more as an independent state than as part and parcel of a mighty empire. How is this check of the Turkish advance to be explained? The Turks accuse Abdi Pasha of treason and have recalled him; and certainly it is very curious that Abdi Pasha is the only Turkish General in Asia, who has been allowed by the Russians to gain local and partial victories. But there are two mistakes on the part of the Turks which explain the want of success in the beginning and the actual defeat in due course afterward. They have spread and divided their army upon all the long line from Batum to Bayazid; their masses are nowhere strong enough for a concentric attack upon Tiflis, though part of them are at the present moment, enjoying the undisputed and useless possession of the city of Erivan. The country is barren and rocky, and it may be difficult to feed a large army there; but quick concentration of all resources and rapid movements are the best means against famine in an army. Two corps, one for covering Batum and attacking on the coastline, another for a direct march upon Tiflis through the valley of the Kura would have been sufficient. But the Turkish forces have been divided and subdivided without any necessity whatever, and to the almost entire disabling of every one of the different corps.

In the second place, the inactivity in which diplomacy held the Turkish fleet allowed the Russians to land two divisions of infantry (of the 5th corps) in Mingrelia, and thus to reenforce Prince Woronzoff's Caucasian army by nearly 20,000 men. Thus strengthened, he not only arrested the Turks on the coast, but has now had the satisfaction of seeing a corps under Gen. Andronnikoff deliver the beleaguered fortress of Akhalzikh, and beat the enemy on the open field near that town. The Russians pretend that with about 10,000 men they have routed 18,000 Turks; of course we cannot rely upon such statements; but must confess that the great number of irregulars in the Turkish Anatolian army and the almost total absence of European officers, particularly in the higher commands and on the staff, must make them but a poor match for an equal number of Russians. The Russians pretend they have taken ten or twelve pieces of cannon, which may be true, as in that impassable country the vanquished party must necessarily abandon most of its guns; at the same time they confess they have made only 120 prisoners. This amounts to a confession that they have massacred almost all the wounded on the field of battle, they being necessarily left in their hands. Besides, they prove that their measures for pursuit and intercepting the retreat of at least part of the enemy, must have been wretchedly planned. They had plenty of cavalry; a bold charge into the midst of the fugitives would have cut off whole battalions. But this action offers, so far as our reports go, but little military or political interest.

On the Danube, the Russians have done nothing more than repeat the affair by which they opened the campaign, at Matchin, a fort, or a projecting rock opposite Braila. They appear to have made little impression. We have also, on good authority, a detailed statement of the Turkish troops concentrated at Widin. They consist of 34,000 infantry, 4,000 cavalry, and 2,000 artillery, with 66 field-guns, besides heavy artillery on the walls of Widin, and on the redoubts of Kalafat. Thus, 40,000 Turks are wasted in order to occupy the direct route from Bucharest into Servia. Forty thousand men, chained down to extensive fortifications which they have to defend, are too few to withstand the attack of a large army, and a great deal too many to defeat roving expeditions of small bodies. With the force already collected at Shumla, these 40,000 men would there be worth twice their number elsewhere. Their absence, next to diplomatic interference, ruined the operation of Oltenitza. It is impossible that Omer Pasha should not know, that if he stands with 100,000 men between Silistra and Rustchuk, the Russians, in numbers sufficient to do mischief, will never attempt to pass by him in order to throw themselves into the mountains of Servia. Such a disposition of his troops cannot accord with his judgment, and he must chafe desperately at the maleficent influences which force it upon him.

Written about December 23, 1853

First published in the *New-York Daily Tribune,* No. 3971, January 9, 1854, as a leader; reprinted in the *New-York Weekly Tribune,* No. 644, January 14, 1854

Reproduced from the *New-York Daily Tribune*

Frederick Engels

THE EUROPEAN WAR[371]

At last, the long-pending question of Turkey appears to have reached a stage where diplomacy will not much longer be able to monopolize the ground for its ever-shifting, ever-cowardly, and ever-resultless movements. The French and British fleets have entered the Black Sea in order to prevent the Russian Navy from doing harm either to the Turkish fleet or the Turkish coast. The Czar Nicholas long since declared that such a step would be, for him, the signal for a declaration of war. Will he now stand it quietly?

It is not to be expected that the combined fleets will at once attack and destroy either the Russian squadron or the fortifications and navy-yards of Sebastopol. On the contrary, we may rest assured that the instructions which diplomacy has provided for the two Admirals[a] are so contrived as to evade, as much as possible, the chance of a collision. But naval and military movements, once ordered, are subject not to the desires and plans of diplomacy, but to laws of their own which cannot be violated without endangering the safety of the whole expedition. Diplomacy never intended the Russians to be beaten at Oltenitza; but a little latitude once given to Omer Pasha, and military movements once begun, the action of the two hostile commanders was carried on in a sphere which was to a great extent uncontrollable by the Ambassadors at Constantinople. Thus, the fleets once removed from their moorings in the Beikoz roads, there is no telling how soon they may find themselves in a position from which Lord Aberdeen's prayers for

[a] J. W. Dundas and F. Hamelin.— *Ed.*

peace, or Lord Palmerston's collusion with Russia cannot draw them, and where they will have to choose between an infamous retreat or a resolute struggle. A narrow land-locked sea like the Euxine, where the opposing navies can hardly contrive to get out of sight of each other, is precisely the locality in which conflicts under such circumstances, may become necessary almost daily. And it is not to be expected that the Czar will allow, without opposition, his fleet to be blockaded in Sebastopol.

If, then, a European war is to follow from this step, it will be in all likelihood a war between Russia on one hand, and England, France and Turkey on the other. The event is probable enough to warrant us in comparing the chances of success and striking the balance of active strength on each side, so far as we can do so.

But will Russia stand alone? What part will Austria, Prussia and the German and Italian States, their dependants, take in a general war? It is reported that Louis Bonaparte has notified the Austrian Government that if in case of a conflict with Russia, Austria should side with that power, the French Government would avail itself of the elements of insurrection which in Italy and Hungary only require a spark to be kindled again into a raging fire, and that then the restoration of Italian and Hungarian nationality would be attempted by France. Such a threat may have its effect upon Austria; it may contribute to keep her neutral as long as possible, but it is not to be expected that Austria will long be enabled to keep aloof from such a struggle, should it come to pass. The very fact of the threat having been uttered, may call forth partial insurrectionary movements in Italy, which could not but make Austria a still more dependant and still more subservient vassal of Russia. And then, after all, has not this Napoleonic game[372] been played once already? Is it to be expected that the man who restored the Pope[a] to his temporal throne,[373] and who has a candidate cut-and-dried for the Neapolitan monarchy,[b] will give to the Italians what they want as much as independence from Austria—unity? Is it to be expected that the Italian people will rush headlong into such a snare? No doubt they are sorely oppressed by Austrian rule, but they will not be very anxious to contribute to the glory of an Empire, which is already tottering in its native soil of France, and of a man who was the first to combat their own revolution. The Austrian Government knows all this, and therefore we may assume that it will be more influenced by its

[a] Pius IX.—*Ed.*

[b] Napoléon Lucien Charles Murat, son of Joachim Murat, Marshal of France and King of Naples.—*Ed.*

own financial embarrassments than by these Bonapartistic threats; we may also be certain that at the decisive moment, the influence of the Czar will be paramount at Vienna, and will entangle Austria on the side of Russia.

Prussia is attempting the same game which she played in 1780, 1800 and 1805.[374] Her plan is to form a league of neutral Baltic, or North German, States, at the head of which she can perform a part of some importance, and turn to whichever side offers her the greatest advantages. The almost comical uniformity with which all these attempts have ended by throwing the greedy, vacillating and pusillanimous Prussian Government into the arms of Russia, belongs to history. It is not to be expected that Prussia will now escape her habitual fate. She will put out feelers in every direction, offer herself at public auction, intrigue in both camps, swallow camels and strain at gnats, lose whatever character may perchance yet be left to her, get beaten, and at last be knocked down to the lowest bidder, who, in this and in every other instance, will be Russia. She will not be an ally, but an incumbrance to Russia, for she will take care to have her army destroyed beforehand, for her own account and gratification.

Until at least one of the German Powers is involved in a European war, the conflict can only rage in Turkey, on the Black Sea and in the Baltic. The naval struggle must, during this period, be the most important. That the allied fleets can destroy Sebastopol and the Russian Black Sea fleet; that they can take and hold the Crimea, occupy Odessa, close the Sea of Azov, and let loose the mountaineers of the Caucasus, there is no doubt. With rapid and energetic action nothing is more easy. Supposing this to occupy the first month of active operations, another month might bring the steamers of the combined fleets to the British Channel, leaving the sailing vessels to follow; for the Turkish fleet would then be capable of doing all the work which might be required in the Black Sea. To coal in the Channel and make other preparations, might take another fortnight; and then, united to the Atlantic and Channel fleets of France and Britain, they might appear before the end of May in the roads of Kronstadt in such a force as to assure the success of an attack. The measures to be taken in the Baltic are as self-evident as those in the Black Sea. They consist in an alliance, at any price, with Sweden; an act of intimidation against Denmark, if necessary; an insurrection in Finland, which would break out upon landing a sufficient number of troops and a guarantee that no peace would be concluded except upon the condition of this province being reunited to

Sweden. The troops landed in Finland would menace Petersburg, while the fleets should bombard Kronstadt. This place is certainly very strong by its position. The channel of deep water leading up to the roads will hardly admit of two men-of-war abreast presenting their broadsides to the batteries, which are established not only on the main island, but on smaller rocks, banks and islands about it. A certain sacrifice, not only of men, but of ships, is unavoidable. But if this be taken into account in the very plan of the attack, if it be once resolved that such and such a ship must be sacrificed, and if the plan be carried out vigorously and unflinchingly, Kronstadt must fall. The masonry of its battlements cannot for any length of time withstand the concentrated fire of heavy Paixhans guns,[375] that most destructive of all arms when employed against stone walls. Large screw-steamers, with a full complement of such guns amid ships, would very soon produce an irresistible effect, though of course they would in the attempt risk their own existence. But what are three or four screw-ships of the line in comparison with Kronstadt, the key of the Russian Empire, whose possession would leave St. Petersburg without defense.

Without Odessa, Kronstadt, Riga, Sebastopol, with Finland emancipated, and a hostile army at the gates of the capital, with all her rivers and harbors closed up, what would Russia be? A giant without arms, without eyes, with no other resource than trying to crush her opponents under the weight of her clumsy torso, thrown here and there at random wherever a hostile battle-cry was heard. If the maritime powers of Europe should act thus resolutely and vigorously, then Prussia and Austria might so far be relieved from the control of Russia that they might even join the allies. For both the German powers, if secure at home, would be ready to profit by the embarrassments of Russia. But it is not to be expected that Lord Aberdeen and M. Drouyn de Lhuys should attempt such energetic steps. The powers that be are not for striking their blows *home,* and if a general war breaks out, the energy of the commanders will be shackled so as to render them innocuous. If nevertheless, decisive victories occur, care will be taken that it is by mere chance, and that their consequences are as harmless as possible for the enemy.

The war on the Asiatic shore of the Black Sea might at once be put an end to by the fleets; that on the European side would go on comparatively uninterrupted. The Russians, beaten out of the Black Sea, deprived of Odessa and Sebastopol, could not cross the Danube without great risk (except in the direction of Servia, for insurrectionary purposes), but they might very well hold the

Principalities, until superior forces and the risk of large bodies of troops being landed on their flank and rear should drive them out of Wallachia. Moldavia they need not evacuate without a general action, for flank and rear demonstrations would there be of little importance, as long as Chotin and Kishinev offered them a safe communication with Russia.

But as long as the war is confined to the Western Powers and Turkey on the one hand, and Russia on the other, it will not be a European war such as we have seen since 1792. However, let it once commence, and the indolence of the Western Powers and the activity of Russia will soon compel Austria and Prussia to decide for the Autocrat. Prussia will probably be of no great account, as it is more than likely that her army, whatever its capacities may be, will be wasted by presumption at some second Jena.[376] Austria, notwithstanding her bankrupt condition, notwithstanding the insurrections that may occur in Italy and Hungary, will be no contemptible opponent. Russia herself obliged to keep up her army in the Principalities, and on the Caucasian frontier, to occupy Poland, to have an army for the defense of the Baltic coast, and especially of St. Petersburg and Finland, will have very few troops to spare for offensive operations. If Austria, Russia and Prussia (always supposing the latter not yet put to rout), can muster five or six hundred thousand men on the Rhine and the Alps, it will be more than can be reasonably expected. And for five hundred thousand allies, the French alone are a match, supposing them to be led by Generals not inferior to those of their opponents, among whom the Austrians alone possess commanders worthy of the name. The Russian Generals are not formidable, and as to the Prussians, they have no Generals at all; their officers are hereditary subalterns.

But we must not forget that there is a sixth power in Europe, which at given moments asserts its supremacy over the whole of the five so-called "Great" Powers and makes them tremble, every one of them. That power is the Revolution. Long silent and retired, it is now again called to action by the commercial crisis, and by the scarcity of food. From Manchester to Rome, from Paris to Warsaw and Pesth, it is omnipresent, lifting up its head and awaking from its slumbers. Manifold are the symptoms of its returning life, everywhere visible in the agitation and disquietude which have seized the proletarian class. A signal only is wanted, and this sixth and greatest European power will come forward, in shining armor, and sword in hand, like Minerva from the head of the Olympian. This signal the impending European war will give, and then all calculations as to the balance of power will be upset by the addition of a new element which, ever buoyant and youthful, will as much baffle the plans of the old European Powers, and their Generals, as it did from 1792 to 1800.

Written on January 8, 1854

First published simultaneously in English in the *New-York Daily Tribune*, No. 3992, February 2, 1854, as a leader, and in German in *Die Reform*, February 3 and 4, 1854

Reproduced from the *New-York Daily Tribune*

Karl Marx

[THE WESTERN POWERS AND TURKEY][377]

London, Tuesday, Jan. 10, 1854

The charge against Mr. Szemere of having revealed the place where the Hungarian crown[378] was concealed, was first brought forward by the Vienna *Soldatenfreund*, the avowed organ of the Austrian police, and this single fact should have sufficed to prove the falsehood of the accusation.

The police is not used to gratuitously denounce its own accomplices, while it is one of its habitual tricks to throw suspicion on the innocent, in order to cover the culpable. A man of the standing and the influence of Mr. Szemere would be the very last to be spontaneously sacrificed by the Austrian police, had they been able to secure his cooperation. If the secret was not betrayed by the indiscretion of one of the agents of Mr. Kossuth—a case by no means improbable—I cannot but suspect the Count K. Batthyány, now resident at Paris, of having been the traitor. He was one of the very few persons initiated into the secret of the place where the regalia were hidden, and he is the only man among them who has applied to the Vienna Court for an *amnesty*. This last fact I have reason to suppose, he will not deny.

Lord Hardinge, the British Commander-in-Chief, has been prevailed upon to withdraw his resignation. As to the Duke of Norfolk, we are informed by the correspondent of *The Dublin Evening Mail*, that

"a bit of Palace gossip has got wind. [...] A certain noble Duke, who holds an office at Court, *in commendam*, with the highest hereditary feudal dignity in the State, made a little too free, it is said, with the champagne at the Royal table, the result of which was the loss of his most noble equilibrium in the dining-room, and the involvement of Majesty itself in the catastrophe. [...] The consequence of this annoying *contretemps* has been the resignation of the noble Duke and the appointment of Earl Spencer as Lord High Steward of her Majesty's Household."[a]

Mr. Sadleir, the broker of the Irish brigade, has again tendered his resignation of his ministerial post, which has this time been accepted by Lord Aberdeen. His position had become untenable after the public disclosures made before an Irish court of law as to the scandalous means by which he had contrived to get into Parliament. The control of the Cabinet of all the Talents over the Irish brigade will not be strengthened by this untoward event.

The bread-riots which occurred on Friday and Saturday at Crediton, Devonshire,[379] were a sort of popular answer to the glowing descriptions of prosperity which the ministerial and free trade papers thought fit to amuse their readers with at the obsequies of the year 1853.

The *Patrie* states from Trebizond that the Russian Chargé d'Affaires at Teheran, having demanded the dismissal of two of the most popular Ministers of the Shah of Persia, the people became excited, and the Commander of the Guard said he would not answer for public tranquillity if this demand were complied with. According to this account, it was the dread of an explosion from the dislike of the people for Russia that induced the Shah to renew his relations with the Chargé d'Affaires of England.

To the huge mass of diplomatic papers, communicated to the public, are now added a *Note of the four Powers* dated the 12th of December and jointly addressed by their respective Ambassadors at Constantinople to the Porte, and a new circular of Mr. Drouyn de Lhuys to the French diplomatic agents, dated Paris, Dec. 30. On perusing the Note of the four Powers, we understand the extreme agitation which prevailed at Constantinople after the acceptance of the Note by the Porte became known, the insurrectionary movement occurring on the 21st, and the necessity the Turkish Ministry was placed in, solemnly to proclaim that the operations of the war would not be interrupted nor interfered with by the renewed peace negotiations. Just nine days after the intelligence of the treacherous and cowardly butchery at Sinope had reached Constantinople and aroused throughout the Ottoman Empire one tremendous cry for revenge, the four Powers coolly invite, and the Ambassadors of Great Britain and France force, the Porte to enter into negotiations with the Czar, the base of which is

[a] "From our Private Correspondent, London, Saturday", *The Dublin Evening Mail,* No. 5466, January 2, 1854.—*Ed.*

that all the *ancient treaties shall be renewed*; that the firmans relative to the spiritual privileges octroyed by the Sultan to his Christian subjects, shall be accompanied by new assurances given to each of these Powers, consequently to the Czar; that the Porte shall name a plenipotentiary to establish an armistice; that it shall allow Russia to erect a church and a hospital at Jerusalem and pledge itself to the Powers, consequently to the Czar, to ameliorate its internal administrative system. The Porte shall not only not receive any indemnity at all for the heavy losses it has undergone consequent on the piratical acts of the Muscovite; all the chains in which Russia has made Turkey dance for a quarter of a century, shall not only be forged anew, but the prisoner shall be kept closer than before; the Porte shall lay itself at the mercy of the Autocrat by giving him humble assurances with regard to the firmans relative to the spiritual privileges of its Christian subjects, and pledging itself to him with regard to its internal administrative system; thus surrendering at once the religious protectorate and the dictation over its civil government to the Czar. In compensation for such a surrender the Porte receives the promise of "the most speedy evacuation possible of the Principalities," the invasion of which Lord Clanricarde declared to be "an act of piracy,"[a] and the assurance that the preamble of the treaty of July 13, 1841[380]—which has proved so trustworthy a safeguard against Russia—shall be formally confirmed.

Although the unfathomable abjectness of these pitiful "Powers" reached its highest possible pitch in frightening, some days after the event of Sinope, the Porte into a negotiation on such bases, they will not get rid of their embarrassment in this sneaking way. The Czar has gone too far to suffer even the appearance of his pretended exclusive protectorate over the Christian subjects of Turkey to be supplanted by a European one, and already we are informed by the Vienna correspondent of *The Times*[b] that

> "Austria has demanded whether the Russian Court would object to a European protectorate over the Christians in Turkey. The reply, in most positive language, was that Russia would permit no other power to meddle in the matter of the Greek Church. Russia had treaties with the Porte, and would settle the question with her alone."

We are also informed by *The Standard* that

---

[a] Quoted from Clanricarde's speech in the House of Lords on August 8, 1853, published by *The Times,* No. 21502, August 9, 1853.—*Ed.*

[b] "Vienna, Sunday afternoon", *The Times,* No. 21633, January 9, 1854.—*Ed.*

"Nicholas will not accept any proposition not proceeding directly from the Turkish sovereign individually, thus rejecting any right of mediation or interference on the part of the European Powers—an insult to those Powers which none can regard as unmerited."

The only important passage of the circular of Monsieur Drouyn de Lhuys is that announcing the entrance of the united squadrons into the Black Sea, with a view to

"combine their movements in such a manner as to prevent the territory or the flag of Turkey from being the object of any fresh attack on the part of the naval forces of Russia."

Non bis in idem. La moutarde après la viande.[a] *The Morning Chronicle* of yesterday published a telegraphic dispatch from its correspondent at Constantinople, dated the 30th, stating that the combined fleets had entered the Black Sea.

"The fleets may enter the Black Sea," says *The Daily News*, "only to do what they have been doing in the Bosphorus—nothing."

According to *The Press*,

"Orders have already been sent out for one ship from the English and one from the French fleet to enter the Black Sea, and under flag of truce to enter Sebastopol. When there they are to inform the Russian Admiral that if he leaves the port of Sebastopol he will be immediately fired into."

Although the Russian fleet, at this not very propitious season, and after their glorious exploit at Sinope, have nothing whatever to call them out into the Black Sea, the Czar will not allow England and France to exclude him, even temporarily, from waters from which he has succeeded in excluding them ever since 1833.[381] His prestige would be gone were he not to answer this communication by a declaration of war.

"A declaration of war of Russia against France and England," says the *Neue Preussische Zeitung*, "is more probable than a speedy peace between Russia and Turkey."

At Newry (Ulster), a great meeting was held for the purpose of taking into consideration the unprovoked aggression of Russia against Turkey. I am glad to be enabled, through the friendly communication from Mr. Urquhart of the Newry report, to give your readers the most remarkable passages of that gentleman's speech. Having explained, on several occasions, my own views of the Oriental question, I need not point out those topics on which I

---

[a] None can be punished twice for the same crime. Mustard after the supper.—*Ed.*

must disagree from Mr. Urquhart. Let me only remark that his views are confirmed by the intelligence that

"the peasants of Lesser Wallachia, assisted by the Wallachian soldiery, have risen against the Russians. The whole country in the environs of Kalafat and along the left shore of the Danube, is in motion. The Russian functionaries have evacuated Turmal."

After some introductory remarks Mr. Urquhart said:

...."In those matters which affect our gravest interests and intercourse with foreign States, there is neither restraint of law, nor guidance of system, there is no responsibility to the nation, no penalties for the omission of any duty, or for the perpetration of any crime; you are entirely destitute of all Constitutional means of restraint, because you are either kept in ignorance or you are misinformed. This system is, therefore, one calculated to pervert the nation, to corrupt the Government and to endanger the State. Meanwhile, you are opposed to a Government, the most crafty and systematic, the most hostile and unscrupulous, and which has worked its way to that preeminence of power by which it threatens the world, through the use which it has been enabled to make of the very Governments which it labors to overthrow—and there is this peculiarity in our condition, as there was formerly in that of Athens—that Russia has found or formed the chief instruments of her greatness in the breast of that State, whose public councils most opposed her policy. There is for this a substantive reason that England in such matters is the black spot of ignorance. The United States has a President, and he exercises the due prerogatives of royalty; there is a Senate which controls the executive, and has prior knowledge of its acts. [Hear, hear and cheers.] In France, there have been repeatedly Committees of Parliament, to investigate the national transactions, calling for documents, and bringing before them the Foreign Minister for examination. There, too, the nation is alert, according, at least, to its knowledge, and so is the Government; for on such matters hinge the existence of ministries and of dynasties. In Austria, there is at least a monarch, and he has knowledge of the acts of his servants. In Turkey and in Russia, you see that in one country the feeling of the people constrains the Government, and in the other the Government represents the will of the nation. England alone remains with a crown without authority, with a Government without system, with a Parliament without control, and a nation without knowledge. [Hear, hear.] Reverting now to the application of this state of things, to the facts before us, I have first to tell you—and it is the salient matter—that Russia has no force to effect her threats, and that she has calculated merely upon the facility of terrifying you by groundless fears, that she has had no purpose whatever of making war on Turkey, that she has no means for doing so, that she has not even made disposition for such an object, that she has calculated upon you restraining Turkey, so that she might occupy her provinces, and calculates further upon you for forcing from that State such compliance with insolent demands as shall break up the Ottoman Empire. [Hear, hear.] It is by your Ambassador in Constantinople[a] and by your squadron in the Bosphorus that she is about to achieve her ends. And here I must advert to a statement made by my gallant friend Colonel Chesney, and at the same time supply an omission which he has made. He stated, that as matters stood before the Pruth was crossed, Turkey was more than a match for Russia, but he did not give you the high estimate he entertains and has expressed of the military qualities of the Turks. He stated, even at the present moment, and with all the immense advantages which you have enabled Russia to acquire, he was still in doubt whether

[a] Stratford de Redcliffe.—*Ed.*

Turkey was not a match for Russia. On this point I have not the shadow of a doubt, if you grant me two conditions—the first, that your Ambassador and your squadron are withdrawn, the second, that Turkey recovers its emasculating reliance on foreigners. But after that came another statement, doubtingly indeed made, but which from his high authority, and there is no higher authority in these matters—may carry an undue weight or bear an unjustifiable interpretation. He said that the moment might be at present favorable for Russia, because the Danube was frozen, and she might push her forces across into Bulgaria. But what forces has she got to push into Bulgaria? Europe has for many months given heed to exaggerated statements; we have been industriously informed of the vast accumulations of her forces prepared to come in action. They were currently rated at 150,000 men, and the people were ready to believe that 150,000 men sufficed for the conquest of Turkey. I received some time ago an official statement which reduced to 80,000 men the whole number that had crossed the Pruth, of which between 20,000 or 30,000 had already perished by disease or were in hospital. The statement was sent by me to one of the newspapers, but was not inserted, being considered incredible. Russia has now published her own statement, reducing the entire number to 70,000 men. [Cheers.] Putting aside then the relative strength of both Empires, if all their forces were brought up, it must be clear that Russia had no intention of making war with such an amount of force as this. Now what was the force which Turkey had to oppose? No less than, at the time referred to, 180,000 men between the Balkan and the Danube, now increased to 200,000 men in strong, fortified positions, with a Russian force reduced to 50,000 men at the outside, and these demoralized by defeat and infected by desertion. As to the qualities of the Turkish troops and their superiority to the Russians, you have heard the testimony of General Bem; you have the living testimony of Colonel Chesney—confirmed by the events which have filled Europe with astonishment and admiration. Observe we are not now upon the point of the relative power of the two Empires but of that of the intention and mode of proceeding of the one—Russia. My argument is that she did not propose making war; because, on the one hand, she had not upon the spot the requisite force, and, on the other, that she could reckon on the Cabinet of England. Russia had no intention of making war—she has no intention now. This is what I have stated before the war—that she would enter and occupy the Principalities by the aid of England. How have I been able to prognosticate? Not, certainly, by the knowledge of Russia's designs, which thousands know as well or better than me, but by the knowledge of England's character. But let us reconsider the case—it is too important to pass it over. Colonel Chesney said that the real question was the reserve which Russia had behind the Pruth. Of that reserve he had heard lately a great deal. Osten-Sacken, with his 50,000 men, was on full march on the Danube to retrieve the disaster of Oltenitza. Now, the 50,000 men dwindled to 18,000, and the best of all is, that even they have not arrived. [Laughter and cheering.] Taking then Colonel Chesney's number, 75,000 reduced by deaths and sickness to 50,000, and throwing into these the 18,000 of ubiquitous reserve, we shall only have, after all, 70,000 men to operate against 200,000 strongly entrenched and in a mountainous region, and at a season of the year when hitherto the Russians have invariably retired from the field.

"Now let me recall the events of the late war in 1828 and '29. Turkey was then in convulsions. Then Mussulman's sword was turned against Mussulmans; the provinces were in revolt, Greece in insurrection, the old military force annihilated, the new conscripts scarcely disciplined, and amounting only to 33,000 men. The command of the Black Sea wrenched from Turkey by British broadsides, delivered in full force in the harbor of Navarino,[382] and then it was that Russia, backed by England and France, made a spring upon Turkey and reached the center of her provinces before she knew that war was declared. And how many men do you think she then judged it prudent to employ? Two hundred and sixteen thousand. [Cheers.] And yet it was only by deception and through the influence of the

English Ambassador, who unfortunately had returned, that she was seduced to sign that treaty of Adrianople that was surprised from her. [Hear, hear.] Look at Turkey now, united in heart and feeling, with a heroism inspired at once by the love of country and detestation of outrages—with united authority, ample resources, able to dispose of 300,000 volunteers, of the most martial character to be found on the face of the earth—of 250,000 disciplined troops—victorious in Asia—with the command of the Black Sea—not lost, be it observed, as I shall presently show, at Sinope—with steam to convey, without loss of men or time, her contingents to the scene of action from the remotest provinces of the Empire, from the snowy heights of the Caucasus to the arid deserts of Arabia, from the wastes of Africa to the Persian Gulf—one spirit of indignation prevails—of manhood has been aroused. [Hear and cheers.] Yes, but as in the former war, a Navarino brought the Cossacks across the Balkan; so now may the screw propellers of Britain, even without war, bring Russian hulks to the Dardanelles. But I am speaking of Russian intentions. That is the point. It is in Downing-st. that this victory is to be achieved, and not in the East. Meanwhile, are you unscathed? Is there a man before me who does not suffer in substance? Is there one the price of whose bread is not enhanced, whose employment, or the employment of his capital is not curtailed? [Hear, hear.] Whose taxes are not increased? Is not Change-alley [a] convulsed? Have we not seen by this movement of Russian troops a disturbance of the money market produced equal to two-thirds of that experienced in 1847—and yet Russia has never intended war. Have we not seen the Governments of Europe degraded and the ground-work laid of insurrections and convulsions—and yet Russia never intended war. Have we not seen the Ottoman Empire exhausting itself by an enormous military establishment of half a million of men, because Russia has displaced 70,000 troops to feed at her expense and at the expense of the operatives of Great Britain? And all this because you have believed people easy of belief that Russia was so strong that she could not be resisted—Turkey so weak that she could not be supported. Really we live in an age of dreams and of fables; we are men not to believe this only, we are men to believe that Russia is more powerful than all the powers of the world banded against her. *The Times* makes light of the army of Moslems, makes equally light of the armies of France and the navies of England, and gravely tells us that all Europe and Turkey to boot may as soon attempt to keep the Russians out of Constantinople, as to keep the north winds from blowing across the Sarmatian Plains. And the argument as regards Europe is just as good as respecting Turkey; yet Turkey will fall, if you persevere. Russia has displaced 70,000 men, and in consequence Turkey is moved with terror and indignation—England convulsed with fear and panic—Russia, too, convulsed with shouts of laughter. [Laughter and prolonged cheering.] I have said I would revert to the affair of Sinope, or as it has been justly termed, the little Navarino. I don't refer to that ungraceful event in reference to our conduct—for we have done in this nothing more disgraceful than in the rest—but I refer to it as bearing upon the relative strength of the two parties. So considered, it has added nothing to Russia's power, and taken nothing from that of Turkey, but the reverse. It has placed in the most unmistakable light the justifiable fears of the Russians of Turkish prowess. Here we have seen a fact without parallel even in our own naval annals—frigates laying themselves alongside line-of-battle ships, and commanders casting the torch into the powder magazine, and offering themselves up for holocaust on their country's shrine. What may not be achieved against a Government which in every act, and especially in this, is the object of abhorrence and disgust to every human being. Observe that the maritime force of Turkey is untouched; not a line-of-battle ship, not a steamer has been sacrificed. Now she is doubly insured in the command of the Black Sea if the diplomatists are withdrawn;

---

[a] A street in London where the Stock Exchange is situated.—*Ed.*

and it is they, and they alone, who have produced the so-called disaster of Sinope. But that disaster was prepared for another end; it was as a rod and a goad to urge the lagging beasts of burden in Paris and in London, and to drive them into enforcing the terms of settlement upon the belligerents. Before I entered this meeting, I heard it stated by a gentleman of the Committee, that it was perfectly competent for England and France to interpose between them if they expected by so doing to secure peace. I know that what he has stated is the general impression throughout this land, but I did not the less on that account listen to him with horror. Who gave you the right to go about the world enforcing peace by arms? It is one thing to resist aggression, it is another thing to commit it. [Hear, hear!] You cannot interpose even to save Turkey, save by declaring war against Russia. Your interposition, however, will be for Russia's behoof, and at her dictation, and with the effect of imposing conditions on Turkey which must bring her fall.... In your negotiations you will propose to Turkey to relieve her from her past treaties with Russia in consideration of an European settlement. This has, indeed, been already put forward, and has been received with acclamation by a nation which has acclaims ready for every perversion. Good Heavens! a European settlement! That is what Turkey has to rely upon. Surely your treaty of Vienna was a European settlement, and what was the result? That settlement was important by its establishment of Poland; and what befell Poland? When Poland had fallen, what did your Minister tell you respecting that treaty? Why, it was this: 'That it had given to England the right to express an opinion regarding the events in Poland.' After going on to state that he had remonstrated on the subject before the event, he says: 'But Russia took another view of the case.' And so it will be with your present settlement; she will take another view of the case. [Loud cheers.] These words were stated in the House of Commons; they were uttered by the very Minister" (Lord Palmerston) "who has now in his hands the fate of Turkey, as he had of Poland. But now you are warned; then you were unconscious.... Let me refer to a piece of intelligence recently published in *The Times* newspaper. It is there stated that our Minister in Persia had had a difference with the Government of the Shah, who was on the point of yielding, when the Minister of Russia interposed to exasperate the quarrel. Thus there you have at the one and at the same moment Russia driving England out of Persia, and England imposing Russia on Turkey. This same letter mentions that an embassy had reached Teheran; that the Afghans were in the greatest state of ferment, and that Dost Mohammed, the implacable enemy of Russia, had much at heart the success of his embassy which was to move Persia to support Turkey. Now, you will recollect that sixteen years ago, England made war against the Afghans, with the purpose of dethroning Dost Mohammed, because he was the enemy of England and the firm ally of Russia. Now, perhaps your Government believed this. If it did, it is very strange that it was not upon Russia they made war, but upon the Afghans, which was exactly the course to throw them into the arms of Russia. But your Government entertained no such belief; it then perfectly knew that Dost Mohammed, as now appears, was the implacable foe of Russia, and it was on that very account that it had attacked him. The fact has been established, and in the House of Commons it has been proved, that documents had been absolutely forged representing Dost Mohammed falsely as the ally of Russia. The Envoy of England himself sent home the original for publication. [Shame.] This is but the legitimate result of the secrecy in the Government and that ignorance in the nation to which I already referred. There is not a man in this assembly upon whom my eyes can rest, who is not by sufferance a participator in this crime, and who by this indifference to his country's acts and honor is not degraded to the position of a slave, while under the delusion that he is a freeman. [Hear, hear.] May I tell you something of what is thought of you by strangers? You have heard recently much of German influences at Court. Perhaps you would like to hear something of the opinions of German cousins of the Queen;

and let me tell you, if Germany is Russian, it is England that has made her so. Listen now to these words:

"'If Turkey is not interfered with by England and France she will conquer. If, on the contrary, the Western Powers, in their infatuated subservience cannot refrain from "mediating," or from meddling with the affairs of the East, Turkey is doomed, and universal dominion of the Muscovy Cossacks will soon sway the destinies of this world! Yet how noble has hitherto been the position and attitude of poor Turkey, in spite of all diplomatic embezzlement, and though she mistook a band of assassins for her friends. Matters look, indeed, gloomy! and I have hourly been expecting a bombardment by the allied fleets of her capital in order to bend her moral heroism to disgraceful submission. The Turks may truly say: "*Longa est injuria, longae ambages, sed summa sequor fatigia rerum!*"[a] What a contrast in their present behavior as compared with that of England on similar occasions! they "make war"—England carries on piracy. Recollect only the "Declaration of Lima" and the invasion of Afghanistan, the bombardment of Copenhagen[383] and the battle of Navarino and then think of Turkey as it stands there at present—abased and threatened, even invaded and provoked by the "civilized world;" she remains amid all her trials, calm and judicious, firm and resolute, but serene.'"

"You may judge by this that there are those in the loftiest station who may sigh in vain for the privilege which your indulgence affords to me of finding a vent for my indignation, and the opportunity of warning of coming events. Suffer me then to tell you the position in which you stand. Britain presents two features, she is an idiot at home, she is a maniac abroad, an armed maniac, endangering her own life and the lives of others. You are not so individually though you are so collectively. Awaken then your individual intelligence and restrain the corporate maniac until you have time to treat the disordered brain—this system from which all the evil proceeds." [Loud and long continued cheering.]

I may add to Mr. Urquhart's speech that Lord Palmerston's last *coup d'éclat*[384] and the favor of the people bestowed upon him, have made him Prime Minister in reality, if not in name.

Written on January 10, 1854

First published in the *New-York Daily Tribune*, No. 3988, January 28, 1854; reprinted in the *New-York Semi-Weekly Tribune*, No. 906, January 31, 1854

Signed: *Karl Marx*

Reproduced from the *New-York Daily Tribune*

[a] Vergilius, *Aeneid*, I, 341.—*Ed.*

Karl Marx

[THE WAR IN THE EAST][385]

London, January 14, 1854

At last, this long-pending "Eastern Question" appears to have reached a step where diplomacy will not much longer be enabled to monopolise this ground for its ever shifting and ever resultless movements. On the 3rd inst. the French and British fleets have entered the Black Sea, in order to prevent the Russian navy from doing harm either to the Turkish fleet or the Turkish coast. Once before the Czar Nicholas has declared that such a step would be, for him, the signal for a declaration of war. Will he now stand it quietly? There is a report to-day that the combined French and English fleets, together with the first division of the Turkish navy, are transporting 17,000 Turks to Batum. If this be correct, it is as much an act of war as if they made a direct attack upon Sebastopol, and the Czar cannot but declare war at once.

But would Russia stand alone? Which part would Austria and Prussia take in a general war?

It is reported that Louis Bonaparte has notified to the Austrian Government that, if in case of a conflict with Russia, Austria allied with this power, the French Government would avail itself of the elements of insurrection, which, in Italy and Poland, only required a spark to be kindled again into a raging fire, and that then the restoration of Italian and Polish nationality would be attempted by France. The Austrian government, however, we may confidently assume, will be more influenced by its own financial embarrassments than by the threats of Bonaparte.

The state of the Austrian Exchequer may be inferred from the late augmentation of its depreciated notes and from the recent expedient of the government enacting a discount of 15 pct. upon the paper money issued by themselves. This device, working the depreciation of their own paper, perhaps carries tax making ingenuity to its perfection, it is putting a tax on the payment of taxes. According to the German papers, the Austrian budget for 1854 will show a deficit of 45,000,000 flrs. on the ordinary service, and 50,000,000 flrs. on the extraordinary. For the 100th time Austria is moving towards a loan, but in a manner which promises no success. It is now proposed to raise a loan of 50,000,000 flrs. for the ostensible purpose of paying interest due and some other pressing demands.

When the news of the intended entrance of the united squadron into the Black Sea reached Vienna, the money changers had enough to do to change paper currency for silver coin. People with 100 and 200 florins thronged to their counting-houses with a view to secure their endangered treasures. Nevertheless, on the decisive moment, the influence of St. Petersburg at Vienna will be paramount and entangle Austria, on the side of Russia, into the coming struggle. As to Prussia, she is attempting the same game as in 1780, in 1800 and 1805,[386] to form a league of neutral Baltic or Northern German States, at the head of which she might play a part of some importance and turn to which side was to offer her the greatest advantages.

That the Turko-European fleets can destroy Sebastopol and the Russian Black Sea fleet, that they can take possession of, and hold the Crimea, occupy Odessa, close the Sea of Azov and let loose the mountaineers of the Caucasus, there is no doubt. The measures to be taken in the Baltic are as self-evident as those in the Black Sea: an alliance at any price with Sweden; an act of intimidation against Denmark, if necessary; an insurrection in Finland, which would break out upon landing a sufficient number of troops, and a guarantee that no peace would be concluded except upon the condition of this province being reunited to Sweden; the troops landed in Finland, to menace Petersburg while the fleet bombards Kronstadt.

All will depend on the maritime powers of Europe acting resolutely and vigorously.

The *New Prussian Gazette* of the 29th ult. confirms the account of the Emperor of Russia having ordered all the forces in his empire to be placed on a war-footing. Not only has he withdrawn his deposits from the banks of England and France, but also ordered voluntary collections to be raised on the part of his nobility, and the railways in progress to be suspended, in order to devote to war all the men and money required for their construction.

On the other hand armaments in France are going on more actively than ever, the second moiety of the contingent of 800,000 men of the class of 1852 having been called out. In France, too, a loan of 200,000,000 frs. (about £8,000,000) has long been contemplated, but the dearth of food, the failure in the wine and silk crops, the prevailing commercial and industrial distress, the great apprehensions entertained about the payments to be made at the end of February, the downward tendency of the funds and railway shares, all these circumstances tend by no means to facilitate such a transaction.

It is the intention of the British Government, as we are informed by *The Times*, to raise the number of seamen and marines for the current year to 53,000 men, which is an increase of about 8,000 on the number voted for last year, and a further addition to the 5,000 men, raised under the orders of Lord Derby's administration.[a] The total increase in the Navy since 1852 may therefore be stated of about 13,000 men. For the force now to be raised for the service of the fleet 38,000 will be seamen and boys, and 15,000 marines.

At last the murder is out, as regards the affair of Sinope. The statements published of the relative strength of Russia and Turkey at that place, show that the Russians had 3 steam two-deckers, one three-decker and 680 guns on their side more than the Turkish forces. So considered the event of Sinope has added nothing to Russia's power, and taken nothing from that of Turkey, but the reverse. Here we have seen a fact without parallel even in our own annals—frigates laying themselves alongside line-of-battle ships, and commanders casting the torch into the powder magazine and offering themselves up for holocaust on their country's shrine. The real maritime force of Turkey is untouched; not a line-of-battle ship, not a steamer having been sacrificed. This is not all. According to the last intelligence received, one of the finest three-deckers of the Russian fleet, the *Rostislav*, 120-gun ship, has been sunk by the Turks. This fact, kept back hitherto under the specious pretext that the *Rostislav* did not sink during the action, but immediately afterwards, is now admitted by the Russians, and forms a good set-off against the destroyed Turkish ships.[387] If one three-decker was actually sunk, we may expect that the other Russian vessels received very serious harm indeed during the action, and after all the victory of Sinope may have more disabled the Russian than the Turkish fleet. When the Pasha

---

[a] *The Times*, No. 21631, January 6, 1854.—*Ed.*

of Egypt[a] heard of the disaster at Sinope, he ordered the immediate armament of 6 frigates, 5 corvettes and 3 brigs, destined to fill up the chasm which has been produced in the material of the Turkish fleet.

The Egyptian steam-frigate *Pervaz-Bahri* disabled and taken after nearly five hours' struggle by the far larger Russian steam-frigate *Vladimir*, was so riddled with shot that she could hardly be brought into Sebastopol, and when there, sank at once. The *Pervaz-Bahri* was only carried into the harbour of Sebastopol by the aid of its chief engineer, Mr. Bell, an Englishman, who was promised on the part of Admiral Korniloff, if he succeeded in taking her there in safety, to be set immediately at liberty. When arrived at Sebastopol, instead of being released, Mr. Bell and his sub-engineers and stokers were put into close confinement, with the miserable allowance of 3d. a-day for their maintenance and given to understand that they would have to march 80 miles on foot, at this inclement season, into the interior. Prince Menchikoff, who commands at Sebastopol, was approved by the Czar and his Ministers, who turned a deaf ear to the representations of our Consul at Odessa[b] and the British Ambassador at St. Petersburg.[c] It was already known that at the battle of Sinope two English merchant men, following private trade, were headlessly and ruthlessly involved in the general destruction. The following is the simple narrative of the destruction of one of those vessels as given by a French paper:

"On the 30th November the brigantine *Howard*, belonging to Bideford, a seaport in the South of England, had finished the discharge of a cargo of coals to the Austrian Consul, Mr. Pirentz, at Sinope, and was then at anchor taking in ballast with a view of sailing to Fatsah for a cargo of corn, which she had engaged to carry to England, when the Russian fleet suddenly came in sight, and without giving any notice whatever, or affording any opportunity for foreign vessels to remove out of danger, commenced a heavy fire of shot and shells on the Turkish fleet lying at anchor and in a few minutes entirely destroyed the *Howard* and other merchant vessels in the harbour."[d]

This atrocious infraction of international law is paraded in the Odessa bulletin, while the Russian journals simultaneously announced in insulting language that, while the English fleets dared not enter the Black Sea, the English Government dared not refuse the use of its dockyards to repair a Russian man-of-war.

---

[a] Abbas Pasha.—*Ed.*
[b] J. James.—*Ed.*
[c] G. H. Seymour.—*Ed.*
[d] "Londres, 5 janvier", *Journal des Débats*, January 7, 1854.—*Ed.*

The latest mails have brought us more supplementary news with regard to the military events which lately took place in Asia. It appears that the Turks have been compelled entirely to evacuate the Russo-Armenian territory, but the precise result of the engagements, which determined this retreat, is not yet known[a]. One Turkish corps had penetrated on the direct road to Akhalzikh from Ardahan, while another body took the more southern road from Kars by Alexandropol (in Georgian, Gümri) to Tiflis. Both these corps, it appears, were met by the Russians. According to the Russian accounts the Turks were routed on either line and lost about 40 pieces of cannon; as to the Turkish accounts, we have nothing official, but in private correspondence the retreat is explained by the necessity of going into winter quarters. Certain it is, that the Turks have evacuated the Russian territory with the exception of Fort St. Nicholas, that the Russians followed them, and that their advanced guard even ventured to within a mile of Kars, where it was repulsed. We know, besides, that the Turkish army of Anatolia, recruited as it is from the Asiatic provinces, the seat of old Moslem barbarism, and counting in its ranks a great number of irregulars, unreliable though generally brave soldiers of adventure, fancy warriors, and filibusters of Kurdistan—that this army of Anatolia, is nothing like the staid, disciplined and drilled army of Rumelia, where the commander knows how many and what men he has from day to day under his command, and where the thirst for independent adventure and private plunder is held under check by articles of war and courts martial. We know that the Russians, very hard up for troops in the beginning of the Asiatic campaign, have been reinforced by the 13th division of infantry (16,000 men) under Lieut.-General Obrucheff II, and by a body of Cossacks from the Don; we know that they have been able to keep the mountaineers in bounds, to maintain their communication as well across the Caucasus by Vladikavkaz as by sea to Odessa and Sebastopol. Under these circumstances, and considering that the Turkish commander Abdi Pasha was either a traitor or a dunce (he has been recalled since and Ahmed Pasha has been sent in his stead), we should not wonder at all if the Turks had been worsted, although there can be no doubt of the exaggeration prevailing in the Russian bulletins.

On the Danube, the Russians have some time ago attacked

---

[a] The description of the engagement at Akhalzikh of November 26, 1853 is given above, on pp. 550-52 of this volume.—*Ed.*

Matchin, a fort situated on an arm of the Danube. A steamer came up with two gunboats; they were met by a hot fire; the gunboats, it is said, were sunk, and the steamer so far damaged that it had to make the best of its way home. Three or four skirmishes occurred, partly between the outposts at Kalafat, partly between the Russian posts on the Danube and small Turkish parties who crossed the river in order to surprise them. The Turks ascribe to themselves the advantage in all the encounters. It is to be regretted that the Turkish irregulars, fit more for this duty than for any other, have not long since been ordered to carry on this war on a small scale with the greatest activity. They would have proved more than a match for the Cossacks, disorganized the necessarily faulty system of outposts of the enemy, faulty because extending over a line 300 miles in length; they would have disturbed the Russian plans, obtained a perfect knowledge of the enemy's movements and might with proper caution and boldness have been victorious in every encounter.

From telegraphic news, received this moment, it appears that

> "on the 6th of this month, a Turkish division, 15,000 strong, with 15 pieces of artillery, attacked the entrenched position of Chetatea, not far from Kalafat, and took it with storm; that the Russians lost 2,500 men, and that a reinforcement of 18,000 Russians marching from Karaul, was forced to retire with a loss of 250 men."[a]

According to another report, the great majority of the population of Lesser Wallachia has risen against, and Krajova been placed in a state of siege by, the Russians.

Meanwhile Russia exhausted herself in efforts to seduce or alarm in all quarters of the world, on our Indian frontiers, in Persia, Servia, Sweden, Denmark, &c. In Persia the British minister had had a difference with the Government of the Shah, who was on the point of yielding, when the Russian Ambassador interposed not only to exasperate the Shah against England, but to drive him into active hostility too, and a declaration of war against the Porte. This intrigue, however, is said to have been baffled by the British Chargé d'Affaires, Mr. Thompson's menace of withdrawing from Teheran, by the dread of an immediate explosion from the dislike of the Persian people for Russia, and by the arrival of an Afghan Embassy, threatening, if Persia formed an alliance with Russia, an invasion of the Persian territory by the Afghans.

A crowd of Russian agents was simultaneously overrunning Servia—seeking out and applying themselves to the places and

---

[a] Marx quotes from the report in *The Times*, No. 21638, January 14, 1854.—*Ed.*

persons formerly known by their attachment to the banished family of the Obrenović—speaking to some of the young Prince Michael—to others of his old father Miloš—now making them hope, through the protection of Russia, for the extension of the limits of Servia—the formation of a new kingdom of Illyria, which should unite all those who spoke the Servian language actually under the domination of Turkey and Austria,—and now announcing to them, in case of resistance, innumerable armies and utter subjugation. Notwithstanding these intrigues, in opposite senses, that Russia ceased not to carry on, she has not succeeded in breaking the bonds between the Servians and the Sultan,[a] but, on the contrary, two firmans were expected from Constantinople at Belgrade, the one suppressing all the relations existing between Servia and Russia, and the other confirming all the privileges conceded, at different epochs, to the Servian people. Then, the Russian Government has actively pursued negotiations at Stockholm and Copenhagen, for the purpose of inducing the governments of Sweden and Denmark to side with her in the approaching European struggle; the great object she has in securing their alliance being to obtain the closing of the passages of the Sound and Belts against the Western Powers. All she has effected till now, is the conclusion of a treaty between Sweden, Denmark and Prussia concerning an armed neutrality, and preparations of armaments, ostensibly directed against herself. Private letters from Sweden exult in the possibility of the Duchy of Finland, so shamefully seized by Russia without a declaration of war, being restored to the Scandinavian Kingdom. As to Denmark, the attitude, not of the people, but of the Court, is more equivocal. It is even rumoured that the present Danish Minister of Foreign Affairs[b] will resign and be replaced by Count Reventlow-Criminil, a man known to be intimately connected with the Court of St. Petersburg. In France the "fusion" of the Orleanists and Legitimists[388] owes to Russia the sort of success it has met with, while that same power is stirring up heaven and earth to destroy the *entente cordiale* existing between the Governments of England and France and to sow distrust between them. Attempts are being made by some of the Paris journals, in the pay of Mr. Kisseleff, to create a belief that the English Government is not sincere, and we see that in England a journal, in the pay of Mr. de Brunnow, in return casts doubts on the sincerity of the French Government.

---

[a] Abdul Mejid.—*Ed.*

[b] Ch. A. Bluhme.—*Ed.*

Another blow, principally aimed against the Western powers, is the Russian prohibition relative to the exportation of Polish corn.

In the meantime the movements of Western diplomacy were by no means hostile to Russia, but exhibited, on the contrary, rather too anxious a tendency to temporise with justice and to compromise with crime. It is now obvious to everyone that their course has been a mistaken and a mischievous one. The resurrection of the Vienna conference and the protocol drawn up by them on the 5th ult., the letter of the French and British Ambassadors at Constantinople to Reshid Pasha,[389] the collective note of the 4 Great Powers presented to the Porte on the 15th, and accepted by the Sultan on the 31st ult., the circular of Mr. Drouyn de Lhuys, announcing the entrance of the united fleets into the Black Sea, to the French diplomatic agents, dated 30th ult., such are the principal events of the diplomatic history of the last 6 weeks.[a] As to the protocol of the Vienna conference, your readers will have been informed of its contents before now. Can there be anything more ludicrous than its assertion that

> "the assurances given on several occasions by the Emperor of Russia exclude the idea that that august Sovereign entertains any wish to interfere with the integrity of the Ottoman Empire,"[b]

and anything more mischievous than its urging on Turkey the propriety of consenting to a month's armistice? Two days after the news of the disgraceful butchery at Sinope had reached Constantinople on the 5th ult., Reshid Pasha addressed a letter to Lord Stratford de Redcliffe and General Baraguay D'Hilliers, communicating the news from Sinope and asking that the fleets might enter the Black Sea. On the 12th, a week after the date of Reshid Pasha's note, he received a very indifferent answer on the part of the two Ambassadors, intimating to him that

> "the presence of the United Squadron had 'a *political* signification,' consequently no *military* one, and that it was a '*moral* support,' consequently no *naval* one."

Thus the Porte was coerced into the acceptance of the joint Note of the 4 Powers presented to her on the 15th December. This note grants the Porte not only no compensation whatever for the losses she has undergone consequent upon the piratical acts of the Autocrat; it insists not only upon the renewal of all the ancient treaties of Kainardji, Adrianople, Unkiar-Skelessi, etc., which have

---

[a] On the note of the four powers and Drouyn de Lhuys' circular see this volume, pp. 560-61.—*Ed.*

[b] Quoted from *The Times*, No. 21615, December 19, 1853.—*Ed.*

furnished, for a century and a half, the arsenal from which Russia has drawn her weapons of fraud, interference, progress and incorporation; but it allows the Czar to carry the point of the religious protectorate and administrative dictation over Turkey by stipulating that

> "the communication of the firmans relative to the spiritual privileges octroyed by the Sublime Porte to all its subjects not Mussulmen, should be made to all the Powers, and accompanied by *suitable* assurances given to each of them,"

and that the Porte shall declare on its part its firm resolution to develop more efficaciously its administrative system and internal reforms.

These new propositions, while in their letter investing the 5 Powers of Europe with a joint protectorate over the Christian subjects of Turkey, give in reality the protectorate to Russia alone. The arrangement is to be, that France and Austria being Roman Catholic countries, are to have the protectorate over the Roman Catholic Christians in Turkey, and England and Prussia being Protestant countries, are to have the protectorate over the Protestant subjects of the Sultan, while Russia is to have the protectorate over those professing the Greek faith. Now, as the Roman Catholics do not number 800,000, nor the Protestants 200,000, while those who profess the Greek religion amount to nearly 10,000,000, it is plain that the Czar would indeed acquire the protectorate over the Christian subjects in Turkey. These proposals of the 4 Powers were not accepted by the Porte till on the 19th ult., when Riza Pasha and Halil Pasha had entered the Ministry, the success of the Peace or Russian party having been thus assured.

On the 21st ult., when it became known that the Council of Ministers had notified to the four Ambassadors the adoption of the propositions, they had suggested, the Saftas (students) assembled to present a petition against the resolution taken by the government, and the outbreak of disturbances was only prevented by the arrest of the ringleaders. So great was the exasperation which prevailed at Constantinople, that the Sultan did not venture to repair on the following day to the Divan, nor proceed, as usual, amidst the thunder of the cannon, and the hurrahs of the foreign war crew, to the mosque of Tophana; and that Reshid Pasha fled for refuge from his own palace in Stambul to the palace contiguous to the residence of the Sultan. On the following day the public mind was somewhat calmed by a proclamation on the part of the Sultan, that no stop should be put to the military operations.

These tortuous, pusillanimous and inexplicable movements of the Western diplomacy, which, throughout the dreary history of the last 9 months, almost exhausted public patience, have thrown doubts upon the sincerity of the British Government, and, as the public feel themselves at a loss to understand the motives that may have caused the long endurance on the part of the Western Powers, secret influences are spoken of, and rumours are industriously spread, that Prince Albert, the husband of the Queen,[a] is interfering in the affairs of the Executive; that he is not only attending on his Sovereign Lady at the meetings of her Council, but is using his influence to control the advice of the responsible advisers; that, while exercising his opportunity to be present at the meeting of the Queen with her Ministers, he is in constant and direct communication with foreign courts, including the Russian one, but except that of France. Another tale is, that the "fusion" of the Orléans and elder Bourbon branches of the late royal family of France receives almost as much countenance from our Court as it does from that of Russia, and the visit of the Duke of Nemours at the Court of Queen Victoria, fresh from the meeting with "Henry the Fifth,"[b] is pointed at as a proof.

A fourth report, that the negotiations in the Eastern question, have, with the assent of Russia, been delegated to the sole intermediation of Count Buol-Schauenstein, brother-in-law of Count Meyendorff, is cited as evidence that this government has never desired independent or effective negotiations, but has, from the first, sought to aid the designs of Russia and her allies, while seeming to oppose her. Mr. Roebuck, it is confidently stated, will bring the whole question of Coburg influence before the House of Commons, while Lord Brougham is said to intend bringing it before the House of Lords. There is no doubt that the Coburg influences form, as this moment, the almost exclusive topic of conversation in the metropolis. Parliament will reassemble on the 31st instant.

So stern a winter as the present one has not been known since 1809. The intensity of the cold has been by no means the most trying incident; the incessant changes both of temperature and of the character of the weather have been far worse. The trains run on the railway with the greatest difficulty; in some parts transit

[a] Victoria.—*Ed.*

[b] Comte de Chambord.—*Ed.*

appears to be quite cut off, and in the means of communication England is thrown back to times forgotten. The electric telegraph has been used to mitigate the inconvenience of commercial documents intercepted by snow drifts, and to prevent the noting of bills for unexplained non-payment. Nevertheless the noting of more than 500 bills in London illustrates the social anarchy occasioned by the uncommon inclemency of the season. The papers are filled with records of the fearful shipwrecks caused by the snow storms and gales, particularly on the Eastern coast. Although the recently published tables of trade, navigation and revenue[a] show a continuance of the prosperity with which 1853 began, the severity of the season, coupled with the rising prices of the first necessaries, principally of corn, coals and tallow, acts as a hard pressure upon the condition of the lower classes. Numerous cases of starvation have occurred. Bread riots in the West are now forming an accompaniment to the lock-outs in the North.

Time, however, compels to defer a detailed account of trade and commerce to a following letter.

Written on January 14, 1854

First published in the *Zuid Afrikaan*, March 6, 1854, in English and Dutch

Reproduced from the newspaper, checked with the Dutch

[a] "Accounts Relating to Trade and Navigation for the Eleven Months Ended December 5, 1853", *The Economist*, No. 541, January 7, 1854.—*Ed.*

Frederick Engels

THE LAST BATTLE IN EUROPE

The letters of our London correspondents and the European journals enable us at last to appreciate in all its bearings the prolonged struggle between the Turks and Russians, of which Chetatea,[390] a small village nine miles north of Kalafat, was the arena. Next to the fact that the series of sanguinary actions in question was characterized by great bravery and that the Turks came off victors, the most striking feature of the whole is that it is without practical result, so far as the expulsion of the Russians from Wallachia is concerned. This comes from a mistake on the part of the Turks to which we have more than once had occasion to direct the attention of our readers. We allude to their sending a separate army to Kalafat, in order to shut up the road to Servia, while the presence of a strong and concentrated force near Rustchuk and Orsova[a] would have been the best guarantee against the Russians venturing into that province. Such a force would have menaced the communications of any Russian army marching westward, while a bridge and bridge-head at Oltenitza or somewhere thereabouts, fortified like that of Kalafat, could have maintained a footing for them on the left bank of the Danube. But even without that, the Russians could not cross the Upper Danube and march into Servia, without leaving the Turks to cross the Lower Danube and march upon Bucharest. Of course, in saying this, we reckon the relative strength of the parties to be what it is in reality, and ascribe a decided superiority of numbers

[a] See this volume, pp. 474, 520-21.—*Ed.*

to the Turkish army of Rumelia, over the Russian army of Wallachia.

Now the fact is that the Turks have used their superiority in the very way to nullify it and provide for being finally beaten. They did not concentrate their forces on the Lower Danube, but divided them. While 30,000 to 35,000 men occupied Widin and Kalafat, the rest of the army remained on the Middle and Lower Danube. They occupy the arc of a circle, while the Russians occupy the chord of this arc. Thus the latter have less space to traverse in order to concentrate all their troops on a given spot. Moreover, the shorter roads of the Russians are through a level country, while the longer ones of the Turks pass over hills and cross many mountain torrents. The Turkish position is, then, as disadvantageous as can be, and yet it has been taken in order to satisfy the old prejudice that there is no better way of barring a road against an enemy than by placing yourself across it.

On the 20th of December Omer Pasha knew at Shumla, that the Russians were preparing a general attack upon Kalafat for the 13th of January. He had twenty-two days' time; yet such is the position of Kalafat with regard to the other stations of the Turkish army, that it does not appear that he could bring on any reenforcements except a few reserves from Sofia. On the other hand, that the Russians, without having received any considerable reenforcements from home—on January 3 Osten-Sacken's ubiquitous corps was not yet at Bucharest—should venture upon a concentration so far west, shows that either the state of the weather and of the Danube did not allow the Turks to cross the river lower down, or that Gorchakoff had other reasons to be assured of their inactivity in that quarter. The Turks at Kalafat were ordered to attack the Russians while yet in the act of concentrating themselves. The best way to do this was to repeat the experiment of Oltenitza.[a] Why was not this done? The bridge at Kalafat stands, in spite of winter and floating ice, and there was no position lower down where a similar bridge and bridge-head could be erected. Or had Omer Pasha been ordered to keep on the right bank of the river? There is so much of a contradictory nature in the Turkish proceedings, bold and clever measures are so regularly followed by the most palpable sins of omission and commission, that diplomatic agency must be at the bottom of it. At all events, Gorchakoff would not have stirred an inch toward

[a] On the progress of the engagement at Oltenitza see this volume, pp. 516-22.—*Ed.*

Kalafat, had he not been certain that the Turks would not repeat the Oltenitza movement.

Altogether some 30,000 Russians must have been sent against Kalafat, for with a lesser force they would hardly have ventured to attack a fortified position, defended by a garrison of 10,000 men, with at least 10,000 more for purposes of reserve or sally. At least one half, then, of the Russian active army in Wallachia was concentrated there. Where and how could the other half, spread over a long line, have resisted a Turkish force crossing at Oltenitza, Silistra or Orsova? And if the communication between Widin and Kalafat could be kept up without difficulty, then there was a possibility of crossing at other points. Thus the Russians by their position on the chord of the arc, the periphery of which was held by the Turks, were enabled to bring a superior force to the field of battle at Chetatea, while the Turks could not reenforce their corps at Kalafat, though aware of the intended attack long beforehand. The Turks, deprived of that movement of diversion which would have prevented the whole battle, deprived of the chance of succor, were reduced to their bravery and to the hope of cutting up the enemy in detail before his concentration was completed. But even this hope was slight, for they could not move very far from Kalafat, and every hostile corps of inferior strength could retire out of the circle of their operations. Thus they fought for five days, generally with success, but at last had to retire again to their entrenchments in the villages around Kalafat, the Russian forces being decidedly superior in strength at the end, when new reenforcements arrived. The result is that the Russian attack upon Kalafat is most probably averted or delayed, and that Turks have shown that in the open field, no less than behind ramparts and ditches, they can fight well. The murderous character of the encounters may be inferred from the statement of a letter from Bucharest, to the effect that in the engagements one whole regiment of Russian rifles, and all but 465 men of a regiment of lancers, were completely annihilated.

At Oltenitza the Turks were attacked in their entrenched positions by the Russians; at Chetatea the Russians were attacked in their entrenched positions by the Turks. On both occasions the Turks have proved victorious, but without reaping any positive results from their victory. The battle of Oltenitza happened just when the proclamation of an armistice was on its way from Constantinople to the Danube. And the battle of Chetatea curiously coincides with the news of the Divan having accepted the lasts proposals of peace, imposed upon them by their Western allies.[391] In the one instance the machinations of diplomacy are nullified in the clash of arms, while in the other the bloody work of war is simultaneously frustrated by some secret diplomatic agency.

Written on January 19, 1854

First published in the *New-York Daily Tribune*, No. 3997, February 8, 1854, as a leader; reprinted in the *New-York Weekly Tribune*, No. 648, February 11, 1854

Reproduced from the *New-York Daily Tribune*

Karl Marx

[THE FIGHTING IN THE EAST.— FINANCES OF AUSTRIA AND FRANCE.— FORTIFICATION OF CONSTANTINOPLE[392]]

London, Friday, Jan. 20, 1854

The latest mails have brought us some supplementary news with regard to the military events which lately took place in Asia. It appears that the Turks have been compelled entirely to evacuate the Russo-Armenian territory, but the precise result of the engagements which determined their retreat, is not known. The Turks had penetrated on the direct road to Akhalzikh from Ardahan, while another body took the more southern road from Kars by Alexandropol (in Georgian, Gümri) to Tiflis. Both these corps, it appears, were met by the Russians; according to the Russian accounts, the Turks were routed on either line and lost about forty pieces of cannon; as to the Turkish accounts, we have nothing official, but in private correspondence the retreat is explained by the necessity of going into winter quarters.

The only thing certain is this, that the Turks have evacuated the Russian territory with the exception of Fort St. Nicholas; that the Russians followed them, and that their advanced guard even ventured to within a mile of Kars, where it was repulsed. We know, besides, that the Turkish army of Anatolia, recruited as it is from the Asiatic provinces, the seat of the old Moslem barbarism, and counting in its ranks a great number of irregulars, unreliable, though generally brave, soldiers of adventure, fancy warriors and filibusters, that this army of Anatolia is nothing like the stern, disciplined and drilled army of Rumelia, whose commander knows how many and what men he has from day to day under his command, and where the thirst for independent adventure and private plunder is held under check by articles of war and courts martial. We know that the Russians, who were very hard up for troops in the beginning of the Asiatic campaign, have been reinforced by 16,000 men under Lieut.-Gen. Obrucheff II, and by a body of Cossacks from the Don; we know that they have been able to keep the mountaineers within bounds, to maintain their communication as well across the Caucasus by Vladikavkaz, as by sea to Odessa and Sebastopol.

Under these circumstances and considering that the Turkish commander Abdi Pasha was either a traitor or a dunce (he has been recalled since and placed under arrest at Kars; Ahmed Pasha was sent in his place), we should not wonder at all if the Turks had been worsted, although there can be no doubt of the exaggeration prevailing in the Russian bulletins. We read in the *Augsburger Zeitung*[a] that

> "towards the end of November, Shamyl made a desperate attempt to force his way to the south, in order to effect a direct communication with the Turks. The strength of his corps was estimated at from 10,000 to 16,000 men, and it is affirmed that the Murides, the flower of his troops, were cut to pieces."

This however wants confirmation.

At last the murder is out, as regards the affair at Sinope. One of the finest three-deckers of the Russian fleet—the *Rostislav*,[393] 120-gun ship—was sunk there by the Turks. This fact—kept back hitherto under the specious pretext that the *Rostislav* did not sink during the action, but immediately afterward—is now admitted by the Russians, and forms a good set-off against the destroyed Turkish ships. If one three-decker was actually sunk, we may suppose that the other Russian vessels received very serious harm indeed during the action—and, after all, the victory of Sinope may have more disabled the Russian than the Turkish fleet. Altogether, the Turks appear to fight like Turks when on the water. The Egyptian steam-frigate *Pervaz-Bahri*, disabled and taken after nearly five hours' struggle by the far larger Russian steam-frigate *Vladimir*, was so riddled with shot that she could hardly be brought into Sebastopol, and when there, sank at once. So far, then, the prizes carried off by the Russians amount to nothing, and indeed the impossibility for them to carry off a single prize from Sinope shows both the obstinacy of the Turkish defense and the mutilated state of the Russian fleet after the action.

There is a report that the combined French and English fleets, together with the first division of the Turkish Navy, are

---

[a] Issue No. 9, January 9, 1854.—*Ed.*

transporting 17,000 Turks to Batum. If this be true, it is as much an act of war as if they made a direct attack upon Sebastopol, and the Czar[a] cannot but declare war at once. Immediately prior to the entrance of the combined fleets into the Black Sea, the Czar is said to have sent his mandate for the withdrawal of all his vessels of war from the waters of the Euxine to Sebastopol. A letter dated Odessa, Dec. 24, reports that

> "the commander of the Russian flotilla in the Sea of Azov had sent one of his *aides-de-camp* to Sebastopol to explain how critical his position was. Two corps of 12,000 men each were ready to be embanked at Sebastopol, when this operation of war was paralyzed by the news of the imminent entrance of the united fleets into the Euxine."[b]

From the last telegraphic news received it appears that the Russians intended attempting a general attack on the Turkish lines at Kalafat, on the 13th inst., the Russian New-Year's day. They had already pushed forward about 10,000 men in entrenchments at Chetatea, a village nine English miles north of Kalafat, but were prevented from concentrating their whole available force by the Turkish General's getting the start of them, storming the enemy's entrenchments with 15,000 or 18,000 men, proving victorious in a series of most murderous encounters that took place on the 6th, 7th, 8th, 9th and 10th inst., and finally forcing the Russians to retire in the direction of Krajova. The Russians themselves confess a loss of 1,000 killed and 4,000 wounded. Gen. Anrep, we are told by the telegraph, "who commanded the Russians, was severely wounded, as well as Gen. Tuinont." On the 10th, it is stated, the Turks who were commanded by Selim Pasha (the Pole Zedlinsky), again *retired* to Kalafat. Thus far the telegraphic news, hitherto the only source of information about these most important events. The report winding up, on the one hand, with the retirement of the Russians on Krajova, and of the Turks, on the other, to Kalafat, evokes a suspicion that great strategical faults have again been committed on both sides. There is one report afloat that Omer Pasha caused a whole corps to pass the [Danube] between the Aluta and the Shil, thus menacing the communications of the Russian corps at Krajova. But how could the Turks cross the Danube, which is filled with floating masses of ice, at any other point than Kalafat, where alone they were prepared for such an emergency?

---

[a] Nicholas I.—*Ed.*

[b] Here and below the facts are cited according to *The Times*, No. 21639, January 16, 1854.—*Ed.*

The defeats the Russians met with at Kalafat are perhaps more important in a political than a military view. Coupled with the entrance of the united fleets into the Black Sea, they cut off the last probability of the Czar's yielding to the humble supplication for peace forwarded by the courier of the Vienna Conference to St. Petersburg. On the other hand they must produce the immediate effect on neighboring Servia of strengthening the National party and intimidating the Russian one, who have lately been lifting up their heads with amazing impudence at Belgrade. Prince Alexander, it is true, and the mass of the Servian people, could not be prevailed upon to break the bonds between their country and the Sultan,[a] although a crowd of Russian agents is simultaneously overrunning Servia, carrying on their intrigues in opposite senses—seeking out and applying themselves to the places and persons formerly known for their attachment to the banished family of the Obrenović—speaking to some of the young Prince Michael—to others of his old father Miloš—now making them hope, through the protection of Russia, for the extension of the limits [of] Servia—the formation of a new kingdom of Illyria, which would unite all those who speak the Servian language now under the domination of Turkey and Austria—and now announcing to them, in case of resistance, innumerable armies and utter subjugation. You are aware that Prince Miloš, residing at Vienna, is the old *protégé* of Metternich, while Michael, his son, is a mere creature of Russia, who in 1842 rendered the princedom vacant by flying from Servia. The Russian defeat at Kalafat will, at the same time, relieve Austria from the fear of a Russian army appearing before Belgrade and evoking among the subjects of Austria, of common origin and faith with herself, the consciousness of their own strength and of the degradation they endure in the domination of the Germans.

As to Austria, I may state *en passant*, that she has at last renounced the long-cherished hope of raising a new loan. The state of her Exchequer may be inferred from the expedient her Government has recently resorted to, of exacting a discount of 15 per cent. upon its own paper money—a financial maneuver only to be compared with the devises of the swindling ingenuity of the French *Rois Faux Monoyeurs*,[b] who appreciated the coin when they had to pay, and depreciated it when they had to receive money. According to the German papers, the Austrian budget for 1854

[a] Abdul Mejid.—*Ed.*
[b] Royal counterfeiters.—*Ed.*

will show a deficit of 45,000,000 florins on the ordinary service, and 50,000,000 florins on the extraordinary. Whenever news of warlike character reaches Vienna, people throng to the banking-houses, in order to change paper currency for silver coin.

France, too, it is known, has long been moving for a loan of 200,000,000 francs (£8,000,000 sterling), but the dearth of food, the failure of the wine and silk crops, the prevailing commercial and industrial distress, the great apprehensions entertained about the payments to be made at the end of February, the downward tendency of the public funds and railway shares, all these circumstances have by no means tended to facilitate such a transaction. Bonaparte could not succeed in finding takers at the Bourse for the new loan. There remained no resource save that recurred to on the eve of the coup d'état—sending Persigny to the Bank of France, forcing out of it 50,000,000 francs ($10,000,000), and leaving in their place that amount of treasury bonds, under the head of "securities." This was actually done on New-Year's day. The fall of the funds to 69 hailed this financial coup d'état. The Government will, as we are now officially informed, obtain a loan from the Bank of France of 2,000,000 or 3,000,000 francs, against treasury bonds. Those not acquainted with what passed on New-Year's day in the parlor of the Bank of France, will be at a loss to understand how the Bank has been prevailed upon to accept a loan rejected at the Bourse.

As to Persia the news continues to be contradictory. According to one report the Persian army is marching upon Erzerum and Bagdad; according to another the Russian intrigue has been baffled by the British Chargé d'Affaires, Mr. Thompson, who menaced withdrawal from Teheran, by the dread of an immediate explosion of the dislike of the Persian people for Russia, and by the arrival of an Afghan Embassy, threatening, if Persia formed an alliance with Russia, an invasion of the Persian territory by the Afghans.

According to private correspondence from Constantinople, published in the *Patrie*, the Divan has resolved to fortify Constantinople on the land side. A mixed commission, consisting of European and Ottoman officers, is said to have already commenced the preparatory survey of the localities. The fortification of Constantinople would altogether change the character of Russo-Turkish warfare, and prove the heaviest blow ever dealt to the eternal dreams of the self-styled heir of the Byzantine Emperors.

The rumor of Austria's concentrating a corps *d'armée* in the Banat, to be placed under the command of Gen. Count Schlick, is contradicted by the German Press.

The *Correspondenz*, of Berlin, states that general orders have been given to the authorities to hold themselves prepared, in case of a mobilization of the Landwehr.[394]

Overtures have been made from St. Petersburg to the Cabinet of Copenhagen for the cession of the Island of Bornholm to Russia.

"Bornholm," as it is justly remarked by *The Daily News*,[a] "might be a Malta or Gibraltar of the Baltic. It is within a day's sail of the Sound and Copenhagen, and [...] placed by nature at the very throat of the Baltic."

In the message sent by Lord Redcliffe to the Governor of Sebastopol, and intimating to him the appearance of the united squadron in the Black Sea, the only object of the movement is stated to be "the protection of the *Ottoman territory* from all aggression or hostile act,"[b] *no mention* being made of the protection of the *Ottoman flag*.

As all the accounts received from Paris, Vienna, Berlin, Constantinople and St. Petersburg, indicate the prospect of war, prices have generally declined in all stock markets on both sides of the Channel.

Written on January 20, 1854

First published in the *New-York Daily Tribune*, No. 3997, February 8, 1854

Signed: *Karl Marx*

Reproduced from the newspaper

[a] Issue No. 2391, January 18, 1854.—*Ed.*

[b] Redcliffe, Baraguay d'Hilliers, "To the Governor of Sebastopol", *The Daily News*, No. 2390, January 17, 1854.—*Ed.*

Karl Marx

[THE CZAR'S VIEWS.—PRINCE ALBERT][395]

London, Tuesday, Jan. 24, 1854

The attempts of the Russian army to cross the Danube simultaneously on the whole line of operations—at Matchin, Giurgevo and Kalafat—are to be considered as reconnoitering maneuvers rather than as serious attacks, which can hardly be ventured upon with the present forces Gen. Gorchakoff has to dispose of.

Last Saturday's *Press*—the Disraeli paper—published a note of a conversation very recently held at Gatchina between the Czar and a "distinguished" Englishman. Almost the whole of the daily London press has reprinted this note, which, besides the known and worn-out commonplaces of Russian diplomacy, contains some interesting statements.

> The Czar "distinctly stated that the ultimatum of Menchikoff had not been disapproved of in London, but that the English Ministry, *having been informed that it would probably be accepted by the Porte*, had recognized it as a satisfactory settlement."

This would only prove that poor John Russell was *falsely informed* by Baron de Brunnow as to the "probable" intentions of the Sublime Porte, and that the Porte's refusing to yield to the Menchikoff ultimatum at once, was by no means the fault of the Coalition Cabinet. The Czar goes on informing "the individual of distinction" that

> "when the news of the victory of Sinope arrived, General Castelbajac" (the French Ambassador) "addressed him a letter beginning something in this way: 'As a Christian and as a soldier, permit me [...] to congratulate your Imperial Majesty on the glorious victory obtained by your Majesty's fleet.'"

Let me remark that Gen. Castelbajac, an old Legitimist and a relative of La Rochejaquelein's, gained his generalship, not by services in the camp, but by less dangerous service in the ante-chambers of the Court, and the ardent confession of exalted royalist principles. Bonaparte appointed him as Ambassador to the Court of St. Petersburg, with a view to give the Czar a proof of deference to his personal wishes, although he was fully aware that Castelbajac was to conspire with the Czar for the restoration of the Bourbons rather than further the interests of his nominal master. This Castelbajac, then, is the very man to have congratulated the Czar "as a soldier and a Christian" on the resultless butchery of Sinope.

"He did not believe," the Czar is stated to have said, "that England, with a *Bourgeois* Parliament, could carry on a war with glory."

There is no doubt that the Czar knows his Cobdens and his Brights, and estimates at its just value the mean and abject spirit of the European middle classes. Finally, the Czar is quite right in stating that, on the one hand, he had not been prepared for war—fully convinced as he was that he should obtain all he cared for by the simple act of bullying—and that, on the other hand, if war were brought about, it would be the "war of incapacities," making it inevitable by their anxious efforts to prevent it, and plunging into it finally in order to cover their blunders and save their places.

"Public opinion is half-inclined to sacrifice Prince Albert at the shrine of rumor. A whisper, which was first insinuated for party uses, has grown into a roar, and a constructive hint has swelled into a positive and monstrous fiction. That those who seek the presence of the Queen[a] should find Prince Albert with her Majesty, is a fact which rather won the sympathy and esteem of the English public; but then it was said that he attended meetings of the Queen with her Ministers; next, that Ministers were made aware of his presence—that, however reluctant to proceed with business before a third party, they found it necessary to do so—that it even became necessary to defend their opinions before the Prince—that the Prince, in fact, interfered with their counsel to their Sovereign—that he not only influenced the Royal mind, but possessing the power of free communication with foreign Courts, he constituted an unlicensed channel for information between the confidential council of the Queen and the Cabinets of foreign potentates, perhaps of the enemies of England—that in short, Prince Albert was a traitor to his Queen, that he had been impeached for high treason, and finally, that on a charge of high treason he had been arrested and committed to the Tower. This was the story not only told in all parts of England a day or two back, but by some believed."

I quote the above passage from *The Spectator*, in order to show your readers how public rumor has been induced by the

[a] Victoria.—*Ed.*

Palmerstonian press to make a poor stupid young man the scapegoat of the responsible Ministers. Prince Albert is a German Prince, connected with most of the absolute and despotic Governments of the Continent. Raised to the rank of Prince-Consort in Great Britain, he has devoted his time partly to fattening pigs, to inventing ridiculous hats for the army, to planning model lodging houses of a peculiarly transparent and uncomfortable kind, to the Hyde Park Exhibition, and to amateur soldiery. He has been considered amiable and harmless, in point of intellect below the general average of human beings, a prolific father and an obsequious husband. Of late, however, he has been deliberately magnified into the most influential man and the most dangerous character of the United Kingdom, said to dispose of the whole State machinery at the secret dictation of Russia. Now there can exist but little doubt that the Prince exercises a direct influence in Court affairs, and, of course, in the interest of despotism. The Prince cannot but act a Prince's part, and who was ever silly enough to suppose he would not? But I need not inform your readers of the utter impotency to which British Royalty itself has been reduced by the British oligarchy, so that, for instance, King William IV, a decided foe to Russia, was forced by his Foreign Minister[a]—a member of the Whig oligarchy—to act as a foe to Turkey. How preposterous, then, to suppose Prince Albert to be able to carry one single point in defiance of the Ministry, except so far as little Court affairs, a dirty riband, or a tinsel star, are concerned! Use is made of his absolutist *penchants* to blind the people's eyes as to the plots and treacheries of the responsible Ministers. If the outcry and attack means anything it means an attack on royalist institutions. If there were no Queen there would be no Prince—if there were no throne there would be no Court influences. Princes would lose their power if thrones were not there to back them, and for them to lean upon. But, now mark! the papers which go the farthest in their "fearful boldness," which cry the loudest and try to make a sort of political capital out of Prince Albert, are the most eager in their assertions of loyalty to the throne and in fulsome adulation of the Queen. As to the Tory papers this proposition is self-evident. As to the radical *Morning Advertiser*, it is the same journal which hailed Bonaparte's coup d'état, and recently attacked an Irish paper for having dared to find fault with the Queen, on the occasion of her presence at Dublin, which reproaches the French Revolutionists with profess-

[a] Palmerston.—*Ed.*

ing Republicanism, and continues to designate Lord Palmerston as the savior of England. The whole is a Palmerstonian trick. Palmerston, by the revelations of his Russianism and his opposition to the new Reform Bill, has become unpopular. The latter act has taken the liberal gilding off his musty gingerbread. Nevertheless, he wants popularity in order to become Premier, or at least Foreign Minister. What an admirable opportunity to stamp himself a Liberal again and to play the part of Brutus, persecuted by secret Court influences. Attack a Prince-Consort—how taking for the people. He'll be the most popular statesman of the age. What an admirable opportunity of casting obloquy on his present colleagues, of stigmatizing them as the tools of Prince Albert, and of convincing the Court that Palmerston must be accepted on his own terms. The Tories, of course, join in the cry, for church and crown are little to them compared with pounds and acres, and these the cotton-lords are winning from them fast. And if the Tories, in the name of "constitution" and "liberty" talk daggers against a Prince, what enlightened Liberal would not throw himself worshipping at their feet!

At the annual meeting of the Manchester Commercial Association the President, Mr. Aspinall Turner, declared with regard to the strikes and lock-outs and the general agitation of the workingmen, which he justly described as "the civil war going on between masters and operatives in Lancashire"—that, "as Manchester had put down royal tyranny and aristocratic tyranny, so it would also deal with the tyranny of Democracy."[a]

> "Here we have," exclaims *The Press*, "an involuntary avowal of the policy of the Manchester school. The crown is in England supreme—then diminish the royal power. The aristocracy stands before us—sweep it from our path. Workingmen agitate—crush them to the earth."

Written on January 24, 1854

First published in the *New-York Daily Tribune*, No. 4000, February 11, 1854; reprinted in the *New-York Semi-Weekly Tribune*, No. 910, February 14, 1854

Signed: *Karl Marx*

Reproduced from the *New-York Daily Tribune*

---

[a] "'The Manchester School' and the Strikes", *The Press*, Vol. I, No. 38, January 21, 1854.—*Ed.*

Karl Marx and Frederick Engels

[FORTIFICATION OF CONSTANTINOPLE.— DENMARK'S NEUTRALITY.— COMPOSITION OF BRITISH PARLIAMENT.— CROP FAILURE IN EUROPE][396]

London, Friday, Jan. 27, 1854

The fortification of Constantinople would be, as I stated in my last letter,[a] the most important step the Turks could take. Constantinople once fortified, with suitable strengthening of the forts on the Bosphorus and Dardanelles, the independence of Turkey, or of any power holding that capital, would require no foreign guarantee. There is no town more easy to be fortified than Constantinople. One single side of the triangle only—the one toward the land—would require a continuous rampart; the second, toward the Sea of Marmora, and the third, toward the Golden Horn, require no fortifications. A line of detached forts, at a convenient distance from the *enceinte*, and continued eastward so as to protect Pera, Galata and the north-eastern bank of the Golden Horn, would both strengthen the *enceinte* and prevent an enemy from turning it and carrying on works of siege on the hills commanding the town from behind Pera and Galata.

Such a fortress would be almost impregnable. Its communications cannot be cut off, unless the Dardanelles or the Bosphorus is forced, and if that were the case the City would be at once lost. But two such narrow passages may easily be fortified so strongly that no hostile fleet can pass through. A Russian army coming from the land side would have to rely upon perilous sea communication with Sebastopol and Odessa, and could hardly hold out for the time required to take the town, while its

[a] See this volume, pp. 587-88.—*Ed.*

continuous falling off in numbers would expose it to defeats from the garrison of the town and the reserves arriving from Asia.

The reply of Russia to the declaration of neutrality[397] on the part of Denmark arrived at Copenhagen on the 20th inst. Russia is stated to refuse to consent to the neutrality, calling on Denmark to take one side or the other. Immediately after this notification, the Ambassadors of France, England and Russia,[a] are said to have had a conference with the Danish Ministers. Now, I am informed from a very trustworthy source, although I can, of course, not vouch for the correctness of the information, that the protest is but a feint on the part of the Cabinet of St. Petersburg calculated to drive the other powers the faster into a formal acknowledgment of the terms on which the Danish neutrality is proposed. I am assured that recent negotiations were going on between Denmark on the one side, and France and England on the other, according to which, in the case of war, England was to occupy the Sound with her men-of-war, and France the Duchy of Schleswig, with a *corps d'armée.* To thwart this combination, communicated to Nesselrode by the Minister Oersted, Russia is said to have intimated to the Copenhagen Cabinet to propose the declaration of neutrality. She now feigns to oppose, and which, if adhered to by France and England, will not only break up their original plan, but also, by exempting from the laws of war, goods carried in neutral vessels, will secure the export of Russian merchandise by the Baltic.

The Czar's protest against the purchase, on the part of Prussia, of an Oldenburg port in the North Sea, is a *bona fide* protest, astonished as the Berlin public is said to have been at this other symptom of the ubiquitous intermeddling of Timur Tamerlane's successor.

The great "Manchester Reform meeting" has "come off, and a great piece of humbug it was," as *The Englishman*[b] justly remarks. The Aberdeen policy extolled, Turkey insulted, Russia glorified, all interference between foreign states disclaimed—these few topics which, as far as foreign policy is concerned, form the regular stock-in-trade of the Manchester School[398]—have again been expatiated on by Messrs. Cobden, Bright and the other "'umble and 'omely men," who want to have a "man of peace" at the Horse Guards, and a "lock-out" at the House of Lords to sell the English and to undersell all other nations.

---

[a] A. Dotézac, A. Buchanan and Baron Ungern-Sternberg.—*Ed.*

[b] A. Richards.—*Ed.*

Mr. Cobden's speech was a mere repetition, and a disingenuous one too, of the speech he made at the closing of Parliament. The only luxury of novelty he indulged in consisted of two arguments—the one directed against France, the other against America. It looks rather suspicious that the same man who took so prominent a part in bringing about the alliance with France at the time when the exploits of the Decembrists had aroused a cry of indignation in England, is now busied in undoing his own work by sneering at that alliance, and denouncing it as "inconsiderate" and "untimely."

As to America, Mr. Cobden declares that it is from the growth of its manufactures and commerce, and not from the warlike policy of Russia, that England may fear to see endangered the grandeur of her commercial and national prosperity. How does this tally with his professional free trade cant, according to which the commercial prosperity of one people depends on the *growth* of the commerce and industry of all other peoples, the notion of any dangerous rivalry between two industrial peoples being disclaimed as a fallacy of protectionist "quacks"? How does this tally with

"England's, by the magic of her machinery, having united forever two remote hemispheres in the bonds of peace, by placing Europe and America in *absolute and inextricable dependence on each other*"?

It is not the first time that Mr. Cobden, in order to divert from Russia the suspicions and the animosity of the English people, is anxious to turn them against the United States of America. In 1836, the seizure of an English vessel on the Circassian coast by a Russian man-of-war, and the fiscal regulations of the St. Petersburg Cabinet with regard to the navigation of the Danube, together with the revelations published in *The Portfolio*, having evoked the wrath of the English people, and, above all, the commercial classes, against Russia,—Mr. Cobden, at that epoch yet "an infant in literary life and unlearned in public speaking," published a small anonymous pamphlet, entitled *Russia: A Cure for Russophobia. By a Manchester Manufacturer.* In this pamphlet it is argued that "in less than twenty years this [namely, the fear of the growth of American prosperity, and not of Russian aggrandizement] will be the sentiment of the people of England generally; and the same convictions *will be forced upon the Government of the country.*" In the same pamphlet he professed that,

"in examining the various grounds upon which those who discuss the subject take up their hostile attitude towards the Russian nation, we have discovered, with infinite surprise and a deep conviction of the truth, that a century of *aristocratic* Government in England has impregnated all classes with the haughty and arrogant spirit of their rulers" (against meek Russia); that "if the Government of St. Petersburg were transferred to the shores of the Bosphorus, a splendid and substantial European city would, in less than twenty years, spring up in the place of those huts which now constitute the capital of Turkey; [...] noble buildings would arise, learned societies flourish, and the arts prosper. [...] If Russia's Government should attain to that actual power, she would cease the wars of the sword and begin the battle with the wilderness, by constructing railroads, building bridges, [...] by fostering the accumulation of capital, *the growth of cities, and the increase of civilization and freedom*.... The slavery which pollutes Constantinople [...] would instantly disappear, and commerce [...] and laws protecting life and property"—(as now exemplified in Moldo-Wallachia)—"take its place."

As a proof of Russia's civilization and consequently her right to appropriate Turkey, Mr. Cobden told his astonished readers that the Russian merchant possessed of 10,000-15,000 roubles, not only engages in foreign commerce, but is "*exempt from corporal punishment, and qualified to drive about in a carriage and pair.*" Are we then to be astonished at the Russian Emperor's recently expressed conviction that "England, with a Bourgeois Parliament, could not carry on a war with glory"?[a] So deeply imbued was Mr. Cobden in 1836 with the "wickedness of the public writers and speakers," who ventured to find fault with the Autocrat of all the Russias, that he wound up his pamphlet with the question:

"And who and what are those writers and speakers? How long shall political quacks be permitted without fear of punishment, [...] to inflame the minds and disorder the understandings of a whole nation?"

Those "public writers and speakers," we presume, who possess 10,000 to 15,000 roubles and are able to drive about in a carriage and pair, to be exempted at least from "corporal *punishment*." Till now, Mr. Cobden's Philo-Russian mania had been considered, by some, as one of the multifarious crotchets he uses to trade in, by others as the necessary offspring of his peace doctrine. Of late, however, the public has been informed by one[b] who justly describes himself as the "literary horse, or ass if you like," of the late Anti-Corn Law League,[399] that when Mr. Cobden wrote his first pamphlet, "he had been to Russia on a commercial errand of his own in 1834-35, and was successful," that his "heart and calico were both in Russia in 1836," and that his anger at the "English

[a] *The Press*, No. 38, January 21, 1854 (see this volume, p. 590).—*Ed.*
[b] A. Somerville.—*Ed.*

writers, speakers, authors and reviewers," originated from their criticising his new customer, Nicholas of Russia.

As the House of Commons is to reassemble in a few days, it seems proper to give, in a condensed form, the statistics of British representation:

	Seats	Percentage of the actual Representation
The relations of Peers possess	103	17,0
Irish Peers	6	
The country gentlemen	266	41,3
Men of letters and science	20	3,0
The army and navy	30	4,6
The commercial and moneyed interest	109	17,1
The lawyers	107	17,0
The workingmen's interest	None	
Total seats occupied	641	

The *Irish Peers* in the House of Commons[400] are: Viscount Palmerston, for Tiverton; Viscount Barrington, for Berkshire; Earl Annesley, for Grimsby; Viscount Monck, for Portsmouth; Viscount Galway, for Retford; and Lord Hotham, for East Yorkshire. The men of literature and science are: Benjamin Disraeli, for Buckinghamshire; Thomas Macaulay, the historian, for Edinburgh; MacGregor, the commercial statist, for Glasgow; William Stirling, author of *Annals of the Artists of Spain, etc.*, for Perthshire; W. Gladstone, author of *The State in its Relations with the Church*, and other works, for Oxford University; Dr. Austen H. Layard, author of *Nineveh and Its Remains, etc.*, for Aylesbury; James Wilson, the editor of *The Economist*, for Westbury; Sir William Molesworth, the Editor of Hobbes' works, etc., for Southwark; Sir E. L. Bulwer-Lytton, poet, dramatist, novelist, for Hertfordshire; William Johnson Fox, Anti-Corn-Law-League writer, for Oldham; W. A. Mackinnon, author of a (very pitiful) *History of Civilization, etc.*, for Rye; R. Monckton Milnes, author of *Memorials of Travel, etc.*, and Benjamin Oliveira, author of a *Tour in the East*, both for Pontefract; Edward Miall, author of several theological and political works, for Rochdale; William Mure, author of a *History of Grecian Literature*, for Renfrewshire, Scotland; W. P. Urquhart, author of *The Life of Francesco Sforza*, for Westmeath County, Ireland; Robert Stephenson, the celebrated railway engineer, for Whitby; William Michell, physician, for Bodmin; John Brady, surgeon, for Leitrim. Whether Lord John Russell may be safely classed under the head of literary gentlemen I dare not decide.

There are, at least, 100 seats, the representatives of which are nominally elected by the constituencies, but really appointed by Dukes, Earls, Marquises, ladies and other persons, who turn their local influence to political account. The Marquis of Westminster, for instance, disposes of two seats for Chester, a town mustering 2,524 electors; the Duke of Norfolk of one seat for Arundel; the Duke of Sutherland of two seats for Newcastle-under-Lyne; the Marquis of Lansdowne of one seat for Calne; the Earl Fitzwilliam of two seats for Malton; the Duke of Richmond of two seats for Chichester; Miss Pierse of one seat for Northallerton, &c.

The disproportion on one side of the electoral body, and on the other of the representatives, when compared with the entire population, may be shown by some few instances:

In Berkshire the entire population amounts to 170,065, and the number of electors to 7,980. It chooses nine representatives for the House, while Leicestershire, with an entire population of 230,308, and a constituency of 13,081 disposes of six seats only; Lincolnshire, with a population of 407,222, and 24,782 electors, disposes of thirteen seats in the House, while Middlesex, with an entire population of 1,886,576, and a constituency of 113,490 elects only fourteen members. Lancashire, with a population of 2,031,236, has a constituency of only 81,786 electors, and disposes of but twenty-six seats in the House, while Buckinghamshire, with an entire population of 163,723, and with 8,125 electors, is represented by eleven members. Sussex, with an entire population of 336,844, and with 18,054 electors, elects eighteen members, while Staffordshire, with a population of 608,716, and with 29,607 electors elects only seventeen.

The relation of the Electoral body to the population is:

In England one County Elector represents 20.7 persons of the County population.

In Wales one County Elector represents 20.0 persons of the County population.

In Scotland one County Elector represents 34.4 persons of the County population.

In England one Borough Elector represents 18.0 persons of the borough population.

In Wales one Borough Elector represents 24.4 persons of the borough population.

In Scotland one Borough Elector represents 23.3 persons of the borough population.

The data for Ireland are not so complete as for England and Scotland; but the following may be taken as a fair approximation for the same period, 1851-52.

One Elector in an Irish County represents 36 persons of the County population.

One Elector in an Irish borough represents 23 persons of the borough population.

The general deficiency of the European Grain markets may be stated as follows: the deficiency of grain in France in place of being ten millions of hectolitres, as stated by the *Moniteur*, to calm the alarm,[a] greatly exceeds twenty millions, that is, more than eight million quarters of English measure; and the deficiency of potatoes is not less than one-fourth of the average of the last five years, while the deficiency in wine, oil and chestnuts is yet greater. The deficiency in the produce of corn in Belgium and Holland is about four millions of hectolitres; that of the Rhine Provinces, Prussia and Switzerland, at a moderate estimate, is taken to exceed ten million hectolitres. The estimated deficiency in Italy is known to be very great, but there is greater difficulty in arriving at even a proximate result. The lowest estimate, however, gives ten millions of hectolitres of grain, or a deficiency throughout the great grain-producing districts of Western Europe of not less than forty-four millions of hectolitres (seventeen million quarters). The deficiency in England is known to exceed five million quarters of grain, and calculations worthy of grave consideration give that amount as the deficiency in wheat alone. Thus there is a fatal deficiency in the last harvest in Western Europe alone of no less than twenty-two million quarters, without taking into account the great inferiority and shortcoming of other cereals, and the general prevalence of the potato-rot—a deficiency which, if valued in wheat, must be equal to at least five million quarters, or a grand total of twenty-seven million quarters of grain.

As to the supplies that may be expected from foreign markets, it is asserted by very competent commercial authority:

"In Poland the crops have been very short; in Russia, deficient, as seen by the high prices asked for grain at the Baltic ports before our deficiencies were known. And though in the Danubian provinces the harvest has not failed, yet the stocks there, as well as at Odessa, are greatly lessened by the immense exportations to the

---

[a] "Paris, le 16 novembre", *Le Moniteur universel,* No. 321, November 17, 1853.—*Ed.*

Mediterranean and to France. As to America, it is unable to supply two million of quarters. All the ships of the world are inadequate to the supply of a quantity near, or even approaching a moiety of the deficiency, which at present is known to all England to exist."

Written on January 26-27, 1854

First published in the *New-York Daily Tribune,* No. 4004, February 16, 1854; reprinted in the *New-York Semi-Weekly Tribune,* No. 911, February 17, and the first half of the article, in the *New-York Weekly Tribune,* No. 650, February 25, 1854

Signed: *Karl Marx*

Reproduced from the *New-York Daily Tribune*

Karl Marx
[COUNT ORLOV'S MISSION.— RUSSIAN FINANCES DURING THE WAR] [401]

London, Friday, Feb. 3, 1854

I was able to see the State procession of the Queen[a] to open Parliament, as it passed the Horse Guards. The Turkish Ambassador was received with loud cheers and hurrahs. Prince Albert, whose countenance was deadly pale, was furiously hissed by the crowds on both sides of the streets, while the Queen was sparing of her usual salutes and morbidly smiled at the unwonted manifestations of popular discontent. In a previous letter I have reduced the anti-Albert movement to its true dimensions, proving it to be a mere party trick.[b] The public demonstration is, nevertheless, of a very grave character, as it proves the ostensible loyalty of the British people to be a mere conventional formality, a ceremonious affectation which cannot withstand the slightest shock. Probably it may induce the Crown to dismiss a Ministry, the anti-national policy of which threatens to endanger its own security.

When the recent mission of Count Orloff to the Vienna Cabinet [402] became known *The Times* informed its credulous readers that Orloff was the very man the Czar used to employ on pacific errands.[c] Now I need not inform you that this same Orloff appeared in the spring of 1833 at Constantinople to squeeze out of the Porte the Treaty of Unkiar-Skelessi.[403] What he now asks from the Cabinet at Vienna is the permission to send a Russian corps from Warsaw, by way of Hungary, to the Danubian seat of

---

[a] Victoria.—*Ed.*
[b] See this volume, pp. 589-92.—*Ed.*
[c] *The Times*, No. 21650, January 28, 1854.—*Ed.*

war. It may be considered as the first result of his presence at Vienna, that Austria now insists upon the Porte's dismissing its present commanders on the Danube—Selim Pasha, Ismail Pasha and Omer Pasha—on the plea that they are renegades[404] and revolutionists. Every one acquainted with the past history of Turkey knows that from the beginning of the Osman power all her great generals, admirals, diplomatists and ministers have always been Christian renegades, Serbs, Greeks, Albanians, etc. Why not ask Russia to dismiss the forty or fifty men she has bought from all parts of Europe, and who constitute her whole stock of diplomatic ingenuity, political intelligence and military ability? In the meantime Austria has concentrated 80,000 men on the Turkish frontiers in Transylvania and Hungary, and ordered a Bohemian corps mustering some 30,000 men to join them. The Prussian Government on its part is stated to have declined to comply with the command of the Czar ordering Frederick William IV to send a corps of 100,000 men to occupy Poland in the name and interest of Russia, and thus set the garrisons there at liberty to march to the south for the prosecution of the campaign in the Principalities.

In a previous letter I called your attention to the recent financial expedient resorted to by the Austrian Government of exacting a discount of 15 per cent. upon their own paper money, when paid for taxes.[a] This ingenious "tax upon the payment of taxes" is now extended to Italy also. The *Milan Gazette* of the 22d inst. publishes a decree from the Austrian Minister of Finance, announcing that

> "in consequence of the fall in the value of paper money it will not be received at the custom-house unless at a discount of 17 per cent."

As to the Russian Exchequer, I had on a previous occasion, at the beginning of what is called the Eastern complication, to warn your readers against the industriously circulated statement of the "hidden" treasures slumbering in the vaults of the Bank of St. Petersburg, and the ridiculous exaggeration of the vast monetary power that Russia can wield at a given moment.[b] My views are fully confirmed by what has happened since. Not only has the Czar been forced to withdraw his metallic deposits from the banks of England and France, but, moreover, to commit an act of fraudulent confiscation. Prince Paskiewich has informed the War-

---

[a] See this volume, pp. 586-87.—*Ed.*
[b] See this volume, p. 117.—*Ed.*

saw mortgage or discount Bank that its capital will be taken as a forced loan, although the statutes of that bank forbid its advancing money upon any security but landed property. We are also informed that the Russian Government intends issuing a sum of 60,000,000 roubles in inconvertible paper, to defray the expenses of the war. This contrivance is no new one on the part of the Petersburg Cabinet. At the close of 1768, Catherine II, in order to meet the expenses of the war with Turkey, founded a bank of assignats, ostensibly instituted on the principle of issuing convertible notes payable to the bearer. But by a well-managed oversight, she forgot to tell the public in what sort of money these notes were to be payable, and some months later the payments were only made in copper coin. By another untoward "accident" it happened that these copper coins were overvalued by 50 per cent. when compared with the uncoined metal, and only circulated at their nominal value in consequence of their great scarcity and the want of small money for retail purposes. The convertibility of the notes was, therefore, a mere trick. In the first instance Catherine limited the whole issue to 40,000,000 roubles, in 25 rouble notes, the rouble representing a silver coin varying from 38 to 40d. British money, according to the rate of exchange, being equivalent to somewhat above 100 copper copeks. At the death of Catherine, in 1796, the mass of this paper money had risen to 157,000,000, nearly four times its original amount. The exchange in London had come down from 41d. in 1787 to 31d. in 1796. During the two subsequent governments, a rapid increase of issues having taken place, in 1810 the paper circulation reached 577,000,000, and the paper rouble was only worth $25^2/_5$ copeks, i.e., one-quarter of its value in 1788; and exchange in London, in the autumn of 1810, sunk to $11^1/_2$d. the rouble, instead of representing 38-40d. In 1817 the amount of notes in circulation was 836,000,000, according to the statement of Count Gurieff. As the custom-house duties and other taxes were calculated in silver roubles, the Government now declared these assignats to be receivable in the proportion of 4 to 1, thus avowing a depreciation of 75 per cent. During the progress of the depreciation, the prices of commodities rose proportionably, subject to very great fluctuations, which commenced troubling the Cabinet itself, and forced it to contract foreign loans in order to withdraw from circulation a portion of the notes. On the lst of January, 1821, their amount was announced to have been reduced to 640,000,000. The subsequent wars with Turkey, Persia, Poland, Khiva, etc., again swelled the mass of the bank assignats, lowered the exchanges anew, and subjected all commodities to extensive and irregular oscillations of prices. It was not till the lst July, 1839, that, the rate of exchange being ameliorated in consequence of an enormous export of grain to England, the Czar issued a manifesto, according to which, from the lst of July, 1840, the huge mass of bank assignats was to be converted into bank notes payable on demand in silver roubles at the full amount of 38d. The Czar Alexander had declared the assignats to be receivable, on the part of the tax-gatherer, at the proportion of 4 to 1; but the Czar Nicholas is said to have restored them, by his conversion, to their full original value again. There was, however, a curious little clause annexed, ordering that for every *one* of such new notes three and a half of the old ones should be delivered up. The old note was not declared to be depreciated to 28 per cent. of its original amount, but $3^1/_2$ of the old notes were declared to be equivalent to a full *new* note. Hence we may infer, on the one hand, that the Russian Cabinet is as conscientious and punctilious in financial as in diplomatic distinctions; and on the other, that the mere danger of an approaching war suffices to throw it back into all the monetary difficulties which Nicholas has tried for about twenty years to emerge from.

One of the European Governments after the other comes forward appealing to the pockets of its beloved subjects. Even the King of sober-minded Holland[a] demands of the States General 600,000 rix-dollars for works of fortification and defense, adding "that circumstances may determine him to mobilize a portion of the army and to send out his fleets."

If it were possible to meet real wants and to fill the general vacuum of money chests by any ingenious art of book-keeping, the contriver of the French budget,[b] as published some days ago in the *Moniteur,* would have done the thing; but there is not the smallest shopkeeper at Paris unaware of the fact that, by the most skilful grouping of figures, one cannot get out of the books of his creditor, and that the hero of the 2d of December,[c] deeming the public pocket to be inexhaustible, has recklessly run into the nation's debt.

There can be imagined nothing more *naïf* than the announcement of the Danish Ministry at the sitting of the Folketing, on the

---

[a] William III.—*Ed.*

[b] Bineau, "Rapport à l'Empereur", *Le Moniteur universel,* No. 27, January 27, 1854.—*Ed.*

[c] Napoleon III.—*Ed.*

17th inst., that the Government intended postponing to a more *expedient* season the proposition to change the fundamental institutions of Denmark, and introduce their much cherished Whole State Constitution (*Gesammtstaatsverfassung*).[405]

Written on February 3, 1854

First published in the *New-York Daily Tribune,* No. 4007, February 20, 1854; reprinted in the *New-York Semi-Weekly Tribune,* No. 912, February 21, 1854

Signed: *Karl Marx*

Reproduced from the *New-York Daily Tribune*

Karl Marx

[BLUE BOOKS.— PARLIAMENTARY DEBATES ON FEBRUARY 6.— COUNT ORLOV'S MISSION.— OPERATIONS OF THE ALLIED FLEET.— THE IRISH BRIGADE.— CONCERNING THE CONVOCATION OF THE LABOR PARLIAMENT][406]

London, Tuesday, Feb. 7, 1854

The "Rights and Privileges of the Greek and Latin Churches," as the ministerial blue book on the Eastern question has been ingeniously baptized, have been subjected by me to a scrutinizing perusal, and I intend shortly to give your readers a condensed survey of this diplomatic labyrinth.[a] For the present, I content myself with the simple assurance that a more monstrous monument of Governmental infamies and imbecility has, perhaps, never been bequeathed to history. And let us remember, what Mr. Baillie said in the House of Commons[b] on the value of these blue books:

"As for information, they had quite as much on this subject as they required—not, he admitted, official information—but [...] quite as much as they were likely to receive from a blue book that had been *carefully prepared*, and had *concealed all that a Government might desire.* [...] He spoke from experience ['hear, hear,' and laughter from the ministerial benches], from a knowledge of how blue books relating to foreign affairs had been prepared for this House."

I know very well that Lord Palmerston, when once accused of having perverted the documents relating to the Afghan war, of having suppressed most important passages in dispatches, and even of having deliberately falsified others,[407] made the following ingenious reply:

"Sir, if any such thing had been done, what was to prevent the two adverse Governments, who succeeded us in power, one of which endured for five years—from proclaiming the fact and producing the real documents?"[c]

---

[a] See this volume, pp. 615-16.—*Ed.*
[b] On January 31, 1854.—*Ed.*
[c] Quoted from Palmerston's speech in the House of Commons on March 1, 1848.—*Ed.*

But I know equally well that the secret of these blue-book dodges is the very secret of the alternate Whig and Tory succession in government, each party having a greater interest to maintain the capability of its opponent for succession, than by ruining their mutual political "honor" to compromise the government of the ruling classes altogether. This is what the British are pleased to call the operation of their glorious constitution.

Lord Clanricarde had given notice that he would move a discussion of the Eastern question in the House of Lords, yesterday. Consequently, great expectations were entertained, and the House almost crowded. Mr. Urquhart did not hesitate even to designate, in yesterday's *Morning Advertiser*, Lord Clanricarde as the future leader of the national party,[a] remembering that he was the only man who opposed, in 1829, the Russians in crossing the Balkan, but forgetting, no doubt, that the same noble Marquis was, during the momentous epoch of 1839-40, Lord Palmerston's Ambassador at the Court of St. Petersburg, and his chief instrument in bringing about the separate treaty of 1840 and the rupture with France.[408]

The public has been decidedly disappointed by the debates, as the Marquis of Clanricarde, inferring from the reports in the public papers, that "there appeared to be something of the semblance of negotiations still going on at Vienna, was extremely sorry to occasion any discussion which might prevent a peaceful termination to those negotiations."[b] Accordingly, he gave notice of his intention to bring forward a motion on the same subject this day week. The noble Marquis contented himself with asking Lord Clarendon "whether any answer had yet been received from the Emperor of Russia to the Vienna proposals?" and "what instructions had been given to the British Minister at St. Petersburg?" Lord Clarendon's reply was, "that he had only received this afternoon an official statement of the facts from Vienna." The Emperor of Russia had rejected the Vienna note, and offered, in its stead, a counter project. On the 2d inst. the Conference had been called together, and had rejected on its part the counter project.

"The new proposals put forward by Russia were wholly unacceptable—they could not be transmitted to Constantinople, and, therefore, there was an end of

[a] D. Urquhart, "How Our Negotiations with Russia Will Conduct Us into a War with France", Letter III, *The Morning Advertiser*, No. 19540, February 6, 1854.—*Ed.*

[b] Marx quotes from Clanricarde's speech, as well as from those of other members of the House of Lords and of the House of Commons, according to *The Times*, No. 21658, February 7, 1854.—*Ed.*

them. He had no reason to think that fresh negotiations on the subject would be renewed. As to the preservation of peace, he held out no such expectation at all."

With regard to the other question put by Lord Clanricarde, he stated that

"on Saturday evening Baron Brunnow called on him at the Foreign Office and placed in his hands a note, in which he announced that the answer he had received from him to the inquiry he was instructed to make by his Government, was not of a kind that permitted him to continue diplomatic relations, and that, therefore, diplomatic relations between Russia and England were suspended. Baron Brunnow had taken leave of him on Saturday evening, but it was then too late to depart from London, and he understood that he was to leave early this morning."

M. de Kisseleff, we are informed by telegraph, left Paris yesterday and is gone to Brussels. The official or Government journals state that all the Embassy at London would be broken up, and every Russian leave England. But I happen to know, from an excellent source, that, on the contrary, the number of Russians in England will only be diminished by the person of the Ambassador, and that the whole *personnel* remains at London under the superintendence of M. de Berg, First Secretary of the Embassy. As to the position of the British Ambassador at the Court of St. Petersburg, Lord Clarendon declared that

"as it was half past 6 o'clock on Saturday when Baron Brunnow called upon him, and as it was necessary [...] to have previous communication with the French Government, it was not possible at the moment to send instructions to the British Minister at St. Petersburg, but they had already held communication with the French Ambassador on the subject, and instructions would be sent to Sir G. Seymour and Gen. de Castelbajac tomorrow, which would place them on exactly the same footing as the Russian Ambassador here, and diplomatic relations between the two countries and Russia would be suspended."

Lord John Russell repeated in the House of Commons the declaration of Lord Clarendon in the Upper House, and Lord Palmerston announced that

"he would bring forward a measure to consolidate the militia laws, in which it was his intention that a militia force should be organized for Scotland and Ireland, the period of enrollment depending upon the votes of the House."

The English army is to be augmented immediately by 11,000 men; 1,500 coast guards are also to be embarked forthwith, intended to form a stock for the crews of the newly commissioned ships. A royal proclamation has been issued forbidding the exportation of any vessels of war, military stores and ammunition to Russia. Embargo has been laid by the naval authorities visiting the private dockyards on the Thames on two vessels in course of construction for Russian account. A contract, on behalf of the British Government, for coal sufficient for steamers of the aggregate amount of 11,000 horse-power, has been concluded at Copenhagen. Admiral Sir Charles Napier is to have command of the Baltic fleet about to be formed.

The official *Wiener Zeitung* announces that

"the Government has received notice that Russia has expressly declared to the four Powers that she regards herself as released from the promise made at Olmütz to remain on the defensive in the Principalities."

Concerning the object of the mission of Count Orloff at Vienna a number of conflicting rumors are afloat; the most credible of which appears to be contained in the Berlin correspondence of to-day's *Times*.

"Russia," says this correspondent, "invites Austria and Prussia to enter with her into a treaty of neutrality for all contingencies; suggests to them to make the declaration of their neutrality the common expression of the neutrality of the German Bund; undertakes to come to the assistance of the Bund should any of its members be attacked; and binds herself, in the case of any territorial changes having to be arranged at the end of the war, to conclude no peace without having due consideration for the interests of the German Powers in such territorial changes. In this proposal for a treaty of neutrality distinct reference is made to the principles and provisions of the Holy Alliance of 1815."

As to the decision probably come to by Austria and Prussia, I can only repeat the convictions already recorded by me on this question.[a] Austria will endeavor by every means to maintain her position of neutrality as long as she will be permitted to do so, and will declare for Russia when the proper time has arrived. Prussia, on the other hand, is likely again to miss the proper time for abandoning her neutrality and will end by calling upon herself the fate of another Jena.[409]

We learn from Constantinople that the combined fleet have returned to their anchorage at Beikoz, notwithstanding the following order, sent out to them, on behalf of the Ambassadors, by the *Samson*:

"The Ambassadors are surprised at the sudden resolution of the Admirals, more particularly at the present moment, when a Turkish steam-flotilla is on the point of starting with ammunition and other stores for the army of Anatolia. The orders of the French and British Governments [...] were formal and precise [they were indeed, but not the original orders with which the Admirals were dispatched, but only those just received], respecting the protection to be afforded by the combined fleets to the Ottoman flag and territory, and the attention of both Admirals is again called to

---

[a] See this volume, pp. 554-55.—*Ed.*

the stringent nature of these instructions which had been duly notified to them. The Admirals, it would appear, consider that the measures entrusted to their execution may be equally well effected, whether the force under their command be stationed at Beikoz or Sinope. [In this case, it would appear to others, that the same instructions might have been carried out by the fleets quietly remaining at Malta and Toulon.] This is a matter which must entirely depend upon their [...] judgment, and on them the responsibility will rest."

The Russian fleet is known to be at Kaffa, near the Strait of Yenikale,[a] whence the distance to Batum is only one-third of the distance between Batum and Beikoz. Will the Admirals be able to prevent a Sinope at Batum, "whether they be stationed at Beikoz or elsewhere?"

You will remember that the Czar's first proclamation accused the Sultan of enlisting under his banner the revolutionary dregs of all Europe. Now, while Lord Stratford de Redcliffe declares to Lord Dudley Stuart that he could not assist him in organizing any of those dregs as a voluntary legion, the Czar has himself been the first to establish a revolutionary corps, the so-called Greco-Slavonian Legion, with the direct intention of provoking the Sultan's subjects to revolt. The corps is being organized in Wallachia and numbers already, according to Russian statements, above 3,000 men, not to be paid in *bons à perpétuité,*[b] as the Wallachians themselves, colonels being promised 5 ducats per day; majors 3 ducats; captains 2; subaltern officers 1, and soldiers 2 zwanzigers, the arms to be supplied by Russia.

Meanwhile the armaments of France seem no longer to be intended to remain on paper. As you know, the reserves of 1851 have been called out and in the last few days immense military stores have been sent from Arras to Metz and Strasbourg. General Pélissier has left for Algiers with orders to select the different corps which are to form the expedition to Constantinople, for which Sir J. Burgoyne and Colonel Ardant have gone to prepare quarters.

The rumored passage of Omer Pasha at the head of a large army, though if attempted it could hardly be executed at a more opportune moment, since the Russians are known to be concentrated at Krajova, between Bucharest and Kalafat, yet needs confirmation.

To return to the doings of the British Parliament, there is, of course, not much to be mentioned, with the exception of the

[a] The Kerch Strait.—*Ed.*
[b] Obligation for all eternity.—*Ed.*

proposition of a bill for throwing open the coast-trade to foreign vessels, a proposition which has not met with a single protest. Protestation must be decidedly dead, since it shows no capacity to make the slightest stand against the universal invasion of the modern principle of commerce: to buy in the cheapest market whatever you require. How far the cheapest crew is qualified to protect life and property, the late catastrophe of the *Tayleur* has shown.[410]

Mr. I. Butt, in yesterday's sitting of the Commons, gave notice

> "that to-morrow he should move that there should be read by the Clerk, at the table of the House, an article published in *The Times* of to-day, and the previous statements of *The Dublin Freeman's Journal*, imputing to the" (*Irish*) "members of the House a trafficking in places for money. He should also move for a Select Committee to inquire into the allegations of such trafficking as contained in these publications."

Why Mr. Butt is indignant only at the trafficking for money will be understood by those who remember that the legality of any other mode of trafficking was settled during last session. Since 1830 Downing-st. has been placed at the mercy of the Irish Brigade.[411] It is the Irish members who have created and kept in place the Ministers to their mind. In 1834 they drove from the Cabinet Sir J. Graham and Lord Stanley. In 1835 they compelled William IV to dismiss the Peel Ministry and to restore the Melbourne Administration. From the general election of 1837 down to that of 1841, while there was a British majority in the Lower House opposed to that Administration, the votes of the Irish Brigade were strong enough to turn the scale and keep it in office. It was the Irish Brigade again who installed the Coalition Cabinet. With all this power of Cabinet-making, the Brigade have never prevented any infamies against their own country nor any injustice to the English people. The period of their greatest power was at the time of O'Connell, from 1834-1841. To what account was it turned? The Irish agitation was never anything but a cry for the Whigs against the Tories, in order to extort places from the Whigs. Nobody who knows anything about the so-called Litchfield-house contract,[412] will differ from this opinion—that contract by which O'Connell was to vote for, but licensed to spout against, the Whigs on condition that he should nominate his own Magistrates in Ireland. It is time for the Irish Brigade to put off their patriotic airs. It is time for the Irish people to put off their dumb hatred of the English and call their own representatives to an account for their wrongs.

The "Society of Arts"[413] and tricks have lately ventured on an escamotage of the Labor Parliament by a countermove intended to "settle" the still enduring struggle between the capitalists and workingmen of England. The meeting was presided over by a noble Lord, and delegates from both parties had been invited to discuss their grievances after the fashion of the Luxembourg conferences of M. Louis Blanc.[414] The humbug was protested against by Mr. Ernest Jones, in the name of the working classes, and old Robert Owen told these enlightened gentlemen that no arbitration, nor device, nor art of any kind, could ever fill the gulf dividing the two great fundamental classes of this or any country. It is superfluous to add that the meeting dissolved under an ample cover of ridicule. The Chartists of London and the Provincial Delegates held a public meeting on the following day, when the proposal of the Labor Parliament was unanimously approved, and the 11th March named for its opening at Manchester.

Written on February 7, 1854

First published in the *New-York Daily Tribune,* No. 4008, February 21, 1854; reprinted in the *New-York Semi-Weekly Tribune,* No. 913, February 24, and the *New-York Weekly Tribune,* No. 650, February 25, 1854

Signed: *Karl Marx*

Reproduced from the *New-York Daily Tribune*

Karl Marx

[RUSSIAN DIPLOMACY.— THE BLUE BOOK ON THE EASTERN QUESTION.— MONTENEGRO][415]

London, Friday, Feb. 10, 1854

At the time when the treaty of neutrality was concluded between Denmark and Sweden, I stated my conviction, contrary to the current opinion in England and France, that it was not by any means to be looked upon as a triumph of the Western Powers, and that the pretended protest of Russia against that treaty was nothing but a feint.[a] The Scandinavian papers, and *The Times'* correspondent, quoting from them, are now unanimous in recording the same opinion, declaring the whole treaty to be the work of Russia.

The propositions submitted by Count Orloff to the Vienna Conference, and rejected by them, were as follows:

1. Renewal of the old treaties.
2. Protectorate of Russia over the Greek Christians of Turkey.
3. Expulsion of all political refugees from the Ottoman Empire.
4. Refusal to admit the mediation of any other Power, and to negotiate otherwise than directly with a Turkish Envoy, to be sent to St. Petersburg.

On the latter point Count Orloff declared his readiness to compromise, but the Conference refused. Why did the Conference refuse? Or why did the Emperor of Russia refuse the last terms of the Conference? The propositions are the same on both sides. The renewal of the old treaties had been stipulated, the Russian Protectorate admitted with only a modification in the form; and, as the last point had been abandoned by Russia herself, the

[a] See this volume, p. 594.—*Ed.*

Austrian demand for the expulsion of the refugees[416] could not have been the cause of a rupture between Russia and the West. It is evident, then, that the position of the Emperor of Russia is now such as to prevent him from accepting *any* terms at the hands of England and France, and that he *must* bring Turkey to his feet either with or without the chance of a European war.

In military circles the latter is now regarded as inevitable, and the preparations for it are going on in every quarter. Admiral Bruat has already left Brest for Algiers, where he is to embark 10,000 men, and sixteen English regiments stationed in Ireland are ordered to hold themselves ready to go to Constantinople. The expedition can only have a twofold object: either to coerce the Turks into submission to Russia, as Mr. Urquhart announces, or to carry on the war against Russia, in real earnest. In both cases the fate of the Turks is equally certain. Once more handed over to Russia, not indeed directly, but to her dissolving agencies, the power of the Ottoman Empire would soon be reduced, like that of the Lower Empire, to the precincts of the capital. Taken under the absolute tutorship of France and England the sovereignty of the Ottomans over their European estates would be no less at an end.

If we are to take the war into our hands, observes *The Times*, we must have the control over all the operations.

In this case, then, the Turkish Ministry would be placed under the direct administration of the Western Ambassadors, the Turkish War Office under the War Offices of England and France, and the Turkish armies under the command of French and English Generals. The Turkish Empire, in its ancient conditions of existence, has ceased to be.

After his complete "failure" at Vienna, Count Orloff is now gone back to St. Petersburg—"with the assurance of the Austrian and Prussian neutrality, under all circumstances." On the other hand, the telegraph reports from Vienna that a change has taken place in the Turkish Ministry, the Seraskier and Kapudan Pasha[a] having resigned. *The Times* cannot understand how the war party could have been defeated at the very time that France and England were going to war. For my part, if the news be true, I can very well understand the "god-sent" occurrence as the work of the

[a] The War Minister and the Minister for the Navy.—*Ed.*

English Coalition representative at Constantinople, whom we find so repeatedly regretting, in his blue-book dispatches, that

"he could hardly yet go so far in his pressure on the Turkish Cabinet as it might be desirable."

The blue books begin with dispatches relating to the demands put forward on the part of France with respect to the Holy Shrines—demands not wholly borne out by the ancient capitulations,[417] and ostensibly made with the view to enforce the supremacy of the Latin over the Greek Church. I am far from participating in the opinion of Mr. Urquhart, according to which the Czar had, by secret influences at Paris, seduced Bonaparte to rush into this quarrel in order to afford Russia a pretext for interfering herself in behalf of the privileges of the Greek Catholics. It is well known that Bonaparte wanted to buy, *coûte que coûte*,[a] the support of the Catholic party, which he regarded from the very first as the main condition for the success of his usurpation. Bonaparte was fully aware of the ascendancy of the Catholic Church over the peasant population of France, and the peasantry were to make him Emperor in spite of the *bourgeoisie* and in spite of the proletariat. M. de Falloux, the Jesuit, was the most influential member of the first ministry he formed, and of which Odilon Barrot, the *soi-disant* Voltairian, was the nominal head. The first resolution adopted by this ministry, on the very day after the inauguration of Bonaparte as President, was the famous expedition against the Roman Republic. M. de Montalembert, the chief of the Jesuit party, was his most active tool in preparing the overthrow of the parliamentary *régime* and the coup d'état of the 2d December. In 1850, the *Univers*, the official organ of the Jesuit party, called day after day on the French Government to take active steps for the protection of the interests of the Latin Church in the East. Anxious to cajole and win over the Pope,[b] and to be crowned by him, Bonaparte had reasons to accept the challenge and make himself appear the "most Catholic"[418] Emperor of France. *The Bonapartist usurpation, therefore, is the true origin of the present Eastern complication.* It is true that Bonaparte wisely withdrew his pretensions as soon as he perceived the Emperor Nicholas ready to make them the pretext for excluding him from the *conclave* of Europe, and Russia was, as

[a] At all costs.—*Ed.*
[b] Pius IX.—*Ed.*

usual, eager to utilise the events which she had not the power to create, as Mr. Urquhart imagines. But it remains a most curious phenomenon in history, that the present crisis of the Ottoman Empire has been produced by the same conflict between the Latin and Greek Churches which once gave rise to the foundation of that Empire in Europe.

It is not my intention to investigate the whole contents of the "Rights and Privileges of the Latin and Greek Churches," before having considered a most important incident entirely suppressed in these blue books, viz.: The Austro-Turkish quarrel about Montenegro.[419] The necessity to previously treat this affair is the more urgent, as it will establish the existence of a concerted plan between Russia and Austria for the subversion and division of the Turkish Empire, and as the very fact of England's putting the subsequent negotiations between the Court of St. Petersburg and the Porte into the hands of Austria, cannot fail to throw a most curious light on the conduct of the English Cabinet throughout this Eastern question. In the absence of any official documents on the Montenegro affair, I refer to a book, which has only just been published on this subject, and is entitled the *Handbook of the Eastern Question*, by L. F. Simpson.[a]

The Turkish fortress of Zabljak (on the frontiers of Montenegro and Albania) was stormed by a band of Montenegrins in December, 1852. It is remembered that Omer Pasha was ordered by the Porte to repel the aggressors. The Sublime Porte declared the whole coast of Albania in a state of blockade, a measure which apparently could be directed only against Austria and her navy, and which indicated the conviction of the Turkish Ministry that Austria had provoked the Montenegrin revolt.

The following article, under date of Vienna, Dec. 29, 1852, appeared then in the *Augsburger Allgemeine Zeitung*:

"If Austria wished to assist the Montenegrins, the blockade could not prevent it. If the Montenegrins descended from their mountains, Austria could provide them with arms and ammunition by Cattaro, in spite of the presence of the Turkish fleet in the Adriatic. Austria does not approve either of the present incursion of the Montenegrins, *nor of the revolution which is on the eve of breaking out in Herzegovina and Bosnia among the Christians.* She has constantly protested against the persecutions of the Christians, and that in the name of humanity; Austria is obliged

[a] L. F. Simpson, *The Eastern Question: a Connected Narrative of Events from the Missions of Count Leiningen and Prince Menschikoff to Constantinople, to the Present Day.* Marx quotes below passages from this book (pp. 3-6 and 8-10).—*Ed.*

to observe neutrality toward the Eastern Church. The last news from Jerusalem will have shown how fiercely religious hatred burned there. The agents of Austria must, therefore, exert all their efforts to maintain peace between the Greek Christians and the Latin Christians of the Empire."

From this article we glean, firstly, that coming revolutions of the Turkish Christians were anticipated as *certain*, that the way for the Russian complaints concerning the oppression of the Greek Church was paved by Austria, and that the religious complication about the Holy Shrines was expected to give occasion for Austria's "neutrality."

In the same month a note was addressed to the Porte by Russia, who offered her mediation in Montenegro, which was declined on the ground that the Sultan[a] was able himself to uphold his own rights. Here we see Russia operating exactly as she did at the time of the Greek revolution[420]—first offering to protect the Sultan against his subjects, with the view of protecting afterward his subjects against the Sultan, if her assistance should not be accepted.

The fact that there existed a concert between Russia and Austria for the occupation of the Principalities, even at this early time, may be gleaned from another extract from the *Augsburger Allgemeine Zeitung*, of 30th December, 1852:

"Russia, which has only recently acknowledged the independence of Montenegro, can scarcely remain an idle spectator of events. Moreover, commercial letters and travelers from Moldavia and Wallachia, mention that from Volhynia down to the mouth of the Pruth, the country swarms with Russian troops, and that reenforcements are continually arriving."

Simultaneously the Vienna journals announced that an Austrian army of observation was assembling on the Austro-Turkish frontiers.

On Dec. 6, 1852, Lord Stanley interpellated Lord Malmesbury with respect to the affairs of Montenegro, and Bonaparte's noble friend made the following declaration:

"The noble lord intimated his desire to ask whether any change had recently taken place in the political relations of that wild country bordering on Albania, called Montenegro. I believe that no change whatever has taken place with respect to its political relations. The chief of that country[b] bears a double title; he is head of the Greek Church in that country, and he is also the temporal sovereign. But with respect to his ecclesiastical position he is *under the jurisdiction of the Emperor of Russia, who is considered to be the head of the whole Greek Church.* The chief of

[a] Abdul Mejid.—*Ed.*
[b] Danilo I Petrović Njegoš.—*Ed.*

Montenegro has been" (as I believe all his ancestors were before him) "accustomed to receive from the sanction and recognition of the Emperor his Episcopal jurisdiction and titles. With respect to the independence of that country, whatever the opinion of different persons may be as to the advantage of such a position, the fact is that *Montenegro has been an independent country for something like 150 years,* and though various attempts have been made by the Porte to bring it into subjection, those attempts have failed one after another, and the country is in the same position now that it was some 200 years ago."

In this speech Lord Malmesbury, the then Tory Secretary for Foreign Affairs, quietly dissects the Ottoman Empire by separating from it a country that had ever belonged to it, recognising at the same time the Emperor of Russia's spiritual pretensions over subjects of the Porte. What are we to say of these two sets of Oligarchs, except that they rival each other in imbecility?

The Porte was, of course, seriously alarmed at this speech of a British Minister, and there appeared, shortly afterward, in an English newspaper the following letter from Constantinople, dated Jan. 5, 1853:

"The Porte has experienced the greatest irritation owing to Lord Malmesbury's declaration in the House of Lords that Montenegro was independent. He thus played into the hands of Russia and Austria, by which England will lose that influence and confidence which she has hitherto enjoyed. In the first article of the treaty of Sistova, concluded between the Porte and Austria in 1791 (to which treaty England, Holland, and Russia were mediating parties), it is expressly stipulated that an amnesty should be granted to the subjects of both Powers who had taken part against their *rightful sovereigns,* viz.: the Servians, *Montenegrins,* Moldavians and Wallachians, named as rebel subjects of the Porte. The Montenegrins who reside in Constantinople, of whom there are 2,000 to 3,000, pay the *haratch* or capitation-tax, and in judicial procedure with subjects of other Powers at Constantinople, the Montenegrins are always considered and treated as Turkish subjects without objection."

In the beginning of January, 1853, the Austrian Government sent Baron Kellner von Köllenstein, an aide-de-camp of the Emperor,[a] to Cattaro to watch the course of events, while Mr. d'Ozeroff, the Russian Envoy at Constantinople, handed in a protest to the Divan against the concessions made to the Latins in the question of the Holy Shrines. At the end of January, Count Leiningen arrived at Constantinople, and was admitted on the 3d February, to a private audience with the Sultan, to whom he delivered a letter from the Austrian Emperor. The Porte refused

[a] Francis Joseph I.—*Ed.*

to comply with his demands, and Count Leiningen thereupon gave in an *ultimatum*, allowing the Porte four days to answer. The Porte immediately placed itself under the protection of England and France, which did not protect her, while Count Leiningen refused their mediation. On Feb. 15, he had obtained everything he had asked for (with the exception of Art. III) and his ultimatum was accepted. It contained the following articles:

"I. Immediate evacuation of Montenegro and the establishment of the *status quo ante bellum*.

"II. A declaration by which the Porte is to engage herself to maintain the *status quo* of the territories of Kleck and Suttorina, and to recognize the *mare clausum* in favor of Austria.

"III. A strict inquiry to take place concerning the acts of Mussulman fanaticism committed against the Christians of Bosnia and Herzegovina.

"IV. Removal of all the political refugees and renegades at present in the provinces adjoining the Austrian frontiers.

"V. Indemnity of 200,000 florins to certain Austrian merchants, whose contracts had been arbitrarily annulled, and the maintenance of those contracts for all the time they were agreed on.

"VI. Indemnity of 56,000 florins to a merchant whose ship and cargo had been unjustly confiscated.

"VII. Establishment of numerous consulates in Bosnia, Servia, Herzegovina and all over Rumelia.

"VIII. Disavowal of the conduct maintained in 1850, in the affair of the refugees."

Before acceding to this ultimatum, the Ottoman Porte, as Mr. Simpson states, addressed a note to the Ambassadors of England and France, demanding a promise from them of positive assistance in the event of a war with Austria. "The two Ministers not being able to pledge themselves in a definite manner," the Turkish Government yielded to the energetic proceedings of Count Leiningen.

On February 28th, Count Leiningen arrived at Vienna, and Prince Menchikoff at Constantinople. On the 3d of March, Lord John Russell had the impudence to declare, in answer to an interpellation of Lord Dudley Stuart, that

"In answer to representations made to the Austrian Government, assurances had been given that the latter held the same views as the English Government on the subject; and, though he could not state the precise terms of the arrangement that had been made, the intervention of France and England had been *successful*, and he trusted the late differences were now over. The course adopted by England had been to give Turkey such advice as would maintain her honor and her independence.... For his own part, he thought that on grounds of right, of international law, of faith toward our ally, and also on grounds of general policy and expediency, *the maintenance of the integrity and independence of Turkey was a great and ruling point of the foreign policy of England.*"

Written on February 10, 1854

First published in the *New-York Daily Tribune,* No. 4013, February 27, 1854; reprinted in the *New-York Semi-Weekly Tribune,* No. 914, February 28, and the *New-York Weekly Tribune,* No. 651, March 4, 1854

Signed: *Karl Marx*

Reproduced from the *New-York Daily Tribune*

APPENDIX

Karl Marx

[APROPOS CAREY][421]

CLUSS' ARTICLE "THE 'BEST PAPER IN THE UNION' AND ITS 'BEST MEN' AND POLITICAL ECONOMISTS" WITH EXTRACTS FROM MARX'S LETTERS

[*Die Reform*, No. 48, September 14, 1853]

The "uneducated" public having ceased to pass judgment on it, the *Neu-England-Zeitung* of Boston has, with commendable modesty and anticipating the significance of its insipid *Grenzboten*[a] radicalism, reached the conclusion that it is the "best newspaper". For some time now, that newspaper has performed some grotesque antics. It resembles an overladen and frail little craft that has put out from the coast of the old world on a voyage of discovery. Suddenly the vessel finds itself out on the high seas and, would you credit it, they have forgotten to bring a compass, a pilot and a captain *who can navigate*! They are now at the mercy of the winds and the waves. At this juncture a worthy old gentleman tries to lecture the unthinking crew on the *seriousness of the situation*; but he is still sermonising when a laughing nymph appears in the distance to chaff at him, and she disturbs the edifying devotions by delighting in the confused doings of those trusty gentlemen.[b] One man after another goes onto the after-deck from amongst this motley rabble, and keeps turning the wheel and trimming the sails. The general confusion is only made worse by the contradictory but always *well-intentioned* instructions of the pseudo-captain,[c] calling for the squaring of the circle, "higher unity", the true, correct course to Canaan, the milk-and-honey world of the future—and this after he had, down in his cabin, just seen himself, and felt like, a second Jean Paul.

Today, as in a final burst of energy, as in death-throes, new and larger sails are suddenly hoisted, while tomorrow fatigue sets in as after the agitation of a consuming fever. Overworked and on the verge of collapse, the crew reef the sails again. They try to put the disorderliness of the chaos from their minds by conjuring up "interesting" family quarrels. Seeking to conceal the contradictions of reality, in the midst of which they feel helpless, they allow that much-vaunted "higher unity" of ideal, free communal activity to go to pieces by decreeing differences between *the European and the American outlook*. The Athenian citizen, whose threadbare probity and woollen rags thrown proudly over his shoulder one has just admired as he delivered his sermon on freedom, steps into the background, and new actors come forward. Can one expect them to understand

[a] An allusion to the German liberal journal *Grenzboten*.—*Ed.*

[b] An allusion to Wilhelm Weitling, an editor of the *Neu-England-Zeitung*, the author of *Das Evangelium eines armen Sünders*.—*Ed.*

[c] An allusion to Eduard Schläger, the publisher of the *Neu-England-Zeitung*.—*Ed.*

that modern *bourgeois* civilisation is based on the slavery of wage-labour, after one of the family had in his stupor completely failed to see yesterday that *ancient* civilisation was founded on absolute slavery? Most certainly not.

In the struggle between the "European and the American outlook" the spokesman for Europe is "Leonidas"-Confucius[a]-Ruge, the Pomeranian *aurora borealis*, representing half a dozen Southern German dictators groping around in a half-light. Everyone knows that he preaches something he has christened *humanism*, and that occasionally he has someone sound his praises to John Bull as the third great German philosopher alongside Strauss and Feuerbach. Ruge's "outlook" can be summed up briefly. In the writings of the philosopher Kant he discerns a *system of limited freedom*, in those of Fichte the *principle of absolute freedom*, and in those of Hegel the *principle and system of absolute freedom through the medium of dialectics*. Herr Ruge has always displayed an instinctive aversion to dialectics and he has always taken up its easier aspect, that of becoming entangled in contradictions, but not that of mastering them. It is therefore natural that he should constantly malign dialectics as being sophistry, as, for example, in the works of Marx. Ruge describes his *humanism* as the *introduction in society of the principle and system of absolute freedom*. So far as we are able to understand it, this humanism of Herr Ruge, his unity of practice and theory, consists in passing off his *de facto* clumsiness as theory to the men of practice and his peculiar and feeble thinking as practice to the theoreticians. Ever since Feuerbach, Bauer, Strauss and others successively dispatched one another from the scene, and no prince of science existed any longer, and since even the materialists pushed their noses in, a state of mind has occurred in old Ruge infected with which, quoting silly Gretchen, his translator into German-American said:

And all this does my brain impair,
As if a mill-wheel were turning there.[b]

For Ruge was in the habit of singing the praises of the reigning prince of science to the public as loudly as possible, in order to win renown himself. Out of all that has come an *olla podrida*[c] of contradictions, which, in the absence of dialectics, has very recently had a democratic gravy poured over it, and, in the form of a *box*[d] *of humanism*, appearing not, it is true, in the world theatre but in *Janus*, blissfully introduced itself to a "very select" public, which unfortunately had almost completely dispersed before the box was constructed.[422]

Of the European press Herr Ruge had in the last few years thrust himself on *The Leader*, edited in London by his friend *Thornton Hunt* who, logically, was extolled in *Janus* as the "most outstanding writer among the English socialists". This unctuous coward had preached communism in order to divert attention from Chartism,[e] and we denounced him in the American press for it at that time. Today

---

[a] A pun on "Confucius" and the German word *Konfusius* (muddler). It was also used, with reference to Ruge, in Marx's letter to Weydemeyer of January 23, 1852, and in the pamphlet *The Great Men of the Exile*, written jointly by Marx and Engels (see present edition, Vols. 39 and 11 resp.).—*Ed.*

[b] Goethe, *Faust*, Part I, Scene 4, Faust's study (a remark of Faust's famulus).—*Ed.*

[c] A Spanish dish, a stew made of one or more meats and several vegetables; figuratively, hodge-podge.—*Ed.*

[d] Marx uses the word *Loge* which means both a lodge in Freemasonry and a box in the theatre.—*Ed.*

[e] An allusion to Hunt's efforts, in *The Northern Star*, No. 734, November 29, 1851, to pass himself off as a champion of the people and Communist.—*Ed.*

that charge is justified before our party. Hunt had forced his way into the Chartists' Executive[423] with the intention of delivering the Chartists into the hands of the finance-reformers (the industrial bourgeoisie). In order to trap *Ernest Jones* he preached physical force and talked of nothing but rifles, at a time of the most splendid prosperity and in the most unfavourable of circumstances. In recognition of his efforts he was thrown out of the official position he held with the workers. Good! Nowadays the scoundrel has thrown off his mask. He has become one of the most respectable gossips of the middle class, and he declares *Bright*, that ideal of the modern English bourgeois, to be a genuine "old Englishman"[a] and the most disinterested of humanitarian enthusiasts with regard to the unfortunate Indian people, and stated recently that he would even prefer despotism to a "raving republic". That is the sort of pitiable figure that the puffed-up "higher unity" cuts. Behind it, whenever *real* conflicts arise, we see bragging arrogance in all its superficiality!

[*Die Reform*, No. 49, September 17, 1853]

Let us now turn to the "American outlook" which represents the counterpart to the family row in the *Neu-England-Zeitung*. For the most part this outlook consists of trivialities and latterly of sententious ideas taken from street ballads which, apparently strung together in public houses under the influence of Philadelphian *lager*, provide the sort of material to fill a cess-pit whose outer walls are cemented with untruths, dirty tricks and platitudes. A few Philadelphian Romans,[b] notably a certain Herr Pösche, currently busy earning his spurs as a cheer-leader for Cushing in Pierce's glorious army of place-hunters, are flourishing as matadors of this school.[424] A bourgeois conservative economic theory, of the kind that *socialists of all parties* are busy fighting—that propounded by the American *Carey* and the Frenchman *Bastiat*—is being trotted out to the credulous public* as the latest German-American discovery, the "*higher unity*" of political economy. We shall see that wherever this grand *higher unity* ventures into contact with real life, it becomes a willing tool in the hands of the *powers that be*. The editors of the *Neu-England-Zeitung* appear not yet to have stained their chaste convictions with studies of such a demanding material nature as those that political economy involves; for we see daily that [...][c] discussion of social questions [...][c] everyone who feels like voiding his bowels. The said doctrine was last demolished, together with M. Bastiat, before the socialist tribunals of Europe in 1849, in the course of a discussion in Proudhon's *Voix du peuple*.[d] As far as European society is concerned, historical

* Judging by the continuing cry of distress from the *Neu-England-Zeitung* and the rumours that are going round, the public would appear, incidentally, to have become something of a rash hypothesis.—*A. C.*

---

[a] Marx uses the English words "old Englishman".—*Ed.*

[b] A pun on the title of the book *The New Rome. The United States of the World* by German petty-bourgeois émigrés Th. Poesche and Ch. Goepp, published in Philadelphia in 1853.—*Ed.*

[c] The text is indecipherable here.—*Ed.*

[d] Published in 1850 as a book, Fr. Bastiat, *Gratuité du crédit. Discussion entre M. Fr. Bastiat et M. Proudhon*, Paris. For Marx's critical analysis of the points of view of the two participants in the discussion see present edition, Vol. 29.—*Ed.*

developments have long since cut the ground from under that particular theoretical representation of a specific historical epoch.

In America, where today the social contradictions are much less sharp than in radically undermined Europe, this theory found its champion in the economist Carey. Its conservative-bourgeois opponent (taking the view of the more recent English school) has already appeared in the person of Professor *Wayland*. His *Principles of Political Economy* has been introduced as a textbook at most of the academies of New England, much to the annoyance of Carey's adherents.

Let us summarise briefly the main points of the doctrine which is compiled by Bastiat in his *Social Harmonies* with grace and in easily comprehensible form, but propagated by Carey without any talent for presentation or for summing up and precision. One cannot deny C. H. Carey a certain amount of positive knowledge and even some original and attractive ideas.[a]

His chief merit is that he has indeed cultivated a native product, grown directly from American soil without any foreign admixtures. His science is of anything but universal character, it is pure *Yankee science*. It attempts to demonstrate that the *economic* conditions of bourgeois society, instead of being conditions for struggle and antagonism, are rather conditions for partnership and harmony. (Very fine in theory, but modern industrial towns demonstrate how things work out in practice!) Those economic conditions can be broken down as follows:

1) *Rent*, the share of the landowner,
2) *Profit*, the share of the capitalist,
3) *Wages*, the share of the worker in the value of the finished product.

We can see that Carey is much too experienced to link the existence of classes with the existence of *political* privileges and monopolies, as for instance the newly-fledged Roman youths at Philadelphia would, or before them s. v.[b] Heinzen, and thus to see social harmony as being unconditionally invented and patented for all time with the great French Revolution.[425] Carey seeks rather for economic reasons behind economic facts, though in so doing he fails to transcend the as yet indistinct, hazy and fluid class relations of America. He therefore only proves that he regards a *point of transition* in the development of society as the *normal condition* of its life. Most characteristic is the argument of Carey's school

[a] For Marx's assessment of Bastiat and Carey see present edition, Vol. 29.—*Ed.*
[b] *Salva venia*—if you please.—*Ed.*

against the English economists. It attacks *Ricardo*, classical champion of the bourgeoisie and most stoic opponent of the proletariat, describing him as a man whose works provide an arsenal for anarchists, socialists, in brief for all "enemies of the bourgeois order". With fanaticism it attacks not only Ricardo but all other leading economists of modern bourgeois Europe, and reproaches these economic heralds of the bourgeoisie with having split society and with forging weapons for civil war by cynically providing the proof that the economic foundations of the various classes are bound to give rise to an inevitable and constantly growing antagonism between them.

The Frenchman Bastiat is an unqualified Free Trader; the Philadelphian Roman youths parrot his views about the "blessings of free trade" with naive credulity. Carey himself began his economic career as a Free Trader, and at the time he would come up with some good jokes, for example that one should couple bourgeois France with China on account of her preference for protective tariffs.[a] As is usually the case with advocates of free trade, he blamed all the discord in society on improper interference by the state in ventures which were the prerogative of private industry and the like. This was all Yankee, Yankee from head to foot. Nowadays Mr. Carey has become sour, he sighs and complains together with the Frenchman *Sismondi* about the destructive effects seen in the centralising big industry of England, which for him engenders the "evil principle" in society.[426]

He would be highly surprised if he knew how German greenhorns saw the avalanche-like growth of the power of big capital as the formation of so many snowballs full of "Anglo-Saxon" enthusiasm for decentralisation and individualism.

Apart from the fact that Carey totally overlooks the transforming, *revolutionary* element in the destructive effects of industry, he is nevertheless again too much of a Yankee to make industry as such *responsible*, yet that would be the only logical conclusion to be drawn from his argument. He makes the English personally responsible for the effects of their industry, not to mention the fact that Ricardo is in his turn made responsible for England. Caught in this contradiction, he must necessarily burrow himself deeper and deeper in the petty-bourgeois element, advocating the long since discarded patriarchal association between agriculture and manufacturing.

---

[a] The reference is to Carey's book *Essay on the Rate of Wages: with an Examination of the Causes of the Differences in the Condition of the Labouring Population Throughout the World*, Philadelphia, 1835, pp. 194-210, 213, 228, 230, etc.—*Ed.*

But the mark of the Yankee with Carey and his adherents is this: under the pretext and, we ought to admit it, with good will and with the conviction of speaking for the "most numerous and the poorest class",[a] they throw down the gauntlet to the English bourgeoisie. Sismondi did that by condemning *modern industry* and expressing his longing to return to the *old method of manufacture*; nowadays, however, they do it by preaching protective tariffs. Accordingly all they are really aiming at with all their philanthropic talk is artificially *accelerating* the ***English*** development of the *industrial bourgeoisie in America*. This is a philanthropic and utopian gesture in the competitive struggle between England and America, this most interesting of phenomena confronting present-day bourgeois economists. The ingenious aspect of economics is revealed here in all its glory.

As this is completely overlooked even by Carey's school, it would of course be unfair of us to assume even an inkling of all this in the thinking of a "State-haemorrhoidarius" and the newly-fledged political economists of the *Neu-England-Zeitung*, since they are stuck in the bourgeois mire right up to their ears and are not even remotely aware of the historical significance of the school of thinking which they themselves have learned by heart.

[*Die Reform*, No. 50, September 21, 1853]

In the competitive struggle between America and England we see the latter pushed increasingly into the position of Venice, Genoa and Holland, which were all forced to lend their capital on interest after the monopoly of their trading power had been broken. Genoa and Venice helped Holland to emerge, Holland provided England with capital, and now England is obliged to do the same for the United States of America. Only today all the conditions in this process are of a much larger scale than they were at that time. England's position differs from that of those countries in that the main factor for them was a monopoly of trade, which is easy to break, whilst she possesses a monopoly of industry as well, which by its very nature is tougher. On the other hand the English bourgeoisie's surfeit of capital is all the more colossal, so that it is obliged to build railways in both continents, and to invest capital in gas-lighting in Berlin, in the vineyards of Bordeaux, and in Russian factories and American steamers. All this provides one with material to support the most interesting observation that the attraction which English central capital exerts necessarily has its complement in a centrifugal force which

[a] A phrase coined by Henri Saint-Simon.— *Ed.*

pours it out again into all the corners of the world. If there were to be a revolution, then the English would have furnished the European continent with all those lines of communication and all that production machinery for nothing. America is not waiting for revolutions. It is settling its accounts in a conservative bourgeois fashion by from time to time liquidating its business with England through bankruptcies. This is one of the secrets of its rapid rise, a regular phenomenon just like railway accidents and shipwrecks. That same lack of concern, that same mad frenzy of production which makes it possible for tens of thousands to be brought into the world who under different circumstances would never see the light of day, cold-bloodedly sends hundreds upon hundreds, propelled by steam, to an early death. The one is simply the complement of the other. *The unscrupulous multiplying of the wealth of capitalist companies accompanied by complete disregard for human life!* That is how the commentary reads on the "victory of individuality amongst the Anglo-Saxons"!

All these are facts which are naturally incomprehensible to the "sober non-violence and homely good sense" of Philadelphian Roman youths who have ingeniously managed to find out from some conservative review or other that the women workers of Lowell today are three times better off as regards their earnings than they were thirty years ago. According to that clever conclusion those women workers of years ago must have eaten only four and a half days a week and must have covered their nakedness with nothing more than a fig-leaf. That Lowell should only have come into existence during the last thirty years, or should have worked its way up from a quietly vegetating population of 200 souls to an industrial town of 36,000 souls; that today approximately a third of that population should consist of women workers* who are living from hand to mouth on an average wage of three dollars a week, that is to say that their wages fluctuate to such an extent above and below this average that they can put a few coppers into the savings bank when times are good, only to use them up again when business stagnates completely or they are laid off for *half the week*; that these women workers should for the most part be condemned to celibacy, not by democratic decree but through pressure of circumstances—these are all things which a "democratic" candidate for high office *must* not see, even if one wanted to assume that he had the necessary powers of vision.

It is true that here in America we cannot deny the existence of that "equality of opportunity for the individual, which is the highest goal one (i.e. the Philadelphian Romans) can perceive". Yellow fever has for long enough been acting as a delegate of the Roman democrats and has demonstrated that principle in New Orleans. However, the possibility of equality, young Sir, lies beyond the range of vision of the bourgeoisie, and only the reformer[a] who has perceived the

* Five-eighths of the population of Lowell is estimated to be women, and only three-eighths men. We believe that *in fact* the disproportion is much more glaring.—*A. C.*

[a] An allusion to Karl Marx.—*Ed.*

full implications of the present conditions of workers has the requisite wider horizon, not hedged round by any kind of prejudice, to include it.

Having now sketched the heroes of both worlds, but, where the hero of the New World was concerned, having preferred to discuss political economy in the original[a] rather than the dull and bloodless imitation which he is always repeating (and we have done this in order to be able to observe the decorum which we owe to the public, and to interrupt the personification of boredom in all its monotony and trite learning in all its gloom), we must add that each of the two parties is accusing the other of gross ignorance in matters of world history (a fact which we simply register), and that the editors occasionally christen these touching, "interesting" scenes a "struggle between materialism and idealism", with Heinzen appearing as godfather in the old disguise of Orlando Furioso.

The feud had become very vehement, and it seemed that the interplay of opposing arguments would end in a brawl rather than resolving itself in that "higher unity" which everyone had so hoped for. They therefore improvised a plan to produce unity through arbitration, a *deus ex machina*,[b] summoned in the person of an "earnest" man,[c] a former diplomat and envoy of some petty republic, unless the solemn protestations of the political sages and grandees of international law are totally deceiving us, betraying to us with their carefully restrained judgments, as they do at every turn, the man who is already groaning under the burden of some future government office. He settles the "struggle" to the satisfaction of both sides, for both parties are adjudged to be at fault, and therefore neither has to make a more dishonourable retreat than the other. Though occasionally still grunting bad-temperedly, "Leonidas" walks peaceably along with his opponents, the "unknown Greeks", whose rôle in the comedy had been taken by the Philadelphian Roman youths. Moved, the choir of the priests of humanism sings "These sacred halls know not what vengeance is!" The curtain falls, but there is no Bengal flame to cast a red light on the patriotic tableau. The final scene is yet to come.

[*Die Reform*, No. 51, September 24, 1853]

Thanks to his manner of a whimpering Heraclitus, the "earnest" arbitrator had gained universal sympathy, extravagantly bestowed upon him by all the treasure-hunters who subscribe to the "science of the future", who were whimpering before him, and who, on their own admission, cast their pearls before the public as Californian gold-diggers would, still rough and unpolished. And lo, full of good cheer and with a happy heart a guest suddenly arrives on the scene, all the more worthy for being uninvited,[d] who chooses, in the rôle of Democritus, to make fun of everything that is funny, and thinks all the evidence indicates that throughout the whole struggle there has been much ado about nothing. He scoffed at the whole fantastic notion of a special democratic mentality, which cannot conceive of

---

[a] As presented by Carey and Bastiat, "hero of the New World" is an allusion to Eduard Schläger.—*Ed.*

[b] Literally "a god from a machine"—a person or thing that appears or is introduced (as into a story) suddenly and unexpectedly and provides an artificial or contrived solution to an apparently insoluble difficulty.—*Ed.*

[c] Karl Blind. In the original the form *ernschte* is used ironically instead of *ernste* (serious).—*Ed.*

[d] Evidently an allusion to the diplomatic mission which Blind carried out in Paris on instructions of the Provisional Government of Baden during the campaign for an imperial constitution in 1849.—*Ed.*

the revolution as anything other than the "fiery hell-hounds" of the wire-pulling European Central Committee.[427] He pacifies their lordships, saying they need have no fear of Bashkirs, and the Prussians and the Bavarians are not so bad either. He explains to them how, without the princehood of its princes, without the customary collection of youths in spiked helmets, with or without monkey-tail cockades, Germany might have stood a chance of Bashkirs. He chuckles at the tender "revolutionary" concern for the national independence of the thirty-six sovereigns, of the Prussian, Bückeburg, Darmstadt or Baden governments, and at the way imperial troops—imperial troops for the "German nation"—are preferred to Bashkirs. He laughs at people's dread of the impending floods of Bashkirs, at the festive bluster, at all the rubbish of political wisdom, the moralising national manifestos addressed to the Prusso-Baden princelings, at the way they are urged faithfully to protect the thirty-six mother-countries with their half-and-half despotism from the Bashkirs, so as to prevent at all costs the premature outbreak of the great conflict, which the democrats do not expect to occur until fifty years after Napoleon's prophecy[a] but which must not occur during their lifetimes. He laughs at the feeble and absurd efforts of democratic sects to reduce all the existing convulsions of European society, the whole enormous historical crisis, and the thousands of difficulties, complications and class problems to a superficial and insipid difference between Cossacks and republicans, and to treat the overthrow of a whole system of production with all the shocks for the world market, with all the class struggles and upheavals in industry that this inevitably entails as if it were just the plainest of pot-house fare, like some fraternal luncheon that has yet to be arranged. He laughs at the barbaric somersaults of Menchikoff, at the diplomatic absurdities of his superiors, Nesselrode-Libinsky,[b] at the top-booted Don Quixote of the European counter-revolution, the mighty and formidable recruiter of Jews Nicholas, and at the "helpless voice" of his politically skilled opponents together with their high-ranking judge. He offers his congratulations on the final extinguishing of the "tiny spark [of revolution] flickering on", and on the final decaying of the whole theatrical apparatus of official democracy, but on the other hand whispers into the ears of the jousters, numb with astonishment at the proletarian audacity they have witnessed, that the *material revolution without hollow-sounding words* is for that very reason more inevitable today than ever, and that *it* was Russia's equal opponent.

Whispering is heard everywhere, and "righteous indignation" manifests itself amongst the democratic notabilities. The agitation grows and nobody notices that, having ended his scornful reprimand, the proletarian rogue has silently turned his back on the sacred halls of "higher unity". People clear their throats. Misunderstood and foundering, political wisdom fires a distress signal, which fades away in melancholy, and there appears the now inevitable factotum of governmental power *in partibus*.[c] Slowly and discreetly, and with *earnest*, ominous demeanour and thoughtfully folded arms, the latter shakes off the fiercely snapping cluster of talents. Resplendent under his arms is the testament of Peter the Great,[428] a history of Russia, bound in pigskin, is borne in and opened at his behest, and bundles of treaties on parchment are piled up round him. He begins to speak. Svyatoslav, Ivan

[a] The reference is to Napoleon's statement: "In fifty years Europe will be either republican or a Cossack one" (see this volume, p. 541).—*Ed.*

[b] The reference is to K. K. Labensky.—*Ed.*

[c] K. Blind. *In partibus* or *in partibus infidelium*—outside the real world, abroad. The phrase means literally "in the country of infidels" and was added to the title of Catholic bishops who were appointed to purely nominal dioceses in non-Christian countries.—*Ed.*

Vasilyevich, Peter I, Catherine II and Nicholas file past, a series of irrefutable signposts pushed successively forward from Moscow to the Danube. What is the direction in which they point? To Constantinople, the fateful city of the Tsar. Is that understood? Tremble Byzantium! Who will save you? And who will save the world from the Cossack flood? Democracy? "It *alone* speaks out* and vainly raises its helpless voice against Russia; the democratic party has got into disrepute in the City, at Westminster Hall and St. James's alike"—thus speaks the factotum himself. The German princes? They are themselves nothing more than the princelings of the Cossacks. Boustrapa[b]? He wants to parade as a Cossack on the Rhine himself. Aberdeen? Has he not once already allowed the Cossacks to get as far as Adrianople?

Who then is left? The Slav revolution? A miserable Montenegrin "Hölperlips".[429] The pessimistic political sages no longer think much of that. What then? There is nothing, nothing else, nowhere is there salvation! Let us cover our heads and hide our tallow candles—*l'Europe sera cosaque.* But wait! Here comes the revolution, the great "mighty people's revolution", the "fourth estate" is on its way, the "estate" which has no more to do than to "launch itself against the Tartar flood of tsarist despotism" if it wishes later to see the "knife and fork question"[c] resolved, an issue which has of course long since been resolved for the people of other estates. Indeed, forward with the "fourth estate", forward with the "people's revolution", forward into battle against Russia! Russia is the seat of "Europe's order based on sceptre, cross, sabre and money"!

The speaker has finished, his "helpless voice" falls silent. He throws back his head, looks about him, triumphant, "earnest", serenely cool.

Where is that other horseman,
His mount has left the stable?

Dumbfounded, they cast an eye round the trusty company. "Thalberg not here?" No answer. The speaker's mournful gaze strays involuntarily out to the blue-vaulted sky. "Paradoxes," he stammers. In resignation he lowers his gaze, and on the street it lights upon the missing intruder, who is playing with a box of matches and laughing away.

Written in September 1853

First published in *Die Reform* Nos. 48, 49, 50 and 51, September 14, 17, 21 and 24, 1853

Signed: *Ad. Cluss*

Printed according to the newspaper

Translated from the German

Published in English for the first time

* Is the "democratic party" suddenly counting old Aunt Voss[a] and Herr Brüggemann of the *Kölnische Zeitung* amongst its number? For during the most recent complications the latter *alone* has gathered at least three score very patriotic, very nationalistic and strongly anti-Russian supporters. Equally all the respectable German press, with the exception of the *Kreuz-*, the *Ostsee-*, the *Augsburger-* and the *Oberpostamts-Zeitung.* The "watchful eye and admonishing words" of these "disreputable people" do then still have sympathisers.—*A. C.*

---

[a] *Königlich privilegirte Berlinische Zeitung von Staats- und gelehrten Sachen.—Ed.*

[b] A nickname of Louis Bonaparte, composed of the first syllables of Boulogne and Strasbourg (centres of Bonapartist putsches of 1836 and 1840), and Paris, where the Bonapartist coup d'état came off on December 2, 1851.—*Ed.*

[c] An expression used in 1838 by Parson J. R. Stephens, a prominent Chartist. It became a symbol of Chartist aspirations.—*Ed.*

NOTES AND INDEXES

NOTES

1 This article is the first in a series on the Eastern question by Marx and Engels published in the *New-York Daily Tribune.* The increase in tension between Russia and the Western Powers in the Near East and the Balkans in 1853 eventually led to the Crimean war. At Marx's request Engels wrote a number of articles from mid-March to early April on the basis of a brief plan suggested to him by Marx in his letter of March 10, 1853 (see present edition, Vol. 39). Marx soon joined in with articles of his own.

Like most articles by Marx and Engels in the *New-York Daily Tribune,* this one was not republished in their lifetime. The section "Turkey", together with the other articles on the Eastern question, was included in a collection compiled by Eleanor Marx and Edward Aveling: *The Eastern Question. A Reprint of Letters written 1853-1856 dealing with the events of the Crimean War,* London, 1897. The collection gave Marx as the author of all the articles, since they had been published in the *New-York Daily Tribune* either anonymously, as editorials, or signed by Marx. Only in 1913, after the publication of the correspondence between Marx and Engels, it was discovered that many articles which Marx had sent to the newspaper were written wholly or in part by Engels.

In this article Marx is the author of the sections "British Politics.—Disraeli.—The Refugees.—Mazzini in London", and Engels of the section "Turkey".

In a leader for the issue that carried this article the editors of the *New-York Daily Tribune* wrote: "In this connection we may properly pay a tribute to the remarkable ability of the correspondent by whom this interesting piece of intelligence is furnished. Mr. Marx has very decided opinions of his own, with some of which we are far from agreeing, but those who do not read his letters neglect one of the most instructive sources of information on the great questions of current European politics."

The *New-York Daily Tribune* was an American newspaper founded in 1841 by Horace Greeley, journalist and politician, and published until 1924. Until the mid-1850s it was a Left-wing Whig paper and after that the organ of the Republican Party. In the forties and the fifties it took a strong stand against slavery. Among its contributors were prominent American writers and journalists. Charles Dana, who was strongly influenced by the ideas of utopian socialism, was one of its editors from the late 1840s. Marx began to write for the newspaper in August 1851 and continued to contribute to it until March 1862. The articles Marx and Engels wrote dealt with key issues of foreign and domestic policy, the working-class movement, the economic development of European countries, colonial expansion, the national liberation movement in the colonial and dependent countries, etc. During the period of reaction in Europe Marx and Engels made use of this widely-read American newspaper to expose the evils of capitalist society, its irreconcilable contradictions and the limitations of bourgeois democracy.

The *New-York Daily Tribune* editors took on occasion considerable liberties with the articles contributed by Marx and Engels, publishing some of them unsigned in the form of editorials or making additions which often contradicted the main text. Marx protested against this repeatedly. In the autumn of 1857, when the economic crisis in the USA affected the finances of the newspaper, Marx was compelled to reduce the number of his articles. His association with the newspaper ceased entirely during the American Civil War, when advocates of a compromise with the slave-owning South gained control over it. p. 3

2 In March 1853 Disraeli, leader of the Tories since 1848, was replaced in this post by Lord Pakington. This was the result of disagreements between Disraeli, who supported certain concessions to the free-trade industrial bourgeoisie, and the Tory advocates of protectionism. The latter won the day, but subsequently the Disraeli line prevailed, reflecting the gradual changing of the old aristocratic Tory Party into a party of the conservative sections of the British bourgeoisie. p. 3

3 At the sitting of the House of Commons on March 1, 1853, Palmerston formally declared that if the continental powers demanded that Britain should expel political refugees, Britain would decline. However, the statement of the Prime Minister, Lord Aberdeen, in the House of Lords on March 4 contained a promise of concessions on this question. Marx had dealt with this subject in a number of his previous reports to the *New-York Daily Tribune.* See also an article on this subject, "The Refugees and the London Police", in *The People's Paper*, No. 47, March 26, 1853. p. 4

4 The *treaties of Tilsit*—peace treaties signed on July 7 and 9, 1807 by Napoleonic France and the members of the fourth anti-French coalition, Russia and Prussia, which were defeated in the campaigns of 1806 and 1807. In an attempt to split the defeated powers, Napoleon made no territorial claims on Russia and even succeeded in transferring part of the Prussian monarchy's eastern lands to Russia. He established an alliance with Alexander I when the two emperors met in Erfurt in the autumn of 1808. The treaties imposed harsh terms on Prussia, which lost nearly half its territory to the German states dependent on France, was made to pay indemnities, and had its army reduced. However, Russia, like Prussia, had to break the alliance with Britain and join Napoleon's Continental System, which was to its disadvantage. Napoleon formed the vassal Duchy of Warsaw on Polish territory seized by Prussia during the partitions of Poland at the end of the eighteenth century, and planned to use the duchy as a springboard in the event of war with Russia.

In Tilsit Alexander I pledged, with France acting as a mediator, to start peace negotiations with Turkey with which Russia had been at war since 1806. In August 1807 Russia and Turkey signed an armistice, but a peace treaty was not concluded and military operations were resumed in 1809. The war ended with the defeat of Turkey in 1812.

Increasingly strained relations between France and Russia led to Napoleon's campaign against Russia in 1812. p. 5

5 At the Congress of the Holy Alliance (an alliance of European monarchs founded on September 26, 1815 on the initiative of the Russian Emperor Alexander I and the Austrian Chancellor Metternich), which began in Troppau in October 1820 and ended in Laibach in May 1821, the principle of intervention in the internal affairs of other states was officially proclaimed. Accordingly, the Laibach Congress decided to send Austrian troops to Italy to crush the revolutionary and national liberation movement there. French intervention in Spain with similar aims was decided on at the Congress of Verona in 1822. p. 5

6 The aggravation of the Eastern question in the early 1840s was caused by the Turko-Egyptian war of 1839-41. In 1839 the Turkish army invaded Syria, which had been conquered in 1831-33 by the Egyptian ruler Mehemet Ali, but it was defeated. Fearing Russian intervention, the Western powers decided to send a joint Note to the Turkish Sultan offering their assistance. However, as a result of the struggle between Britain and France over spheres of influence in the Near East, the London Convention on military assistance to the Sultan was signed on July 15, 1840 by Britain, Russia, Austria and Prussia, without France. The latter was counting on Mehemet Ali, but was soon compelled to abandon him to his fate. After the military intervention of Britain and Austria, Mehemet Ali was forced to renounce all his possessions outside Egypt and submit to the supreme power of the Turkish Sultan. p. 5

7 The principle of legitimacy was proclaimed by Talleyrand at the Vienna Congress of European monarchs and their Ministers held in 1814-15. It actually meant the restoration of the "legitimate" dynasties and monarchies overthrown during the French revolution of 1789-94 and the Napoleonic wars, and was made the cornerstone of the treaties of Vienna. However, in recarving the map of Europe, the governments which had defeated Napoleonic France were prompted more by their own, frequently conflicting, interests than by the claims of the "legitimate" monarchs who were being restored. p. 6

8 Turkish armies laid siege to Vienna in 1529 and 1683 but in both cases failed to take it. In 1683 it was saved by the army of the Polish King John Sobieski.

The *battle of Kulevcha* (Bulgaria) took place on May 30, 1829, during the Russo-Turkish war of 1828-29. The Turkish army was defeated. p. 7

9 The word "race" is used here in accordance with its meaning at the time: it meant both "races of the second order" (groups within the main races) and linguistic and ethnic groups. p. 7

10 Transylvania became part of Hungary under the Austrian rule of the Habsburgs in the late seventeenth century. During the 1848-49 revolution the Hungarian revolutionary Government refused to recognise the right of the Transylvanian Wallachians to national independence. As a result, the Austrian counter-revolutionary forces were able to draw the insurgent army of Transylvanian Wallachians into the struggle against the Hungarian revolutionary army. The defeat of the Hungarian bourgeois revolution had deplorable consequences for the people of Transylvania, where the rule of the Hungarian magnates was restored. p. 9

[11] The *Ruthenians*—the name given in nineteenth-century West-European ethnographical and historical works to the Ukrainian population of Galicia and Bukovina, which was separated at the time from the rest of the Ukrainian people. During the national liberation uprising in Cracow in 1846 the Austrian authorities provoked clashes between Ukrainian peasants and insurgent Polish detachments. However, after the suppression of the uprising, the participants in the peasant movement in Galicia were subjected to brutal reprisals. p. 9

[12] In the summer of 1848, the anti-feudal movement and the struggle for complete liberation from the rule of the Turkish Sultan gained strength in the Danubian Principalities of Moldavia and Wallachia, which formally remained autonomous possessions of Turkey. The movement in Wallachia grew into a bourgeois revolution. In June 1848, a Constitution was proclaimed, a liberal Provisional Government was formed and George Bibesco, the ruler of Wallachia, abdicated and fled the country.

On June 28, 1848, 12,000 Russian soldiers entered Moldavia and in July Turkish troops invaded the country. The Russian and Turkish intervention helped restore feudal rule, and the subsequent entry of Turkish troops into Wallachia with the consent of the Tsarist Government brought about the defeat of the bourgeois revolution there. p. 9

[13] The *Cyrillic alphabet*, one of the two ancient Slav alphabets (the other is called the Glagolitic alphabet), is named after Cyril, a missionary monk of the mid-ninth century, who, together with his brother Methodius, translated several religious texts from Greek into Slavonic. The Russian, Bulgarian and many other Slavonic languages use a modified form of the Cyrillic alphabet. p. 10

[14] A reference to the reactionary bourgeois and landowner elements of the national movement in Croatia and Bohemia, who during the 1848-49 revolution opposed the revolutionary-democratic solution of the national question and advocated uniting the oppressed Slav peoples within the framework of the Habsburg Empire. This standpoint was reflected in the decisions of the Croatian Sábors held in 1848 in Agram (Zagreb), and in the efforts of the moderately liberal wing of the 1848 Slav Congress in Prague (Palacký, Šafařík) to maintain and strengthen the Habsburg monarchy. The Left, radical wing (Sabina, Frič, Libelt and others), on the other hand, wanted to act in alliance with the revolutionary-democratic movement in Germany and Hungary. p. 11

[15] The *New-York Daily Tribune* has: "the Russian war of 1809". The reference is to the Russo-Turkish war of 1806-12, which ended in the defeat of Turkey and the signing in May 1812 of the Bucharest peace treaty, according to which Bessarabia was joined to Russia. The treaty provided for Serbian autonomy in domestic affairs, thus laying the foundation for Serbia's future independence (see Note 26). In 1807 Russia and Turkey concluded an armistice with the mediation of France, but the peace negotiations were interrupted and military operations resumed in 1809. p. 11

[16] The anti-Russian party in Serbia, headed by Garašanin, sought support from the Western powers. In response to a demand from the Russian Ambassador Extraordinary to Constantinople, Prince Menshikov, Prince Alexander of Serbia dismissed Garašanin from the post of the head of government and Foreign

Minister. The struggle between the different parties led to an aggravation of the political situation in Serbia in 1853. p. 11

17 This article was published in the collection: Karl Marx, *The Eastern Question*, London, 1897. The collection gave Marx as the author of the article. However, it was later discovered that this article, as well as "The Turkish Question" and "What Is to Become of Turkey in Europe?", were written by Engels. This is confirmed by Engels' letter to Marx of March 11, 1853, in which he agreed, in response to Marx's request, to write a series of articles on the subject, and also by his letter to Marx of May 1, 1854, in which he referred to these articles in connection with future plans for writing on the Eastern question for the press (see present edition, Vol. 39). p. 13

18 The first Anglo-Afghan War of 1838-42, started by the British with the aim of seizing Afghanistan, ended in total failure for the British colonialists.

In 1843 the British colonialists seized Sind, a region in the north-western part of India bordering on Afghanistan. During the Anglo-Afghan war the East India Company resorted to threats and violence to obtain the consent of the feudal rulers of Sind to the passage of British troops across their territory. Taking advantage of this, the British demanded in 1843 that the local feudal princes proclaim themselves vassals of the Company. After crushing the rebel Baluch tribes (the natives of Sind), the annexation of the entire region by British India was announced.

The *Punjab* (North-West India) was conquered in British campaigns against the Sikhs in 1845-46 and 1848-49. In the sixteenth century, the Sikhs were a religious sect in the Punjab. Their teaching of equality became the ideology of the peasants and lower urban strata who fought against the Empire of the Great Moguls and the Afghan invaders in the late seventeenth century. Subsequently a local aristocracy emerged among the Sikhs, whose representatives ruled the Sikh state established in the latter half of the eighteenth century. In 1845, the British authorities in India provoked an armed conflict with the Sikhs and in 1846 succeeded in turning the Sikh state into a vassal. In 1848 the Sikhs revolted, but were totally subjugated in 1849. The conquest of the Punjab turned all India into a British colony. p. 14

19 A reference to the Milan insurrection started on February 6, 1853 by the followers of the Italian revolutionary Mazzini and supported by Hungarian revolutionary refugees. The aim of the insurgents, who were mostly Italian workers, was to overthrow Austrian rule, but their conspiratorial tactics led them to failure. Marx analysed it in a number of articles (see present edition, Vol. 11, pp. 508-09, 513-16 and 535-37). p. 17

20 This article was published in *The Eastern Question*. p. 18

21 A reference to a coin with an imprint of the Egyptian sacred bull Apis; such coins with imprints of animals were used in Greece until the fifth century B.C. p. 19

22 A reference to the cordial agreement (*entente cordiale*) between France and England in the early period of the July monarchy (1830-35). The agreement proved ineffectual, however, and was soon followed by increased friction between the two powers. p. 20

23 This article was published in *The Eastern Question* which gave Marx as its author (see Note 17). p. 22

[24] The Greek insurrection was prepared by secret societies of Greek patriots (Hetaeria). It was sparked off in spring 1821 by a march of a detachment under Alexander Ypsilanti—a Greek officer in the Russian army and leader of a secret society in Odessa—to the Danubian Principalities across the Pruth in order thence to enter Greece. The campaign was a failure, but it marked the beginning of a mass movement in Greece which soon spread throughout the country. In January 1822 the National Assembly in Epidaurus proclaimed the independence of Greece and adopted a Constitution. Initially the powers of the Holy Alliance strongly opposed the insurrection. However, the great sympathy aroused everywhere for the Greek struggle against Turkish domination, and especially the opportunity of using this struggle to strengthen their influence in the south of the Balkans, caused Britain, Russia and France to recognise Greece as a belligerent and render her armed assistance. Russia's victory in the Russo-Turkish war of 1828-29 was of major importance in helping Greece to acquire independence. Turkey was compelled to recognise Greece as an independent state. However, the European powers imposed a monarchical form of government on the Greek people. p. 22

[25] *Fanariote Greeks*—inhabitants of Fanar (a district in Constantinople), most of whom were descendants of aristocratic Byzantine families. Owing to their wealth and political connections they held important posts in the administration of the Ottoman Empire. p. 22

[26] The Serbian insurrection, which flared up in February 1804 against the arbitrary rule and brutal reprisals of the Turkish janissaries, developed into an armed struggle for the country's independence from Turkey. During the insurrection a national government was set up and Georgi Petrović (Karageorge), the leader of the insurgents, was proclaimed the hereditary supreme ruler of the Serbian people in 1808. The Serbian movement was greatly advanced by the successful operations of the Russian army in the Balkans during the Russo-Turkish war of 1806-12. According to the Bucharest peace treaty of 1812 Turkey was to give Serbia autonomy in domestic affairs. Taking advantage of Napoleon's invasion into Russia, however, the Turkish Sultan organised a punitive expedition to Serbia in 1813 and restored his rule there. As a result of a new insurrection by the Serbs in 1815 and also diplomatic assistance from Russia, Turkish rule was overthrown. After the Russo-Turkish war of 1828-29, which ended with the signing of a peace treaty in Adrianople in 1829, Turkey recognised the autonomy, i.e., the virtual independence, of the Serbian Principality in a special order issued by the Sultan in 1830. p. 23

[27] The *battle of Navarino* took place on October 20, 1827. It was fought by the Turko-Egyptian fleet, on the one side, and the allied British, French and Russian fleet commanded by Vice-Admiral Codrington, on the other. The latter was sent by the European powers to Greek waters for the purpose of armed mediation in the war between Turkey and the Greek insurgents. The battle ended in a crushing defeat for the Turko-Egyptian fleet. p. 24

[28] *Magna Charta* (*Magna Carta Libertatum*)—a charter signed by King John of England on June 15, 1215, under pressure from the rebellious barons, who were supported by the knights and burghers. It restricted the rights of the King, mainly in the interests of the big feudal magnates, and contained some concessions to the knights and burghers. p. 24

29 In 1849 the Russian and Austrian governments demanded that Turkey should extradite Hungarian and Polish refugees who had taken part in the revolution in Hungary. The Turkish Government, which hoped to make use of the refugees in reorganising the army, refused to comply with this demand. The conflict became especially acute after the intervention of the Western powers, which decided to oppose Russia for fear of her growing influence in the Near East and in Central Europe. The British Government sent a squadron to the Dardanelles. Nicholas I was compelled to give way and be content with the Turkish Government's promise to expel the refugees from Turkey. p. 24

30 The *will of Peter the Great*—a spurious document circulated by enemies of Russia. The idea of the existence of the "will" was advanced in the West as early as 1797. In 1812 Ch. L. Lesur described the contents of this pseudo-will in his book *Des progrès de la puissance russe, depuis son origine jusqu'au commençement du XIXe siècle*, and in 1836 it was reproduced as a document in T. F. Gaillardet's book *Mémoires du Chevalier d'Eon*. In Marx's and Engels' lifetime many people in Western Europe regarded this document as authentic. p. 25

31 A reference to the three partitions of Poland (1772, 1793 and 1795) by Prussia, Tsarist Russia and Austria (which did not take part in the second one). As a result of the third partition the Polish state ceased to exist. p. 25

32 A reference to the actions of the Austrian police in connection with the Milan insurrection in February 1853 (see Note 19) and the attempt of the Hungarian tailor János Libényi to assassinate the Austrian Emperor Francis Joseph on February 18, 1853 (see present edition, Vol. 11, p. 513). These events were used by the Austrian authorities as a pretext for mass arrests and trials of persons suspected of conspiracy against the government and participation in the national liberation movement in Hungary and Italy. Marx compares these reprisals with the measures taken by the governments of German states against participants in the opposition movement after the Napoleonic wars, which were carried out on the pretext of fighting against "demagogical machinations". p. 28

33 The *Cologne communist trial* (October 4-November 12, 1852) was a trial of a group of Communist League members charged with "treasonable conspiracy". The trial was rigged by the Prussian police on the basis of forged documents and fabricated evidence, which were used not only against the accused but also to discredit the whole proletarian organisation. Such evidence included, for instance, the so-called Original Minute-book of the Communist League Central Authority meetings and other documents forged by police agents, but also genuine documents of the Willich-Schapper adventurist faction which was responsible for the split in the Communist League. Seven of the twelve accused were sentenced to imprisonment for terms of three to six years. Marx guided the defence from London by sending material revealing the provocative methods of the prosecution, and after the trial he exposed its organisers (see Engels' article "The Late Trial at Cologne", published in the *New-York Daily Tribune*, and Marx's pamphlet *Revelations Concerning the Communist Trial in Cologne*, present edition, Vol. 11, pp. 388-93 and 395-457). p. 29

34 Marx is referring to Napoleon III's claims to the left bank of the Rhine, which representatives of French ruling circles had regarded as France's "natural border" in the east ever since the seventeenth century. p. 29

[35] The *Treaty of Adrianople*—a peace treaty signed between Turkey and Russia in September 1829 to end the Russo-Turkish war of 1828-29. By the treaty Russia obtained the Danube Delta with its islands and a considerable portion of the eastern Black Sea coast south of the Kuban estuary. Turkey was to recognise the autonomy of Moldavia and Wallachia, granting them the right to elect their Hospodars independently; their autonomy was to be guaranteed by Russia. The Turkish Government also pledged to recognise Greece as an independent state, whose only obligation to Turkey was to pay an annual tribute to the Sultan, and to observe the previous treaties with regard to Serbian autonomy, issuing a special order in official recognition of it.

Marx's notebook with excerpts for 1853 contains, on page 18, a passage in French from the Adrianople treaty. The text of the treaty was published in many collections of documents, in works by various authors quoted by Marx, and in periodicals p. 33

[36] See Note 26. p. 33

[37] Ali Pasha of Janina, who ruled over a vast territory in the south-west of the Balkans (Epirus, Albania, South Macedonia and other lands, with Janina as the centre), had been at war with the Turkish Sultan since 1820, a fact which contributed to the success of the Greek uprising. However, unlike the national liberation movement of the Greeks, this struggle was of a feudal-separatist nature and ended in his defeat in 1822.

For the *battle of Navarino* see Note 27.

When war broke out between Turkey and Russia in the spring of 1828, French troops under the command of General Maison landed in Morea (the Peloponnesus) in Southern Greece in August and occupied the peninsula. The aim of the expedition, which was organised on the pretext of rendering assistance to the Greeks, was to counteract growing Russian influence in the Balkans and consolidate the position of France in the region. p. 33

[38] The *London conferences* of the representatives of Britain, Russia and France were held in 1827-29 and discussed the Greek question. On July 6, 1827, the three powers signed a Convention which confirmed the Protocol on Greek autonomy signed by Britain and Russia in St. Petersburg on April 4, 1826. Both the Protocol and the Convention contained clauses on the diplomatic recognition of Greece as an independent state and armed mediation in the Turko-Greek conflict. On the basis of this Convention the allied fleet was sent into Greek waters and took part in the battle of Navarino. A number of other documents concerning Greece were also signed, including a Protocol of March 22, 1829, which established the borders of the Greek state and provided for a monarchical form of government in Greece. However, these agreements and the steps taken by Britain and France, who hoped to settle the conflict through diplomacy, without a defeat for Turkey in the Russo-Turkish war, could not make Turkey change her attitude on the Greek question. It was only after the victory of the Russian army under General Diebich in the 1829 campaign that Turkey agreed to make some concessions. p. 33

[39] The editors of the *New-York Daily Tribune* inserted the following passage at the end of the article (which was also reproduced in the *New-York Weekly Tribune*): "For the present, the duty of those who would forward the popular cause in Europe is to lend all possible aid to the development of industry, education, obedience to law, and the instinct of freedom and independence in the Christian dependencies of Turkey. The future peace and progress of the world

are concerned in it. If there is to be a harvest, too much care cannot be given to the preparation of the soil and the sowing of the seed." p. 36

40 An allusion to the swing to the right of the liberal bourgeoisie already in the early days of the March 1848 revolution in Prussia. Immediately after the uprising in Berlin (March 18) the bourgeoisie hastily organised a civic militia to counterbalance the revolutionary insurgent workers. Engels described the situation in Prussia at the time in his work *Revolution and Counter-Revolution in Germany*, pointing out that "the alliance between the bourgeoisie and the supporters of the overturned system was concluded upon the very barricades of Berlin" (see present edition, Vol. 11, p. 36). p. 38

41 Clippings from the *Belletristisches Journal und New-Yorker Criminal-Zeitung* of April 1, 8, 15 and 22, 1853 containing Hirsch's article "Die Opfer der Moucharderie" with Marx's notes and underlinings have been preserved. p. 40

42 The books by Adolphe Chenu and Lucien de la Hodde are analysed in a review by Marx and Engels, published in the fourth issue of the *Neue Rheinische Zeitung. Politisch-ökonomische Revue*, 1850 (see present edition, Vol. 10, pp. 311-25). p. 40

43 A reference to the so-called Original Minute-book of the Communist League Central Authority fabricated by Prussian agent-provocateurs in London and presented at the Cologne trial as official proof of the defendants' guilt. Concerning this forged document see Marx's *Revelations Concerning the Communist Trial in Cologne* (present edition, Vol. 11, pp. 420-24). p. 41

44 According to most recent research, Bangya passed on to the Prussian police information he happened to learn from German refugees in France. The police used it to arrest a number of Communist League members in Germany and stage a trial in Cologne. See E. Schraepler, *Handwerkerbünde und Arbeitervereine. 1830-1853*, Berlin-New York, 1972, S. 462 et al. p. 41

45 This article is the first in a series by Marx on the budget of Aberdeen's Coalition Ministry, published in the London weekly *The People's Paper*, the organ of the revolutionary wing of Chartists founded in May 1852. He wrote them at the same time as his articles on the subject for the *New-York Daily Tribune*, and in places the text is almost identical.

Marx contributed his articles to *The People's Paper* without payment, and frequently assisted with editing articles and helped Ernest Jones, the editor-in-chief, with matters of organisation. He also enlisted his close colleagues, Georg Eccarius, Wilhelm Pieper and Adolph Cluss, to write for the newspaper as permanent contributors. Eccarius, in particular, wrote with Marx's assistance a review of the literature on the coup d'état in France on December 2 (see present edition, Vol. 11, Appendices). This review was the first in the English press to popularise Marx's ideas that were set forth in *The Eighteenth Brumaire of Louis Bonaparte*.

Apart from publishing Marx's articles, written specially for it, *The People's Paper* from October 1852 to December 1856 reprinted the most important articles by Marx and Engels from the *New-York Daily Tribune*. In 1856, as a result of Jones' rapprochement with the bourgeois radicals, Marx and Engels ceased their work for *The People's Paper* and temporarily broke off relations with Jones. In June 1858 the newspaper passed into the hands of bourgeois businessmen. p. 44

46 Following William Cobbett, Marx gives the year 1701 as the beginning of Queen Anne's reign, in accordance with the calendar in operation in England before 1752, when the new year began with March 25. According to the new style, Anne's reign began in 1702. p. 44

47 The *South Sea Company* was founded in England about 1712 officially for trade with South America and the Pacific islands, but its real purpose was speculation in state bonds. The government granted several privileges and monopoly rights to the Company, including the right to issue state securities. The Company's large-scale speculation brought it to bankruptcy in 1720 and greatly increased Britain's national debt. p. 46

48 A reference to Russell's motion for the "removal of some disabilities of Her Majesty's Jewish subjects", introduced in the House of Commons on February 24, 1853. The motion aimed at granting the Jews the right to be elected to the House of Commons. It passed through the Commons but was turned down by the House of Lords. Marx gave an appraisal of this bill in his article "Parliamentary Debates.—The Clergy Against Socialism.—Starvation" (see present edition, Vol. 11).

The *Canada Clergy Reserves* (1791-1840) consisted of a seventh of the revenue from the sale of lands in Canada and were used chiefly for subsidising the Established and the Presbyterian Churches. In 1853 the British Parliament passed a law authorising the legislative bodies in Canada to distribute the funds independently and grant subsidies to other churches also according to the proportion of the population professing this or that religion. When Peel's Bill, introduced on February 15, 1853, was passing through the House of Commons, the members, on Russell's initiative, voted against the clause on the withdrawal of subsidies to various churches in Canada, which were granted in years when their share of the revenue from the sale of lands was below a fixed sum. p. 49

49 See Note 48. p. 50

50 In accordance with parliamentary procedure, the House of Commons, when discussing certain important questions, declares itself a Committee of the whole House. The functions of the Chairman of the Committee at such sittings are performed by one of the persons on a list of chairmen who is specially appointed by the Speaker. p. 50

51 See Note 47. p. 53

52 This refers to the debates on the system of education in the Catholic College in Maynooth (Ireland) in the House of Commons in February and March 1853. The College was founded in 1795 with the support of Pitt the Younger, who secured the granting of considerable subsidies for it by the British Parliament. This policy, pursued in following years also, aimed at winning support for the British Government from the upper strata of the Irish landlords, bourgeoisie and clergy, and thereby causing a split in the Irish national movement. p. 56

53 The *Irish Brigade*—the Irish faction in the British Parliament from the 1830s to the 1850s. It was led by Daniel O'Connell until 1847. As neither the Tories nor the Whigs had a decisive majority the Irish Brigade, alongside the Free

Traders, could tip the balance in Parliament and in some cases decide the fate of the government.

In the early 1850s, a number of M.P.s belonging to this faction entered into an alliance with the radical Irish Tenant-Right League and formed the so-called Independent Opposition in the House of Commons. However, the leaders of the Irish Brigade soon concluded an agreement with British ruling circles and refused to support the League's demands, which led to the demoralisation and final dissolution of the Independent Opposition in 1859. p. 58

54 The *Manchester School*—a trend in economic thinking which reflected the interests of the industrial bourgeoisie. Its supporters, known as Free Traders, advocated removal of protective tariffs and non-intervention by the government in economic life. The centre of the Free Traders' agitation was Manchester, where the movement was headed by two textile manufacturers, Richard Cobden and John Bright, who founded the Anti-Corn Law League in 1838. In the 1840s and 1850s the Free Traders were a separate political group, which later formed the Left wing of the Liberal Party. p. 58

55 The *Taxes on Knowledge* in Britain were the advertisement duty, the stamp duty on newspapers and the tax on paper. p. 58

56 In a conversation with the French Ambassador, shortly after the Bonapartist coup d'état on December 2, 1851, the British Foreign Secretary Palmerston approved of Louis Bonaparte's usurpation. (Marx calls the latter "the hero of the plain of Satory", referring to a review that he held near Versailles in the autumn of 1850 which was actually a Bonapartist demonstration.) Palmerston did this without consulting the other members of the Ministry, however, which led to his dismissal in December 1851. The British Government was nevertheless the first to recognise Bonaparte.

As Home Secretary in Aberdeen's Coalition Government formed in December 1852, Palmerston instigated police persecutions, harassment in the press and lawsuits against political refugees in Britain. His department communicated information about their activities to the police of Austria and other continental powers. While carrying on this policy, Palmerston professed loyalty to constitutional and democratic principles. p. 59

57 The editors of the *New-York Daily Tribune* published the following note to this article in the same issue of May 6, 1853: "Our readers will find a masterly exposition of Mr. Gladstone's budget, and of its bearing on the present stated parties in England, in the letter of our London Correspondent, Dr. Marx, published in this morning's *Tribune*. We have seen nowhere an abler criticism on the budget or on its author, and do not expect to see one." p. 67

58 A reference to the London Protocol of May 8, 1852 on the integrity of the Danish monarchy, signed by the representatives of Austria, Denmark, England, France, Prussia, Russia and Sweden. It was based on the Protocol adopted by the above-mentioned countries (except Prussia) at the London Conference on August 2, 1850, which supported the indivisibility of the lands belonging to the Danish Crown, including the Duchy of Schleswig-Holstein. The 1852 Protocol mentioned the Russian Emperor (as a descendant of Duke Charles Peter Ulrich of Holstein-Gottorp who reigned in Russia as Peter III) among the lawful claimants to the Danish throne who had waived their rights in favour of Duke Christian of Glücksburg who was proclaimed successor to King Frederick VII.

This provided an opportunity for the Russian Tsar to claim the Danish Crown in the event of the Glücksburg dynasty dying out. p. 67

59 A reference to attempts by the Pope in 1850 to assume the right of appointing Catholic bishops for Britain. This was opposed by the Church of England and the government. A law was passed in 1851 which decreed the Pope's appointments invalid. p. 67

60 A reference to the Holy Roman Empire of the German Nation (962-1806), which at different periods included the German, Italian, Austrian, Hungarian and Bohemian lands, Switzerland and the Netherlands. It was a motley conglomeration of feudal kingdoms and principalities, church lands and free towns with different political structures, legal standards and customs. p. 67

61 See Note 54. p. 69

62 See Note 53. p. 73

63 In 1845-47 there was famine in Ireland due to the ruin of farms and the pauperisation of the peasants. Although blight had caused a great shortage of potatoes, the principal diet of the Irish peasants, the English landlords continued to export food from the country, condemning the poorest sections of the population to starvation. About a million people starved to death and the new wave of emigration caused by the famine carried away another million. As a result, large areas of Ireland were depopulated and the abandoned land was turned into pastures by the Irish and English landlords. p. 73

64 The *Mayfair-men*, or *Mayfair Radicals*—the name given to a group of aristocratic politicians (Molesworth, Bernal Osborne and others), who flirted with democratic circles. Mayfair is an upper-class residential district in London bordering Hyde Park. p. 74

65 An allusion to the attitude of Aberdeen's Coalition Ministry, especially of Palmerston as Home Secretary, to political refugees in Britain and the services which the Home Office rendered to the police authorities of Austria and other powers in the struggle against the revolutionary-democratic movement (see Note 56). p. 74

66 In accordance with parliamentary procedure, the House of Commons, when discussing important questions concerning the national budget, declares itself a Committee of Ways and Means. This is one of the cases when the House sits as a committee (see Note 50). p. 76

67 A reference to the eighth Kaffir war waged by Britain in 1850-53 against the Xhosa tribes. (The name "Kaffir" is wrongly applied to members of all the tribes inhabiting South-Eastern Africa.) In accordance with the peace treaty of 1853 the Xhosa tribes ceded some of their lands to the British. p. 76

68 See Note 53. p. 80

69 See Note 54. p. 80

70 Marx sent this article to the *New-York Daily Tribune* together with Engels' article on Switzerland, written at his request and posted to him from Manchester on

April 26, 1853, as one report. The editors divided the material into two parts and published them as separate articles. (Marx later wrote of this in his letters to Engels of June 2 and 29, 1853.) The first article comprised the text written by Marx after he had received Engels' article and the beginning of Engels' report describing the separatist putsch of clerical and conservative elements in the Freiburg canton in the spring of 1853. The bulk of Engels' report was published as a separate article, signed by Marx, in another issue (see below "Political Position of the Swiss Republic"). In this volume the articles are given as published in the afternoon and evening editions of the *New-York Daily Tribune*. p. 82

71 This letter has not come to light. It is possible that the words "the substance of which I have already communicated to you" were inserted by the editors of the *New-York Daily Tribune*, and refer to some other material, such as the article by A.P.C. (Aurelius Pulszky), "Oriental Affairs.—Austria and Radetzky.—The Gunpowder Plot", in the newspaper issue of May 6, 1853, which mentioned Hale's letter published in *The Daily News* on April 18, 1853. This article said that the letter denied Kossuth's participation in the production of rockets. p. 84

72 The *Sonderbund*—a separatist union formed by the seven economically backward Catholic cantons of Switzerland in 1843 to resist progressive bourgeois reforms and defend the privileges of the Church and the Jesuits. The decree of the Swiss Diet of July 1847 on the dissolution of the Sonderbund served as a pretext for the latter to commence hostilities against the other cantons early in November. On November 23, 1847, the Sonderbund army was defeated by the federal forces. Even after the defeat of the Sonderbund its adherents among the Catholic clergy, the patrician upper strata in the towns, and the conservative section of the peasantry made attempts to seize power in separate cantons. p. 84

73 This article constitutes the main part of Engels' correspondence included by Marx in their common report (see Note 70). The editors of the *New-York Daily Tribune* published the article under the date-line "May 1", but actually it was written not later than April 26 and sent by Marx to New York on the 29th of that month. The article was printed under the heading "Switzerland" and entitled "Political Position of This Republic". In this edition the title of the article has been changed in accordance with its publication in the German and Russian editions of the *Collected Works* of Marx and Engels.

The article was published in German with slight abridgements, under the title "Switzerland", in the New York newspaper *Die Reform* of June 1 and 4, 1853. The editorial note to the article gave Marx as its author. Following this *Die Reform* began to publish translations or renderings of Marx's articles printed in the *New-York Daily Tribune*. The main part in popularising Marx's articles through *Die Reform* was played by Joseph Weydemeyer and Adolph Cluss, former members of the Communist League. p. 86

74 A reference to the Vienna Congress (September 1814-June 1815). On March 20, 1815 the main powers participating in the Congress signed a declaration guaranteeing "permanent neutrality" to Switzerland. p. 86

75 Switzerland was drawn into a conflict with France (December 1851-January 1852) over Louis Bonaparte's demand for the expulsion from Switzerland of French republican refugees, opponents of the Bonapartist coup d'état of December 2, 1851. As in 1836, when the July monarchy staged military demonstrations threatening Switzerland with war for granting asylum to French refugees—Louis Bonaparte among them—the Swiss Government was again compelled to make major concessions to France.

In the eighteenth century the principality of Neuchâtel and Valangin (in German: Neuenburg and Vallendis) was under Prussian rule. It was ceded to France in 1806, during the Napoleonic wars. In 1815, by a decision of the Vienna Congress, it was incorporated into the Swiss Confederation as the 21st canton, while remaining a vassal of Prussia. On February 29, 1848 a bourgeois revolution in Neuchâtel put an end to Prussian rule and a republic was proclaimed. Prussia, however, laid constant claims to Neuchâtel up to 1857, which led to a sharp conflict with the Swiss Republic, and only pressure from France forced her to renounce these claims officially.

In 1853 a dispute arose between Switzerland and Austria over the Italian refugees residing in the Swiss canton of Tessin (Ticino), who had taken part in the national liberation movement in Italy and fled to Switzerland from the Italian provinces under Austrian rule after the unsuccessful uprising in Milan of February 6, 1853 (see Note 19). p. 87

76 From the fifteenth to the mid-nineteenth century the Swiss cantons concluded agreements with the European states for the supply of Swiss mercenaries. The reference here is to agreements signed in 1848 by the canton of Berne and some other cantons with the counter-revolutionary government of Ferdinand II, King of Naples. The use of Swiss troops against the revolutionary movement in Italy aroused profound indignation among the Swiss progressive public, which eventually led to the annulment of these agreements. p. 88

77 See Note 72. p. 89

78 A reference to the Constitution of the Swiss Confederation adopted on September 12, 1848. The new Constitution ensured a measure of centralisation, changing a confederation of cantons (the confederation treaty of 1814 sanctioned by the Congress of Vienna greatly restricted the power of central government) into a federative state. In place of the former Swiss Diet a new legislative body, a Federal Assembly (Bundesversammlung) was set up consisting of two chambers—the National Council and the Council of States. Executive power was vested in the Federal Council whose Chairman acted as President of the Republic. p. 89

79 In 1850 popular unrest spread over a number of Southern provinces in China (Kwangsi, etc.), and developed into a powerful peasant war. The insurgents established a state of their own over a considerable part of Chinese territory. The state was called Taiping Tankuo, hence the name of the movement—the Taiping uprising. The leaders of the movement put forward a utopian programme calling for China's feudal social order to be transformed into a semi-military patriarchal system based on the egalitarian principle in the sphere of production and consumption. The movement, which was also directed

against foreign invaders, was weakened by internal strife and the formation of its own feudal top strata in the Taiping state. It was dealt a crushing blow by the armed intervention of Britain, the USA and France, who initially aided the Manchu dynasty under cover of neutrality. The Taiping uprising was put down in 1864. p. 93

80 A reference to the Anglo-Chinese war of 1840-42, known as the First Opium War. It was started over the confiscation of foreign merchants' stocks of opium by the Chinese authorities. As a result of the war, the British imposed the Nanking Treaty on China in 1842, the first of a series of treaties concluded by the Western powers with China, which reduced it to the level of a semi-colony. The Nanking Treaty made China open five of its ports to British commerce—Canton, Shanghai, Amoy, Ningpo, and Foochow, cede the Island of Hongkong to Great Britain "in perpetuity" and pay a large indemnity. In 1843 a supplementary treaty was signed by which extraterritoriality was granted to foreigners in China. Similar treaties with China were also signed by the USA and France in 1844. p. 93

81 Rich deposits of gold were discovered in California in 1848 and in Australia in 1851. These discoveries were of great importance for the development of the European and American states. p. 94

82 Early in the seventeenth century China was threatened by the united Manchu tribes (known together with the Mongols as Tartars, the name of a Mongol tribe in North-Eastern Mongolia and Manchuria at the time of the formation of Genghis Khan's Empire in the early thirteenth century). The invasion by the Manchus led to the rule of the Ch'ing dynasty in the country (1644-1912), which constantly aroused the anger and opposition of the Chinese people. p. 98

83 *Hong*—a privileged merchants' guild, founded in China in 1721, whose members, on paying a large entrance fee to the treasury, obtained a monopoly of trade with foreigners. After the conclusion of the Nanking Treaty it was dissolved. p. 98

84 This article is the first of a series written by Marx in 1853 dealing with the British conquest of India, Britain's colonial rule in that country, and its consequences for the peoples of Hindustan. The articles were based on detailed study, especially of the history and socio-economic conditions of India and certain other countries in the East. Marx copied a great deal of information on the subject from books and various other sources, which can be found in three of his notebooks with excerpts marked XXI, XXII and XXIII, which also contain passages copied from works on European history and political economy. The material on India and other countries of the East contains passages from parliamentary Blue Books, parliamentary reports, various reference-books on statistics, commerce, railway construction in India, etc., European travellers' notes including those of the French physician and writer François Bernier: *Voyages contenant la description des états du Grand Mogol, de l'Indoustan*, Paris, 1830, and the Russian traveller A. D. Soltykov: *Lettres sur l'Inde*, Paris, 1849. Marx paid great attention to the works of English orientalists, among them R. Patton, *The Principles of Asiatic Monarchies*, London, 1801; M. Wilks, *Historical Sketches of the South of*

India, London, 1810-17; and Th. S. Raffles, *The History of Java*, London, 1817. Marx obtained a great deal of information from the series of works (by John Dickinson and other authors) published by the Free Traders' India Reform Association, and also from the books: G. Campbell, *Modern India; a Sketch of the System of Civil Government*, London, 1852, and *A Scheme for the Government of India*, London, 1853; J. Chapman, *The Cotton and Commerce of India*, London, 1851, and others. Some of the works Marx used are cited or mentioned in his articles. In the course of his research Marx frequently discussed his ideas on the subject with Engels, who was also studying Oriental history at the time (see Marx's letters to Engels of June 2 and 14, 1853 and Engels' reply of June 6, 1853 to the first letter). The results of their discussions were also used by Marx for his articles.

The text of the last section in the article ("Turkey and Russia") was published under this title in *The Eastern Question*. p. 101

85 See Note 58. p. 101

86 Marx is referring to a series of articles published in the *Neue Rheinische Zeitung* in 1848-49 in connection with the Danish-German war over Schleswig and Holstein.

By a decision of the Vienna Congress (1815), the duchies of Schleswig and Holstein remained in the possession of the Danish monarchy (the personal union of Schleswig, Holstein and Denmark had existed since 1499), even though the majority of the population in Holstein and in Southern Schleswig were Germans. Under the impact of the March 1848 revolution in Prussia, the national movement among the German population of the duchies grew, and became radical and democratic, forming part of the struggle for the unification of Germany. Volunteers from all over the country rushed to the aid of the local population when it took up arms against Danish rule. Prussia and other states of the German Confederation also sent federal troops to the duchies. However, the Prussian ruling circles, which had declared war against Denmark, fearing a popular upsurge and an intensification of the revolution, sought an agreement with the Danish monarchy at the expense of the common interests of the German states. An armistice between Prussia and Denmark was concluded on August 26, 1848, at Malmö. On March 2, 1849, Prussia resumed hostilities, but under pressure from England and Russia, who supported Denmark, was forced to conclude a peace treaty (July 2, 1850), temporarily relinquishing its claims to Schleswig and Holstein and abandoning them to continue fighting alone. The Schleswig-Holstein troops were defeated and ceased to offer resistance.

The position of the proletarian wing of German democracy on the Schleswig-Holstein issue was set forth in a number of articles by Engels published in the *Neue Rheinische Zeitung*, in particular "The War Comedy", "The Armistice with Denmark", "The Armistice 'Negotiations'", "The Danish Armistice", "The Danish-Prussian Armistice", "European War Inevitable", and "From the Theatre of War.—The German Navy" (see present edition, Vol. 7, pp. 42-44, 266-69, 270, 411-15 and 421-25; Vol. 8, pp. 456-57; Vol. 9, pp. 259-60). Marx refers to several publications on this question in his Notebook XXII for 1853. p. 101

87 See Note 47. p. 102

88 *Downing Street*—a side-turning off Whitehall, where the main government buildings in London are situated; it contains the residences of the Prime Minister (at No. 10) and the Chancellor of the Exchequer (at No. 11).

The *Presidencies*—Bengal, Bombay and Madras, the three divisions of the East India Company's territory which were originally governed by the Presidents of the Company's three factories. The Regulating Act of 1773 raised the Governor of Bengal to the rank of Governor-General of all Britain's possessions in India. He was called Governor-General of Bengal until 1833 and then Governor-General of India. p. 104

89 A reference to the India Reform Association, founded by the Free Trader John Dickinson in March 1853. p. 104

90 The long-standing dispute between the Greek Orthodox Church and the Roman Catholic Church over rights to the Christian Holy Places in Palestine was resumed in 1850 on Louis Bonaparte's initiative. It soon developed into a serious diplomatic conflict between Russia, which upheld the privileges of the Greek Orthodox clergy, and France, which supported the Roman Catholics. Both sides made use of this conflict in their struggle for hegemony in the Middle East. The vacillating Turkish Government at first yielded to the French demand but on May 4, 1853, during Menshikov's visit to Turkey, it agreed to guarantee special rights and privileges to the Greek Orthodox Church (a special order to this effect was issued by the Sultan a month later). At the same time the Sultan, supported by the British and French ambassadors, rejected Nicholas I's demand that he should be recognised as the protector of the Orthodox population in the Ottoman Empire. p. 105

91 The *Treaty of Kuchuk Kainarji*, signed between Russia and Turkey on July 21, 1774, put an end to the Russo-Turkish war of 1768-74, in which Turkey was defeated. By that treaty Russia obtained the section of the Black Sea coast between the Southern Bug and the Dnieper, with the fortress of Kinburn, and also Azov, Kerch and Jenikale, and secured independent status for the Crimea facilitating its incorporation into Russia. Russian merchant ships were granted the right of free passage through the Bosporus and the Dardanelles. The Sultan was to grant a number of privileges to the Greek Orthodox Church in Turkey, in particular Article 14 of the treaty provided for the construction of an Orthodox church in Constantinople.

For the *Treaty of Adrianople* see Note 35. p. 105

92 For the *Laibach* and *Verona congresses of the Holy Alliance* see Note 5.

For the *treaties of Tilsit* see Note 4. p. 106

93 A section of this article was published under the title "The Ultimatum and After" in *The Eastern Question*. p. 107

94 In 1853 Austria broke off diplomatic relations with Piedmont (Sardinia) after the Piedmontese authorities had granted asylum to a number of refugees from Lombardy (which was under Habsburg rule), who had participated in the national liberation movement of 1848-49 in Italy and the Milan insurrection of February 6, 1853. p. 108

95 In addressing Louis Bonaparte, who was proclaimed Emperor of the French in December 1852, Nicholas I, by agreement with the Austrian and Prussian courts, used the expression "Your Majesty and dear friend", instead of the usual "Your Majesty and dear brother", and called him "Emperor Louis Napoleon" and not "Emperor Napoleon III". The Austrian and Prussian courts, however, used the accepted form of address for him, but in referring to the need to observe the Vienna Congress decisions, they also hinted at the illegality of his rule since the Congress had prohibited the Bonaparte dynasty from occupying the French throne. p. 108

96 *Bujukdere*—a holiday resort on the shore of the Bosporus, near Constantinople, where the Russian embassy in Turkey had its summer residence. p. 109

97 This article was published in *The Eastern Question* under the title "The English and French Fleets.— *The Times.*—Russian Aggrandizement". p. 112

98 This article was published in *The Eastern Question.* p. 115

99 Marx's article, to which he refers in citing this fact, has not been discovered in the *New-York Daily Tribune.* Judging by the notes made by Jenny Marx on the dispatch of articles to the newspaper, it was written by Marx on June 3, 1853, but for some reason was not published. The report on the recall of the Prussian officers appeared in the Augsburg *Allgemeine Zeitung* on June 1, 1853. p. 115

100 The article which Marx intended to write was not published in the *New-York Daily Tribune.* p. 118

101 See Note 47. p. 118

102 *Wesleyans* or *Methodists*—a religious sect founded by John Wesley in Britain in the eighteenth century. At the end of the century it split off from the Church of England and also became popular, as a form of Protestantism, in the USA and Canada. Its distinguishing feature was its demand for a strict and methodical adherence to Christian doctrines, concerning which divisions arose between Wesleyan Methodists and "Primitive" Methodists. p. 119

103 For the preparatory materials for Marx's articles on India see Note 84. In writing this article, Marx made use of some of Engels' ideas which the latter set forth in his letter to Marx of June 6, 1853. p. 125

104 A reference to the rule in India, mainly in the north, of the Mohammedan invaders who came from Central Asia, Afghanistan and Persia. Early in the thirteenth century the Delhi Sultanate became the bulwark of Moslem domination but at the end of the fourteenth century it declined and was subsequently conquered by the Moguls, new invaders of Turkish descent, who came to India from the east of Central Asia in the early sixteenth century and in 1526 founded the Empire of the Great Moguls (named after the ruling dynasty of the Empire) in Northern India. Contemporaries regarded them as the direct descendants of the

Mongol warriors of Genghis Khan's time, hence the name "Moguls". In the mid-seventeenth century the Mogul Empire included the greater part of India and part of Afghanistan. Later on, however, the Empire began to decline due to peasant rebellions, the growing resistance of the Indian people to the Mohammedan conquerors and increasing separatist tendencies. In the early half of the eighteenth century the Empire of the Great Moguls practically ceased to exist. p. 125

105 *Religion of the Lingam*—the cult of the God Shiva, particularly widespread among the southern Indian sect of the Lingayat (from the word "linga"—the emblem of Shiva), a Hindu sect which does not recognise distinctions of caste and rejects fasts, sacrifices and pilgrimages.

Juggernaut (*Jagannath*)—a title of Krishna, the eighth avatar of Vishnu. The cult of Juggernaut was marked by sumptuous ritual and extreme religious fanaticism which manifested itself in the self-torture and suicide of believers. On feast days some believers threw themselves under the wheels of the chariot bearing the idol of Vishnu-Juggernaut. p. 126

106 *Heptarchy* (government by seven rulers)—a term used by English historiographers to describe the political system in England from the sixth to eighth centuries, when the country was divided into seven highly unstable Anglo-Saxon kingdoms, which, in their turn, frequently split up and reunited. Marx uses this term by analogy to describe the disunity of the Deccan (Central and South India) before its conquest by the Mohammedans at the beginning of the fourteenth century. p. 126

107 The island of Salsette, north of Bombay, was famous for its 109 Buddhist cave temples. p. 126

108 The text of the section "The Turkish Question" was published in *The Eastern Question* under the title "Brunnow and Clarendon.—Armenian Proclamation". p. 134

109 The Ten Hours' Bill, which applied to women and children only, was passed by the British Parliament on June 8, 1847. The Truck Act was passed in 1831. However many manufacturers evaded these laws in practice. p. 135

110 In 1824, under mass pressure, the British Parliament lifted the ban on the trade unions. In 1825, however, it passed a Bill on workers' combinations, which, while confirming the raising of the ban on trade unions, greatly restricted their activity. In particular, any agitation for workers to join unions and take part in strikes was regarded as compulsion and violence and punished as a crime. p. 135

111 A reference to the Blackstone-Edge meeting organised by the Chartists on August 2, 1846. The meeting in which Ernest Jones took part was held on June 19, 1853. p. 135

112 The *People's Charter*, the Chartist programme document, contained a demand for universal suffrage (for men of 21 and over), annual elections to Parliament, secret ballot, equal constituencies, abolition of property qualifications for candidates to Parliament, and salaries for M.P.s. p. 136

113 This article, without the sections "The Budget" and "Tax on Newspaper Supplements", was published in *The Eastern Question* under the title "Aberdeen, Clarendon, Brunnow.—Connivance of the Aberdeen Ministry with Russia". p. 142

114 A reference to the draft convention between Russia and Turkey which Menshikov laid as an ultimatum before the Porte after the settlement of the question of the Holy Places on May 4, 1853 (see Note 90). The draft provided not only for freedom of religion for Orthodox believers in the Turkish Empire but also for the Russian Tsar's protectorate over them and was rejected by the Sultan (see this volume, pp. 105-06 and 109-11). p. 143

115 The Bucharest Treaty, concluded between Russia and Turkey in 1812, confirmed certain autonomous rights of Moldavia and Wallachia and the right of Russia, laid down in the Treaty of Kuchuk Kainarji in 1774, to defend the interests of the Orthodox Christians in the Danubian Principalities against the Porte. Under the Adrianople Treaty of 1829 Moldavia and Wallachia were granted autonomy in domestic affairs and were actually placed under the protectorate of Russia. p. 144

116 The *Balta-Liman Convention* was concluded between Russia and Turkey on May 1, 1849, following the occupation of Moldavia and Wallachia by Russian and Turkish troops for the purpose of suppressing the revolutionary movement. According to the Convention the occupation was to continue until the danger of revolution was completely removed (the occupation troops were withdrawn in 1851), the Hospodars were to be appointed temporarily by the Sultan in agreement with the Tsar, and a number of measures, including an occupation, to be taken by Russia and Turkey in the event of a new revolution were laid down. p. 144

117 The *Convention of 1841* on the Black Sea Straits was signed by Austria, Britain, France, Prussia, Russia and Turkey in London on July 13, 1841. According to the Convention the Bosporus and the Dardanelles were to be closed in peacetime to all foreign warships. The Convention said nothing about wartime, leaving Turkey to decide the question at her own discretion. p. 145

118 An allusion to the recall of Colonel Rose from Constantinople in February 1853, and the appointment of Lord Stratford de Redcliffe in his place as British Ambassador to Turkey. p. 145

119 A reference to Chancellor Nesselrode's letter to the Turkish Foreign Minister Reshid Pasha of May 31, 1853. The letter was written in the form of ultimatum. It laid the responsibility for Menshikov's unsuccessful mission on the Turkish Government and called for acceptance of Russian demands to guarantee the privileges of the Orthodox Christian subjects of the Sultan, which actually meant the establishment of the Tsar's protectorate over them. Nesselrode threatened to resort to military action, i.e., the occupation of Moldavia and Wallachia, if the ultimatum was rejected. Turkey, supported by Britain and France, rejected the demands of the Tsarist Government in Reshid Pasha's letter of June 16, 1853. p. 146

120 The *Bank of England* was founded by private persons in 1694. The founders loaned its fixed capital to the government, which explains the origin of the British national debt. The Bank was actually controlled by the government and

functioned as the state bank, e.g. it was entitled to issue money. It remained nominally a private establishment, however, until the end of the Second World War. p. 148

121 A reference to the overthrow of the Stuart dynasty and the enthronement of William III of Orange, after which constitutional monarchy was consolidated in England on the basis of a compromise between the landed aristocracy and the financial bourgeoisie. p. 149

122 The *Seven Years' War* (1756-63)—a war between the Anglo-Prussian and the Franco-Russo-Austrian coalitions. One of the chief causes of the war was the colonial and commercial rivalry between England and France. The main theatre of operations in the East was India where the French and their puppets among the local princes were opposed by the British East India Company, which took advantage of the war to seize new Indian territories. The war ended with France losing almost all her possessions in India (except five coastal towns whose fortifications she was compelled to demolish), while England considerably strengthened her colonial might. p. 149

123 A reference to the Reform Bill which was passed by Parliament in June 1832. The Bill was directed against the political monopoly of the landed and financial aristocracy and gave representatives of the industrial bourgeoisie access to Parliament. The proletariat and the petty bourgeoisie, the main forces in the struggle for the reform, received no electoral rights. p. 151

124 Marx lists a number of wars of conquest waged by the British East India Company. The war in the Carnatic (a principality in South-Eastern India) lasted at intervals from 1746 to 1763. The warring sides—the British and French East India Companies—sought to subjugate the Carnatic under the guise of supporting different local pretenders to the principality. The British, who in January 1761 took possession of Pondichery, the principal French bastion in the south, ultimately won the day.

In 1756, in an effort to avert a British invasion, the Nawab of Bengal started a war, seizing Calcutta, the British base in North-Eastern India. But the armed forces of the British East India Company under Robert Clive's command soon recaptured the city, demolished the Bengal fortifications of the French, who supported the Nawab, and defeated him at Plassey on June 23, 1757. In 1763 they crushed the uprising that broke out in Bengal against British rule. Along with Bengal, the British took possession of Bihar, a region on the Ganges, which was under the rule of the Nawab of Bengal. In 1803, the British completed the conquest of several feudal principalities of Orissa situated south of Bengal. p. 151

125 In 1790-92 and 1799 the British East India Company waged wars with Mysore, an independent feudal state in South India. Its ruler Tippoo Saib had taken part in previous Mysore campaigns against the British and was a sworn enemy of the British colonialists. In the first of these wars Mysore lost half of its dominions, which were seized by the East India Company and its allied feudal princes. The second war ended with the total defeat and the death of Tippoo. Mysore became a vassal principality.

The *subsidiary system*, or the system of so-called *subsidiary agreements*—a method of turning the potentates of Indian principalities into vassals of the East India Company. Most widespread were agreements under which the princes had to maintain (subsidise) the Company's troops stationed on their territory and agreements which saddled the princes with loans on exorbitant terms. Failure to fulfil them resulted in the confiscation of their possessions. p. 151

126 See Note 18. p. 152

127 Marx's preparatory materials on India (Notebook XXI) include passages from J. R. MacCulloch's *The Literature of Political Economy*, London, 1845. The book contains extracts from the works of English economists of an earlier period on British trade with India, among them the above-mentioned treatises of J. Child, Th. Mun and J. Pollexfen. p. 153

128 In the first Burmese war of 1824-26 the troops of the East India Company seized the Province of Assam, bordering on Bengal, and the coastal districts of Arakan and Tenasserim. The second Burmese war (1852) resulted in the seizure by the British of the Province of Pegu. Burma did not sign a peace treaty, however, and refused to recognise the seizure of Pegu. In 1853 the British authorities threatened to resume military operations but abstained from this step, largely due to the guerrilla warfare in Pegu against the foreign invaders, which continued until 1860. In the 1860s Britain imposed on Burma a number of unequal treaties and in 1885, as a result of the third Burmese war, annexed the whole territory of Burma. p. 155

129 A reference to the debate in the House of Commons (June 24, 1853) on the Bill on Irish landlords and tenants introduced by the Aberdeen Ministry.

The government hoped to normalise relations between landlords and tenants by granting the latter certain rights and thereby mitigating the agrarian struggle in the country. After more than two years of debates Parliament rejected the Bill. p. 157

130 *Tenancy-at-will*—a form of tenancy, inherited from the Middle Ages, which did not guarantee a definite term of lease for the tenant and under which the contract could be broken or modified by the landlord at any time, depending on his will. p. 158

131 After the Act of Union was passed in 1801, the British Parliament abolished the protective tariffs shielding Ireland's young and weak industry from foreign competition. This resulted in the collapse of local enterprises, which were unable to compete with British industry, and in Ireland's transformation into an agrarian appendage of Britain. p. 159

132 Marx's excerpts from F. W. Newman's *Lectures on Political Economy* and H. Spencer's *Social Statics* are contained in his Notebook XXI. p. 162

133 The title under which the article appeared in the *New-York Semi-Weekly Tribune*. The *New-York Daily Tribune* entitled it "Russian Policy Against Turkey", and under this title the first section of the article, bearing on the Russo-Turkish conflict, was published in *The Eastern Question*.

In his work on this article and other reports dealing with the history of international relations, Marx made use of materials and documents usually translated into English and published in *The Portfolio; or a Collection of State Papers.* His excerpts from this source are contained in Notebook XXII. p. 163

134 "*Pacification of Greece*"—an expression used in the diplomatic documents of the European powers with reference to their intervention in the Turko-Greek conflict caused by the liberation struggle of the Greek people against Turkish rule in the 1820s. p. 163

135 See Note 38. p. 164

136 A reference to Nesselrode's Note (a circular letter of June 11, 1853) to Russian diplomats abroad. The Note criticised the Porte's actions and gave grounds for presenting a new ultimatum to Turkey demanding that the Russian Tsar be recognised as the protector of the Christian subjects of the Sultan and threatening to resort to "decisive measures" if these demands were rejected. This ultimatum, which Marx calls below an "ultimatissimum", was presented to the Porte on June 16, 1853. p. 166

137 A reference to the Executive Committee of the National Charter Association founded in July 1840. The Association was the first mass workers' party in the history of the working-class movement and had up to 50,000 members at the height of the Chartist movement. However, a lack of ideological and tactical unity and a certain looseness in its organisation affected its activities. After the defeat of the Chartists in 1848 and the ensuing split in their ranks the Association lost its mass character. Nevertheless, under the leadership of Ernest Jones and other revolutionary Chartists it fought for the revival of Chartism on a socialist basis, which found its expression in the programme adopted by the Chartist Convention in 1851. The Association ceased its activities in 1858. p. 170

138 See Note 111. p. 172

139 The first section of this article, entitled "Austria and Russia", was published in *The Eastern Question.*

On the use by Marx of facts and materials published in *The Portfolio* for his articles on the history of international relations, see Note 133. p. 174

140 See Note 130. p. 178

141 The *Suttee*—a custom by which a Hindu widow immolates herself on the funeral pyre with her husband's body. p. 181

142 The first section of this article was published in *The Eastern Question* under the title "Layard.—Gladstone.—Aberdeen.—Palmerston". p. 185

143 A reference to the excavations of Nineveh, the capital of ancient Assyria, directed by the English archaeologist Austen Henry Layard in 1845-51. p. 185

144 Under the Poor Law of 1834 the only relief available to the poor who were fit for work was admission to a workhouse. These were dubbed "Poor Law Bastilles". p. 188

145 A reference to the Bill passed by Parliament on August 5, 1850, in response to workers' protest against the verdict of the Court of Exchequer, which on February 8, 1850 acquitted a group of manufacturers accused of violating the Ten Hours' Bill. This ruling created a precedent and was tantamount to a repeal of the Bill. The workers were also incensed by the relay system practised by British manufacturers. Under the relay system, women and juveniles stayed at work for the full length of the working day for adult men (up to 15 hours), but worked at intervals. The length of their actual work was not outwardly to exceed the legal limit. The manufacturers began to make especially wide use of this system after 1847, in an attempt to circumvent the Ten Hours' Bill.

The new Bill prohibited the relay system but fixed a $10^1/_2$-hour working day for women and juveniles. Marx makes a more detailed analysis of the British workers' struggle for a shorter working day in Volume I of *Capital.* p. 190

146 This article, excluding the section "The East India Question", was published in *The Eastern Question.* p. 192

147 The *Peace Society* (the Society for Promoting Permanent and Universal Peace)—a pacifist organisation founded by the Quakers in London in 1816. It was strongly supported by the Free Traders, who believed that, given peace, free trade would enable Britain to make full use of her industrial superiority and thus gain economic and political supremacy. p. 192

148 An allusion to Palmerston's speech during a parliamentary debate on the Anglo-Greek conflict in June 1850. In January 1850 the British Government presented Greece with an ultimatum and sent ships to blockade Piraeus using as a pretext the burning (in Athens in 1847) of the house of the Portuguese merchant Pacifico, who was a British subject. The real object of the move, however, was to make Greece surrender several strategically important islands in the Aegean Sea. In his speech of June 25, 1850 Palmerston justified Britain's action by the need to safeguard the prestige of British subjects, and drew an analogy between them and Roman citizens. The Latin phrase he cited: "civis Romanus sum" ("I am a Roman citizen"), was used to indicate the high status and privileges afforded by British citizenship. p. 192

149 A reference to the Smyrna incident caused by the arrest of Martin Koszta, a Hungarian refugee and US subject, by order of the Austrian consul, who had him put on board the Austrian warship *Hussar.* This led to an armed clash between the refugees and Austrian naval officers. Ingraham, the captain of the American warship *Saint Louis,* had to intervene and demanded the release of Koszta. Thanks to the mediation of the consuls of other powers an armed conflict was averted. After the negotiations, which lasted for several months, Koszta was released and left for the USA. p. 193

150 See Note 91. p. 195

[151] See Note 27. p. 195

[152] In the spring of 1833 Russian troops were landed in Unkiar-Skelessi, near the Bosporus, to render assistance to the Turkish Sultan against the army of the insurgent Egyptian ruler Mehemet Ali. In May 1833 the Porte, with the mediation of Britain and France, signed a peace treaty with Mehemet Ali, ceding him Syria and Palestine. However, Russian diplomats took advantage of the strained situation and the presence of Russian troops in Turkey and prevailed upon the Porte to sign, on July 8, 1833, the *Unkiar-Skelessi Treaty* on a defensive alliance with Russia. On the insistence of Russia a secret clause was included in the treaty prohibiting all foreign warships, except those of Russia, to pass through the Bosporus and the Dardanelles. This clause remained in force until the new Egyptian crisis of 1839-41 (see Note 6). In negotiating with Britain and other powers on joint operations against Mehemet Ali, Nicholas I had to comply with their demand that in peacetime the Straits be closed to warships of all foreign states without exception. p. 195

[153] *Furcae Caudinae*—a gorge near the Roman town of Caudium, where in 321 B.C., during the second Samnite war, the Samnites defeated the Roman legions and made them pass under the "yoke", which was considered a terrible disgrace to a defeated army. Hence the expression "to pass under furcae Caudinae", that is to be subjected to extreme humiliation. p. 196

[154] Until 1872 candidates to the British Parliament were nominated by a show of hands and even persons without the right to vote could take part in the nomination. But only a very small section of the population could take part in the election, the franchise being restricted by a high property qualification, residence qualification, etc. Candidates turned down by open vote could also stand for election. Marx described these features of the British electoral system in his article "The Chartists" (1852), citing as an example the nomination of candidates in Halifax where Ernest Jones' candidacy was proposed (see present edition, Vol. 11, pp. 333-41). p. 196

[155] See Note 89. p. 197

[156] '*Change Alley*—a street in London containing many banks and usurers' offices; it was famous for all kinds of financial transactions and speculative deals. p. 197

[157] See Note 125. p. 197

[158] *Jagirdars*—representatives of the Moslem feudal gentry in the Great Mogul Empire who received for temporary use large estates (jagirs) in return for which they rendered military service and supplied contingents of troops. When the Empire began to disintegrate the jagirdars became hereditary feudal owners. p. 198

[159] Babur (1483-1530), the founder of the Great Mogul Empire (see Note 104), was a descendant of Tamerlane, who in his turn considered himself the

successor of Genghis Khan. In the eighteenth century, after the disintegration of the Empire, the Mogul emperors became the puppets of the regional governors and Indian feudal lords. After the seizure of Delhi in 1803 by the British they became figureheads of the East India Company and received pensions from it. In 1858, when India was declared a possession of the British Crown, the last formal vestiges of Mogul power were abolished. p. 199

160 This article, excluding the first section "War in Burma", was published under the title "The Russian Question.—Curious Diplomatic Correspondence" in *The Eastern Question.* p. 201

161 See Note 128. p. 201

162 See Note 148. p. 202

163 See Note 22. p. 202

164 See Note 54. p. 202

165 A reference to Nesselrode's circular letter to Russian diplomats abroad of July 2, 1853. (Below Marx cites the date as June 20, 1853, according to the old style accepted in Russia.) The text of it was published in *The Times*, No. 21418, July 12, 1853. Written in the spirit of the previous Note of June 11, 1853 (see Note 136), it supported the Tsarist Government's demands on Turkey and criticised the policy of the Western powers. In referring to the French Minister's reply to the Note, Marx made a slight error, which was due to the lack of clarity in the text of the telegram from Paris published in *The Morning Post.* He quoted from Drouyn de Lhuys' reply to Nesselrode's first Note of June 11, 1853, the text of which together with the text of the French Government's reply of June 25, 1853 was published in the official newspaper *Le Moniteur universel*, No. 195, on July 14, 1853. Nesselrode's Note of July 2 and Drouyn de Lhuys' reply to it of July 15 were published in *Le Moniteur universel*, No. 198 for July 17, 1853, after Marx had written his article. In the second Note, the French Government likewise expressed its disapproval of the Tsar's position in the Eastern question and professed to stand for a peaceful solution of the conflict. p. 203

166 A reference to the London Convention of July 13, 1841 (see Note 117). The Convention annulled the Treaty of Unkiar-Skelessi (1833), which was advantageous to Russia because it opened the Black Sea Straits to Russian warships. Nevertheless, the Tsarist Government, which had taken part since 1840 in the joint military operations of the four powers (Austria, Britain, Prussia and Russia) against Mehemet Ali, who was supported by France, was compelled to adhere to the principle of neutralising the Straits advanced by the Western powers. Yielding to threats of an anti-French coalition, France abandoned Mehemet Ali and signed the Convention. p. 203

167 Taking advantage of the Turko-Egyptian conflict of 1839 (see Note 6) and increasing tension between Britain and France, the Tsarist Government proposed to Palmerston, in September 1839, the conclusion of an agreement,

which, under the guise of joint assistance to the Sultan, would provide for a division of spheres of influence in the Middle East between the two powers. The British Government, which was striving for complete domination in Turkey, rejected the proposal on the pretext that the Eastern question should be settled by a general agreement of European powers. p. 205

168 The first section of this article was published under the title "Russia and the Western Powers" in *The Eastern Question.* p. 209

169 Nesselrode's Note of July 2, 1853 and the reply of the French Foreign Minister Drouyn de Lhuys sent on July 15, 1853 (see Note 165) contained mutual accusations of the French and Russian governments of provoking a conflict. Nesselrode asserted that Britain and France had been the first to demonstrate hostility by sending their squadrons to the Straits before the Russian army entered the Danubian Principalities. Drouyn de Lhuys' Note laid the whole responsibility for the conflict on Russia. p. 209

170 A reference to the conspiracy against the Sultan Abdul Mejid organised by opponents of the policy of reforms (tansimat). The foundation of this policy was laid by Abdul Mejid's rescript of 1839, which proclaimed the introduction of certain changes, e.g. reform of the taxation system, a guarantee of the inviolability of life and property, and some others. Despite the highly limited nature of these reforms, they were violently opposed by reactionaries grouped around the Sultan's brother Abdul Aziz. p. 211

171 A reference to the proclamation issued by Gorchakov, the commander of the Russian army on the Danube, to the inhabitants of Moldavia and Wallachia in the summer of 1853 and published in *The Times,* No. 21477, July 11, 1853. The proclamation declared that the object of the Russian army's entry into the Danubian Principalities was not to change the political institutions and the order guaranteed for the Principalities by former treaties. p. 211

172 The *Zemindari* and *Ryotwari systems*—two systems of land taxation introduced by the British colonial authorities. The Zemindari system was introduced in Bengal and then in other provinces in North-Eastern and Central India at the end of the eighteenth century. The Ryotwari system was established in the Madras Presidency (first in two districts in 1792, and then throughout the region in 1818-23) and in the Presidency of Bombay (1818-28). In both cases the colonial power was recognised as the supreme owner of the land. Under the Zemindari system the tax from the agricultural population was collected, in return for a certain share, by zemindars, hereditary tax-collectors, who formed a new stratum of feudal landowners. To help them perform this function they enlisted the services of agricultural middlemen of lower rank. Under the Ryotwari system the Indian peasants, the ryots, were directly dependent on the East India Company, to whom they paid tax. The tax was collected by company officials and its rate depended on the harvest. p. 214

173 *Collector*—the British chief official of a district in India who acted as a magistrate and collected taxes. p. 214

174 *Mahrattas* (Marathas)—a people who lived in the North-Western Deccan. In the mid-seventeenth century they began an armed struggle against the Empire of the Great Moguls, thus contributing to its decline. In the course of the struggle the Mahrattas formed an independent state of their own, whose rulers soon embarked on wars of conquest. At the close of the seventeenth century their state was weakened by internal feudal strife, but early in the eighteenth century a powerful confederation of Mahratta principalities was formed under a supreme governor, the peshwa. In 1761 they suffered a crushing defeat at the hands of the Afghans in the struggle for supremacy in India. Weakened by this struggle and internal feudal strife, the Mahratta principalities fell prey to the East India Company and were subjected by it as a result of the Anglo-Mahratta war of 1803-05. p. 217

175 See Note 172. p. 218

176 *Jats*—a caste group in Northern India which consisted mainly of peasants, but also included the military. In the seventeenth century the Jat peasants repeatedly rose in revolt against the rule of the Mogul feudals. p. 221

177 *Brahmins*—one of the four ancient Indian castes which originally consisted mainly of privileged priests; like other Indian castes, it subsequently also contained people of different trades and social standing, including impoverished peasants and artisans. p. 221

178 *Rajah*—title of the Indian princes. In the Middle Ages it was given to Hindu feudal lords and in British India to certain big landowners. p. 221

179 The *temple of Juggernaut* in Orissa (Eastern India)—the centre of worship of Vishnu-Juggernaut, one of the chief Hindu deities (see Note 105). The priests of the temple, who were under the protection of the East India Company, obtained vast sums of money from mass pilgrimages, while encouraging the temple women to engage in prostitution, and from organising sumptuous festivals which were accompanied by the suicide and self-torture of fanatic believers. p. 222

180 The final section of this article was published under the title "Traditional Policy of Russia" in *The Eastern Question.* p. 223

181 See Note 47. p. 223

182 Marx ironically compares the adherents of lowering cabmen's payment to sixpence per mile with a leading figure of the English revolution in the seventeenth century, John Hampden, who was tried in 1637 for refusal to pay the King's tax-collectors "ship money", a tax which had not been authorised by the House of Commons. p. 224

183 *Mons Sacer*—a sacred mountain where, as the legend goes, plebeians retired in protest against patrician oppression in 494 B.C. p. 225

184 See Note 63. p. 226

185 Jonathan Swift bequeathed all his fortune for the building of a lunatic asylum in Dublin. The asylum was opened in 1757. p. 226

186 On April 10, 1848, a Chartist demonstration was organised in London to present the Chartist petition to Parliament. The government banned the demonstration and troops and police were brought to London to prevent it. The Chartist leaders, many of whom vacillated, decided to call off the demonstration and persuaded the participants to disperse. This failure was used by reactionary forces to launch an offensive against the workers and repress the Chartists. p. 226

187 A reference to amendments to the Danish Constitution of June 5, 1849 to give more powers to the Crown, drafted in 1853. The new Constitution was promulgated on October 2, 1855.

Lex Regia—the law of Danish succession promulgated on November 14, 1665 by King Frederick III of Denmark extended to women the right of succeeding to the throne. Under the London Protocol of May 8, 1852 (see Note 58) and the new law of succession of July 31, 1853 this right was abolished. Thus, Duke Christian of Glücksburg was proclaimed successor to King Frederick VII as the latter had no heir. The new law indirectly confirmed the right of members of the Russian imperial dynasty to succeed to the Danish throne. p. 227

188 See Note 91. p. 229

189 See Note 30. p. 230

190 In his "political testament" (1633) Richelieu expounded the principles of the domestic and foreign policy of French absolutism, in an attempt to substantiate its claims for an extension of France's boundaries and French hegemony in Europe.

Capitularies—the name given from the time of Charlemagne (768-814) to the collections of ordinances of the Frankish kings of the Carolingian dynasty; some of them dealt with the administration of the conquered lands. p. 230

191 At the end of the eleventh century a Turkish feudal state sprang up in the east of Asia Minor as a result of its conquest by the Ogyz Turks. Its capital was the town of Iconium (Konia). The Iconian Sultanate under the ruling Seljukian dynasty waged a struggle against Byzantium and the crusaders. In the second half of the thirteenth century under the impact of the Mongolian invaders it disintegrated into independent principalities. One of them, headed by the tribal chief Osman, was situated in the north-west of Anatolia and bordered on Byzantium. It became the nucleus of the newly formed Turkish state—the Ottoman (Osman) Empire. In the fourteenth century the new state included the old possessions of the Iconian sultans and the conquered territories of the neighbouring countries. In 1453 under Mehemed II the Osman Turks captured Constantinople, the last stronghold of the Byzantine emperors, and turned it into the capital of the Ottoman Empire. p. 231

[192] The New York *Crystal Palace* was built for the World Industrial Exhibition of 1853. It was opened on July 15; later it was used to house various exhibitions. It was destroyed by fire in 1856. p. 232

[193] This article, entitled "The Press on Eastern Affairs.—Notes of England and Russia", was published in abridged form in *The Eastern Question.* p. 233

[194] See Note 129. p. 234

[195] On July 24, 1853 a conference of the representative of Austria and the ambassadors of Britain, France and Prussia on mediation between Russia and Turkey was opened in Vienna. It drafted a conciliatory Note (the so-called Vienna Note) which laid down that Turkey observe the Kuchuk Kainarji and Adrianople treaties and respect the rights and privileges of the Greek Orthodox Church. The conference ruled that the Note be sent first to the Tsar and, in the event of his approval, to the Sultan.

Nicholas I approved the Note, but Abdul Mejid made his agreement to sign it conditional on the insertion of a number of amendments and reservations, which the Tsarist Government thought unacceptable. p. 234

[196] *Odnodvortsi*—a special group of state peasants in the Russian Empire formed from the lower ranks of the servicemen (*sluzhiliye lyudi*) who had originally performed the service of guarding the outlying areas of the State of Muscovy, where they settled in separate households and were soldiers and farmers at one and the same time. p. 236

[197] *Eidermen* or *Eider Danes*—the Danish liberal party of the middle of the nineteenth century whose members supported the union of Schleswig (up to the River Eider) with Denmark. The party favoured the separation of Denmark and Holstein, where the population consisted mainly of Germans; it shared the Danish bourgeoisie's fear of the competition of Holstein's industry. Therefore the Eider Danes opposed any Danish succession law which applied to all parts of the Kingdom of Denmark. p. 237

[198] A reference to a party which was founded in Denmark in 1846. It demanded the transfer of lands which peasants used as feudal tenants into their private ownership, and also the abolition of feudal obligations and the introduction of universal suffrage and other reforms in the interests of the wealthy peasants. p. 237

[199] See Note 58. p. 237

[200] See Note 187. p. 237

[201] This article, excluding the section "Advertisement Duty", was published under the title "Russian Movements.—Denmark.—United States and Europe" in *The Eastern Question.* p. 239

202 See Note 116. p. 239

203 See Note 187. p. 241

204 A reference to the law excluding succession by the female line, which existed in a number of West-European monarchies. This was based on Salic law (Lex Salica), the law of the Salian Franks, which dated back to the sixth century. Chapter LIX of the Lex Salica allowed succession by the male line only. p. 242

205 See Note 86. p. 242

206 The *Treaty of Westphalia of 1648* ended the European Thirty Years' War (1618-48) in which the Pope, the Spanish and Austrian Habsburgs and the Catholic German princes fought the Protestant countries of Bohemia, Denmark, Sweden, the Netherlands and a number of German Protestant states. The rulers of Catholic France—rivals of the Habsburgs—supported the Protestant camp. The treaty as a whole sealed the victory of the anti-Habsburg coalition, promoted the establishment of France's hegemony in Europe and added to the political disunity of Germany. Under the terms of the Treaty of Westphalia the Swiss Confederation was recognised as an independent state. p. 244

207 The first section of the article was published under the title "To Withdraw or Not to Withdraw" in *The Eastern Question.* p. 245

208 An ironical allusion by Marx to the methods used by Louis Bonaparte and his entourage in preparing the coup d'état of December 2, 1851, when they were trying to win the support of officers and soldiers. During the receptions and after the military parades organised by Louis Bonaparte, then President of the Republic, officers and men were usually treated to sausage-meat, cold fowl, champagne, etc. p. 245

209 Marx is summing up his comments (see pp. 209, 228, 234-35 and 240) on the attempts of the Western powers at mediation in the Turkish conflict at the conference of diplomats in Vienna in the last decade of July 1853 and on its conciliatory Note (see Note 195). However, it is highly probable that this refers to an article mailed to the *New-York Daily Tribune* between August 5 and 12, 1853, which was either lost on the way to New York or was not published due to reasons unknown. p. 246

210 See Note 110. p. 249

211 The *Encumbered Estates Act* was adopted by the Irish Parliament in 1849 and was later supplemented by the Acts of 1852-53 and others. This Act provided for the sale of mortgaged estates by auction if their owners were proved to be insolvent. It resulted in the lands of ruined landlords passing into the hands of usurers, middlemen and rich tenants. p. 251

212 By a tradition dating back to the Middle Ages the members of the House of Lords are obliged to swear a solemn oath (the oath of allegiance) to the Crown. At the same time the medieval Magna Carta Libertatum (1215) gave English feudal lords the right to revolt against the throne in cases of infringement of their feudal privileges. p. 251

213 A reference to Britain's support of the Portuguese branch of the Coburg dynasty during the popular uprising of 1846-47. The uprising was brutally suppressed. p. 254

214 This article was published under the same title in *The Eastern Question.* p. 257

215 This article has not been found. p. 257

216 A reference to Nesselrode's circular letters of June 11 and July 2, 1853 (see Notes 136 and 165). p. 258

217 In 1852 a conflict arose between Turkey and Montenegro, which demanded complete independence of the Sultan, whose vassal it remained nominally. The Porte rejected Russia's mediation on this issue, and at the beginning of 1853 the Turkish army under the command of Omer Pasha invaded Montenegro. The Austrian Government feared that if Russia entered the war to defend the Montenegrins that would cause unrest in the Slav regions of the Habsburg Empire, so it hastily dispatched Count Leiningen on a special mission to Constantinople (Marx mentions this mission below) to demand the withdrawal of Turkish troops from Montenegro and the restoration of the status quo. The concentration of Austrian troops on the Montenegrin border compelled the Porte to accept these demands. p. 261

218 This article was published under the same title in *The Eastern Question.* p. 265

219 Together with a draft Russo-Turkish agreement which recognised the Tsar as the protector of Orthodox Christians in Turkey, Prince Menshikov proposed that the Turkish Government should sign a secret document on a defence alliance which would provide for Russian military assistance to the Sultan in the event of a third power attempting to violate the above-mentioned agreement on the privileges of the Greek Orthodox Church in Turkey. The Turkish Government, supported by the British and French Ambassadors to Constantinople, rejected the draft agreement and the secret defence treaty. p. 266

220 A reference to the reply of the Turkish Foreign Minister Reshid Pasha of June 16, 1853 to Chancellor Nesselrode's letter of May 31, 1853 (see Note 119). In his reply Reshid Pasha rejected Nesselrode's ultimatum. At the same time he wrote that the Porte was willing to send a special mission to St. Petersburg to settle the dispute in such a way that the rights of the Greek Orthodox Church in Turkey could be confirmed without damage to the Sultan's sovereignty. p. 267

221 In 1839 the Serbian Prince Miloš Obrenović, whose attempts to establish autocratic rule were firmly opposed by the commercial bourgeoisie, was

compelled to abdicate. However, his successor Mihailo Obrenović strove to continue his father's policy. In August 1842 the so-called defenders of the statute, who supported a moderate Constitution and bourgeois reforms, revolted against him and proclaimed Alexander Karageorgević Prince of Serbia. In effect a regime of the merchant oligarchy was established, the representatives of which (Garašanin and others) made plans for uniting the lands of the Southern Slavs under Serbia. p. 269

222 See Note 116. p. 269

223 *Navigation Acts* were passed in Britain to protect British shipping against foreign competition. The best known was that of 1651, directed mainly against the Dutch, who controlled most of the sea trade. It prohibited the importation of any goods not carried by British ships or the ships of the country where the goods were produced, and laid down that British coasting trade and commerce with the colonies were to be carried on only by British ships. The Navigation Acts were modified in the early nineteenth century and repealed in 1849 except for a reservation regarding coasting trade, which was revoked in 1854. p. 275

224 The first section of this article was published under the same title in *The Eastern Question.* p. 277

225 The aristocratic wing of the Polish emigration centred around Prince Adam Czartoryski who resided in the Hôtel Lambert in Paris. Polish aristocratic émigrés also lived in Britain and other countries. Polish patriots organised a national liberation uprising in the Cracow Republic which, by a decision of the Vienna Congress, was controlled jointly by Austria, Russia and Prussia—the countries who had taken part in the partitions of Poland at the end of the eighteenth century. On February 22, 1846 the insurgents managed to take power, formed a National Government of the Polish Republic and issued a manifesto on the abolition of feudal obligations. The Cracow uprising was suppressed in early March 1846, and in November 1846 Austria, Prussia and Russia signed a treaty on the annexation of the free city of Cracow to the Austrian Empire. Palmerston, who became Foreign Secretary in July 1846, rejected the French proposal for a collective protest against this action and in a letter of November 23, 1846 notified the Vienna Cabinet that Britain would not defend the Cracow Republic, while hypocritically calling on Austria, Prussia and Russia to renounce their intentions with regard to Cracow. p. 280

226 See Note 48. p. 281

227 A reference to an agreement reached between the Peelites, the Whigs and the so-called Mayfair Radicals (see Note 64) who met at the private residence of Lord John Russell in Chesham Place, London, in the spring of 1852. The agreement provided for joint opposition to Derby's Tory Cabinet and also the formation of a Coalition Ministry in case of its resignation. It remained in force until December 1852 when the Aberdeen Coalition Ministry was formed. The key posts in the new Ministry were held by the Whig and Peelite leaders, while the

representatives of the Mayfair Radicals were given a number of administrative appointments. p. 281

228 See Note 48. p. 282

229 On August 23, 1853 *The Morning Advertiser* published a note under the heading "The Russian Agent Bakunin" signed with the initials F. M. (the author was Francis Marx, an English conservative journalist, and supporter of Urquhart); it accused Bakunin of being connected with the Tsarist Government. On the following day, August 24, the paper published a letter by Golovin (the author of the anonymous article on Bakunin in *The Morning Advertiser* for August 14 which prompted F. M.'s note), Herzen and the Polish refugee Worcell refuting F. M.'s note. On August 27 the latter replied with a statement in which he said that revolutions in Europe were always fomented by Tsarist agents. On August 29 Golovin and Herzen published another letter entitled "Who Is F. M.?" Herzen abstained from further polemic on the subject, which was carried on by Golovin alone.

In the letter of August 24 a "certain German newspaper" was mentioned, in which Bakunin had allegedly been first accused. The authors of the letter hinted at the *Neue Rheinische Zeitung.* In this connection Marx decided to send his letter to the editor of *The Morning Advertiser.* p. 284

230 From May 3 to 9, 1849 Dresden, the capital of Saxony, was the scene of an armed uprising caused by the refusal of the King of Saxony to approve the Imperial Constitution drafted by the Frankfurt National Assembly. The insurgents, among whom the workers played a prominent part in barricade fighting, gained control of a considerable section of the town and formed a provisional government headed by the radical democrat Samuel Tzschirner. An active part in the uprising was played by Mikhail Bakunin, the Russian revolutionary, Stephan Born, a workers' leader, and Richard Wagner, the composer. The uprising was suppressed by Saxon and Prussian troops. p. 286

231 In all probability the editors of the *New-York Daily Tribune* omitted the part of the article concerning the Russo-Turkish conflict. In his next newspaper report of September 9, 1853, Marx refers to the passage in his article written on August 30, 1853 (i.e., this article) in which he wrote about the actual rejection of the Vienna Note; this passage is not given in the text included in the present publication. The comparatively short length of the article testifies to the fact that it was abridged. The editors may have had other material at hand on the subject (Ferenc Pulszky's article) ready for publication in the same number (September 15, 1853). It is also possible that the omitted part was used by the editors for the leader which read, in part, as follows: "The news from Europe would seem to leave the Eastern question as far from actual settlement as ever. The Czar had accepted the Vienna propositions on the express condition that the Sultan should make no modification in them, and without any stipulation as to the withdrawal of his troops from the Turkish dominions. The Porte has, however, made some modifications in these proposals, and one or two of them are sufficiently shrewd and important, as our reader may see by reference to another column. Now it remains to be seen whether the Czar will allow these changes, or will go to war. To us it is by no means certain that he will not, after sufficient time for consideration, and after the season for naval operations has fully passed, reply that he can submit to no such indignities, and that he will now proceed to take further guarantees by

annexing as much of Turkey as he may judge proper. We are no believers in a long maintenance of peace, and shall admit there has been a settlement of the Turkish question only when the papers have been signed on both sides, and the Russian army marched back to its own side of the Pruth" (*New-York Daily Tribune*, No. 3873, September 15, 1853). p. 287

232 See Note 223. p. 288

233 The text of the declaration of the Seamen's United Friendly Association, which may have been quoted by Marx from a leaflet, was published later in *The People's Paper*, No. 80, November 12, 1853. p. 289

234 Marx's statement to the editor of *The People's Paper* was written in connection with the anonymous article (by Golovin) "How to Write History", published in *The Morning Advertiser* on September 3, 1853. This article, which attacked Marx, was a reply to Marx's letter to the editor of *The Morning Advertiser* of August 30, 1853 (see this volume, pp. 284-86).

On August 31 *The Morning Advertiser* published Arnold Ruge's letter in which Marx and the *Neue Rheinische Zeitung* were openly accused of slandering Bakunin. In his reply to Golovin Marx also exposed Ruge's false arguments. Details connected with this statement are given by Marx in his letter to Engels of September 3, 1853, in which he also includes the first draft of his reply. On September 7, 1853 Marx wrote to Engels that he had sent his reply to *The People's Paper* because the editors of *The Morning Advertiser* had refused to publish it.

In October the editors of *The Morning Advertiser* announced that the matter was closed. p. 290

235 A reference to the Convention decrees adopted in 1793 (spring-autumn) at the height of the struggle against counter-revolutionary conspiracies and revolts. The law on suspects (*lois des suspects*), promulgated on September 17, 1793, provided for the arrest of all persons "who by their conduct or their connections, their talks or writings proved to be adherents of tyranny". p. 291

236 This article was published in the *New-York Daily Tribune* unsigned and without a title. In selecting a title for it the editors of the present edition had regard to the entry "9. September. Kritik des Peel acts etc. Schumla Briefe" in Marx's notebook.

The first two sections of this article were published under the title "The Vienna Note" in *The Eastern Question*. p. 292

237 This part of the article mentioned was omitted by the editors of the *New-York Daily Tribune* (see Note 231). p. 292

238 The Bank Act of 1844 passed by Peel's government established the maximum quantity of bank-notes in circulation guaranteed by definite reserve funds of gold and silver. The additional issue of bank-notes was allowed only if precious metal reserves were increased proportionally. The Act was violated several times by the government itself, in particular, during the monetary crises of 1847 and 1857. Besides this article, Marx gave an analysis of the meaning and significance of the

1844 Act in a series of articles written in 1857-58 for the *New-York Daily Tribune* (see present edition, Vols. 15 and 16). A detailed description of the Act is given in Marx's *Capital*, Vol. III, Ch. XXIV. p. 296

239 See Note 165. p. 302

240 A reference to the closure of the Capuchin monastery in Locarno in the autumn of 1852 and the expulsion of 22 Italian-born Capuchins from Ticino to Lombardy. The actions of the Swiss authorities against the Capuchin Order, which enjoyed Austrian protection, aggravated Austro-Swiss relations, which were further strained by the fact that participants in the Italian national liberation movement resided on Swiss territory. p. 302

241 See Note 19. p. 302

242 Th. Carlyle, *Latter-Day Pamphlets,* No. II, *Model Prisons*, London, 1850. A critical analysis of this work was given in one of the reviews published by Marx and Engels in the fourth issue of the journal *Neue Rheinische Zeitung. Politisch-ökonomische Revue*, 1850 (see present edition, Vol. 10, pp. 301-09). p. 303

243 The first section of this article concerning the Russo-Turkish conflict was published under the title "The Vienna Note (continued)" in *The Eastern Question.* p. 309

244 A reference to the London Convention of July 15, 1840 signed by Britain, Austria, Prussia and Russia on support to the Turkish Sultan against the Egyptian ruler Mehemet Ali, and also to the London Convention of 1841 (see Note 117) and the Balta-Liman Convention of 1849 (see Note 116). France, which supported Mehemet Ali, did not sign the first Convention, but the threat of an anti-French coalition made it deny its support to the Egyptian ruler and take part in the drawing up of the London Convention of 1841. Besides the clauses on armed intervention in the Turko-Egyptian conflict and an ultimatum to Mehemet Ali to give up all his possessions except Egypt to the Sultan, the 1840 Convention had a clause on the joint protection of the Straits, which served as a prerequisite for the stipulation in the 1841 Convention that the Straits should be closed to men-of-war of all states. p. 312

245 In response to Marx's request Engels sent him material on the economic situation in Lancashire and other industrial regions of England which Marx used in this and the following article. Marx wrote about it in his letter to Engels of September 28, 1853 (see present edition, Vol. 39).

The first section of this article was published under the title "The English Ministry Outwitted.—Panic" in *The Eastern Question.* p. 318

246 The *ulema* (*ulama*)—a body of the theologians and legalists of Islam; it provided teachers for the mosques and schools, supervised law and the courts and had a great influence on the political life of the Turkish Empire. p. 325

247 A reference to a strike of engineering workers that started in late December 1851 and involved several towns in South-East and Central England. The strike was organised by the Amalgamated Society of Engineers with the aim of abolishing overtime and improving working conditions. The employers responded with a

lockout. After three months' struggle the workers lost and were compelled to resume work on former terms. The employers suffered considerable material losses, however, as a result of the strike and lockout. p. 326

248 On the use of Engels' material in this article see Note 245.

In selecting a title for the article the editors of the present edition made use of the entry in Marx's notebook: "Dienstag. 27. September. Turkey. Strikes. Manchester Geschichte."An abridged translation into German was published in *Die Reform* under the title "Der Stand der Arbeiterbewegung in England".

An excerpt from the first section of the article together with the beginning of the following article: "The Russians in Turkey", was published under the title "The English Ministry Outwitted.—Panic" in *The Eastern Question.* p. 329

249 In the latter period Marx and Engels substituted the more precise terms "value of labour power" and "price of labour power" for "value of labour" and "price of labour" as Marx concluded that the worker sells the capitalist his labour power and not his labour (see F. Engels, Introduction to a separate edition of Marx's "Wage Labour and Capital" of 1891, present edition, Vol. 28). p. 333

250 This article was the first in a series in the *New-York Daily Tribune* on the preparation and course of the Crimean war. (Turkey declared war on Russia at the beginning of October 1853.) The articles were written by Engels, who gave a systematic account of the campaign drawing on available information, mostly from the West-European press. Many articles were published unsigned by the newspaper editors, as leaders.

The beginning of this article was combined with part of the first section of the article "Panic on the London Stock Exchange.—Strikes" and published under the title "The English Ministry Outwitted.— Panic" in *The Eastern Question.* p. 335

251 A reference to the leader "Russian Designs in Turkey" published in the *New-York Daily Tribune* on September 17, 1853. The reference would appear to have been inserted by the newspaper editors. p. 336

252 A reference to the Turkish military expedition under Omer Pasha to Kurdistan in 1846 to suppress an uprising against the Sultan. On the expedition of Omer Pasha to Montenegro see Note 217. p. 336

253 See Note 8. p. 338

254 Alexander Suvorov took part in the siege of Ochakov but not in the storming of it on December 17, 1788 due to a wound received during the siege and also to disagreement with the commander-in-chief of the Russian army, Prince Potemkin, as to the conduct of the siege. On December 22, 1790 the Russian army commanded by Suvorov took the Turkish fortress of Izmail by storm and this contributed greatly to the victory of the Russians in the Russo-Turkish war of 1787-91. p. 339

255 The capture of Warsaw by Russian troops on September 8, 1831 was one of the

final acts of Tsarist Russia, which together with Prussia and Austria suppressed the Polish national liberation insurrection of 1830-31. The majority of its participants were revolutionary nobles (the *szlachcics*) and most of its leaders came from the ranks of the aristocracy. In spite of its defeat, it was of major international significance because it diverted the forces of counter-revolution and thwarted their plans regarding the bourgeois revolution of 1830 in France and the 1830-31 revolution in Belgium. p. 339

256 The pamphlet *Lord Palmerston* was planned by Marx as a series of articles for the *New-York Daily Tribune.* When he started working on it in early October 1853 Marx gave his consent to its simultaneous publication in the Chartist *People's Paper.* However, whereas the Chartist paper started publishing Marx's articles as a series entitled "Lord Palmerston" and prefaced each article with the editorial note: "Written for the *New-York Tribune* by Dr. Marx, and communicated by him to us", the editors of the *Tribune* published the first article as a leader without mentioning the author's name. This determined the subsequent publication of the work as articles outwardly not connected with each other. Eight articles appeared in *The People's Paper* between October 22 and December 24, 1853, and the last, like the preceding ones, ended with the words: "To be continued". As can be seen from Marx's letter to Engels of December 14, 1853, Marx intended to write additional articles on Palmerston's policy in 1840-41, when the London Conventions were concluded, and also to analyse Palmerston's stand during the 1848-49 revolutions. However, these plans were not realised.

The *New-York Daily Tribune* did not publish all of Marx's articles and its final publication was at the beginning of 1854, although Marx dispatched the last article to New York as early as December 6, 1853. In all, the newspaper published four articles as leaders and under different titles. On October 19, 1853, the *Tribune* published the leader "Palmerston" which corresponded to the first and second articles published in *The People's Paper*; on November 4, 1853, the leader "Palmerston and Russia" corresponding to the third article of the series; on November 21, 1853, the leader "A Chapter of Modern History" corresponding to the fourth and fifth articles; and on January 11, 1854, the leader "England and Russia" corresponding to the seventh article. The first three leaders were also reprinted in the *New-York Weekly Tribune* on October 22, November 12 and December 3, 1853. The sixth and eighth articles of the series were never published by the *Tribune* and in its special issues. The texts of the articles in *The People's Paper* and the *New-York Daily Tribune* are not identical. When Marx sent his articles to the *Tribune* and *The People's Paper* he evidently modified them in accordance with the different form of publication in these newspapers. There are also signs that the *Tribune* editors altered Marx's text.

The pamphlet against Palmerston was widely circulated. On November 26, 1853, the *Glasgow Sentinel* reprinted from the *Tribune* the article "Palmerston and Russia" (the third of the *People's Paper* series). In December 1853 the London publisher Tucker published this article under the same title in pamphlet form. (Marx mentions this edition in his article "Palmerston's Resignation", see this volume, p. 546). At the beginning of February 1854 a second edition of this pamphlet was put out with Marx's participation: Marx made some amendments and additions on the basis of the *People's Paper* publication.

Shortly afterwards Tucker published another pamphlet, *Palmerston and the Treaty of Unkiar Skelessi* (the title-page bearing the title: "Palmerston, What Has He Done?"); with slight amendments the pamphlet reproduced the text of the fourth (excluding the first four paragraphs) and the fifth articles of the *People's Paper* series. Both pamphlets were included as Nos. 1 and 2 in the *Political Fly-Sheets* series published by Tucker, and in the first half of 1855 they were again reprinted together with pamphlets by other authors. Tucker mentioned Marx's name in the preface to that edition as the author of pamphlets Nos. 1 and 2 (in the table of contents pamphlet No. 1 was entitled differently: "Palmerston and Poland"). Marx himself prevented the rest of his articles from being published in Tucker's edition because Urquhart's articles had also been published in the *Political Fly-Sheets* series. On this score Marx wrote to Lassalle on June 1, 1854: "I have no desire to be numbered among the associates of this gentleman; the estimation of Palmerston is the only point we have in common. In the rest I have a diametrically opposite point of view. This became evident during our first meeting."

On November 17, 1855 and January 5, 1856, the Urquhart *Sheffield Free Press*, which was in opposition to Palmerston, published two of Marx's articles (the third and the sixth from the *People's Paper* publication). The first of them was also reprinted as No. 4a of *The Free Press Serials* published in Sheffield. Almost simultaneously all eight articles of the series appeared in the five issues (Nos. 12, 13, 14, 18 and 19 of December 29, 1855, January 5 and 12 and February 9 and 16, 1856) of the London Urquhart *Free Press* and were published as No. 5 of *The Free Press Serials* entitled "The Story of the Life of Lord Palmerston". The author's name was mentioned in the editorial introduction to this edition.

An abridged translation of the *Tribune* text into German by Adolph Cluss was printed in New York in *Die Reform* as early as November 2, 1853. The publishers' note to it stated the following: "The great interest aroused by Palmerston's name at the present time has induced us to print this rendering from the *Tribune*. The essay reveals a more than average knowledge of British affairs by the author, and though it bears no signature it is easy to tell who the author is." The article "Palmerston", published in instalments in *Die Reform* on November 2, 3, 4, 8 and 9, corresponds to the first and second articles in the *People's Paper* series. In February 1855 Marx published two articles entitled "Lord Palmerston" in the Breslau (Wrocław) *Neue Oder-Zeitung* which were in the main a summary of the *People's Paper* and the *Tribune* publications. Excerpts from Marx's pamphlet (his name was mentioned in the editors' note) were published in Berlin in 1859-60 by the German journalist E. Fischel in *Das Neue Portfolio. Eine Sammlung wichtiger Dokumente und Aktenstücke zur Zeitgeschichte,* Hefte 1-2, under the title "Der 'wahrhaft' englische Minister und Russland am Bosporus. Lord Palmerston und die polnische Insurrection 1831".

In 1893, after Marx's death, the third article of the series appeared in Polish in the seventh issue of the journal *Przedświt*, published in London by Polish socialists connected with Engels. The seventh article was reprinted from the *Tribune* under the same title, "England and Russia", in the collection: Karl Marx, *The Eastern Question*, London, 1897. In 1899 a separate edition of all the articles of the series: Karl Marx, *The Story of the Life of Lord Palmerston*, was published in London. It was prepared by Eleanor Marx and reproduced the London *Free Press* series.

In his work on the pamphlet Marx used a great deal of material, in particular, the Blue Books, periodical publications of British parliamentary and Foreign Office documents. In addition he drew on parliamentary reports, various collections of international treaties and diplomatic documents, satirical pamphlets and the press. Several notebooks with excerpts made by Marx from various books are extant. These books include: *The Russians in Moldavia and Wallachia*, London, 1849; Heinrich Brandt, *Russlands Politik und Heer in den letzten Jahren*, Berlin, 1852; *The Greek and Eastern Churches. Their History, Faith, and Worship*, London, 1852; J. M. Neale, *Introduction to the History of the Holy Eastern Church*, London,

1851; V. Krasinski, *Sketch of the Religious History of the Slavonic Nations*, Edinburgh, 1851; A. Theiner, *Die Staatskirche Russlands im Jahre 1839*, Schaffhausen, 1844; D. Urquhart, *Progress of Russia in the West, North, and South*, London, 1853, *Reasons for Demanding Investigation into the Charges Against Lord Palmerston*, Glasgow, 1840, *An Appeal Against Faction*, London, 1843, and *La Crise*, Paris, 1840; G. Francis, *Opinions and Policy of Palmerston*, London, 1852. Marx used the last book as well as *Hansard* when citing from Palmerston's speeches. (The sources of quotations are given in the Index of Quoted and Mentioned Literature.)

In this volume the text of the pamphlet is reproduced according to *The People's Paper*. The main differences between the *People's Paper* text and that of the *New-York Daily Tribune* are given in footnotes. Misprints which occurred in *The People's Paper* are corrected on the basis of later authorised editions and factual data. p. 341

257 *Carbonari*—members of bourgeois and aristocratic revolutionary secret societies which appeared in Italy in the early nineteenth century. They fought for national independence and unification of Italy and at the same time demanded liberal-constitutional reforms. The Carbonari played an important role in the revolutionary developments in the kingdoms of Naples and Sardinia early in the 1820s and also during the revolutionary struggle in Italy against Austrian rule and local feudal monarchies in the 1830s. p. 347

258 In the course of the parliamentary debates in June 1850 on the Anglo-Greek conflict connected with the Pacifico incident (see Note 148) the government's foreign policy was approved by the House of Commons; the House of Lords, however, rejected by a majority of 37 the stand taken by the Foreign Secretary Palmerston on this issue. France and Russia also disapproved of this stand; as a sign of protest the French Ambassador left London and the Russian Ambassador refused Palmerston's invitation to dinner. p. 347

259 In 1815 a law was passed prohibiting grain imports when grain prices in England fell below 80 shillings per quarter. In 1822 the law was modified slightly and in 1828 a sliding scale was introduced—a system of raising or lowering tariffs in proportion to the fall or rise of grain prices on the home market. The Corn Laws were introduced by Tory cabinets in the interests of the big landowners. The industrial bourgeoisie who opposed the Corn Laws under the slogan of free trade secured their repeal in 1846. p. 348

260 Marx has in mind the presence of foreign mercenaries in Britain, who were recruited by the British army during the Napoleonic wars mostly from small German states, in particular Hanover, the ancestral land of the British kings of the Hanover dynasty. p. 348

261 A reference to the bombardment of Copenhagen by the British in September 1807 with the aim of preventing Denmark from joining the continental blockade inaugurated by Napoleon, which forbade the countries of the Continent to trade with Britain. p. 348

262 A *Mutiny Act* was passed annually by Parliament from 1689 to 1881. By this Act the Crown was invested with the authority to have a standing army and navy of

a certain strength, to introduce rules and regulations in the army and navy, to court-martial and establish a system of punishment for mutiny, disobedience of orders, breach of discipline, etc. p. 350

263 Under the *Corporation Act* passed by the British Parliament in 1661 persons who held elected posts (this applied mainly to municipal administration) were required to accept the dogmas of the Church of England.

The *Test Act* of 1673 required the same of all persons holding government posts. p. 350

264 *Dissenters*—members of Protestant sects and trends which departed from the dogmas of the official Church of England; in a broader sense those who disagree with any opinion. p. 350

265 *Catholic Emancipation*—the abolition by the British Parliament in 1829 as a result of the mass movement in Ireland of restrictions on the political rights of Catholics. Catholics were granted the right to stand for election to Parliament and to hold certain government offices. Simultaneously, the property qualification was raised fivefold. The British ruling classes hoped that this manoeuvre would bring the élite of the Irish bourgeoisie and Catholic landowners to their side and cause a split in the Irish national movement. p. 351

266 *Absentees*—landlords who owned estates in Ireland but lived permanently in England. Their estates were managed by realty agents who robbed the Irish peasants, or were leased to speculator-middlemen, who subleased small plots to the peasants. p. 351

267 A reference to the broad campaign for a Reform Bill (see Note 123) which started some years before the Bill was passed in 1832. p. 352

268 See Note 5. p. 353

269 See Note 27. p. 354

270 A reference to the London Convention of July 6, 1827 (see Note 38). p. 354

271 The *Treaty of Turkmanchai*, which ended the Russo-Persian war of 1826-28, was signed on February 22, 1828. Under this treaty Russia received the territories of the Yerevan and Nakhichevan khanates (Eastern Armenia), and Russia's exclusive right to have a navy in the Caspian Sea was confirmed. Persia was to pay war indemnities of 20 million rubles. At the same time the treaty marked a turning point in the destiny of the Armenian people who were suffering from Persian and Turkish despotism. The Persian Government was required to let Armenians leave the country freely and soon more than 40,000 people moved to the Armenian region which was joined to Russia, and to other Russian Transcaucasian territories. Turkish Armenians also moved to the region. p. 355

272 One of the points at issue in the conflict over the "Holy Places" (see Note 90) which France and Russia used as a pretext in the struggle for hegemony in the Middle East, was the question of whether the Catholic or Orthodox Church should have the keys to the Holy Sepulchre in Jerusalem and the right to take care of its dome. p. 356

273 The *Treaty of Akkerman* was signed by Russia and Turkey on October 7, 1826. Under this treaty the Turkish Government was to observe the former treaties signed with Russia, the Russian merchant fleet obtained the right to sail in Turkish waters and Russian merchants to trade throughout the whole of Turkey. The treaty confirmed the recognition of Serbian autonomy by the Sultan and provided for the election of Hospodars in Moldavia and Wallachia from the local Boyards. The Akkerman Treaty did not touch upon the Greek question. In this connection on the eve of the Russo-Turkish war of 1828-29 Turkish official circles violated the treaty and asserted that by it Russia had pledged non-interference in Greek affairs and broken this pledge by her assistance to the Greeks. However, in fact the Tsarist Government's declaration of its "disinterestedness in Greek affairs" was made several months before it signed the treaty. p. 356

274 See Note 35. p. 357

275 In the *New-York Daily Tribune* of October 19, 1853 this article was concluded with the following words, evidently added by the editors: "This was a plain way of saying he was not the representative of liberty, or honesty, or what makes the best character of England. Such as the noble lord was then, and in the earlier part of his career which we have reviewed, he is at this, and none who know him can expect at his hands any but false service to the cause of justice and human rights in the present momentous crisis. What remains of his public history we leave for another day; we are sorry to say that is not the better half." p. 358

276 The refusal of the Milanese to pay homage to Frederick I Barbarossa took place in 1159 and was prompted by Frederick's attempts to abolish the free towns in Northern Italy and subjugate them to his rule. The prolonged struggle that ensued culminated in the victory of the towns although the city of Milan was destroyed in 1162. p. 359

277 A reference to the *London Convention of July 15, 1840* (see Note 244). p. 365

278 For the *Cracow insurrection* see Note 225; for the developments in Galicia mentioned below see Note 11. p. 366

279 In 1846 the Guizot Government managed to arrange the marriage of the Spanish infanta Maria Luisa Fernanda to Louis Philippe's youngest son, the Duke of Montpensier, and thwart Britain's plans to marry Leopold of Coburg to Isabella II of Spain. The tension between the British and French

governments became very acute and after the failure of British diplomacy Palmerston sought a pretext to take revenge. p. 367

280 The *Treaty of Utrecht of 1713* was one of a series of peace treaties concluding the war of the Spanish succession which began in 1701 between France and Spain, on the one hand, and the countries of the anti-French coalition—Britain, the Netherlands, Portugal, Prussia, Savoy and Habsburg Austria—on the other; Austria did not sign the treaty and made peace with France at Rastatt in 1714. Under the terms of the treaty, Philip V, the Bourbon King of Spain and Louis XIV's grandson, kept Spain. The King of France was to renounce his right and that of his successors from the Bourbon dynasty to the Spanish Crown. Several French and Spanish possessions in the West Indies and North America, as well as Gibraltar, were obtained by Britain.

When he accused France in 1846 of violating the Treaty of Utrecht, Palmerston had in mind Louis Philippe's plans to unite the two monarchies through the marriage of his youngest son and the Spanish infanta. p. 367

281 Under the pretext of protecting French subjects in Mexico a French squadron started to blockade the Mexican ports on April 16, 1838; after the bombardment, the port of Vera Cruz was occupied on November 27-28. On March 9, 1839 Mexico was compelled to sign a treaty and an agreement with France.

The blockade of Buenos Aires and the littoral territory by the Anglo-French fleet (1845-50) was aimed at making the Argentine Government open the Paraná and Uruguay to foreign ships (they had been closed since 1841 as a result of the war between Argentina and Uruguay) and recognise Uruguay's independence. In 1850-51 these demands were accepted. p. 367

282 The relations established between Britain and France after the July revolution of 1830 and known in history as the *entente cordiale* were not confirmed by treaty until April 1834, when the so-called Quadruple Alliance was concluded between Britain, France, Spain and Portugal. But when this treaty was being concluded disagreements between Britain and France became apparent and they subsequently led to the aggravation of relations between the two countries. Formally directed against the absolutist "northern states" (Russia, Austria and Prussia), the treaty in fact allowed Britain to strengthen her position in Spain and Portugal under the pretext of rendering armed assistance to both governments in their struggle against pretenders to the throne (Don Carlos in Spain and Dom Miguel in Portugal). p. 371

283 A reference to the battle of Beilan (Syria) which took place at the end of July 1832. Egyptian troops commanded by Ibrahim Pasha defeated the Sultan's army and drove it out of Syria. The subsequent entry of Egyptian troops into Asia Minor and the defeat of the Turkish army in December 1832 at Konia (the battle is mentioned several times above) led to the victory of Egypt in the Turko-Egyptian war of 1831-33. In April 1833 under a treaty signed at Kutaiah the Egyptian Pasha Mehemet Ali was recognised as independent ruler of Egypt and Syria. p. 375

[284] The *Organic Statute of the Kingdom of Poland of 1832* was introduced by the Tsarist Government after the suppression of the Polish national liberation insurrection of 1830-31. The statute abolished the remnants of national autonomy of the Polish lands which were under Tsarist Russia's rule. It also abolished the 1815 Constitution, the Polish Diet and the Polish army; the Russian system of administration was extended to the kingdom. p. 378

[285] A reference to the Russo-Turkish Treaty of January 29, 1834 which amended certain articles of the 1829 Treaty of Adrianople. The annual payments of indemnities by Turkey under the Adrianople Treaty were curtailed, the total sum of indemnities being reduced by two million ducats. p. 380

[286] See Note 148. p. 383

[287] In the *New-York Daily Tribune* of January 11, 1854 the article began as follows: "Lord Palmerston's resignation seems to be working in England all the marvels he could have hoped from it. While the public indignation is becoming more and more active against the Cabinet he has abandoned, and whose policy he had on all occasions, up to the last moment of his connection with them, emphatically endorsed, the very parties loudest in their denunciations of the Coalition, vie with each other in the praise of Palmerston. And while they call for energetic and honorable resistance to the encroachments of Russia, on the one hand, they seem to desire nothing so much as the restoration of their favorite statesman to high office on the other. Thus this accomplished and relentless actor deludes the world. It would be an amusing spectacle were the interests involved less momentous. How deep is the delusion we have already had occasion to show, and now add below a new demonstration of the truth that, for some reason or other, Lord Palmerston has steadily labored for the advancement of Russia, and has used England for that purpose. Those who seek to look behind the scenes of current history and to judge events and men at their real value will, we think, find our exposure instructive."

These words could not be by Marx, as the last articles of the series "Lord Palmerston" were sent by him to the *New-York Daily Tribune* not later than December 6, 1853, not less than ten days prior to Palmerston's resignation (December 16, 1853). The editors of the *Tribune* delayed publication of this article until January 11, 1854, and the passage which they inserted in it may have been borrowed from another article by Marx, which he sent later (Marx's notebook gives the date December 20, 1853), on English press comments on Palmerston's resignation. The article of December 20, 1853 has not been discovered in the *New-York Daily Tribune* and the manuscript is not extant. p. 391

[288] For the *St. Petersburg Protocol of April 4, 1826* and the *London Convention of July 6, 1827* see Note 38.

Britain and Russia, who signed the Protocol, tried to conceal the real aims of their intervention in the Greco-Turkish conflict on the side of Greece and declared that they had no intention of expanding their territory at Turkey's expense, or of seeking exceptional influence or special commercial privileges in the Sultan's possessions. Similar declarations were made when Britain, Russia and France signed the London Convention of July 6, 1827. p. 392

289 This article has not been discovered in the *New-York Daily Tribune* although, according to Marx's notebook, it was posted by Marx to New York on December 6, 1853. *The People's Paper* published it on December 24, 1853 as the eighth in the "Lord Palmerston" series. p. 398

290 Marx is alluding to the so-called Potemkin villages—an expression which symbolises sham prosperity. It was said that the Empress Catherine II's favourite, Prince Potemkin, who was Governor-General of the southern provinces of Russia, built sham villages on Catherine's route to the south in 1787 to convince her that the territory entrusted to him was flourishing. p. 404

291 *Lloyd's*—a company founded in London in the seventeenth century specialising in marine insurance and shipping information. p. 406

292 A reference to the war of the mountain-dwellers of the Northern Caucasus against Tsarist Russia which began at the end of the 1820s. It was caused by the Tsarist colonisation policy and the oppressive rule of local feudal lords who were supported by the Tsarist Government. This movement was led mainly by the adherents of Muridism—a fanatical and militant trend in Islam. Using the support of the Moslem clergy and the discontent of the mountain-dwellers they were able to muster considerable forces and to set up a religious-military state headed by Shamyl in Daghestan and Chechnya in the 1830s. The war waged by Tsarist troops against Shamyl, who had captured the mountain fortresses, was very arduous and continued for decades. The Russian troops won decisive victories over Shamyl's forces after the end of the Crimean war; in 1859 Gunib, the last stronghold of the mountain-dwellers, fell. Shamyl's defeat was also due to the fact that the peasants oppressed by the local nobility which consisted of the upper stratum of Murids, deserted the movement. p. 406

293 On November 3, 1853 the *New-York Daily Tribune* (No. 3915) published a comment from Buffalo on this article. It was written in the form of a letter to the editors, entitled "Workmen's Strike in England" and signed "An Old English Factory Clerk". The writer of the letter stressed, in particular, that "every word of 'Karl Marx's' letter of the 7th inst., is true, touching the intentions of bad men, to provoke the operatives to overt acts". In their note the editors argued the importance of strikes in the struggle for the workers' economic interests, advising the latter to fight for protectionist tariffs, and concluded with "but let every one act as to him shall seem advisable".

The article, entitled "Die Lage England", was published in an abridged form in the New York newspaper *Die Reform*.

The first section of this article was published under the title "The War Question" in *The Eastern Question*. p. 407

294 A reference to Reshid Pasha's Note of August 19, 1853 to the representatives of Britain, France and Prussia, which stated that the Turkish Government would accept the Vienna Note (see Note 195) only if certain amendments and reservations were made in it, and if the Russian troops withdrew from the Danubian Principalities. p. 407

295 In September 1853 a meeting between Nicholas I and the Austrian Emperor Francis Joseph took place in Olmütz as a result of which the Austrian Government made an unsuccessful attempt to encourage the Western powers to take a new step towards settling the Russo-Turkish conflict on the basis of unconditional acceptance of the Vienna Note by the Sultan. During the talks Nicholas I sought to convince Francis Joseph that the operations of Russian troops in the Danubian Principalities would be limited to defence of the left bank of the Danube. p. 409

296 A reference to an anonymous political pamphlet published in France in 1594. It was written by supporters of religious peace closely associated with King Henry IV (Jacques Gillot, Florent Chrestien, P. Le Roy and others). The pamphlet was directed against the Catholic League (which was founded in 1576 during the Huguenot wars and operated with intervals up to 1596), whose aristocratic leaders strove to reduce the power of the monarchy and gain unrestricted privileges for the Catholic feudal nobility. The title of the pamphlet was borrowed from the Roman author Varro (lst century B.C.) who wrote his Menippean Satires in imitation of the Greek philosopher Menippus. p. 412

297 A description follows of the initial stages of the major social clash between workers and employers which is known in the history of the working-class movement as the *Preston strike.* The weavers and spinners of the textile mills in and around Preston went on strike in August 1853 demanding a ten per cent wage rise; they were supported by workers of other trades. In September of the same year the Manufacturers' Association responded with a lockout. Twenty-five thousand workers out of thirty thousand were without work. The lockout lasted until February 1854, but the strike continued after that date. To break the strike the Manufacturers' Association started bringing workers to Preston from Ireland and English workhouses. In March 1854 the leaders of the strike were arrested, and as funds were low the workers were compelled to return to work. The strike ended in May.

In his reports to the *New-York Daily Tribune* Marx wrote about different episodes of the strike; at the end of March 1854 he devoted a whole article to this event, "British Finances.—The Troubles at Preston" (see present edition, Vol. 13). p. 412

298 A reference to the heroic uprising of the Paris workers in June 1848. The uprising was the first great civil war between the proletariat and the bourgeoisie in history. p. 414

299 The first section of this article was published under the title "The Turkish Manifesto" in *The Eastern Question.* p. 416

300 *Crank*—a revolving disc which criminals sentenced to hard labour are required to turn a certain number of times each day. p. 419

301 A section of this article was published under the title "The Northern Powers" in *The Eastern Question.* p. 421

302 The so-called trial of Risquons-Tout which was held from August 9 to 30, 1848 in Antwerp was rigged by the government of the Belgian King Leopold against the

democrats. The pretext for it was a clash which took place not far from the French border near the village of Risquons-Tout on March 29, 1848, between a Belgian republican legion which was on its way home from France and a detachment of soldiers. The principal among the accused (Mellinet, Ballin, Tedesco) were sentenced to death, later commuted to thirty years imprisonment; subsequently they were pardoned.

Delescluze was at that time government commissioner of the Département du Nord, bordering on Belgium, through which the Belgian legion passed. p. 421

303 Among the entries in Marx's notebook made on October 19, 1853 there is a passage in German from the draft Constitution of Schleswig and in French from an article on the draft Constitution of Denmark published in *L'Indépendance.* p. 421

304 A reference to the fortified lines near the town of Torres Vedras (Portugal) built in 1810 on Wellington's orders to protect Lisbon from the French troops. p. 426

305 During the 1815 campaign in Belgium Napoleon hoped by defeating the Prussians at Ligny on June 16 to isolate them from Wellington's Anglo-Dutch army and rout the allied armies separately. However, when the French attacked Wellington's army and tried to outflank it at Waterloo on June 18, 1815, Prussian troops commanded by Blücher, who had evaded pursuit, joined in the battle and decided the outcome in favour of the allies. p. 427

306 This article was published under the same title in *The Eastern Question.* p. 430

307 The beginning of this article was published under the title "War" in *The Eastern Question.* p. 435

308 On October 23, 1853, during the transfer of part of the Russian Danubian fleet from Izmail to the region of Brăila and Galatz, Russian ships and gunboats passing the fort of Isakchea exchanged artillery fire with the Turkish garrison there. The garrison suffered heavy losses as a result. p. 435

309 A reference to the *Committee at rue de Poitiers*—the leading body of the so-called Party of Order which was a coalition of two monarchist factions in France: the Legitimists (supporters of the Bourbon dynasty) and the Orleanists (those of the Orleans dynasty). This party of the wealthy conservative bourgeoisie, formed in 1848, held key posts in the Legislative Assembly of the Second Republic from 1849 until the coup d'état of December 2, 1851. The failure of its policy was used by supporters of Louis Bonaparte in the Bonapartist interests. General Baraguay d'Hilliers, who supported the Committee during the Republic, sided with the Bonapartists on the eve of the coup. p. 435

310 In October 1853 a strike began in Wigan in which several thousand factory workers and miners took part. The employers responded with a lockout. At their meeting on October 28 the mine and factory owners decided to resume work on October 31 using as strikebreakers workers they had brought from Wales. On learning of this a thousand-strong crowd of strikers stoned the premises of the

meeting, the Chamber of Commerce and the houses of some employers. The workers were dispersed by troops summoned for the purpose. On October 31, the day when the mines were opened, disturbances broke out again in Wigan, with clashes between strikers and strikebreakers. The military opened fire, and some strikers were killed. p. 436

311 In August 1842, at a time of economic crisis and growing poverty, workers' strikes and disturbances started in several industrial regions of England. In Lancashire, large areas of Cheshire, Yorkshire and other counties the strikes grew into spontaneous uprisings. The government responded with mass reprisals and severe court sentences for the Chartist leaders. The bourgeoisie who shared the Free Traders' views tried to use the workers' movement to bring pressure to bear on the government to repeal the Corn Laws. In many instances they incited the workers to action. However, the bourgeoisie became alarmed at the scope of the strikes and disturbances and, convinced that the workers were pursuing their own ends, supported the brutal reprisals against them. For details see Engels' work *The Condition of the Working-Class in England* and his article "History of the English Corn Laws" (present edition, Vol. 4, pp. 520-23 and 656-61). p. 436

312 A reference to the speeches by Bright and Cobden at the conference in Edinburgh organised by the Peace Society (see Note 147). p. 437

313 The part of the article published in *Die Reform* was entitled "Persien, Russland und Dänemark (*Tribune*-Korrespondenz von Karl Marx)".

The text of the first two sections was published under the title "Persia.—Denmark" in *The Eastern Question.* p. 444

314 Persian ruling circles made several attempts to annex Herat, a trade-route junction. Afghanistan and Persia fought incessant wars for possession of the town. The capture of Herat by Persian troops in October 1856 was used by Britain to unleash war against Persia, as a result of which the Shah had to evacuate Herat. In 1863 Herat was annexed by the Afghan Emir.

In 1853 the Tsarist Government organised a military expedition to Kazakhstan up the Syr Darya. It was led by the Orenburg Governor-General V. A. Perovsky (his unsuccessful Khivan expedition of 1839-40 is mentioned below). The expedition was sent against the Kokand Khanate which had captured Kazakh lands (Marx's article mistakenly gives "Khiva"). This led to the setting up of the Syr Darya military line by the Russians, which served as a bridgehead for a subsequent offensive against the Kokand, Bukhara and Khiva khanates. p. 444

315 See Note 187. p. 444

316 See Note 198. p. 445

317 A reference to the Danish Government formed on March 22, 1848 as a result of the revolutionary upsurge in the country which found expression in mass demonstrations in the Copenhagen theatre Casino. As well as conservatives, the new government included representatives of the liberal party of Eidermen (or Eider Danes) (see Note 197). The Government took a chauvinist stand on the

national liberation movement in the duchies of Schleswig and Holstein and fought against the unification of these German regions with Germany. On the war for Schleswig-Holstein in 1848-50 see Note 86. p. 445

318 The *Anti-Corn Law League* was founded in 1838 by the Manchester factory owners Richard Cobden and John Bright. The League demanded unrestricted free trade and fought for abolition of the Corn Laws, which placed high tariffs on imported agricultural produce. In this way, the League sought to weaken the economic and political position of the landed aristocracy, as well as to cut workers' wages.

The struggle between the industrial bourgeoisie and the landed aristocracy over the Corn Laws culminated in their repeal in 1846 (see Note 259). p. 448

319 In the *battle of Jena* on October 14, 1806 the Prussian troops were defeated by Napoleon's army. This resulted in Prussia's capitulation. p. 452

320 On September 25-26, 1799 the French Army commanded by Masséna defeated the Russian corps under General Rimsky-Korsakov at Zurich. This defeat put the Russian troops commanded by Suvorov which were marching from Northern Italy to join Rimsky-Korsakov's corps in a very difficult position. However, despite the considerable numerical superiority of the enemy troops, Suvorov's army succeeded in dealing them several blows and reached the Upper Rhine region. In his work "Po and Rhine" written in 1859 Engels calls Suvorov's march over the Alps during this campaign "the most remarkable of all the Alpine crossings" (see this edition, Vol. 16). p. 455

321 This article by Engels, as can be seen from the entry in Marx's notebook, was dispatched to the *New-York Daily Tribune* together with Marx's article "The Labor Question" (see this volume, pp. 460-63) as a single report. However, the newspaper editors divided it in two parts and published Engels' text as a leader and the text written by Marx as a separate article under his signature in the issue of November 28.

From Engels' article it is evident that he had at his disposal inaccurate information on the balance of forces on the Danube during the battles of Kalafat and Oltenitza and some other facts; the Russian troops at Oltenitza were commanded by Dannenberg, not Pavlov; General Guyon and Ismail Pasha are two different people and not the same person as is stated in the article. Later when he obtained more reliable information Engels reassessed the balance of forces and also the qualities of the Turkish military command and the results of the battles of Kalafat and Oltenitza (see this volume, pp. 471-76 and 516-22). p. 457

322 On March 23, 1849 the Austrian army commanded by Radetzky inflicted a decisive defeat upon the Piedmontese army at Novara, which led to the restoration of Austrian rule in Northern Italy. In the course of the campaign the Austrian commander-in-chief made use of the dispersal of Piedmontese forces under the command of General Ramorino. p. 459

[323] See Note 321.

The fact that Marx used the material published in *The People's Paper* for November 12, 1853 in his article datelined November 11, 1853 shows that either this issue of the newspaper appeared earlier than the date which it bears or, which is more likely, Marx had access to this and other material in advance.
p. 460

[324] *Comité du Salut Public* (The Committee of Public Safety)—the central body of the revolutionary government in France during the Jacobin dictatorship (June 2, 1793-July 27, 1794).
p. 468

[325] In connection with an upsurge in the strike movement in 1853 a group of Chartists headed by Ernest Jones proposed the setting up of a broad workers' organisation "The Mass Movement" which was to unite trade unionists and unorganised workers with the primary aim of co-ordinating strikes in various parts of the country. The organisation was to be headed by a regularly convened Labour Parliament consisting of delegates elected at meetings of unorganised workers and at trade union meetings. The Labour Parliament assembled in Manchester on March 6, 1854 and was in session until March 18. It discussed and adopted the programme of the Mass Movement and set up an Executive of five members. Marx, who was elected an honorary delegate to the Parliament, sent it a letter (see this edition, Vol. 13) in which he formulated the task of creating an independent political party of the proletariat. Marx saw the convocation of the Labour Parliament as an attempt to lead the labour movement out of narrow trade unionism and to unite the economic and political struggle. Most of the trade union leaders, however, did not support the idea of creating a single mass workers' organisation. The abatement of the strike movement by the summer of 1854 also affected the campaign. The Labour Parliament was never convened after March 1854.
p. 470

[326] See Note 186.
p. 470

[327] This article published by Adolph Cluss in the New York newspaper *Die Reform* is a reproduction of Marx's comments on Urquhart that he made in the non-extant part of his letter to Cluss written in mid-November. In his letter to Joseph Weydemeyer of December 7, 1853, in which he quotes part of the above-mentioned letter (see present edition, Vol. 39), Cluss wrote: "Marx added some notes on Urquhart because Jones, in a paper I am to receive, characterises him in a tactless way as a Russian ally. Marx writes that he gave Jones a dressing down for this. I have made up a short article out of the 'Urquhartiade'." When the article was being prepared for the press Cluss evidently changed the opening sentence. The rest of Marx's text appears not to be touched by him and is authentic or nearly authentic. For his criticism of Urquhart's views Marx draws from the book: D. Urquhart, *Progress of Russia in the West, North, and South,* London, 1853. As far back as June 1853 he planned to write a special article for the *New-York Daily Tribune* devoted to a critical analysis of this book (see this volume, p. 118).
p. 477

[328] A reference to articles by the Hungarian journalist Aurelius Ferenc Pulszky, who was a supporter of Kossuth. Residing in London as a refugee, he contributed to the *New-York Daily Tribune* from 1853 to 1860. His reports were published unsigned or under the initials A. P. C. (which evidently stood for

Aurelius Pulszky's Correspondence). Marx got to know about Pulszky contributing to the *New-York Daily Tribune* much later. It is still unclear whether Marx knew that reports signed with the initials A. P. C. belonged to Pulszky. p. 478

329 Marx's pamphlet *The Knight of the Noble Consciousness* written in November 1853 and published with Adolph Cluss' and Joseph Weydemeyer's assistance in pamphlet form in New York in January 1854 was a reply to the slanderous article by August Willich, "Doktor Karl Marx und seine Enthüllungen", which was published in the *Belletristisches Journal und New-Yorker Criminal-Zeitung* on October 28 and November 4, 1853. Soon after Willich's article appeared supporters of Marx and Engels in the USA, Joseph Weydemeyer, Adolph Cluss and Abraham Jacobi, sent a refutation to the newspaper which was published on November 25, 1853. However, Marx thought it expedient to answer himself. A clipping from the *Belletristisches Journal* with Marx's underlinings, etc., is extant. In his pamphlet Marx refutes Willich's attempts to cast doubt on the fairness of Marx's criticism of the activity of the Willich-Schapper sectarian and adventurist group in his work *Revelations Concerning the Communist Trial in Cologne.* Marx included Engels' letter-statement of November 23, 1853 which he wrote at Marx's request (this letter is not otherwise extant) and also statements of revolutionary refugees who testified to the slanderous character of Willich's assertions (on this see Marx's letter to Engels of December 2, 1853, present edition, Vol. 39). Marx borrowed some passages for his pamphlet from the work *The Great Men of the Exile* which he wrote jointly with Engels in May-June 1852 but which was not published (see present edition, Vol. 11, pp. 227-326). p. 479

330 *Revelations Concerning the Communist Trial in Cologne* (see present edition, Vol. 11, pp. 395-457), which Marx wrote between late October and early December 1852, was published in pamphlet form in Basle in January 1853. Almost all its copies (2,000) were confiscated by the police in Baden while being transported from Switzerland to Germany. In the USA the work was initially reprinted in March and April in instalments in the Boston *Neu-England Zeitung*, and at the end of April 1853 it was published by this newspaper as a pamphlet. In *The Knight of the Noble Consciousness* Marx cites the *Revelations* from a separate Boston edition. p. 481

331 The editors gave the following footnote to this passage: "Mr. Blum is in Philadelphia, not in Australia, and when the American Workers' Union was formed he sat on its board as Willich's agent." p. 482

332 The *Black Bureau*—a secret institution established at postal departments in France, Prussia, Austria and several other states to inspect private correspondence. It existed at the time of absolute monarchies in Europe. p. 485

333 A reference to the Communist League, the first German and international communist organisation of the proletariat, formed under the leadership of Marx and Engels in London early in June 1847, as a result of the reorganisation of the League of the Just (a secret association of workers and

artisans that appeared in the 1830s and had communities in Germany, France, Switzerland and England). The programme and organisational principles of the Communist League were drawn up with the direct participation of Marx and Engels. The League's members took an active part in the bourgeois-democratic revolution in Germany in 1848-49. Though the defeat of the revolution dealt a blow at the League, it was reorganised in 1849-50 and continued its activities. In the summer of 1850 disagreements arose in the League between the supporters of Marx and Engels and the Willich-Schapper sectarian group which tried to impose on the League its adventurist tactics of starting a revolution immediately without taking into account the actual situation and the practical possibilities. The discord resulted in a split within the League. Owing to police persecutions and arrests of League members in May 1851, the activities of the Communist League as an organisation in Germany practically ceased. On November 17, 1852, on a motion by Marx, the London District announced the dissolution of the League.

The Communist League played an important historical role as the first proletarian party based on scientific principles of communism, as a school of proletarian revolutionaries, and as the historical forerunner of the International Working Men's Association. p. 485

334 *Synoptics*—the writers of the first three Gospels. Marx is referring to Bruno Bauer's book which points out contradictions between the different Gospel versions and also between actual historical events and the Gospels. p. 487

335 A reference to the *German Workers' Educational Society* in London which was founded in February 1840 by Karl Schapper, Joseph Moll and other leaders of the League of the Just. After the reorganisation of the League of the Just in the summer of 1847 and the founding of the Communist League (see Note 333), the League's local communities played a leading role in the Society. During various periods of its activity, the Society had branches in working-class districts in London. In 1847 and 1849-50 Marx and Engels took an active part in the Society's work, but on September 17, 1850 Marx, Engels and a number of their followers withdrew because the Willich-Schapper sectarian and adventurist faction had temporarily increased its influence in the Society, causing a split in the Communist League. In the late 1850s Marx and Engels resumed their work in the Educational Society, which existed up to 1918, when it was closed down by the British Government. p. 488

336 The tasks of these two organisations, both with small memberships and headed mainly by petty-bourgeois democrats, were to collect money for starting an "immediate revolution" in Germany. Willich and other Communist League members who belonged to his faction joined the Émigré Club. Shortly afterwards these two organisations broke up. For details on the disputes between them see: Karl Marx and Frederick Engels, *The Great Men of the Exile* (present edition, Vol. 11, pp. 227-326). p. 488

337 A reference to the attempts by Johann Gottfried Kinkel and other leaders of the Émigré Club to organise a so-called German-American revolutionary loan. To this end Kinkel went to the USA in September 1851. The loan was to be floated among the German-born Americans and used to begin an immediate

revolution in Germany. The Agitation Union, headed by Arnold Ruge, was in rivalry with the Émigré Club and also sent a representative to the USA to canvass for revolutionary funds. The attempt to distribute the "revolutionary loan" failed. Marx and Engels in a number of works and letters denounced the undertaking as an adventurist attempt to produce a revolution artificially during a period when the revolutionary movement was on the wane. p. 488

338 The *Holy Grail*—according to medieval legend, the cup or chalice used by Christ at the Last Supper. p. 488

339 *Demagogues*—members of the opposition movement among German intellectuals. The word has been in use since the Carlsbad Conference of Ministers of German States in August 1819, which adopted a special resolution against the demagogues' intrigues. p. 490

340 A reference to the detachment formed by Willich in Besançon, France, in November 1848 from German emigrant workers and artisans. The members of the detachment received allowances from the French Government until the beginning of 1849. Later the detachment merged with a volunteer corps which took part in the Baden-Palatinate uprising of 1849 under the command of Willich. p. 491

341 Engels is referring to the Spartan King Leonidas and his troop of three hundred men who fought the battle of Thermopylae in 480 B.C., defending the mountain pass against an army of Persians during the Greco-Persian wars. King Leonidas and his men were all killed during the battle. p. 492

342 In September 1849 Marx was elected to the German Relief Committee formed by the German Workers' Educational Society in London. With a view to counteracting the attempts of petty-bourgeois refugee democrats to influence the proletarian refugees, the Committee was reorganised into the Social-Democratic Refugee Committee, as suggested by Marx and other Communist League leaders. Engels was among the leaders of the new committee. In mid-September 1850 Marx and Engels withdrew from the Refugee Committee because the majority of its members were under the influence of the Willich-Schapper group. p. 492

343 Marx is referring to the Central Committee of the Willich-Schapper sectarian and adventurist faction which split away from the Communist League in September 1850 and formed an independent organisation. Marx and Engels ironically called this organisation the Sonderbund by analogy with the separatist union of the seven economically backward Catholic cantons of Switzerland formed in the 1840s to resist progressive bourgeois reforms. p. 499

344 A reference to the workers' society founded in London in January 1852 with Marx's support and a Hanoverian refugee, the carpenter G. L. Stechan, as President. It included workers who broke away from the German Workers' Educational Society which had come under the influence of the Willich-

Schapper group. The Communist League member Georg Lochner, a worker close to Marx and Engels, also took an active part in organising this society. Later, many of its members, including Stechan himself, came under the influence of the Willich-Schapper group and re-joined the Educational Society. p. 500

345 A reference to the articles by Marx and Engels on the uprising of Paris workers in June 1848, the anti-revolutionary policy of the liberal majority in the Frankfurt National Assembly, the collaborationist position of the liberal deputies in the Prussian National Assembly, and the wavering of the petty-bourgeois leaders of the March Associations (see present edition, Vols. 7-9).

March Associations, which were organised at the end of November 1848 by representatives of the Left wing of the Frankfurt National Assembly, existed in a number of German towns and were headed by the Central March Association in Frankfurt. They were named after the March revolution of 1848 in Germany. Their leaders, Fröbel, Simon, Wesendock, Raveaux, Eizenmann, Ruge, Vogt and others, all petty-bourgeois democrats, confined themselves to revolutionary bluster and were hesitant and inconsistent in their struggle against counter-revolution. In December 1848 Marx and Engels, writing in the *Neue Rheinische Zeitung*, began to criticise the hesitant and ambivalent policy of the leaders of the March Associations, pointing out that such a policy aided the enemies of the revolution. p. 501

346 A reference to the conflict between Prussia and Austria which arose in the autumn of 1850 as a result of their struggle for supremacy in Germany. Prussia and Austria both demanded the right to intervene in the internal affairs of the Hesse-Cassel electorate to suppress the growing movement for a Constitution directed against Frederick William I and his reactionary Ministers. Austria received diplomatic support from Nicholas I, the Russian Tsar. Prussia was obliged to surrender and let the Austrians carry out a punitive mission in Hesse-Cassel. p. 503

347 On February 24, 1851 an international meeting, the so-called banquet of the equal, was organised in London by some French emigrants headed by Louis Blanc and the Blanquist refugees Barthélemy, Adam and others, together with the Willich-Schapper faction, to celebrate the anniversary of the February revolution of 1848. Marx and Engels sent their supporters, Konrad Schramm and Wilhelm Pieper, to the banquet, who were assaulted and turned out by Willich and Schapper's followers. Blanqui, who was in prison at the time, sent the text of a toast to London to be read out at the banquet. In the toast he denounced Louis Blanc and other members of the Provisional Government of the French Republic. The text was deliberately withheld from those present at the banquet by its organisers. However, it was published in a number of French newspapers. Marx and Engels translated it into English and German and provided it with a preface (see present edition, Vol. 10, pp. 537-39). The German version was printed in a large edition and distributed in Germany and England. The fate of the English translation is unknown. p. 505

348 A reference to Frederick William IV breaking his solemn promise to the people during the March revolution of 1848 in Prussia to establish a constitutional order. p. 509

349 Before the revolution of 1848-49 representatives of religious trends in Germany, so-called German Catholicism and the Protestant Free Communities, tried to establish a German National Church. German Catholicism, which appeared in 1844 in a number of German states, was aimed against the obscurantism and ritualism of the Catholic Church. While rejecting the Papacy and many dogmas and rituals of the Catholic Church, the German Catholics tried to apply Catholicism to the needs of the German bourgeoisie. The Free Communities broke away from the official Protestant Church in 1846 under the influence of the so-called Friends of Light, who were against Pietism, a mystical and self-righteous trend which dominated the Protestant Church. These two forms of religious opposition reflected the discontent of the bourgeoisie in the 1840s with the reactionary order in Germany and its striving for political unification of the country. The Free Communities and the German Catholics united in 1859. p. 510

350 The conflict concerning the religious denomination of children of mixed marriages between Catholics and Protestants arose in 1837 with the arrest of C. A. Droste-Vischering, Archbishop of Cologne, who was accused of high treason for refusing to obey the orders of Frederick William III, the King of Prussia. It ended in 1841 under Frederick William IV with the Prussian Government yielding to the Catholic Church. p. 510

351 This article was published in *The Eastern Question* and attributed to Marx. At the beginning of the article Engels would seem to be referring to his article "Progress of the Turkish War", which appeared as a leader in the *New-York Daily Tribune* of December 7, 1853 (see this volume, pp. 471-76). p. 516

352 The beginning of the article was published under the title "Diplomacy Again" in *The Eastern Question.* p. 523

353 See Notes 114 and 119. p. 523

354 This article was published in *The Eastern Question.* p. 527

355 See Note 195. p. 527

356 In Marx's notebook of excerpts for 1853 there is a passage from Palmerston's letter to Bulwer dated September 10, 1839. As a source Marx used the *Correspondence Relative to the Affairs of the Levant*, London, 1841. p. 530

357 In the known and published articles by Marx written for the *New-York Daily Tribune* during this period this fact is not mentioned. It is possible that this material was left out by the editors. p. 533

358 In 1844 the British Home Secretary, Sir James Graham, to please the Austrian Government, ordered the Post Office to allow the police to open the correspondence of Italian revolutionary immigrants.

Marx is referring to the Bandiera brothers, members of a conspiratorial organisation, who landed in June 1844 on the Calabrian coast at the head of a small detachment of Italian patriots, with the intention of sparking off an insurrection against the Bourbons of Naples and Austrian rule. The members of the expedition were betrayed by one of their number, however, and taken prisoner. The Bandiera brothers were shot. p. 533

359 Passages from this article were published in *The Eastern Question.* p. 536

360 The battle of Sinope was fought on November 30, 1853. The Turkish fleet on its way to deliver troops and arms to the Caucasian coast, was detected and attacked by the Russian Black Sea squadron, under the command of Vice-Admiral P. S. Nakhimov. The Russian fleet included six battleships and two frigates; the Turks, supported by coastal batteries, had sixteen ships, including two steamships. The Russian armament was superior, however, and during the battle fifteen Turkish ships were sunk and their commander, Admiral Osman Pasha, was taken prisoner. The Sinope victory consolidated Russia's position on the Black Sea and at the same time precipitated a declaration of war on Russia by Britain and France. p. 536

361 The Manifesto issued by Nicholas I on June 26, 1853 in connection with the Tsarist Government's decision to bring troops into the Danubian Principalities, and also a number of Russian diplomatic documents, stated that the aim of occupying the Principalities was to create "material guarantees" to safeguard the rights and privileges of the Greek Orthodox Church in Turkey and ensure that the Sultan fulfilled his obligations to Russia. p. 537

362 *Claremont*—a house near London, the residence of Louis Philippe after his escape from France. p. 538

363 A reference to the commission of seventeen Orleanist and Legitimist deputies of the Legislative Assembly, notorious for their reactionary views, appointed by the Minister of the Interior in May 1850 to draft a new electoral law. The name is borrowed from the title of an historical drama by Victor Hugo set in medieval Germany where the *Burggraf* was governor, appointed by the Emperor, of a *Burg* (city) or district. p. 539

364 An allusion to General Malet's unsuccessful plot against Napoleon I in October 1812. The organisers of the plot, in which both extreme Royalists and Republicans took part, were counting on Napoleon's defeat in Russia and tried to make use of a rumour of his death during the Russian campaign. p. 540

365 See Note 309. p. 541

366 This article was published in *The Eastern Question.* p. 543

367 Palmerston announced his resignation from the Aberdeen Coalition Ministry on December 16, 1853. It was not accepted, however, and he soon returned to the post of Home Secretary. p. 543

368 An allusion to the hasty recognition by Palmerston of the Bonapartist coup of December 2, 1851 (see Note 56). p. 545

369 This article was written by Engels on the basis of material in the British and French official press (*The Times, The Morning Herald, Le Moniteur universel*) which was biased in its appraisal of the military operations on the eve of the Western powers declaring war on Russia and in its comments on Russian reports during the Crimean war. This accounts for the inaccuracies in Engels' description of the battle of Sinope and his analysis of the balance of forces and the fighting power and actions of the Russian fleet in the Black Sea. Drawing on British newspapers Engels used information which stated incorrectly that the Black Sea fleet was tactically weak and its personnel consisted mainly of "fresh water sailors" and non-Russians. A considerable role in belittling the importance of the battle of Sinope was played by the political bias of this article directed against Russian Tsarism as the bulwark of reaction. The article was published in *The Eastern Question.* p. 547

370 The battle of Akhalzikh in the Caucasian theatre of military operations took place on November 26, 1853. p. 547

371 This article was published in *The Eastern Question.* p. 553

372 During his Italian campaigns of 1795-96 and 1800, Napoleon Bonaparte took advantage of the Italian republican and national liberation movement against Austrian feudal-absolutist rule in order to establish French supremacy in some of the Italian states; some Italian regions were annexed to France. p. 554

373 A reference to the abolition of the Roman Republic and the restoration of the secular power of the Pope in July 1849, as a result of French military intervention initiated by Louis Bonaparte after he had been elected President of the French Republic. p. 554

374 During the war of the Bavarian succession (1778-79), waged between Austria and the allied Prussia and Saxony, the Prussian Government made attempts to gain Tsarist Russia's support, and this enabled the latter to play the role of arbiter during the Teschen peace negotiations. However, Prussia's plans were frustrated by the defence alliance concluded in 1780 between Russia and Austria.

In 1800, during the war of France against the second anti-French coalition, Prussia tried to act as the mediator between the belligerent powers, but as a result was itself isolated.

In 1805, during the war of the third coalition (Austria, Britain, Sweden and Russia) against Napoleonic France, Prussia took a neutral stand, waiting to see how the situation developed. After Austria's defeat and withdrawal from the war, Prussia joined the allies, who formed a fourth anti-French coalition in September 1806, but in October was routed by Napoleon's troops. p. 555

375 The Paixhans guns were used in the navy. They were invented by the French General Paixhans in 1822 to fire hollow explosive shells. They are described by Engels in his article "Navy" (see present edition, Vol. 18). p. 556

376 See Note 319. p. 557

377 Part of this article was published under the title "More Documents" in *The Eastern Question.* p. 559

378 After the defeat of the 1848-49 Hungarian revolution, Kossuth and his supporters hid the regalia of the first King, Stephen, in the vicinity of Orsova, including his crown by which the Austrian emperors were crowned kings of Hungary. On September 8, 1853 the hiding place was discovered, and rumours spread about who had given away the secret to the Austrian authorities. Drawing on the information of their London correspondent A. Pulszky, the editors of the *New-York Daily Tribune* on October 19, 1853 wrongly accused Bertalan Szemere, a participant in the Hungarian revolution. p. 559

379 On January 6-9, 1854 food riots began in several towns in Devonshire; they were caused by the rise in bread prices, and soon spread throughout the county. The main participants were women and children who looted foodshops. The disturbances were suppressed by the army. p. 560

380 See Note 117. p. 561

381 A reference to the secret article in the Russo-Turkish treaty of friendship and mutual defence signed in Unkiar-Skelessi on July 8, 1833 (see Note 152). p. 562

382 See Note 27. p. 564

383 The first Anglo-Afghan war of 1838-42 started with the invasion of Afghanistan by British occupation troops in Sind. The invasion was carried out under the pretext of rendering assistance to the pretender, the Emir Dost Mohammed's brother Shuja. However, a popular uprising in November 1841 against the British invaders and Shuja compelled the British, who sustained a severe defeat, to withdraw.

For the *bombardment of Copenhagen* see Note 261. p. 567

384 See Note 367. p. 567

385 This article was written by Marx for the newspaper *Zuid Afrikaan* published in Capetown simultaneously in English and Dutch. In December 1853 Marx received an invitation to contribute to this paper through the husband of his younger sister Louise, the Dutch businessman J. K. Juta. Only one of the three articles Marx sent to *Zuid Afrikaan* was published. p. 568

386 See Note 374. p. 569

387 The report on the sinking of the Russian battleship *Rostislav* published in *The Times,* No. 21631, on January 9, 1854 was incorrect. According to Russian official documents, after the battle of Sinope the *Rostislav* returned safely to Sevastopol for repairs. p. 570

388 A reference to the meeting of Count Chambord, the pretender to the French throne, with the Orleanist Duke Louis de Nemours, which took place at the end of 1853, and also Chambord's visit to Louis Philippe's widow at the beginning of 1854. However, this fresh attempt at merging the junior and senior branches of the Bourbon dynasty was unsuccessful. p. 574

389 A reference to the Protocol signed on December 5, 1853 at the conference in Vienna by the representatives of Britain, France and Prussia and the Austrian Foreign Minister Buol. In this Protocol as in the subsequent Notes the four powers offered their mediation in the conflict between Russia and Turkey.

The letter of December 12, 1853, from the French and British ambassadors to Constantinople, Baraguay d'Hilliers and Stratford de Redcliffe, to the Turkish Foreign Minister Reshid Pasha, stated that the presence of the French and British fleets in the Bosporus testified to the friendly intentions of the British and French governments towards Turkey and that in the event of the Tsarist Government landing its troops on Turkish territory their fleets would aid the Ottoman Empire. p. 575

390 After Oltenitza in early November 1853 the battle of Chetatea was the second most important battle between the Turkish and Russian armies in the Danubian theatre during the early period of the Crimean war. The main military operations took place in January 1854 when the Turks attempted to launch an offensive in the vicinity of Kalafat at the junction of the borders of Wallachia, Serbia and Bulgaria. After staunch resistance the Russian detachment abandoned its position at Chetatea in the face of a large Turkish force (about 18,000 men). However, the arrival of Russian reinforcements put the Turks on the defensive and subsequently caused them to withdraw to Kalafat. p. 579

391 A reference to the Note to Constantinople signed by the British, French, Austrian and Prussian ambassadors on December 12, 1853 (see this volume, p. 560). The Note contained a fresh offer of mediation in the Russo-Turkish conflict. In a reply sent on December 31, 1853, Turkey stated her conditions for peace negotiations: 1) the preservation and guarantee of her territorial integrity; 2) Russian evacuation of the Danubian Principalities; 3) the renewal and observance of the 1841 treaty; 4) respect of the Sultan's sovereignty. These conditions were approved by a new Vienna Conference of the ambassadors on January 13, 1854 and forwarded to the Tsarist Government. p. 582

392 A part of this article was published under the title "The War in Asia" in *The Eastern Question.* p. 583

393 See Note 387. p. 584

394 *Landwehr*—the army reserve formed in Prussia during the struggle against Napoleon. In the 1840s the army reserve consisted of men under forty who had done three years active service and not less than two years in the reserve. In contrast to the regular army, conscription to the army reserve took place in cases of extreme necessity (war, or the threat of war). p. 588

395 In his description of the campaign against Albert, the Prince Consort, Marx used material published in the Chartist *People's Paper* on January 21, 1854.

This article, excluding the last paragraph, was published under the same title in *The Eastern Question.* p. 589

396 The description of the fortification of Constantinople was apparently written by Engels. In his letter to Engels of January 25, 1854, Marx asked his opinion on the subject (see present edition, Vol. 39). Presumably Marx received a note or a letter from Engels, which is not extant, with the relevant material and included it in his report for the *New-York Daily Tribune* dated January 27, 1854. The rest of the article is probably by Marx. The first two sections of this article were published under the title "Cobden and Russia" in *The Eastern Question.*

Cobden's pamphlet is quoted below from A. Somerville's *Cobdenic Policy the International Enemy of England*, London, 1854. p. 593

397 A reference to the declaration by Sweden and Denmark (December 1853) that if hostilities commenced in the Baltic Sea they would remain neutral. p. 594

398 See Note 54. p. 594

399 See Note 318. p. 596

400 According to a tradition that grew up after the Act of Union, twenty-six Irish peers out of approximately a hundred (the title of peer was conferred on many members of the British aristocracy possessing large landed estates in Ireland) were elected to the House of Lords; the rest could stand for election to the House of Commons. p. 597

401 An abridged version of this article was published under the title "War Finance" in *The Eastern Question.* p. 601

402 On the instructions of Nicholas I, A. F. Orlov negotiated with Emperor Francis Joseph in Vienna in late January and early February 1854. The Russian Government sought to secure Austria's benevolent neutrality in the war, in return for a guarantee of the inviolability of Austrian possessions. It also advanced a plan for a joint Russo-Austrian protectorate over states which would be formed in the Balkans if Turkey disintegrated. Orlov's mission was unsuccessful, however, owing to disagreements between Russia and Austria on the Eastern question. p. 601

403 As Ambassador Extraordinary to Constantinople and commander-in-chief of the Russian troops sent to assist the Turkish Sultan Mahmud II to defeat Mehemet Ali of Egypt, Orlov played a major part in the conclusion of the Unkiar-Skelessi Treaty between Russia and Turkey in 1833 (see Note 152). p. 601

404 *Renegades* was the name given in the Middle Ages to Christians in Moslem Spain who embraced Islam. Among Christians in Europe the word was afterwards applied generally to Christians in the Eastern countries who became Mohammedans. p. 602

405 A reference to the new Danish Constitution drafted in 1853 (see Note 187). It restricted the autonomy of Denmark proper, Schleswig, Holstein and Lauenburg and made them more dependent on the Danish Crown. This Constitution, which came into force on October 2, 1855, met with strong opposition and was replaced in 1863 with a more liberal one. p. 605

406 Excerpts from this article were published under the title "Blue Books.—Ambassadors Withdrawing" in *The Eastern Question.*

The blue book on the Eastern question mentioned in this article is *Correspondence respecting the Rights and Privileges of the Latin and Greek Churches in Turkey. Presented to both Houses of Parliament by Command of Her Majesty,* London, 1854. p. 606

407 A reference to the reports submitted to Parliament on the negotiations between Alexander Burnes, the British representative in Kabul, and the Emir of Afghanistan, Dost Mohammed. As a result of the negotiations the British Government, at Palmerston's insistence, declared war on Afghanistan in 1838. The reports were submitted to Parliament in 1839 but, as subsequently transpired, the most important papers were not produced, which made it possible to claim that Dost Mohammed was the initiator of the Anglo-Afghan conflict. Palmerston's opponents raised this question in the House of Commons in 1848. p. 606

408 See Note 6. p. 607

409 See Note 319. p. 609

410 The British ship *Tayleur* bound for Melbourne was wrecked and sank near the island of Lambey not far from Dublin. Investigations revealed that the ship's crew consisted of untrained, inexperienced sailors. p. 611

411 For *Downing Street* see Note 88; for the *Irish Brigade* see Note 53. p. 611

412 The *Litchfield-house contract* (or compact) was concluded between the Whig leaders and Daniel O'Connell, leader of the Liberal wing of the Irish national liberation movement, who headed the Irish faction in Parliament. The negotiations were conducted at Lord Litchfield's house in London. Under the contract the Irish Liberal leaders were promised some posts in the government. In his turn, O'Connell pledged to stop the mass campaign for the repeal of the Union and to support the Whigs in Parliament. p. 611

413 The *"Society of Arts" and tricks*—an ironical name given by Marx to the cultural and philanthropic Society of Arts founded in 1754; in the 1850s its President was Prince Albert. The Society tried to prevent the development of the mass strike movement in Britain and the convocation of the Labour Parliament (see Note 325), and sought to play the part of arbitrator between workers and employers. At its meeting in January 1854 Ernest Jones tried to propose a resolution recognising the workers' right to strike and condemning lockouts, but the meeting would not let him speak. His comrades-in-arms walked out in protest. Robert Owen also spoke against the view, supported by a majority at the meeting, that the labour question could be solved by philanthropic measures and arbitration. p. 612

414 A reference to the Labour Commission that met at the Luxembourg Palace under the chairmanship of Louis Blanc. It was set up on February 28, 1848 by the Provisional Government under pressure from the workers who demanded a Ministry of Labour. The Commission, in which both workers and employers were represented, acted as mediator in labour conflicts, often taking the side of the employers. The revolutionary action of the masses on May 15, 1848 put an end to the Luxembourg Commission, which the government disbanded on May 16, 1848. p. 612

415 This article was published in *The Eastern Question.* p. 613

416 For the Austrian and Russian demands for extradition of Hungarian and Polish revolutionary refugees in Turkey see Note 29. p. 614

417 *Capitulations*—documents that granted commercial advantages and privileges to the subjects of West-European states in Oriental countries, including Turkey. p. 615

418 Marx is ironically dubbing Louis Bonaparte with the title the Pope conferred on Ferdinand, King of Aragon (1479-1516), for the banishment of the Moors from Spain and which was subsequently used by the Pope in addressing the Spanish kings. p. 615

419 See Note 217. p. 616

420 See Note 24. p. 617

421 These notes by Marx on Henry Charles Carey's views consist of fragments from Marx's letters to his pupil and comrade-in-arms Adolph Cluss, that were inserted by the latter in his article "The 'Best Paper in the Union' and Its 'Best Men' and Political Economists". The article by Cluss was published in the American working-class newspaper *Die Reform.* It contained criticism of the ideological discord among the German petty-bourgeois émigrés and their infatuation with the theories of bourgeois economists. Cluss reproduced whole passages from Marx's letters, making some changes or additions evidently for the sake of coherence, of which he wrote to Marx on September 11, 1853, referring jokingly to his own work as a plagiarism. Marx's authorship is also evident from their similarity to and frequently full coincidence with what Marx wrote on Carey's views to Engels (June 14, 1853) and Weydemeyer (March 5, 1852) (see present edition, Vol. 39). In his letter to Engels of October 8, 1853, Marx took a favourable view of Cluss' work but at the same time he stated definitely: "In his attack upon the *Neu-England Zeitung* he—aptly as I think—makes use of sundry passages from my letters about Carey, etc." (Ibid.) Since the text belonging to Cluss is also based on Marx's advice and instructions and his description of petty-bourgeois émigrés, and also because this form is more convenient for the reader, in this edition the article is published in full, and Cluss' text is given in smaller type.

Marx's notes, as a separate publication, appeared in Russian in the journal *The U.S.A.*, No. 5, 1977. p. 623

422 An allusion to the fact that the German refugee newspaper *Janus*, published by Karl Heinzen in New York, ceased publication at the end of 1852. Its issues for 1852 contained articles by Arnold Ruge, which Marx, in his letter to Engels of April 30, 1852, described as follows: "...in the *Janus* we sent you, Ruge seeks—and *how* he seeks, *mon Dieu!*—to appropriate communism as the latest product of his 'humanist thought'" (see present edition, Vol. 39). p. 624

423 See Note 137. p. 625

424 Marx's criticism of the *Neu-England Zeitung* was evidently prompted by Poesche's article "Die 'Klassenkämpfer'", published in that newspaper on September 3, 1853. In connection with the article Marx wrote to Adolph Cluss on September 15, 1853 that Poesche makes "insipid would-be jokes about cranky proponents of the class struggle", etc., and further, "I think it is time you made a fresh start in the polemic and picked a few holes in the jejune arguments of Goepp-Poesche, discoverers of the *material view* though their materialism is that of the man-in-the-street" (see present edition, Vol. 39). p. 625

425 A similar idea is expressed in Marx's letter to Weydemeyer of March 5, 1852: "He [Carey] tries to refute them [Ricardo, Malthus, Mill, Say, etc.], not, it is true, like the fatuous Heinzen, by relating the existence of classes to the existence of *political* privileges and *monopolies*, but by seeking to demonstrate that *economic* conditions—rent (landed property), *profit* (capital) and wages (wage labour), rather than being conditions of struggle and antagonism, are conditions of association and harmony." In reproducing Marx's notes in his article, Cluss possibly made some editorial changes in this passage, as suggested by his letter to Marx of September 11, 1853. p. 626

426 Marx is referring to Carey's book *The Slave Trade, Domestic and Foreign: Why It Exists, and How It May Be Extinguished*, published in Philadelphia in 1853. (In the same year a stereotyped edition of the book came out in London.) In his book (pp. 202-04), Carey quoted from Marx's article "Elections.—Financial Clouds.—The Duchess of Sutherland and Slavery" published in the *New-York Daily Tribune* on February 9, 1853 (see present edition, Vol. 11, pp. 486-94). Marx read Carey's book when he received a copy from the author, and gave a brief critical review of it in his letter to Engels of June 14, 1853. The main points of this criticism are reproduced in this article. p. 627

427 A reference to the Central Committee of European Democracy set up in London in June 1850 on the initiative of Giuseppe Mazzini. It included bourgeois and petty-bourgeois refugees from various countries. Extremely heterogeneous in composition and ideological principles, the Central Committee of European Democracy had practically disintegrated by March 1852 because of strained relations between the Italian and French democratic refugees. Its inaugural manifesto "Aux peuples!" of July 3, 1850 was criticised by Marx and Engels in their international review (from May to October) published in the autumn of 1850 in the *Neue Rheinische Zeitung. Politisch-ökonomische Revue* (see present edition, Vol. 10, pp. 490-532). p. 631

428 See Note 30. p. 631

429 See Note 217. p. 632

NAME INDEX

A

Abbas I (1813-1854)—Pasha of Egypt (1849-54).—571

Abd-el-Kader (1808-1883)—Emir of Algeria, a leader in the national liberation war of 1832-47 in Morocco and Algeria against the French invaders; was taken prisoner in 1847; with Napoleon III's permission emigrated to Turkey in 1852.—423

Abdi Pasha (b. 1801)—Turkish general, commander of the Turkish army in the Caucasus in 1853.—432, 433, 550, 572, 584

Abdul Aziz (1830-1876)—Sultan of Turkey (1861-76), brother of Abdul Mejid.—211

Abdul Mejid (1823-1861)—Sultan of Turkey (1839-61).—18, 105, 110, 138, 163, 165, 194, 209-12, 228, 235, 245, 254, 257, 261, 263, 267-69, 272, 277-79, 309-13, 318, 321-23, 340, 407-08, 416-17, 423, 458, 523, 528-30, 532, 537, 561, 574-76, 586, 617-18

Aberdeen, George Hamilton Gordon, Earl of (1784-1860)—British statesman, Tory, leader of the Peelites from 1850; Foreign Secretary (1828-30 and 1841-46) and Prime Minister of the Coalition Ministry (1852-55).—3, 4, 20, 32, 33, 80, 103, 118, 120, 138, 142-46, 167, 175, 177, 186, 192, 196, 202, 230, 235, 252, 254-55, 263, 268-69, 272, 301-02, 309-10, 311-12, 321, 325, 354-55, 366, 381, 386, 392-93, 398, 400, 419, 523, 527, 537, 543, 553, 556, 560, 594, 632

A'Court, William, Baron Heytesbury (1779-1860)—British diplomat, ambassador to Russia (1828-32).—393

Adam—French worker, Blanquist; after the June 1848 uprising in Paris emigrated to Belgium and later to London; member of the Société des proscrits démocrates et socialistes in London in 1850.—508

Adélaide (1777-1847)—Princess of Orleans, sister of Louis Philippe, King of the French.—203, 206

Aesop (6th century B.C.)—semi-legendary Greek fabulist.—53

Agha Mohammed (1742-1797)—Shah of Persia (1794-97), founder of the Qajar dynasty.—113

Ahmed (d. 1855)—Bey of Tunisia (1837-55).—408

Ahmed Pasha—Turkish general, commander of the Turkish army in the Caucasus at the end of 1853.—572, 584

Ahmet Pasha—Turkish general, commander of the Turkish troops on the Danube in 1853-54.—294

Albano—English architect.—256

Albemarle, George Thomas Keppel, 6th Earl of (1799-1891)—British politi-

B

Backhouse, John (1772-1845)—British official, Under-Secretary for Foreign Affairs (1827-42).—387, 396

Baillie, Henry James (b. 1804)—British M.P., Tory.—606

Bahadur Shah II (1767-1862)—last nominal ruler of the Grand Mogul Empire in India.—199

Bakunin, Mikhail (1814-1876)—Russian democrat, journalist; participant in the 1848-49 revolutions in Germany; subsequently an ideologist of Narodism and anarchism.—284-86, 290, 291

Balcarres—see *Crawford, James*

Bandiera brothers, *Attilio* (1810-1844) and *Emilio* (1819-1844)—Austrian naval officers, leaders of the national liberation movement in Italy, members of the Young Italy society; executed for their attempt to stir up an insurrection in Calabria (1844).—533

Bangya, Janos (1817-1868)—Hungarian journalist and officer, participant in the 1848-49 revolution in Hungary; Kossuth's emissary abroad and at the same time an agent-provocateur; later served in the Turkish army under the name of Mehemed bey.—40, 42

Baraguay d'Hilliers, Achille, comte (1795-1878)—French general, since 1854 marshal, Bonapartist; ambassador to Constantinople (1853-54); commander of the French expeditionary corps in the Baltic in 1854.—531, 560, 575, 588, 619

Baring Alexander, 1st Baron Ashburton (1774-1848)—head of a banking house in London, Tory M.P.—300

Barrington, William Keppel, Viscount (b. 1793)—Irish peer, M.P.—597

Barrot, Camille Hyacinthe Odilon (1791-1873)—French politician and lawyer; leader of the liberal dynastic opposition until February 1848; from December 1848 to October 1849 headed the monarchist coalition ministry.—615

Barthélemy, Emmanuel (c. 1820-1855)—French worker, Blanquist, member of secret revolutionary societies during the July monarchy and participant in the June 1848 uprising in Paris; a leader of the Société des proscrits démocrates et socialistes in London; executed in 1855 on a criminal charge.—494, 496, 506-07

Basilius Haivalian—Patriarch of the Armenian Church in Aleppo (1853-54).—279

Bastiat, Frédéric (1801-1850)—French economist; preached harmony of class interests in bourgeois society.—625, 627, 630

Batthyány, Kázmér, Count of (1807-1854)—Hungarian statesman, liberal aristocrat; Minister of Foreign Affairs in the Hungarian revolutionary Government of Szemere (1849); after the suppression of the revolution emigrated to Turkey and then to France.—559

Bauer, Bruno (1809-1882)—German philosopher, Young Hegelian.—42, 487, 624

Beaumont, Miles Thomas Stapleton, Baron (1805-1854)—English landowner, member of the House of Lords, Liberal.—211, 263

Beaumont-Vassy, Edouard Ferdinand de la Bonninière, vicomte de (1816-1876)—French writer and historian; monarchist.—117

Becker, Hermann Heinrich (1820-1885)—German lawyer and journalist, member of the Communist League (from 1850); sentenced to five years' imprisonment at the Cologne Communist trial in 1852; subsequently a national-liberal.—482, 485, 487, 502-04

Becker, Nicolaus (1809-1845)—German poet.—67

Bell—chief engineer on the Egyptian frigate *Pervaz Bahri*, an Englishman.—571

Bell, George—British merchant, brother and partner of James Bell.—398, 402-06

other European states.—254, 308, 370, 371, 544, 577

Coburg—see *Albert*

Codrington, Sir Edward (1770-1851)—British admiral, commander of the combined Russian, British and French fleet in the battle of Navarino (1827).—354, 376

Cola, M.—Russian consul in Galatz (1853).—116

Colbert, Jean Baptiste (1619-1683)—French statesman, Controller-General of Finance (1665-83); virtually directed France's home and foreign policy.—70

Collier, Robert Porrett, 1st Baron Monkswell (1817-1886)—English lawyer and radical politician, M.P.—50

Confucius (550 or 551-479 B.C.)—Chinese philosopher and statesman.—624

Constantine (*Konstantin*) *Pavlovich* (1779-1831)—Russian Grand Duke, commander of the Polish army from 1814; virtual Viceroy of Poland (1814-31).—113, 386

Cooper, James Fenimore (1789-1851)—American novelist.—40

Coppock, James (1798-1857)—English lawyer, electoral agent.—304

Corry, Armar Lawry (1792-1855)—British admiral.—112

Cowell, George—English worker, Chartist; one of the leaders of the Preston strike in 1853-54.—446, 462

Cowley, Henry Wellesley, 1st Earl of (1804-1884)—British diplomat, ambassador to Paris (1852-67).—4

Craufurd, Edward Henry John (b. 1816)—English judge; M.P. (1852-53).—176, 177

Crawford, James Lindsay Balcarres, Earl of (1783-1869)—English landlord and mine-owner.—331, 436, 447

Cromwell, Oliver (1599-1658)—leader of the English revolution; from 1653 Lord Protector of England, Scotland and Ireland.—148, 273

Crossley, Sir Francis (1817-1872)—English manufacturer, radical M.P.—196

Cushing, Caleb (1800-1879)—American lawyer and politician, Attorney-General (1853-57).—625

Czartoryski, Adam Jerzy, Prince (1770-1861)—Polish magnate, friend of Alexander I; Russian Foreign Minister (1804-06); head of the Provisional Government during the Polish insurrection of 1830-31, later leader of Polish conservative-monarchist émigrés in Paris.—280, 386

D

Dalhousie, James Andrew Broun Ramsay, Marquess and Earl of (1812-1860)—British statesman, Peelite; Governor-General of India (1848-56); pursued a policy of colonial conquests.—121, 122, 199, 282

Danilo I Petrović Njegoš (1826-1860)—Prince of Montenegro (1852-60).—446, 617

Dannenberg, Pyotr Andreyevich (1792-1872)—Russian general, commander of Russian forces on the Danube and in the Crimea during the Crimean war.—458, 472

Danton, Georges Jacques (1759-1794)—prominent figure in the French Revolution, leader of the Right-wing Jacobins.—291

Decker, Karl von (1784-1844)—German general and military writer.—481

Delacour (*De la Cour*), *Edmond* (1805-1873)—French diplomat, ambassador to Constantinople (1853).—21, 109, 110, 194, 259, 278

Delahodde (de la Hodde), Lucien (1808-1865)—French journalist, member of secret revolutionary societies during the Restoration and the July monarchy, police agent-provocateur.—40

Delasusse, Aaron Louis Frédéric Regnault, Baron de (1788-1860)—French admiral.—109

Delescluze, Louis Charles (1809-1871)—French revolutionary, participant in the revolutions of 1830 and 1848 and member of the Paris Commune of 1871.—421

Delius—Prussian official, deputy to the Second Chamber of the Prussian Diet (1852-53), brother of Karl Delius.—30

Delius, Karl—Magdeburg merchant.—30

Demetrius Antachi—Patriarch of the Greek Church in Aleppo (1853-54).—279

Democritus (c. 460-c. 370 B.C.)—Greek philosopher, a founder of the atomistic theory.—630

Demosthenes (384-322 B.C.)—Greek orator and politician; Athens leader of the Anti-Macedonian Party; champion of democracy in slave-owning society.—20

Derby, Edward Geoffrey Smith Stanley, Earl of (1799-1869)—British statesman, Tory leader, Prime Minister (1852, 1858-59 and 1866-68).—3, 186, 252, 280, 281, 377, 401, 406, 413, 570, 611, 617

Desmoulins, Lucie Simplice Camille Benoist (1760-1794)—French journalist; leader in the French Revolution; Right-wing Jacobin.—291

Dickens, Charles John Huffam (1812-1870)—English novelist.—79, 360

Dickinson—owner of iron works in Blackburn, Lancashire.—331

Dickinson, John (1815-1876)—English writer, Free Trader, author of several books on India, a founder of India Reform Society.—155, 180, 183, 184, 219

Diebich-Zabalkansky, Ivan Ivanovich, Count (Diebitsch, Hans Karl Friedrich Anton) (1785-1831)—Russian field marshal, commander-in-chief of the Russian army during the Russo-Turkish war of 1828-29 and of the troops which crushed the Polish uprising of 1830-31.—7, 33, 457

Dietz, Oswald (c. 1824-1864)—German architect; participated in the 1848-49 revolution; emigrated to London; member of the Central Authority of the Communist League; after the split of the League in 1850 joined the sectarian Willich-Schapper group, member of its Central Committee; subsequently took part in the American Civil War on the side of the North.—499, 500

Disraeli, Benjamin, Earl of Beaconsfield (1804-1881)—British statesman and author, a Tory leader; Chancellor of the Exchequer (1852, 1858-59 and 1866-68) and Prime Minister (1868 and 1874-80).—3, 46, 48, 53, 54, 55, 58-60, 63, 69, 70, 72, 73, 75, 80, 81, 137, 177, 178, 186, 202, 240, 253, 265, 295, 589, 597

Dolgorukoff (Dolgorukov), Vasily Andreyevich, Prince (1803-1868)—Russian statesman; War Minister (1853-56); Chief of the gendarmes (1856-66).—240, 241

Dornbush.—409

Dost Mohammed Khan (1793-1863)—Afghan Emir (1826-39 and 1842-63).—566

Dotézac, Adolphe (1808-1889)—French diplomat, envoy to Copenhagen (1848-69).—594

Dronke, Ernst (1822-1891)—German writer, at first a "true socialist", later member of the Communist League and an editor of the *Neue Rheinische Zeitung*; after the 1848-49 revolution emigrated to England; supported Marx and Engels.—41, 42, 485, 486

Drouyn de Lhuys, Edouard (1805-1881)—French diplomat and politician, in the 1840s Orleanist and after 1851 Bonapartist; Minister of Foreign Affairs (1848-49, 1851, 1852-55, 1862-66).—203, 209, 211, 258, 267, 301, 321, 556, 560, 562, 575

Druey, Henri (1799-1855)—Swiss radical statesman; member of the Federal Council (1848-54), and President of the Swiss Confederation in 1850.—91

Dundas, Sir James Whitley Deans (1785-1862)—British admiral, commander-in-chief of the British navy in the Mediterranean from 1852 to January 1855.—5, 112, 118, 553

Duplat, Gustavus Charles—British diplomat, consul at Warsaw (1841-54).—365

Durham, John George Lambton, 1st Earl of (1792-1840)—British politician,

Whig; ambassador to St. Petersburg (1835-37).—389, 394, 403

E

Eccarius, Johann Friedrich—German tailor, member of the Communist League; emigrated to London in 1851; supported Marx and Engels during the split in the Communist League.—500

Eccarius Johann Georg (1818-1889)—German tailor, brother of Johann Friedrich Eccarius; prominent figure in the German and international working-class movement; member of the League of the Just and later of the Communist League; member of the General Council of the First International; subsequently took part in the British trade union movement.—500

Edward IV (1442-1483)—King of England (1461-83).—251

Elizabeth I (1533-1603)—Queen of England (1558-1603).—148, 152

Ellenborough, Edward Law, 1st Earl of (1790-1871)—British Tory statesman; Governor-General of India (1842-44); First Lord of the Admiralty (1846); President of the Board of Control for India (1858).—181, 186, 198, 263

Ellice, Edward (1781-1863)—British politician, M.P. (1818, 1820, 1830 and 1831-63).—48, 55

Elphinstone, Mountstuart (1779-1859)—governor of Bombay (1819-27), author of a *History of India*.—199

Emmanuel, Georgy Arsenyevich (1775-1837)—Russian general of Magyar descent, Russian commander in the Caucasus (1826-31).—392

Engelhardt—Russian general, commander of Russian troops on the Danube in 1853.—472

Engels, Frederick (1820-1895).—41, 42, 82, 87, 232, 285, 450-52, 457, 474, 486, 496, 497, 507, 516

Ersch, Johann Samuel (1766-1828)—German bibliographer, professor of geography and statistics in Halle.—59

Esterházy of Galántha, Paul Anton (*Pál Antál*), *Prince* (1786-1866)—Hungarian magnate, diplomat in the service of Austria, Minister of Foreign Affairs in the Hungarian government (March-September 1848).—205-06

Evans, Sir George de Lacy (1787-1870)—English general; participant in the Crimean war; M.P.—357, 362, 382

Ewerbeck, August Hermann (1816-1860)—German physician and man of letters; member of the Communist League until 1850.—284, 291

F

Falloux, Frédéric Alfred Pierre, comte de (1811-1886)—French politician and writer, Legitimist and clerical; in 1848 inspired the suppression of the June uprising in Paris; Minister of Education (1848-49).—615

Ferdinand II (1810-1859)—King of Naples (1830-59).—243

Ferdinand VII (1784-1833)—King of Spain (1808 and 1814-33).—353

Ferdinand August Franz Anton (1816-1885)—Prince Saxe-Coburg-Saalfeld-Kohary, husband of Queen Maria II da Gloria of Portugal, King of Portugal under the name of Ferdinand II (1837-53) and regent from 1853 to 1855.—370

Ferdinando Alberto Amedeo (1822-1855)—Duke of Genoa, brother of Victor Emmanuel II, King of Sardinia.—108

Feuerbach, Ludwig Andreas von (1804-1872)—German materialist philosopher.—624

Fichte, Johann Gottlieb (1762-1814)—German philosopher.—624

Fickler, Joseph (1808-1865)—German journalist, democrat; a leader of the 1848-49 democratic movement in Baden; after the revolution emigrated to Switzerland and then to Britain and America.—488

Filmore, L.—Berlin correspondent of *The Times* (1853-54).—609

Fischbach—Russian general, commander of Russian troops on the Danube in 1853.—473

Fitzroy, Henry (1807-1859)—English politician, Peelite, Under-Secretary for Home Affairs from 1852 to 1855.—224, 225

Fitzwilliam, Charles William Wentworth, 3rd Earl of (1786-1857)—English politician, Whig M.P.—186, 295, 598

Fletcher Ann.—469

Fletcher Margaret.—469

Fleury, Charles (real name: *Carl Friedrich August Krause*) (b. 1824)—London businessman, Prussian spy and police agent.—40, 82

Forbes, Charles—Scottish landowner.—415

Fox, Charles James (1749-1806)—British statesman, Whig leader; in 1783 Foreign Secretary in Portland's Coalition Ministry (the Fox-North Ministry).—120, 150

Fox, William Johnson (1786-1864)—English politician and author, Free Trader, M.P.—597

Francis I (1494-1547)—King of France (1515-47).—59

Francis Joseph I (1830-1916)—Emperor of Austria (1848-1916).—108, 174, 418, 618

Frederick I (1826-1907)—virtual ruler of Baden from 1852, Grand Duke of Baden from 1856.—510

Frederick I ("Barbarossa" or "Redbeard") (c. 1123-1190)—King of Germany from 1152, Holy Roman Emperor (1155-90).—105, 359

Frederick III (1609-1670)—King of Denmark (1648-70).—238

Frederick VII (1808-1863)—King of Denmark (1848-63).—168, 227, 238, 241, 445

Frederick William IV (1795-1861)—King of Prussia (1840-61).—29, 30, 108, 209, 314, 509, 511, 602

Fuad Pasha, Mehemmed (1814-1869)—Turkish statesman; in the 1850s and 1860s repeatedly held the posts of Grand Vizier and Minister of Foreign Affairs.—5, 18, 106

G

Galway, George Edward Arundell (Monckton-Arundell), Viscount (1805-1876)—Irish peer, Tory M.P.—597

Gammage, Robert George (1815-1888)—shoemaker, a Chartist leader, author of *The History of the Chartist Movement* (1854).—170, 171

Garašanin, Iliya (1812-1874)—Serbian liberal statesman; Minister of the Interior (1843-52 and 1858-59), Prime Minister and Minister of Foreign Affairs (1852-53 and 1861-67).—11, 228, 269

Gebert, August—Mecklenburg joiner, member of the Communist League first in Switzerland and then in London; after the split in the League in 1850 joined the separatist Willich-Schapper group, member of its Central Committee.—500

George I (1660-1727)—King of Great Britain and Ireland (1714-27).—44, 45, 153

George II (1683-1760)—King of Great Britain and Ireland (1727-1760).—44, 45, 153

George III (1738-1820)—King of Great Britain and Ireland (1760-1820).—44, 45, 150, 153

Gerbex, Charles Léopold Dominique (1816-1879)—Swiss army officer, chief of the National Guard in the canton of Fribourg from 1852 onwards; directed the suppression of the putsch in Fribourg in 1853.—85

Gerlach, Wilhelm—German refugee in London, a worker at Hale's rocket factory in a London suburb.—84

Germanos—Patriarch of the Greek Church in Constantinople (1852-53).—163

Géza (Gaysa) (c. 949-997)—ruler of Hungary (972-997); spread Christianity.—56

Ghica, Grigore Alexandru, Prince (1807-1857)—hospodar of Moldavia (1849-

Secretary of State for the Colonies (1846-52); son of Charles Grey.—186

Grillenzoni, Giovanni (1796-1868)—Italian revolutionary; follower of Mazzini.—302

Grosvenor, Lord Robert, 1st Baron Ebury (1801-1893)—British politician, Whig, later Liberal.—62

Gruber, Johann Gottfried (1774-1851)—German scientist, historian of literature.—59

Grundtvig, Nikolai Frederik Severin (1783-1872)—Danish theologian and poet; deputy to the Folketing.—101

Guizot, François Pierre Guillaume (1787-1874)—French historian and statesman; virtually directed France's foreign and home policy from 1840 to the February revolution of 1848.—20, 32, 87, 89, 203

Gurieff (Guriev), Dmitry Alexandrovich, Count (1751-1825)—Russian statesman, Minister of Finance (1810-23).—603

Guyon—see *Khourschid Pasha*

Gümpel—German democrat; refugee in London in the early 1850s.—500

Gyulay, Ferenc, Count (1798-1868)—Austrian general, War Minister (1849-50).—174

H

Habsburgs (*or Hapsburgs*)—imperial dynasty of the Holy Roman Empire from 1273 to 1806 (with intervals), of Austria (from 1804) and of Austria-Hungary (1867-1918).—16

Hackelberg, Otto, Baron von—Austrian naval officer, killed in Smyrna in 1853.—211

Hale, Robert—son and partner of William Hale.—82, 83, 84, 107

Hale, William—owner of a rocket factory in a London suburb.—82-84, 107

Halil Pasha (d. 1856)—Turkish military figure and statesman; kapudan Pasha (Naval Minister) (1854-55).—576

Halliday, Sir Frederick James (1806-1901)—East India Company official, Governor of Bengal (1854-59).—177

Hamelin, François Alphonse (1796-1864)—French admiral, commander-in-chief of the French fleet in the Mediterranean and the Black Sea (1853-54); Minister of the Navy (1855-60).—553

Hamilton—see *Seymour, George Hamilton*

Hammer-Purgstall, Joseph, Baron von (1774-1856)—Austrian orientalist, author of works on the history of Turkey.—22, 229

Hampden, John (1595-1643)—prominent figure in the English revolution, a leader of the Parliamentary opposition to the absolutist regime.—224

Hardinge, Sir Henry, Viscount (1785-1856)—British general, field marshal from 1855, Tory; Secretary for War (1828-30 and 1841-44); Governor-General of India (1844-47); commander-in-chief of the British army (1852-56).—559

Hardwicke, Charles Philip Yorke, 4th Earl of (1799-1873)—British naval officer and politician, Tory; admiral from 1854.—263

Hasenclever, Johann Peter (1810-1853)—German artist.—232

Hegel, Georg Wilhelm Friedrich (1770-1831)—German philosopher.—93, 481, 487, 624

Heinzen, Karl (1809-1880)—German radical journalist, participant in the 1849 uprising in Baden and the Palatinate; refugee in Switzerland and later in England; emigrated to the USA in autumn 1850.—626, 630

Heise, Hermann (d. 1860)—German democratic journalist, participant in the revolution of 1848-49, later a refugee in England.—502

Henry V (of France)—see *Chambord*

Henry, Sir Thomas (1807-1876)—British judge.—82, 84

Hentze, A.—German army officer, member of the Communist League; after the split in the League in 1850 joined the sectarian Willich-Schapper group; witness for the prosecution

at the Cologne Communist trial (1852).—501, 502, 503
Heraclitus (c. 540-c. 480 B.C.)—Greek philosopher, a founder of dialectics.—630
Herbert, Sidney, Baron of Lea (1810-1861)—British statesman, Tory at the beginning of his career and later a Peelite; Secretary-at-War (1845-46 and 1852-55) and Secretary for War (1859-60).—58, 192
Herries, John Charles (1778-1855)—British statesman, Tory.—177, 368
Herzen, Alexander Ivanovich (1812-1870)—Russian revolutionary democrat, materialist philosopher and writer.—284
Heytesbury—see *A'Court, William*
Hinckeldey, Karl Ludwig Friedrich von (1805-1856)—Prussian official, Police President of Berlin from 1848: President of the Police Department in the Ministry of the Interior from 1853.—28-30
Hirsch, Wilhelm—commercial clerk from Hamburg, Prussian police agent in London in the early 1850s.—40, 41, 43, 82, 481, 498, 500
Hobbes, Thomas (1588-1679)—English philosopher.—597
Hobhouse, John Cam, Baron Broughton de Gyfford (1786-1869)—British Whig statesman, President of the Board of Control for India (1835-41 and 1846-52).—139, 183
Hogg, Sir James Weir (1790-1876)—British politician, Peelite; President of the Court of Directors of the East India Company (1846-47 and 1852-53).—123, 125, 223
Holland, Henry Richard Fox Vassall, Baron (1773-1840)—British Whig politician, member of the Ministries of Granville (1806-07), Grey (1830-34) and Melbourne (1834, 1835-40).—206, 207
Homer—semi-legendary Greek epic poet.—140, 488
Hooson, Edward—British worker, prominent Chartist.—170, 172
Horace (*Quintus Horatius Flaccus*) (65-8 B.C.)—Roman poet.—86
Horsfall, Thomas Berry (b. 1805)—British mine-owner and politician, Tory M.P.—413
Hotham, Beaumont, Baron (1794-1870)—British general; Tory M.P.—597
Hsien Fêng (c. 1831-1861)—Emperor of China (1850-61).—95, 98
Hume, Joseph (1777-1855)—British politician, radical leader, M.P.—51, 69, 76, 125, 196, 358, 367, 369, 401, 405, 447
Hunt, Henry (1773-1835)—British politician, radical M.P.—358
Hunt, Thornton Leigh (1810-1873) —English radical journalist, participant in the Chartist movement in the 1840s and 1850s; co-founder with G. H. Lewes of the newspaper *The Leader* (1850).—525, 624

I

Ibrahim Pasha (1789-1848)—foster-son of the Viceroy of Egypt Mehemet Ali; Egyptian commander-in-chief during the war against Turkey (1831-33 and 1839-41); virtual ruler of Egypt from 1847.—360, 375, 376, 377, 379
Inglis, Sir Robert Harry (1786-1855)—British politician, Tory M.P.—177, 379
Ingraham, Duncan Nathaniel (1802-1891)—American naval officer, captain of the warship *St. Louis* which was anchored at Smyrna in 1853.—212, 293
Ioanidis—official of the Wallachian Ministry of Home Affairs in 1853.—277
Iskander-bey (1810-1861)—Turkish colonel of Polish descent; participant in the 1848-49 revolution in Hungary; emigrated to Turkey after the defeat of the revolution; commanded Turkish troops on the Danube (1853-54), in the Crimea (1855), and in the Caucasus (1855-56).—294
Ismail Pasha (1805-1861)—Turkish general of Circassian descent.—458
Ismail Pasha (*György Kmety*) (1810-1865)—Turkish general of Magyar

descent; participant in the 1848-49 revolution in Hungary; Turkish commander on the Danube (1853-54) and in the Caucasus (1854-55).—602
Ivan IV (*Ivan Vasilyevich, Ivan the Terrible*) (1530-1584)—the first tsar of Russia (1547-84).—631-32
Izylmetieff (*Izylmetyev*) *Ivan Nikolayevich* (1813-1870)—Russian rear admiral, commander of the frigate *Aurora* in 1853-54.—533, 534
Izzet Pasha—Turkish general.—295

J

James, J.—British consul in Odessa in 1853-54.—571
Jean Paul (pen-name of *Richter, Johann Paul Friedrich*) (1763-1825)—German satirist.—623
Jocelyn, Robert, Viscount (1816-1854)—British officer, M.P.; secretary of the Board of Control for India (1845-46).—196, 197
John (*Lackland*) (c. 1167-1216)—King of England (1199-1216).—24
Jones, Ernest Charles (1819-1869)—prominent figure in the English working-class movement; proletarian poet and journalist, Left-wing Chartist leader; friend of Marx and Engels.—57, 58, 135, 136, 170-72, 196, 226, 414, 448, 462, 463, 470, 513, 514, 525, 612, 625

K

Kant, Immanuel (1724-1804)—German philosopher.—624
Kara George (*Karageorge*) (1752-1817)—leader of the Serbs in the struggle against Turkish oppression in 1804-13, ruler of independent Serbia (1811-13); in 1813 was forced to leave Serbia and returned incognito in 1817; assassinated by order of Milosh Obrenovich.—36, 458
Karnicki, Wladislaw, Count—Austrian diplomat, chargé d'affaires in Berne in 1853.—107, 108
Kellner von Köllenstein, Friedrich, Baron (b. 1802)—Austrian general, aide-de-camp of Emperor Francis Joseph I from 1849.—618
Keogh, William Nicholas (1817-1878)—Irish lawyer and politician, a leader of the Irish group in Parliament; repeatedly held high judicial posts in Ireland.—120
Kepler, Johannes (1571-1630)—German astronomer.—93
Khalchinsky, Ivan Dmitrievich (1810-1856)—Russian diplomat, consul-general in Moldavia and Wallachia in 1853.—235
Khourschid Pasha (*Gyuon, Richard Debaufre*) (1803-1856)—Turkish general of British descent, participant in the 1848-49 revolution in Hungary; Turkish commander in the Caucasus in 1853.—458
Khuli-Khan—see *Nadir Shah*
Kinkel, Johann Gottfried (1815-1882)—German poet and journalist, democrat; participant in the 1849 uprising in Baden and the Palatinate; sentenced to life imprisonment by Prussian court; escaped from prison and emigrated to England; a leader of petty-bourgeois émigrés in London; opposed Marx and Engels.—43, 485, 488, 489, 500, 502
Kinkel, Johanna (*née Mockel*) (1810-1858)—German writer, wife of Gottfried Kinkel.—485
Kisseleff (*Kiselev*), *Nikolai Dmitrievich* (1800-1869)—Russian diplomat, ambassador to Paris (1851-54).—115, 574, 608
Knight, Henry Gally (1786-1846)—English traveller and writer, M.P.—362
Korniloff (*Kornilov*), *Vladimir Alexeyevich* (1806-1854)—Russian admiral, Chief of Staff of the Black Sea Fleet (1849-53); organised the defence of Sevastopol.—5, 549, 571
Kościelski, Wladyslaw (b. 1820)—Polish democrat; emigrant; later a general in the Turkish army.—285
Kossuth, Lajos (1802-1894)—leader of the Hungarian national liberation

movement, headed bourgeois-democratic elements during the 1848-49 revolution; head of the Hungarian revolutionary government; after the defeat of the revolution emigrated first to Turkey and then to England and the USA.—42, 57, 68, 83, 84, 390, 494, 559

Koszta, Martin (d. 1858)—participant in the 1848-49 revolution in Hungary; after the defeat of the revolution emigrated to Turkey and then to the USA, where he became a US citizen; the attempt of the Austrian authorities to arrest him in Smyrna in 1853 led to a clash with Hungarian refugees.—193, 211, 243, 258, 293

Kraemer, Georgi—Russian consul-general in London (1853).—82

Kupffer, Adolf Yakovlevich (1799-1865)—Russian physicist and mineralogist; headed a scientific expedition to the Elbrus in 1829.—392

L

Labensky, Ksavery Ksaveryevich (1800-1855)—Russian diplomat, Councillor of the Department of Foreign Affairs (1841-55).—631

Labouchere, Henry, 1st Baron Taunton (1798-1869) — British statesman, Whig; President of the Board of Trade (1839-41 and 1847-52); Secretary of State for the Colonies (1855-58).—188, 207

La Fayette, Marie Joseph Paul Yves Roch Gilbert du Motier, marquis de (1757-1834)—prominent figure in the French Revolution, a leader of the moderate constitutionalists (Feuillants); took part in the July revolution of 1830.—58

Lagrené, Théodose Marie Melchior Joseph de (1800-1862)—French diplomat; official of the French legation in St. Petersburg in 1831-34; for some time performed the functions of the chargé d'affaires.—383

La Guéronnière, Louis Étienne Arthur Dubreuil Hélion, vicomte de (1816-1875)—French political writer, Bonapartist in the 1850s.—209

Lamarche, Hippolyte Dumas de (b. 1789)—French journalist; contributed to *Le Siècle*.—110

Lamartine, Alphonse Marie Louis de (1790-1869)—French poet, historian and politician; a moderate republican leader in the 1840s; Minister of Foreign Affairs and virtually head of the Provisional Government in 1848.—58

Landolphe—French petty-bourgeois socialist, refugee in London; after the split in the Communist League in 1850 joined the sectarian Willich-Schapper group.—506

Lansdowne, Sir Henry Petty-Fitzmaurice, Marquis of (1780-1863)—British statesman, Whig; Chancellor of the Exchequer (1806-07); President of the Council (1830-41, 1846-52); Minister without portfolio (1852-63).—252, 598

Larochejaquelein (La Rochejaquelein), Henri Auguste Georges Du Vergier, marquis de (1805-1867)—French politician, a Legitimist leader; deputy to the Constituent Assembly during the Second Republic, senator during the Second Empire.—589

Lavalette (La Valette), Charles Jean Marie Félix, marquis de (1806-1881)—French statesman, Bonapartist; ambassador to Constantinople (1851-53); Minister of the Interior (1865-67); Minister of Foreign Affairs (1868-69).—269

Layard, Sir Austen Henry (1817-1894)—British archaeologist and politician; Radical, subsequently Liberal; M.P.—185, 186, 192, 202, 266, 268-71, 597

Lazareff (Lazarev), Mikhail Petrovich (1788-1851)—Russian admiral, Antarctic explorer; commander-in-chief of the Black Sea Fleet from 1833.—398

Ledru-Rollin, Alexandre Auguste (1807-1874)—French journalist and politician, a petty-bourgeois democrat leader; editor of *La Réforme*; Minister of the Interior in the Provisional Government (1848); deputy to the Constituent and Legislative Assemblies (leader of the Montagnards); emigrated to England after the demonstration of June 13, 1849.—421, 495, 505, 540

Leeds—see *Osborne, Sir Thomas*

Leiningen-Westerburg, Christian Franz Seraphin Vincenz, Count (1812-1856)—Austrian general; sent on a diplomatic mission to Constantinople in 1853.—18, 262, 616, 618, 619

Leonidas (c. 508-480 B.C.)—King of Sparta (c. 488-480 B.C.), hero of the battle of Thermopylae during the Greco-Persian war.—624, 630

Leopold I (1790-1865)—King of the Belgians (1831-65).—108, 204, 254, 538

Léopold Louis Philippe Marie Victor (1835-1909)—eldest son of Leopold I, King of Belgium under the name of Leopold II (1865-1909).—254

Letellier, A.—French journalist.—210

Libeny (Libényi), János (c. 1832-1853)—Hungarian tailor; attempted to assassinate the Emperor Francis Joseph of Austria in 1853.—30

Liddell, Henry George, 2nd Earl of Ravensworth (1821-1903)—British politician, M.P.—187

Lieven, Darya (Dorothea) Khristoforovna, Princess (1785-1857)—wife of Russian diplomat Khristofor Lieven, hostess of political salons in London and Paris.—21

Lieven, Khristofor Andreyevich, Prince (1774-1839)—Russian diplomat, envoy to Berlin (1810-12); ambassador to London (1812-34).—165, 167, 230, 355, 374, 379, 381

Lieven, Wilhelm Karlovich, Baron (1800-1880)—Russian general, sent on diplomatic missions abroad.—314

Liprandi, Pavel Petrovich (1796-1864)—Russian general, commander of Russian troops on the Danube and in the Crimea during the Crimean war.—472

Liverpool, Robert Banks Jenkinson, 2nd Earl of (1770-1828)—British statesman, a Tory leader; Home Secretary (1804-09); Secretary for War and the Colonies (1809-12); Prime Minister (1812-27).—348

Lizius—book-publisher in Frankfurt am Main.—43

Lochner, Georg (born c. 1824) — prominent figure in the German working-class movement, joiner by trade; member of the Communist League and of the General Council of the First International, friend and associate of Marx and Engels.—499

Louis XIV (1638-1715)—King of France (1643-1715).—70

Louis Bonaparte—see *Napoleon III*

Louis Napoleon—see *Napoleon III*

Louis Philippe I (1773-1850)—Duke of Orleans, King of the French (1830-48).—4, 148, 149, 166, 203, 254

Louise (1817-1898)—Princess of Hesse, wife of Prince Christian of Glücksburg, later King of Denmark.—238

Loustallot, Elisée (1762-1790)—French democratic journalist, a Jacobin leader in the French Revolution.—108

Lowe, Robert, 1st Viscount Sherbrooke (1811-1892)—British statesman and journalist, contributor to *The Times*; Whig and later Liberal; M.P., Chancellor of the Exchequer (1868-73); Home Secretary 1873-74).—223

Lucas, Frederick (1812-1855)—Irish journalist and politician, a leader of the Irish Tenant-Right movement; M.P. (1852-55).—119

Lüders, Alexander Nikolayevich, Count (1790-1874)—Russian general, commander of a corps on the Danube (1853-54) and of the Southern army (1855); in December 1855 commander-in-chief of the Russian army in the Crimea.—455, 473

Lund—Yorkshire manufacturer.—413

Lusignan, Levon—Armenian prince, political adventurer; in 1853 a refugee in England.—138

Lytton, Edward George Earle Lytton Bulwer-Lytton, 1st Baron (1803-

M.P.; flirted with the Chartists in the 1840s.—597

Michell, William—English physician, M.P.—598

Miguel, Maria Evarist (1802-1866)—King of Portugal (1828-34).—355

Mill, James (1773-1836)—British economist and philosopher.—150

Miller, Joseph or *Josias* (commonly called *Joe Miller*) (1684-1738)—English comic actor.—68

Milner Gibson—see *Gibson, Thomas Milner*

Milnes, Richard Monckton, 1st Baron Haughton (1809-1885)—English author and politician, M.P.; at the beginning of his career a Tory, in the latter half of the 19th century a Liberal.—272, 280, 366, 597

Mindon—Burmese King (1853-78).—282, 283

Minié, Claude Étienne (1804-1879)—French army officer and military inventor.—475

Minto, Gilbert Elliot, 2nd Earl of (1782-1859)—British diplomat and statesman, Whig; First Lord of the Admiralty (1835-41); Lord Privy Seal (1846-52).—207

Miskowsky, Henryk Ludvic (d. 1854)—Polish army officer, participant in the 1848-49 revolution in Hungary; emigrated to Turkey after the revolution and later to London.—494, 495

Mitchell, John (1815-1875)—Irish revolutionary democrat, Left-wing leader of Young Ireland; deported to a penal colony in 1848; escaped in 1853 and emigrated to the USA.—302

Molesworth, Sir William (1810-1855)—British statesman, Liberal; First Commissioner of the Board of Works (1853); Secretary of State for the Colonies (1855).—50, 192, 256, 597

Monck, Sir Charles Stanley, Fourth Viscount Monck in Irish peerage, First Baron Monck in peerage of the United Kingdom (1819-1894)—British statesman, Liberal; Lord of the Treasury (1855-58).—597

Monrad, Ditlev Gothard (1811-1887)—Danish bishop, Minister of Worship (1848 and 1859-63), Prime Minister and Minister of Finance (1863-64); leader of the National-Liberal Party in the 1850s.—445

Monsell, William, Baron Emly (1812-1894)—Irish Liberal, a leader of the Irish faction in Parliament; clerk of ordnance (1852-57).—120

Montalembert, Charles Forbes René de Tryon, comte de (1810-1870)—French politician and writer; deputy to the Constituent and Legislative Assemblies during the Second Republic; Orleanist.—615

Montpensier, Antoine Marie Philippe Louis d'Orleans, duc de (1824-1890)—son of King Louis Philippe of the French, and husband of the Spanish Infanta Maria Luisa Fernanda; pretender to the Spanish throne in 1868-69.—367

Morison, James (1770-1840)—English quack who made a fortune selling "Morison's pills".—482

Mozart, Wolfgang Amadeus (1756-1791)—Austrian composer.—372

Müllner, Amadeus Gottfried Adolf (1774-1829)—German poet, playwright and literary critic.—43

Mun, Thomas (1571-1641)—English merchant and economist, mercantilist; a Director of the East India Company from 1615.—152

Munro, Sir Thomas (1761-1827)—British general, governor of Madras (1819-27).—197-98

Muntz, George Frederick (1794-1857)—English radical, M.P.; organised a number of mass meetings in support of the campaign for the Reform Bill of 1832.—273

Murat, Joachim (1767-1815)—Marshal of France (1804); King of Naples (1808-15).—554

Murat, Napoléon Lucien Charles, Prince (1803-1878)—French politician, Bonapartist, cousin of Napoleon III.—554

Tory statesman; Prime Minister (1674-79 and 1690-95); charged with bribery by Parliament in 1695.—149, 390

Osman Pasha (c. 1785-c. 1860)—Turkish admiral; commander of the Turkish squadron at the battle of Sinope.—550

Osman Pasha—governor of Aleppo in 1853.—279

Osten-Sacken, Dmitry Yerofeyevich, Count (1789-1881)—Russian general; commander in the South of Russia during the Crimean war (1853-54) and of the Sevastopol garrison (late 1854 and 1855).—473, 564, 580

Otto I (1815-1867)—Prince of Bavaria, King of Greece (1832-62).—371

Owen, Robert (1771-1858)—British utopian socialist.—612

Ozeroff (*Ozerov*)—Russian diplomat, acting chargé d'affaires in Constantinople in 1853.—18, 618

P

Paixhans, Henri Joseph (1783-1854)—French general, military engineer and inventor.—556

Pakington, Sir John Somerset (1799-1880)—British statesman, Tory, later Conservative; Secretary for War and the Colonies (1852); First Lord of the Admiralty (1858-59 and 1866-67) and Secretary for War (1867-68).—3, 58, 74, 223, 265, 271

Palmerston, Henry John Temple, 3rd Viscount (1784-1865)—British statesman; at the beginning of his career a Tory, from 1830 onwards a Whig leader; Foreign Secretary (1830-34, 1835-41 and 1848-51); Home Secretary (1852-55), and Prime Minister (1855-58 and 1859-65).—3, 20, 26, 32, 33, 58, 59, 68, 144-46, 188, 189, 192, 205-08, 226, 234, 246, 255, 256, 276, 277, 280, 295, 303, 304, 309, 310, 311, 312, 325, 345-87, 388, 389, 390, 393, 395, 396, 397, 398, 399, 401, 402, 403, 404, 405, 406, 419, 470, 477, 525, 527, 529, 531, 533, 534, 537, 543-46, 554, 566, 567, 591, 592, 597, 606, 607, 608

Paradis, Jean Baptiste (b. 1827)—French journalist, contributed to *La Presse* in 1853.—228

Paskiewich (*Paskevich*), *Ivan Fyodorovich, Prince* (1782-1856)—Russian field marshal-general; from June 1831, commander-in-chief of the Tsarist army suppressing the Polish insurrection; governor of the Kingdom of Poland from 1832; commander-in-chief of the army suppressing the revolution in Hungary (1849), and of the Russian forces on the Danube (1854).—424, 429, 602

Pawloff (*Pavlov*), *Prokofy Yakovlevich* (1796-1868)—Russian general; Russian commander on the Danube and in the Crimea during the Crimean war.—458, 472

Peace—employee of the Earl of Crawford, a mine-owner.—447

Peacock, Sir Barnes (1810-1890)—English lawyer; held high posts in the Indian colonial administration and justice department in the 1850s and 1860s.—122-23

Pedro I (1798-1834)—Emperor of Brazil (1822-31); King of Portugal under the name of Pedru IV (1826); abdicated in favour of his daughter, Maria II da Gloria.—370

Peel, Sir Robert (1788-1850)—British statesman; moderate Tory; Prime Minister (1834-35 and 1841-46); repealed the Corn Laws in 1846.—60, 71, 181, 254, 292, 296-97, 298, 299, 300, 314, 358, 365, 369, 371, 375, 376, 382, 384, 404, 405, 406, 409, 436, 611

Peel, Sir Robert (1822-1895)—British politician and diplomat, son of Prime Minister Sir Robert Peel; in the early 1850s a Peelite; M. P.—137

Pélissier, Aimable Jean Jacques (1794-1864)—French general, marshal from 1855; participated in the conquest of Algeria in 1830-50; commander-in-chief of the French army in the Crimea (May 1855-July 1856).—610

R

a founder of the "German-Catholics" movement; participated in the revolution of 1848-49; after its defeat emigrated to Britain.—488

Rose, Hugh Henry, Baron Strathnairn (1801-1885)—British officer, later field marshal; chargé d'affaires in Constantinople (1852-53); took part in the Crimean war; organised the suppression of the national liberation movement in India (1857-59).—5, 145, 261, 266

Rothacker, Wilhelm—German democrat, member of the Communist League; emigrated to the USA after the defeat of the revolution of 1848-49.—486, 487

Roussin, Albin Reine, baron (1781-1854)—French admiral, Minister of the Navy (1840, 1843); ambassador to Constantinople (1832-34).—372

Ruge, Arnold (1802-1880)—German radical journalist, Young Hegelian; Left-wing deputy to the Frankfurt National Assembly in 1848; a leader of German petty-bourgeois émigrés in Britain in the 1850s; national-liberal after 1866.—488, 624

Ruriks—dynasty of Russian princes and subsequently tsars (912-1598), descended from Rurik, a semi-legendary Varangian leader.—230

Russell, Sir Henry (1751-1836)—English lawyer, judge in India (1798-1813).—198

Russell, John Russell, 1st Earl (1792-1878)—British statesman, Whig leader; Prime Minister (1846-52 and 1865-66); Foreign Secretary (1852-53 and 1859-65).—50-52, 56, 58, 78, 103, 119-20, 137, 138, 139, 143, 175, 177, 186, 188, 193, 202, 206, 207, 211, 235, 240, 265, 266, 267, 268, 271, 272, 309, 312, 325, 350, 509, 512, 543, 589, 608, 619

Ruston, Benjamin (d. 1853)—English worker, Chartist.—172, 173

S

Sadleir, John (1814-1856)—Irish banker and politician, a leader of the Irish group in Parliament; Junior Lord of Treasury (1853).—120, 560

Saint-Marc, Girardin (1801-1873)—French journalist and literary critic, Orleanist.—117

Saint-Simon, Claude Henri de Rouvroy, comte de (1760-1825)—French utopian socialist.—628

Salt, Sir Titus (1803-1876)—English manufacturer.—327, 414

Sand, George (pen-name of *Amandine Aurore Lucie Dupin, baronne Dudevant*) (1804-1876)—French novelist, representative of the democratic trend in romanticism.—284, 285

Sardanapalus—see *Assurbanipal*

Saunders, John—London police-sergeant.—83

Schapper, Karl (c. 1812-1870)—prominent figure in the German and international working-class movement; a leader of the League of the Just; member of the Central Authority of the Communist League; participant in the revolution of 1848-49; a leader of the sectarian group during the split in the Communist League in 1850; again became a close associate of Marx in 1856; member of the General Council of the First International.—482, 485, 493, 497, 505

Schärttner, August—a Hanau cooper, participant in the 1848 revolution and the Baden-Palatinate uprising of 1849; emigrated to London; member of the Communist League; after its split in 1850 joined the Willich-Schapper sectarian group, and became a member of its Central Committee.—489

Schiller, Charles—French journalist.—109, 236, 240, 407

Schily, Viktor (1810-1875)—German lawyer, democrat; participant in the Baden-Palatinate uprising of 1849, then a refugee in France; member of the First International.—486, 502

Schimmelpfennig, Alexander (1824-1865)—Prussian army officer, democrat; took part in the Baden-Palatinate uprising of 1849 and later emigrated to the USA; adhered to the Willich-Schapper sectarian group; fought in the American Civil War on the side of the Northerners.—501, 505

Schläger, Eduard—German journalist, petty-bourgeois democrat; a refugee in the USA in the 1850s-1870s; editor of the *Neu-England-Zeitung*.—623, 630

Schlick, Franz Heinrich, Count (1789-1862)—Austrian general; took part in suppressing the revolution of 1848-49 in Hungary; commanded the Austrian forces in Galicia and Bukovina (1854-59).—587

Schneider II, Karl—German lawyer, democrat, participant in the 1848-49 revolution; defence counsel at the Cologne Communist trial (1852).—485, 502

Schramm, Konrad (c. 1822-1858)—prominent figure in the German working-class movement, member of the Communist League; a refugee in London from 1849; responsible editor of the *Neue Rheinische Zeitung. Politisch-ökonomische Revue*; friend and associate of Marx and Engels.—492, 493, 494, 496, 503

Schwarzenberg, Friedrich, Prince (1800-1870)—Austrian army officer and later general; took part in suppressing the peasant riots in Galicia (1846) and the revolution in Hungary (1849).—366

Scully, Francis (b. 1820)—Irish politician; Liberal M. P. (1847-57).—253

Sébastiani, Horace François Bastien, comte (1772-1851)—French marshal and diplomat, Orleanist; Foreign Minister (1830-32), ambassador to London (1835-40).—203-08

Selim Pasha (*Zedlinsky*)—Turkish general of Polish descent; commanded Turkish forces on the Danube in 1853-54.—585, 602

Seymour, George Hamilton (1797-1880)—British diplomat, envoy to St. Petersburg in 1851-54.—239, 263, 266, 301, 571, 607, 608

Shafi Khan—Persian diplomat; envoy to London in 1853.—444

Shakespeare, William (1564-1616)—English poet and dramatist.—103, 272, 276, 327, 345, 373, 385, 508

Shamyl (c. 1798-1871)—leader of the Daghestan and Chechen mountaineers' struggle against the Tsarist colonisers from the 1830s to the 1850s.—146, 422, 446, 455, 456, 584

Sheil, Richard Lalor (1791-1851)—Irish playwright and politician; Whig M. P.—381, 382, 390

Sidmouth, Henry Addington, 1st Viscount (1757-1844)—British statesman, Tory; Prime Minister and Chancellor of the Exchequer (1801-04); Home Secretary (1812-21).—348

Sidney—see *Herbert, Sidney*

Sidney, Sir Philip (1554-1586)—English poet and diplomat.—276

Sieyès, Emmanuel Joseph, comte de (1748-1836)—French abbot, took an active part in the French Revolution; moderate constitutionalist (Feuillant).—70

Sigel, Franz (1824-1902)—Baden army officer; democrat, one of the military leaders of the Baden-Palatinate uprising in 1849; then a refugee in Switzerland, Britain, and from 1852 in the USA; took part in the American Civil War on the side of the Northerners.—486, 491

Simpson, Leonard Francis—English man of letters.—616, 619

Sismondi, Jean Charles Léonard Simonde de (1773-1842)—Swiss economist, representative of economic romanticism.—627, 628

Slade, Sir Adolphus (1804-1877)—British naval officer, subsequently admiral; was in the Turkish service from 1849 to 1866.—428

Slaney, Robert Aglionby (1792-1862)—British politician, M. P. (1826-35 1837-41, 1847-62); advocate of reforms to improve the living conditions of the poor.—171

Soltykoff (*Soltykov*), *Alexei Dmitrievich, Prince* (1806-1859)—Russian travel-

T

U

V

W

Winkelried, Arnold von (d. 1386)—semi-legendary hero of the Swiss war of liberation against the Habsburgs; according to legend he secured the victory over the Austrian Duke Leopold in the battle of Sempach at the price of his life.—488

Wise, John Ayshford—British M.P. (1853).—256

Wiseman, Nicholas (1802-1865)—English Catholic priest; became first Archbishop of Westminster and Cardinal in 1850.—302

Wood, Sir Charles, 1st Viscount Halifax (1800-1885)—British statesman, Whig; Chancellor of the Exchequer (1846-52), President of the Board of Control for India (1852-55); First Lord of the Admiralty (1855-58); Secretary of State for India (1859-66).—77, 103; 104, 115, 120-23, 125, 126, 139, 140, 177, 180, 184, 186, 223, 260, 265

Woronzoff (Vorontsov), Mikhail Semyonovich, Prince (1782-1856)—Russian statesman and general; in 1844-54 commander-in-chief of the Transcaucasian Russian army in the Caucasus and governor of the Caucasus.—446, 455, 456, 476, 551

Wuilleret, Louis (1815-1898)—Swiss lawyer and politician, a leader of the Conservative Party in the canton of Fribourg; clericalist.—85

Z

Zamoyski, Wladyslaw, Count—Polish magnate, participant in the insurrection of 1830-31; later a leader of the Polish conservative monarchist refugees in Paris.—386

Zhigmont (Tuinont), Semyon Iosifovich (1812-1886)—Russian general, commander of the Odessa regiment of chàsseurs in 1852-53.—585

INDEX OF LITERARY AND MYTHOLOGICAL NAMES

Achilles (Gr. Myth.)—the bravest Greek warrior in the Trojan War, hero of Homer's *Iliad*, the first song of which describes Achilles' quarrel with Agamemnon, the Greeks' leader, and his withdrawal into his tent.—110

Ahriman—Greek name of the ancient Persian Anra Mainyu, the principle of evil.—487

Aladdin—a character from the *Arabian Nights*, owner of a magic lamp.—223

Alcina—a character from Lodovico Ariosto's poem *L'Orlando furioso* and Matteo Bojardo's *Orlando innamorato*, a sorceress.—345, 390

Birch, Harvey—the main character of Fenimore Cooper's novel *The Spy*, who considered spying as his duty to his country.—40

Cerberus (Gr. Myth.)—a never sleeping dog guarding the entrance of Hades.—72, 631

Christ, Jesus (Bib.).—490, 497

Don Quixote—hero of Cervantes' novel of the same name.—77, 201, 348, 353, 631

Epimenides (Gr. Myth.)—a Cretan prophet who, according to legend, spent more than half a century in sleep.—160

Falstaff, Sir John—a fat, merry ribald and boastful knight in Shakespeare's *Merry Wives of Windsor* and *Henry IV*.—373

INDEX OF QUOTED AND MENTIONED LITERATURE

WORKS BY KARL MARX AND FREDERICK ENGELS[a]

Marx, Karl

Advertisement Duty.— Russian Movements.—Denmark.— The United States in Europe (this volume). In: *New-York Daily Tribune*, No. 3850, August 19, 1853.—246

Affairs Continental and English (this volume). In: *New-York Daily Tribune*, No. 3864, August 23, 1853.—419

Affairs in Holland.—Denmark.—Conversion of the British Debt.—India, Turkey and Russia (this volume). In: *New-York Daily Tribune*, No. 3790, June 9, 1853.—109, 118

The Attack on Francis Joseph.—The Milan Riot.—British Politics.—Disraeli's Speech.— Napoleon's Will (present edition, Vol. 11). In: *New-York Daily Tribune*, No. 3710, March 8, 1853.—39

Bakunin (present edition, Vol. 7). In: *Neue Rheinische Zeitung*, No. 64, August 3, 1848.—285

The Berlin Conspiracy (this volume). In: *New-York Daily Tribune*, No. 3745, April 18, 1853.—37

[*The Czar's Views.—Prince Albert*] (this volume). In: *New-York Daily Tribune*, No. 4000, February 11, 1854.—601

Elections.—Financial Clouds.— The Duchess of Sutherland and Slavery (present edition, Vol. 11). In: *New-York Daily Tribune*, No. 3686, February 8, 1853.—188, 414

English Prosperity.—Strikes.— The Turkish Question.—India (this volume). In: *New-York Daily Tribune*, No. 3809, July 1, 1853.—142, 169-70

Feargus O'Connor.—Ministerial Defeats.— The Budget (this volume). In: *New-York Daily Tribune*, No. 3758, May 3, 1853.—68

[a] Editions in the language of the original are given only in case when they were published during the author's lifetime.—*Ed.*

Marx, Karl and Engels, Frederick
Adress of the Central Authority to the League, March 1850 (present edition, Vol. 10)
— Die Centralbehörde an den Bund. In: *Dresdner Journal und Anzeiger,* No. 177, June 28, 1851; *Allgemeiner Polizei-Anzeiger,* No. 52, June 30, 1851; *Kölnishe Zeitung,* No. 156, July 1, 1851; *Schwäbischer Merkur,* No. 158, July 4, 1851.—497

[*Fortification of Constantinople.—Denmark's Neutrality.—Composition of British Parliament.—Crop Failure in Europe*] (this volume). In: *New-York Daily Tribune,* No. 4004, February 16, 1854.—613

The Great Men of the Exile (present edition, Vol. 11).—41, 42

WORKS BY DIFFERENT AUTHORS

Aberdeen, G. [Speeches in the House of Lords]
— March 4, 1853. In: *The Times,* No. 21368, March 5, 1853.—3
— July 7, 1853. In: *The Times,* No. 21475, July 8, 1853.—186
— August 9, 1853. In: *The Times,* No. 21503, August 10, 1853.—252
— August 12, 1853. In: *The Times,* No. 21506, August 13, 1853.—263, 268
— Lord Aberdeen to Mr. Monsell, June 3, 1853. In: *The Times,* No. 21447, June 6, 1853.—120

Albemarle, G. [Speech in the House of Lords, July 1, 1853.] In: *The Times,* No. 21470, July 2, 1853.—215

Anstey, Th. [Speeches in the House of Commons]
— February 8, 1848. In: *Hansard's Parliamentary Debates.* 3d series, Vol. XCVI, London, 1848.—379-80
— February 23, 1848. In: *Hansard's Parliamentary Debates.* 3d series, Vol. XCVI, London, 1848.—361, 381, 385, 387-90, 398, 400

Antoine, G. *A. M. le rédacteur du journal la "Patrie".* In: *La Patrie,* No. 66, March 7, 1851.—506

Aquinas, Thomas. *Summa Theologica.*—49, 55

Ariosto, L. *L'Orlando furioso.*—345

Attwood, Th. [Speeches in the House of Commons]
— August 28, 1833. In: *Hansard's Parliamentary Debates.* 3d series, Vol. XX, London, 1833.—389-90
— December 14, 1837. In: *Hansard's Parliamentary Debates.* 3d series, Vol. XXXIX, London, 1838.—405

Augier, J. *Une dépêche du 16 Mai....* In: *Le Pays,* No. 146, May 26, 1853.—109

Baillie, H. J. [Speech in the House of Commons, January 31, 1854.] In: *The Times,* No. 21653, February 1, 1854.—606

Bakunin, M. *Aufruf an die Slaven,* Leipzig, 1848.—285
— *Erklärung.* In: *Ostdeutsches Athenäum,* supplement to the *Neue Oder-Zeitung für*

Kunst, Wissenschaft und Literatur, No. 151, 1848.—284, 285; *Neue Rheinische Zeitung,* No. 47 (supplement), July 17, 1848.—285

Barthélemy, E. *Au rédacteur en chef du journal La Patrie.* In: *La Patrie,* No. 71, March 12, 1851.—506-07

Basset, A. *Nos lettres....* In: *La Patrie,* No. 190, July 9, 1853.—193

Bastiat, Fr. *Gratuité du crédit. Discussion entre M. Fr. Bastiat et M. Proudhon,* Paris, 1850.—625

— *Harmonies économiques. 2-me édition augmentée des manuscripts laissés par auteur,* Paris, 1851.—626

Battle of the Frogs and Mice (Batrachomyomachia).—488

Bauer, B. *Kritik der evangelischen Geschichte der Synoptiker,* Bd. 1-2, Leipzig, 1841; Bd. 3, Braunschweig, 1842.—487

Beaumont, M. Th. S. [Speeches in the House of Lords]

— July 18, 1853. In: *The Times,* No. 21484, July 19, 1853.—211

— August 12, 1853. In: *The Times,* No. 21506, August 13, 1853.—263

Beaumont-Vassy [, E. de la Bonninière, de]. *Histoire des États Européens depuis le Congrès de Vienne.—Empire Russe,* Paris, 1853.—117

Becker, N. *Der deutsche Rhein.*—67

Benson, J. *Highly Important Meeting at Manchester.* In: *The People's Paper,* No. 82, November 26, 1853.—514-15

Béranger, P. de. *Les Mirmidons, ou les funérailles d'Achille.*—6

Berkeley, F. [Speech in the House of Commons, June 14, 1853.] In: *The Times,* No. 21455, June 15, 1853.—137

Blackett, J. F. B. [Speeches in the House of Commons]

— June 9, 1853. In: *The Times,* No. 21451, June 10, 1853.—125

— August 16, 1853. In: *The Times,* No. 21509, August 17, 1853.—273

Blanc, L. *To the Editor of the Times.* In: *The Times,* No. 20741, March 5, 1851.—506

[Blanqui, L. A.] *Toste envoyé par le citoyen L. A. Blanqui à la commission près les réfugiés de Londres, pour le banquet anniversaire du 24 février.* In: *La Patrie,* No. 58, February 27, 1851.—506

Bojardo, M. M. *Orlando Innamorato.*—488

Boniface, L. [Articles.] In: *Le Constitutionnel,* No. 146, May 26, 1853.—111; No. 231, August 19, 1853.—278; September 5, 1853.—294

Bright, J. [Speeches in the House of Commons]

— June 14, 1853. In: *The Times,* No. 21455, June 15, 1853.—137

— June 27, 1853. In: *The Times,* No. 21466, June 28, 1853.—182

— July 1, 1853. In: *The Times,* No. 21470, July 2, 1853.—175-76

— July 8, 1853. In: *The Times,* No. 21476, July 9, 1853.—192, 197

— July 14, 1853. In: *The Times,* No. 21481, July 15, 1853.—202

— [Speech at the Peace Conference in Edinburgh, October 12, 1853.] In: *The Times,* No. 21559, October 14, 1853.—419, 437

Brougham, H. P. [Speech in the House of Lords, July 7, 1853.] In: *The Times,* No. 21475, July 8, 1853.—185

Bulwer, W. [Speech in the House of Commons, July 11, 1833.] In: *Hansard's Parliamentary Debates.* 3d series, Vol. XIX, London, 1833.—389

Butt, I. [Speeches in the House of Commons]
— April 12, 1853. In: *The Times,* No. 21401, April 13, 1853.—58
— February 6, 1854. In: *The Times,* No. 21658, February 7, 1854.—611

Campbell, G. *Modern India: a Sketch of the System of Civil Government. To Which Is Prefixed, Some Account of the Natives and Native Institutions,* London, 1852.—181, 184, 199, 214, 220

Canning, S. [Speech in the House of Commons, June 21, 1838.] In: *Hansard's Parliamentary Debates.* 3d series, Vol. XCIII, London, 1838.—405

Carey, H. Ch. *Essay on the Rate of Wages: with an Examination of the Causes of the Differences in the Condition of the Labouring-Population Throughout the World,* Philadelphia, 1835.—627
— *Principles of Political Economy. Part the First: Of the Laws of the Production and Distribution of Wealth,* Philadelphia, 1837.—551-53
— *The Slave trade, domestic and foreign: Why It Exists, and How It May Be Extinguished,* Philadelphia, 1853.—627

Carlyle, Th. *Latter-Day Pamphlets.* No. II: *Model Prisons,* London, 1850.—303

Cervantes Saavedra, Miguel de. *Don Quixote.*—77, 348, 478

Chapman, J. *The Cotton and Commerce of India, Considered in Relation to the Interests of Great Britain; with Remarks on Railway Communication in the Bombay Presidency,* London, 1851.—220

Chenu, A. *Les Conspirateurs. Les sociétés secrètes. La préfecture de police sous Caussidière. Les corps francs,* Paris, 1850.—40

[Child, J.] *A Treatise Wherein is Demonstrated I. That the East-India Trade is the Most National of all Foreign Trades. II. That the Clamors, Aspersions, and Objections made against the present East-India Company, are Sinister, Selfish, or Groundless. III. That since the discovery of the East-Indies, the Dominion of the Sea depends much upon the Wane or Increase of that Trade, and consequently the Security of the Liberty, Property, and Protestant Religion of this Kingdom. IV. That the Trade of the East-Indies cannot be carried on to National advantage, in any other way than by a General Joynt-Stock. V. That the East-India Trade is more profitable and necessary to the Kingdom of England, than to any other Kingdom or Nation in Europe,* London, 1681.—152

Clanricarde, U. J. [Speeches in the House of Lords]
— August 8, 1853. In: *The Times,* No. 21502, August 9, 1853.—561
— August 9, 1853. In: *The Times,* No. 21503, August 10, 1853.—251
— August 12, 1853. In: *The Times,* No. 21506, August 13, 1853.—263
— February 6, 1854. In: *The Times,* No. 21658, February 7, 1854.—607

Clarendon, G. W. F. [Speeches in the House of Lords]
— July 7, 1853. In: *The Times,* No. 21475, July 8, 1853.—186
— July 18, 1853. In: *The Times,* No. 21484, July 19, 1853.—211
— August 2, 1853. In: *The Times,* No. 21497, August 3, 1853.—239
— August 8, 1853. In: *The Times,* No. 21502, August 9, 1853.—324
— August 12, 1853. In: *The Times,* No. 21506, August 13, 1853.—261, 262-63
— February 6, 1854. In: *The Times,* No. 21658, February 7, 1854.—607-08

Cobbett, J. M. [Speech in the House of Commons, July 5, 1853.] In: *The Times*, No. 21473, July 6, 1853.—187-88

Cobbet, W. *Paper against Gold; or, the History and Mystery of the Bank of England, of the Debt, of the Stocks, of the Sinking Fund, and of All the Other Tricks and Contrivances, Carried on by the Means of Paper Money*, London, 1828.—44

Cobden, R. *How Wars Are Got Up in India. The Origin of the Burmese War*, 4th edition, London, 1853.—234
— (anon.) *Russia. By a Manchester Manufacturer; Author of "England, Ireland, and America"*, Edinburgh, 1836.—595, 596
— [Speeches in the House of Commons]
— April 14, 1853. In: *The Times*, No. 21403, April 15, 1853.—58
— June 14, 1853. In: *The Times*, No. 21455, June 15, 1853.—137
— June 27, 1853. In: *The Times*, No. 21466, June 28, 1853.—177
— July 1, 1853. In: *The Times*, No. 21470, July 2, 1853.—175, 176
— August 16, 1853. In: *The Times*, No. 21509, August 17, 1853.—274-76
— [Speech at the Peace Conference in Edinburgh, October 12, 1853.] In: *The Times*, No. 21559, October 14, 1853.—419, 437
— [Speech at the Meeting in Manchester, January 24, 1854.] In: *The Times*, No. 21647, January 25, 1854.—595

Codrington, E. [Speech in the House of Commons, April 20, 1836.] In: *Hansard's Parliamentary Debates*. 3d series, Vol. XXXII, London, 1836.—376

Collier, R. P. [Speech in the House of Commons, March 1, 1853.] In: *The Times*, No. 21365, March 2, 1853.—50-51

Cooper, F. *The Spy*.—40

Craufurd, E. H. [Speech in the House of Commons, July 1, 1853.] In: *The Times*, No. 21470, July 2, 1853.—176

Decker, C. von. *Der kleine Krieg, im Geiste der neueren Kriegführung. Oder: Abhandlung über die Verwendung und den Gebrauch aller drei Waffen im kleinen Kriege*, Berlin und Posen, 1822.—481

Derby, E. G. (see also Stanley, E. G.) [Speech in the House of Lords, July 7, 1853.] In: *The Times*, No. 21475, July 8, 1853.—186

Dickens, Ch. *The Life and Adventures of Martin Chuzzlewit*.—79
— *The Posthumous Papers of the Pickwick Club*.—360

Dickinson, J. *The Government of India under a Bureaucracy*. In: *India Reform*, No. VI, London, Manchester, 1853.—155, 180, 183, 184, 219

The Disputed Question of the Danish Succession; or What Is to Be Done by the Powers of Europe.—101

Disraeli, B. [Speeches in the House of Commons]
— March 3, 1853. In: *The Times*, No. 21367, March 4, 1853.—69
— April 8, 1853. In: *The Times*, No. 21398, April 9, 1853.—46, 48-49, 53, 54, 55, 63
— July 7, 1853. In: *The Times*, No. 21475, July 8, 1853.—185
— July 14, 1853. In: *The Times*, No. 21481, July 15, 1853.—202
— August 2, 1853. In: *The Times*, No. 21497, August 3, 1853.—240

Ellenborough, E. L. [Speeches in the House of Lords]
— July 7, 1853. In: *The Times*, No. 21475, July 8, 1853.—185
— August 12, 1853. In: *The Times*, No. 21506, August 13, 1853.—263

Ellice, E. [Speech in the House of Commons, April 8, 1853.] In: *The Times*, No. 21398, April 9, 1853.—48, 55

[Ersch, J. S. und Gruber, J. G.] *Allgemeine Encyclopädie der Wissenschaften und Künste*, Bd. 22, Leipzig, 1832.—59

Evans, G. [Speech in the House of Commons, March 17, 1834.] In: *Hansard's Parliamentary Debates.* 3d series, Vol. XXII, London, 1834.—382

[Ewerbeck, A.] *Bakunin.* In: *Neue Rheinische Zeitung*, No. 36, July 6, 1848.—284

Fitzwilliam, Ch. W. [Speech in the House of Lords, July 7, 1853.] In: *The Times*, No. 21475, July 8, 1853.—186

Forbes, Ch. *To the Editor of the Times.* In: *The Times*, No. 21544, September 27, 1853.—415

Gammage, R. [Speech at the Blackstone-Edge meeting, June 19, 1853.] In: *The People's Paper*, No. 60, June 25, 1853.—170-71

Gibson, Th. M. [Speeches in the House of Commons]
— April 14, 1853. In: *The Times*, No. 21403, April 15, 1853.—58, 62, 69
— July 1, 1853. In: *The Times*, No. 21470, July 2, 1853.—175

Girardin, E. de. *Est-ce la paix, est-ce la guerre?* In: *La Presse*, May 27, 1853.—109

Gladstone, W. [Speeches in the House of Commons]
— March 1, 1853. In: *The Times*, No. 21365, March 2, 1853.—69
— March 3, 1853. In: *The Times*, No. 21367, March 4, 1853.—69-70
— April 8, 1853. In: *The Times*, No. 21398, April 9, 1853.—48-49, 53-55, 63
— April 14, 1853. In: *The Times*, No. 21403, April 15, 1853.—69
— April 18, 1853. In: *The Times*, No. 21406, April 19, 1853.—59-66, 69, 71, 76-80
— July 1, 1853. In: *The Times*, No. 21470, July 2, 1853.—175
— July 7, 1853. In: *The Times*, No. 21475, July 8, 1853.—185-86
— July 28, 1853. In: *The Times*, No. 21493, July 29, 1853.—223
— [Speech at the meeting in Manchester, October 12, 1853.] In: *The Times*, No. 21558, October 13, 1853.—419
— *The State in Its Relations with the Church.* Fourth edition, revised and enlarged. In two volumes, Vols. I-II, London, 1841.—597

Goethe, J. W. von. *An Suleika (Westöstlicher Diwan).*—133
— *Faust.*—624

Golovine, J., Herzen, A. *Who Is F. M.?* In: *The Morning Advertiser*, August 29, 1853.—284

Golovine, J., Herzen, A., Worcell, S. *The Russian Agent, Bakunin.* In: *The Morning Advertiser*, August 24, 1853.—284

[Golovine, J.] (anon.) *How to Write History.* [*From a Foreign Correspondent.*] In: *The Morning Advertiser*, No. 12389, September 3, 1853.—290, 291

Granier de Cassagnac, A. *Paris. 23 mars. Des affaires d'Orient.* In: *Le Constitutionnel,* No. 83, March 24, 1853.—20

Grey, Ch. [Speech in the House of Lords, February 4, 1834.] In: *Hansard's Parliamentary Debates.* 3d series, Vol. XXI, London, 1834.—393

Grey, G. [Speech in the House of Commons, July 5, 1853.] In: *The Times,* No. 21473, July 6, 1853.—188

Grey, H. G. [Speech in the House of Lords, July 7, 1853.] In: *The Times,* No. 21475, July 8, 1853.—185

Grosvenor, R. [Speech in the House of Lords, April 14, 1853.] In: *The Times,* No. 21403, April 15, 1853.—62

Grundtvig, N. *Dissolution of Parliament Explained to the Danish People,* 1853.—101

[Hammer, J. von.] *Geschichte des Osmanischen Reiches, grossentheils aus bisher unbenützten Handschriften und Archiven durch Joseph von Hammer,* Bd. 1-10, Pest, 1827-1835.—22, 229

Hardwicke, Ch. Ph. Y. [Speech in the House of Lords, August 12, 1853.] In: *The Times,* No. 21506, August 13, 1853.—263

Hegel, G. W. F. *Phänomenologie des Geistes.*—481, 487

Herbert, S. [Speech in the House of Commons, April 12, 1853.] In: *The Times,* No. 21401, April 13, 1853.—58

Herries, J. Ch. [Speech in the House of Commons, January 26, 1836.] In: *Hansard's Parliamentary Debates.* 3d series, Vol. IX, London, 1832.—368

Hirsch, W. *Die Opfer der Moucharderie, Rechtfertigungsschrift.* In: *Belletristisches Journal und New-Yorker Criminal-Zeitung,* April 1, 8, 15, 22, 1853.—40-43, 481

[Hobbes, Th.] *The English Works of Thomas Hobbes of Malmesbury; Now First Collected and Edited by Sir William Molesworth.* In 16 volumes, London, 1839-1844.—597

Hodde, L. de la. *La naissance de la république en février 1848,* Paris, 1850.—40

Hogg, J. [Speeches in the House of Commons]
— June 6, 1853. In: *The Times,* No. 21448, June 7, 1853.—123, 125
— July 28, 1853. In: *The Times,* No. 21493, July 29, 1853.—223

Horatius Flacci. *Epistolarum.* Liber primus.—86

Hume, J. [Speeches in the House of Commons]
— August 8, 1831. In: *Hansard's Parliamentary Debates.* 3d series, Vol. V, London, 1831.—358
— July 16, 1832. In: *Hansard's Parliamentary Debates.* 3d series, Vol. XIV, London, 1832.—369
— March 17, 1837. In: *Hansard's Parliamentary Debates.* 3d series, Vol. XXXVII, London, 1837.—401
— August 17, 1846. In: *Hansard's Parliamentary Debates.* 3d series, Vol. LXXXVIII, London, 1846.—367
— March 3 1853. In: *The Times,* No. 21367, March 4, 1853.—51, 69
— June 9 1853. In: *The Times,* No. 21451, June 10, 1853.—125
— July 8, 1853. In: *The Times,* No. 21476, July 9, 1853.—196-97

Hunt, H. [Speech in the House of Commons, August 8, 1831.] In: *Hansard's Parliamentary Debates.* 3d series, Vol. V, London, 1831.—358

Hunt, Th. L. *To the Members of the National Charter Association.* In: *The Northern Star,* No. 734, November 29, 1851.—624

Inglis, R. H. [Speech in the House of Commons, August 24, 1833.] In: *Hansard's Parliamentary Debates.* 3d series, Vol. XX, London, 1833.—379

Jocelyn, R. [Speech in the House of Commons, July 8, 1853.] In: *The Times,* No. 21476, July 9, 1853.—196

Jones, E. *The Cruelties of the Rich. The Highland Lady.—The Yorkshire Factory Prince.* In: *The People's Paper,* No. 74, October 1, 1853.—414
— *A Parliament of Labour. To the Trades and Working Men in General.* In: *The People's Paper,* No. 80, November 12, 1853.—470
— *The People's Friend.* In: *The People's Paper,* No. 50, April 16, 1853.—57-58
— [Speech at the Blackstone-Edge meeting, June 19, 1853.] In: *The People's Paper,* No. 60, June 25, 1853.—171-73
— [Speech at the meeting in Preston, November 4, 1853.] In: *The People's Paper,* No. 80, November 12, 1853.—462
— [Speech at the meeting in Manchester, November 20, 1853.] In: *The People's Paper,* No. 82, November 26, 1853.—514-15
— [Speech at the meeting of the Society of Arts, January 30, 1854.] In: *The People's Paper,* No. 92, February 4, 1854.—612

Knight, H. [Speech in the House of Commons, July 13, 1840.] In: *Hansard's Parliamentary Debates.* 3d series, Vol. LV, London, 1840.—362

Kossuth, L. *The Lord Dudley Stuart, April 15, 1853.* In: *The Times,* No. 21412, April 26, 1853.—84

[Kupffer, A. Y.] *Voyage dans les environs du Mont Elbrouz dans le Caucase, entrepris par ordre de Sa Majesté l'Empereur; en 1829. Rapport fait à l'Académie Impériale des Sciences de St.-Pétersbourg, par M. Kupffer, membre de cette Académie,* St.-Pétersbourg, 1830.—392

Labouchere, H. [Speech in the House of Commons, July 5, 1853.] In: *The Times,* No. 21473, July 6, 1853.—188

La Guéronnière, L. [Article.] In: *Le Pays,* July 19, 1853.—209

Lamarche, H. *Affaires d'Orient.—Rejet de l'Ultimatum Russe.* In: *Le Siècle,* May 26, 1853.—110-11
— *Affaires d'Orient.* In: *Le Siècle,* No. 6417, July 20, 1853.—254

Landolphe, Blanc, L., Barthélemy, E., Shapper, C., Willich, A., Mihaloski, Simonyi, E. *Londres, le 1er mars 1851.* In: *La Patrie,* No. 66, March 7, 1851.—506

Layard, A. H. *Nineveh and Its Remains: with an Account of a Visit to the Chaldaean Christians of Kurdistan, and the Yezidis, or Devil-Worshippers; and an Enquiry into the Manners and Arts of the Ancient Assyrians.* In two volumes, London, 1849.—597
— [Speeches in the House of Commons]

— July 7, 1853. In: *The Times*, No. 21475, July 8, 1853.—185, 186
— August 16, 1853. In: *The Times*, No. 21509, August 17, 1853.—266, 268-71

Letellier, A. [Article.] In: *L'Assemblée nationale*, No. 198, July 17, 1853.—210

Liddell, H. G. [Speech in the House of Commons, July 7, 1853.] In: *The Times*, No. 21475, July 8, 1853.—187

Lowe, R. [Speech in the House of Commons, July 28, 1853.] In: *The Times*, No. 21493, July 29, 1853.—223

Mackinnon, W. A. *History of Civilisation.* In two volumes, Vols. I-II, London, 1846.—597

Maddock, Th. H. [Speech in the House of Commons, July 28, 1853.] In: *The Times*, No. 21493, July 29, 1853.—223

Mahon, Ph. H. [Speech in the House of Commons, April 20, 1836.] In: *Hansard's Parliamentary Debates.* 3d series, Vol. XXXII, London, 1836.—377, 393

Malmesbury, J. H. [Speeches in the House of Lords]
— December 6, 1852. In: L. Simpson, *The Eastern Question...*, London, 1854.—617, 618
— July 7, 1853. In: *The Times*, No. 21475, July 8, 1853.—186
— July 18, 1853. In: *The Times*, No. 21484, July 19, 1853.—211
— August 9, 1853. In: *The Times*, No. 21503, August 10, 1853.—252
— August 12, 1853. In: *The Times*, No. 21506, August 13, 1853.—258-62

M[arx], F. *The Russian Agent, Bakunin. To the Editor of the Morning Advertiser.* In: *The Morning Advertiser*, August 23, 1853.—284

Mayer, P. [Preface of the Editors to E. Barthélemy's letter.] In: *La Patrie*, No. 71, March 12, 1851.—506-07

[McNeill, J.] *Progress and Present Position of Russia in the East*, London, 1836.—357

Mill, J. *The History of British India*, London, 1818.—150

Milnes, R. M. [Speeches in the House of Commons]
— August 16, 1853. In: *The Times*, No. 21509, August 17, 1853.—272-73
— August 20, 1853. In: *The Times*, No. 21513, August 22, 1853.—280
— *Memorials of a Tour in Some Parts of Greece*, London, 1834.—597

Molesworth, W.—see [Hobbes, Th.] *The English Works of Thomas Hobbes....*
— [Speech in the House of Commons, August 4, 1853.] In: *The Times*, No. 21499, August 5, 1853.—256

Molinari, G. de. *Le banket....* In: *La Patrie*, No. 58, February 27, 1851.—506

Monsell, W. *To the Editor of the Times.* In: *The Times*, No. 21447, June 6, 1853.—120

Müllner, A. *Die Schuld.*—43

M [un], T. *A Discourse of Trade, From England into the East-Indies: Answering to diverse Objections which are usually made against the same*, London, 1621.—152

Muntz, G. F. [Speech in the House of Commons, August 16, 1853.] In: *The Times*, No. 21509, August 17, 1853.—273

Mure, W. *A Critical History of the Language and Literature of Antient Greece*, Vols. I-II, London, 1850.—597

Nefftzer, A. *Bulletin du Jour.* In: *La Presse*, August 4, 1853.—243

Newcastle, H. P. [Speech in the House of Lords, August 9, 1853.] In: *The Times*, No. 21503, August 10, 1853.—252

Newman, F. W. *Lectures on Political Economy*, London, 1851.—161

O'Brien, W. S. [Speech in the House of Commons, March 16, 1847.] In: *Hansard's Parliamentary Debates.* 3d series, Vol. XCI, London, 1847.—367

O'Connell, D. [Speech in the House of Commons, March 17, 1837.] In: *Hansard's Parliamentary Debates.* 3d series, Vol. XXXVII, London, 1837.—402

Oliveira, B. *Tour in the East.*—597

Owen, R. [Speech at the meeting of the Society of Arts, January 30, 1854.] In: *The People's Paper*, No. 92, February 4, 1854.—612

Pakington, J. [Speeches in the House of Commons]
— July 28, 1853. In: *The Times*, No. 21493, July 29, 1853.—223
— August 16, 1853. In: *The Times*, No. 21509, August 17, 1853.—271, 272

Palmerston, J. [Speeches in the House of Commons]
— February 3, 1808. In: *The Parliamentary Debates from the Year 1803 to the Present Time* [Ser. I], Vol. X, London, 1812; G. H. Francis, *Opinions and Policy of the Right Honourable Viscount Palmerston, G. C. B., M. P., &c. as Minister, Diplomatist, and Statesman, during More Than Forty Years of Public Life*, London, 1852.—347
— March 10, 1812. In: *The Parliamentary Debates* [Ser. I], Vol. XXI, London, 1812; G. H. Francis, *Opinions and Policy of the Right Honourable Viscount Palmerston...*, London, 1852.—349
— March 1, 1813. In: *The Parliamentary Debates* [Ser. I], Vol. XXIV, London, 1813; G. H. Francis, *Opinions and Policy of the Right Honourable Viscount Palmerston...*, London, 1852.—351
— March 8, 1816. In: *The Parliamentary Debates* [Ser. I], Vol. XXXIII, London, 1816; G. H. Francis, *Opinions and Policy of the Right Honourable Viscount Palmerston...*, London, 1852.—349
— April 25, 1816. In: *The Parliamentary Debates* [Ser. I], Vol. XXXIII, London, 1816; G. H. Francis, *Opinions and Policy of the Right Honourable Viscount Palmerston...*, London, 1852.—349
— May 16, 1820. In: *The Parliamentary Debates.* New series [2], Vol. I, London, 1820; G. H. Francis, *Opinions and Policy of the Right Honourable Viscount Palmerston...*, London, 1852.—349-50
— June 14, 1820. In: *The Parliamentary Debates.* New series [2], Vol. I, London, 1820; G. H. Francis, *Opinions and Policy of the Right Honourable Viscount Palmerston...*, London, 1852.—350
— April 30, 1823. In: G. H. Francis, *Opinions and Policy of the Right Honourable Viscount Palmerston...*, London, 1852.—354, 397
— March 5, 1824. In: *The Parliamentary Debates.* New series [2], Vol. X, London,

1824; G. H. Francis, *Opinions and Policy of the Right Honourable Viscount Palmerston...*, London, 1852.—350
— April 9, 1824. In: *The Parliamentary Debates.* New series [2], Vol. XI, London, 1825; G. H. Francis, *Opinions and Policy of the Right Honourable Viscount Palmerston...*, London, 1852.—350
— March 11, 1825. In: *The Parliamentary Debates.* New series [2], Vol. XII, London, 1825; G. H. Francis, *Opinions and Policy of the Right Honourable Viscount Palmerston...*, London, 1852.—350
— January 31, 1828. In: G. H. Francis, *Opinions and Policy of the Right Honourable Viscount Palmerston...*, London, 1852.—354
— February 26, 1828. In: *The Parliamentary Debates.* New series [2], Vol. XVIII, London, 1828; G. H. Francis, *Opinions and Policy of the Right Honourable Viscount Palmerston...*, London, 1852.—350
— March 10, 1828. In: *The Parliamentary Debates.* New series [2], Vol. XVIII, London, 1828; G. H. Francis, *Opinions and Policy of the Right Honourable Viscount Palmerston...*, London, 1852.—350
— March 12, 1828. In: *The Parliamentary Debates.* New series [2], Vol. XVIII, London, 1828; G. H. Francis, *Opinions and Policy of the Right Honourable Viscount Palmerston...*, London, 1852.—350
— March 31, 1828. In: *The Parliamentary Debates.* New series [2], Vol. XVIII, London, 1828.—354
— June 27, 1828. In: *The Parliamentary Debates.* New series [2], Vol. XIX, London, 1829.—353
— February 10, 1829. In: *The Parliamentary Debates.* New series [2], Vol. XX, London, 1829.—351
— March 18, 1829. In: *The Parliamentary Debates.* New series [2], Vol. XX, London, 1829; G. H. Francis, *Opinions and Policy of the Right Honourable Viscount Palmerston...*, London, 1852.—351
— May 7, 1829. In: G. H. Francis, *Opinions and Policy of the Right Honourable Viscount Palmerston...*, London, 1852.—352
— June 1, 1829. In: G. H. Francis, *Opinions and Policy of the Right Honourable Viscount Palmerston...*, London, 1852.—354
— February 5, 1830. In: G. H. Francis, *Opinions and Policy of the Right Honourable Viscount Palmerston...*, London, 1852.—355
— February 16, 1830. In: G. H. Francis, *Opinions and Policy of the Right Honourable Viscount Palmerston...*, London, 1852.—355, 357
— March 24, 1831. In: G. H. Francis, *Opinions and Policy of the Right Honourable Viscount Palmerston...*, London, 1852.—353
— August 8, 1831. In: *Hansard's Parliamentary Debates.* 3d series, Vol. V, London, 1831.—357-58
— August 16, 1831. In: *Hansard's Parliamentary Debates.* 3d series, Vol. VI, London, 1832.—362
— January 26, 1832. In: *Hansard's Parliamentary Debates.* 3d series, Vol. IX, London, 1832.—360
— June 28, 1832. In: G. H. Francis, *Opinions and Policy of the Right Honourable Viscount Palmerston...*, London, 1852.—360
— July 16, 1832. In: G. H. Francis, *Opinions and Policy of the Right Honourable Viscount Palmerston...*, London, 1852.—368
— August 7, 1832. In: G. H. Francis, *Opinions and Policy of the Right Honourable Viscount Palmerston...*, London, 1852.—358, 359
— April 2, 1833. In: G. H. Francis, *Opinions and Policy of the Right Honourable Viscount Palmerston...*, London, 1852.—350

— July 12, 1832. In: *Hansard's Parliamentary Debates.* 3d series, Vol. XIV, London, 1833.—369
— March 17, 1834. In: *Hansard's Parliamentary Debates.* 3d series, Vol. XXII, London, 1834.—375, 382, 384
— June 21, 1838. In: *Hansard's Parliamentary Debates.* 3d series, Vol. XCIII, London, 1838.—404, 405-06
— July 13, 1840. In: *Hansard's Parliamentary Debates.* 3d series, Vol. LV, London, 1840.—365

Peel, R. [Speech in the House of Commons, June 14, 1853.] In: *The Times,* No. 21455, June 15, 1853.—137

Pellier, Am. *Paris, 19 septembre.* In: *L'Assemblée nationale,* No. 263, September 20, 1853.—318

Phillimore, J. G. [Speech in the House of Commons, June 14, 1853.] In: *The Times,* No. 21455, June 15, 1853.—137

[Pollexfen, J.] *England and East-India Inconsistent in Their Manufactures, Being an Answer to a Treatise, Intituled, an Essay on the East-India Trade,* London, 1697.—153

Poesche, Th., Goepp, Ch. *The New Rome. The United States of the World,* New York, 1852, Philadelphia, 1853.—625

Pösche, Th. *Die "Klassenkämpfer".* In: *Neu-England Zeitung,* September 3, 1853.—625

Raffles, Th. S. *The History of Java.* In two volumes, Vol. I, London, 1817.—126, 131

Raymond, X. [Article.] In: *Journal des Débats,* May 23, 1853.—105

[Richards, A.] *The New Battle of Navarino.* In: *The Morning Advertiser,* December 13, 1853.—536-37
— *"The Times" and the New Gunpowder plot.* In: *The Morning Advertiser,* No. 19291, April 21, 1853.—68
— *The Demand for Explanations.* In: *The Morning Advertiser,* No. 19382, August 5, 1853.—240
— *A Word to the Morning Post.* In: *The Morning Advertiser,* No. 19366, July 18, 1853.—212

Roden, R. J. [Speech in the House of Lords, August 9, 1853.] In: *The Times,* No. 21503, August 10, 1853.—251

Roebuck, J. A. [Speech in the House of Commons, March 17, 1837.] In: *Hansard's Parliamentary Debates.* 3d series, Vol. XXXVII, London, 1837.—401

Russell, J. [Speeches in the House of Commons]
— February 10, 1853. In: *The Times,* No. 21349, February 11, 1853.—51
— March 3, 1853. In: L. F. Simpson, *The Eastern Question...,* London, 1854.—619-20
— March 18, 1853. In: *The Times,* No. 21380, March 19, 1853.—50, 56
— April 4, 1853. In: *The Times,* No. 21394, April 5, 1853.—51, 52
— May 31, 1853. In: *The Times,* No. 21443, June 1, 1853.—119-20
— July 1, 1853. In: *The Times,* No. 21470, July 2, 1853.—177
— July 5, 1853. In: *The Times,* No. 21473, July 6, 1853.—188
— July 11, 1853. In: *The Times,* No. 21478, July 12, 1853.—193
— July 14, 1853. In: *The Times,* No. 21481, July 15, 1853.—202
— July 18, 1853. In: *The Times,* No. 21484, July 19, 1853.—211
— July 28, 1853. In: *The Times,* No. 21493, July 29, 1853.—223

Stanley, E. H. [Speech in the House of Commons, June 13, 1853.] In: *The Times*, No. 21454, June 14, 1853.—138-39

Stewart, P. [Speech in the House of Commons, April 20, 1836.] In: *Hansard's Parliamentary Debates*. 3d series, Vol. XXXII, London, 1836.—363-64, 394, 395, 398

Stirling, W. *Annals of the Artists of Spain*, Vols. I-III, London, 1848.—597

St. Leonards. [Speech in the House of Lords, August 9, 1853.] In: *The Times*, No. 21503, August 10, 1853.—252

Stowe, H. E. Beecher. *Uncle Tom's Cabin*.—80

Stuart, D. [Speeches in the House of Commons]
— March 17, 1837. In: *Hansard's Parliamentary Debates*. 3d series, Vol. XXXVII, London, 1837.—392, 403
— March 22, 1837. In: *Hansard's Parliamentary Debates*. 3d series, Vol. XXXVII, London, 1837.—364
— August 2, 1853. In: *The Times*, No. 21497, August 3, 1853.—240
— August 16, 1853. In: *The Times*, No. 21509, August 17, 1853.—272

Sugden, E. [Speech in the House of Commons, January 16, 1832.] In: *Hansard's Parliamentary Debates*. 3d series, Vol. IX, London, 1832.—369

Thousand and One Nights.—22, 198, 223

Tooke, Th. *A History of Prices, and of the State of the Circulation, from 1793 to 1837; Preceded by a Brief Sketch of the State of the Corn Trade in the Last Two Centuries*, Vols. I-II, London, 1838.—524
— *A History of Prices, and of the State of the Circulation, in 1838 and 1839, with remarks on the Corn Laws, and on some of the alterations proposed in our banking system*, London, 1840.—524
— *A History of Prices, and of the State of the Circulation, from 1839 to 1847 inclusive*, London, 1848.—524

Urquhart, D. *How Our Negotiations with Russia will Conduct Us into a War with France*. Letter III. In: *The Morning Advertiser*, No. 19540, February 6. 1854.—607
— (anon.) *The Kaiser and the Czar*. In: *The Morning Advertiser*, August 23, 1853.—279
— (anon.) *The Political Malefactors*. In: *The Morning Advertiser*, September 20, 1853.—309, 312, 325
— *Progress of Russia in the West, North, and South, by Opening the Sources of Opinion and Appropriating the Channels of Wealth and Power*. Second edition, London, 1853.—118, 390, 394, 396, 397, 398, 404, 545
— *The Relative Power of Russia and Great Britain*. In: *The Morning Advertiser*, August 15, 1853.—257
— *The Spirit of the East, Illustrated in a Journal of Travels Through Roumeli during an Eventful Period*, Vols. I-II, London, 1838.—26
— *Time in Diplomacy—The "European Recognition". To the Editor of the Morning Advertiser*. In: *The Morning Advertiser*, August 12, 1853.—257
— (anon.) *Turkey and Its Resources: Its municipal Organization and free trade; the state and prospects of English commerce in the East, the new administration of Greece, Its revenue and national possessions*, London, 1833.—26

— *War between England and France. To the editor of the Morning Advertiser.* In: *The Morning Advertiser,* August 16, 1853.—257
— *What Means "Protection" of the Greek Church? To the Editor of the Morning Advertiser.* In: *The Morning Advertiser,* August 11, 1853.—257

Urquhart, W. P. *Life and Times of Francesco Sforza, Duke of Milan, with a Preliminary Sketch of the History of Italy,* Vols. I-II, Edinburgh and London, 1852.—597

Vidil, J. [Letter to the editors of *La Patrie.*] In: *La Patrie,* No. 69, March 10, 1851.—506

[Vidocq, F. E.] *Mémoires de Vidocq,* T. I-IV, Paris, 1828-1829.—40

Walmsley, J. [Speech in the House of Commons, July 18, 1853.] In: *The Times,* No. 21484, July 19, 1853.—211

Wayland, Fr. *The Elements of Political Economy,* Boston, 1837.—626

Weitling, W. *Das Evangelium eines armen Sünders,* Bern, 1845.—623

Wellington, A. [Speech in the House of Lords, February 4, 1834.] In: *Hansard's Parliamentary Debates.* 3d series, vol. XXI, London, 1834.—376

Williams, W. [Speech in the House of Commons, March 1, 1853.] In: *The Times,* No. 21365, March 2, 1853.—51, 69

Willich, A. *Doctor Karl Marx und seine Enthüllungen.* In: *Belletristisches Journal und New-Yorker Criminal-Zeitung,* October 28, November 4, 1853.—481-87, 489, 490, 491-503, 506

Wise, J. A. [Speech in the House of Commons, August 4, 1853.] In: *The Times,* No. 21499, August 5, 1853.—255-56

Wood, Ch. [Speeches in the House of Commons]
— June 3, 1853. In: *The Times,* No. 21446, June 4, 1853.—120-23, 125, 126
— July 7, 1853. In: *The Times,* No. 21475, July 8, 1853.—186
— August 15, 1853. In: *The Times,* No. 21508, August 16, 1853.—265

DOCUMENTS

[Abdul Mejid.] [*The Firman Accorded by the Sultan to the Patriarch of the Greek Orthodox Church.*] In: *The Times,* No. 21467, June 29, 1853.—194
— *To General Baraguay d'Hilliers.* In: *The Times,* No. 21605, December 7, 1853.—532

Accounts Relating to Trade and Navigation. For the Six Months ended July 5, 1853. In: *The Economist,* No. 519, August 6, 1853.—247-49

Accounts Relating to Trade and Navigation. For the Eleven Months ended December 5, 1853. In: *The Economist,* No. 541, January 7, 1854.—578

Alexander Georgiewitsch. [*The reply of Prince Alexander of Servia to the application of the Ottoman Porte to declare himself on the conflict between it and Russia.*] In: *The Times*, No. 21601, December 2, 1853.—523-24

The Ambassadors at Constantinople to Redschid Pasha. In: *The Times*, No. 21630, January 5, 1854.—575

Backhouse, J. [Letter to Messrs. Bell.] *Foreign Office, May 5th, 1836.* In: D. Urquhart, *Progress of Russia in the West, North, and South...*, 2nd ed., London, 1853.—396
— *Correspondence between Mr. Backhouse and Mr. Urquhart.* In: *The Times*, No. 16948, January 25, 1839; *The Portfolio*, 1844, Vol. II, No. VI.—387, 388

Bineau, J. M. *Rapport à l'Empereur.* In: *Le Moniteur universel*, No. 27, January 27, 1854.—604

Clarendon, G. *The Earl of Clarendon to Sir G. H. Seymour. Foreign-office*, 16th July, 1853. In: *Sunday Times*, September 11, 1853.—301

Commission to Examine into the State of Mind of Feargus O'Connor, Esq., Late M.P. for Nottingham. In: *The People's Paper*, No. 50, April 16, 1853.—57

Correspondence relative to the affairs of Hungary. 1847-1849. Presented to both Houses of Parliament by Command of Her Majesty. August 15, 1850, London.—391

Correspondence respecting the Rights and Privileges of the Latin and Greek Churches in Turkey. Part I. *Presented to both Houses of Parliament by Command of Her Majesty*, London, 1854.—606, 615, 616

Declaration of Circassian Independence, addressed to the Courts of Europe. In: *The Portfolio; or a Collection of State Papers, Illustrative of the History of Our Times*, 1836, Vol. I, No. IV.—401

Directions and Regulations of the General Board of Health, Whitehall, September 20, 1853. In: *The Times*, No. 21540, September 22, 1853.—326

Drouyn-de-Lhuys, E. *Circulaire du Gouvernement de l'Empereur. Paris, le 25 juin 1853.* In: *Le Moniteur universel*, No. 195, July 14, 1853.—203
— *Circulaire. Paris, le 15 juillet 1853.* In: *Le Moniteur universel*, No. 198, July 17, 1853.—209
— *Circulaire. Paris, le 30 décembre 1853.* In: *Le Moniteur universel*, No. 6, January 6, 1854; *The Times*, No. 21632, January 7, 1854.—560-62, 575

An expository Statement to accompany the Resolutions, London, 1853.—68

[Ferdinand.] *Proclamation de l'Empereur Ferdinand d'Autriche en date de Vienne, le 11 Novembre 1846.* In: G. Fr. Martens, *Recueil de traités d'Alliance, de paix, de neutralité....* [Pt. IV.] Nouveau recueil général. T. X. Pour 1847. Gottingue, 1852.—367

(*From the Quarterly Return of the Registrar-General.*) In: *The Times*, No. 21498, August 4, 1853.—246

Gladstone, W. *The [...] resolutions are to be proposed by Mr. Chancellor of the Exchequer in Committee on Acts relating to the National Debt....* In: *The Times*, No. 21397, April 8, 1853.—46, 52-55

Gortschakoff, M. D. *The [...] proclamation to the inhabitants of Moldavia and Wallachia.* In: *The Times,* No. 21477, July 11, 1853.—211, 240

Lagrené, T. *Note to Count Nesselrode.* In: *Hansard's Parliamentary Debates,* 3d series, Vol. XXII, London, 1834.—383

Letters from the Black Sea and the Caucasus.—The Vixen Again. In: *The Portfolio,* London, [1844], Vol. II, No. VIII.—403

[Lieven, K.] *Copy of a Despatch from Prince Lieven, and Count Matuszevich, addressed to Count Nesselrode, dated London, 1st (13th) June, 1829.* In: *The Portfolio. Diplomatic Review* (new series), London, 1843, Vol. I, No. I.—165, 167

Marieni, L. R. *Intendeza Prov. delle Finanze in Pavia Avviso d'Asia.* In: *Gazzetta ufficiale di Milano,* No. 22, 1854.—602

Memoir on the Means Possessed by Russia for Breaking up the Alliance Between France and England, April, 1834. In: *The Portfolio; or a Collection of State Papers, etc. etc. Illustrative of the History of Our Times,* London, 1836, Vol. II, No. XIV.—166

Menschikoff, A. S. *His Highness Redschid Pasha, Minister of Foreign Affairs.* In: *The Times,* No. 21506, August 13, 1853.—261-62

Napoleon. *Décret fixant le Prix des tabacs à livrer aux troupes de la marine.* In: *Le Moniteur universel,* No. 223, August 11, 1853.—245

Nesselrode, Ch. *Circular Note [May 30 (June 11), 1853].* In: *Le Moniteur universel,* No. 195, July 14, 1853.—203, 237-38, 242; *The Times,* No. 21461, June 22, 1853.—166, 167, 258; *Journal de Saint-Pétersbourg,* No. 122, June 12, 1853.—258
- *Circulaire. St.-Pétersbourg, le 20 juin (2d of July), 1853.* In: *The Times,* No. 21478, July 12, 1853.—193, 195, 196, 258, 301; *Le Moniteur universel,* No. 198, July 17, 1853.—209; *Journal de Saint-Pétersbourg,* No. 139, July 3, 1853.—258
- *Despatch from Count Nesselrode to M. De Tatistcheff. [d.d.] St. Petersburg, Feb. 12, 1829.* In: *The Portfolio; a Collection of State Papers, and Other Documents and Correspondence, Historical, Diplomatic, and Commercial,* London, 1836, Vol. IV, No. 27.—174-75
- *To Meyendorf, Sept. 7 (August 26), 1853.* In: *Die Zeit,* No. 218, September 18, 1853; *The Times,* No. 21540, September 22, 1853.—323-24
- [*Reply to the note by M. Lagrené, October 1833.*] In: *Hansard's Parliamentary Debates.* 3d series, Vol. XXII, London, 1834.—383

Nicholas I. *Rescript Sarskoje-Zelo, Oct. 27 (Nov. 8) 1853.* In: *The Times,* No. 21610, December 13, 1853.—538
- *Imperial manifesto. Ukase to the Governing Senate.* In: *Hamburger Nachrichten,* July 29, 1853; *Le Moniteur universel,* No. 214, August 2, 1853.—235
- [Declaration of war of April 26, 1828.] In: *The Portfolio; or a Collection of State Papers, Illustrative of the History of Our Times,* London, 1836, Vol. I, No. VII.—164
- [Manifesto of October 1, 1829.] In: *The Portfolio; or a Collection of State Papers, Illustrative of the History of Our Times,* London, 1836, Vol. I, No. 7.—164

The Note approved by the Powers represented at the Vienna Conference, and proposed simultaneously for the acceptance of Russia and Turkey. In: *The Times,* No. 21523, September 1, 1853.—292, 309, 409, 416

[*The Note presented to the Divan by the Ambassadors of the four European Powers on the 15th Dec., 1853.*] *Pera, Dec. 12, 1853.* Signed: S. de Redcliffe, Baraguay d'Hilliers, L. de Wildenbruck, De Bruck. In: *The Times*, No. 21635, January 11, 1854; *The Leader*, No. 199, January 14, 1854.—560, 575, 576

Pozzo di Borgo. *Copy of a Despatch from Count Pozzo di Borgo, dated Paris, 22nd Dec. 1826.* In: *The Portfolio; Diplomatic Review* (new series), London, 1843, Vol. I, No. II.—164, 203
— *Copy of a Very Secret Despatch from Count Pozzo di Borgo, Dated Paris, the 28th November, 1828.* In: *The Portfolio; or a Collection of State Papers, Illustrative of the History of Our Times*, London, 1836, Vol. I, Nos. VII-IX.—164, 165, 166, 167, 227
— *Copy of a Very Secret Despatch from Count Pozzo di Borgo, Dated Paris, December 14th, 1828.* In: *The Portfolio; or a Collection of State Papers, Illustrative of the History of Our Times*, London, 1836, Vol. II, No. XIII.—166

Preston Manufacturers' Manifesto. In: *The Times*, No. 21576, November 3, 1853.—447, 448

The protocol signed on the 5th of December at Vienna by the representatives of the Four Great Powers. In: *The Times*, No. 21615, December 19, 1853; *The Morning Herald*, No. 22345, December 19, 1853.—575

Redcliffe, Baraguay d'Hilliers. *To the governor of Sevastopol.* In: *The Daily News*, No. 2390, January 17, 1854.—588

Redschid Pasha. [*The Note addressed by Turkey to the Four Powers.*] In: *The Times*, No. 21528, September 8, 1853.—292
— *To Lord Stratford de Redcliffe and General Baraguay d'Hilliers.* In: *The Times*, No. 21622, December 27, 1853.—575
— *Sublime Porte.—Department of Foreign Affairs. To his Excellency the Count De Nesselrode.* In: *The Leader*, No. 172, July 9, 1853.—267
— *To the representatives of England, France, Austria, and Prussia.* In: *The Leader*, No. 181, September 10, 1853.—407

[Sébastiani, H. *Correspondence with Mme Adélaide, sister of Louis-Philippe.*] In: *La Presse*, July 15, 1853.—203-08

Traité de paix entre la Russie et la Perse, conclu et signé à Tourkmantchai, le 22 février 1828. In: G. Fr. Martens, *Recueil de Traités d'Alliance, de Paix, de Neutralité....* Tome VII, Seconde Partie, 1824-1828, Gottingue, 1830.—355

Traité de paix entre la Russie et Porte Ottomane signé à Adrianople le 2/14 Septembre 1829. In: G. Fr. Martens, *Recueil de Traités d'Alliance, de Paix, de Neutralité....* [Pt. II.] T. VIII, 1825-1830, Gottingue, 1831.—392

Traité d'Unkiar-Iskelessi entre la Russie et la Porte Ottomanne, signé à Constantinople le 8 Juillet 1833. In: G. Fr. Martens, *Recueil de Traités d'Alliance, de Paix, de Neutralité....* [Pt. II.] T. 11, 1830-1834. Goettingue, 1837.—372, 601; *The Morning Herald*, August 21, 1833.—379

The Treaty of Balta Liman, dated May 1, 1849. In: *The Times*, No. 21458, June 18, 1853.—144

Vice-Chancellor's Court, Saturday, Sept. 3. (Before Sir W. P. Wood.) The Shrewsbury and Birmingham Railway Company v. the Directors of the Said Company and Others. In: *The Times,* No. 21525, September 5, 1853.—303-04

Victoria. [Speech from the throne at the opening of Parliament, January 19, 1847.] In: *Hansard's Parliamentary Debates.* 3d series, Vol. LXXXIX, London, 1847.—367

William IV. [Speech from the throne at the proroguing of Parliament, August 29, 1833.] In: *Hansard's Parliamentary Debates.* 3d series, Vol. XX, London, 1833.—380

ANONYMOUS ARTICLES AND REPORTS
PUBLISHED IN PERIODIC EDITIONS

Allgemeine Zeitung, No. 1, January 1, 1853: *Wien, 29 Dec.*—616-17
— No. 337, December 3, 1853: *Der neue Vorschlag der Machte der Wiener Konferenz.*—528
— No. 9, January 9, 1854: *Der Kriegsschauplatz in Asien.*—584

L'Assemblée nationale, No. 251, September 8, 1853.—292-93

Der Bund, No. 141, May 23, 1853: *Die österreichische Gesandtschaft in Bern.*—107

Le Constitutionnel, No. 231, August 19, 1853: *Le Journal de Constantinople....*—278
— No. 288, October 15, 1853: *Nous avons lieu....*—417-18

Courrier de Marseille, No. 2928, March 20, 1853: *Affaires d'Orient* (signed: Esprit Privat).—18

The Daily News, No. 2133, March 25, 1853.—20
— No. 2207, June 17, 1853: *The Armenians in Turkey.*—138
— No. 2352, December 3, 1853: *Portsmouth, Dec. 2.*—533
— No. 2356, December 8, 1853: *The Russians at Portsmouth. Portsmouth, Dec. 7.*—534
— No. 2391, January 18, 1854: *Great despots and great conquerors are never satisfied....*—588

The Dublin Evening Mail, No. 5466, January 2, 1854: *From Our Private Correspondent. London, Saturday.*—559-60

The Economist. Weekly Commercial Times, Bankers' Gazette, and Railway Monitor: a Political, Literary, and General Newspaper, Vol. XI, No. 498, March 12, 1853: *Turkey and Its Value.*—15
— No. 505, April 30, 1853: *China.*—95
— No. 507, May 14, 1853: *Backwardness of the Season.*—98
— No. 508, May 21, 1853: *China and the Tea Trade.*—97
— No. 516, July 16, 1853: *Bank Returns and Money Market.*—210
— No. 518, July 30, 1853: *The Corn Trade Under Protection.*—234; *The Eastern Question.*—237
— No. 519, August 6, 1853: *Accounts Relating to Trade and Navigation.*—247; *(From Messrs. J. and C. Sturge's Circular.) Birmingham, Aug. 3, 1853.*—249

The Morning Post, No. 24726, March 22, 1853: *False colouring....*—20
— No. 24734, March 31, 1853: *Prussia.*—28
— April 18, 1853: *London, Monday, April 18, 1853.*—58
— May 27, 1853: *Truth is confined within strict limits....*—109
— No. 24821, July 11, 1853: *Vienna, Saturday Afternoon*—193; *Constantinople, June 26.*—194
— No. 24825, July 15, 1853: *Paris, Thursday Night.*—203
— No. 24827, July 18, 1853: *The Week.*—210
— No. 24835, July 27, 1853: *The working classes in many parts....*—225-26
— No. 24836, July 28, 1853: *Many an occurrence of national importance....*—226
— August 2, 1853: *On Tuesday last we announced....*—234, 235
— August 11, 1853: *London, Thursday, August 11, 1853.*—246
— No. 24877, September 14, 1853: *Manchester Trade Report. From Our Own Correspondent. Manchester, Sept. 13.*—315
— No. 24878, September 15, 1853: *London, Thursday, Sept. 15, 1853.*—322
— No. 24881, September 19, 1853: *London, Monday, Sept. 19, 1853.*—318, 321
— No. 24883, September 21, 1853: *London, Wednesday, Sept. 21, 1853.*—322
— No. 24887, September 26, 1853: *Money Market and City News. City, Saturday Evening.*—330
— October 19, 1853: *Paris, Monday.*—422
— October 21, 1853.—422
— November 14, 1853: *The Week.*—470
— November 17, 1853: *War and its probabilities....*—526
— December 6, 1853: *London, Tuesday, December 6, 1853.*—527-28; *The Russians at Portsmouth.—Singular Affair. Portsmouth, Dec. 5.*—534
— December 8, 1853: *London, Thursday, December 8, 1853.*—531-32
— December 13, 1853: *London, Tuesday, December 13, 1853.*—537

National-Zeitung, No. 340, July 7, 1853.—235
— No. 384, August 19, 1853.—280

Neue Preussische Zeitung, No. 177, August 2, 1853: *Wien, 29. Juli.*—240
— No. 304, December 29, 1853.—569

Neue Rheinische Zeitung, No. 115, October 13, 1848: *Berlin, 10 Oktbr.*—285

New-York Daily Tribune, No. 3761, May 6, 1853: *The American Art-Union Investigation.*—181; *Mrs. Stowe at Edinburgh.*—176; *The Dress Makers of London.*—176; *Debate on the Fisheries in the House of Lords on the 21st.*—176; *Greece.*—176; *John P. Hale.*—176; *Spain.*—176; *Athlone Election.*—176
— No. 3839, August 6, 1853: *Peace or War.*—293

The Observer, May 22, 1853: *London, Sunday, May 22.*—103
— September 4, 1853: *The Funds-city, Saturday, Sept. 3.*—305
— September 11, 1853: *The Banks of England Directors....*—305
— September 19, 1853: *The Beginning of the End.*—316
— September 26, 1853: *The Funds-city, Saturday, Sept. 24.*—329, 330

Œsterreichische Correspondenz, October 31, 1853.—445

Il Parlamento, No. 178, July 29, 1853: *Torino, 28 luglio. La Politica Americana in Europa.*—243-44

— No. 21658, February 7, 1854: *Prussia (From Our Own Correspondent). Berlin, Feb. 3.*—609
— No. 21661, February 10, 1854: *Vienna, Thursday Morning.*—614

Der Wanderer, September 4, 1853: *Aus Odessa.*—293
— No. 498, October 28, 1853: *Wien, 27 October.*—446

Weekly Dispatch, No. 2707, October 30, 1853: *Town Talk.*—440

The Weekly Times, Vol. VII, No. 345, August 21, 1853: *The Parliamentary Doings of '53.*—283
— Vol. VII, No. 355, October 30, 1853: *The War Mania.—Thickening of the Plot.*—443

Die Zeit, No. 77, April 3, 1853: *Die Contre-Revolution.*—37

INDEX OF PERIODICALS

Courrier de Marseille—18

Criminal-Zeitung—see *Belletristisches Journal und New-Yorker Criminal-Zeitung*

The Daily News—English liberal newspaper, organ of the industrial bourgeoisie, published in London from 1846 to 1928.—19, 25-26, 80, 138, 272, 295, 304, 436, 462, 533, 534, 562, 584, 588

Deutsche-Brüsseler-Zeitung—newspaper founded by German refugees in Brussels and published from January 1847 to February 1848. From September 1847 Marx and Engels regularly contributed to it and under their influence it became an organ of revolutionary communist propaganda.—87

The Dublin Evening Mail—liberal daily published from 1823.—559, 560

Dublin Freeman's Journal—see *The Freeman's Journal*

The Economist. Weekly Commercial Times, Bankers' Gazette, and Railway Monitor: a Political, Literary, and General Newspaper—English journal published in London since 1843.—15, 26, 95-98, 114, 161, 210, 234, 237, 247, 248, 299, 305, 409, 419, 438, 441, 442, 460-61, 464-68, 513, 525, 542, 578, 597

L'Emancipation—Belgian daily, organ of Catholic clerical circles, founded in Brussels in 1830.—38, 243

The Examiner—English liberal weekly published in London from 1808 to 1881.—255, 438

Frankfurter Journal—German daily published in Frankfurt am Main from the seventeenth century to 1903; voiced liberal views in the 1840s and 1850s.—67, 422

Frankfurter Postzeitung—German newspaper published in Frankfurt am Main from 1619 to 1866; organ of the Federal Diet in the 1850s; appeared under this title from 1852.—246, 632

The Freeman's Journal—Irish liberal daily published in Dublin from 1763 to 1924; supported the demand for the repeal of the Union and defended the Irish tenants' rights in the 1840s and 1850s.—611

Gazette—see *The London Gazette*

Gazette—see *Oesterreichisch Kaiserliche Wiener Zeitung*

Gazzetta ufficiale di Milano—daily published in Milan from 1816 to 1875, organ of the Austrian authorities in Northern Italy; it changed its title several times.—602

The Globe and Traveller—English daily published in London from 1803 to 1921; mouthpiece of the Whigs up to 1866, and later a Conservative newspaper.—135, 145, 310, 314-15, 318, 322, 381, 534-35

Die Grenzboten, Zeitschrift für Politik und Literatur—German liberal weekly published in Leipzig from 1841 to 1922.—623

The Guardian—English weekly, organ of the Established Church, published in London since 1846.—530, 531

The Mark Lane Express, and Agricultural Journal, etc.—English weekly, organ of the commercial bourgeoisie, published in London from 1832 to 1924.—307, 330

Le Moniteur universel—French daily published in Paris from 1789; official organ of the government from 1799.—5, 21, 108, 209, 236, 245, 307, 316, 318, 536, 549, 599, 604

The Morning Advertiser—English daily published in London from 1794 to 1934; mouthpiece of the radical bourgeoisie in the 1850s.—20, 38, 58, 68, 72, 192, 210, 212, 240, 255, 257, 279, 284, 286, 290, 291, 310, 312-13, 325, 532-33, 536, 591, 592, 607

The Morning Chronicle—English daily published in London from 1770 to 1862; organ of the Whigs (1840s), of the Peelites (early 1850s) and later of the Conservative Party.—20, 46, 52, 80, 140, 145, 236, 292, 306, 310, 315, 407, 408, 527, 532, 534, 537, 562

The Morning Herald—English conservative daily published in London from 1780 to 1869.—18, 19-20, 80, 112, 143, 147, 242, 379, 417, 436, 525, 533, 538, 547

The Morning Post—English conservative daily published in London from 1772 to 1937; organ of the Right wing of the Whigs led by Palmerston in the mid-nineteenth century.—19-20, 28, 58, 80, 109, 145, 193, 194, 203, 210, 225-26, 234, 246, 310, 315, 318, 321, 322, 330, 422, 470, 525-29, 530, 532, 534, 537

La Nation, organe quotidien démocrate socialiste—newspaper of the Belgian petty-bourgeois democrats published in Brussels from 1848 to 1856.—255, 293

National-Zeitung—German daily published in Berlin from 1848 to 1915; voiced liberal views in the 1850s.—235, 280

Neu-England Zeitung—democratic weekly published by German petty-bourgeois émigrés in Boston (USA) from 1846 to 1853.—481, 623, 625, 628

Neue Oder-Zeitung—German daily published in Breslau (Wrocław); from 1846 to March 1849 it came out under the title *Allgemeine Oder-Zeitung* as the organ of Catholic opposition circles. From March 1849 to the end of 1855 it appeared as *Neue Oder-Zeitung* and was the organ of the German bourgeois democrats; in 1855 Marx was its London correspondent.—284, 285

Neue Preussische Zeitung—German daily published in Berlin from June 1848; mouthpiece of Junkers and Court circles; also known as *Kreuz-Zeitung* because the heading contained a cross bearing the device "Forward with God for King and Fatherland".—240, 505, 562, 569

Neue Rheinische Zeitung. Organ der Democratie—German daily, organ of the revolutionary-proletarian wing of the democrats during the 1848-49 revolution in Germany; it was published in Cologne under the editorship of Marx from June 1, 1848 to May 19, 1849 (with an interval between September 27 and October 12, 1848).—101, 284, 285, 501

Neue Rheinische Zeitung. Politisch-ökonomische Revue—journal, theoretical organ of the Communist League, founded by Marx and Engels in December 1849 and published until November 1850.—41, 490

SUBJECT INDEX

A

D

F

N

O

P

S

T